The Ephemeris of
TRANS-NEPTUNIAN KBO PLANETS

The Ephemeris of
TRANS-NEPTUNIAN KBO PLANETS

Henry Seltzer

Published by ACS Publications, Starcrafts LLC
68 A Fogg Rd., Epping, NH 03042

First Printing 2021

Cover and layout design by Molly Sullivan

The design shown on the cover is a triangle of the proposed glyphs for new planets by Henry Seltzer, with Nature and starry sky background. The glyphs for Eris, Haumea, and Makemke were either designed (Eris, Haumea) or adopted (Makemake) by Henry as symbolic for these new KBO planets, with the latter two, called "plutoids," being represented by variations on the Pluto chalice glyph.

ISBN: 978-1-934976-69-2

Printed in the United States of America

Acknowledgments

Nothing of any importance takes place in a vacuum; it takes a village not only to raise a child but to make advances in our understanding of the universe that we live in. Many figures from the evolution of modern 21st-century Western Astrology have contributed to my knowledge of its basic principles, which in turn has informed my study of these new archetypes that have so recently swum into view as this climactic century was getting underway. I must therefore express my gratitude to Dane Rudhyar and Marc Edmund Jones, the founders of the modern humanistic approach, as well as to many other contributors to new developments in our ancient art, including Jeff Green, Steven Forrest, Robert Hand, Liz Greene, Alan Oken, Stephen Arroyo, Melanie Reinhart, and Richard Tarnas. This is of course to name but a few of the beacons along the path of my astrological education. I must also give a shout-out to Jonathon Tenney, who helped me come to a better understanding of what I was trying to achieve when I created the TimePassages software with the express purpose of furthering astrology's development and street cred by making a tool that would be easy to use and provide accurate information for professionals, while also allowing as many as possible to see for themselves the incredible information provided by the interpretation of their birth chart.

As far as the company that was formed for distributing this compendium of basic astrological wisdom that is in TimePassages, called AstroGraph Software, incorporated in 2006, I am very grateful to my son, Asia Seltzer, who has enabled it to shine, and to Stephanie Shaffer, Lisa Stutey, and Leslie Benson, who have also been instrumental in making this organization that I still lead the success that it has become today. This in turn has allowed me to be able to do the research among these novel KBO planets that has fleshed out at least a good start on the delineation of these fascinating astrological archetypes.

It is a truism, proven in recent centuries, that when the astronomers speak and name, the astrologers investigate and delineate. It is my honor and privilege to mention all of our debt to the lead astronomer for all three of these KBO "dwarf" planets, namely Mike Brown, of Cal Tech, who not only discovered and traced the orbits of these newly officially-named planetary objects, but also has been open to the task of the astrologers in further elucidating their meaning.

These ephemeris calculations presented herein have been enabled by the terrific work of the folks at Astrodienst, who created in the '80s the Swiss Ephemeris calculations that power TimePassages, along with many other software projects, and who maintain it to this day, principally Alois Treindl and Dieter Koch. The circulation of my initial take on Eris as Feminine Warrior in support of soul intention, amply proven out over the intervening years and now gaining ground, published in 2015 as *The Tenth Planet*, from The Wessex Astrologer, has been greatly facilitated by the able editorial assistance of Margaret Cahill who is the principal there.

Bringing us up to the present moment of 2021, this Ephemeris of KBO planets was initially proposed by Maria Kay Simms, who conceived and commissioned it, and eventually saw it come to pass. In the details of its execution should also of course be mentioned the leadership of Thomas Canfield, and the able expertise of Molly Sullivan, also of ACS Publications, who is responsible for its professional look and feel, including the formatting of the Introduction. The layout of the ephemeris pages themselves was beautifully designed and engineered by David Eyes.

INTRODUCTION

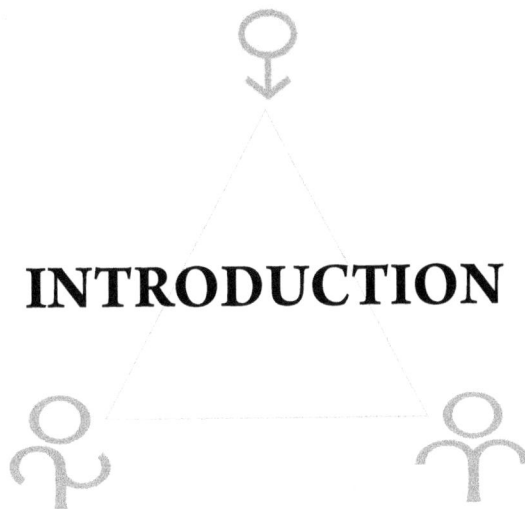

Eris ⚴   Makemake ♁   Haumea ♁

In the ephemeris pages that follow, the positions of the four Kuiper Belt Object (hereafter KBO) planets **Pluto, Eris, Makemake,** and **Haumea,** are given from 1900 to 2050, once a week at midnight on Sundays. The calculations are for Greenwich, England, and are based on the Swiss Ephemeris from Astrodienst, version 2.10, as of March 2021.

Although major feminine asteroid Ceres is also now labeled 'dwarf planet,' she resides in the Asteroid belt and her meaning in Western Astrology is relatively well-known, so that she will not be part of this discussion. Also, while it is possible that other KBOs will eventually be named as planets, the IAU as of this writing has no plans to do so.[1] The meaning of Pluto is well-known, so we will concentrate on these three new ones. Eris is of a size, density, and brightness to rival Pluto and has been shown to be quite significant in chart work. Makemake and Haumea are smaller, but still these four are the largest known Kuiper Belt Objects. In this Introduction we will provide evidence for the astrological significance of all three of these new KBO planets. After many years of study into these very interesting

bodies as they relate to Western Astrology, I have been able to come to the conclusion that they are all quite significant in charts. My earlier research focused on Eris and resulted in the idea that this new outer planet represents a Feminine Warrior archetype in support of soul intention. This is related to life purpose, references deep inner values, and represents as well a dedication to principle that is so strong that it can border on the violent at times. All this has been documented in my book, *The Tenth Planet*, published by The Wessex Astrologer. Since the publication date of this work in the spring of 2015, the evidence along these lines continues to pile up, so that I am more confirmed than ever in this delineation. Over and over, I have found Eris to be incredibly powerful in both natal and forecasting astrology. In the first section of this introduction, I will share key example charts that testify to her astrological meaning.

In turning my attention to the other two designated "dwarf" planets residing in the Kuiper Belt that complete this ephemeris collection, namely, Makemake and Haumea, I initially assumed that they, too, would prove to be powerful in charts, and indeed I have been able to confirm this assumption.

[1] Personal communication, Mike Brown.

Please note that in my research thus far, I have not tried to understand the relationship in terms of meaning of other KBOs not designated by the IAU as planets, to these ones officially named. Those others are potentially significant, and astrologers have been writing about them in interesting ways, but my focus has been on the three new KBOs named as planets.

Because Makemake and Haumea are the first officially designated planets to be named for indigenous gods and goddesses, I felt that they would prove to represent in some form a "profound connection to Nature." After looking at hundreds of charts, I can now report that this indeed seems to be the case. Makemake and Haumea can be seen as representing Nature connection, also Nature as spiritual path, and adherence to concepts of natural law. With strong Haumea, there is a love of nature and of right action, along with a natural charisma that is almost always present, while Makemake represents the more activist of these two Nature archetypes, associated with doing something about humanitarian and earth issues. Most particularly in this current decade – due to the magnitude of the topic – this could reference activism with regard to the growing existential threat of climate change.

A good exemplar of Makemake in an activist context, and one that came along after my initial characterization of Makemake as the more "activist" of these two Nature archetypes, is **Greta Thunberg**. At the tender age of 15, and speaking for her generation, she addressed the U.N. regarding climate change, courageously and unflinchingly telling the leaders of the world that they were screwing up. She does, as was signaled by her actions, possess prominent Eris, indicating her warrior-like stance in speaking truth to power. Thunberg's Eris is in a close grand trine with Jupiter and Pluto, widely square her Sun, and likely square her Moon. She is undeniably

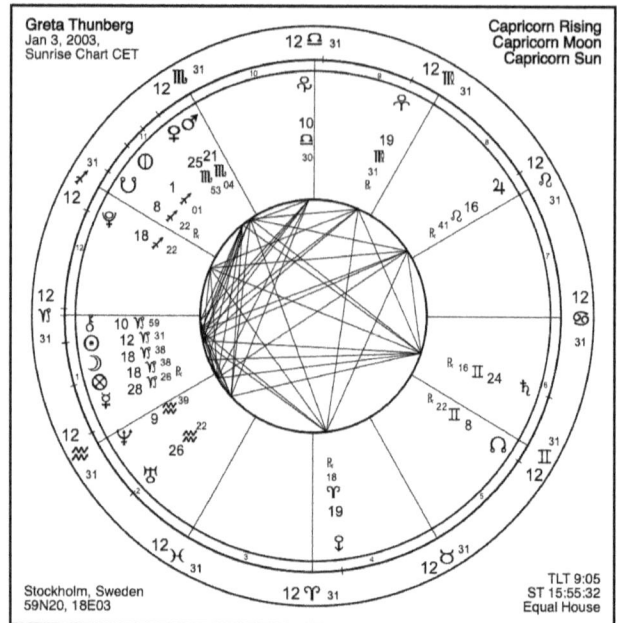

Greta Thunberg
Jan 3, 2003,
Sunrise Chart CET
Capricorn Rising
Capricorn Moon
Capricorn Sun
Stockholm, Sweden
59N20, 18E03
TLT 9:05
ST 15:55:32
Equal House

activist in her agenda, and Eris is additionally the focus of a yod from Makemake and Mars in sextile, featuring a partile or same-degree quincunx from Makemake to Eris, both at 19 degrees of their respective signs. She therefore makes a good example case of both strong Eris, implying implacable spiritual warrior energy, and also the participation in the Eris configuration of prominent Makemake, indicating her environmental activism (see chart).

The first section below will delineate Eris in my description of her as Feminine Warrior, based on the research leading up to the original publication, nearly six years ago as of this writing. There will also be examples from the many pertinent charts that have come to light since that time and that provide evidence along these same lines.

The second section will describe the delineations of Makemake and Haumea. These two new astrological factors seem to share a commonality of archetypal meaning, as representing a planetary archetype of 'Profound connection to Nature.' Note that these two planetary objects have relatively quite similar orbital periods of 306 and 284 years, respectively, which could contribute to their similarity of meaning in astrological charts. There are also some notable symbolic differences between them. While focusing on natal factors, I will as well explore some transits of these new "Nature" planets for a broader outline of their potential usefulness. The information presented herein will hopefully serve astrologers as a basis for further research.

Relationship to the Pluto Archetype

A brief mention of the Pluto archetype in relationship to these new ones might be in order here. Pluto represents deep transformation; death and rebirth; compulsion or unevolved power urge. In all these ramifications of astrological meaning, the Pluto archetype goes to great depth within the psyche, to soul-level, and I have found this as well to be true of these twenty-first-century archetypes. Details will follow. The indications from the research are that to the astrological adage "as above, so below" must be added the psychological corollary "as farthest out, so deepest within."

Eris ⚵

I'll start with a simple story of how the archetype became defined for me in the way that it did. In Greek mythology, Eris was the sister of the God of War, who "followed him willingly into the battle, and delighted in the groans of the dying," and this idea from her mythology informed my initial characterization as "woman warrior." When I sought evidence for this characterization, I began by looking at the charts of female warriors on screen, like Angelina Jolie, plus all the feminist leaders that I could find, and they all had prominent Eris. With feminists, in many cases I detected a certain ruthless style, as well as taking on a cause that they felt profoundly concerned about, namely women's rights and suffrage. Eris in Greek mythology was also named goddess of Chaos and Discord, which has thrown some astrologers off. Eris is not merely a discord-inducer. There is chaos, at times, cer-

tainly, and that is so for Pluto as well. Oftentimes, those with strong Eris bring a new way of seeing, which represents a different order of organization, which seems like chaos to the existing status quo. Examples are of course the feminists and suffragettes as well as paradigm shifters like Copernicus, Newton, and Einstein, all possessing strong Eris. The higher octave here is the need for these strong-minded people to search inside and become crystal clear on their deepest principles, those that they are willing to completely stand behind, to articulate and to act upon – rather than being swayed by impulse or allowing violent outbreaks to surface without underlying ideals to make them relevant.

To take an example almost at random, consider the chart of **Ti-Grace Atkinson**. (See chart). She was an early member of NOW (the National Organization of Women), left it because it was not radical enough, and founded her own "October 17th Movement" group, later renamed Radical Feminists, active from 1968 to 1973. Her book is entitled *Amazon Odyssey*. Logically, she would be possessed of strong Eris. Her chart does not disappoint; we find Eris in a close grand trine in Fire with feisty Pluto and Mercury in

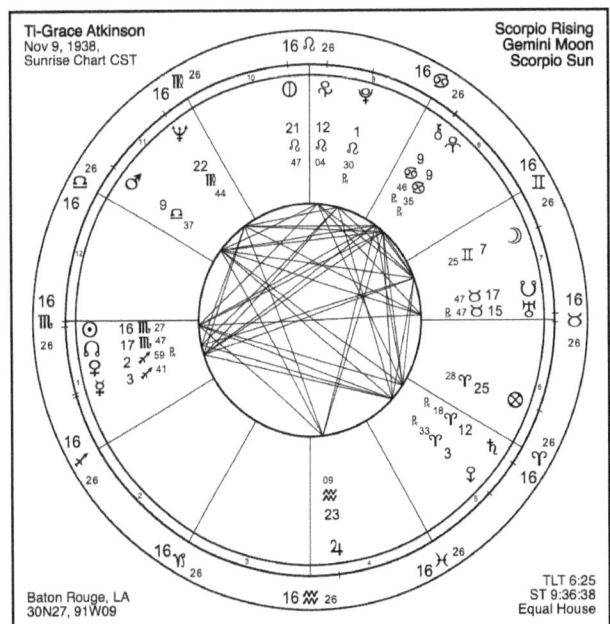

Ti-Grace Atkinson
Nov 9, 1938,
Sunrise Chart CST

Scorpio Rising
Gemini Moon
Scorpio Sun

Baton Rouge, LA
30N27, 91W09

TLT 6:25
ST 9:36:38
Equal House

Sagittarius, the trine between Eris and Mercury being partile. The Eris/Saturn midpoint participates with Mars in a close T-square to Chiron, bespeaking a call to action based on painful awareness of a social situation. Eris is additionally parallel to Mercury within a tenth of a degree, and just as closely contra-parallel to Pluto as well, making this a particularly strong grand trine. In my research, I have found that the combination of Eris with Mercury invariably signals a writer.

Or consider the chart of **Emmeline Pankhurst**, born July 14, 1858, at 9:30 PM according to original collection data, or perhaps July 15, corrected later from official records. She was a strong proponent of suffrage in the early 1900s U.K., as referenced in the 2015 movie *Suffragette*. As in all the feminist leaders that I was able to research, she has strong Eris, and the aspects to Eris suggest that the July 14 date is the correct one. In the July 14th chart, Eris is closely sesquiquadrate Sun, bi-quintile Saturn within six minutes of a degree, and square both Uranus and Jupiter, which are about 9 degrees apart in Gemini. The square to their midpoint is exact within eight minutes of a degree (see chart). One day later, these aspects are not so precise – so that the original

birth data is probably correct. On either date, she would have Eris in the first house, which does make sense for this dedicated feminine warrior who did not eschew violence in pursuit of her goal. Her methods were criticized but her work is recognized as being crucial in achieving women's suffrage in the U.K. She founded the Woman's Social and Political Union, whose members smashed windows and assaulted police officers in pursuit of what they considered their God-given right to vote. A statue honoring her – and the suffrage movement she founded – was erected in London, near the Houses of Parliament.

I have found, in researching literally hundreds of charts, that Eris seems to always light up the house that she occupies. In the first house, there is an identification with the spiritual warrior role, and there is a bulldozer of energy available for whatever is sensed as a deeply felt principle. In the second, matters of this house such as resources take on an extra intensity and are oriented toward the same factor of deep-seated values. In the third, communication and learning are involved. In the fourth, these people have almost a separate life that they lead deep down inside themselves that is connected to their soul mission. In the fifth house, creativity must come directly from the wellspring of deep principle or a feeling of falsity ensues. In the end, they might be able to come into themselves more fully. In the sixth house, a principle of service to the greater good and to the surrounding society is almost always present. In the seventh, this Eris placement becomes the quest for partnership and for a partner to match them, or more than match them, in depth of purpose. Similarly, in the eighth house, it is a quest for intimacy and deep connection with others – and also with self – that is implied. In the ninth house, a love of higher learning makes for an important component of life purpose. When Eris is found in the tenth house, the native is destined

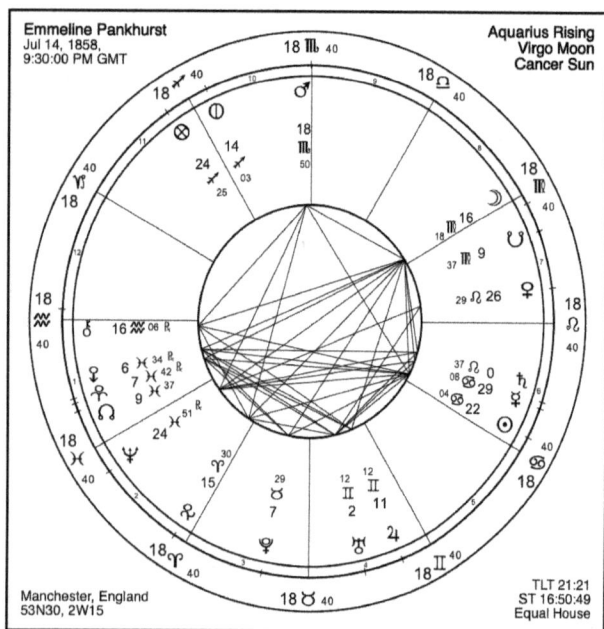

Emmeline Pankhurst
Jul 14, 1858,
9:30:00 PM GMT

Aquarius Rising
Virgo Moon
Cancer Sun

Manchester, England
53N30, 2W15

TLT 21:21
ST 16:50:49
Equal House

for recognition and for learning to use that spotlight for principled action. In the eleventh house, it is the society that is the more direct beneficiary of an earnest depth of character and of will that moves strongly through them. Finally, in the twelfth house, it is the vast unconscious portion of the Self which is very present to the native, and which represents an important facet of their own unique sense of mission; there is also the potential for an almost fantasy world to be created that contains or sidetracks the impulses of a strong will and a deeply earnest life intention that goes against the grain of consensus thinking.

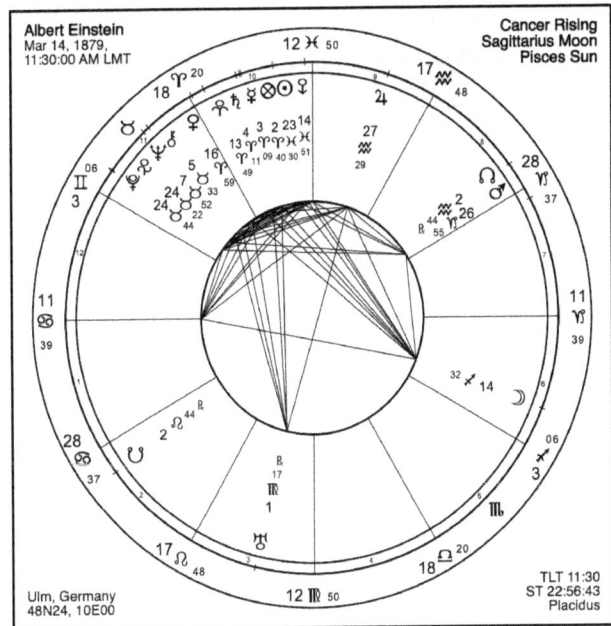

The chart of **Albert Einstein** is interesting in regard to his Eris placement. With Eris in his tenth house, near the MC, he became the most recognized scientist in the world (see chart). Eris is partile square the Moon, which often reflects a different mode of thought than the prevailing consensus orientation of solar logic would dictate; "thinking outside the box," as it were. Copernicus has Eris in close sesquiquadrate to a Moon-Jupiter conjunction, for example, while Newton has a partile Eris-Moon conjunction in early Cancer. The noted twentieth-century psychologist C. G. Jung, who also displayed a distinct departure from the psychology of his day, has Moon within two degrees of a sextile to his first-house Eris (see chart on page 12).

In an extremely interesting transiting example with Eris, involving Albert Einstein, there is the transit of Eris to Einstein's Sun, also being located in his tenth house, with the angular distance from Eris to his Sun only about 8 ½ degrees. As transiting Eris got closer, touching and then in a final pass crossing his Sun in February of 1905, only to retrograde back to station directly upon it, to the minute, by the end of that year, he had what is known as his "miracle year" of 1905, when he, while working as a patent examiner, published four physics papers that overturned the founda-

tions of 19th-century physics, including on the photoelectric effect, for which he won the Nobel Prize, the "E=mc²" law, and the general theory of relativity. When Eris was within one degree of the Sun, in 1899, he was beginning to write letters about relativity, and when it had reached the one-degree boundary on the other side, he no longer worked for the Swiss Patent Office but had become a professor of physics at the University of Bern.

I arrived at many examples of strong Eris from suspecting the presence of the archetype in the life; one of these being the case of **Terence McKenna**. For those who might not know of him, Terence McKenna, when he lectured, was positive and passionate about his point of view, clearly articulated and unique to himself, especially regarding the psychedelic experience. When asked, in a San Francisco lecture, if McKenna would be another likely exemplar of this maverick archetype, I replied "yes" immediately, not having seen the chart, but rather based on his personality. When McKenna's birth data was located and displayed to the audience, it did indeed portray strong Eris (see chart on page 6). McKenna's Eris is alone in her own hemisphere, quincunx his Moon, and in close trine with his Mars-Mercury conjunction, as is quite appropriate given his sharp articulation of his own unique point of view.

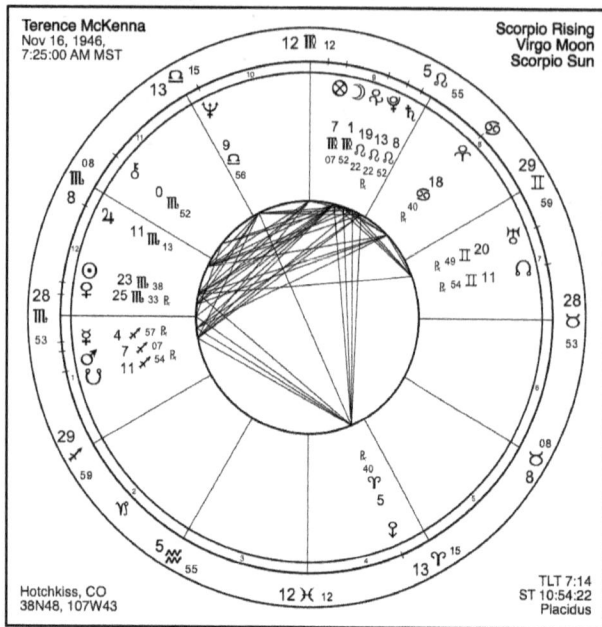

For a glimpse of a more complex assessment of Eris in action, in both natal astrology and also in transit, let me present the example of **Herman Melville**, another chart of consequence. Melville's map demonstrates an unusually charged presence of outer planet energies, with Saturn-Pluto in conjunction, as noted by Rick Tarnas in his seminal *Cosmos and Psyche*, and also, quite tellingly, with

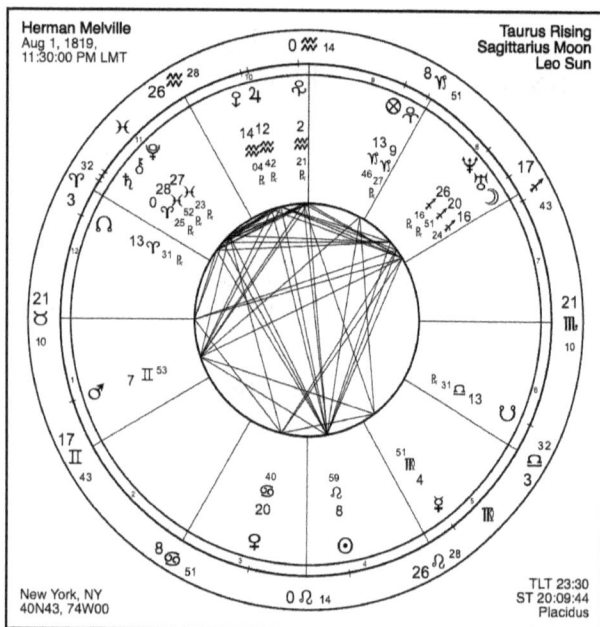

Neptune-Pluto, in close square within about a degree. His masterpiece, *Moby Dick*, is of course a dark story of almost Shakespearean psychological complexity (symbolized by Pluto and Neptune) taking place in an ocean setting (Neptune). Highlighting both natal archetypes is the presence of Chiron closely conjunct Pluto, and Eris with Jupiter at the Neptune/Pluto midpoint (see chart). Great emphasis is provided in this chart by Eris, in the tenth house, closely conjunct Jupiter and opposed to Melville's Sun. Jupiter-Eris is additionally emblematic of the joyous descriptions of the whaling industry that grace the novel's pages, and also symbolizes the expansiveness of this book with its great density and length. Regarding the tenth house placement of Eris, in connection to Jupiter, Neptune, and Pluto, it is the Shakespearean depths of this tale celebrating life on the high seas in search of the whale that made Melville's reputation for the ages. For those interested in a longer description of the relationship of Melville's Eris placement to his art, see chapter 4 of my book, *The Tenth Planet*.

One important feature of the transits of the summer of 1850 when Melville was hard at work on *Moby Dick* was that the transiting midpoint of Eris and Neptune, characteristic of the oceanic tale he was composing, opposed Melville's Mercury within minutes of a degree. Another interesting factor relates to the turn-around in his writing, when, influenced by his neighbor, luminary author Nathaniel Hawthorne, he decided to delve into a more complex and sinister plot than he had originally contemplated. That August 1850 moment was of great consequence in changing the direction of Melville's masterwork. Up until that month, he planned a more ordinary tale of the high seas like those that he had already produced, "as a sawyer saws wood,"[2] as he had described the pop novels that had come before. As I looked into this important timing, I was startled to dis-

[2] Charles Olsen, "Call Me Ishmael," p. 24, reprinted in *Modern Critical Interpretations, Moby Dick*, ed. Harold Bloom, 1986 Chelsea House.

cover there happened to take place on August 7th of that year a solar eclipse in partile opposition to his natal Eris. The simultaneous long-term transit of the Neptune/Eris midpoint in partile opposition to Melville's natal Mercury was concurrent with the more dramatic astrological event featuring his Eris. Finding that eclipse so perfectly placed in the timing of Melville's great artistic production, for which he was to eventually become famous as a classic early American novelist, thereby fulfilling his life purpose, confirmed my understanding that the Eris archetype was significant in these areas. This example, as well as other research, has also shown that Eris can be quite significant by transit, as well as in her natal placements.

♀ Makemake and Haumea ♀

Turning to these other two new KBO planets, Haumea and Makemake, these can be characterized as representing "profound connection to Nature." This is so in a way that, just as with Pluto and with Eris, goes to depth within the psyche. This then obviously adds an important factor to concepts regarding who and what we really are.

The starting point, for me, of this archetypal characterization of Haumea and Makemake lay in recognizing that these two planets are currently the only officially designated planets named for indigenous gods and goddesses. Again note that I am going by the significance of these being officially named by the astronomers as a variety of planet. As well, along with Pluto and Eris, these are the four largest Kuiper Belt Objects, and the IAU has no current plans to extend this list. My first thought, whether by deduction or somehow channeled, was "profound connection to Nature," and that has proven to be accurate, with Makemake being the more activist of the two. It is high time for Western culture to recognize that we humans are essentially a cog in

a wheel, a semi-unconscious part of Nature that surrounds us, and in which we have our being. Nature itself resides deep within us, and her processes: birth, growth, flowering, decay, and death, are fundamental to us as well, beyond just the physical, operating on many levels. Awareness of this factor has been flagrantly missing from the prevailing increasingly materialistic philosophy of past centuries. Only now, in the midst of the twenty-first-century societal transformation in which we as a culture are now engaged, is this basic fact of life – well-known to indigenous societies – beginning to be acknowledged, namely the primacy of Nature as a fundamental part of our very being.

Regarding these two Nature planets, a mention of the mythology of their naming might be in order here, as a starting point, noting that the mythology is not the final determinant of their astrological meaning, which must come from research. Haumea, the creation goddess of the Hawaiian mythology, is in fact a powerful symbol for nature herself, as indicated earlier. After giving birth from all different parts of her body, she was characterized by her ability to regenerate as a young woman. In mimicry of her mythological shape-shifting characteristics, her physical shape as a planetary object is coincidentally a match, elongated from its rapid rotational speed. Note that the orbital period of these two KBO planets is only a little longer than the 248-year period of Pluto; Haumea being 284 years, while Makemake takes 306 years to circle the sun.

The glyph that I am using in these charts for Haumea is a variation of the Pluto chalice, designed to represent a pregnant woman, while the glyph that I have proposed for Makemake, another variation of the Pluto glyph, is an outline of a Birdman, which is significant in the Rapa Nui culture. This latter design was suggested by astrologer Philip Sedgwick. These glyphs, which you will find in the ephemeris pages that follow, and in the example charts of this Introduction, are ♔ for Makemake and ⯓ for Haumea.

As the creation goddess of the Hawaiian people, Haumea is the mother of all of the other gods and goddesses of Hawaiian mythology. She had a magic wand that could make food appear and was constantly giving off new forms, constantly regenerating, constantly changing, in a fitting symbol for the processes of Nature herself. She was the mother of Pele, goddess of the volcanic action that is even now creating more landmass on the Big Island. I was incidentally able at times to correlate prominent Haumea in lunation cycles associated with the recent lava outbreaks there.

Turning to Makemake, he was named for the creation god of the Rapa Nui people of Easter Island, and we find again in the mythology of his naming the huge importance of the cycles of Nature among indigenous cultures. The legend of the Birdman reflects this. Once a year, in the spring, the return of the bird population to a nearby rocky landmass signaled the contest for the reigning "Birdman" for that year, the spiritual leader of the community. This was through a competition amongst young men, each a champion for an older candidate. In a kind of triathlon event they were to swim the strait and swim back with the first egg of the season in their headdress, climbing a rocky cliff in the process. The Birdman chosen for the year would then go into retreat, and would be the de facto leader of the island tribes, responsible for having the big dreams that would provide their guidance. This is a fascinating reflection of the process of Nature being fundamental to their cultural realities, and that is also the reason that the glyph of Makemake I chose to utilize resembles a "birdman."

As far as example charts, there are many. To summarize, those with strong Haumea have indeed a deep connection with Nature either overt or subtle. For example, I examined the chart of **Henry David Thoreau**, who was an early originator of the idea of a "back to Nature" movement within Western culture. He made his dwelling place for a time in the woods near his hometown of Concord, Massachusetts, memorializing these experiences in his classic, *Walden*. I found that Thoreau exhibited a strong dose of Haumea and Makemake in both his natal chart and for his transits on the date when he established his temporary residence on the shores of Walden Pond. Note that Thoreau was an iconoclast, and an inherent paradigm shifter, and that his natal Eris is quintile Jupiter, partile (same degree) sextile to Uranus, bi-quintile Moon, and partile quincunx his Moon/Sun midpoint. Haumea resides in the last degree of Capricorn closely quincunx his natal Mercury – and he wrote about Nature his entire life. Haumea is also sextile and closely parallel Jupiter, sextile Pluto, and widely opposite his Sun degree in late Cancer. Makemake is opposite his Moon, trine his Mars, quincunx Venus, quintile Chiron, and sextile Saturn (see chart).

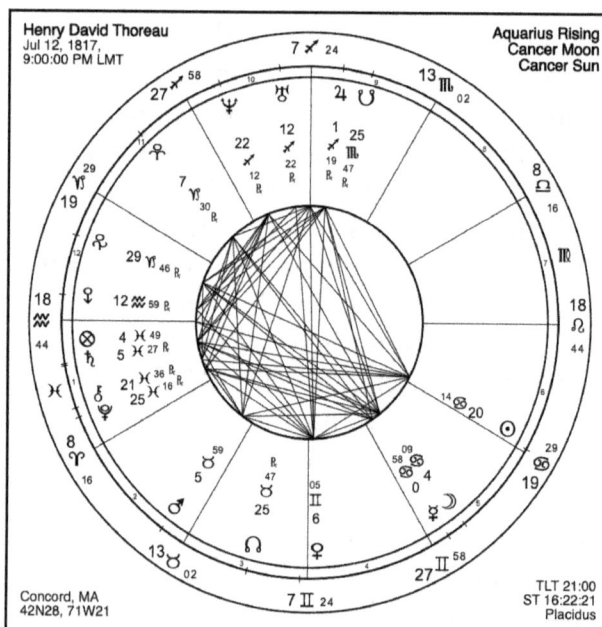

Henry David Thoreau
Jul 12, 1817,
9:00:00 PM LMT

Aquarius Rising
Cancer Moon
Cancer Sun

Concord, MA
42N28, 71W21

TLT 21:00
ST 16:22:21
Placidus

When Thoreau moved to his cabin on Walden Pond, on July 4th, 1845, it was on a New Moon, at 12 degrees of Cancer. Thoreau has both Moon and Sun in Cancer, and the transiting New Moon was in partile conjunction with his Moon/Sun midpoint and in partile quincunx to his natal Eris (signifying important life mission). These two nature planets, as I am calling them, were also quite active in the transits for that July 4th. Transiting Makemake (ruling nature activism) in conjunction with transiting Saturn (signifying major life events, earned accolades, and fame) were on his Ascendant, conjunct his natal Eris, and quincunx his Sun. Haumea (love of nature) was one sign ahead of Makemake, in Pisces, and trine his Sun, quintile his natal Makemake, and semi-sextile his ascendant. Interestingly, transiting Jupiter on this significant date was precisely conjunct Thoreau's natal Mars, to the minute of a degree, and therefore trine his natal Makemake, while transiting Mars was in partile semi-sextile to his natal Haumea.

When considering Nature as spiritual path, another iconic figure who comes to mind is James Lovelock, who enunciated the Gaia Principle in the early 1970s. This was the idea that the earth is an entity with her own agenda for transformation and for resolution of issues such as species survival and those associated with climate change. We would expect strong Haumea, as well as Makemake, since this principle is fundamentally an activist approach, a template for respecting and taking better care of our earthly home. We have his birth time, and Lovelock has Haumea in a one-degree conjunction with the Moon, indicating nurturing and caring for Nature, as well as a novel way of thinking about Nature. Haumea is additionally parallel to Neptune, which is elevated in his chart, another indication of the fundamentally spiritual principle that he annunciated with respect to Mother Earth. Makemake is also quite strong, making aspects to his Sun, MC,

and his Venus, ruler of his mystical twelfth house, quintile his Saturn-Mercury partile conjunction, plus being septile Neptune.

Celebrity actors like **Leonardo DiCaprio** and **Rachel McAdams** who have used their star power to espouse environmental causes can also be shown to possess strong Haumea and Makemake placements. When transiting Saturn was on her natal Makemake, McAdams created the website "Green is Sexy."[3]

Leonardo DiCaprio is a United Nations Messenger for Peace – with a focus on climate change – and famously addressed the U.N. on this topic on April 22, 2016, to bring awareness to this issue. He also produced and narrated the film *Before The Flood*, which documents the extremity of the global warming problem. I was interested to see his chart, and in fact, we have his birth time.

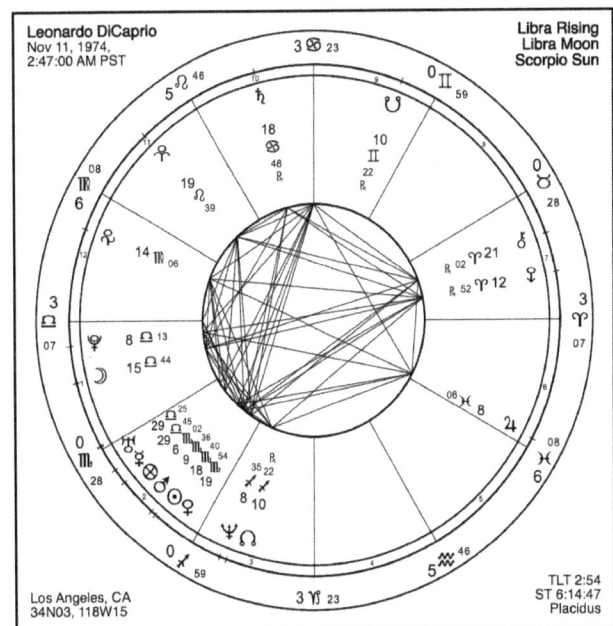

Leonardo DiCaprio
Nov 11, 1974,
2:47:00 AM PST
Libra Rising
Libra Moon
Scorpio Sun
Los Angeles, CA
34N03, 118W15
TLT 2:54
ST 6:14:47
Placidus

DiCaprio's Haumea in the twelfth aspects his Moon-Eris opposition, by semi-sextile and quincunx, with Eris in his seventh, signifying a nurturing attitude toward others as an important component of his makeup. Haumea is also bi-quintile to Chiron, and precisely semi-square his tight Mercury-Uranus conjunction, thus indicating that he is conscious

[3] https://en.wikipedia.org/wiki/Rachel_McAdams#Environmental_activism

of the current painful state of the environment, and well recognizes the spiritual within the natural world. With Uranus so closely involved, he is willing to be innovative in describing and attempting to solve that situation.

His Makemake in the eleventh house symbolizes quite well his environmental activism, as does also its close trine to Chiron. Makemake is very prominent, being closely square his Sun-Venus conjunction in the second house of resources. This latter aspect symbolizes his values, the planet's survival that he remains so greatly concerned with, and as well the money that DiCaprio is willing to bring to the table in his efforts to help.

When he addressed the U.N. on the eve of the Paris Accords, on Earth Day, 2016, he had Makemake on his Ascendant and square his MC, while the Sun in early Taurus was sextile MC and opposed to his Mercury-Uranus conjunction. Remarkably, transiting Uranus, transiting Venus, and transiting Eris in a tight triple conjunction, opposed by transiting Haumea, were all three quintile his MC, conjunct his Chiron, and trine his natal Makemake. Jupiter was conjunct within one degree his natal Haumea as

transiting Saturn closely squared this point. This is, all-in-all, quite a good showing of these new nature planets in transit, bringing in as well his Chiron, Ascendant and MC (see transit chart).

Later that same year, his film *Before the Flood* premiered in London on October 21, 2016, with the Sun directly on his natal Mercury-Uranus, and transiting Makemake in even closer aspect to his Ascendant and MC. Saturn squared his natal Haumea by less than a degree while transiting Chiron, in partile semi-sextile to his natal Chiron, was quincunx his natal Makemake. Moreover, transiting Haumea, in tight conjunction with transiting Mercury, was opposed to an Eris-Uranus conjunction in the sky of less than a degree, all four aligned with his natal Chiron. This is another set of dramatic transits.

Rachel McAdams' natal placements are also particularly precise, with her Haumea in partile sextile to Uranus located in her first house, and in partile square to her partile conjunction of Mercury and Neptune, all at 17 degrees of their respective signs, while Makemake lies in a one-degree square to her Scorpio Sun (see chart).

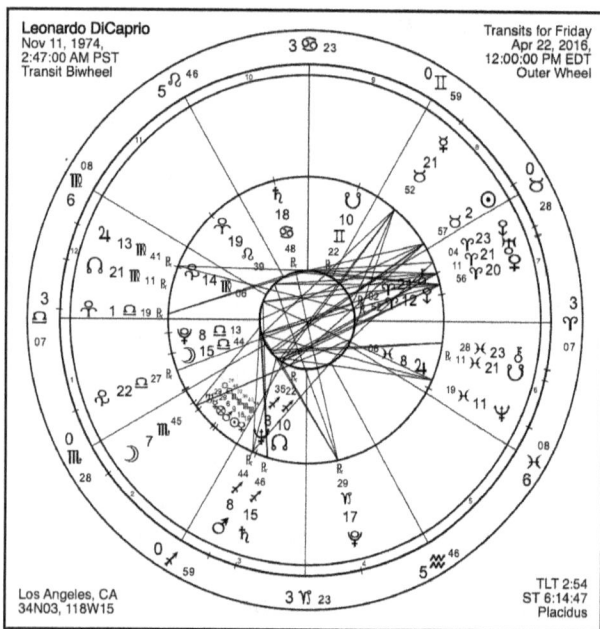

Leonardo DiCaprio
Nov 11, 1974,
2:47:00 AM PST
Transit Biwheel

Transits for Friday
Apr 22, 2016,
12:00:00 PM EDT
Outer Wheel

Los Angeles, CA
34N03, 118W15

TLT 2:54
ST 6:14:47
Placidus

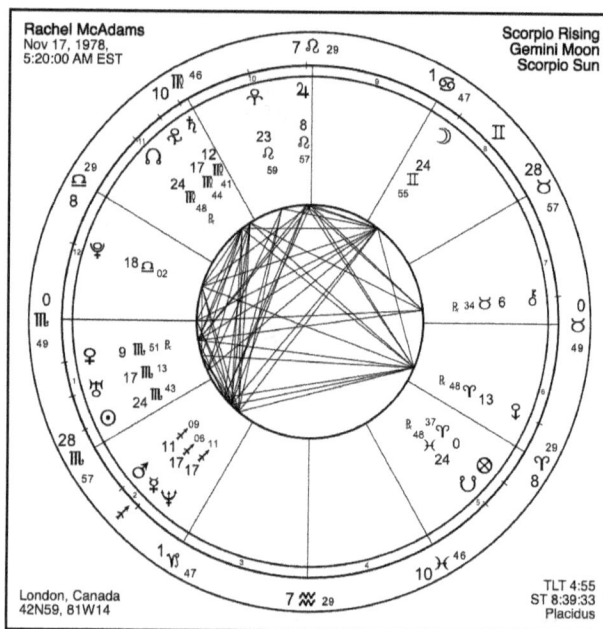

Rachel McAdams
Nov 17, 1978,
5:20:00 AM EST

Scorpio Rising
Gemini Moon
Scorpio Sun

London, Canada
42N59, 81W14

TLT 4:55
ST 8:39:33
Placidus

David Bowie, another iconic figure of popular culture with strong Haumea, has her in close quincunx with Sun and Mars, parallel the Moon, square Jupiter, partile sextile Uranus, septile Neptune, and conjunct and closely parallel Pluto (see chart). He was not primarily a dweller in Nature, but as appropriate to the Haumea archetype, he made his own environment wherever he went, continually shape-shifting in order to do so. He thus created new worlds within the existing culture by the transformative style of his musical and dramatic art.

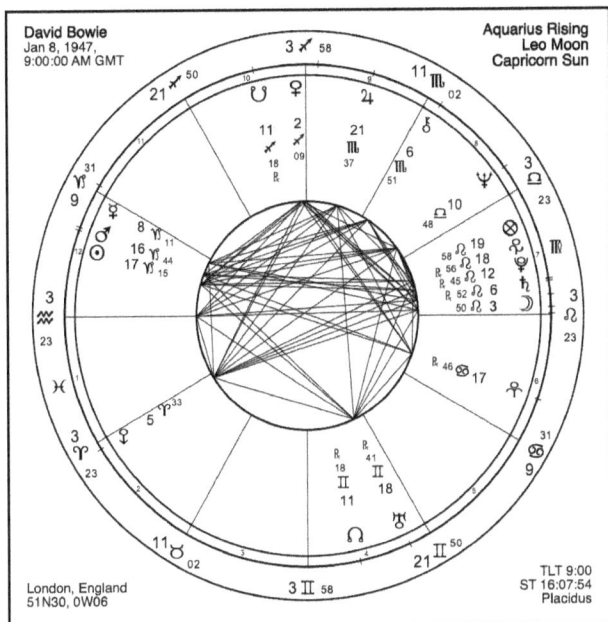

Many times, as his career continued to blossom, he essentially created new facets of culture by turning on his imagination, and then proceeding to inhabit the worlds that he had imagined. In this way, he is similar to psychedelic explorers like Timothy Leary, Ram Dass, and Albert Hoffman, all with strong Haumea. Investigating these psychonauts from the 1960s made for an important clue to the Haumea archetype, which includes the ability to see the world in a spiritually evolved manner, including its other dimensions, which go to transpersonal planes of existence above and beyond our ordinary 3-D sense of physical reality, and to depth within the psyche.

David Bowie freely gave the great gift of himself to late 20th-century culture, and we are the richer for it. Those with strong Haumea almost always possess a natural charisma together with an upbeat attitude that tends to do well by doing good.

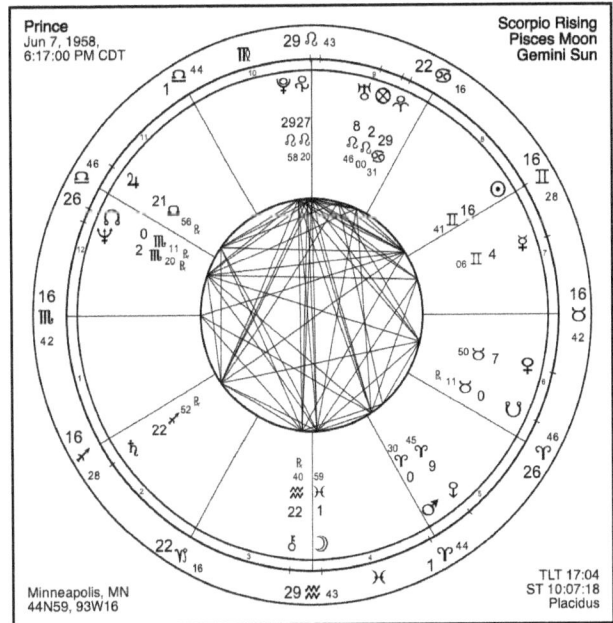

The chart of **Prince** is another that displays noticeably strong Haumea, being conjunct Pluto and coincident with his MC, quincunx Mars and as well opposed both his Chiron and his Moon, in partile opposition of their midpoint to within one minute of a degree (see chart). Of course, similar to David Bowie, Prince too was a shape-shifting artist with tons of charisma and creative style that changed the face of the society. He was also a secret philanthropist who helped many people anonymously.

C. G. Jung is also an iconic exemplar for paradigm-shifting breakthrough in the scientific discipline of psychology and for Western culture in general. Jung has Eris partile trine Mercury, as his prolific written output would testify to, and is also in possession of a powerful Haumea presence at very nearly the midpoint of his Moon-Pluto eight-degree conjunction (see chart on page 12).

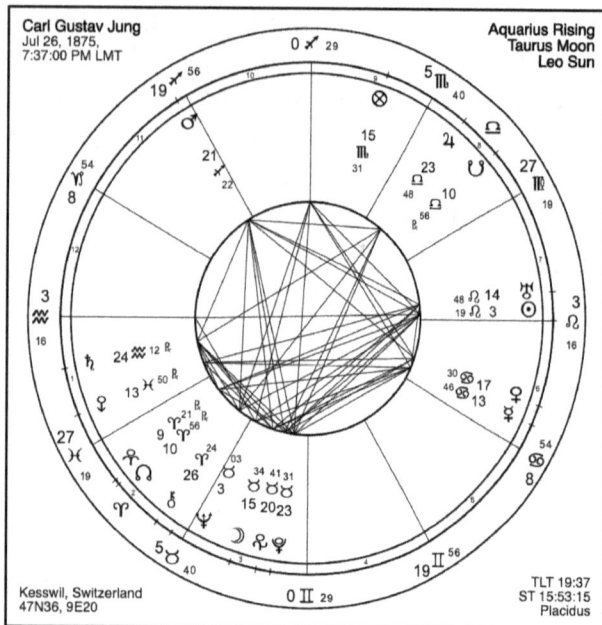

Carl Gustav Jung
Jul 26, 1875,
7:37:00 PM LMT

Aquarius Rising
Taurus Moon
Leo Sun

Kesswil, Switzerland
47N36, 9E20

TLT 19:37
ST 15:53:15
Placidus

Haumea is also closely parallel to Jupiter, square Saturn, quintile his Sun, sextile his Venus, and the focal point of a yod from Jupiter and Mars. Of course, he dwelled deep within his psyche and was charismatic. I also find it quite telling that he identified with natural process. He was known to have remarked that people who were leading an artificial life tended to be afraid of him:

> It is the truth, a force of nature that expresses itself through me—I am only a channel—I can imagine in many instances where I would become sinister to you. For instance, if life had led you to take up an artificial attitude, then you wouldn't be able to stand me, because I am a natural being. By my very presence I crystallize; I am a ferment. The unconscious of people who live in an artificial manner senses me as a danger. Everything about me irritates them, my way of speaking, my way of laughing. They sense nature.[4]

With regard to this characterization of Haumea as "profound connection to Nature" in the sense of going to hidden depths within the psyche, there is also the chart of **Friedrich von Schelling,** an eighteenth-century philosopher who was known as a "nature philosopher." He is considered a precursor of Jung and spoke of human subjectivity as being a part of Nature. When I sought out his chart, I was looking for it to potentially exhibit a strong presence of Haumea, and it does. We have his time (see chart). Haumea is partile conjunct his natal Moon, at 6 degrees of Cancer, and sextile his Sun within one degree. Von Schelling's Haumea also aspects by sextile and trine his Saturn-Chiron opposition, and is semi-sextile and quincunx, within 1 degree, his natal Eris trine Jupiter. Essentially, this "Nature" philosopher has Haumea all over his chart, which to me greatly confirmed the delineation that I had hypothesized of Haumea as "profound connection with Nature." It is also helpful to recognize, as with David Bowie, C. G. Jung, and others, that connection to Nature can be seen as embracing elements that go to depth within the human psyche.

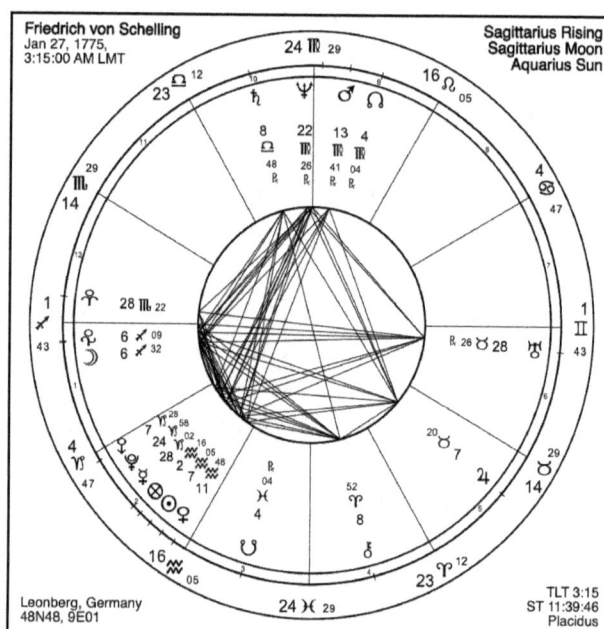

Friedrich von Schelling
Jan 27, 1775,
3:15:00 AM LMT

Sagittarius Rising
Sagittarius Moon
Aquarius Sun

Leonberg, Germany
48N48, 9E01

TLT 3:15
ST 11:39:46
Placidus

[4] https://www.goodreads.com/quotes/8377400-it-is-the-truth-a-force-of-nature-that-expresses

As far as Makemake, this planet, too, seems to have nature connection in its symbolic makeup, both literally and also metaphorically in the sense of adherence to natural law. For the activism implied in the archetype, we have the example already given of Greta Thunberg, who notably exhibits a strong configuration in the partile inconjunct to Eris, part of a yod to Eris from Mars and Makemake (see chart on page 2). Another iconic example is **Edward Abbey**, author of *Desert Solitaire*, who wrote convincingly about the adverse changes to his beloved desert environment brought about by development and the extraction industries. In another well-known work of his, *The Monkey Wrench Gang*, he wrote that the best way to handle this would be to simply sabotage the bulldozers. I saw that his Makemake, although not his Haumea, was in close configuration with his Mercury, and it originally got me thinking along the lines of a more activist delineation for Makemake (see chart). I have since expanded this characterization of Makemake to include other kinds of pragmatic application of the profound impulse toward Nature exhibited by these two new KBO planets.

Another terrific example chart for Eris, as well as Makemake and Haumea, is **Julia Butterfly Hill**. She famously climbed the redwood tree she called Luna when it was threatened by loggers and lived in it for two years, through two difficult winters, in 1997-1999, ultimately saving the tree and several surrounding acres. In this, she obviously displayed pluck and courage, plus an enormous love of Nature and a courageous self-sacrificial stance in defending it; or more personal than that, in defending her friend, the tree. Hill has Eris conjunct Chiron, trine Neptune, and semi-square both Sun and Jupiter within 2 degrees, with Eris precisely semi-square, within minutes of a degree, their midpoint. Eris is also in partile aspect to her Haumea, a quincunx that is exact to within 1 minute of a degree. As far as Makemake, we find him in partile trine with Chiron in Aries, quintile Uranus, and septile Saturn (see chart). When she climbed the tree on December 10, 1997, the transits of both Makemake and Haumea were fascinating. Transiting Makemake was conjunct her natal Haumea while transiting Haumea was in bi-quintile aspect to her natal Sun within 2 minutes of a degree. In an equally rare alignment, Sun in Sagittarius,

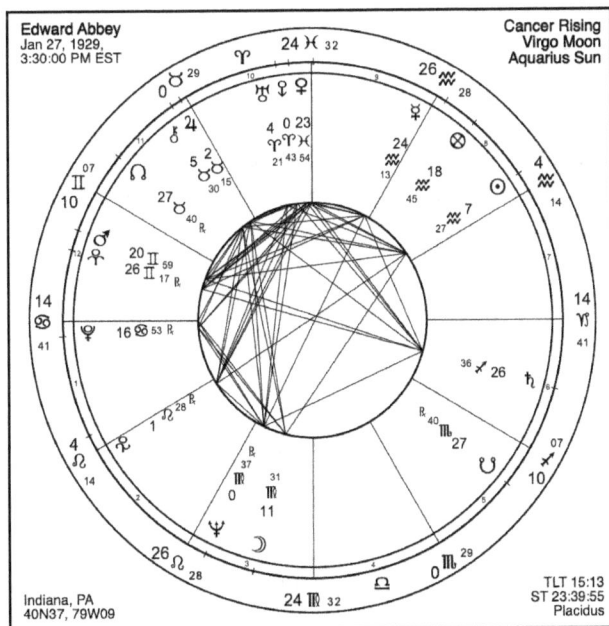

Edward Abbey
Jan 27, 1929,
3:30:00 PM EST

Cancer Rising
Virgo Moon
Aquarius Sun

Indiana, PA
40N37, 79W09

TLT 15:13
ST 23:39:55
Placidus

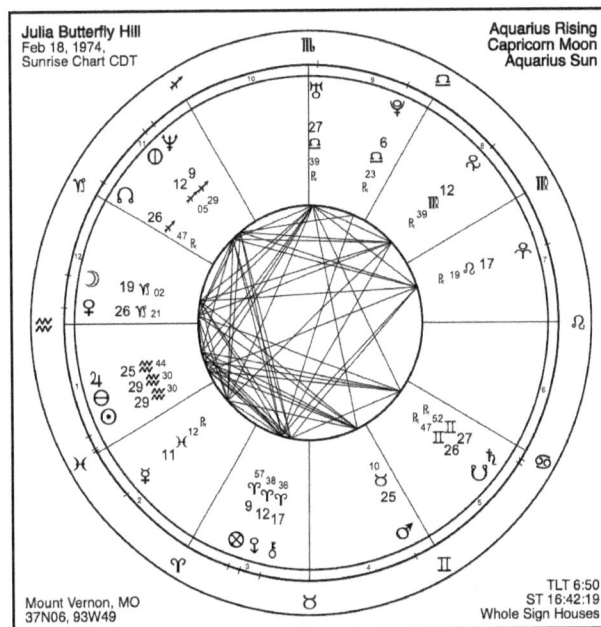

Julia Butterfly Hill
Feb 18, 1974,
Sunrise Chart CDT

Aquarius Rising
Capricorn Moon
Aquarius Sun

Mount Vernon, MO
37N06, 93W49

TLT 6:50
ST 16:42:19
Whole Sign Houses

transiting Jupiter in Aquarius, and transiting Eris in Aries were all at 18 degrees of their respective signs, with Sun trine Eris in the sky and transiting Jupiter at their midpoint, all three making one-degree aspects to her natal Makemake plus forming a grand trine between transiting Sun, transiting Eris, and her natal Makemake.

For another example of Nature activism, consider the chart of Elon Musk. He has a partile Eris-Chiron conjunction that happens to be in partile trine to Makemake (chart not shown, see chart data on page 19). True to his Nature activist astrological credentials, he is a practicing climate change engineer and extended nature explorer in the sense that he is building electric cars and outer space exploration vehicles.

For yet another example of how these new planets can arise in transit, contemporary to the time of this writing, consider Robin Wright's movie *Land*, released on February 12, 2021, to theaters, and to streaming on March 5th. This highlights an extreme back-to-nature situation of a depressed woman, including the survival techniques necessary to live completely off the grid. This was the project of actor and director Robin Wright, in her directorial debut, and I sought the strong presence of these two Nature planets, particularly Makemake because of this back-to-the-land survival theme. Also, I actually wondered about what was, at the time, a very prominent transiting Makemake at 7 degrees of Libra. In that transiting placement as of late February, through mid-March of that year, Makemake was in partile opposition to Chiron, and partile quincunx to Uranus, all three of them at 7 degrees of their respective signs.

Somewhat to my surprise, when I looked at her chart, she herself had Makemake at 7 Leo, thus partile sextiled, trined, and squared by transiting Makemake, Chiron, and Uranus, all located at 7 degrees in the timing of the film's streaming release. It is not very often that you go looking for a 7-degree placement in a natal chart and then find it (see chart data on page 19). As for her Haumea, it is sesquiquadrate her Aries Sun, bi-quintile Eris, and opposed to her Pisces Venus. Her Makemake is the stronger of the two, being trine Eris and participating in a close sesquiquadrate to her partile triple conjunction of Saturn-Mercury-Chiron, at 23 degrees of Pisces, the same degree of Pisces, incidentally, of the mid-month New Moon of March, 2021, the month when her movie was released to a wider audience.

As far as the explorers of psychedelics, all the ones I looked at had strong presences of these new Nature planets. A good example chart would be that of Ram Dass, born Richard Alpert, who took part in the famous Harvard Psilocybin Project with Timothy Leary, and was fired along with him. He would go on to seek a spiritual meaning for his life with Hindu guru Neem Karoli Baba, in India, returning to the Western World as Ram Dass meaning "servant of god." My thrust here is that these early psychedelic pioneers were explorers and lovers of an extended sense of Nature that was to be found in the other-dimensional worlds that they encountered and popularized.

We have his birth time (see chart). Ram Dass has Haumea strongly located in his first house, in partile trine to Eris, very telling in and of itself, closely conjunct Mars, square Mercury, trine Moon, and semi-sextile Neptune, plus closely contra-parallel his Saturn. This is a powerful placement. As far as Makemake, that too is strong in the chart of Ram Dass, being closely square his MC and quintile his partile Sun-Uranus conjunction in the tenth house. This speaks to his essentially activist agenda, to bring a form of spiritual enlightenment to Western culture.

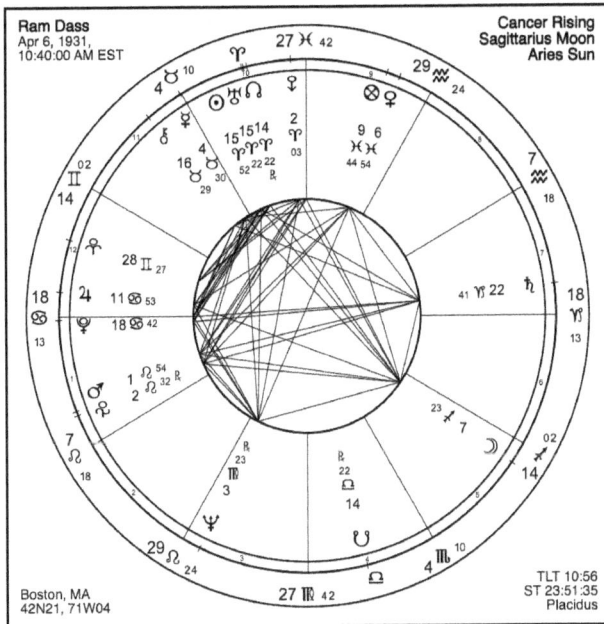

Ram Dass
Apr 6, 1931,
10:40:00 AM EST

Cancer Rising
Sagittarius Moon
Aries Sun

Boston, MA
42N21, 71W04

TLT 10:56
ST 23:51:35
Placidus

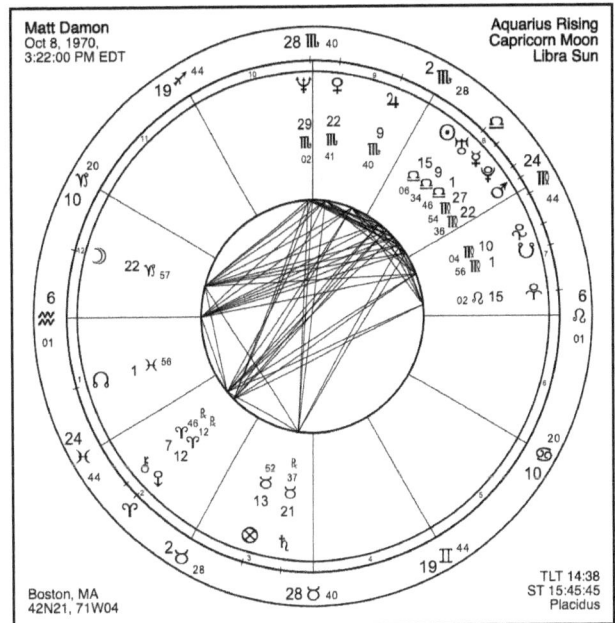

Matt Damon
Oct 8, 1970,
3:22:00 PM EDT

Aquarius Rising
Capricorn Moon
Libra Sun

Boston, MA
42N21, 71W04

TLT 14:38
ST 15:45:45
Placidus

In seeking a somewhat wider set of meanings for these new Nature planets, we must note that Haumea can also symbolize an inherent sense of goodness, of right action and right relationship, and the activism implied by strong Makemake does not have to be environmentally aligned. When I looked at the charts of two well-known actors and filmmakers, **Matt Damon** and **Ben Affleck**, I found the presence of both Haumea and Makemake. I initially sought to confirm Haumea in their charts, because the screenplay for *Good Will Hunting* that they created as unknowns exhibited, as it seemed to me, a sense of goodness of heart, as the very name implies, and as would be indicative of strong Haumea. The quote from one critic is "*Good Will Hunting* is stuffed — indeed, overstuffed — with heart, soul, audacity, and blarney."[5]

I have in general found that movies with almost cliché happy endings, which in fact exhibit a sense of natural goodness inherent in the human condition, were often created by those with strong Haumea, and this, therefore, represents an expanded idea of the qualities of this new planetary archetype.

Matt Damon and Ben Affleck are born two years apart. They were childhood friends, and when Damon wrote the original screenplay for *Good Will Hunting*, he asked Affleck for help in getting it produced. I found that while Damon's chart has quite a strong dose of Haumea, being quintile Venus, sextile Jupiter, semi-sextile Uranus, sesquiquadrate Moon, and quincunx his Chiron-Eris conjunction to within a few minutes of a degree of their midpoint, there was not so much Makemake,

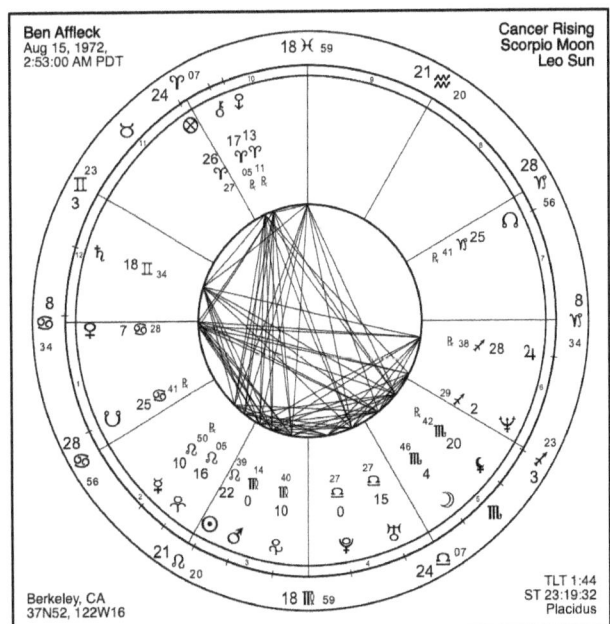

Ben Affleck
Aug 15, 1972,
2:53:00 AM PDT

Cancer Rising
Scorpio Moon
Leo Sun

Berkeley, CA
37N52, 122W16

TLT 1:44
ST 23:19:32
Placidus

5 https://ew.com/article/1997/12/05/good-will-hunting-3/

except for a partile sextile to the Sun (see chart). On the other hand, in Affleck's chart there was not much Haumea but quite a lot of Makemake. This indeed accords with their different roles in the creation of the screenplay, with Damon more the originator.

Ben Affleck's Makemake is widely conjunct his Sun, quincunx his MC , sesquiquadrate Jupiter, sextile Uranus, sextile Saturn, semi-square Pluto and closely trine his Chiron-Eris conjunction. Prior to this research, I had no idea of activism in Ben Affleck's career. I found when I looked him up that he has had a variety of political and philanthropic activism to his credit, although not particularly environmental. The example of these two charts speaks to the wider understanding of the concept of Nature, as symbolized by Makemake and Haumea, in far more general terms, as participating in a sense of innate goodness that is fundamental to the human condition.

It should be mentioned that these example charts are not exceptional. I literally have dozens of others, all concurring with my take on Haumea and Makemake, that of profound connection to Nature, to nature

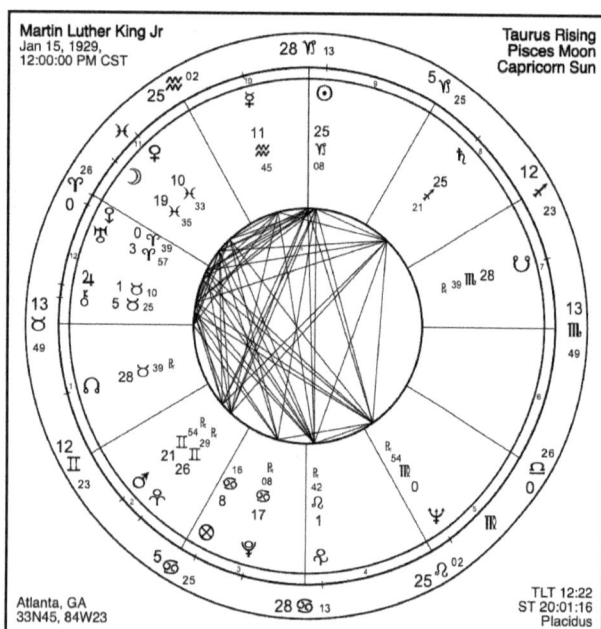

Martin Luther King Jr
Jan 15, 1929,
12:00:00 PM CST

Taurus Rising
Pisces Moon
Capricorn Sun

Atlanta, GA
33N45, 84W23

TLT 12:22
ST 20:01:16
Placidus

as spiritual path and to concepts of natural law, natural goodness, and right action. This applies to both of these new archetypes, with Makemake the more activist of the two.

As another example of a do-the-right-thing activist bent as revealed by the strong presence of both Haumea and Makemake, consider the chart of **Martin Luther King, Jr.** He is obviously known as an activist, extremely so, although not so much as Nature advocate or aficionado. King was obviously a rather busy man in the years of his maturity, from age 25 until his untimely late-sixties death at age 39. He was up to his eyebrows in the struggle for civil rights, of which he is the iconic emblem. On the subject of Nature and natural law, however, there are notable MLK quotes:

> *It really boils down to this: that all life is interrelated. We are all caught in an inescapable network of mutuality, tied into a single garment of destiny. Whatever affects one destiny, affects all indirectly.*
>
> *We must rapidly begin the shift from a 'thing-oriented' society to a 'person-oriented' society. When machines and computers, profit motives and property rights are considered more important than people, the giant triplets of racism, materialism, and militarism are incapable of being conquered.*[6]

The above might remind us of some of the broader considerations of adherence to natural law that we have seen as a significant counterpart to the fondness for and acceptance of Nature that is inherent in the two new indigenous-based archetypes. Indeed, when I examined the chart of MLK, Jr. I was impressed by the strength of both of these new 'nature' archetypes (see chart).

---

[6] https://baynature.org/2013/01/20/was-mlk-an-environmentalist/

MLK's Haumea is in close trine with his Eris, similar to Ram Das, born about two years later. Additionally, Haumea is partile square to Jupiter, square Chiron, trine Uranus, bi-quintile Venus, and bi-quintile Saturn, themselves in wide quintile with each other, and contra-parallel the Sun. Makemake is also strongly placed in MLK's chart, as would be indicated by his activism, being closely opposed to Saturn, closely inconjunct (quincunx) his Sun, septile Chiron, and sesquiquadrate his Mercury within a mere 20 minutes of a degree. Noting that King was the author of multiple books, as well as a gifted speaker, perhaps the most remarkable of his generation, and addressing the painful problem of racism, these close aspects from activist Makemake to Chiron and to articulate Mercury make a great deal of sense for his life. Makemake is also square both Moon and Eris, being square to the Moon/Eris midpoint within less than one and a half degrees.

As a final example of strong Haumea and Makemake, and one that is consistent with the primary characteristics of these new Nature archetypes, including love of nature, strong moral compass, and the activism that I associate more with Makemake, I would like to bring forward the chart of **Robert Redford**. In addition to his being a dynamite actor and box-office heartthrob, as to which some earlier examples given equally attest, Redford has been a strong voice for beneficial social change and for environmental activism. He was an early promoter of the NRDC when it was forming and an advocate for many other liberal causes, not least of which wound up preserving the area of the Provo Canyon in Utah that he saved from housing development in order to create the resort and independent film center that became Sundance.

Born and raised in the Los Angeles region, early on in his life he longed for more natural settings and went to Colorado for school. An early film choice as well was the making of the movie *Jerimiah Johnson*, about a confirmed mountain man who lived on his own in Western nature married a Native American bride. As his film career began to get off the ground, he fell in love with Provo Canyon and built a home there. He followed his initial two-acre purchase with another two thousand, in the early 1970s, taking over and expanding an existing small ski resort and ultimately establishing the Sundance Institute for teaching independent film development. He has in addition always been a truth-teller in his craft as actor and also as director, with an extremely stubborn attitude about telling the story in the way that he wanted it to be told, emphasizing transformative character development, choosing the right thing, and uplifting denouement.

Given his iconic stature as an independent filmmaker, and as an environmentalist, making his own way and damn the torpedoes, I sought the presence of all three of these new archetypes and found a quite interesting configuration (see chart). His Eris is powerfully placed, being near the Ascendant in the first house, trine Mars, and closely contra-parallel Pluto. Eris with Pluto always signals a bulldozer of

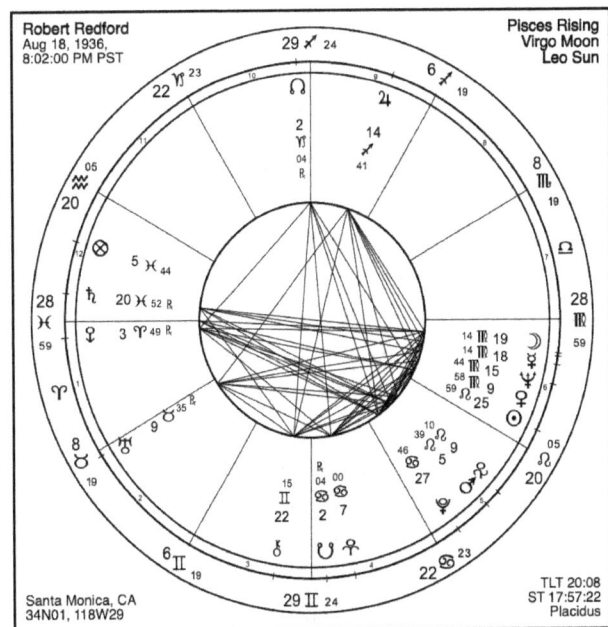

Robert Redford
Aug 18, 1936,
8:02:00 PM PST

Pisces Rising
Virgo Moon
Leo Sun

Santa Monica, CA
34N01, 118W29

TLT 20:08
ST 17:57:22
Placidus

a doer, someone with the reputation of "look out! do not get in his way;" and this is pretty much the way his collaborators and business associates describe him. These two Nature planets are involved in several partile aspects. Haumea, representing his great love of nature, and his carefully honed internal concept of natural law, makes a perfect square to Uranus in the second house, stressing his well-documented unpredictable side, and a partile semi-sextile to Venus, his second house ruler, while Makemake lies in partile semi-sextile to his Mars/Haumea midpoint. Haumea is conjunct Mars within four degrees, parallel Pluto, and closely contra-parallel Jupiter. Uranus being highlighted along with Jupiter in his Haumea configuration brings an aura of brilliant ideas to his love of nature, as he has amply demonstrated. He has been in fact a genius multi-career individual, as actor, director, environmental activist, and founder/leader of the Sundance Institute. Makemake is square Eris, and indicates his activist prominence by being also sextile Venus and Uranus, septile Sun, and closely quintile the Moon and Mercury in their sixth house conjunction.

Robert Redford, therefore, makes another terrific example of how these new planetary archetypes can show up in a chart and shed greater light on the subject's biography and life purpose.

Over and over again, as I believe these example charts amply demonstrate, I have found evidence for these new Kuiper Belt planets, in the same category, now, as Pluto, to be quite as significant in chart work – in quite specific ways – as the Lord of Death and Rebirth. These named KBO planets can be shown to go to depth within the psyche and to point to important contents, as we have seen. As we have come to better and better know Pluto, over the nearly one hundred years since his initial discovery, so too will we come to know these others, and our civilization will be the richer for it.

In closing, let me remark that the astronomers' categories do not entirely match those of our astrological craft. Pluto may be small, and designated a 'dwarf' or a KBO planet, as I prefer the term, but yet is still mighty in interpretative symbolism for us. The same is true, I believe, for these other ones so particularly designated as KBO planets by the astronomical scientists.

Eris as Feminine Warrior in support of soul intention has the implicit message for us of discovering what is deep within, underlying our outer beliefs and values, and proceeding to stand up for these depth principles and for these alone, to the exclusion of conditioning and consensus thought. In this way, we rise to embody the most authentic version of ourselves that we can muster; and just in time, for our culture has need of this activity in all of us. This is indeed an archetype whose time has come for Western and, indeed, for global culture. The era is now upon us of the fully developed and powerful, yet softer and more feminine exemplar of this ideal of right action. As the plentiful evidence from the current zeitgeist indicates, including the March on Washington and the many capable woman leaders now emerging, not to mention the #MeToo and Time's Up movements, these Feminine Warrior leaders are more than ready to arise and begin to effect meaningful change. Earth issues too, and a new merger with Nature, and with the beleaguered natural environment, are key to our very survival in these difficult and transformational twenty-first-century times. That the archetype arises when the culture has need of it is an astrological truism; it is very much the case with Makemake and Haumea as we are coming to understand these symbols. It might also be that the animal and the plant kingdoms and what we know of indigenous cosmology have something to teach us concerning natural law and how to live softly upon the earth. And it seems as though these ambassadors from the farthest yet-discovered reaches of our solar system miraculously have as well.

CHART DATA

- Rodden Rating (AA birth certificate, A memory, C conflicted, B bio, X, unknown)

Greta Thunberg - Jan 3, 2003, CET, Stockholm, Sweden (RR: X, ADB = AstroDataBank)

Ti-Grace Atkinson - Nov 9, 1938, Baton Rouge, LA (RR:X, Wikipedia)

Emmeline Pankhurst - July 14, 1858, 9:30 pm, Manchester, England (RR: DD, ADB)

Albert Einstein - March 14, 1879, 11:30 am, Ulm, Germany (RR: AA, ADB)

Isaac Newton - January 4, 1643, 1:38 am, LMT, Wolsingham, England (RR: C, ADB)

Terence McKenna - November 16, 1946, 7:25 am, Hotchkiss, CO (RR: AA, ADB)

Herman Melville - August 1, 1819, 11:30 pm LMT, New York, NY (RR: ΛA, ADB)

Henry David Thoreau - July 12, 1817, 9:00 pm LMT, Concord, MA (RR: A, ADB)

James Lovelock - July 26, 1919, 2:00 PM GDT, Letchworth, England (RR: B, ADB)

Leonardo DiCaprio - November 11, 1974, 2:47 am, Los Angeles, CA (RR:AA, ADB)

Rachel McAdams - November 17, 1978, 5:20 am, London, Canada (RR: B, Bio **)

David Bowie - Jan 8, 1947, 9:00 am GMT, Brixton, England (RR:A, ADB)

Prince - June 7, 1958, 6:17 pm, Minneapolis, MN (RR: AA, ADB)

C. G. Jung - July 26, 1875, 7:37 pm LMT, Kesswil, Switzerland (RR: C, ADB)

Friedrich von Schelling - Jan 27, 1775, 3:15 am LMT, Leonberg, Germany (RR:AA, ADB)

Edward Abbey - Jan 29, 1927, 10:30 pm, Indiana, PA (RR:AA, ADB)

Julia Butterfly Hill - Feb 18, 1974, Mount Vernon, MO (RR:X, Wikipedia)

Elon Musk - Jun 28, 1971, Pretoria, South Africa (RR:X, ADB)

Robin Wright - April 8, 1966, Dallas, TX (RR: X, Wikipedia)

Ram Dass – April 6, 1931, 10:40 am, Boston, MA (RR: B, ADB)

Matt Damon - October 8, 1970, 3:22 pm, Boston, MA (RR:AA, ADB)

Ben Affleck - August 15, 1972, 2:53 am, Berkeley, CA (RR:AA , ADB)

Martin Luther King Jr. – January 15, 1929, 12:00 pm, Atlanta, GA (RR:A, ADB)

Robert Redford – August 18, 1936, 8:02 PM, Santa Monica, CA (RR:AA, ADB)

** See https://www.astro-theme.com/astrology/Rachel_McAdams

IN SUMMARY

♀ Eris – Feminine Warrior in support of soul intention; taking a determined stand for what you most deeply believe.

Makemake – Profound connection to Nature, involving eco activism or acting out of concern for social welfare.

Haumea – Profound connection to Nature and to natural law; principles right-action and right-relationship; a natural charisma.

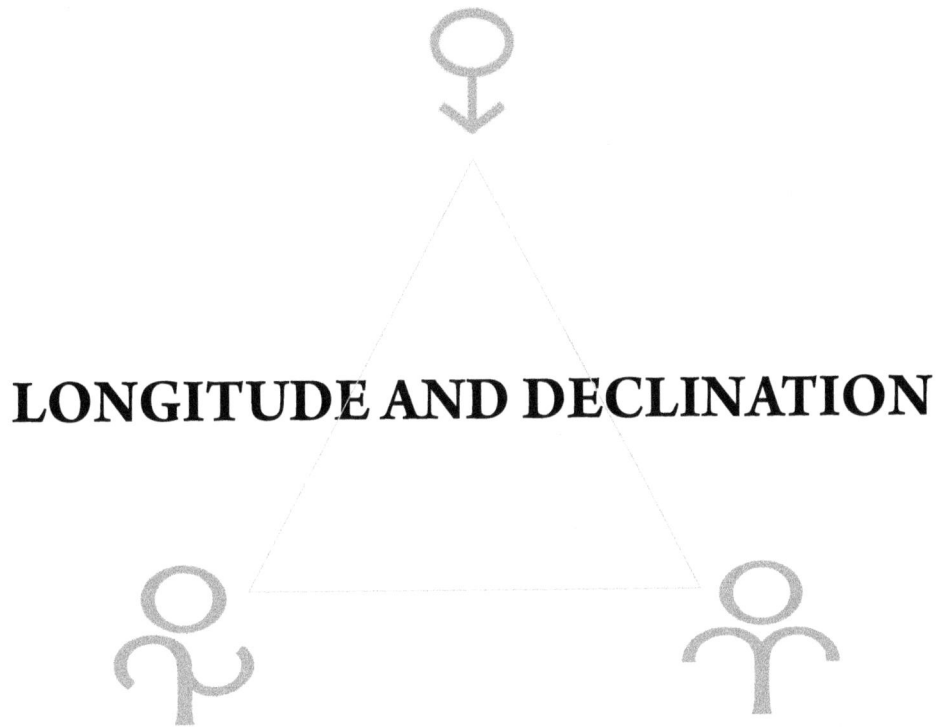

LONGITUDE AND DECLINATION

		[symbol 1]	[symbol 2]	[symbol 3]	[symbol 4]
1899	12/31 Su	15♊16 ℞	21♓34 D	17♉42 ℞	28♊32 ℞
1900	1/07 Su	15♊09	21♓36	17♉37	28♊23
	1/14 Su	15♊02	21♓39	17♉34	28♊14
	1/21 Su	14♊56	21♓43	17♉31	28♊06
	1/28 Su	14♊51	21♓47	17♉30	27♊59
	2/04 Su	14♊47	21♓51	17♉31 D	27♊52
	2/11 Su	14♊44	21♓56	17♉32	27♊47
	2/18 Su	14♊42	22♓01	17♉35	27♊42
	2/25 Su	14♊41	22♓06	17♉40	27♊39
	3/04 Su	14♊41 D	22♓12	17♉45	27♊37
	3/11 Su	14♊43	22♓18	17♉52	27♊37
	3/18 Su	14♊45	22♓23	18♉00	27♊37 D
	3/25 Su	14♊48	22♓29	18♉09	27♊39
	4/01 Su	14♊53	22♓35	18♉18	27♊42
	4/08 Su	14♊58	22♓40	18♉29	27♊46
	4/15 Su	15♊04	22♓45	18♉40	27♊52
	4/22 Su	15♊11	22♓50	18♉51	27♊58
	4/29 Su	15♊19	22♓54	19♉03	28♊06
	5/06 Su	15♊27	22♓58	19♉16	28♊14
	5/13 Su	15♊36	23♓02	19♉28	28♊23
	5/20 Su	15♊45	23♓04	19♉40	28♊33
	5/27 Su	15♊54	23♓07	19♉52	28♊44
	6/03 Su	16♊04	23♓09	20♉04	28♊55
	6/10 Su	16♊14	23♓10	20♉15	29♊06
	6/17 Su	16♊23	23♓10	20♉26	29♊18
	6/24 Su	16♊33	23♓10 ℞	20♉36	29♊29
	7/01 Su	16♊42	23♓10	20♉45	29♊41
	7/08 Su	16♊51	23♓08	20♉53	29♊52
	7/15 Su	17♊00	23♓07	21♉01	0♋03
	7/22 Su	17♊08	23♓04	21♉07	0♋14
	7/29 Su	17♊15	23♓01	21♉12	0♋24
	8/05 Su	17♊21	22♓58	21♉16	0♋33
	8/12 Su	17♊27	22♓54	21♉19	0♋42
	8/19 Su	17♊32	22♓50	21♉20	0♋50
	8/26 Su	17♊36	22♓45	21♉20 ℞	0♋57
	9/02 Su	17♊39	22♓40	21♉19	1♋02
1900	9/09 Su	17♊41 D	22♓36 ℞	21♉17 ℞	1♋07 D
	9/16 Su	17♊41	22♓31	21♉13	1♋11
	9/23 Su	17♊41 ℞	22♓26	21♉09	1♋13
	9/30 Su	17♊40	22♓21	21♉03	1♋14
	10/07 Su	17♊37	22♓16	20♉56	1♋14 ℞
	10/14 Su	17♊34	22♓11	20♉48	1♋12
	10/21 Su	17♊30	22♓07	20♉40	1♋10
	10/28 Su	17♊25	22♓03	20♉31	1♋06
	11/04 Su	17♊19	22♓00	20♉22	1♋01
	11/11 Su	17♊12	21♓57	20♉12	0♋55
	11/18 Su	17♊05	21♓55	20♉03	0♋48
	11/25 Su	16♊57	21♓53	19♉53	0♋40
	12/02 Su	16♊49	21♓52	19♉44	0♋32
	12/09 Su	16♊41	21♓51	19♉35	0♋23
	12/16 Su	16♊33	21♓51 D	19♉27	0♋14
	12/23 Su	16♊25	21♓52	19♉20	0♋05
	12/30 Su	16♊17	21♓54	19♉14	29♊55
1901	1/06 Su	16♊10	21♓56	19♉09	29♊46
	1/13 Su	16♊03	21♓59	19♉05	29♊37
	1/20 Su	15♊57	22♓02	19♉02	29♊29
	1/27 Su	15♊52	22♓06	19♉00	29♊22
	2/03 Su	15♊48	22♓10	19♉00 D	29♊15
	2/10 Su	15♊44	22♓15	19♉01	29♊09
	2/17 Su	15♊42	22♓20	19♉04	29♊04
	2/24 Su	15♊41	22♓25	19♉08	29♊01
	3/03 Su	15♊41 D	22♓31	19♉13	28♊58
	3/10 Su	15♊42	22♓36	19♉19	28♊57
	3/17 Su	15♊43	22♓42	19♉26	28♊57 D
	3/24 Su	15♊46	22♓48	19♉35	28♊58
	3/31 Su	15♊51	22♓53	19♉44	29♊01
	4/07 Su	15♊56	22♓59	19♉54	29♊05
	4/14 Su	16♊01	23♓04	20♉05	29♊10
	4/21 Su	16♊08	23♓09	20♉16	29♊16
	4/28 Su	16♊16	23♓13	20♉28	29♊23
	5/05 Su	16♊24	23♓17	20♉40	29♊31
	5/12 Su	16♊32	23♓21	20♉52	29♊40
	5/19 Su	16♊41	23♓24	21♉04	29♊49

Astro Data

1900

1/29 Mo	13:47	[symbol 3]	SD	17♉30	2.5	(2:28)
2/27 Tu	14:50	[symbol 1]	SD	14♊41	13.0	(13:02)
3/11 Su	08:41	[symbol 4]	SD	27♊37	7.7	(7:41)
6/19 Tu	19:42	[symbol 2]	SR	23♓10	-32.6	(-32:35)
8/23 Th	10:12	[symbol 3]	SR	21♉20	3.8	(3:50)

1900

9/17 Mo	19:23	[symbol 1]	SR	17♊41	13.5	(13:28)
10/02 Tu	10:41	[symbol 4]	SR	1♋14	8.0	(8:02)
12/10 Mo	08:57	[symbol 2]	SD	21♓51	-33.1	(-33:03)

1901

1/31 Th	07:43	[symbol 3]	SD	19♉00	3.5	(3:30)
2/28 Th	18:17	[symbol 1]	SD	15♊41	13.4	(13:22)
3/13 We	00:53	[symbol 4]	SD	28♊57	8.3	(8:15)
5/25 Sa	22:07	[symbol 4]	→ ♋		8.7	(8:44)

LONGITUDE

		♇	♀	⯓	⯔
1901	5/26 Su	16 ♊ 51 D	23 ♓ 26 D	21 ♉ 16 D	0 ♋ 00 D
	6/02 Su	17 ♊ 00	23 ♓ 28	21 ♉ 28	0 ♋ 10
	6/09 Su	17 ♊ 10	23 ♓ 30	21 ♉ 39	0 ♋ 21
	6/16 Su	17 ♊ 20	23 ♓ 30	21 ♉ 50	0 ♋ 33
	6/23 Su	17 ♊ 30	23 ♓ 30 R	22 ♉ 00	0 ♋ 44
	6/30 Su	17 ♊ 39	23 ♓ 30	22 ♉ 10	0 ♋ 56
	7/07 Su	17 ♊ 48	23 ♓ 29	22 ♉ 19	1 ♋ 07
	7/14 Su	17 ♊ 57	23 ♓ 27	22 ♉ 26	1 ♋ 18
	7/21 Su	18 ♊ 05	23 ♓ 25	22 ♉ 33	1 ♋ 29
	7/28 Su	18 ♊ 12	23 ♓ 22	22 ♉ 39	1 ♋ 39
	8/04 Su	18 ♊ 19	23 ♓ 19	22 ♉ 43	1 ♋ 49
	8/11 Su	18 ♊ 25	23 ♓ 15	22 ♉ 46	1 ♋ 58
	8/18 Su	18 ♊ 30	23 ♓ 11	22 ♉ 48	2 ♋ 06
	8/25 Su	18 ♊ 34	23 ♓ 06	22 ♉ 49	2 ♋ 13
	9/01 Su	18 ♊ 38	23 ♓ 02	22 ♉ 48 R	2 ♋ 19
	9/08 Su	18 ♊ 40	22 ♓ 57	22 ♉ 46	2 ♋ 24
	9/15 Su	18 ♊ 41	22 ♓ 52	22 ♉ 43	2 ♋ 28
	9/22 Su	18 ♊ 41 R	22 ♓ 47	22 ♉ 39	2 ♋ 31
	9/29 Su	18 ♊ 40	22 ♓ 42	22 ♉ 34	2 ♋ 32
	10/06 Su	18 ♊ 38	22 ♓ 37	22 ♉ 27	2 ♋ 32 R
	10/13 Su	18 ♊ 35	22 ♓ 32	22 ♉ 20	2 ♋ 31
	10/20 Su	18 ♊ 31	22 ♓ 28	22 ♉ 12	2 ♋ 29
	10/27 Su	18 ♊ 26	22 ♓ 24	22 ♉ 03	2 ♋ 26
	11/03 Su	18 ♊ 20	22 ♓ 21	21 ♉ 54	2 ♋ 21
	11/10 Su	18 ♊ 14	22 ♓ 18	21 ♉ 45	2 ♋ 16
	11/17 Su	18 ♊ 07	22 ♓ 15	21 ♉ 35	2 ♋ 09
	11/24 Su	17 ♊ 59	22 ♓ 13	21 ♉ 25	2 ♋ 02
	12/01 Su	17 ♊ 52	22 ♓ 12	21 ♉ 16	1 ♋ 54
	12/08 Su	17 ♊ 43	22 ♓ 11	21 ♉ 07	1 ♋ 45
	12/15 Su	17 ♊ 35	22 ♓ 12 D	20 ♉ 59	1 ♋ 36
	12/22 Su	17 ♊ 27	22 ♓ 12	20 ♉ 52	1 ♋ 27
	12/29 Su	17 ♊ 19	22 ♓ 14	20 ♉ 45	1 ♋ 17
1902	1/05 Su	17 ♊ 12	22 ♓ 16	20 ♉ 39	1 ♋ 08
	1/12 Su	17 ♊ 05	22 ♓ 18	20 ♉ 35	0 ♋ 59
	1/19 Su	16 ♊ 59	22 ♓ 21	20 ♉ 31	0 ♋ 51
	1/26 Su	16 ♊ 53	22 ♓ 25	20 ♉ 29	0 ♋ 43
	2/02 Su	16 ♊ 49	22 ♓ 29	20 ♉ 29	0 ♋ 36
1902	2/09 Su	16 ♊ 45 R	22 ♓ 34 D	20 ♉ 29 D	0 ♋ 30 R
	2/16 Su	16 ♊ 42	22 ♓ 39	20 ♉ 31	0 ♋ 25
	2/23 Su	16 ♊ 41	22 ♓ 44	20 ♉ 35	0 ♋ 21
	3/02 Su	16 ♊ 40	22 ♓ 50	20 ♉ 39	0 ♋ 18
	3/09 Su	16 ♊ 41 D	22 ♓ 55	20 ♉ 45	0 ♋ 16
	3/16 Su	16 ♊ 42	23 ♓ 01	20 ♉ 52	0 ♋ 16 D
	3/23 Su	16 ♊ 45	23 ♓ 06	21 ♉ 00	0 ♋ 17
	3/30 Su	16 ♊ 49	23 ♓ 12	21 ♉ 09	0 ♋ 19
	4/06 Su	16 ♊ 53	23 ♓ 17	21 ♉ 18	0 ♋ 22
	4/13 Su	16 ♊ 59	23 ♓ 23	21 ♉ 29	0 ♋ 27
	4/20 Su	17 ♊ 06	23 ♓ 28	21 ♉ 40	0 ♋ 32
	4/27 Su	17 ♊ 13	23 ♓ 32	21 ♉ 51	0 ♋ 39
	5/04 Su	17 ♊ 21	23 ♓ 36	22 ♉ 03	0 ♋ 47
	5/11 Su	17 ♊ 29	23 ♓ 40	22 ♉ 15	0 ♋ 55
	5/18 Su	17 ♊ 38	23 ♓ 43	22 ♉ 27	1 ♋ 05
	5/25 Su	17 ♊ 48	23 ♓ 46	22 ♉ 39	1 ♋ 14
	6/01 Su	17 ♊ 57	23 ♓ 48	22 ♉ 51	1 ♋ 25
	6/08 Su	18 ♊ 07	23 ♓ 49	23 ♉ 03	1 ♋ 36
	6/15 Su	18 ♊ 17	23 ♓ 50	23 ♉ 14	1 ♋ 47
	6/22 Su	18 ♊ 26	23 ♓ 50 R	23 ♉ 24	1 ♋ 58
	6/29 Su	18 ♊ 36	23 ♓ 50	23 ♉ 34	2 ♋ 10
	7/06 Su	18 ♊ 45	23 ♓ 49	23 ♉ 43	2 ♋ 21
	7/13 Su	18 ♊ 54	23 ♓ 47	23 ♉ 51	2 ♋ 32
	7/20 Su	19 ♊ 02	23 ♓ 45	23 ♉ 58	2 ♋ 43
	7/27 Su	19 ♊ 10	23 ♓ 42	24 ♉ 04	2 ♋ 53
	8/03 Su	19 ♊ 17	23 ♓ 39	24 ♉ 09	3 ♋ 03
	8/10 Su	19 ♊ 23	23 ♓ 36	24 ♉ 13	3 ♋ 12
	8/17 Su	19 ♊ 29	23 ♓ 32	24 ♉ 15	3 ♋ 20
	8/24 Su	19 ♊ 33	23 ♓ 27	24 ♉ 16	3 ♋ 28
	8/31 Su	19 ♊ 37	23 ♓ 23	24 ♉ 16 R	3 ♋ 34
	9/07 Su	19 ♊ 39	23 ♓ 18	24 ♉ 15	3 ♋ 40
	9/14 Su	19 ♊ 41	23 ♓ 13	24 ♉ 12	3 ♋ 44
	9/21 Su	19 ♊ 41 R	23 ♓ 08	24 ♉ 08	3 ♋ 47
	9/28 Su	19 ♊ 41	23 ♓ 03	24 ♉ 03	3 ♋ 49
	10/05 Su	19 ♊ 39	22 ♓ 58	23 ♉ 57	3 ♋ 50
	10/12 Su	19 ♊ 36	22 ♓ 53	23 ♉ 50	3 ♋ 49 R
	10/19 Su	19 ♊ 33	22 ♓ 49	23 ♉ 43	3 ♋ 47
	10/26 Su	19 ♊ 28	22 ♓ 45	23 ♉ 34	3 ♋ 44
	11/02 Su	19 ♊ 22	22 ♓ 41	23 ♉ 25	3 ♋ 40
	11/09 Su	19 ♊ 16	22 ♓ 38	23 ♉ 16	3 ♋ 35

Astro Data

1901							
	6/20 Th	10:57	♀	SR	23 ♓ 30	-32.3	(-32:17)
	8/25 Su	03:58	⯓	SR	22 ♉ 48	4.8	(4:49)
	9/19 Th	00:36	♇	SR	18 ♊ 41	13.8	(13:49)
	10/04 Fr	00:31	⯔	SR	2 ♋ 32	8.6	(8:36)
	12/10 Tu	21:08	♀	SD	22 ♓ 11	-32.8	(-32:47)
1902							
	2/02 Su	04:01	⯓	SD	20 ♉ 28	4.6	(4:33)
1902							
	3/02 Su	01:05	♇	SD	16 ♊ 40	13.8	(13:45)
	3/14 Fr	15:25	⯔	SD	0 ♋ 16	8.8	(8:48)
	6/21 Sa	04:08	♀	SR	23 ♓ 50	-32.0	(-32:01)
	8/26 Tu	21:51	⯓	SR	24 ♉ 16	5.8	(5:50)
	9/20 Sa	06:48	♇	SR	19 ♊ 41	14.1	(14:08)
	10/05 Su	09:56	⯔	SR	3 ♋ 50	9.1	(9:07)

LONGITUDE

		♇	⯰	⯲	⯳
1902	11/16 Su	19♊09 ℞	22♓36 ℞	23♉06 ℞	3♋29 ℞
	11/23 Su	19♊02	22♓34	22♉57	3♋22
	11/30 Su	18♊54	22♓32	22♉48	3♋14
	12/07 Su	18♊46	22♓32	22♉39	3♋06
	12/14 Su	18♊38	22♓32 D	22♉30	2♋57
	12/21 Su	18♊30	22♓32	22♉22	2♋48
	12/28 Su	18♊22	22♓33	22♉15	2♋39
1903	1/04 Su	18♊14	22♓35	22♉09	2♋29
	1/11 Su	18♊07	22♓38	22♉04	2♋20
	1/18 Su	18♊01	22♓41	22♉01	2♋12
	1/25 Su	17♊55	22♓44	21♉58	2♋04
	2/01 Su	17♊50	22♓48	21♉57	1♋57
	2/08 Su	17♊46	22♓53	21♉57 D	1♋50
	2/15 Su	17♊43	22♓58	21♉58	1♋45
	2/22 Su	17♊41	23♓03	22♉01	1♋40
	3/01 Su	17♊40	23♓08	22♉05	1♋37
	3/08 Su	17♊40 D	23♓14	22♉10	1♋35
	3/15 Su	17♊42	23♓19	22♉17	1♋34
	3/22 Su	17♊44	23♓25	22♉24	1♋34 D
	3/29 Su	17♊47	23♓31	22♉33	1♋36
	4/05 Su	17♊52	23♓36	22♉42	1♋39
	4/12 Su	17♊57	23♓41	22♉52	1♋43
	4/19 Su	18♊03	23♓46	23♉03	1♋48
	4/26 Su	18♊10	23♓51	23♉14	1♋54
	5/03 Su	18♊18	23♓55	23♉26	2♋02
	5/10 Su	18♊26	23♓59	23♉38	2♋10
	5/17 Su	18♊35	24♓02	23♉50	2♋19
	5/24 Su	18♊45	24♓05	24♉02	2♋28
	5/31 Su	18♊54	24♓07	24♉14	2♋38
	6/07 Su	19♊04	24♓09	24♉25	2♋49
	6/14 Su	19♊14	24♓10	24♉37	3♋00
	6/21 Su	19♊23	24♓10	24♉47	3♋11
	6/28 Su	19♊33	24♓10 ℞	24♉57	3♋23
	7/05 Su	19♊42	24♓09	25♉06	3♋34
	7/12 Su	19♊51	24♓07	25♉15	3♋45
	7/19 Su	20♊00	24♓05	25♉22	3♋56
	7/26 Su	20♊08	24♓03	25♉29	4♋06

		♇	⯰	⯲	⯳
1903	8/02 Su	20♊15 D	24♓00 ℞	25♉34 D	4♋16 D
	8/09 Su	20♊22	23♓56	25♉38	4♋25
	8/16 Su	20♊28	23♓52	25♉41	4♋34
	8/23 Su	20♊32	23♓48	25♉42	4♋42
	8/30 Su	20♊36	23♓43	25♉43 ℞	4♋48
	9/06 Su	20♊39	23♓39	25♉42	4♋54
	9/13 Su	20♊41	23♓34	25♉40	4♋59
	9/20 Su	20♊42	23♓29	25♉36	5♋02
	9/27 Su	20♊41 ℞	23♓24	25♉32	5♋05
	10/04 Su	20♊40	23♓19	25♉26	5♋06
	10/11 Su	20♊38	23♓14	25♉20	5♋06 ℞
	10/18 Su	20♊34	23♓10	25♉12	5♋04
	10/25 Su	20♊30	23♓06	25♉04	5♋02
	11/01 Su	20♊25	23♓02	24♉56	4♋58
	11/08 Su	20♊19	22♓59	24♉46	4♋53
	11/15 Su	20♊12	22♓56	24♉37	4♋48
	11/22 Su	20♊05	22♓54	24♉27	4♋41
	11/29 Su	19♊57	22♓53	24♉18	4♋33
	12/06 Su	19♊49	22♓52	24♉09	4♋25
	12/13 Su	19♊41	22♓51 D	24♉00	4♋17
	12/20 Su	19♊33	22♓52	23♉52	4♋08
	12/27 Su	19♊25	22♓53	23♉45	3♋58
1904	1/03 Su	19♊17	22♓55	23♉39	3♋49
	1/10 Su	19♊10	22♓57	23♉33	3♋40
	1/17 Su	19♊03	23♓00	23♉29	3♋32
	1/24 Su	18♊57	23♓03	23♉26	3♋24
	1/31 Su	18♊52	23♓07	23♉24	3♋16
	2/07 Su	18♊48	23♓12	23♉24 D	3♋09
	2/14 Su	18♊44	23♓16	23♉25	3♋04
	2/21 Su	18♊42	23♓22	23♉27	2♋59
	2/28 Su	18♊41	23♓27	23♉31	2♋55
	3/06 Su	18♊40 D	23♓32	23♉35	2♋53
	3/13 Su	18♊41	23♓38	23♉41	2♋51
	3/20 Su	18♊43	23♓44	23♉48	2♋51 D
	3/27 Su	18♊47	23♓49	23♉57	2♋52
	4/03 Su	18♊51	23♓55	24♉05	2♋55
	4/10 Su	18♊56	24♓00	24♉15	2♋58

Astro Data

1902							
12/11 Th	13:28	⯰	SD	22♓31	-32.5	(-32:31)
1903							
2/03 Tu	22:07	⯲	SD	21♉56	5.6	(5:34)
3/03 Tu	07:12	♇	SD	17♊40	14.1	(14:04)
3/16 Mo	08:07	⯳	SD	1♋34	9.4	(9:24)
6/21 Su	16:15	⯰	SR	24♓10	-31.8	(-31:46)
8/28 Fr	11:57	⯲	SR	25♉43	6.8	(6:50)
9/21 Mo	12:39	♇	SR	20♊42	14.5	(14:28)
10/06 Tu	20:31	⯳	SR	5♋06	9.7	(9:40)
12/12 Sa	06:10	⯰	SD	22♓51	-32.2	(-32:15)
1904							
2/05 Fr	16:56	⯲	SD	23♉24	6.6	(6:34)
3/03 Th	13:41	♇	SD	18♊40	14.4	(14:25)
3/16 We	22:41	⯳	SD	2♋51	9.9	(9:56)

1904						1905					
4/17 Su	19 ♊ 02 D	24 ♓ 05 D	24 ♉ 26 D	3 ♋ 03 D		1/01 Su	20 ♊ 20 R	23 ♓ 14 D	25 ♉ 07 R	5 ♋ 08 R
4/24 Su	19 ♊ 08	24 ♓ 10	24 ♉ 37	3 ♋ 09		1/08 Su	20 ♊ 13	23 ♓ 16	25 ♉ 02	4 ♋ 59
5/01 Su	19 ♊ 16	24 ♓ 14	24 ♉ 48	3 ♋ 16		1/15 Su	20 ♊ 06	23 ♓ 19	24 ♉ 57	4 ♋ 51
5/08 Su	19 ♊ 24	24 ♓ 18	25 ♉ 00	3 ♋ 23		1/22 Su	20 ♊ 00	23 ♓ 21	24 ♉ 54	4 ♋ 42
5/15 Su	19 ♊ 33	24 ♓ 21	25 ♉ 12	3 ♋ 32		1/29 Su	19 ♊ 54	23 ♓ 26	24 ♉ 51	4 ♋ 35
5/22 Su	19 ♊ 42	24 ♓ 24	25 ♉ 24	3 ♋ 41		2/05 Su	19 ♊ 50	23 ♓ 30	24 ♉ 50	4 ♋ 28
5/29 Su	19 ♊ 52	24 ♓ 26	25 ♉ 36	3 ♋ 51		2/12 Su	19 ♊ 46	23 ♓ 35	24 ♉ 51 D	4 ♋ 12
6/05 Su	20 ♊ 01	24 ♓ 28	25 ♉ 47	4 ♋ 02		2/19 Su	19 ♊ 43	23 ♓ 40	24 ♉ 53	4 ♋ 16
6/12 Su	20 ♊ 11	24 ♓ 29	25 ♉ 59	4 ♋ 12		2/26 Su	19 ♊ 42	23 ♓ 45	24 ♉ 56	4 ♋ 12
6/19 Su	20 ♊ 21	24 ♓ 30	26 ♉ 09	4 ♋ 23		3/05 Su	19 ♊ 41 D	23 ♓ 51	25 ♉ 00	4 ♋ 09
6/26 Su	20 ♊ 31	24 ♓ 29 R	26 ♉ 20	4 ♋ 35		3/12 Su	19 ♊ 42	23 ♓ 56	25 ♉ 05	4 ♋ 08
7/03 Su	20 ♊ 40	24 ♓ 29	26 ♉ 29	4 ♋ 46		3/19 Su	19 ♊ 43	24 ♓ 02	25 ♉ 12	4 ♋ 07 D
7/10 Su	20 ♊ 49	24 ♓ 27	26 ♉ 38	4 ♋ 57		3/26 Su	19 ♊ 46	24 ♓ 08	25 ♉ 20	4 ♋ 08
7/17 Su	20 ♊ 58	24 ♓ 26	26 ♉ 46	5 ♋ 08		4/02 Su	19 ♊ 50	24 ♓ 13	25 ♉ 28	4 ♋ 10
7/24 Su	21 ♊ 06	24 ♓ 23	26 ♉ 52	5 ♋ 18		4/09 Su	19 ♊ 55	24 ♓ 18	25 ♉ 38	4 ♋ 13
7/31 Su	21 ♊ 14	24 ♓ 20	26 ♉ 58	5 ♋ 28		4/16 Su	20 ♊ 00	24 ♓ 23	25 ♉ 48	4 ♋ 17
8/07 Su	21 ♊ 21	24 ♓ 17	27 ♉ 02	5 ♋ 38		4/23 Su	20 ♊ 07	24 ♓ 28	25 ♉ 58	4 ♋ 23
8/14 Su	21 ♊ 27	24 ♓ 13	27 ♉ 06	5 ♋ 47		4/30 Su	20 ♊ 14	24 ♓ 32	26 ♉ 10	4 ♋ 29
8/21 Su	21 ♊ 32	24 ♓ 09	27 ♉ 08	5 ♋ 55		5/07 Su	20 ♊ 22	24 ♓ 36	26 ♉ 21	4 ♋ 36
8/28 Su	21 ♊ 36	24 ♓ 04	27 ♉ 09	6 ♋ 02		5/14 Su	20 ♊ 31	24 ♓ 40	26 ♉ 33	4 ♋ 45
9/04 Su	21 ♊ 39	23 ♓ 59	27 ♉ 08 R	6 ♋ 08		5/21 Su	20 ♊ 40	24 ♓ 43	26 ♉ 45	4 ♋ 54
9/11 Su	21 ♊ 41	23 ♓ 55	27 ♉ 07	6 ♋ 13		5/28 Su	20 ♊ 49	24 ♓ 45	26 ♉ 57	5 ♋ 03
9/18 Su	21 ♊ 43	23 ♓ 50	27 ♉ 04	6 ♋ 17		6/04 Su	20 ♊ 59	24 ♓ 47	27 ♉ 09	5 ♋ 13
9/25 Su	21 ♊ 43 R	23 ♓ 45	27 ♉ 00	6 ♋ 19		6/11 Su	21 ♊ 09	24 ♓ 48	27 ♉ 20	5 ♋ 24
10/02 Su	21 ♊ 42	23 ♓ 40	26 ♉ 55	6 ♋ 21		6/18 Su	21 ♊ 19	24 ♓ 49	27 ♉ 31	5 ♋ 35
10/09 Su	21 ♊ 40	23 ♓ 35	26 ♉ 48	6 ♋ 21 R		6/25 Su	21 ♊ 29	24 ♓ 49 R	27 ♉ 41	5 ♋ 46
10/16 Su	21 ♊ 36	23 ♓ 31	26 ♉ 41	6 ♋ 20		7/02 Su	21 ♊ 38	24 ♓ 48	27 ♉ 51	5 ♋ 57
10/23 Su	21 ♊ 32	23 ♓ 27	26 ♉ 33	6 ♋ 18		7/09 Su	21 ♊ 47	24 ♓ 47	28 ♉ 00	6 ♋ 08
10/30 Su	21 ♊ 27	23 ♓ 23	26 ♉ 25	6 ♋ 15		7/16 Su	21 ♊ 56	24 ♓ 45	28 ♉ 08	6 ♋ 19
11/06 Su	21 ♊ 22	23 ♓ 19	26 ♉ 16	6 ♋ 11		7/23 Su	22 ♊ 05	24 ♓ 43	28 ♉ 15	6 ♋ 30
11/13 Su	21 ♊ 15	23 ♓ 17	26 ♉ 07	6 ♋ 05		7/30 Su	22 ♊ 13	24 ♓ 40	28 ♉ 21	6 ♋ 40
11/20 Su	21 ♊ 08	23 ♓ 14	25 ♉ 57	5 ♋ 59		8/06 Su	22 ♊ 20	24 ♓ 37	28 ♉ 26	6 ♋ 49
11/27 Su	21 ♊ 00	23 ♓ 13	25 ♉ 48	5 ♋ 52		8/13 Su	22 ♊ 26	24 ♓ 33	28 ♉ 30	6 ♋ 58
12/04 Su	20 ♊ 52	23 ♓ 12	25 ♉ 39	5 ♋ 44		8/20 Su	22 ♊ 31	24 ♓ 29	28 ♉ 32	7 ♋ 06
12/11 Su	20 ♊ 44	23 ♓ 11	25 ♉ 30	5 ♋ 35		8/27 Su	22 ♊ 36	24 ♓ 25	28 ♉ 34	7 ♋ 14
12/18 Su	20 ♊ 36	23 ♓ 12 D	25 ♉ 22	5 ♋ 27		9/03 Su	22 ♊ 40	24 ♓ 20	28 ♉ 34 R	7 ♋ 20
12/25 Su	20 ♊ 28	23 ♓ 13	25 ♉ 14	5 ♋ 17		9/10 Su	22 ♊ 42	24 ♓ 15	28 ♉ 33	7 ♋ 26
						9/17 Su	22 ♊ 44	24 ♓ 10	28 ♉ 30	7 ♋ 30
						9/24 Su	22 ♊ 44 R	24 ♓ 05	28 ♉ 27	7 ♋ 33
						10/01 Su	22 ♊ 43	24 ♓ 01	28 ♉ 22	7 ♋ 35

Astro Data

1904

6/21 Tu	02:13	♀ SR	24 ♓ 30	-31.5	(-31:29)
8/29 Mo	03:40	♇ SR	27 ♉ 08	7.8	(7:49)
9/21 We	10:45	♀ SR	21 ♊ 43	14.8	(14:48)
10/07 Fr	08:02	♇ SR	6 ♋ 21	10.2	(10:11)
12/11 Su	16:50	♀ SD	23 ♓ 11	-32.0	(-31:57)

1905

2/06 Mo	09:31	♇ SD	24 ♉ 50	7.6	(7:36)
3/04 Sa	18:30	♀ SD	19 ♊ 41	14.8	(14:45)
3/18 Sa	10:18	♇ SD	4 ♋ 07	10.5	(10:28)
6/21 We	18:41	♀ SR	24 ♓ 49	-31.2	(-31:12)
8/30 We	19:20	♇ SR	28 ♉ 34	8.8	(8:49)
9/23 Sa	07:12	♀ SR	22 ♊ 44	15.1	(15:07)
10/08 Su	19:12	♇ SR	7 ♋ 36	10.7	(10:41)

		⚷	♀	⚵	⚶
1905	10/08 Su	22 ♊ 42 R	23 ♓ 56 R	28 ♉ 16 R	7 ♋ 36 D
	10/15 Su	22 ♊ 39	23 ♓ 51	28 ♉ 09	7 ♋ 35 R
	10/22 Su	22 ♊ 35	23 ♓ 47	28 ♉ 02	7 ♋ 34
	10/29 Su	22 ♊ 30	23 ♓ 43	27 ♉ 54	7 ♋ 31
	11/05 Su	22 ♊ 25	23 ♓ 40	27 ♉ 45	7 ♋ 27
	11/12 Su	22 ♊ 19	23 ♓ 37	27 ♉ 36	7 ♋ 22
	11/19 Su	22 ♊ 12	23 ♓ 35	27 ♉ 26	7 ♋ 16
	11/26 Su	22 ♊ 04	23 ♓ 33	27 ♉ 17	7 ♋ 09
	12/03 Su	21 ♊ 56	23 ♓ 32	27 ♉ 08	7 ♋ 01
	12/10 Su	21 ♊ 48	23 ♓ 31	26 ♉ 59	6 ♋ 53
	12/17 Su	21 ♊ 40	23 ♓ 31 D	26 ♉ 50	6 ♋ 44
	12/24 Su	21 ♊ 32	23 ♓ 32	26 ♉ 42	6 ♋ 35
	12/31 Su	21 ♊ 24	23 ♓ 33	26 ♉ 35	6 ♋ 26
1906	1/07 Su	21 ♊ 16	23 ♓ 35	26 ♉ 29	6 ♋ 17
	1/14 Su	21 ♊ 09	23 ♓ 38	26 ♉ 24	6 ♋ 09
	1/21 Su	21 ♊ 03	23 ♓ 41	26 ♉ 20	6 ♋ 00
	1/28 Su	20 ♊ 57	23 ♓ 45	26 ♉ 18	5 ♋ 52
	2/04 Su	20 ♊ 52	23 ♓ 49	26 ♉ 16	5 ♋ 45
	2/11 Su	20 ♊ 48	23 ♓ 54	26 ♉ 16 D	5 ♋ 39
	2/18 Su	20 ♊ 45	23 ♓ 59	26 ♉ 17	5 ♋ 33
	2/25 Su	20 ♊ 43	24 ♓ 04	26 ♉ 20	5 ♋ 29
	3/04 Su	20 ♊ 42	24 ♓ 09	26 ♉ 24	5 ♋ 26
	3/11 Su	20 ♊ 42 D	24 ♓ 15	26 ♉ 29	5 ♋ 23
	3/18 Su	20 ♊ 44	24 ♓ 20	26 ♉ 35	5 ♋ 22
	3/25 Su	20 ♊ 46	24 ♓ 26	26 ♉ 42	5 ♋ 23 D
	4/01 Su	20 ♊ 50	24 ♓ 31	26 ♉ 50	5 ♋ 24
	4/08 Su	20 ♊ 54	24 ♓ 37	26 ♉ 59	5 ♋ 27
	4/15 Su	21 ♊ 00	24 ♓ 42	27 ♉ 09	5 ♋ 31
	4/22 Su	21 ♊ 06	24 ♓ 46	27 ♉ 20	5 ♋ 36
	4/29 Su	21 ♊ 13	24 ♓ 51	27 ♉ 31	5 ♋ 42
	5/06 Su	21 ♊ 21	24 ♓ 55	27 ♉ 42	5 ♋ 49
	5/13 Su	21 ♊ 29	24 ♓ 58	27 ♉ 54	5 ♋ 56
	5/20 Su	21 ♊ 38	25 ♓ 02	28 ♉ 05	6 ♋ 05
	5/27 Su	21 ♊ 48	25 ♓ 04	28 ♉ 17	6 ♋ 14
	6/03 Su	21 ♊ 57	25 ♓ 06	28 ♉ 29	6 ♋ 24
	6/10 Su	22 ♊ 07	25 ♓ 07	28 ♉ 40	6 ♋ 35
	6/17 Su	22 ♊ 17	25 ♓ 08	28 ♉ 51	6 ♋ 45
	6/24 Su	22 ♊ 27	25 ♓ 08 R	29 ♉ 02	6 ♋ 56

		⚷	♀	⚵	⚶
1906	7/01 Su	22 ♊ 36 D	25 ♓ 08 R	29 ♉ 12 D	7 ♋ 07 D
	7/08 Su	22 ♊ 46	25 ♓ 07	29 ♉ 21	7 ♋ 18
	7/15 Su	22 ♊ 55	25 ♓ 05	29 ♉ 29	7 ♋ 29
	7/22 Su	23 ♊ 04	25 ♓ 03	29 ♉ 37	7 ♋ 40
	7/29 Su	23 ♊ 12	25 ♓ 00	29 ♉ 43	7 ♋ 50
	8/05 Su	23 ♊ 19	24 ♓ 57	29 ♉ 49	8 ♋ 00
	8/12 Su	23 ♊ 26	24 ♓ 53	29 ♉ 53	8 ♋ 09
	8/19 Su	23 ♊ 31	24 ♓ 49	29 ♉ 56	8 ♋ 17
	8/26 Su	23 ♊ 36	24 ♓ 45	29 ♉ 58	8 ♋ 25
	9/02 Su	23 ♊ 40	24 ♓ 41	29 ♉ 58 R	8 ♋ 32
	9/09 Su	23 ♊ 43	24 ♓ 36	29 ♉ 58	8 ♋ 37
	9/16 Su	23 ♊ 45	24 ♓ 31	29 ♉ 56	8 ♋ 42
	9/23 Su	23 ♊ 46	24 ♓ 26	29 ♉ 52	8 ♋ 46
	9/30 Su	23 ♊ 45 R	24 ♓ 21	29 ♉ 48	8 ♋ 48
	10/07 Su	23 ♊ 44	24 ♓ 16	29 ♉ 43	8 ♋ 49
	10/14 Su	23 ♊ 42	24 ♓ 12	29 ♉ 36	8 ♋ 49 R
	10/21 Su	23 ♊ 38	24 ♓ 07	29 ♉ 29	8 ♋ 48
	10/28 Su	23 ♊ 34	24 ♓ 04	29 ♉ 21	8 ♋ 45
	11/04 Su	23 ♊ 29	24 ♓ 00	29 ♉ 13	8 ♋ 42
	11/11 Su	23 ♊ 22	23 ♓ 57	29 ♉ 04	8 ♋ 37
	11/18 Su	23 ♊ 16	23 ♓ 55	28 ♉ 54	8 ♋ 32
	11/25 Su	23 ♊ 08	23 ♓ 53	28 ♉ 45	8 ♋ 25
	12/02 Su	23 ♊ 01	23 ♓ 51	28 ♉ 36	8 ♋ 18
	12/09 Su	22 ♊ 53	23 ♓ 51	28 ♉ 27	8 ♋ 10
	12/16 Su	22 ♊ 44	23 ♓ 51 D	28 ♉ 18	8 ♋ 01
	12/23 Su	22 ♊ 36	23 ♓ 51	28 ♉ 10	7 ♋ 52
	12/30 Su	22 ♊ 28	23 ♓ 52	28 ♉ 03	7 ♋ 43
1907	1/06 Su	22 ♊ 20	23 ♓ 54	27 ♉ 56	7 ♋ 34
	1/13 Su	22 ♊ 13	23 ♓ 57	27 ♉ 51	7 ♋ 26
	1/20 Su	22 ♊ 06	24 ♓ 00	27 ♉ 47	7 ♋ 17
	1/27 Su	22 ♊ 00	24 ♓ 04	27 ♉ 43	7 ♋ 09
	2/03 Su	21 ♊ 55	24 ♓ 08	27 ♉ 42	7 ♋ 02
	2/10 Su	21 ♊ 51	24 ♓ 12	27 ♉ 41 D	6 ♋ 55
	2/17 Su	21 ♊ 47	24 ♓ 17	27 ♉ 42	6 ♋ 49
	2/24 Su	21 ♊ 45	24 ♓ 21	27 ♉ 44	6 ♋ 45
	3/03 Su	21 ♊ 44	24 ♓ 27	27 ♉ 47	6 ♋ 41
	3/10 Su	21 ♊ 44 D	24 ♓ 33	27 ♉ 51	6 ♋ 38

Astro Data

1905

12/12 Tu	05:17	♀	SD	23 ♓ 31	-31.7	(-31:40)

1906

2/08 Th	00:45	⚶	SD	26 ♉ 16	8.6	(8:35)
3/05 Mo	21:25	⚷	SD	20 ♊ 42	15.1	(15:06)
3/19 Mo	23:47	⚶	SD	5 ♋ 12	11.0	(11:02)
6/22 Fr	10:45	♀	SR	25 ♓ 08	-30.9	(-30:55)

1906

9/01 Sa	11:36	⚶	SR	29 ♉ 58	9.8	(9:47)
9/24 Mo	14:12	⚷	SR	23 ♊ 46	15.4	(15:26)
10/10 We	08:17	⚶	SR	8 ♋ 49	11.2	(11:12)
12/12 We	22:37	♀	SD	23 ♓ 50	-31.4	(-31:25)

1907

2/09 Sa	17:08	⚶	SD	27 ♉ 41	9.6	(9:34)
3/07 Th	04:17	⚷	SD	21 ♊ 44	15.4	(15:26)

	♇	♀	⚷	⚸			♇	♀	⚷	⚸
1907	3/17 Su	21 ♊ 45 D	24 ♓ 38 D	27 ♉ 57 D	6 ♋ 37 R	**1907**	12/22 Su	23 ♊ 41 R	24 ♓ 10 D	29 ♉ 37 R	9 ♋ 08 R
	3/24 Su	21 ♊ 47	24 ♓ 44	28 ♉ 04	6 ♋ 37 D		12/29 Su	23 ♊ 33	24 ♓ 12	29 ♉ 29	9 ♋ 00
	3/31 Su	21 ♊ 50	24 ♓ 49	28 ♉ 12	6 ♋ 38						
	4/07 Su	21 ♊ 54	24 ♓ 55	28 ♉ 20	6 ♋ 40						
	4/14 Su	21 ♊ 59	25 ♓ 00	28 ♉ 30	6 ♋ 43						
	4/21 Su	22 ♊ 05	25 ♓ 05	28 ♉ 40	6 ♋ 48	**1908**	1/05 Su	23 ♊ 25	24 ♓ 13	29 ♉ 23	8 ♋ 51
	4/28 Su	22 ♊ 12	25 ♓ 09	28 ♉ 51	6 ♋ 53		1/12 Su	23 ♊ 17	24 ♓ 16	29 ♉ 17	8 ♋ 42
	5/05 Su	22 ♊ 20	25 ♓ 13	29 ♉ 02	7 ♋ 00		1/19 Su	23 ♊ 10	24 ♓ 19	29 ♉ 12	8 ♋ 33
	5/12 Su	22 ♊ 28	25 ♓ 17	29 ♉ 13	7 ♋ 07		1/26 Su	23 ♊ 04	24 ♓ 22	29 ♉ 08	8 ♋ 25
	5/19 Su	22 ♊ 37	25 ♓ 20	29 ♉ 25	7 ♋ 16		2/02 Su	22 ♊ 59	24 ♓ 26	29 ♉ 06	8 ♋ 17
	5/26 Su	22 ♊ 46	25 ♓ 23	29 ♉ 37	7 ♋ 25		2/09 Su	22 ♊ 54	24 ♓ 30	29 ♉ 05	8 ♋ 10
	6/02 Su	22 ♊ 56	25 ♓ 25	29 ♉ 49	7 ♋ 34		2/16 Su	22 ♊ 50	24 ♓ 35	29 ♉ 05 D	8 ♋ 04
	6/09 Su	23 ♊ 06	25 ♓ 26	0 ♊ 00	7 ♋ 45		2/23 Su	22 ♊ 48	24 ♓ 40	29 ♉ 07	7 ♋ 59
	6/16 Su	23 ♊ 15	25 ♓ 27	0 ♊ 11	7 ♋ 55		3/01 Su	22 ♊ 46	24 ♓ 45	29 ♉ 09	7 ♋ 55
	6/23 Su	23 ♊ 25	25 ♓ 28 R	0 ♊ 22	8 ♋ 06		3/08 Su	22 ♊ 46 D	24 ♓ 51	29 ♉ 13	7 ♋ 52
	6/30 Su	23 ♊ 35	25 ♓ 27	0 ♊ 32	8 ♋ 17		3/15 Su	22 ♊ 46	24 ♓ 56	29 ♉ 19	7 ♋ 51
	7/07 Su	23 ♊ 45	25 ♓ 26	0 ♊ 41	8 ♋ 28		3/22 Su	22 ♊ 48	25 ♓ 02	29 ♉ 25	7 ♋ 50
	7/14 Su	23 ♊ 54	25 ♓ 25	0 ♊ 50	8 ♋ 39		3/29 Su	22 ♊ 51	25 ♓ 07	29 ♉ 32	7 ♋ 50 D
	7/21 Su	24 ♊ 03	25 ♓ 23	0 ♊ 58	8 ♋ 49		4/05 Su	22 ♊ 55	25 ♓ 13	29 ♉ 41	7 ♋ 52
	7/28 Su	24 ♊ 11	25 ♓ 20	1 ♊ 05	9 ♋ 00		4/12 Su	22 ♊ 59	25 ♓ 18	29 ♉ 50	7 ♋ 55
	8/04 Su	24 ♊ 19	25 ♓ 17	1 ♊ 10	9 ♋ 10		4/19 Su	23 ♊ 05	25 ♓ 23	0 ♊ 00	7 ♋ 59
	8/11 Su	24 ♊ 26	25 ♓ 14	1 ♊ 15	9 ♋ 19		4/26 Su	23 ♊ 12	25 ♓ 27	0 ♊ 10	8 ♋ 04
	8/18 Su	24 ♊ 32	25 ♓ 10	1 ♊ 19	9 ♋ 27		5/03 Su	23 ♊ 19	25 ♓ 31	0 ♊ 21	8 ♋ 11
	8/25 Su	24 ♊ 37	25 ♓ 05	1 ♊ 21	9 ♋ 35		5/10 Su	23 ♊ 27	25 ♓ 35	0 ♊ 33	8 ♋ 18
	9/01 Su	24 ♊ 41	25 ♓ 01	1 ♊ 22	9 ♋ 42		5/17 Su	23 ♊ 36	25 ♓ 39	0 ♊ 44	8 ♋ 26
	9/08 Su	24 ♊ 44	24 ♓ 56	1 ♊ 21 R	9 ♋ 48		5/24 Su	23 ♊ 45	25 ♓ 41	0 ♊ 56	8 ♋ 34
	9/15 Su	24 ♊ 47	24 ♓ 51	1 ♊ 20	9 ♋ 53		5/31 Su	23 ♊ 55	25 ♓ 43	1 ♊ 07	8 ♋ 44
	9/22 Su	24 ♊ 48	24 ♓ 46	1 ♊ 17	9 ♋ 57		6/07 Su	24 ♊ 04	25 ♓ 45	1 ♊ 19	8 ♋ 54
	9/29 Su	24 ♊ 48 R	24 ♓ 41	1 ♊ 13	10 ♋ 00		6/14 Su	24 ♊ 14	25 ♓ 46	1 ♊ 30	9 ♋ 04
	10/06 Su	24 ♊ 47	24 ♓ 37	1 ♊ 09	10 ♋ 01		6/21 Su	24 ♊ 24	25 ♓ 47	1 ♊ 41	9 ♋ 15
	10/13 Su	24 ♊ 45	24 ♓ 32	1 ♊ 03	10 ♋ 02 R		6/28 Su	24 ♊ 34	25 ♓ 46 R	1 ♊ 51	9 ♋ 25
	10/20 Su	24 ♊ 42	24 ♓ 28	0 ♊ 56	10 ♋ 01		7/05 Su	24 ♊ 44	25 ♓ 46	2 ♊ 01	9 ♋ 36
	10/27 Su	24 ♊ 37	24 ♓ 24	0 ♊ 48	9 ♋ 59		7/12 Su	24 ♊ 53	25 ♓ 44	2 ♊ 10	9 ♋ 47
	11/03 Su	24 ♊ 32	24 ♓ 20	0 ♊ 40	9 ♋ 56		7/19 Su	25 ♊ 02	25 ♓ 42	2 ♊ 18	9 ♋ 58
	11/10 Su	24 ♊ 27	24 ♓ 17	0 ♊ 31	9 ♋ 52		7/26 Su	25 ♊ 11	25 ♓ 40	2 ♊ 25	10 ♋ 08
	11/17 Su	24 ♊ 20	24 ♓ 14	0 ♊ 22	9 ♋ 46		8/02 Su	25 ♊ 19	25 ♓ 37	2 ♊ 31	10 ♋ 18
	11/24 Su	24 ♊ 13	24 ♓ 12	0 ♊ 12	9 ♋ 40		8/09 Su	25 ♊ 26	25 ♓ 33	2 ♊ 36	10 ♋ 28
	12/01 Su	24 ♊ 05	24 ♓ 11	0 ♊ 03	9 ♋ 33		8/16 Su	25 ♊ 32	25 ♓ 30	2 ♊ 40	10 ♋ 36
	12/08 Su	23 ♊ 57	24 ♓ 10	29 ♉ 54	9 ♋ 25		8/23 Su	25 ♊ 38	25 ♓ 25	2 ♊ 43	10 ♋ 45
	12/15 Su	23 ♊ 49	24 ♓ 10 D	29 ♉ 45	9 ♋ 17		8/30 Su	25 ♊ 42	25 ♓ 21	2 ♊ 44	10 ♋ 52

Astro Data

1907

3/21 Th	11:32	⚸	SD	6 ♋ 37	11.5	(11:32)
6/08 Sa	19:00	⚷	→ ♊		10.5	(10:31)
6/23 Sa	21:29	♀	SR	25 ♓ 28	-30.7	(-30:39)
9/03 Tu	03:58	⚷	SR	1 ♊ 22	10.8	(10:45)
9/25 We	20:53	♇	SR	24 ♊ 48	15.8	(15:46)
10/11 Fr	17:37	⚸	SR	10 ♋ 02	11.7	(11:42)
12/03 Tu	12:30	⚷	→ ♉ R		10.4	(10:26)
12/13 Fr	14:01	♀	SD	24 ♓ 10	-31.1	(-31:08)

1908

2/11 Tu	09:46	⚷	SD	29 ♉ 05	10.6	(10:34)
3/07 Sa	11:13	♇	SD	22 ♊ 46	15.8	(15:46)
3/22 Su	02:19	⚸	SD	7 ♋ 50	12.1	(12:05)
4/19 Su	01:09	⚷	→ ♊		11.1	(11:07)
6/22 Mo	08:27	♀	SR	25 ♓ 47	-30.4	(-30:24)
9/03 Th	17:28	⚷	SR	2 ♊ 44	11.7	(11:41)

LONGITUDE

Year	Date	♇	♀	☂	♔
1908	9/06 Su	25♊46 D	25♓16 ℞	2♊44 ℞	10♋58 D
	9/13 Su	25♊48	25♓11	2♊43	11♋03
	9/20 Su	25♊50	25♓07	2♊41	11♋08
	9/27 Su	25♊50 ℞	25♓02	2♊38	11♋11
	10/04 Su	25♊50	24♓57	2♊33	11♋13
	10/11 Su	25♊48	24♓52	2♊28	11♋14
	10/18 Su	25♊45	24♓48	2♊21	11♋13 ℞
	10/25 Su	25♊41	24♓44	2♊14	11♋12
	11/01 Su	25♊37	24♓40	2♊06	11♋09
	11/08 Su	25♊31	24♓37	1♊57	11♋05
	11/15 Su	25♊25	24♓34	1♊48	11♋00
	11/22 Su	25♊18	24♓32	1♊39	10♋54
	11/29 Su	25♊10	24♓30	1♊30	10♋47
	12/06 Su	25♊02	24♓30	1♊20	10♋40
	12/13 Su	24♊54	24♓29	1♊11	10♋32
	12/20 Su	24♊46	24♓29 D	1♊03	10♋23
	12/27 Su	24♊38	24♓30	0♊55	10♋15
1909	1/03 Su	24♊30	24♓32	0♊48	10♋06
	1/10 Su	24♊22	24♓34	0♊42	9♋57
	1/17 Su	24♊15	24♓37	0♊37	9♋48
	1/24 Su	24♊08	24♓40	0♊33	9♋40
	1/31 Su	24♊02	24♓44	0♊30	9♋32
	2/07 Su	23♊57	24♓48	0♊28	9♋25
	2/14 Su	23♊53	24♓53	0♊28 D	9♋19
	2/21 Su	23♊50	24♓58	0♊29	9♋13
	2/28 Su	23♊49	25♓03	0♊31	9♋09
	3/07 Su	23♊48	25♓09	0♊35	9♋06
	3/14 Su	23♊48 D	25♓14	0♊40	9♋03
	3/21 Su	23♊49	25♓20	0♊45	9♋02
	3/28 Su	23♊52	25♓25	0♊52	9♋02 D
	4/04 Su	23♊55	25♓31	1♊00	9♋04
	4/11 Su	24♊00	25♓36	1♊09	9♋06
	4/18 Su	24♊05	25♓41	1♊19	9♋10
	4/25 Su	24♊12	25♓45	1♊29	9♋15
	5/02 Su	24♊19	25♓50	1♊40	9♋21
	5/09 Su	24♊27	25♓53	1♊51	9♋27
	5/16 Su	24♊35	25♓57	2♊02	9♋35
1909	5/23 Su	24♊44 D	26♓00 D	2♊14 D	9♋43 D
	5/30 Su	24♊54	26♓02	2♊26	9♋52
	6/06 Su	25♊04	26♓04	2♊37	10♋02
	6/13 Su	25♊14	26♓05	2♊48	10♋12
	6/20 Su	25♊24	26♓05	2♊59	10♋23
	6/27 Su	25♊33	26♓05 ℞	3♊10	10♋33
	7/04 Su	25♊43	26♓05	3♊20	10♋44
	7/11 Su	25♊53	26♓04	3♊29	10♋55
	7/18 Su	26♊02	26♓02	3♊37	11♋06
	7/25 Su	26♊11	25♓59	3♊45	11♋16
	8/01 Su	26♊19	25♓57	3♊51	11♋26
	8/08 Su	26♊26	25♓53	3♊56	11♋36
	8/15 Su	26♊33	25♓49	4♊01	11♋45
	8/22 Su	26♊39	25♓45	4♊04	11♋53
	8/29 Su	26♊44	25♓41	4♊06	12♋00
	9/05 Su	26♊48	25♓36	4♊06	12♋07
	9/12 Su	26♊51	25♓32	4♊06 ℞	12♋13
	9/19 Su	26♊52	25♓27	4♊04	12♋17
	9/26 Su	26♊53	25♓22	4♊01	12♋21
	10/03 Su	26♊53 ℞	25♓17	3♊57	12♋23
	10/10 Su	26♊51	25♓12	3♊52	12♋24
	10/17 Su	26♊49	25♓08	3♊46	12♋24 ℞
	10/24 Su	26♊46	25♓04	3♊39	12♋23
	10/31 Su	26♊41	25♓00	3♊31	12♋21
	11/07 Su	26♊36	24♓57	3♊22	12♋17
	11/14 Su	26♊30	24♓54	3♊13	12♋13
	11/21 Su	26♊23	24♓52	3♊04	12♋07
	11/28 Su	26♊15	24♓50	2♊55	12♋01
	12/05 Su	26♊08	24♓49	2♊46	11♋54
	12/12 Su	25♊59	24♓48	2♊37	11♋46
	12/19 Su	25♊51	24♓49 D	2♊28	11♋37
	12/26 Su	25♊43	24♓49	2♊20	11♋29
1910	1/02 Su	25♊35	24♓51	2♊13	11♋20
	1/09 Su	25♊27	24♓53	2♊06	11♋11
	1/16 Su	25♊20	24♓56	2♊01	11♋02
	1/23 Su	25♊13	24♓59	1♊56	10♋54
	1/30 Su	25♊07	25♓02	1♊53	10♋46

Astro Data

Year	Date	Time	Body	Station	Position	Value
1908	9/26 Su	02:04	♇	SR	25♊50	16.1 (16:05)
	10/12 Mo	02:38	♔	SR	11♋14	12.2 (12:10)
	12/13 Su	02:06	♀	SD	24♓29	-30.9 (-30:51)
1909	2/12 Fr	04:43	☂	SD	0♊28	11.5 (11:32)
	3/08 Mo	19:55	♇	SD	23♊48	16.1 (16:07)
	3/23 Tu	15:13	♔	SD	9♋02	12.6 (12:34)
1909	6/22 Tu	22:32	♀	SR	26♓05	-30.1 (-30:07)
	9/05 Su	08:11	☂	SR	4♊06	12.6 (12:38)
	9/27 Mo	10:44	♇	SR	26♊53	16.4 (16:23)
	10/13 We	09:42	♔	SR	12♋24	12.7 (12:39)
	12/13 Mo	11:49	♀	SD	24♓48	-30.6 (-30:35)

1910		♇	♇	♇	♇
	2/06 Su	25♊01 R	25♓07 D	1♊51 R	10♋39 R
	2/13 Su	24♊57	25♓11	1♊50	10♋32
	2/20 Su	24♊54	25♓16	1♊51 D	10♋26
	2/27 Su	24♊52	25♓21	1♊53	10♋22
	3/06 Su	24♊50	25♓27	1♊56	10♋18
	3/13 Su	24♊50 D	25♓32	2♊00	10♋15
	3/20 Su	24♊51	25♓37	2♊05	10♋14
	3/27 Su	24♊53	25♓43	2♊12	10♋14 D
	4/03 Su	24♊57	25♓48	2♊19	10♋15
	4/10 Su	25♊01	25♓54	2♊28	10♋17
	4/17 Su	25♊06	25♓59	2♊37	10♋20
	4/24 Su	25♊12	26♓03	2♊47	10♋24
	5/01 Su	25♊19	26♓08	2♊57	10♋30
	5/08 Su	25♊27	26♓11	3♊08	10♋36
	5/15 Su	25♊35	26♓15	3♊20	10♋43
	5/22 Su	25♊44	26♓18	3♊31	10♋51
	5/29 Su	25♊53	26♓20	3♊43	11♋00
	6/05 Su	26♊03	26♓22	3♊54	11♋10
	6/12 Su	26♊13	26♓24	4♊06	11♋19
	6/19 Su	26♊23	26♓24	4♊17	11♋30
	6/26 Su	26♊33	26♓24 R	4♊27	11♋40
	7/03 Su	26♊43	26♓24	4♊37	11♋51
	7/10 Su	26♊53	26♓23	4♊47	12♋02
	7/17 Su	27♊02	26♓21	4♊55	12♋12
	7/24 Su	27♊11	26♓19	5♊03	12♋23
	7/31 Su	27♊19	26♓16	5♊10	12♋33
	8/07 Su	27♊27	26♓13	5♊16	12♋43
	8/14 Su	27♊34	26♓09	5♊20	12♋52
	8/21 Su	27♊40	26♓05	5♊24	13♋00
	8/28 Su	27♊45	26♓01	5♊26	13♋08
	9/04 Su	27♊50	25♓56	5♊27	13♋15
	9/11 Su	27♊53	25♓52	5♊27 R	13♋21
	9/18 Su	27♊55	25♓47	5♊26	13♋26
	9/25 Su	27♊56	25♓42	5♊23	13♋29
	10/02 Su	27♊56 R	25♓37	5♊20	13♋32
	10/09 Su	27♊55	25♓32	5♊15	13♋34
	10/16 Su	27♊53	25♓28	5♊09	13♋34 R
	10/23 Su	27♊50	25♓24	5♊02	13♋33
	10/30 Su	27♊46	25♓20	4♊55	13♋31
	11/06 Su	27♊41	25♓16	4♊47	13♋28

1910		♇	♇	♇	♇
	11/13 Su	27♊35 R	25♓14 R	4♊38 R	13♋24 R
	11/20 Su	27♊28	25♓11	4♊29	13♋19
	11/27 Su	27♊21	25♓09	4♊20	13♋13
	12/04 Su	27♊13	25♓08	4♊11	13♋06
	12/11 Su	27♊05	25♓07	4♊02	12♋59
	12/18 Su	26♊57	25♓07 D	3♊53	12♋50
	12/25 Su	26♊49	25♓08	3♊45	12♋42
1911	1/01 Su	26♊40	25♓09	3♊37	12♋33
	1/08 Su	26♊32	25♓11	3♊30	12♋24
	1/15 Su	26♊25	25♓14	3♊24	12♋16
	1/22 Su	26♊18	25♓17	3♊20	12♋07
	1/29 Su	26♊12	25♓21	3♊16	11♋59
	2/05 Su	26♊06	25♓25	3♊13	11♋52
	2/12 Su	26♊01	25♓29	3♊12	11♋45
	2/19 Su	25♊58	25♓34	3♊12 D	11♋39
	2/26 Su	25♊55	25♓39	3♊13	11♋34
	3/05 Su	25♊53	25♓44	3♊16	11♋30
	3/12 Su	25♊53 D	25♓50	3♊20	11♋27
	3/19 Su	25♊54	25♓55	3♊25	11♋25
	3/26 Su	25♊55	26♓01	3♊31	11♋24
	4/02 Su	25♊58	26♓06	3♊38	11♋25 D
	4/09 Su	26♊02	26♓11	3♊46	11♋26
	4/16 Su	26♊07	26♓16	3♊55	11♋29
	4/23 Su	26♊13	26♓21	4♊04	11♋33
	4/30 Su	26♊20	26♓25	4♊15	11♋38
	5/07 Su	26♊27	26♓29	4♊25	11♋44
	5/14 Su	26♊35	26♓33	4♊37	11♋51
	5/21 Su	26♊44	26♓36	4♊48	11♋59
	5/28 Su	26♊53	26♓39	4♊59	12♋07
	6/04 Su	27♊03	26♓41	5♊11	12♋16
	6/11 Su	27♊13	26♓42	5♊22	12♋26
	6/18 Su	27♊23	26♓43	5♊33	12♋36
	6/25 Su	27♊33	26♓43 R	5♊44	12♋46
	7/02 Su	27♊43	26♓43	5♊54	12♋57
	7/09 Su	27♊53	26♓42	6♊04	13♋08
	7/16 Su	28♊02	26♓40	6♊13	13♋18
	7/23 Su	28♊11	26♓38	6♊21	13♋29

Astro Data

1910

2/13 Su	10:34	♇	SD	1♊50	12.5 (12:31)
3/10 Th	01:15	♇	SD	24♊50	16.5 (16:27)
3/25 Fr	03:50	♇	SD	10♋14	13.1 (13:03)
6/23 Th	17:09	♇	SR	26♓24	-29.9 (-29:51)
9/06 Tu	18:53	♇	SR	5♊27	13.6 (13:34)
9/28 We	20:28	♇	SR	27♊56	16.7 (16:42)
10/14 Fr	19:05	♇	SR	13♋34	13.1 (13:07)

1910

12/14 We	03:10	♇	SD	25♓07	-30.3 (-30:19)

1911

2/15 We	12:38	♇	SD	3♊12	13.5 (13:27)
3/11 Sa	05:17	♇	SD	25♊53	16.8 (16:46)
3/26 Su	14:09	♇	SD	11♋24	13.6 (13:33)
6/24 Sa	06:28	♇	SR	26♓43	-29.6 (-29:34)

1911 – 1912

		Ψ	♇	♇	♇
1911	7/30 Su	28 Ⅱ 20 D	26 ♓ 36 R	6 Ⅱ 28 D	13 ♋ 39 D
	8/06 Su	28 Ⅱ 28	26 ♓ 32	6 Ⅱ 34	13 ♋ 49
	8/13 Su	28 Ⅱ 35	26 ♓ 29	6 Ⅱ 39	13 ♋ 58
	8/20 Su	28 Ⅱ 42	26 ♓ 25	6 Ⅱ 43	14 ♋ 07
	8/27 Su	28 Ⅱ 47	26 ♓ 21	6 Ⅱ 46	14 ♋ 15
	9/03 Su	28 Ⅱ 52	26 ♓ 16	6 Ⅱ 47	14 ♋ 22
	9/10 Su	28 Ⅱ 55	26 ♓ 12	6 Ⅱ 48 R	14 ♋ 28
	9/17 Su	28 Ⅱ 58	26 ♓ 07	6 Ⅱ 47	14 ♋ 33
	9/24 Su	29 Ⅱ 00	26 ♓ 02	6 Ⅱ 45	14 ♋ 37
	10/01 Su	29 Ⅱ 00 R	25 ♓ 57	6 Ⅱ 42	14 ♋ 40
	10/08 Su	28 Ⅱ 59	25 ♓ 52	6 Ⅱ 37	14 ♋ 42
	10/15 Su	28 Ⅱ 57	25 ♓ 48	6 Ⅱ 32	14 ♋ 43
	10/22 Su	28 Ⅱ 55	25 ♓ 44	6 Ⅱ 25	14 ♋ 43 R
	10/29 Su	28 Ⅱ 51	25 ♓ 40	6 Ⅱ 18	14 ♋ 41
	11/05 Su	28 Ⅱ 46	25 ♓ 36	6 Ⅱ 10	14 ♋ 39
	11/12 Su	28 Ⅱ 40	25 ♓ 33	6 Ⅱ 02	14 ♋ 35
	11/19 Su	28 Ⅱ 34	25 ♓ 31	5 Ⅱ 53	14 ♋ 30
	11/26 Su	28 Ⅱ 27	25 ♓ 29	5 Ⅱ 44	14 ♋ 24
	12/03 Su	28 Ⅱ 19	25 ♓ 27	5 Ⅱ 35	14 ♋ 18
	12/10 Su	28 Ⅱ 11	25 ♓ 27	5 Ⅱ 25	14 ♋ 10
	12/17 Su	28 Ⅱ 03	25 ♓ 26 D	5 Ⅱ 17	14 ♋ 02
	12/24 Su	27 Ⅱ 55	25 ♓ 27	5 Ⅱ 08	13 ♋ 54
	12/31 Su	27 Ⅱ 46	25 ♓ 28	5 Ⅱ 00	13 ♋ 45
1912	1/07 Su	27 Ⅱ 38	25 ♓ 30	4 Ⅱ 53	13 ♋ 37
	1/14 Su	27 Ⅱ 31	25 ♓ 32	4 Ⅱ 47	13 ♋ 28
	1/21 Su	27 Ⅱ 23	25 ♓ 35	4 Ⅱ 42	13 ♋ 19
	1/28 Su	27 Ⅱ 17	25 ♓ 39	4 Ⅱ 38	13 ♋ 11
	2/04 Su	27 Ⅱ 11	25 ♓ 43	4 Ⅱ 35	13 ♋ 03
	2/11 Su	27 Ⅱ 06	25 ♓ 47	4 Ⅱ 33	12 ♋ 56
	2/18 Su	27 Ⅱ 02	25 ♓ 52	4 Ⅱ 33 D	12 ♋ 50
	2/25 Su	26 Ⅱ 59	25 ♓ 57	4 Ⅱ 33	12 ♋ 45
	3/03 Su	26 Ⅱ 57	26 ♓ 02	4 Ⅱ 36	12 ♋ 40
	3/10 Su	26 Ⅱ 56	26 ♓ 07	4 Ⅱ 39	12 ♋ 37
	3/17 Su	26 Ⅱ 57 D	26 ♓ 13	4 Ⅱ 43	12 ♋ 35
	3/24 Su	26 Ⅱ 58	26 ♓ 18	4 Ⅱ 49	12 ♋ 34
	3/31 Su	27 Ⅱ 01	26 ♓ 24	4 Ⅱ 56	12 ♋ 34 D
	4/07 Su	27 Ⅱ 04	26 ♓ 29	5 Ⅱ 03	12 ♋ 35
	4/14 Su	27 Ⅱ 09	26 ♓ 34	5 Ⅱ 12	12 ♋ 37

		Ψ	♇	♇	♇
1912	4/21 Su	27 Ⅱ 14 D	26 ♓ 39 D	5 Ⅱ 21 D	12 ♋ 41 D
	4/28 Su	27 Ⅱ 21	26 ♓ 43	5 Ⅱ 31	12 ♋ 46
	5/05 Su	27 Ⅱ 28	26 ♓ 47	5 Ⅱ 42	12 ♋ 51
	5/12 Su	27 Ⅱ 36	26 ♓ 51	5 Ⅱ 53	12 ♋ 58
	5/19 Su	27 Ⅱ 45	26 ♓ 54	6 Ⅱ 04	13 ♋ 05
	5/26 Su	27 Ⅱ 54	26 ♓ 57	6 Ⅱ 15	13 ♋ 13
	6/02 Su	28 Ⅱ 03	26 ♓ 59	6 Ⅱ 27	13 ♋ 22
	6/09 Su	28 Ⅱ 13	27 ♓ 01	6 Ⅱ 38	13 ♋ 32
	6/16 Su	28 Ⅱ 23	27 ♓ 01	6 Ⅱ 49	13 ♋ 41
	6/23 Su	28 Ⅱ 33	27 ♓ 02	7 Ⅱ 00	13 ♋ 52
	6/30 Su	28 Ⅱ 43	27 ♓ 02 R	7 Ⅱ 10	14 ♋ 02
	7/07 Su	28 Ⅱ 53	27 ♓ 01	7 Ⅱ 20	14 ♋ 13
	7/14 Su	29 Ⅱ 03	26 ♓ 59	7 Ⅱ 29	14 ♋ 23
	7/21 Su	29 Ⅱ 12	26 ♓ 57	7 Ⅱ 38	14 ♋ 34
	7/28 Su	29 Ⅱ 21	26 ♓ 55	7 Ⅱ 45	14 ♋ 44
	8/04 Su	29 Ⅱ 29	26 ♓ 52	7 Ⅱ 52	14 ♋ 54
	8/11 Su	29 Ⅱ 37	26 ♓ 48	7 Ⅱ 57	15 ♋ 03
	8/18 Su	29 Ⅱ 43	26 ♓ 45	8 Ⅱ 01	15 ♋ 12
	8/25 Su	29 Ⅱ 49	26 ♓ 40	8 Ⅱ 05	15 ♋ 20
	9/01 Su	29 Ⅱ 54	26 ♓ 36	8 Ⅱ 07	15 ♋ 28
	9/08 Su	29 Ⅱ 58	26 ♓ 31	8 Ⅱ 07	15 ♋ 34
	9/15 Su	0 ♋ 01	26 ♓ 27	8 Ⅱ 07 R	15 ♋ 40
	9/22 Su	0 ♋ 03	26 ♓ 22	8 Ⅱ 05	15 ♋ 44
	9/29 Su	0 ♋ 04	26 ♓ 17	8 Ⅱ 03	15 ♋ 48
	10/06 Su	0 ♋ 04 R	26 ♓ 12	7 Ⅱ 59	15 ♋ 50
	10/13 Su	0 ♋ 02	26 ♓ 08	7 Ⅱ 54	15 ♋ 51
	10/20 Su	0 ♋ 00	26 ♓ 03	7 Ⅱ 48	15 ♋ 51 R
	10/27 Su	29 Ⅱ 56	25 ♓ 59	7 Ⅱ 41	15 ♋ 50
	11/03 Su	29 Ⅱ 52	25 ♓ 56	7 Ⅱ 33	15 ♋ 48
	11/10 Su	29 Ⅱ 46	25 ♓ 53	7 Ⅱ 25	15 ♋ 44
	11/17 Su	29 Ⅱ 40	25 ♓ 50	7 Ⅱ 16	15 ♋ 40
	11/24 Su	29 Ⅱ 33	25 ♓ 48	7 Ⅱ 07	15 ♋ 34
	12/01 Su	29 Ⅱ 26	25 ♓ 46	6 Ⅱ 58	15 ♋ 28
	12/08 Su	29 Ⅱ 18	25 ♓ 46	6 Ⅱ 49	15 ♋ 21
	12/15 Su	29 Ⅱ 09	25 ♓ 45 D	6 Ⅱ 40	15 ♋ 13
	12/22 Su	29 Ⅱ 01	25 ♓ 46	6 Ⅱ 31	15 ♋ 05
	12/29 Su	28 Ⅱ 53	25 ♓ 47	6 Ⅱ 23	14 ♋ 57

Astro Data

1911

9/08 Fr	09:04	♇	SR	6 Ⅱ 48	14.5 (14:29)
9/30 Sa	04:37	Ψ	SR	29 Ⅱ 00	17.0 (17:01)
10/16 Mo	05:59	♇	SR	14 ♋ 43	13.6 (13:34)
12/14 Th	21:24	♇	SD	25 ♓ 26	-30.1 (-30:03)

1912

2/17 Sa	02:08	♇	SD	4 Ⅱ 32	14.4 (14:23)
3/11 Mo	12:46	Ψ	SD	26 Ⅱ 56	17.1 (17:06)
3/26 Tu	22:02	♇	SD	12 ♋ 34	14.0 (14:01)

1912

6/23 Su	13:32	♇	SR	27 ♓ 02	-29.3 (-29:19)
9/10 Tu	16:27	Ψ	→ ♋		17.4 (17:21)
9/09 Mo	00:35	♇	SR	8 Ⅱ 07	15.4 (15:23)
9/30 Mo	13:09	Ψ	SR	0 ♋ 04	17.3 (17:19)
10/16 We	13:51	♇	SR	15 ♋ 51	14.0 (14:01)
10/20 Su	08:22	♇	→ Ⅱ R		17.3 (17:17)
12/14 Sa	08:11	♇	SD	25 ♓ 45	-29.8 (-29:47)

1913		♇	♀	♅	♆
	1/05 Su	28 II 45 R	25 H 48 D	6 II 16 R	14 S 48 R
	1/12 Su	28 II 37	25 H 51	6 II 09	14 S 39
	1/19 Su	28 II 29	25 H 53	6 II 04	14 S 31
	1/26 Su	28 II 21	25 H 57	5 II 59	14 S 22
	2/02 Su	28 II 16	26 H 01	5 II 56	14 S 15
	2/09 Su	28 II 11	26 H 05	5 II 54	14 S 07
	2/16 Su	28 II 07	26 H 10	5 II 53	14 S 01
	2/23 Su	28 II 03	26 H 14	5 II 53 D	13 S 55
	3/02 Su	28 II 01	26 H 20	5 II 55	13 S 50
	3/09 Su	28 II 00	26 H 25	5 II 58	13 S 47
	3/16 Su	28 II 00 D	26 H 30	6 II 02	13 S 44
	3/23 Su	28 II 01	26 H 36	6 II 07	13 S 43
	3/30 Su	28 II 03	26 H 41	6 II 13	13 S 42 D
	4/06 Su	28 II 06	26 H 47	6 II 20	13 S 43
	4/13 Su	28 II 11	26 H 52	6 II 29	13 S 45
	4/20 Su	28 II 16	26 H 56	6 II 38	13 S 48
	4/27 Su	28 II 22	27 H 01	6 II 47	13 S 52
	5/04 Su	28 II 29	27 H 05	6 II 57	13 S 58
	5/11 Su	28 II 37	27 H 09	7 II 08	14 S 04
	5/18 Su	28 II 45	27 H 12	7 II 19	14 S 11
	5/25 Su	28 II 54	27 H 15	7 II 31	14 S 19
	6/01 Su	29 II 04	27 H 17	7 II 42	14 S 27
	6/08 Su	29 II 14	27 H 19	7 II 53	14 S 37
	6/15 Su	29 II 24	27 H 20	8 II 05	14 S 46
	6/22 Su	29 II 34	27 H 20	8 II 16	14 S 56
	6/29 Su	29 II 44	27 H 20 R	8 II 26	15 S 07
	7/06 Su	29 II 54	27 H 20	8 II 36	15 S 17
	7/13 Su	0 S 04	27 H 18	8 II 45	15 S 28
	7/20 Su	0 S 13	27 H 17	8 II 54	15 S 38
	7/27 Su	0 S 22	27 H 14	9 II 02	15 S 48
	8/03 Su	0 S 31	27 H 11	9 II 08	15 S 58
	8/10 Su	0 S 38	27 H 08	9 II 14	16 S 08
	8/17 Su	0 S 45	27 H 04	9 II 19	16 S 17
	8/24 Su	0 S 52	27 H 00	9 II 23	16 S 25
	8/31 Su	0 S 57	26 H 56	9 II 25	16 S 33
	9/07 Su	1 S 01	26 H 51	9 II 26	16 S 40
	9/14 Su	1 S 05	26 H 46	9 II 26 R	16 S 45
	9/21 Su	1 S 07	26 H 42	9 II 25	16 S 50
	9/28 Su	1 S 08	26 H 37	9 II 23	16 S 54
	10/05 Su	1 S 08 R	26 H 32	9 II 19	16 S 57

1913		♇	♀	♅	♆
	10/12 Su	1 S 07 R	26 H 28 R	9 II 15 R	16 S 58 D
	10/19 Su	1 S 05	26 H 23	9 II 09	16 S 59 R
	10/26 Su	1 S 02	26 H 19	9 II 02	16 S 58
	11/02 Su	0 S 58	26 H 15	8 II 55	16 S 56
	11/09 Su	0 S 52	26 H 12	8 II 47	16 S 53
	11/16 Su	0 S 46	26 H 09	8 II 38	16 S 49
	11/23 Su	0 S 40	26 H 07	8 II 30	16 S 44
	11/30 Su	0 S 32	26 H 06	8 II 20	16 S 38
	12/07 Su	0 S 25	26 H 05	8 II 11	16 S 31
	12/14 Su	0 S 16	26 H 04	8 II 02	16 S 24
	12/21 Su	0 S 08	26 H 04 D	7 II 54	16 S 16
	12/28 Su	0 S 00	26 H 05	7 II 45	16 S 07

1914		♇	♀	♅	♆
	1/04 Su	29 II 51	26 H 07	7 II 38	15 S 59
	1/11 Su	29 II 43	26 H 09	7 II 31	15 S 50
	1/18 Su	29 II 36	26 H 12	7 II 25	15 S 41
	1/25 Su	29 II 29	26 H 15	7 II 20	15 S 33
	2/01 Su	29 II 22	26 H 19	7 II 16	15 S 25
	2/08 Su	29 II 17	26 H 23	7 II 14	15 S 18
	2/15 Su	29 II 12	26 H 27	7 II 12	15 S 11
	2/22 Su	29 II 09	26 H 32	7 II 12 D	15 S 05
	3/01 Su	29 II 06	26 H 37	7 II 13	15 S 00
	3/08 Su	29 II 04	26 H 43	7 II 16	14 S 56
	3/15 Su	29 II 04 D	26 H 48	7 II 19	14 S 53
	3/22 Su	29 II 05	26 H 53	7 II 24	14 S 51
	3/29 Su	29 II 06	26 H 59	7 II 30	14 S 50
	4/05 Su	29 II 09	27 H 04	7 II 37	14 S 51 D
	4/12 Su	29 II 13	27 H 09	7 II 45	14 S 52
	4/19 Su	29 II 18	27 H 14	7 II 53	14 S 55
	4/26 Su	29 II 24	27 H 19	8 II 03	14 S 59
	5/03 Su	29 II 31	27 H 23	8 II 13	15 S 04
	5/10 Su	29 II 39	27 H 27	8 II 23	15 S 09
	5/17 Su	29 II 47	27 H 30	8 II 34	15 S 16
	5/24 Su	29 II 56	27 H 33	8 II 45	15 S 24
	5/31 Su	0 S 05	27 H 35	8 II 57	15 S 32
	6/07 Su	0 S 15	27 H 37	9 II 08	15 S 41
	6/14 Su	0 S 25	27 H 38	9 II 19	15 S 50
	6/21 Su	0 S 35	27 H 39	9 II 30	16 S 00

Astro Data

1913

2/17 Mo	13:42	♎ SD	5 II 53	15.3 (15:20)
3/12 We	20:19	♇ SD	28 II 00	17.4 (17:25)
3/28 Fr	10:21	♌ SD	13 S 42	14.5 (14:27)
6/24 Tu	04:21	♀ SR	27 H 20	-29.1 (-29:03)
7/09 We	22:24	♇ → S		17.7 (17:41)
9/10 We	13:46	♎ SR	9 II 26	16.3 (16:17)
10/01 We	19:26	♇ SR	1 S 08	17.6 (17:37)

1913

10/17 Fr	21:25	♌ SR	16 S 59	14.5 (14:27)
12/14 Su	16:38	♀ SD	26 H 04	-29.5 (-29:30)
12/28 Su	04:19	♇ → II R		17.6 (17:34)

1914

2/19 Th	05:34	♎ SD	7 II 12	16.2 (16:14)
3/14 Sa	05:02	♇ SD	29 II 04	17.7 (17:43)
3/29 Su	22:07	♌ SD	14 S 50	14.9 (14:56)
5/26 Tu	20:43	♇ → S		17.9 (17:56)
6/24 We	22:48	♀ SR	27 H 39	-28.8 (-28:46)

1914		⚳	⚴	⚵	⚶
	6/28 Su	0♋45 D	27♓39 R	9♊41 D	16♋10 D
	7/05 Su	0♋55	27♓38	9♊51	16♋21
	7/12 Su	1♋05	27♓37	10♊01	16♋31
	7/19 Su	1♋15	27♓36	10♊09	16♋42
	7/26 Su	1♋24	27♓33	10♊17	16♋52
	8/02 Su	1♋33	27♓31	10♊25	17♋02
	8/09 Su	1♋41	27♓27	10♊31	17♋12
	8/16 Su	1♋48	27♓24	10♊36	17♋21
	8/23 Su	1♋54	27♓20	10♊40	17♋29
	8/30 Su	2♋00	27♓15	10♊43	17♋37
	9/06 Su	2♋05	27♓11	10♊44	17♋44
	9/13 Su	2♋09	27♓06	10♊45 R	17♋50
	9/20 Su	2♋11	27♓01	10♊44	17♋55
	9/27 Su	2♋13	26♓57	10♊42	18♋00
	10/04 Su	2♋13 R	26♓52	10♊39	18♋03
	10/11 Su	2♋13	26♓47	10♊35	18♋04
	10/18 Su	2♋11	26♓43	10♊30	18♋05
	10/25 Su	2♋08	26♓39	10♊23	18♋05 R
	11/01 Su	2♋04	26♓35	10♊16	18♋03
	11/08 Su	1♋59	26♓32	10♊08	18♋01
	11/15 Su	1♋53	26♓29	10♊00	17♋57
	11/22 Su	1♋47	26♓27	9♊51	17♋52
	11/29 Su	1♋40	26♓25	9♊42	17♋47
	12/06 Su	1♋32	26♓24	9♊33	17♋40
	12/13 Su	1♋24	26♓23	9♊24	17♋33
	12/20 Su	1♋16	26♓23 D	9♊15	17♋25
	12/27 Su	1♋07	26♓24	9♊07	17♋17
1915	1/03 Su	0♋59	26♓25	8♊59	17♋08
	1/10 Su	0♋51	26♓27	8♊52	17♋00
	1/17 Su	0♋43	26♓30	8♊46	16♋51
	1/24 Su	0♋36	26♓33	8♊41	16♋43
	1/31 Su	0♋29	26♓37	8♊37	16♋35
	2/07 Su	0♋23	26♓41	8♊34	16♋27
	2/14 Su	0♋18	26♓45	8♊32	16♋20
	2/21 Su	0♋14	26♓50	8♊31 D	16♋14
	2/28 Su	0♋11	26♓55	8♊32	16♋09
	3/07 Su	0♋09	27♓00	8♊34	16♋04

1915		⚳	⚴	⚵	⚶
	3/14 Su	0♋09 R	27♓05 D	8♊37 D	16♋01 R
	3/21 Su	0♋09 D	27♓11	8♊41	15♋59
	3/28 Su	0♋10	27♓16	8♊46	15♋58
	4/04 Su	0♋13	27♓22	8♊53	15♋58 D
	4/11 Su	0♋17	27♓27	9♊00	15♋59
	4/18 Su	0♋21	27♓32	9♊09	16♋01
	4/25 Su	0♋27	27♓36	9♊18	16♋04
	5/02 Su	0♋33	27♓41	9♊28	16♋09
	5/09 Su	0♋41	27♓45	9♊38	16♋14
	5/16 Su	0♋49	27♓48	9♊49	16♋21
	5/23 Su	0♋58	27♓51	10♊00	16♋28
	5/30 Su	1♋07	27♓53	10♊11	16♋36
	6/06 Su	1♋16	27♓55	10♊22	16♋45
	6/13 Su	1♋26	27♓57	10♊34	16♋54
	6/20 Su	1♋36	27♓57	10♊45	17♋04
	6/27 Su	1♋47	27♓58 R	10♊55	17♋14
	7/04 Su	1♋57	27♓57	11♊06	17♋24
	7/11 Su	2♋07	27♓56	11♊15	17♋34
	7/18 Su	2♋17	27♓55	11♊24	17♋45
	7/25 Su	2♋26	27♓52	11♊33	17♋55
	8/01 Su	2♋35	27♓50	11♊40	18♋05
	8/08 Su	2♋43	27♓47	11♊47	18♋15
	8/15 Su	2♋51	27♓43	11♊52	18♋24
	8/22 Su	2♋58	27♓39	11♊56	18♋33
	8/29 Su	3♋04	27♓35	12♊00	18♋41
	9/05 Su	3♋09	27♓31	12♊02	18♋48
	9/12 Su	3♋13	27♓26	12♊03	18♋54
	9/19 Su	3♋16	27♓21	12♊02 R	19♋00
	9/26 Su	3♋18	27♓16	12♊01	19♋04
	10/03 Su	3♋19	27♓12	11♊58	19♋08
	10/10 Su	3♋18 R	27♓07	11♊54	19♋10
	10/17 Su	3♋17	27♓02	11♊49	19♋11
	10/24 Su	3♋14	26♓58	11♊44	19♋11 R
	10/31 Su	3♋11	26♓55	11♊37	19♋10
	11/07 Su	3♋06	26♓51	11♊29	19♋08
	11/14 Su	3♋01	26♓48	11♊21	19♋04
	11/21 Su	2♋55	26♓46	11♊13	19♋00
	11/28 Su	2♋48	26♓44	11♊04	18♋55
	12/05 Su	2♋40	26♓43	10♊55	18♋48
	12/12 Su	2♋32	26♓42	10♊46	18♋41

Astro Data

1914

9/12 Sa	04:10	⚵	SR	10♊45	17.2 (17:10)
10/03 Sa	03:15	⚳	SR	2♋13	17.9 (17:55)
10/19 Mo	03:19	⚶	SR	18♋05	14.9 (14:52)
12/15 Tu	07:21	⚴	SD	26♓23	-29.2 (-29:13)

1915

2/20 Sa	20:24	⚵	SD	8♊31	17.1 (17:08)

1915

3/15 Mo	12:31	⚳	SD	0♋08	18.1 (18:03)
3/31 We	09:34	⚶	SD	15♋57	15.4 (15:22)
6/25 Fr	13:36	⚴	SR	27♓58	-28.5 (-28:30)
9/13 Mo	15:09	⚵	SR	12♊03	18.0 (18:02)
10/04 Mo	14:44	⚳	SR	3♋19	18.2 (18:12)
10/20 We	09:58	⚶	SR	19♋11	15.3 (15:18)
12/16 Th	01:20	⚴	SD	26♓42	-29.0 (-28:58)

1915		♇	♀	⚷	♇
	12/19 Su	2♋24 ℞	26♓42 D	10♊37 ℞	18♋34 ℞
	12/26 Su	2♋15	26♓42	10♊28	18♋26
1916	1/02 Su	2♋07	26♓44	10♊20	18♋17
	1/09 Su	1♋59	26♓45	10♊13	18♋09
	1/16 Su	1♋51	26♓48	10♊06	18♋00
	1/23 Su	1♋43	26♓51	10♊01	17♋52
	1/30 Su	1♋36	26♓54	9♊56	17♋44
	2/06 Su	1♋30	26♓58	9♊53	17♋36
	2/13 Su	1♋25	27♓03	9♊51	17♋29
	2/20 Su	1♋21	27♓07	9♊49	17♋22
	2/27 Su	1♋17	27♓12	9♊50 D	17♋17
	3/05 Su	1♋15	27♓17	9♊51	17♋12
	3/12 Su	1♋14	27♓23	9♊54	17♋08
	3/19 Su	1♋14 D	27♓28	9♊58	17♋06
	3/26 Su	1♋15	27♓34	10♊03	17♋04
	4/02 Su	1♋17	27♓39	10♊09	17♋04 D
	4/09 Su	1♋20	27♓44	10♊16	17♋05
	4/16 Su	1♋25	27♓49	10♊24	17♋07
	4/23 Su	1♋30	27♓54	10♊33	17♋10
	4/30 Su	1♋36	27♓58	10♊42	17♋14
	5/07 Su	1♋43	28♓02	10♊52	17♋19
	5/14 Su	1♋51	28♓06	11♊03	17♋25
	5/21 Su	2♋00	28♓09	11♊14	17♋32
	5/28 Su	2♋09	28♓11	11♊25	17♋40
	6/04 Su	2♋19	28♓13	11♊36	17♋48
	6/11 Su	2♋28	28♓15	11♊47	17♋57
	6/18 Su	2♋39	28♓16	11♊58	18♋06
	6/25 Su	2♋49	28♓16 ℞	12♊09	18♋16
	7/02 Su	2♋59	28♓16	12♊19	18♋26
	7/09 Su	3♋09	28♓15	12♊29	18♋37
	7/16 Su	3♋19	28♓13	12♊39	18♋47
	7/23 Su	3♋29	28♓11	12♊47	18♋57
	7/30 Su	3♋38	28♓09	12♊55	19♋07
	8/06 Su	3♋46	28♓06	13♊02	19♋17
	8/13 Su	3♋54	28♓02	13♊08	19♋27
	8/20 Su	4♋01	27♓59	13♊12	19♋35
	8/27 Su	4♋08	27♓54	13♊16	19♋44

1916		♇	♀	⚷	♇
	9/03 Su	4♋13 D	27♓50 ℞	13♊19 D	19♋51 D
	9/10 Su	4♋18	27♓45	13♊20	19♋58
	9/17 Su	4♋21	27♓41	13♊20 ℞	20♋03
	9/24 Su	4♋23	27♓36	13♊19	20♋08
	10/01 Su	4♋25	27♓31	13♊17	20♋12
	10/08 Su	4♋25 ℞	27♓26	13♊13	20♋15
	10/15 Su	4♋24	27♓22	13♊09	20♋16
	10/22 Su	4♋21	27♓18	13♊03	20♋17 ℞
	10/29 Su	4♋18	27♓14	12♊57	20♋16
	11/05 Su	4♋14	27♓10	12♊50	20♋14
	11/12 Su	4♋09	27♓07	12♊42	20♋11
	11/19 Su	4♋03	27♓05	12♊33	20♋07
	11/26 Su	3♋56	27♓03	12♊25	20♋02
	12/03 Su	3♋49	27♓01	12♊16	19♋56
	12/10 Su	3♋41	27♓01	12♊07	19♋49
	12/17 Su	3♋32	27♓00 D	11♊58	19♋42
	12/24 Su	3♋24	27♓01	11♊49	19♋34
	12/31 Su	3♋16	27♓02	11♊41	19♋26
1917	1/07 Su	3♋07	27♓04	11♊33	19♋17
	1/14 Su	2♋59	27♓06	11♊26	19♋09
	1/21 Su	2♋51	27♓09	11♊21	19♋00
	1/28 Su	2♋44	27♓12	11♊16	18♋52
	2/04 Su	2♋38	27♓16	11♊12	18♋44
	2/11 Su	2♋32	27♓20	11♊09	18♋37
	2/18 Su	2♋28	27♓25	11♊08	18♋30
	2/25 Su	2♋24	27♓30	11♊07 D	18♋24
	3/04 Su	2♋21	27♓35	11♊08	18♋19
	3/11 Su	2♋20	27♓40	11♊10	18♋15
	3/18 Su	2♋19 D	27♓45	11♊14	18♋12
	3/25 Su	2♋20	27♓51	11♊18	18♋11
	4/01 Su	2♋22	27♓56	11♊24	18♋10
	4/08 Su	2♋25	28♓01	11♊31	18♋10 D
	4/15 Su	2♋29	28♓06	11♊38	18♋12
	4/22 Su	2♋34	28♓11	11♊47	18♋14
	4/29 Su	2♋40	28♓16	11♊56	18♋18
	5/06 Su	2♋47	28♓20	12♊06	18♋23
	5/13 Su	2♋55	28♓23	12♊16	18♋29
	5/20 Su	3♋03	28♓26	12♊27	18♋35

Astro Data

1916

2/21 Tu	12:36	⚷	SD	9♊49	18.0 (18:02)
3/15 We	16:59	♇	SD	1♋14	18.4 (18:21)
3/31 Fr	19:37	♇	SD	17♋04	15.8 (15:47)
6/24 Sa	21:10	♀	SR	28♓16	-28.2 (-28:13)

1916

9/14 Th	03:13	⚷	SR	13♊20	18.9 (18:53)
10/05 Th	01:22	♇	SR	4♋25	18.5 (18:29)
10/20 Fr	19:43	♇	SR	20♋17	15.7 (15:41)
12/15 Fr	16:05	♀	SD	27♓00	-28.7 (-28:42)

1917

2/23 Fr	02:09	⚷	SD	11♊07	18.9 (18:54)
3/16 Fr	23:11	♇	SD	2♋19	18.7 (18:39)
4/02 Mo	02:21	♇	SD	18♋10	16.2 (16:13)

		♇	♇	♇	♇				♇	♇	♇	♇
1917	5/27 Su	3 ♋ 12 D	28 ♓ 29 D	12 Ⅱ 38 D	18 ♋ 43 D	1918	2/10 Su	3 ♋ 40 ℞	27 ♓ 38 D	12 Ⅱ 27 ℞	19 ♋ 44 ℞
	6/03 Su	3 ♋ 21	28 ♓ 31	12 Ⅱ 49	18 ♋ 51		2/17 Su	3 ♋ 35	27 ♓ 42	12 Ⅱ 25	19 ♋ 38
	6/10 Su	3 ♋ 31	28 ♓ 33	13 Ⅱ 00	18 ♋ 59		2/24 Su	3 ♋ 31	27 ♓ 47	12 Ⅱ 24	19 ♋ 31
	6/17 Su	3 ♋ 41	28 ♓ 34	13 Ⅱ 11	19 ♋ 09		3/03 Su	3 ♋ 28	27 ♓ 52	12 Ⅱ 25 D	19 ♋ 26
	6/24 Su	3 ♋ 52	28 ♓ 34	13 Ⅱ 22	19 ♋ 18		3/10 Su	3 ♋ 26	27 ♓ 57	12 Ⅱ 27	19 ♋ 22
	7/01 Su	4 ♋ 02	28 ♓ 34 ℞	13 Ⅱ 33	19 ♋ 28		3/17 Su	3 ♋ 26	28 ♓ 02	12 Ⅱ 30	19 ♋ 19
	7/08 Su	4 ♋ 12	28 ♓ 33	13 Ⅱ 43	19 ♋ 39		3/24 Su	3 ♋ 26 D	28 ♓ 08	12 Ⅱ 34	19 ♋ 16
	7/15 Su	4 ♋ 21	28 ♓ 32	13 Ⅱ 52	19 ♋ 49		3/31 Su	3 ♋ 27	28 ♓ 13	12 Ⅱ 39	19 ♋ 15
	7/22 Su	4 ♋ 32	28 ♓ 30	14 Ⅱ 01	19 ♋ 59		4/07 Su	3 ♋ 30	28 ♓ 18	12 Ⅱ 45	19 ♋ 15 D
	7/29 Su	4 ♋ 41	28 ♓ 28	14 Ⅱ 09	20 ♋ 09		4/14 Su	3 ♋ 34	28 ♓ 23	12 Ⅱ 53	19 ♋ 16
	8/05 Su	4 ♋ 50	28 ♓ 25	14 Ⅱ 16	20 ♋ 19		4/21 Su	3 ♋ 39	28 ♓ 28	13 Ⅱ 01	19 ♋ 19
	8/12 Su	4 ♋ 58	28 ♓ 21	14 Ⅱ 23	20 ♋ 29		4/28 Su	3 ♋ 44	28 ♓ 33	13 Ⅱ 10	19 ♋ 22
	8/19 Su	5 ♋ 06	28 ♓ 18	14 Ⅱ 28	20 ♋ 38		5/05 Su	3 ♋ 51	28 ♓ 37	13 Ⅱ 19	19 ♋ 26
	8/26 Su	5 ♋ 12	28 ♓ 14	14 Ⅱ 32	20 ♋ 46		5/12 Su	3 ♋ 58	28 ♓ 41	13 Ⅱ 29	19 ♋ 32
	9/02 Su	5 ♋ 18	28 ♓ 09	14 Ⅱ 35	20 ♋ 54		5/19 Su	4 ♋ 06	28 ♓ 44	13 Ⅱ 40	19 ♋ 38
	9/09 Su	5 ♋ 23	28 ♓ 05	14 Ⅱ 36	21 ♋ 00		5/26 Su	4 ♋ 15	28 ♓ 47	13 Ⅱ 51	19 ♋ 45
	9/16 Su	5 ♋ 27	28 ♓ 00	14 Ⅱ 37 ℞	21 ♋ 07		6/02 Su	4 ♋ 25	28 ♓ 49	14 Ⅱ 02	19 ♋ 53
	9/23 Su	5 ♋ 29	27 ♓ 55	14 Ⅱ 36	21 ♋ 12		6/09 Su	4 ♋ 34	28 ♓ 51	14 Ⅱ 13	20 ♋ 01
	9/30 Su	5 ♋ 31	27 ♓ 51	14 Ⅱ 34	21 ♋ 16		6/16 Su	4 ♋ 44	28 ♓ 52	14 Ⅱ 24	20 ♋ 10
	10/07 Su	5 ♋ 31 ℞	27 ♓ 46	14 Ⅱ 31	21 ♋ 19		6/23 Su	4 ♋ 55	28 ♓ 52	14 Ⅱ 35	20 ♋ 20
	10/14 Su	5 ♋ 31	27 ♓ 41	14 Ⅱ 27	21 ♋ 21		6/30 Su	5 ♋ 05	28 ♓ 52 ℞	14 Ⅱ 46	20 ♋ 30
	10/21 Su	5 ♋ 29	27 ♓ 37	14 Ⅱ 22	21 ♋ 21		7/07 Su	5 ♋ 15	28 ♓ 52	14 Ⅱ 56	20 ♋ 40
	10/28 Su	5 ♋ 26	27 ♓ 33	14 Ⅱ 16	21 ♋ 21 ℞		7/14 Su	5 ♋ 26	28 ♓ 50	15 Ⅱ 05	20 ♋ 50
	11/04 Su	5 ♋ 22	27 ♓ 30	14 Ⅱ 09	21 ♋ 19		7/21 Su	5 ♋ 35	28 ♓ 49	15 Ⅱ 15	21 ♋ 00
	11/11 Su	5 ♋ 17	27 ♓ 26	14 Ⅱ 02	21 ♋ 17		7/28 Su	5 ♋ 45	28 ♓ 46	15 Ⅱ 23	21 ♋ 10
	11/18 Su	5 ♋ 11	27 ♓ 24	13 Ⅱ 53	21 ♋ 13		8/04 Su	5 ♋ 54	28 ♓ 44	15 Ⅱ 30	21 ♋ 20
	11/25 Su	5 ♋ 05	27 ♓ 22	13 Ⅱ 45	21 ♋ 08		8/11 Su	6 ♋ 02	28 ♓ 40	15 Ⅱ 37	21 ♋ 30
	12/02 Su	4 ♋ 58	27 ♓ 20	13 Ⅱ 36	21 ♋ 03		8/18 Su	6 ♋ 10	28 ♓ 37	15 Ⅱ 42	21 ♋ 39
	12/09 Su	4 ♋ 50	27 ♓ 19	13 Ⅱ 27	20 ♋ 56		8/25 Su	6 ♋ 17	28 ♓ 33	15 Ⅱ 47	21 ♋ 48
	12/16 Su	4 ♋ 42	27 ♓ 19 D	13 Ⅱ 18	20 ♋ 49		9/01 Su	6 ♋ 23	28 ♓ 28	15 Ⅱ 50	21 ♋ 55
	12/23 Su	4 ♋ 33	27 ♓ 19	13 Ⅱ 09	20 ♋ 42		9/08 Su	6 ♋ 28	28 ♓ 24	15 Ⅱ 52	22 ♋ 03
	12/30 Su	4 ♋ 25	27 ♓ 20	13 Ⅱ 01	20 ♋ 33		9/15 Su	6 ♋ 33	28 ♓ 19	15 Ⅱ 53	22 ♋ 09
							9/22 Su	6 ♋ 36	28 ♓ 14	15 Ⅱ 53 ℞	22 ♋ 14
							9/29 Su	6 ♋ 38	28 ♓ 10	15 Ⅱ 52	22 ♋ 19
							10/06 Su	6 ♋ 39	28 ♓ 05	15 Ⅱ 49	22 ♋ 22
1918	1/06 Su	4 ♋ 16	27 ♓ 22	12 Ⅱ 53	20 ♋ 25		10/13 Su	6 ♋ 38 ℞	28 ♓ 00	15 Ⅱ 45	22 ♋ 24
	1/13 Su	4 ♋ 08	27 ♓ 24	12 Ⅱ 46	20 ♋ 17		10/20 Su	6 ♋ 37	27 ♓ 56	15 Ⅱ 40	22 ♋ 25
	1/20 Su	4 ♋ 00	27 ♓ 26	12 Ⅱ 40	20 ♋ 08		10/27 Su	6 ♋ 34	27 ♓ 52	15 Ⅱ 35	22 ♋ 25 ℞
	1/27 Su	3 ♋ 53	27 ♓ 30	12 Ⅱ 34	20 ♋ 00		11/03 Su	6 ♋ 31	27 ♓ 48	15 Ⅱ 28	22 ♋ 24
	2/03 Su	3 ♋ 46	27 ♓ 33	12 Ⅱ 30	19 ♋ 52		11/10 Su	6 ♋ 26	27 ♓ 45	15 Ⅱ 21	22 ♋ 22

Astro Data

1917

6/25 Mo	07:21	♀	SR	28 ♓ 34	-28.0 (-27:59)
9/15 Sa	14:58	♇	SR	14 Ⅱ 37	19.7 (19:44)
10/06 Sa	12:13	♇	SR	5 ♋ 31	18.8 (18:46)
10/22 Mo	04:16	♇	SR	21 ♋ 21	16.1 (16:05)
12/15 Sa	23:47	♀	SD	27 ♓ 19	-28.5 (-28:27)

1918

2/24 Su	14:33	♇	SD	12 Ⅱ 24	19.8 (19:47)
3/18 Mo	06:18	♇	SD	3 ♋ 26	19.0 (18:58)
4/03 We	10:29	♇	SD	19 ♋ 15	16.6 (16:37)
6/26 We	01:44	♀	SR	28 ♓ 52	-27.7 (-27:43)
9/17 Tu	04:31	♇	SR	15 Ⅱ 53	20.6 (20:34)
10/07 Mo	19:12	♇	SR	6 ♋ 39	19.0 (19:02)
10/23 We	12:34	♇	SR	22 ♋ 25	16.5 (16:28)

		♇	♀	♇	♇
1918	11/17 Su	6 ♋ 21 R	27)(42 R	15 II 13 R	22 ♋ 19 R
	11/24 Su	6 ♋ 14	27)(40	15 II 04	22 ♋ 14
	12/01 Su	6 ♋ 07	27)(39	14 II 55	22 ♋ 09
	12/08 Su	6 ♋ 00	27)(37	14 II 46	22 ♋ 03
	12/15 Su	5 ♋ 52	27)(37	14 II 38	21 ♋ 56
	12/22 Su	5 ♋ 43	27)(37 D	14 II 29	21 ♋ 48
	12/29 Su	5 ♋ 35	27)(38	14 II 20	21 ♋ 41
1919	1/05 Su	5 ♋ 26	27)(39	14 II 12	21 ♋ 32
	1/12 Su	5 ♋ 18	27)(41	14 II 05	21 ♋ 24
	1/19 Su	5 ♋ 10	27)(44	13 II 58	21 ♋ 15
	1/26 Su	5 ♋ 02	27)(47	13 II 53	21 ♋ 07
	2/02 Su	4 ♋ 55	27)(51	13 II 48	20 ♋ 59
	2/09 Su	4 ♋ 49	27)(55	13 II 45	20 ♋ 51
	2/16 Su	4 ♋ 44	27)(59	13 II 42	20 ♋ 44
	2/23 Su	4 ♋ 39	28)(04	13 II 41	20 ♋ 38
	3/02 Su	4 ♋ 36	28)(09	13 II 41 D	20 ♋ 32
	3/09 Su	4 ♋ 34	28)(14	13 II 42	20 ♋ 18
	3/16 Su	4 ♋ 33	28)(19	13 II 45	20 ♋ 24
	3/23 Su	4 ♋ 33 D	28)(25	13 II 49	20 ♋ 12
	3/30 Su	4 ♋ 34	28)(30	13 II 54	20 ♋ 20
	4/06 Su	4 ♋ 36	28)(35	13 II 59	20 ♋ 20 D
	4/13 Su	4 ♋ 39	28)(40	14 II 06	20 ♋ 21
	4/20 Su	4 ♋ 44	28)(45	14 II 14	20 ♋ 22
	4/27 Su	4 ♋ 49	28)(50	14 II 23	20 ♋ 25
	5/04 Su	4 ♋ 55	28)(54	14 II 32	20 ♋ 29
	5/11 Su	5 ♋ 03	28)(58	14 II 42	20 ♋ 34
	5/18 Su	5 ♋ 11	29)(01	14 II 52	20 ♋ 40
	5/25 Su	5 ♋ 19	29)(04	15 II 03	20 ♋ 47
	6/01 Su	5 ♋ 28	29)(06	15 II 14	20 ♋ 55
	6/08 Su	5 ♋ 38	29)(08	15 II 25	21 ♋ 03
	6/15 Su	5 ♋ 48	29)(09	15 II 36	21 ♋ 12
	6/22 Su	5 ♋ 58	29)(10	15 II 47	21 ♋ 21
	6/29 Su	6 ♋ 09	29)(10 R	15 II 58	21 ♋ 31
	7/06 Su	6 ♋ 19	29)(10	16 II 08	21 ♋ 41
	7/13 Su	6 ♋ 29	29)(09	16 II 18	21 ♋ 51
	7/20 Su	6 ♋ 39	29)(07	16 II 27	22 ♋ 01
	7/27 Su	6 ♋ 49	29)(05	16 II 36	22 ♋ 11

		♇	♀	♇	♇
1919	8/03 Su	6 ♋ 58 D	29)(02 R	16 II 43 D	22 ♋ 21 D
	8/10 Su	7 ♋ 07	28)(59	16 II 50	22 ♋ 31
	8/17 Su	7 ♋ 15	28)(55	16 II 56	22 ♋ 40
	8/24 Su	7 ♋ 22	28)(52	17 II 01	22 ♋ 49
	8/31 Su	7 ♋ 29	28)(47	17 II 05	22 ♋ 57
	9/07 Su	7 ♋ 34	28)(43	17 II 07	23 ♋ 04
	9/14 Su	7 ♋ 39	28)(38	17 II 09	23 ♋ 11
	9/21 Su	7 ♋ 42	28)(33	17 II 09 R	23 ♋ 16
	9/28 Su	7 ♋ 45	28)(29	17 II 08	23 ♋ 21
	10/05 Su	7 ♋ 46	28)(24	17 II 06	23 ♋ 25
	10/12 Su	7 ♋ 46 R	28)(19	17 II 02	23 ♋ 27
	10/19 Su	7 ♋ 45	28)(15	16 II 58	23 ♋ 29
	10/26 Su	7 ♋ 43	28)(11	16 II 53	23 ♋ 29 R
	11/02 Su	7 ♋ 40	28)(07	16 II 46	23 ♋ 28
	11/09 Su	7 ♋ 36	28)(04	16 II 39	23 ♋ 26
	11/16 Su	7 ♋ 30	28)(01	16 II 31	23 ♋ 23
	11/23 Su	7 ♋ 24	27)(59	16 II 23	23 ♋ 19
	11/30 Su	7 ♋ 17	27)(57	16 II 14	23 ♋ 14
	12/07 Su	7 ♋ 10	27)(56	16 II 06	23 ♋ 09
	12/14 Su	7 ♋ 02	27)(55	15 II 57	23 ♋ 02
	12/21 Su	6 ♋ 54	27)(55 D	15 II 48	22 ♋ 55
	12/28 Su	6 ♋ 45	27)(56	15 II 39	22 ♋ 47
1920	1/04 Su	6 ♋ 37	27)(57	15 II 31	22 ♋ 39
	1/11 Su	6 ♋ 28	27)(59	15 II 23	22 ♋ 30
	1/18 Su	6 ♋ 20	28)(01	15 II 17	22 ♋ 22
	1/25 Su	6 ♋ 12	28)(04	15 II 11	22 ♋ 14
	2/01 Su	6 ♋ 05	28)(08	15 II 06	22 ♋ 05
	2/08 Su	5 ♋ 59	28)(12	15 II 02	21 ♋ 58
	2/15 Su	5 ♋ 53	28)(16	14 II 59	21 ♋ 50
	2/22 Su	5 ♋ 48	28)(21	14 II 57	21 ♋ 44
	2/29 Su	5 ♋ 44	28)(26	14 II 57 D	21 ♋ 38
	3/07 Su	5 ♋ 42	28)(31	14 II 58	21 ♋ 33
	3/14 Su	5 ♋ 40	28)(36	15 II 00	21 ♋ 29
	3/21 Su	5 ♋ 40 D	28)(41	15 II 03	21 ♋ 26
	3/28 Su	5 ♋ 40	28)(47	15 II 08	21 ♋ 25
	4/04 Su	5 ♋ 42	28)(52	15 II 13	21 ♋ 24
	4/11 Su	5 ♋ 45	28)(57	15 II 20	21 ♋ 24 D

Astro Data

1918

12/16 Mo	13:08	♀	SD	27)(37	-28.2 (-28:09)

1919

2/26 We	02:47	♎	SD	13 II 41	20.6 (20:37)
3/19 We	17:34	♀	SD	4 ♋ 32	19.3 (19:16)
4/04 Fr	18:18	♎	SD	20 ♋ 20	17.0 (17:00)
6/26 Th	16:29	♀	SR	29)(10	-27.5 (-27:27)

1919

9/18 Th	18:00	♎	SR	17 II 09	21.4 (21:23)
10/09 Th	04:02	♀	SR	7 ♋ 46	19.3 (19:19)
10/24 Fr	16:05	♎	SR	23 ♋ 29	16.9 (16:51)
12/17 We	08:29	♀	SD	27)(55	-27.9 (-27:53)

1920

2/27 Fr	14:30	♎	SD	14 II 57	21.5 (21:27)
3/20 Sa	02:47	♀	SD	5 ♋ 40	19.5 (19:32)
4/05 Mo	05:57	♎	SD	21 ♋ 24	17.4 (17:25)

1920		♇	♀	♠	♠
	4/18 Su	5♋49 D	29♓02 D	15♊27 D	21♋26 D
	4/25 Su	5♋55	29♓07	15♊35	21♋28
	5/02 Su	6♋01	29♓11	15♊44	21♋32
	5/09 Su	6♋08	29♓15	15♊54	21♋36
	5/16 Su	6♋15	29♓18	16♊04	21♋42
	5/23 Su	6♋24	29♓21	16♊15	21♋48
	5/30 Su	6♋33	29♓24	16♊26	21♋56
	6/06 Su	6♋42	29♓26	16♊37	22♋04
	6/13 Su	6♋52	29♓27	16♊48	22♋12
	6/20 Su	7♋03	29♓28	16♊59	22♋21
	6/27 Su	7♋13	29♓28 R	17♊09	22♋31
	7/04 Su	7♋23	29♓28	17♊20	22♋41
	7/11 Su	7♋34	29♓27	17♊30	22♋51
	7/18 Su	7♋44	29♓25	17♊39	23♋01
	7/25 Su	7♋54	29♓23	17♊48	23♋11
	8/01 Su	8♋03	29♓20	17♊56	23♋21
	8/08 Su	8♋12	29♓17	18♊03	23♋31
	8/15 Su	8♋21	29♓14	18♊09	23♋40
	8/22 Su	8♋28	29♓10	18♊14	23♋49
	8/29 Su	8♋35	29♓06	18♊19	23♋57
	9/05 Su	8♋41	29♓02	18♊21	24♋05
	9/12 Su	8♋46	28♓57	18♊23	24♋11
	9/19 Su	8♋50	28♓52	18♊24	24♋17
	9/26 Su	8♋52	28♓48	18♊23 R	24♋22
	10/03 Su	8♋54	28♓43	18♊21	24♋26
	10/10 Su	8♋55 R	28♓38	18♊19	24♋29
	10/17 Su	8♋54	28♓34	18♊15	24♋31
	10/24 Su	8♋52	28♓30	18♊10	24♋32
	10/31 Su	8♋49	28♓26	18♊04	24♋31 R
	11/07 Su	8♋45	28♓22	17♊57	24♋30
	11/14 Su	8♋40	28♓20	17♊49	24♋27
	11/21 Su	8♋35	28♓17	17♊41	24♋24
	11/28 Su	8♋28	28♓15	17♊33	24♋19
	12/05 Su	8♋21	28♓14	17♊24	24♋13
	12/12 Su	8♋13	28♓13	17♊15	24♋07
	12/19 Su	8♋05	28♓13 D	17♊06	24♋00
	12/26 Su	7♋56	28♓13	16♊57	23♋52

1921		♇	♀	♠	♠
	1/02 Su	7♋47 R	28♓15 D	16♊49 R	23♋44 R
	1/09 Su	7♋39	28♓16	16♊41	23♋36
	1/16 Su	7♋31	28♓19	16♊34	23♋28
	1/23 Su	7♋23	28♓21	16♊28	23♋19
	1/30 Su	7♋15	28♓25	16♊23	23♋11
	2/06 Su	7♋08	28♓29	16♊18	23♋03
	2/13 Su	7♋02	28♓33	16♊15	22♋56
	2/20 Su	6♋57	28♓37	16♊13	22♋49
	2/27 Su	6♋53	28♓42	16♊12	22♋43
	3/06 Su	6♋50	28♓47	16♊13 D	22♋38
	3/13 Su	6♋48	28♓53	16♊14	22♋34
	3/20 Su	6♋48	28♓58	16♊17	22♋31
	3/27 Su	6♋48 D	29♓03	16♊21	22♋28
	4/03 Su	6♋49	29♓08	16♊26	22♋27
	4/10 Su	6♋52	29♓14	16♊32	22♋27 D
	4/17 Su	6♋56	29♓19	16♊39	22♋28
	4/24 Su	7♋00	29♓23	16♊47	22♋30
	5/01 Su	7♋06	29♓28	16♊56	22♋34
	5/08 Su	7♋13	29♓31	17♊05	22♋38
	5/15 Su	7♋20	29♓35	17♊15	22♋43
	5/22 Su	7♋29	29♓38	17♊26	22♋49
	5/29 Su	7♋38	29♓41	17♊37	22♋56
	6/05 Su	7♋47	29♓43	17♊47	23♋04
	6/12 Su	7♋57	29♓44	17♊58	23♋12
	6/19 Su	8♋07	29♓45	18♊09	23♋21
	6/26 Su	8♋18	29♓45	18♊20	23♋31
	7/03 Su	8♋28	29♓45 R	18♊31	23♋40
	7/10 Su	8♋39	29♓44	18♊41	23♋50
	7/17 Su	8♋49	29♓43	18♊50	24♋00
	7/24 Su	8♋59	29♓41	18♊59	24♋11
	7/31 Su	9♋09	29♓39	19♊08	24♋20
	8/07 Su	9♋18	29♓36	19♊15	24♋30
	8/14 Su	9♋26	29♓32	19♊22	24♋40
	8/21 Su	9♋34	29♓29	19♊27	24♋49
	8/28 Su	9♋41	29♓25	19♊32	24♋57
	9/04 Su	9♋48	29♓20	19♊35	25♋05
	9/11 Su	9♋53	29♓16	19♊37	25♋12
	9/18 Su	9♋57	29♓11	19♊38	25♋18
	9/25 Su	10♋00	29♓06	19♊38 R	25♋23
	10/02 Su	10♋02	29♓02	19♊37	25♋27

Astro Data

1920

6/25 Fr	12:58	♀	SR	29♓28	-27.2 (-27:10)
9/19 Su	04:04	♠	SR	18♊24	22.2 (22:11)
10/09 Sa	14:24	♇	SR	8♋55	19.6 (19:34)
10/24 Su	20:51	♠	SR	24♋32	17.2 (17:12)
12/16 Th	21:52	♀	SD	28♓13	-27.6 (-27:38)

1921

2/28 Mo	06:03	♠	SD	16♊12	22.3 (22:16)
3/21 Mo	10:00	♇	SD	6♋47	19.9 (19:51)
4/06 We	15:58	♠	SD	22♋27	17.8 (17:47)
6/26 Su	11:01	♀	SR	29♓45	-26.9 (-26:55)
9/20 Tu	14:38	♠	SR	19♊38	23.0 (22:58)

	♀	♀	♀	♀
1921				
10/09 Su	10 ⊗ 03 D	28 ♓ 57 ℞	19 ♊ 34 ℞	25 ⊗ 31 D
10/16 Su	10 ⊗ 03 ℞	28 ♓ 52	19 ♊ 31	25 ⊗ 33
10/23 Su	10 ⊗ 02	28 ♓ 48	19 ♊ 26	25 ⊗ 34
10/30 Su	9 ⊗ 59	28 ♓ 44	19 ♊ 20	25 ⊗ 34 ℞
11/06 Su	9 ⊗ 56	28 ♓ 41	19 ♊ 14	25 ⊗ 33
11/13 Su	9 ⊗ 51	28 ♓ 38	19 ♊ 07	25 ⊗ 30
11/20 Su	9 ⊗ 45	28 ♓ 35	18 ♊ 59	25 ⊗ 27
11/27 Su	9 ⊗ 39	28 ♓ 33	18 ♊ 50	25 ⊗ 23
12/04 Su	9 ⊗ 32	28 ♓ 32	18 ♊ 41	25 ⊗ 18
12/11 Su	9 ⊗ 24	28 ♓ 31	18 ♊ 33	25 ⊗ 12
12/18 Su	9 ⊗ 16	28 ♓ 31 D	18 ♊ 24	25 ⊗ 05
12/25 Su	9 ⊗ 08	28 ♓ 31	18 ♊ 15	24 ⊗ 57
1922				
1/01 Su	8 ⊗ 59	28 ♓ 32	18 ♊ 07	24 ⊗ 49
1/08 Su	8 ⊗ 50	28 ♓ 34	17 ♊ 59	24 ⊗ 41
1/15 Su	8 ⊗ 42	28 ♓ 36	17 ♊ 51	24 ⊗ 33
1/22 Su	8 ⊗ 34	28 ♓ 38	17 ♊ 45	24 ⊗ 25
1/29 Su	8 ⊗ 26	28 ♓ 42	17 ♊ 39	24 ⊗ 16
2/05 Su	8 ⊗ 19	28 ♓ 45	17 ♊ 34	24 ⊗ 08
2/12 Su	8 ⊗ 13	28 ♓ 50	17 ♊ 31	24 ⊗ 01
2/19 Su	8 ⊗ 07	28 ♓ 54	17 ♊ 28	23 ⊗ 54
2/26 Su	8 ⊗ 03	28 ♓ 59	17 ♊ 27	23 ⊗ 48
3/05 Su	7 ⊗ 59	29 ♓ 04	17 ♊ 27 D	23 ⊗ 42
3/12 Su	7 ⊗ 57	29 ♓ 09	17 ♊ 28	23 ⊗ 38
3/19 Su	7 ⊗ 56	29 ♓ 14	17 ♊ 31	23 ⊗ 34
3/26 Su	7 ⊗ 56 D	29 ♓ 20	17 ♊ 34	23 ⊗ 32
4/02 Su	7 ⊗ 57	29 ♓ 25	17 ♊ 39	23 ⊗ 30
4/09 Su	7 ⊗ 59	29 ♓ 30	17 ♊ 45	23 ⊗ 30 D
4/16 Su	8 ⊗ 03	29 ♓ 35	17 ♊ 51	23 ⊗ 30
4/23 Su	8 ⊗ 07	29 ♓ 40	17 ♊ 59	23 ⊗ 32
4/30 Su	8 ⊗ 13	29 ♓ 44	18 ♊ 07	23 ⊗ 35
5/07 Su	8 ⊗ 19	29 ♓ 48	18 ♊ 16	23 ⊗ 39
5/14 Su	8 ⊗ 26	29 ♓ 52	18 ♊ 26	23 ⊗ 44
5/21 Su	8 ⊗ 34	29 ♓ 55	18 ♊ 36	23 ⊗ 50
5/28 Su	8 ⊗ 43	29 ♓ 58	18 ♊ 47	23 ⊗ 56
6/04 Su	8 ⊗ 52	0 ♈ 00	18 ♊ 58	24 ⊗ 04
6/11 Su	9 ⊗ 02	0 ♈ 01	19 ♊ 09	24 ⊗ 12
6/18 Su	9 ⊗ 12	0 ♈ 02	19 ♊ 20	24 ⊗ 21

	♀	♀	♀	♀
1922				
6/25 Su	9 ⊗ 23 D	0 ♈ 03 D	19 ♊ 31 D	24 ⊗ 30 D
7/02 Su	9 ⊗ 33	0 ♈ 03 ℞	19 ♊ 41	24 ⊗ 39
7/09 Su	9 ⊗ 44	0 ♈ 02	19 ♊ 51	24 ⊗ 49
7/16 Su	9 ⊗ 54	0 ♈ 01	20 ♊ 01	24 ⊗ 59
7/23 Su	10 ⊗ 04	29 ♓ 59	20 ♊ 10	25 ⊗ 09
7/30 Su	10 ⊗ 14	29 ♓ 57	20 ♊ 19	25 ⊗ 19
8/06 Su	10 ⊗ 24	29 ♓ 54	20 ♊ 26	25 ⊗ 29
8/13 Su	10 ⊗ 33	29 ♓ 51	20 ♊ 33	25 ⊗ 38
8/20 Su	10 ⊗ 41	29 ♓ 47	20 ♊ 39	25 ⊗ 48
8/27 Su	10 ⊗ 48	29 ♓ 43	20 ♊ 44	25 ⊗ 56
9/03 Su	10 ⊗ 55	29 ♓ 39	20 ♊ 48	26 ⊗ 04
9/10 Su	11 ⊗ 00	29 ♓ 34	20 ♊ 50	26 ⊗ 11
9/17 Su	11 ⊗ 05	29 ♓ 30	20 ♊ 52	26 ⊗ 18
9/24 Su	11 ⊗ 09	29 ♓ 25	20 ♊ 52 ℞	26 ⊗ 23
10/01 Su	11 ⊗ 11	29 ♓ 20	20 ♊ 51	26 ⊗ 28
10/08 Su	11 ⊗ 12	29 ♓ 15	20 ♊ 49	26 ⊗ 31
10/15 Su	11 ⊗ 13 ℞	29 ♓ 11	20 ♊ 46	26 ⊗ 34
10/22 Su	11 ⊗ 12	29 ♓ 07	20 ♊ 42	26 ⊗ 35
10/29 Su	11 ⊗ 09	29 ♓ 03	20 ♊ 36	26 ⊗ 36 ℞
11/05 Su	11 ⊗ 06	28 ♓ 59	20 ♊ 30	26 ⊗ 35
11/12 Su	11 ⊗ 02	28 ♓ 56	20 ♊ 23	26 ⊗ 33
11/19 Su	10 ⊗ 57	28 ♓ 53	20 ♊ 15	26 ⊗ 30
11/26 Su	10 ⊗ 51	28 ♓ 51	20 ♊ 07	26 ⊗ 26
12/03 Su	10 ⊗ 44	28 ♓ 50	19 ♊ 59	26 ⊗ 21
12/10 Su	10 ⊗ 36	28 ♓ 49	19 ♊ 50	26 ⊗ 15
12/17 Su	10 ⊗ 28	28 ♓ 48	19 ♊ 41	26 ⊗ 09
12/24 Su	10 ⊗ 20	28 ♓ 48 D	19 ♊ 32	26 ⊗ 01
12/31 Su	10 ⊗ 11	28 ♓ 49	19 ♊ 23	25 ⊗ 54
1923				
1/07 Su	10 ⊗ 02	28 ♓ 51	19 ♊ 15	25 ⊗ 46
1/14 Su	9 ⊗ 54	28 ♓ 53	19 ♊ 08	25 ⊗ 37
1/21 Su	9 ⊗ 45	28 ♓ 55	19 ♊ 01	25 ⊗ 29
1/28 Su	9 ⊗ 38	28 ♓ 59	18 ♊ 55	25 ⊗ 21
2/04 Su	9 ⊗ 30	29 ♓ 02	18 ♊ 50	25 ⊗ 13
2/11 Su	9 ⊗ 24	29 ♓ 06	18 ♊ 46	25 ⊗ 05
2/18 Su	9 ⊗ 18	29 ♓ 11	18 ♊ 43	24 ⊗ 58
2/25 Su	9 ⊗ 13	29 ♓ 15	18 ♊ 42	24 ⊗ 52
3/04 Su	9 ⊗ 09	29 ♓ 20	18 ♊ 41 D	24 ⊗ 46
3/11 Su	9 ⊗ 07	29 ♓ 25	18 ♊ 42	24 ⊗ 41

Astro Data

1921

10/11 Tu	01:05	♀	SR	10 ⊗ 03	19.8 (19:50)
10/26 We	04:24	♀	SR	25 ⊗ 34	17.6 (17:34)
12/17 Sa	07:10	♀	SD	28 ♓ 31	-27.4 (-27:22)

1922

3/01 We	19:51	♀	SD	17 ♊ 27	23.1 (23:04)
3/22 We	18:40	♀	SD	7 ⊗ 56	20.1 (20:07)
4/07 Fr	22:15	♀	SD	23 ⊗ 30	18.1 (18:08)
6/03 Sa	01:38	♀	→ ♈		-26.6 (-26:35)

1922

6/27 Tu	03:30	♀	SR	0 ♈ 03	-26.7 (-26:39)
7/21 Fr	04:44	♀	→ ♓ ℞		-26.8 (-26:45)
9/22 Fr	00:10	♀	SR	20 ♊ 52	23.7 (23:43)
10/12 Th	14:08	♀	SR	11 ⊗ 13	20.1 (20:05)
10/27 Fr	10:13	♀	SR	26 ⊗ 36	17.9 (17:54)
12/17 Sa	19:47	♀	SD	28 ♓ 48	-27.1 (-27:05)

1923

3/03 Sa	08:24	♀	SD	18 ♊ 41	23.9 (23:52)

1923		♀	♀	♠	♠
	3/18 Su	9♋05 R	29♓31 D	18♊44 D	24♋37 R
	3/25 Su	9♋05 D	29♓36	18♊47	24♋34
	4/01 Su	9♋05	29♓41	18♊51	24♋32
	4/08 Su	9♋07	29♓46	18♊56	24♋32
	4/15 Su	9♋10	29♓51	19♊03	24♋32 D
	4/22 Su	9♋14	29♓56	19♊10	24♋33
	4/29 Su	9♋19	0♈01	19♊18	24♋36
	5/06 Su	9♋26	0♈05	19♊27	24♋40
	5/13 Su	9♋33	0♈08	19♊36	24♋44
	5/20 Su	9♋40	0♈12	19♊46	24♋50
	5/27 Su	9♋49	0♈14	19♊57	24♋56
	6/03 Su	9♋58	0♈17	20♊08	25♋03
	6/10 Su	10♋08	0♈18	20♊19	25♋11
	6/17 Su	10♋18	0♈20	20♊29	25♋19
	6/24 Su	10♋28	0♈20	20♊40	25♋28
	7/01 Su	10♋39	0♈20 R	20♊51	25♋38
	7/08 Su	10♋49	0♈20	21♊01	25♋48
	7/15 Su	11♋00	0♈19	21♊11	25♋57
	7/22 Su	11♋10	0♈17	21♊21	26♋07
	7/29 Su	11♋20	0♈15	21♊29	26♋17
	8/05 Su	11♋30	0♈12	21♊37	26♋27
	8/12 Su	11♋39	0♈09	21♊44	26♋37
	8/19 Su	11♋48	0♈05	21♊51	26♋46
	8/26 Su	11♋55	0♈01	21♊56	26♋55
	9/02 Su	12♋02	29♓57	22♊00	27♋03
	9/09 Su	12♋08	29♓53	22♊03	27♋10
	9/16 Su	12♋13	29♓48	22♊05	27♋17
	9/23 Su	12♋17	29♓43	22♊05	27♋23
	9/30 Su	12♋20	29♓39	22♊05 R	27♋27
	10/07 Su	12♋22	29♓34	22♊03	27♋31
	10/14 Su	12♋23	29♓29	22♊00	27♋34
	10/21 Su	12♋22 R	29♓25	21♊56	27♋36
	10/28 Su	12♋20	29♓21	21♊52	27♋37
	11/04 Su	12♋17	29♓18	21♊46	27♋36 R
	11/11 Su	12♋13	29♓14	21♊39	27♋35
	11/18 Su	12♋08	29♓11	21♊31	27♋32
	11/25 Su	12♋03	29♓09	21♊23	27♋28
	12/02 Su	11♋56	29♓08	21♊15	27♋24
	12/09 Su	11♋48	29♓06	21♊06	27♋18
	12/16 Su	11♋41	29♓06	20♊57	27♋12

1923		♀	♀	♠	♠
	12/23 Su	11♋32 R	29♓06 D	20♊48 R	27♋05 R
	12/30 Su	11♋24	29♓07	20♊40	26♋57
1924	1/06 Su	11♋15	29♓08	20♊32	26♋49
	1/13 Su	11♋06	29♓10	20♊24	26♋41
	1/20 Su	10♋58	29♓12	20♊17	26♋33
	1/27 Su	10♋50	29♓15	20♊11	26♋25
	2/03 Su	10♋42	29♓19	20♊05	26♋17
	2/10 Su	10♋35	29♓23	20♊01	26♋09
	2/17 Su	10♋29	29♓27	19♊58	26♋02
	2/24 Su	10♋24	29♓32	19♊56	25♋55
	3/02 Su	10♋20	29♓37	19♊55	25♋49
	3/09 Su	10♋17	29♓42	19♊55 D	25♋44
	3/16 Su	10♋15	29♓47	19♊56	25♋40
	3/23 Su	10♋14	29♓52	19♊59	25♋36
	3/30 Su	10♋14 D	29♓58	20♊03	25♋34
	4/06 Su	10♋16	0♈03	20♊08	25♋33
	4/13 Su	10♋18	0♈08	20♊14	25♋33 D
	4/20 Su	10♋22	0♈12	20♊21	25♋34
	4/27 Su	10♋27	0♈17	20♊29	25♋36
	5/04 Su	10♋33	0♈21	20♊37	25♋40
	5/11 Su	10♋40	0♈25	20♊46	25♋44
	5/18 Su	10♋47	0♈28	20♊56	25♋49
	5/25 Su	10♋56	0♈31	21♊06	25♋55
	6/01 Su	11♋05	0♈34	21♊17	26♋02
	6/08 Su	11♋14	0♈35	21♊28	26♋10
	6/15 Su	11♋24	0♈37	21♊39	26♋18
	6/22 Su	11♋35	0♈37	21♊50	26♋27
	6/29 Su	11♋45	0♈38 R	22♊00	26♋36
	7/06 Su	11♋56	0♈37	22♊11	26♋45
	7/13 Su	12♋06	0♈36	22♊21	26♋55
	7/20 Su	12♋17	0♈35	22♊30	27♋05
	7/27 Su	12♋27	0♈32	22♊39	27♋15
	8/03 Su	12♋37	0♈30	22♊47	27♋25
	8/10 Su	12♋46	0♈27	22♊55	27♋34
	8/17 Su	12♋55	0♈23	23♊01	27♋44
	8/24 Su	13♋03	0♈20	23♊07	27♋52
	8/31 Su	13♋10	0♈15	23♊11	28♋01

Astro Data

1923

3/24 Sa	02:07	♀	SD	9♋05	20.4 (20:23)
4/09 Mo	06:24	♠	SD	24♋32	18.5 (18:31)
4/27 Fr	07:46	♀	→ ♈		-26.4 (-26:21)
6/27 We	18:14	♀	SR	0♈20	-26.4 (-26:23)
8/28 Tu	22:29	♀	→ ♓ R		-26.7 (-26:43)
9/23 Su	11:16	♠	SR	22♊05	24.5 (24:30)
10/14 Su	00:01	♀	SR	12♋23	20.3 (20:20)
10/28 Su	17:07	♠	SR	27♋37	18.2 (18:15)
12/18 Tu	12:26	♀	SD	29♓06	-26.8 (-26:49)

1924

3/03 Mo	19:54	♠	SD	19♊54	24.6 (24:38)
3/24 Mo	12:43	♀	SD	10♋14	20.7 (20:40)
4/01 Tu	17:11	♀	→ ♈		-26.2 (-26:09)
4/09 We	12:54	♠	SD	25♋33	18.9 (18:51)
6/27 Fr	03:08	♀	SR	0♈38	-26.1 (-26:07)

Year	Date	♆	♀	⚴	⚵
1924	9/07 Su	13♋17 D	0♈11 ℞	23♊15 D	28♋08 D
	9/14 Su	13♋22	0♈06	23♊17	28♋15
	9/21 Su	13♋27	0♈02	23♊18	28♋21
	9/28 Su	13♋30	29♓57	23♊18 ℞	28♋26
	10/05 Su	13♋32	29♓52	23♊17	28♋31
	10/12 Su	13♋33	29♓48	23♊14	28♋34
	10/19 Su	13♋33 ℞	29♓44	23♊11	28♋36
	10/26 Su	13♋31	29♓40	23♊06	28♋37
	11/02 Su	13♋29	29♓36	23♊01	28♋37 ℞
	11/09 Su	13♋25	29♓32	22♊54	28♋36
	11/16 Su	13♋21	29♓30	22♊47	28♋33
	11/23 Su	13♋15	29♓27	22♊39	28♋30
	11/30 Su	13♋09	29♓25	22♊31	28♋26
	12/07 Su	13♋01	29♓24	22♊22	28♋21
	12/14 Su	12♋54	29♓23	22♊13	28♋14
	12/21 Su	12♋45	29♓23 D	22♊05	28♋08
	12/28 Su	12♋37	29♓24	21♊56	28♋00
1925	1/04 Su	12♋28	29♓25	21♊47	27♋53
	1/11 Su	12♋19	29♓27	21♊40	27♋44
	1/18 Su	12♋11	29♓29	21♊32	27♋36
	1/25 Su	12♋02	29♓32	21♊26	27♋28
	2/01 Su	11♋55	29♓36	21♊20	27♋20
	2/08 Su	11♋48	29♓39	21♊15	27♋12
	2/15 Su	11♋41	29♓44	21♊12	27♋05
	2/22 Su	11♋36	29♓48	21♊09	26♋58
	3/01 Su	11♋31	29♓53	21♊08	26♋52
	3/08 Su	11♋28	29♓58	21♊08 D	26♋46
	3/15 Su	11♋25	0♈03	21♊09	26♋42
	3/22 Su	11♋24	0♈09	21♊11	26♋38
	3/29 Su	11♋24 D	0♈14	21♊14	26♋36
	4/05 Su	11♋25	0♈19	21♊19	26♋34
	4/12 Su	11♋27	0♈24	21♊25	26♋34 D
	4/19 Su	11♋31	0♈29	21♊31	26♋35
	4/26 Su	11♋35	0♈33	21♊39	26♋36
	5/03 Su	11♋41	0♈38	21♊47	26♋39
	5/10 Su	11♋47	0♈42	21♊56	26♋43
	5/17 Su	11♋55	0♈45	22♊05	26♋48
1925	5/24 Su	12♋03 D	0♈48 D	22♊16 D	26♋54 D
	5/31 Su	12♋12	0♈50	22♊26	27♋00
	6/07 Su	12♋21	0♈52	22♊37	27♋08
	6/14 Su	12♋31	0♈54	22♊48	27♋16
	6/21 Su	12♋41	0♈55	22♊58	27♋24
	6/28 Su	12♋52	0♈55 ℞	23♊09	27♋33
	7/05 Su	13♋03	0♈55	23♊20	27♋43
	7/12 Su	13♋13	0♈54	23♊30	27♋52
	7/19 Su	13♋24	0♈52	23♊39	28♋02
	7/26 Su	13♋34	0♈50	23♊49	28♋12
	8/02 Su	13♋44	0♈48	23♊57	28♋22
	8/09 Su	13♋54	0♈45	24♊05	28♋32
	8/16 Su	14♋03	0♈42	24♊12	28♋41
	8/23 Su	14♋11	0♈38	24♊17	28♋50
	8/30 Su	14♋19	0♈34	24♊22	28♋58
	9/06 Su	14♋26	0♈29	24♊26	29♋06
	9/13 Su	14♋31	0♈25	24♊29	29♋13
	9/20 Su	14♋36	0♈20	24♊30	29♋19
	9/27 Su	14♋40	0♈16	24♊31 ℞	29♋25
	10/04 Su	14♋42	0♈11	24♊30	29♋29
	10/11 Su	14♋44	0♈06	24♊28	29♋33
	10/18 Su	14♋44 ℞	0♈02	24♊25	29♋35
	10/25 Su	14♋43	29♓58	24♊20	29♋37
	11/01 Su	14♋41	29♓54	24♊15	29♋37 ℞
	11/08 Su	14♋38	29♓51	24♊09	29♋36
	11/15 Su	14♋34	29♓48	24♊02	29♋34
	11/22 Su	14♋28	29♓45	23♊54	29♋31
	11/29 Su	14♋22	29♓43	23♊46	29♋27
	12/06 Su	14♋15	29♓42	23♊38	29♋22
	12/13 Su	14♋07	29♓41	23♊29	29♋16
	12/20 Su	13♋59	29♓41 D	23♊20	29♋10
	12/27 Su	13♋51	29♓41	23♊11	29♋03
1926	1/03 Su	13♋42	29♓42	23♊03	28♋55
	1/10 Su	13♋33	29♓44	22♊55	28♋47
	1/17 Su	13♋25	29♓46	22♊47	28♋39
	1/24 Su	13♋16	29♓49	22♊41	28♋31
	1/31 Su	13♋08	29♓52	22♊35	28♋23

Astro Data

Year	Date	Time	Planet	Event	Position	Value
1924	9/24 We	09:11	♀	→ ♓ ℞		-26.6 (-26:34)
	9/24 We	00:27	⚴	SR	23♊18	25.2 (25:13)
	10/14 Tu	09:40	♆	SR	13♋33	20.6 (20:34)
	10/28 Tu	20:51	⚵	SR	28♋37	18.6 (18:34)
	12/18 Th	02:36	♀	SD	29♓23	-26.6 (-26:34)
1925	3/05 Th	05:43	⚴	SD	21♊08	25.4 (25:23)
	3/09 Mo	22:31	♀	→ ♈		-26.0 (-26:01)
	3/25 We	23:07	♆	SD	11♋24	20.9 (20:55)
	4/10 Fr	22:02	⚵	SD	26♋34	19.2 (19:12)
1925	6/27 Sa	14:02	♀	SR	0♈55	-25.9 (-25:51)
	9/25 Fr	11:37	⚴	SR	24♊30	25.9 (25:56)
	10/15 Th	20:16	♆	SR	14♋44	20.8 (20:49)
	10/22 Th	03:19	♀	→ ♓ ℞		-26.4 (-26:23)
	10/30 Fr	00:35	⚵	SR	29♋37	18.9 (18:53)
	12/18 Fr	09:40	♀	SD	29♓41	-26.3 (-26:18)

Date	⚳	⚴	⚵	⚶
1926 2/07 Su	13♋01 ℞	29♓56 D	22♊30 ℞	28♋15 ℞
2/14 Su	12♋54	0♈00	22♊26	28♋07
2/21 Su	12♋48	0♈05	22♊23	28♋00
2/28 Su	12♋43	0♈09	22♊21	27♋54
3/07 Su	12♋39	0♈14	22♊20 D	27♋48
3/14 Su	12♋37	0♈20	22♊21	27♋43
3/21 Su	12♋35	0♈25	22♊23	27♋39
3/28 Su	12♋35 D	0♈30	22♊26	27♋37
4/04 Su	12♋35	0♈35	22♊30	27♋35
4/11 Su	12♋37	0♈40	22♊35	27♋34
4/18 Su	12♋40	0♈45	22♊41	27♋34 D
4/25 Su	12♋44	0♈50	22♊48	27♋36
5/02 Su	12♋50	0♈54	22♊56	27♋38
5/09 Su	12♋56	0♈58	23♊05	27♋42
5/16 Su	13♋03	1♈02	23♊15	27♋46
5/23 Su	13♋11	1♈05	23♊24	27♋52
5/30 Su	13♋19	1♈07	23♊35	27♋58
6/06 Su	13♋29	1♈09	23♊45	28♋05
6/13 Su	13♋39	1♈11	23♊56	28♋13
6/20 Su	13♋49	1♈12	24♊07	28♋21
6/27 Su	13♋59	1♈12	24♊18	28♋30
7/04 Su	14♋10	1♈12 ℞	24♊28	28♋40
7/11 Su	14♋21	1♈11	24♊38	28♋49
7/18 Su	14♋32	1♈10	24♊48	28♋59
7/25 Su	14♋42	1♈08	24♊58	29♋09
8/01 Su	14♋52	1♈06	25♊06	29♋19
8/08 Su	15♋02	1♈03	25♊14	29♋28
8/15 Su	15♋11	1♈00	25♊21	29♋38
8/22 Su	15♋20	0♈56	25♊28	29♋47
8/29 Su	15♋28	0♈52	25♊33	29♋55
9/05 Su	15♋35	0♈48	25♊37	0♌03
9/12 Su	15♋41	0♈43	25♊40	0♌10
9/19 Su	15♋47	0♈39	25♊42	0♌17
9/26 Su	15♋51	0♈34	25♊43	0♌23
10/03 Su	15♋54	0♈29	25♊42 ℞	0♌28
10/10 Su	15♋55	0♈25	25♊41	0♌31
10/17 Su	15♋56	0♈20	25♊38	0♌34
10/24 Su	15♋56 ℞	0♈16	25♊34	0♌36
10/31 Su	15♋54	0♈12	25♊29	0♌36
11/07 Su	15♋51	0♈09	25♊23	0♌36 ℞

Date	⚳	⚴	⚵	⚶
1926 11/14 Su	15♋47 ℞	0♈06 ℞	25♊17 ℞	0♌34 ℞
11/21 Su	15♋42	0♈03	25♊09	0♌32
11/28 Su	15♋36	0♈01	25♊01	0♌28
12/05 Su	15♋29	0♈00	24♊53	0♌23
12/12 Su	15♋22	29♓59	24♊44	0♌18
12/19 Su	15♋14	29♓58 D	24♊36	0♌12
12/26 Su	15♋06	29♓59	24♊27	0♌05
1927 1/02 Su	14♋57	0♈00	24♊18	29♋57
1/09 Su	14♋48	0♈01	24♊10	29♋49
1/16 Su	14♋39	0♈03	24♊02	29♋41
1/23 Su	14♋31	0♈06	23♊55	29♋33
1/30 Su	14♋22	0♈09	23♊49	29♋25
2/06 Su	14♋15	0♈13	23♊44	29♋17
2/13 Su	14♋08	0♈17	23♊39	29♋09
2/20 Su	14♋02	0♈21	23♊36	29♋02
2/27 Su	13♋56	0♈26	23♊34	28♋55
3/06 Su	13♋52	0♈31	23♊33	28♋50
3/13 Su	13♋49	0♈36	23♊33 D	28♋45
3/20 Su	13♋47	0♈41	23♊34	28♋40
3/27 Su	13♋46	0♈46	23♊37	28♋37
4/03 Su	13♋46 D	0♈51	23♊41	28♋35
4/10 Su	13♋48	0♈57	23♊46	28♋34
4/17 Su	13♋51	1♈01	23♊51	28♋34 D
4/24 Su	13♋54	1♈06	23♊58	28♋35
5/01 Su	13♋59	1♈11	24♊06	28♋37
5/08 Su	14♋05	1♈15	24♊14	28♋40
5/15 Su	14♋12	1♈18	24♊23	28♋45
5/22 Su	14♋20	1♈21	24♊33	28♋50
5/29 Su	14♋28	1♈24	24♊43	28♋56
6/05 Su	14♋37	1♈26	24♊54	29♋03
6/12 Su	14♋47	1♈28	25♊04	29♋10
6/19 Su	14♋57	1♈29	25♊15	29♋18
6/26 Su	15♋08	1♈30	25♊26	29♋27
7/03 Su	15♋18	1♈29 ℞	25♊37	29♋36
7/10 Su	15♋29	1♈29	25♊47	29♋46
7/17 Su	15♋40	1♈28	25♊57	29♋55
7/24 Su	15♋51	1♈26	26♊06	0♌05

Astro Data

1926

Date	Time	Body	Event	Position	Decl.
2/12 Fr	22:25	⚴	→ ♈		-26.0 (-25:57)
3/06 Sa	18:23	⚵	SD	22♊20	26.1 (26:08)
3/27 Sa	08:09	⚳	SD	12♋35	21.2 (21:10)
4/12 Mo	06:25	⚶	SD	27♋34	19.5 (19:32)
6/28 Mo	08:38	⚴	SR	1♈12	-25.6 (-25:36)
9/01 We	17:08	⚶	→ ♌		19.3 (19:16)
9/26 Su	22:53	⚵	SR	25♊43	26.7 (26:39)
10/17 Su	08:51	⚳	SR	15♋56	21.0 (21:02)
10/31 Su	06:58	⚶	SR	0♌36	19.2 (19:12)

1926

Date	Time	Body	Event	Position	Decl.
12/05 Su	14:30	⚴	→ ♓ ℞		-26.1 (-26:04)
12/18 Sa	22:02	⚴	SD	29♓58	-26.0 (-26:02)

1927

Date	Time	Body	Event	Position	Decl.
1/01 Sa	11:19	⚴	→ ♈		-26.0 (-25:58)
12/30 Th	21:13	⚶	→ ♋ ℞		19.4 (19:22)
3/08 Tu	05:24	⚵	SD	23♊33	26.9 (26:51)
3/28 Mo	16:01	⚳	SD	13♋46	21.4 (21:26)
4/13 We	12:17	⚶	SD	28♋34	19.9 (19:51)
6/28 Tu	23:34	⚴	SR	1♈30	-25.3 (-25:20)
7/20 We	02:08	⚶	→ ♌		19.7 (19:43)

		♇	♀	♎	♌
1927	7/31 Su	16♋01 D	1♈24 R	26♊15 D	0♌15 D
	8/07 Su	16♋11	1♈21	26♊23	0♌24
	8/14 Su	16♋21	1♈18	26♊31	0♌34
	8/21 Su	16♋30	1♈14	26♊37	0♌43
	8/28 Su	16♋38	1♈10	26♊43	0♌52
	9/04 Su	16♋45	1♈06	26♊47	1♌00
	9/11 Su	16♋52	1♈02	26♊51	1♌07
	9/18 Su	16♋57	0♈57	26♊53	1♌14
	9/25 Su	17♋02	0♈52	26♊54	1♌20
	10/02 Su	17♋05	0♈48	26♊54 R	1♌25
	10/09 Su	17♋08	0♈43	26♊53	1♌29
	10/16 Su	17♋09	0♈39	26♊51	1♌32
	10/23 Su	17♋09 R	0♈35	26♊47	1♌34
	10/30 Su	17♋07	0♈31	26♊43	1♌35
	11/06 Su	17♋05	0♈27	26♊37	1♌35 R
	11/13 Su	17♋01	0♈24	26♊31	1♌34
	11/20 Su	16♋57	0♈21	26♊24	1♌32
	11/27 Su	16♋51	0♈19	26♊16	1♌28
	12/04 Su	16♋45	0♈17	26♊08	1♌24
	12/11 Su	16♋37	0♈16	25♊59	1♌19
	12/18 Su	16♋30	0♈16	25♊51	1♌13
	12/25 Su	16♋21	0♈16 D	25♊42	1♌06
1928	1/01 Su	16♋12	0♈17	25♊33	0♌59
	1/08 Su	16♋04	0♈18	25♊25	0♌51
	1/15 Su	15♋55	0♈20	25♊17	0♌43
	1/22 Su	15♋46	0♈23	25♊10	0♌35
	1/29 Su	15♋38	0♈26	25♊03	0♌27
	2/05 Su	15♋30	0♈29	24♊57	0♌19
	2/12 Su	15♋23	0♈33	24♊53	0♌11
	2/19 Su	15♋16	0♈38	24♊49	0♌04
	2/26 Su	15♋11	0♈42	24♊47	29♋57
	3/04 Su	15♋06	0♈47	24♊45	29♋51
	3/11 Su	15♋02	0♈52	24♊45 D	29♋46
	3/18 Su	15♋00	0♈57	24♊46	29♋41
	3/25 Su	14♋59	1♈03	24♊48	29♋38
	4/01 Su	14♋58 D	1♈08	24♊51	29♋35
	4/08 Su	15♋00	1♈13	24♊56	29♋34

		♇	♀	♎	♌
1928	4/15 Su	15♋02 D	1♈18 D	25♊01 D	29♋33 D
	4/22 Su	15♋05	1♈22	25♊08	29♋34
	4/29 Su	15♋10	1♈27	25♊15	29♋36
	5/06 Su	15♋15	1♈31	25♊23	29♋39
	5/13 Su	15♋22	1♈35	25♊32	29♋43
	5/20 Su	15♋29	1♈38	25♊42	29♋47
	5/27 Su	15♋38	1♈41	25♊52	29♋53
	6/03 Su	15♋47	1♈43	26♊02	0♌00
	6/10 Su	15♋56	1♈45	26♊12	0♌07
	6/17 Su	16♋06	1♈46	26♊23	0♌15
	6/24 Su	16♋17	1♈47	26♊34	0♌23
	7/01 Su	16♋27	1♈47 R	26♊45	0♌32
	7/08 Su	16♋38	1♈46	26♊55	0♌42
	7/15 Su	16♋49	1♈45	27♊05	0♌51
	7/22 Su	17♋00	1♈44	27♊15	1♌01
	7/29 Su	17♋11	1♈41	27♊24	1♌11
	8/05 Su	17♋21	1♈39	27♊32	1♌20
	8/12 Su	17♋31	1♈36	27♊40	1♌30
	8/19 Su	17♋40	1♈32	27♊47	1♌39
	8/26 Su	17♋49	1♈28	27♊53	1♌48
	9/02 Su	17♋56	1♈24	27♊58	1♌56
	9/09 Su	18♋03	1♈20	28♊01	2♌04
	9/16 Su	18♋09	1♈15	28♊04	2♌11
	9/23 Su	18♋14	1♈11	28♊06	2♌17
	9/30 Su	18♋18	1♈06	28♊06 R	2♌23
	10/07 Su	18♋21	1♈02	28♊05	2♌27
	10/14 Su	18♋22	0♈57	28♊03	2♌30
	10/21 Su	18♋23 R	0♈53	28♊00	2♌33
	10/28 Su	18♋22	0♈49	27♊56	2♌34
	11/04 Su	18♋20	0♈45	27♊51	2♌34 R
	11/11 Su	18♋17	0♈42	27♊45	2♌33
	11/18 Su	18♋12	0♈39	27♊38	2♌31
	11/25 Su	18♋07	0♈37	27♊31	2♌28
	12/02 Su	18♋01	0♈35	27♊22	2♌24
	12/09 Su	17♋54	0♈34	27♊14	2♌19
	12/16 Su	17♋46	0♈33	27♊05	2♌14
	12/23 Su	17♋38	0♈33 D	26♊57	2♌07
	12/30 Su	17♋29	0♈34	26♊48	2♌00

Astro Data

1927

9/28 We	06:23	♎	SR		26♊54	27.3 (27:10)
10/18 Tu	23:12	♇	SR		17♋09	21.3 (21:15)
11/01 Tu	13:51	♌	SR		1♌35	19.5 (19:30)
12/19 Mo	16:25	♀	SD		0♈16	-25.8 (-25:45)

1928

1/23 Th	04:32	♎	→ ♋ R			20.0 (19:59)
3/08 Th	18:45	♎	SD		24♊45	27.6 (27:34)
3/28 We	23:46	♇	SD		14♋58	21.7 (21:40)
4/13 Fr	16:49	♌	SD		29♋33	20.2 (20:09)

1928

6/02 Sa	19:46	♌	→ ♌			20.2 (20:09)
6/28 Th	06:32	♀	SR	1♈47		-25.1 (-25:04)
9/28 Fr	16:51	♎	SR	28♊06		28.0 (28:00)
10/19 Fr	12:07	♇	SR	18♋23		21.5 (21:28)
11/01 Th	21:36	♌	SR	2♌34		19.8 (19:47)
12/19 We	05:37	♀	SD	0♈33		-25.5 (-25:30)

LONGITUDE

	♇	♀	♇	♇
1929				
1/06 Su	17♋20 R	0♈35 D	26♊39 R	1♌53 R
1/13 Su	17♋11	0♈37	26♊31	1♌45
1/20 Su	17♋03	0♈40	26♊24	1♌36
1/27 Su	16♋54	0♈42	26♊17	1♌28
2/03 Su	16♋46	0♈46	26♊11	1♌20
2/10 Su	16♋38	0♈50	26♊06	1♌12
2/17 Su	16♋32	0♈54	26♊02	1♌05
2/24 Su	16♋26	0♈59	25♊59	0♌58
3/03 Su	16♋21	1♈03	25♊57	0♌52
3/10 Su	16♋17	1♈08	25♊57	0♌46
3/17 Su	16♋14	1♈14	25♊57 D	0♌42
3/24 Su	16♋12	1♈19	25♊59	0♌38
3/31 Su	16♋12 D	1♈24	26♊02	0♌35
4/07 Su	16♋12	1♈29	26♊06	0♌33
4/14 Su	16♋14	1♈34	26♊11	0♌33
4/21 Su	16♋17	1♈39	26♊17	0♌33 D
4/28 Su	16♋21	1♈43	26♊24	0♌34
5/05 Su	16♋27	1♈47	26♊32	0♌37
5/12 Su	16♋33	1♈51	26♊41	0♌40
5/19 Su	16♋40	1♈55	26♊50	0♌45
5/26 Su	16♋48	1♈57	27♊00	0♌50
6/02 Su	16♋57	2♈00	27♊10	0♌57
6/09 Su	17♋06	2♈02	27♊20	1♌04
6/16 Su	17♋16	2♈03	27♊31	1♌11
6/23 Su	17♋27	2♈04	27♊42	1♌20
6/30 Su	17♋37	2♈04 R	27♊51	1♌28
7/07 Su	17♋48	2♈04	28♊03	1♌38
7/14 Su	17♋59	2♈03	28♊13	1♌47
7/21 Su	18♋10	2♈01	28♊23	1♌57
7/28 Su	18♋21	1♈59	28♊32	2♌06
8/04 Su	18♋31	1♈57	28♊41	2♌16
8/11 Su	18♋42	1♈54	28♊49	2♌26
8/18 Su	18♋51	1♈50	28♊56	2♌35
8/25 Su	19♋00	1♈47	29♊02	2♌44
9/01 Su	19♋08	1♈42	29♊07	2♌52
9/08 Su	19♋15	1♈38	29♊11	3♌00
9/15 Su	19♋22	1♈34	29♊15	3♌07
9/22 Su	19♋27	1♈29	29♊17	3♌14
9/29 Su	19♋31	1♈24	29♊17	3♌20
10/06 Su	19♋35	1♈20	29♊17 R	3♌24

	♇	♀	♇	♇
1929				
10/13 Su	19♋37 D	1♈15 R	29♊15 R	3♌28 D
10/20 Su	19♋37	1♈11	29♊13	3♌31
10/27 Su	19♋37 R	1♈07	29♊09	3♌32
11/03 Su	19♋35	1♈03	29♊04	3♌33 R
11/10 Su	19♋32	1♈00	28♊58	3♌32
11/17 Su	19♋29	0♈57	28♊52	3♌31
11/24 Su	19♋24	0♈55	28♊45	3♌28
12/01 Su	19♋18	0♈53	28♊37	3♌24
12/08 Su	19♋11	0♈52	28♊28	3♌20
12/15 Su	19♋03	0♈51	28♊20	3♌14
12/22 Su	18♋55	0♈51 D	28♊11	3♌08
12/29 Su	18♋47	0♈51	28♊02	3♌01
1930				
1/05 Su	18♋38	0♈52	27♊54	2♌54
1/12 Su	18♋29	0♈54	27♊46	2♌46
1/19 Su	18♋20	0♈56	27♊38	2♌38
1/26 Su	18♋11	0♈59	27♊31	2♌30
2/02 Su	18♋03	1♈02	27♊25	2♌22
2/09 Su	17♋55	1♈06	27♊19	2♌14
2/16 Su	17♋48	1♈10	27♊15	2♌06
2/23 Su	17♋42	1♈15	27♊12	1♌59
3/02 Su	17♋37	1♈20	27♊09	1♌53
3/09 Su	17♋32	1♈25	27♊08	1♌47
3/16 Su	17♋29	1♈30	27♊09 D	1♌42
3/23 Su	17♋27	1♈35	27♊10	1♌38
3/30 Su	17♋26	1♈40	27♊12	1♌35
4/06 Su	17♋26 D	1♈45	27♊16	1♌33
4/13 Su	17♋28	1♈50	27♊21	1♌31
4/20 Su	17♋30	1♈55	27♊27	1♌32 D
4/27 Su	17♋34	1♈59	27♊33	1♌33
5/04 Su	17♋39	2♈04	27♊41	1♌35
5/11 Su	17♋45	2♈07	27♊49	1♌38
5/18 Su	17♋52	2♈11	27♊58	1♌41
5/25 Su	18♋00	2♈14	28♊08	1♌47
6/01 Su	18♋08	2♈16	28♊18	1♌53
6/08 Su	18♋17	2♈18	28♊28	2♌00
6/15 Su	18♋27	2♈20	28♊39	2♌08
6/22 Su	18♋38	2♈21	28♊49	2♌16

Astro Data

1929

3/10 Su	05:08	♇	SD	25♊57	28.3 (28:15)
3/30 Sa	11:50	♀	SD	16♋12	21.9 (21:54)
4/14 Su	20:23	♇	SD	0♌33	20.5 (20:28)
6/28 Fr	17:54	♀	SR	2♈04	-24.8 (-24:47)
9/30 Mo	04:48	♇	SR	29♊17	28.7 (28:40)

1929

10/21 Mo	02:07	♇	SR	19♋37	21.7 (21:40)
11/02 Sa	23:46	♇	SR	3♌33	20.1 (20:03)
12/19 Th	14:47	♀	SD	0♈51	-25.2 (-25:15)

1930

3/11 Tu	13:00	♇	SD	27♊08	28.9 (28:55)
3/31 Mo	23:39	♀	SD	17♋26	22.1 (22:08)
4/16 We	04:56	♇	SD	1♌32	20.8 (20:45)
6/29 Su	09:50	♀	SR	2♈21	-24.6 (-24:33)

		♇	♀	♠	♠			♇	♀	♠	♠
1930	6/29 Su	18♋48 D	2♈21 D	29♊00 D	2♌24 D	1931	3/15 Su	18♋45 R	1♈46 D	28♊20 D	2♌42 R
	7/06 Su	18♋59	2♈21 R	29♊11	2♌33		3/22 Su	18♋42	1♈51	28♊21	2♌38
	7/13 Su	19♋10	2♈20	29♊21	2♌43		3/29 Su	18♋41	1♈56	28♊23	2♌34
	7/20 Su	19♋21	2♈19	29♊31	2♌52		4/05 Su	18♋41 D	2♈01	28♊26	2♌32
	7/27 Su	19♋32	2♈17	29♊40	3♌02		4/12 Su	18♋42	2♈06	28♊30	2♌30
	8/03 Su	19♋43	2♈14	29♊49	3♌12		4/19 Su	18♋44	2♈11	28♊36	2♌30 D
	8/10 Su	19♋53	2♈11	29♊57	3♌21		4/26 Su	18♋48	2♈15	28♊42	2♌31
	8/17 Su	20♋03	2♈08	0♋05	3♌31		5/03 Su	18♋52	2♈20	28♊49	2♌33
	8/24 Su	20♋12	2♈05	0♋11	3♌40		5/10 Su	18♋58	2♈24	28♊57	2♌36
	8/31 Su	20♋21	2♈01	0♋17	3♌48		5/17 Su	19♋04	2♈27	29♊06	2♌39
	9/07 Su	20♋28	1♈56	0♋21	3♌56		5/24 Su	19♋12	2♈30	29♊15	2♌44
	9/14 Su	20♋35	1♈52	0♋25	4♌04		5/31 Su	19♋20	2♈33	29♊25	2♌50
	9/21 Su	20♋41	1♈47	0♋27	4♌10		6/07 Su	19♋29	2♈35	29♊35	2♌56
	9/28 Su	20♋46	1♈43	0♋28	4♌16		6/14 Su	19♋39	2♈37	29♊46	3♌04
	10/05 Su	20♋49	1♈38	0♋28 R	4♌21		6/21 Su	19♋49	2♈38	29♊57	3♌11
	10/12 Su	20♋52	1♈34	0♋27	4♌25		6/28 Su	20♋00	2♈38	0♋07	3♌20
	10/19 Su	20♋53	1♈29	0♋25	4♌28		7/05 Su	20♋11	2♈38 R	0♋18	3♌29
	10/26 Su	20♋53 R	1♈25	0♋21	4♌30		7/12 Su	20♋22	2♈37	0♋28	3♌38
	11/02 Su	20♋52	1♈21	0♋17	4♌31		7/19 Su	20♋33	2♈36	0♋38	3♌47
	11/09 Su	20♋49	1♈18	0♋12	4♌31 R		7/26 Su	20♋44	2♈34	0♋48	3♌57
	11/16 Su	20♋46	1♈15	0♋05	4♌30		8/02 Su	20♋55	2♈32	0♋57	4♌07
	11/23 Su	20♋41	1♈12	29♊58	4♌27		8/09 Su	21♋05	2♈29	1♋05	4♌16
	11/30 Su	20♋35	1♈10	29♊51	4♌24		8/16 Su	21♋16	2♈26	1♋13	4♌26
	12/07 Su	20♋29	1♈09	29♊43	4♌19		8/23 Su	21♋25	2♈22	1♋20	4♌35
	12/14 Su	20♋22	1♈08	29♊34	4♌14		8/30 Su	21♋34	2♈18	1♋26	4♌44
	12/21 Su	20♋14	1♈08 D	29♊25	4♌08		9/06 Su	21♋42	2♈14	1♋31	4♌52
	12/28 Su	20♋05	1♈08	29♊17	4♌02		9/13 Su	21♋49	2♈10	1♋34	4♌59
							9/20 Su	21♋55	2♈05	1♋37	5♌06
							9/27 Su	22♋00	2♈01	1♋39	5♌12
							10/04 Su	22♋04	1♈56	1♋39 R	5♌18
1931	1/04 Su	19♋56	1♈09	29♊08	3♌54		10/11 Su	22♋07	1♈52	1♋38	5♌21
	1/11 Su	19♋47	1♈11	29♊00	3♌47		10/18 Su	22♋09	1♈47	1♋37	5♌25
	1/18 Su	19♋38	1♈13	28♊52	3♌39		10/25 Su	22♋09 R	1♈43	1♋34	5♌28
	1/25 Su	19♋30	1♈16	28♊45	3♌31		11/01 Su	22♋09	1♈39	1♋29	5♌29
	2/01 Su	19♋21	1♈19	28♊38	3♌23		11/08 Su	22♋07	1♈36	1♋24	5♌29 R
	2/08 Su	19♋13	1♈23	28♊32	3♌15		11/15 Su	22♋04	1♈33	1♋18	5♌28
	2/15 Su	19♋06	1♈27	28♊28	3♌07		11/22 Su	21♋59	1♈30	1♋12	5♌26
	2/22 Su	18♋59	1♈31	28♊24	3♌00		11/29 Su	21♋54	1♈28	1♋04	5♌23
	3/01 Su	18♋53	1♈36	28♊21	2♌53		12/06 Su	21♋48	1♈26	0♋56	5♌19
	3/08 Su	18♋49	1♈41	28♊20	2♌47		12/13 Su	21♋41	1♈25	0♋48	5♌14

Astro Data

1930

8/12 Tu	02:05	♇ → ♋		29.1	(29:06)
10/01 We	15:46	♇ SR	0♋28	29.3	(29:17)
10/22 We	13:32	♀ SR	20♋53	21.9	(21:51)
11/04 Tu	02:11	♠ SR	4♌31	20.3	(20:20)
11/21 Fr	20:54	♇ → ♊ R		29.5	(29:28)
12/20 Sa	01:51	♀ SD	1♈08	-25.0	(-24:59)

1931

3/13 Fr	00:47	♇ SD	28♊20	29.6	(29:34)

1931

4/02 Th	11:25	♀ SD	18♋41	22.4	(22:21)
4/17 Fr	13:34	♠ SD	2♌30	21.0	(21:01)
6/22 Mo	21:45	♇ → ♋		29.6	(29:36)
6/30 Tu	01:35	♀ SR	2♈38	-24.3	(-24:17)
10/03 Sa	03:47	♠ SR	1♋39	29.9	(29:53)
10/24 Sa	01:48	♀ SR	22♋09	22.0	(22:02)
11/05 Th	08:05	♠ SR	5♌29	20.6	(20:35)
12/20 Su	18:57	♀ SD	1♈25	-24.7	(-24:42)

LONGITUDE

		♇	⯰	⯲	⯳
1931	12/20 Su	21 ♋ 33 ℞	1 ♈ 25 ℞	0 ♋ 39 ℞	5 ♌ 08 ℞
	12/27 Su	21 ♋ 25	1 ♈ 25 D	0 ♋ 30	5 ♌ 02
1932	1/03 Su	21 ♋ 16	1 ♈ 26	0 ♋ 22	4 ♌ 55
	1/10 Su	21 ♋ 07	1 ♈ 28	0 ♋ 13	4 ♌ 47
	1/17 Su	20 ♋ 58	1 ♈ 30	0 ♋ 05	4 ♌ 39
	1/24 Su	20 ♋ 49	1 ♈ 32	29 ♊ 58	4 ♌ 31
	1/31 Su	20 ♋ 40	1 ♈ 35	29 ♊ 51	4 ♌ 23
	2/07 Su	20 ♋ 32	1 ♈ 39	29 ♊ 45	4 ♌ 15
	2/14 Su	20 ♋ 24	1 ♈ 43	29 ♊ 40	4 ♌ 07
	2/21 Su	20 ♋ 17	1 ♈ 47	29 ♊ 36	4 ♌ 00
	2/28 Su	20 ♋ 11	1 ♈ 52	29 ♊ 33	3 ♌ 53
	3/06 Su	20 ♋ 06	1 ♈ 56	29 ♊ 31	3 ♌ 47
	3/13 Su	20 ♋ 02	2 ♈ 02	29 ♊ 31	3 ♌ 42
	3/20 Su	19 ♋ 59	2 ♈ 07	29 ♊ 31 D	3 ♌ 37
	3/27 Su	19 ♋ 57	2 ♈ 12	29 ♊ 33	3 ♌ 33
	4/03 Su	19 ♋ 57 D	2 ♈ 17	29 ♊ 36	3 ♌ 31
	4/10 Su	19 ♋ 57	2 ♈ 22	29 ♊ 40	3 ♌ 29
	4/17 Su	19 ♋ 59	2 ♈ 27	29 ♊ 45	3 ♌ 28
	4/24 Su	20 ♋ 02	2 ♈ 31	29 ♊ 51	3 ♌ 29 D
	5/01 Su	20 ♋ 06	2 ♈ 36	29 ♊ 57	3 ♌ 30
	5/08 Su	20 ♋ 12	2 ♈ 40	0 ♋ 05	3 ♌ 33
	5/15 Su	20 ♋ 18	2 ♈ 43	0 ♋ 14	3 ♌ 36
	5/22 Su	20 ♋ 25	2 ♈ 47	0 ♋ 23	3 ♌ 41
	5/29 Su	20 ♋ 33	2 ♈ 49	0 ♋ 33	3 ♌ 46
	6/05 Su	20 ♋ 42	2 ♈ 51	0 ♋ 43	3 ♌ 52
	6/12 Su	20 ♋ 52	2 ♈ 53	0 ♋ 53	3 ♌ 59
	6/19 Su	21 ♋ 02	2 ♈ 54	1 ♋ 04	4 ♌ 07
	6/26 Su	21 ♋ 13	2 ♈ 55	1 ♋ 14	4 ♌ 15
	7/03 Su	21 ♋ 23	2 ♈ 55 ℞	1 ♋ 25	4 ♌ 24
	7/10 Su	21 ♋ 35	2 ♈ 54	1 ♋ 35	4 ♌ 33
	7/17 Su	21 ♋ 46	2 ♈ 53	1 ♋ 45	4 ♌ 42
	7/24 Su	21 ♋ 57	2 ♈ 51	1 ♋ 55	4 ♌ 52
	7/31 Su	22 ♋ 08	2 ♈ 49	2 ♋ 04	5 ♌ 02
	8/07 Su	22 ♋ 19	2 ♈ 47	2 ♋ 13	5 ♌ 11
	8/14 Su	22 ♋ 29	2 ♈ 44	2 ♋ 21	5 ♌ 21
	8/21 Su	22 ♋ 39	2 ♈ 40	2 ♋ 28	5 ♌ 30
	8/28 Su	22 ♋ 48	2 ♈ 36	2 ♋ 34	5 ♌ 39

		♇	⯰	⯲	⯳
1932	9/04 Su	22 ♋ 56 D	2 ♈ 32 ℞	2 ♋ 39 D	5 ♌ 47 D
	9/11 Su	23 ♋ 04	2 ♈ 28	2 ♋ 44	5 ♌ 55
	9/18 Su	23 ♋ 10	2 ♈ 23	2 ♋ 47	6 ♌ 02
	9/25 Su	23 ♋ 16	2 ♈ 19	2 ♋ 49	6 ♌ 08
	10/02 Su	23 ♋ 20	2 ♈ 14	2 ♋ 50	6 ♌ 14
	10/09 Su	23 ♋ 24	2 ♈ 10	2 ♋ 49 ℞	6 ♌ 18
	10/16 Su	23 ♋ 26	2 ♈ 05	2 ♋ 48	6 ♌ 22
	10/23 Su	23 ♋ 27	2 ♈ 01	2 ♋ 45	6 ♌ 24
	10/30 Su	23 ♋ 27 ℞	1 ♈ 57	2 ♋ 41	6 ♌ 26
	11/06 Su	23 ♋ 25	1 ♈ 53	2 ♋ 37	6 ♌ 27 ℞
	11/13 Su	23 ♋ 22	1 ♈ 50	2 ♋ 31	6 ♌ 26
	11/20 Su	23 ♋ 18	1 ♈ 48	2 ♋ 25	6 ♌ 24
	11/27 Su	23 ♋ 13	1 ♈ 45	2 ♋ 17	6 ♌ 22
	12/04 Su	23 ♋ 08	1 ♈ 44	2 ♋ 09	6 ♌ 18
	12/11 Su	23 ♋ 01	1 ♈ 43	2 ♋ 01	6 ♌ 13
	12/18 Su	22 ♋ 53	1 ♈ 42	1 ♋ 53	6 ♌ 08
	12/25 Su	22 ♋ 45	1 ♈ 42 D	1 ♋ 44	6 ♌ 01
1933	1/01 Su	22 ♋ 36	1 ♈ 43	1 ♋ 35	5 ♌ 55
	1/08 Su	22 ♋ 27	1 ♈ 44	1 ♋ 27	5 ♌ 47
	1/15 Su	22 ♋ 18	1 ♈ 46	1 ♋ 19	5 ♌ 39
	1/22 Su	22 ♋ 09	1 ♈ 49	1 ♋ 11	5 ♌ 31
	1/29 Su	22 ♋ 00	1 ♈ 51	1 ♋ 04	5 ♌ 23
	2/05 Su	21 ♋ 52	1 ♈ 55	0 ♋ 58	5 ♌ 15
	2/12 Su	21 ♋ 44	1 ♈ 59	0 ♋ 52	5 ♌ 08
	2/19 Su	21 ♋ 37	2 ♈ 03	0 ♋ 48	5 ♌ 00
	2/26 Su	21 ♋ 30	2 ♈ 08	0 ♋ 45	4 ♌ 53
	3/05 Su	21 ♋ 25	2 ♈ 12	0 ♋ 42	4 ♌ 47
	3/12 Su	21 ♋ 20	2 ♈ 17	0 ♋ 41	4 ♌ 41
	3/19 Su	21 ♋ 17	2 ♈ 22	0 ♋ 41 D	4 ♌ 36
	3/26 Su	21 ♋ 15	2 ♈ 28	0 ♋ 43	4 ♌ 32
	4/02 Su	21 ♋ 14	2 ♈ 33	0 ♋ 45	4 ♌ 29
	4/09 Su	21 ♋ 14 D	2 ♈ 38	0 ♋ 49	4 ♌ 27
	4/16 Su	21 ♋ 15	2 ♈ 43	0 ♋ 53	4 ♌ 26
	4/23 Su	21 ♋ 18	2 ♈ 47	0 ♋ 59	4 ♌ 26 D
	4/30 Su	21 ♋ 22	2 ♈ 52	1 ♋ 05	4 ♌ 27
	5/07 Su	21 ♋ 27	2 ♈ 56	1 ♋ 13	4 ♌ 30
	5/14 Su	21 ♋ 33	2 ♈ 59	1 ♋ 21	4 ♌ 33

Astro Data

1932

1/22 Fr	11:23	⯲	→ ♊ ℞		30.2 (30:14)
3/13 Su	11:38	⯲	SD	29 ♊ 31	30.2 (30:13)
4/02 Sa	22:59	♇	SD	19 ♋ 57	22.5 (22:32)
4/17 Su	19:14	⯳	SD	3 ♌ 28	21.3 (21:18)
5/02 Mo	22:14	⯲	→ ♋		30.2 (30:10)
6/29 We	10:13	⯰	SR	2 ♈ 55	-24.0 (-24:01)

1932

10/03 Mo	12:11	⯲	SR	2 ♋ 50	30.5 (30:31)
10/24 Mo	17:44	♇	SR	23 ♋ 27	22.2 (22:13)
11/05 Sa	12:42	⯳	SR	6 ♌ 27	20.8 (20:50)
12/20 Tu	11:38	⯰	SD	1 ♈ 42	-24.5 (-24:27)

1933

3/15 We	00:31	⯲	SD	0 ♋ 41	30.8 (30:50)
4/04 Tu	07:29	♇	SD	21 ♋ 14	22.8 (22:45)
4/19 We	01:01	⯳	SD	4 ♌ 26	21.6 (21:34)

		♇	♀	⚶	♠
1933	5/21 Su	21 ♋ 40 D	3 ♈ 03 D	1 ♋ 30 D	4 ♌ 37 D
	5/28 Su	21 ♋ 47	3 ♈ 06	1 ♋ 40	4 ♌ 42
	6/04 Su	21 ♋ 56	3 ♈ 08	1 ♋ 49	4 ♌ 48
	6/11 Su	22 ♋ 05	3 ♈ 10	2 ♋ 00	4 ♌ 55
	6/18 Su	22 ♋ 15	3 ♈ 11	2 ♋ 10	5 ♌ 02
	6/25 Su	22 ♋ 26	3 ♈ 12	2 ♋ 21	5 ♌ 10
	7/02 Su	22 ♋ 37	3 ♈ 12 ℞	2 ♋ 31	5 ♌ 19
	7/09 Su	22 ♋ 48	3 ♈ 11	2 ♋ 42	5 ♌ 28
	7/16 Su	22 ♋ 59	3 ♈ 10	2 ♋ 52	5 ♌ 37
	7/23 Su	23 ♋ 10	3 ♈ 09	3 ♋ 02	5 ♌ 46
	7/30 Su	23 ♋ 22	3 ♈ 07	3 ♋ 11	5 ♌ 56
	8/06 Su	23 ♋ 32	3 ♈ 04	3 ♋ 20	6 ♌ 06
	8/13 Su	23 ♋ 43	3 ♈ 01	3 ♋ 28	6 ♌ 15
	8/20 Su	23 ♋ 53	2 ♈ 58	3 ♋ 36	6 ♌ 24
	8/27 Su	24 ♋ 02	2 ♈ 54	3 ♋ 42	6 ♌ 33
	9/03 Su	24 ♋ 11	2 ♈ 50	3 ♋ 48	6 ♌ 42
	9/10 Su	24 ♋ 19	2 ♈ 45	3 ♋ 52	6 ♌ 50
	9/17 Su	24 ♋ 26	2 ♈ 41	3 ♋ 56	6 ♌ 57
	9/24 Su	24 ♋ 32	2 ♈ 36	3 ♋ 58	7 ♌ 03
	10/01 Su	24 ♋ 37	2 ♈ 32	3 ♋ 59	7 ♌ 09
	10/08 Su	24 ♋ 41	2 ♈ 27	3 ♋ 59 ℞	7 ♌ 14
	10/15 Su	24 ♋ 44	2 ♈ 23	3 ♋ 58	7 ♌ 18
	10/22 Su	24 ♋ 45	2 ♈ 19	3 ♋ 56	7 ♌ 21
	10/29 Su	24 ♋ 45 ℞	2 ♈ 15	3 ♋ 53	7 ♌ 23
	11/05 Su	24 ♋ 44	2 ♈ 11	3 ♋ 48	7 ♌ 24
	11/12 Su	24 ♋ 42	2 ♈ 08	3 ♋ 43	7 ♌ 23 ℞
	11/19 Su	24 ♋ 38	2 ♈ 05	3 ♋ 37	7 ♌ 22
	11/26 Su	24 ♋ 34	2 ♈ 03	3 ♋ 30	7 ♌ 20
	12/03 Su	24 ♋ 28	2 ♈ 01	3 ♋ 22	7 ♌ 16
	12/10 Su	24 ♋ 21	2 ♈ 00	3 ♋ 14	7 ♌ 12
	12/17 Su	24 ♋ 14	1 ♈ 59	3 ♋ 06	7 ♌ 07
	12/24 Su	24 ♋ 06	1 ♈ 59 D	2 ♋ 57	7 ♌ 01
	12/31 Su	23 ♋ 57	2 ♈ 00	2 ♋ 48	6 ♌ 54
1934	1/07 Su	23 ♋ 49	2 ♈ 01	2 ♋ 40	6 ♌ 47
	1/14 Su	23 ♋ 39	2 ♈ 03	2 ♋ 31	6 ♌ 39
	1/21 Su	23 ♋ 30	2 ♈ 05	2 ♋ 24	6 ♌ 31
	1/28 Su	23 ♋ 21	2 ♈ 08	2 ♋ 16	6 ♌ 23
	2/04 Su	23 ♋ 13	2 ♈ 11	2 ♋ 10	6 ♌ 15

		♇	♀	⚶	♠
1934	2/11 Su	23 ♋ 04 ℞	2 ♈ 15 D	2 ♋ 04 ℞	6 ♌ 07 ℞
	2/18 Su	22 ♋ 57	2 ♈ 19	2 ♋ 00	6 ♌ 00
	2/25 Su	22 ♋ 50	2 ♈ 23	1 ♋ 56	5 ♌ 53
	3/04 Su	22 ♋ 44	2 ♈ 28	1 ♋ 53	5 ♌ 46
	3/11 Su	22 ♋ 39	2 ♈ 33	1 ♋ 52	5 ♌ 40
	3/18 Su	22 ♋ 36	2 ♈ 38	1 ♋ 51 D	5 ♌ 35
	3/25 Su	22 ♋ 33	2 ♈ 43	1 ♋ 52	5 ♌ 31
	4/01 Su	22 ♋ 31	2 ♈ 48	1 ♋ 54	5 ♌ 28
	4/08 Su	22 ♋ 31 D	2 ♈ 53	1 ♋ 57	5 ♌ 25
	4/15 Su	22 ♋ 32	2 ♈ 58	2 ♋ 02	5 ♌ 24
	4/22 Su	22 ♋ 34	3 ♈ 03	2 ♋ 07	5 ♌ 24 D
	4/29 Su	22 ♋ 38	3 ♈ 07	2 ♋ 13	5 ♌ 24
	5/06 Su	22 ♋ 42	3 ♈ 12	2 ♋ 20	5 ♌ 26
	5/13 Su	22 ♋ 48	3 ♈ 15	2 ♋ 28	5 ♌ 29
	5/20 Su	22 ♋ 55	3 ♈ 19	2 ♋ 37	5 ♌ 33
	5/27 Su	23 ♋ 02	3 ♈ 22	2 ♋ 46	5 ♌ 38
	6/03 Su	23 ♋ 11	3 ♈ 24	2 ♋ 56	5 ♌ 43
	6/10 Su	23 ♋ 20	3 ♈ 26	3 ♋ 06	5 ♌ 50
	6/17 Su	23 ♋ 30	3 ♈ 27	3 ♋ 16	5 ♌ 57
	6/24 Su	23 ♋ 40	3 ♈ 28	3 ♋ 27	6 ♌ 05
	7/01 Su	23 ♋ 51	3 ♈ 28 ℞	3 ♋ 38	6 ♌ 13
	7/08 Su	24 ♋ 02	3 ♈ 28	3 ♋ 48	6 ♌ 22
	7/15 Su	24 ♋ 13	3 ♈ 27	3 ♋ 58	6 ♌ 31
	7/22 Su	24 ♋ 25	3 ♈ 26	4 ♋ 08	6 ♌ 40
	7/29 Su	24 ♋ 36	3 ♈ 24	4 ♋ 18	6 ♌ 50
	8/05 Su	24 ♋ 47	3 ♈ 21	4 ♋ 27	7 ♌ 00
	8/12 Su	24 ♋ 58	3 ♈ 18	4 ♋ 35	7 ♌ 09
	8/19 Su	25 ♋ 08	3 ♈ 15	4 ♋ 43	7 ♌ 18
	8/26 Su	25 ♋ 18	3 ♈ 11	4 ♋ 50	7 ♌ 27
	9/02 Su	25 ♋ 27	3 ♈ 07	4 ♋ 56	7 ♌ 36
	9/09 Su	25 ♋ 35	3 ♈ 03	5 ♋ 01	7 ♌ 44
	9/16 Su	25 ♋ 43	2 ♈ 59	5 ♋ 04	7 ♌ 52
	9/23 Su	25 ♋ 49	2 ♈ 54	5 ♋ 07	7 ♌ 58
	9/30 Su	25 ♋ 54	2 ♈ 50	5 ♋ 09	8 ♌ 04
	10/07 Su	25 ♋ 59	2 ♈ 45	5 ♋ 09 ℞	8 ♌ 10
	10/14 Su	26 ♋ 02	2 ♈ 41	5 ♋ 09	8 ♌ 14
	10/21 Su	26 ♋ 04	2 ♈ 36	5 ♋ 07	8 ♌ 17
	10/28 Su	26 ♋ 04	2 ♈ 32	5 ♋ 04	8 ♌ 19
	11/04 Su	26 ♋ 04 ℞	2 ♈ 29	5 ♋ 00	8 ♌ 20
	11/11 Su	26 ♋ 02	2 ♈ 25	4 ♋ 55	8 ♌ 20 ℞

Astro Data

1933

6/29 Th	17:48	♀	SR	3 ♈ 12	-23.8 (-23:45)
10/04 We	19:44	⚶	SR	4 ♋ 00	31.1 (31:05)
10/26 Th	08:09	♇	SR	24 ♋ 45	22.4 (22:21)
11/06 Mo	19:30	♠	SR	7 ♌ 24	21.1 (21:05)
12/20 We	10:23	♀	SD	1 ♈ 59	-24.2 (-24:11)

1934

3/16 Fr	12:14	⚶	SD	1 ♋ 51	31.4 (31:26)
4/05 Th	19:22	♇	SD	22 ♋ 31	22.9 (22:55)
4/20 Fr	03:49	♠	SD	5 ♌ 24	21.8 (21:49)
6/30 Sa	10:06	♀	SR	3 ♈ 28	-23.5 (-23:29)
10/06 Sa	04:34	⚶	SR	5 ♋ 09	31.6 (31:38)
10/28 Su	00:34	♇	SR	26 ♋ 04	22.5 (22:31)
11/07 We	22:17	♠	SR	8 ♌ 20	21.3 (21:19)

	Date	♇	♀	⚶	⚷
1934	11/18 Su	25♋59 ℞	2♈22 ℞	4♋49 ℞	8♌19 ℞
	11/25 Su	25♋54	2♈20	4♋42	8♌17
	12/02 Su	25♋49	2♈18	4♋35	8♌14
	12/09 Su	25♋43	2♈17	4♋27	8♌10
	12/16 Su	25♋36	2♈16	4♋18	8♌05
	12/23 Su	25♋28	2♈16 D	4♋10	7♌59
	12/30 Su	25♋20	2♈16	4♋01	7♌53
1935	1/06 Su	25♋11	2♈17	3♋52	7♌46
	1/13 Su	25♋02	2♈19	3♋44	7♌38
	1/20 Su	24♋52	2♈21	3♋36	7♌31
	1/27 Su	24♋43	2♈24	3♋29	7♌23
	2/03 Su	24♋34	2♈27	3♋22	7♌15
	2/10 Su	24♋26	2♈31	3♋16	7♌07
	2/17 Su	24♋18	2♈35	3♋11	6♌59
	2/24 Su	24♋11	2♈39	3♋07	6♌52
	3/03 Su	24♋05	2♈44	3♋04	6♌45
	3/10 Su	24♋00	2♈49	3♋02	6♌39
	3/17 Su	23♋55	2♈54	3♋01	6♌34
	3/24 Su	23♋52	2♈59	3♋02 D	6♌29
	3/31 Su	23♋50	3♈04	3♋03	6♌25
	4/07 Su	23♋50	3♈09	3♋06	6♌23
	4/14 Su	23♋50 D	3♈14	3♋10	6♌21
	4/21 Su	23♋52	3♈19	3♋15	6♌21
	4/28 Su	23♋55	3♈23	3♋21	6♌21 D
	5/05 Su	23♋59	3♈27	3♋27	6♌23
	5/12 Su	24♋04	3♈31	3♋35	6♌25
	5/19 Su	24♋11	3♈35	3♋43	6♌29
	5/26 Su	24♋18	3♈38	3♋53	6♌33
	6/02 Su	24♋26	3♈40	4♋02	6♌38
	6/09 Su	24♋35	3♈42	4♋12	6♌45
	6/16 Su	24♋45	3♈44	4♋22	6♌51
	6/23 Su	24♋55	3♈45	4♋33	6♌59
	6/30 Su	25♋06	3♈45	4♋43	7♌07
	7/07 Su	25♋17	3♈45 ℞	4♋54	7♌16
	7/14 Su	25♋28	3♈44	5♋04	7♌25
	7/21 Su	25♋40	3♈43	5♋14	7♌34
	7/28 Su	25♋51	3♈41	5♋24	7♌44

	Date	♇	♀	⚶	⚷
1935	8/04 Su	26♋02 D	3♈38 ℞	5♋33 D	7♌53 D
	8/11 Su	26♋13	3♈36	5♋42	8♌03
	8/18 Su	26♋24	3♈32	5♋50	8♌12
	8/25 Su	26♋34	3♈29	5♋57	8♌21
	9/01 Su	26♋43	3♈25	6♋03	8♌30
	9/08 Su	26♋52	3♈21	6♋08	8♌38
	9/15 Su	27♋00	3♈16	6♋12	8♌46
	9/22 Su	27♋07	3♈12	6♋16	8♌53
	9/29 Su	27♋12	3♈07	6♋18	8♌59
	10/06 Su	27♋17	3♈03	6♋18	9♌04
	10/13 Su	27♋21	2♈58	6♋18 ℞	9♌09
	10/20 Su	27♋23	2♈54	6♋17	9♌12
	10/27 Su	27♋24	2♈50	6♋14	9♌15
	11/03 Su	27♋24 ℞	2♈46	6♋10	9♌16
	11/10 Su	27♋23	2♈43	6♋06	9♌17 ℞
	11/17 Su	27♋20	2♈40	6♋00	9♌16
	11/24 Su	27♋16	2♈37	5♋54	9♌14
	12/01 Su	27♋11	2♈35	5♋47	9♌12
	12/08 Su	27♋05	2♈34	5♋39	9♌08
	12/15 Su	26♋58	2♈33	5♋31	9♌03
	12/22 Su	26♋51	2♈33 D	5♋22	8♌58
	12/29 Su	26♋43	2♈33	5♋13	8♌51
1936	1/05 Su	26♋34	2♈34	5♋05	8♌45
	1/12 Su	26♋25	2♈35	4♋56	8♌37
	1/19 Su	26♋15	2♈37	4♋48	8♌30
	1/26 Su	26♋06	2♈40	4♋41	8♌22
	2/02 Su	25♋57	2♈43	4♋34	8♌14
	2/09 Su	25♋49	2♈47	4♋27	8♌06
	2/16 Su	25♋40	2♈51	4♋22	7♌58
	2/23 Su	25♋33	2♈55	4♋17	7♌51
	3/01 Su	25♋26	2♈59	4♋14	7♌44
	3/08 Su	25♋21	3♈04	4♋12	7♌37
	3/15 Su	25♋16	3♈09	4♋11	7♌32
	3/22 Su	25♋13	3♈14	4♋11 D	7♌27
	3/29 Su	25♋10	3♈19	4♋12	7♌23
	4/05 Su	25♋09	3♈24	4♋14	7♌20
	4/12 Su	25♋09 D	3♈29	4♋18	7♌18

Astro Data

1934						
12/21 Fr	05:42	♀	SD	2♈16	-23.9 (-23:55)
1935						
3/17 Su	22:00	⚶	SD	3♋01	32.0 (32:00)
4/07 Su	07:54	♇	SD	23♋50	23.1 (23:06)
4/21 Su	10:28	⚷	SD	6♌21	22.1 (22:03)
7/01 Mo	02:12	♀	SR	3♈45	-23.2 (-23:15)

1935					
10/07 Mo	15:14	⚶	SR	6♋18	32.2 (32:12)
10/29 Tu	14:18	♇	SR	27♋24	22.7 (22:39)
11/08 Fr	23:51	⚷	SR	9♌17	21.5 (21:32)
12/21 Sa	21:47	♀	SD	2♈32	-23.7 (-23:40)
1936					
3/18 We	06:31	⚶	SD	4♋11	32.6 (32:34)
4/07 Tu	23:25	♇	SD	25♋09	23.3 (23:16)

	♇	♀	♇	♇
1936				
4/19 Su	25♋10 D	3♈34 D	4♋22 D	7♌17 ℞
4/26 Su	25♋13	3♈39	4♋28	7♌17 D
5/03 Su	25♋17	3♈43	4♋34	7♌18
5/10 Su	25♋22	3♈47	4♋42	7♌21
5/17 Su	25♋28	3♈50	4♋50	7♌24
5/24 Su	25♋35	3♈54	4♋59	7♌28
5/31 Su	25♋43	3♈56	5♋08	7♌33
6/07 Su	25♋51	3♈58	5♋18	7♌39
6/14 Su	26♋01	4♈00	5♋28	7♌46
6/21 Su	26♋11	4♈01	5♋38	7♌53
6/28 Su	26♋22	4♈01	5♋49	8♌01
7/05 Su	26♋33	4♈01 ℞	6♋00	8♌09
7/12 Su	26♋44	4♈01	6♋10	8♌18
7/19 Su	26♋56	4♈00	6♋20	8♌28
7/26 Su	27♋07	3♈58	6♋30	8♌37
8/02 Su	27♋18	3♈56	6♋39	8♌46
8/09 Su	27♋30	3♈53	6♋48	8♌56
8/16 Su	27♋40	3♈50	6♋56	9♌05
8/23 Su	27♋51	3♈46	7♋04	9♌14
8/30 Su	28♋00	3♈42	7♋10	9♌23
9/06 Su	28♋10	3♈38	7♋16	9♌32
9/13 Su	28♋18	3♈34	7♋20	9♌40
9/20 Su	28♋25	3♈29	7♋24	9♌47
9/27 Su	28♋31	3♈25	7♋26	9♌53
10/04 Su	28♋36	3♈20	7♋27	9♌59
10/11 Su	28♋40	3♈16	7♋27 ℞	10♌04
10/18 Su	28♋43	3♈11	7♋26	10♌07
10/25 Su	28♋45	3♈07	7♋34	10♌10
11/01 Su	28♋45 ℞	3♈04	7♋21	10♌12
11/08 Su	28♋44	3♈00	7♋16	10♌13
11/15 Su	28♋42	2♈57	7♋11	10♌12 ℞
11/22 Su	28♋39	2♈54	7♋05	10♌11
11/29 Su	28♋34	2♈52	6♋58	10♌09
12/06 Su	28♋18	2♈51	6♋50	10♌05
12/13 Su	28♋22	2♈50	6♋41	10♌01
12/20 Su	28♋14	2♈49	6♋34	9♌55
12/27 Su	28♋06	2♈49 D	6♋25	9♌49

	♇	♀	♇	♇
1937				
1/03 Su	27♋58 ℞	2♈50 D	6♋17 ℞	9♌43 ℞
1/10 Su	27♋49	2♈52	6♋08	9♌36
1/17 Su	27♋39	2♈53	6♋00	9♌28
1/24 Su	27♋30	2♈56	5♋52	9♌20
1/31 Su	27♋21	2♈59	5♋45	9♌12
2/07 Su	27♋12	3♈02	5♋38	9♌04
2/14 Su	27♋04	3♈06	5♋33	8♌56
2/21 Su	26♋56	3♈10	5♋28	8♌49
2/28 Su	26♋49	3♈15	5♋24	8♌42
3/07 Su	26♋43	3♈20	5♋22	8♌35
3/14 Su	26♋38	3♈25	5♋20	8♌30
3/21 Su	26♋34	3♈30	5♋20 D	8♌24
3/28 Su	26♋31	3♈35	5♋21	8♌20
4/04 Su	26♋30	3♈40	5♋22	8♌17
4/11 Su	26♋29 D	3♈45	5♋26	8♌15
4/18 Su	26♋30	3♈50	5♋30	8♌14
4/25 Su	26♋32	3♈54	5♋35	8♌13 D
5/02 Su	26♋36	3♈59	5♋41	8♌14
5/09 Su	26♋40	4♈03	5♋48	8♌16
5/16 Su	26♋46	4♈06	5♋56	8♌19
5/23 Su	26♋52	4♈09	6♋05	8♌23
5/30 Su	27♋00	4♈12	6♋14	8♌27
6/06 Su	27♋09	4♈14	6♋13	8♌33
6/13 Su	27♋18	4♈16	6♋33	8♌40
6/20 Su	27♋28	4♈17	6♋44	8♌47
6/27 Su	27♋38	4♈18	6♋54	8♌54
7/04 Su	27♋49	4♈18 ℞	7♋05	9♌03
7/11 Su	28♋01	4♈17	7♋15	9♌11
7/18 Su	28♋12	4♈16	7♋25	9♌21
7/25 Su	28♋24	4♈15	7♋35	9♌30
8/01 Su	28♋35	4♈13	7♋45	9♌39
8/08 Su	28♋47	4♈10	7♋54	9♌49
8/15 Su	28♋58	4♈07	8♋02	9♌58
8/22 Su	29♋08	4♈04	8♋10	10♌07
8/29 Su	29♋18	4♈00	8♋17	10♌16
9/05 Su	29♋28	3♈56	8♋13	10♌25
9/12 Su	29♋36	3♈51	8♋17	10♌33
9/19 Su	29♋44	3♈47	8♋31	10♌40
9/26 Su	29♋51	3♈42	8♋34	10♌47
10/03 Su	29♋56	3♈38	8♋36	10♌53

Astro Data

1936

4/21 Tu	17:18	♌	SD	7♌17	22.3	(22:17)
6/30 Tu	11:59	♀	SR	4♈01	-23.0	(-22:59)
10/08 Th	02:24	♈	SR	7♋17	31.7	(31:43)
10/30 Fr	05:20	♇	SR	28♋45	21.8	(21:46)
11/09 Mo	03:19	♌	SR	10♌13	21.8	(21:46)
12/21 Mo	12:50	♀	SD	2♈49	-23.4	(-23:23)

1937

3/19 Fr	14:55	♈	SD	5♋20	33.1	(33:07)
4/09 Fr	13:47	♇	SD	16♋29	23.4	(23:25)
4/23 Fr	00:01	♌	SD	8♌13	22.5	(22:31)
6/30 We	21:24	♀	SR	4♈18	-23.7	(-22:43)
10/07 Th	12:14	♇	→ ♌		12.9	(12:52)
10/09 Sa	10:35	♈	SR	8♋36	33.2	(33:12)

		♇	♀	♣	♠
1937	10/10 Su	0♌01 D	3♈33 R	8♋36 R	10♌58 D
	10/17 Su	0♌04	3♈29	8♋35	11♌02
	10/24 Su	0♌06	3♈25	8♋34	11♌05
	10/31 Su	0♌07	3♈21	8♋31	11♌07
	11/07 Su	0♌07 R	3♈17	8♋27	11♌08
	11/14 Su	0♌05	3♈14	8♋22	11♌08 R
	11/21 Su	0♌02	3♈11	8♋16	11♌07
	11/28 Su	29♋58	3♈09	8♋09	11♌05
	12/05 Su	29♋53	3♈08	8♋02	11♌02
	12/12 Su	29♋46	3♈06	7♋54	10♌58
	12/19 Su	29♋39	3♈06	7♋46	10♌53
	12/26 Su	29♋31	3♈06 D	7♋37	10♌47
1938	1/02 Su	29♋23	3♈07	7♋28	10♌41
	1/09 Su	29♋14	3♈08	7♋20	10♌34
	1/16 Su	29♋04	3♈10	7♋12	10♌26
	1/23 Su	28♋55	3♈12	7♋04	10♌18
	1/30 Su	28♋46	3♈15	6♋56	10♌10
	2/06 Su	28♋37	3♈18	6♋49	10♌02
	2/13 Su	28♋28	3♈22	6♋43	9♌55
	2/20 Su	28♋20	3♈26	6♋38	9♌47
	2/27 Su	28♋13	3♈31	6♋34	9♌40
	3/06 Su	28♋06	3♈35	6♋31	9♌33
	3/13 Su	28♋01	3♈40	6♋29	9♌27
	3/20 Su	27♋57	3♈45	6♋29	9♌22
	3/27 Su	27♋53	3♈50	6♋29 D	9♌17
	4/03 Su	27♋51	3♈55	6♋31	9♌14
	4/10 Su	27♋50	4♈00	6♋33	9♌11
	4/17 Su	27♋51 D	4♈05	6♋37	9♌10
	4/24 Su	27♋53	4♈10	6♋42	9♌09
	5/01 Su	27♋55	4♈14	6♋48	9♌10 D
	5/08 Su	28♋00	4♈18	6♋54	9♌11
	5/15 Su	28♋05	4♈22	7♋02	9♌14
	5/22 Su	28♋11	4♈25	7♋10	9♌17
	5/29 Su	28♋19	4♈28	7♋19	9♌22
	6/05 Su	28♋27	4♈30	7♋29	9♌27
	6/12 Su	28♋36	4♈32	7♋39	9♌33
	6/19 Su	28♋46	4♈33	7♋49	9♌40

		♇	♀	♣	♠
1938	6/26 Su	28♋56 D	4♈34 D	7♋59 D	9♌48 D
	7/03 Su	29♋07	4♈34 R	8♋10	9♌56
	7/10 Su	29♋18	4♈34	8♋20	10♌04
	7/17 Su	29♋30	4♈33	8♋31	10♌13
	7/24 Su	29♋42	4♈31	8♋41	10♌23
	7/31 Su	29♋53	4♈29	8♋50	10♌32
	8/07 Su	0♌05	4♈27	8♋59	10♌41
	8/14 Su	0♌16	4♈24	9♋08	10♌51
	8/21 Su	0♌27	4♈21	9♋16	11♌00
	8/28 Su	0♌37	4♈17	9♋23	11♌09
	9/04 Su	0♌47	4♈13	9♋29	11♌18
	9/11 Su	0♌56	4♈09	9♋34	11♌26
	9/18 Su	1♌04	4♈04	9♋39	11♌33
	9/25 Su	1♌11	4♈00	9♋42	11♌40
	10/02 Su	1♌17	3♈55	9♋44	11♌47
	10/09 Su	1♌23	3♈51	9♋45	11♌52
	10/16 Su	1♌26	3♈46	9♋44 R	11♌56
	10/23 Su	1♌29	3♈42	9♋43	12♌00
	10/30 Su	1♌30	3♈38	9♋40	12♌02
	11/06 Su	1♌30 R	3♈35	9♋37	12♌03
	11/13 Su	1♌29	3♈31	9♋32	12♌04 R
	11/20 Su	1♌26	3♈29	9♋27	12♌03
	11/27 Su	1♌23	3♈26	9♋20	12♌01
	12/04 Su	1♌18	3♈24	9♋13	11♌58
	12/11 Su	1♌12	3♈23	9♋05	11♌55
	12/18 Su	1♌05	3♈23	8♋57	11♌50
	12/25 Su	0♌57	3♈12 D	8♋49	11♌44
1939	1/01 Su	0♌49	3♈23	8♋40	11♌38
	1/08 Su	0♌40	3♈24	8♋31	11♌31
	1/15 Su	0♌31	3♈26	8♋23	11♌24
	1/22 Su	0♌21	3♈28	8♋15	11♌16
	1/29 Su	0♌12	3♈31	8♋07	11♌08
	2/05 Su	0♌03	3♈34	8♋00	11♌00
	2/12 Su	29♋54	3♈38	7♋54	10♌52
	2/19 Su	29♋46	3♈42	7♋49	10♌45
	2/26 Su	29♋38	3♈46	7♋44	10♌37
	3/05 Su	29♋31	3♈51	7♋41	10♌31

Astro Data

1937

10/31 Su	20:07	♇	SR	0♌07	22.9	(22:53)
11/10 We	07:55	♠	SR	11♌08	22.0	(21:58)
11/25 Th	09:07	♇	→ ♋ R		23.0	(22:58)
12/22 We	00:47	♀	SD	3♈06	-23.1	(-23:08)

1938

3/21 Mo	03:11	♣	SD	6♋29	33.6	(33:38)
4/11 Mo	01:54	♇	SD	27♋50	23.6	(23:33)
4/24 Su	04:52	♠	SD	9♌09	22.7	(22:44)

1938

7/01 Fr	10:31	♀	SR	4♈34	-22.5	(-22:17)
8/03 We	17:58	♇	→ ♌		23.2	(23:09)
10/10 Mo	19:22	♣	SR	9♋45	33.7	(33:43)
11/02 We	12:19	♇	SR	1♌30	23.0	(22:59)
11/11 Fr	14:40	♠	SR	12♌04	22.2	(22:09)
12/22 Th	09:04	♀	SD	3♈12	-22.9	(-22:52)

1939

2/07 Tu	12:57	♇	→ ♋ R		23.5	(23:30)

1939	♇	♀	♁	♆		1939	♇	♀	♁	♆
3/12 Su	29♋25 ℞	3♈56 D	7♋39 ℞	10♌24 ℞		12/17 Su	2♌32 ℞	3♈39 ℞	10♋08 ℞	12♌46 ℞
3/19 Su	29♋20	4♈01	7♋37	10♌19		12/24 Su	2♌24	3♈39 D	10♋00	12♌41
3/26 Su	29♋17	4♈06	7♋37 D	10♌14		12/31 Su	2♌16	3♈39	9♋51	12♌35
4/02 Su	29♋14	4♈11	7♋39	10♌10						
4/09 Su	29♋13	4♈16	7♋41	10♌07		1940				
						1/07 Su	2♌07	3♈40	9♋43	12♌29
4/16 Su	29♋13 D	4♈21	7♋44	10♌06		1/14 Su	1♌58	3♈42	9♋34	12♌21
4/23 Su	29♋14	4♈25	7♋49	10♌05		1/21 Su	1♌49	3♈44	9♋26	12♌14
4/30 Su	29♋17	4♈30	7♋54	10♌05 D		1/28 Su	1♌39	3♈47	9♋18	12♌06
5/07 Su	29♋20	4♈34	8♋01	10♌06		2/04 Su	1♌30	3♈50	9♋11	11♌58
5/14 Su	29♋25	4♈38	8♋08	10♌08						
						2/11 Su	1♌21	3♈53	9♋05	11♌50
5/21 Su	29♋31	4♈41	8♋16	10♌12		2/18 Su	1♌12	3♈57	8♋59	11♌42
5/28 Su	29♋38	4♈44	8♋25	10♌16		2/25 Su	1♌04	4♈02	8♋54	11♌35
6/04 Su	29♋46	4♈46	8♋34	10♌21		3/03 Su	0♌57	4♈06	8♋50	11♌28
6/11 Su	29♋55	4♈48	8♋44	10♌27		3/10 Su	0♌51	4♈11	8♋48	11♌22
6/18 Su	0♌05	4♈50	8♋54	10♌33						
						3/17 Su	0♌46	4♈16	8♋46	11♌16
6/25 Su	0♌15	4♈50	9♋04	10♌41		3/24 Su	0♌42	4♈21	8♋46 D	11♌11
7/02 Su	0♌26	4♈51	9♋15	10♌49		3/31 Su	0♌39	4♈26	8♋47	11♌07
7/09 Su	0♌37	4♈50 ℞	9♋25	10♌57		4/07 Su	0♌37	4♈31	8♋48	11♌04
7/16 Su	0♌49	4♈50	9♋35	11♌06		4/14 Su	0♌36 D	4♈36	8♋51	11♌01
7/23 Su	1♌00	4♈48	9♋46	11♌15						
						4/21 Su	0♌37	4♈41	8♋56	11♌00
7/30 Su	1♌12	4♈46	9♋55	11♌24		4/28 Su	0♌39	4♈45	9♋01	11♌00 D
8/06 Su	1♌24	4♈44	10♋05	11♌34		5/05 Su	0♌42	4♈49	9♋07	11♌01
8/13 Su	1♌35	4♈41	10♋14	11♌43		5/12 Su	0♌47	4♈53	9♋14	11♌03
8/20 Su	1♌46	4♈38	10♋22	11♌53		5/19 Su	0♌53	4♈57	9♋22	11♌06
8/27 Su	1♌57	4♈34	10♋29	12♌02						
						5/26 Su	0♌59	5♈00	9♋30	11♌10
9/03 Su	2♌07	4♈30	10♋35	12♌10		6/02 Su	1♌07	5♈02	9♋39	11♌14
9/10 Su	2♌17	4♈26	10♋41	12♌19		6/09 Su	1♌16	5♈04	9♋49	11♌20
9/17 Su	2♌25	4♈22	10♋46	12♌26		6/16 Su	1♌25	5♈06	9♋59	11♌26
9/24 Su	2♌33	4♈17	10♋49	12♌33		6/23 Su	1♌35	5♈07	10♋09	11♌34
10/01 Su	2♌39	4♈13	10♋51	12♌40						
						6/30 Su	1♌46	5♈07	10♋19	11♌41
10/08 Su	2♌45	4♈08	10♋53	12♌45		7/07 Su	1♌57	5♈07 ℞	10♋30	11♌50
10/15 Su	2♌49	4♈04	10♋53 ℞	12♌50		7/14 Su	2♌09	5♈06	10♋40	11♌58
10/22 Su	2♌52	4♈00	10♋52	12♌54		7/21 Su	2♌20	5♈05	10♋51	12♌07
10/29 Su	2♌54	3♈56	10♋50	12♌57		7/28 Su	2♌31	5♈03	11♋00	12♌17
11/05 Su	2♌54 ℞	3♈52	10♋46	12♌58						
						8/04 Su	2♌44	5♈01	11♋10	12♌26
11/12 Su	2♌54	3♈49	10♋42	12♌59		8/11 Su	2♌56	4♈58	11♋19	12♌35
11/19 Su	2♌52	3♈46	10♋37	12♌58 ℞		8/18 Su	3♌07	4♈55	11♋27	12♌45
11/26 Su	2♌48	3♈43	10♋31	12♌57		8/25 Su	3♌18	4♈51	11♋35	12♌54
12/03 Su	2♌44	3♈41	10♋24	12♌54		9/01 Su	3♌28	4♈48	11♋42	13♌03
12/10 Su	2♌38	3♈40	10♋16	12♌51						

Astro Data

1939

3/22 We	14:10	♁	SD	7♋37	34.2 (34:09)
4/12 We	15:16	♇	SD	29♋13	23.7 (23:40)
4/25 Tu	06:10	♆	SD	10♌05	21.9 (22:56)
6/14 We	04:49	♇	→♌		23.5 (23:31)
7/02 Su	03:10	♀	SR	4♈51	-22.2 (-22:13)
10/12 Th	03:36	♁	SR	10♋53	34.2 (34:10)
11/04 Sa	08:07	♇	SR	2♌54	23.1 (23:04)
11/12 Su	17:12	♆	SR	12♌59	22.4 (22:21)

1939

12/22 Fr	23:06	♀	SD	3♈39	-22.6 (-22:37)

1940

3/22 Fr	23:58	♁	SD	8♋46	34.6 (34:38)
4/13 Sa	09:15	♇	SD	0♌36	23.8 (23:47)
4/25 Th	11:32	♆	SD	11♌00	23.1 (23:08)
7/01 Mo	14:38	♀	SR	5♈07	-22.0 (-21:57)

1940	Date	♀	♀	♇	♇
	9/08 Su	3 ♌ 38 D	4 ♈ 43 ℞	11 ♋ 47 D	13 ♌ 11 D
	9/15 Su	3 ♌ 47	4 ♈ 39	11 ♋ 52	13 ♌ 19
	9/22 Su	3 ♌ 55	4 ♈ 35	11 ♋ 56	13 ♌ 26
	9/29 Su	4 ♌ 02	4 ♈ 30	11 ♋ 59	13 ♌ 33
	10/06 Su	4 ♌ 08	4 ♈ 26	12 ♋ 01	13 ♌ 39
	10/13 Su	4 ♌ 13	4 ♈ 21	12 ♋ 01 ℞	13 ♌ 44
	10/20 Su	4 ♌ 16	4 ♈ 17	12 ♋ 01	13 ♌ 48
	10/27 Su	4 ♌ 19	4 ♈ 13	11 ♋ 59	13 ♌ 51
	11/03 Su	4 ♌ 20	4 ♈ 09	11 ♋ 56	13 ♌ 53
	11/10 Su	4 ♌ 20 ℞	4 ♈ 06	11 ♋ 52	13 ♌ 54
	11/17 Su	4 ♌ 18	4 ♈ 03	11 ♋ 47	13 ♌ 54 ℞
	11/24 Su	4 ♌ 15	4 ♈ 00	11 ♋ 41	13 ♌ 52
	12/01 Su	4 ♌ 11	3 ♈ 58	11 ♋ 35	13 ♌ 50
	12/08 Su	4 ♌ 06	3 ♈ 57	11 ♋ 27	13 ♌ 47
	12/15 Su	4 ♌ 00	3 ♈ 56	11 ♋ 19	13 ♌ 43
	12/22 Su	3 ♌ 53	3 ♈ 55	11 ♋ 11	13 ♌ 38
	12/29 Su	3 ♌ 45	3 ♈ 56 D	11 ♋ 03	13 ♌ 32
1941	1/05 Su	3 ♌ 36	3 ♈ 56	10 ♋ 54	13 ♌ 26
	1/12 Su	3 ♌ 27	3 ♈ 58	10 ♋ 45	13 ♌ 19
	1/19 Su	3 ♌ 18	4 ♈ 00	10 ♋ 37	13 ♌ 11
	1/26 Su	3 ♌ 08	4 ♈ 02	10 ♋ 29	13 ♌ 03
	2/02 Su	2 ♌ 59	4 ♈ 05	10 ♋ 22	12 ♌ 56
	2/09 Su	2 ♌ 49	4 ♈ 09	10 ♋ 15	12 ♌ 48
	2/16 Su	2 ♌ 41	4 ♈ 13	10 ♋ 09	12 ♌ 40
	2/23 Su	2 ♌ 32	4 ♈ 17	10 ♋ 04	12 ♌ 32
	3/02 Su	2 ♌ 25	4 ♈ 21	10 ♋ 00	12 ♌ 25
	3/09 Su	2 ♌ 18	4 ♈ 26	9 ♋ 57	12 ♌ 19
	3/16 Su	2 ♌ 12	4 ♈ 31	9 ♋ 55	12 ♌ 13
	3/23 Su	2 ♌ 08	4 ♈ 36	9 ♋ 54	12 ♌ 08
	3/30 Su	2 ♌ 04	4 ♈ 41	9 ♋ 55 D	12 ♌ 03
	4/06 Su	2 ♌ 02	4 ♈ 46	9 ♋ 56	12 ♌ 00
	4/13 Su	2 ♌ 01	4 ♈ 51	9 ♋ 59	11 ♌ 57
	4/20 Su	2 ♌ 02 D	4 ♈ 56	10 ♋ 02	11 ♌ 56
	4/27 Su	2 ♌ 03	5 ♈ 00	10 ♋ 07	11 ♌ 55 D
	5/04 Su	2 ♌ 06	5 ♈ 05	10 ♋ 13	11 ♌ 56
	5/11 Su	2 ♌ 10	5 ♈ 08	10 ♋ 20	11 ♌ 57
	5/18 Su	2 ♌ 15	5 ♈ 12	10 ♋ 27	12 ♌ 00

1941	Date	♀	♀	♇	♇
	5/25 Su	2 ♌ 22 D	5 ♈ 15 D	10 ♋ 35 D	12 ♌ 03 D
	6/01 Su	2 ♌ 29	5 ♈ 18	10 ♋ 44	12 ♌ 08
	6/08 Su	2 ♌ 37	5 ♈ 20	10 ♋ 54	12 ♌ 13
	6/15 Su	2 ♌ 47	5 ♈ 21	11 ♋ 04	12 ♌ 19
	6/22 Su	2 ♌ 57	5 ♈ 23	11 ♋ 14	12 ♌ 26
	6/29 Su	3 ♌ 07	5 ♈ 23	11 ♋ 24	12 ♌ 34
	7/06 Su	3 ♌ 18	5 ♈ 23 ℞	11 ♋ 35	12 ♌ 42
	7/13 Su	3 ♌ 30	5 ♈ 22	11 ♋ 45	12 ♌ 51
	7/20 Su	3 ♌ 42	5 ♈ 21	11 ♋ 55	12 ♌ 59
	7/27 Su	3 ♌ 53	5 ♈ 20	12 ♋ 05	13 ♌ 09
	8/03 Su	4 ♌ 05	5 ♈ 18	12 ♋ 15	13 ♌ 18
	8/10 Su	4 ♌ 17	5 ♈ 15	12 ♋ 24	13 ♌ 27
	8/17 Su	4 ♌ 29	5 ♈ 12	12 ♋ 33	13 ♌ 37
	8/24 Su	4 ♌ 40	5 ♈ 08	12 ♋ 40	13 ♌ 46
	8/31 Su	4 ♌ 51	5 ♈ 05	12 ♋ 48	13 ♌ 55
	9/07 Su	5 ♌ 01	5 ♈ 01	12 ♋ 54	14 ♌ 04
	9/14 Su	5 ♌ 10	4 ♈ 56	12 ♋ 59	14 ♌ 12
	9/21 Su	5 ♌ 19	4 ♈ 52	13 ♋ 03	14 ♌ 19
	9/28 Su	5 ♌ 26	4 ♈ 47	13 ♋ 06	14 ♌ 26
	10/05 Su	5 ♌ 33	4 ♈ 43	13 ♋ 08	14 ♌ 32
	10/12 Su	5 ♌ 38	4 ♈ 38	13 ♋ 09	14 ♌ 37
	10/19 Su	5 ♌ 42	4 ♈ 34	13 ♋ 09 ℞	14 ♌ 41
	10/26 Su	5 ♌ 45	4 ♈ 30	13 ♋ 08	14 ♌ 45
	11/02 Su	5 ♌ 46	4 ♈ 26	13 ♋ 05	14 ♌ 47
	11/09 Su	5 ♌ 47 ℞	4 ♈ 23	13 ♋ 02	14 ♌ 48
	11/16 Su	5 ♌ 46	4 ♈ 20	12 ♋ 57	14 ♌ 49 ℞
	11/23 Su	5 ♌ 43	4 ♈ 17	12 ♋ 51	14 ♌ 48
	11/30 Su	5 ♌ 40	4 ♈ 15	12 ♋ 45	14 ♌ 46
	12/07 Su	5 ♌ 35	4 ♈ 13	12 ♋ 38	14 ♌ 43
	12/14 Su	5 ♌ 29	4 ♈ 12	12 ♋ 30	14 ♌ 39
	12/21 Su	5 ♌ 22	4 ♈ 12	12 ♋ 22	14 ♌ 34
	12/28 Su	5 ♌ 14	4 ♈ 12 D	12 ♋ 14	14 ♌ 29
1942	1/04 Su	5 ♌ 06	4 ♈ 12	12 ♋ 05	14 ♌ 23
	1/11 Su	4 ♌ 57	4 ♈ 14	11 ♋ 57	14 ♌ 16
	1/18 Su	4 ♌ 48	4 ♈ 16	11 ♋ 48	14 ♌ 08
	1/25 Su	4 ♌ 38	4 ♈ 18	11 ♋ 40	14 ♌ 01
	2/01 Su	4 ♌ 29	4 ♈ 21	11 ♋ 33	13 ♌ 53

Astro Data

1940

10/12 Sa	12:56	♇ SR	12 ♋ 01	34.6 (34:36)
11/05 Tu	01:31	♀ SR	4 ♌ 20	23.1 (23:08)
11/12 Tu	18:36	♇ SR	13 ♌ 54	22.5 (22:31)
12/22 Su	15:55	♀ SD	3 ♈ 55	-22.3 (-22:20)

1941

3/24 Mo	09:13	♇ SD	9 ♋ 54	35.1 (35:05)
4/14 Mo	18:25	♀ SD	2 ♌ 01	23.9 (23:52)
4/26 Sa	18:02	♇ SD	11 ♌ 55	23.3 (23:19)

1941

7/01 Tu	22:01	♀ SR	5 ♈ 23	-21.7 (-21:41)
10/14 Tu	01:13	♇ SR	13 ♋ 09	35.1 (35:04)
11/06 Th	20:45	♀ SR	5 ♌ 47	23.2 (23:11)
11/13 Th	23:05	♇ SR	14 ♌ 49	22.7 (22:42)
12/23 Tu	02:36	♀ SD	4 ♈ 12	-22.1 (-22:05)

1942		☿	♀	⚷	⚸	1942		☿	♀	⚷	⚸
	2/08 Su	4 ♌ 19 R	4 ♈ 24 D	11 ♋ 26 R	13 ♌ 45 R		11/15 Su	7 ♌ 14 R	4 ♈ 36 R	14 ♋ 07 R	15 ♌ 43 D
	2/15 Su	4 ♌ 10	4 ♈ 28	11 ♋ 19	13 ♌ 37		11/22 Su	7 ♌ 13	4 ♈ 34	14 ♋ 02	15 ♌ 43 R
	2/22 Su	4 ♌ 02	4 ♈ 32	11 ♋ 14	13 ♌ 30		11/29 Su	7 ♌ 09	4 ♈ 31	13 ♋ 55	15 ♌ 41
	3/01 Su	3 ♌ 54	4 ♈ 37	11 ♋ 10	13 ♌ 22		12/06 Su	7 ♌ 05	4 ♈ 30	13 ♋ 49	15 ♌ 39
	3/08 Su	3 ♌ 47	4 ♈ 41	11 ♋ 06	13 ♌ 16		12/13 Su	7 ♌ 00	4 ♈ 28	13 ♋ 41	15 ♌ 35
	3/15 Su	3 ♌ 41	4 ♈ 46	11 ♋ 04	13 ♌ 10		12/20 Su	6 ♌ 53	4 ♈ 28	13 ♋ 33	15 ♌ 31
	3/22 Su	3 ♌ 36	4 ♈ 51	11 ♋ 03	13 ♌ 04		12/27 Su	6 ♌ 46	4 ♈ 28 D	13 ♋ 25	15 ♌ 25
	3/29 Su	3 ♌ 32	4 ♈ 56	11 ♋ 03 D	13 ♌ 00						
	4/05 Su	3 ♌ 29	5 ♈ 01	11 ♋ 04	12 ♌ 56						
	4/12 Su	3 ♌ 28	5 ♈ 06	11 ♋ 06	12 ♌ 53						
						1943					
	4/19 Su	3 ♌ 27 D	5 ♈ 11	11 ♋ 09	12 ♌ 51		1/03 Su	6 ♌ 37	4 ♈ 28	13 ♋ 16	15 ♌ 19
	4/26 Su	3 ♌ 29	5 ♈ 16	11 ♋ 14	12 ♌ 50		1/10 Su	6 ♌ 29	4 ♈ 30	13 ♋ 08	15 ♌ 13
	5/03 Su	3 ♌ 31	5 ♈ 20	11 ♋ 19	12 ♌ 51 D		1/17 Su	6 ♌ 19	4 ♈ 31	12 ♋ 59	15 ♌ 06
	5/10 Su	3 ♌ 35	5 ♈ 24	11 ♋ 26	12 ♌ 52		1/24 Su	6 ♌ 10	4 ♈ 34	12 ♋ 51	14 ♌ 58
	5/17 Su	3 ♌ 39	5 ♈ 27	11 ♋ 33	12 ♌ 54		1/31 Su	6 ♌ 00	4 ♈ 36	12 ♋ 43	14 ♌ 50
	5/24 Su	3 ♌ 45	5 ♈ 31	11 ♋ 41	12 ♌ 57		2/07 Su	5 ♌ 51	4 ♈ 40	12 ♋ 36	14 ♌ 42
	5/31 Su	3 ♌ 52	5 ♈ 33	11 ♋ 49	13 ♌ 02		2/14 Su	5 ♌ 41	4 ♈ 43	12 ♋ 30	14 ♌ 34
	6/07 Su	4 ♌ 01	5 ♈ 36	11 ♋ 59	13 ♌ 07		2/21 Su	5 ♌ 33	4 ♈ 47	12 ♋ 24	14 ♌ 27
	6/14 Su	4 ♌ 09	5 ♈ 37	12 ♋ 08	13 ♌ 13		2/28 Su	5 ♌ 24	4 ♈ 52	12 ♋ 19	14 ♌ 19
	6/21 Su	4 ♌ 19	5 ♈ 38	12 ♋ 18	13 ♌ 19		3/07 Su	5 ♌ 17	4 ♈ 56	12 ♋ 15	14 ♌ 13
	6/28 Su	4 ♌ 30	5 ♈ 39	12 ♋ 29	13 ♌ 26		3/14 Su	5 ♌ 11	5 ♈ 01	12 ♋ 13	14 ♌ 06
	7/05 Su	4 ♌ 41	5 ♈ 39 R	12 ♋ 39	13 ♌ 34		3/21 Su	5 ♌ 05	5 ♈ 06	12 ♋ 11	14 ♌ 01
	7/12 Su	4 ♌ 52	5 ♈ 39	12 ♋ 50	13 ♌ 43		3/28 Su	5 ♌ 01	5 ♈ 11	12 ♋ 11 D	13 ♌ 56
	7/19 Su	5 ♌ 04	5 ♈ 38	13 ♋ 00	13 ♌ 52		4/04 Su	4 ♌ 57	5 ♈ 16	12 ♋ 11	13 ♌ 52
	7/26 Su	5 ♌ 16	5 ♈ 36	13 ♋ 10	14 ♌ 01		4/11 Su	4 ♌ 56	5 ♈ 21	12 ♋ 13	13 ♌ 49
	8/02 Su	5 ♌ 28	5 ♈ 34	13 ♋ 20	14 ♌ 10		4/18 Su	4 ♌ 55	5 ♈ 26	12 ♋ 16	13 ♌ 47
	8/09 Su	5 ♌ 40	5 ♈ 32	13 ♋ 29	14 ♌ 19		4/25 Su	4 ♌ 56 D	5 ♈ 31	12 ♋ 20	13 ♌ 46
	8/16 Su	5 ♌ 52	5 ♈ 29	13 ♋ 38	14 ♌ 29		5/02 Su	4 ♌ 57	5 ♈ 35	12 ♋ 25	13 ♌ 45 D
	8/23 Su	6 ♌ 03	5 ♈ 25	13 ♋ 46	14 ♌ 38		5/09 Su	5 ♌ 01	5 ♈ 39	12 ♋ 31	13 ♌ 46
	8/30 Su	6 ♌ 14	5 ♈ 22	13 ♋ 53	14 ♌ 47		5/16 Su	5 ♌ 05	5 ♈ 43	12 ♋ 38	13 ♌ 48
	9/06 Su	6 ♌ 25	5 ♈ 18	14 ♋ 00	14 ♌ 56		5/23 Su	5 ♌ 11	5 ♈ 46	12 ♋ 46	13 ♌ 51
	9/13 Su	6 ♌ 34	5 ♈ 13	14 ♋ 05	15 ♌ 04		5/30 Su	5 ♌ 17	5 ♈ 49	12 ♋ 54	13 ♌ 55
	9/20 Su	6 ♌ 43	5 ♈ 09	14 ♋ 10	15 ♌ 12		6/06 Su	5 ♌ 25	5 ♈ 51	13 ♋ 03	14 ♌ 00
	9/27 Su	6 ♌ 51	5 ♈ 04	14 ♋ 13	15 ♌ 19		6/13 Su	5 ♌ 34	5 ♈ 53	13 ♋ 13	14 ♌ 06
	10/04 Su	6 ♌ 58	5 ♈ 00	14 ♋ 16	15 ♌ 25		6/20 Su	5 ♌ 43	5 ♈ 54	13 ♋ 23	14 ♌ 12
	10/11 Su	7 ♌ 04	4 ♈ 55	14 ♋ 17	15 ♌ 30		6/27 Su	5 ♌ 54	5 ♈ 55	13 ♋ 33	14 ♌ 19
	10/18 Su	7 ♌ 09	4 ♈ 51	14 ♋ 17 R	15 ♌ 35		7/04 Su	6 ♌ 04	5 ♈ 55 R	13 ♋ 44	14 ♌ 27
	10/25 Su	7 ♌ 12	4 ♈ 47	14 ♋ 16	15 ♌ 39		7/11 Su	6 ♌ 16	5 ♈ 55	13 ♋ 54	14 ♌ 35
	11/01 Su	7 ♌ 14	4 ♈ 43	14 ♋ 14	15 ♌ 41		7/18 Su	6 ♌ 28	5 ♈ 54	14 ♋ 04	14 ♌ 44
	11/08 Su	7 ♌ 15	4 ♈ 40	14 ♋ 11	15 ♌ 43		7/25 Su	6 ♌ 40	5 ♈ 52	14 ♋ 15	14 ♌ 53

Astro Data

1942

3/25 We	16:10	♎	SD	11 ♋ 03	35.5 (35:32)
4/16 Th	11:02	☿	SD	3 ♌ 27	24.0 (23:57)
4/27 Mo	22:59	♌	SD	12 ♌ 50	23.5 (23:30)
7/02 Th	12:23	♀	SR	5 ♈ 39	-21.4 (-21:25)
10/15 Th	10:28	♎	SR	14 ♋ 17	35.5 (35:28)
11/08 Su	14:42	☿	SR	7 ♌ 15	23.2 (23:14)
11/15 Su	03:03	♌	SR	15 ♌ 43	21.9 (21:53)

1942

12/13 We	12:07	☿	SD	4 ♈ 28	-21.8 (-21:50)

1943

3/27 Sa	02:39	♎	SD	12 ♋ 11	36.0 (35:58)
4/18 Su	03:04	☿	SD	4 ♌ 55	24.0 (24:01)
4/29 Th	03:24	♎	SD	13 ♌ 45	23.7 (23:41)
7/03 Sa	03:41	☿	SR	5 ♈ 55	-21.2 (-21:09)

	♇	♀	♋	♌
1943 8/01 Su	6 Ω 52 D	5 ♈ 51 R	14 ♋ 24 D	15 Ω 02 D
8/08 Su	7 Ω 04	5 ♈ 48	14 ♋ 34	15 Ω 11
8/15 Su	7 Ω 16	5 ♈ 45	14 ♋ 43	15 Ω 21
8/22 Su	7 Ω 28	5 ♈ 42	14 ♋ 51	15 Ω 30
8/29 Su	7 Ω 39	5 ♈ 38	14 ♋ 59	15 Ω 39
9/05 Su	7 Ω 50	5 ♈ 34	15 ♋ 06	15 Ω 48
9/12 Su	8 Ω 00	5 ♈ 30	15 ♋ 12	15 Ω 56
9/19 Su	8 Ω 09	5 ♈ 26	15 ♋ 16	16 Ω 04
9/26 Su	8 Ω 18	5 ♈ 21	15 ♋ 20	16 Ω 11
10/03 Su	8 Ω 25	5 ♈ 17	15 ♋ 23	16 Ω 18
10/10 Su	8 Ω 31	5 ♈ 12	15 ♋ 25	16 Ω 23
10/17 Su	8 Ω 37	5 ♈ 08	15 ♋ 25 R	16 Ω 28
10/24 Su	8 Ω 40	5 ♈ 04	15 ♋ 25	16 Ω 32
10/31 Su	8 Ω 43	5 ♈ 00	15 ♋ 23	16 Ω 35
11/07 Su	8 Ω 44	4 ♈ 56	15 ♋ 20	16 Ω 37
11/14 Su	8 Ω 44 R	4 ♈ 53	15 ♋ 16	16 Ω 38
11/21 Su	8 Ω 43	4 ♈ 50	15 ♋ 11	16 Ω 38 R
11/28 Su	8 Ω 40	4 ♈ 48	15 ♋ 06	16 Ω 37
12/05 Su	8 Ω 37	4 ♈ 46	14 ♋ 59	16 Ω 34
12/12 Su	8 Ω 31	4 ♈ 45	14 ♋ 52	16 Ω 31
12/19 Su	8 Ω 25	4 ♈ 44	14 ♋ 44	16 Ω 27
12/26 Su	8 Ω 18	4 ♈ 44 D	14 ♋ 36	16 Ω 22
1944 1/02 Su	8 Ω 10	4 ♈ 44	14 ♋ 27	16 Ω 16
1/09 Su	8 Ω 02	4 ♈ 45	14 ♋ 19	16 Ω 10
1/16 Su	7 Ω 52	4 ♈ 47	14 ♋ 10	16 Ω 03
1/23 Su	7 Ω 43	4 ♈ 49	14 ♋ 02	15 Ω 55
1/30 Su	7 Ω 33	4 ♈ 52	13 ♋ 54	15 Ω 47
2/06 Su	7 Ω 24	4 ♈ 55	13 ♋ 46	15 Ω 39
2/13 Su	7 Ω 14	4 ♈ 59	13 ♋ 40	15 Ω 32
2/20 Su	7 Ω 05	5 ♈ 03	13 ♋ 34	15 Ω 24
2/27 Su	6 Ω 57	5 ♈ 07	13 ♋ 29	15 Ω 16
3/05 Su	6 Ω 49	5 ♈ 11	13 ♋ 25	15 Ω 09
3/12 Su	6 Ω 42	5 ♈ 16	13 ♋ 22	15 Ω 03
3/19 Su	6 Ω 36	5 ♈ 21	13 ♋ 20	14 Ω 57
3/26 Su	6 Ω 31	5 ♈ 26	13 ♋ 19	14 Ω 52
4/02 Su	6 Ω 27	5 ♈ 31	13 ♋ 19 D	14 Ω 48
4/09 Su	6 Ω 25	5 ♈ 36	13 ♋ 21	14 Ω 44

	♇	♀	♋	♌
1944 4/16 Su	6 Ω 24 R	5 ♈ 41 D	13 ♋ 23 D	14 Ω 42 R
4/23 Su	6 Ω 24 D	5 ♈ 46	13 ♋ 27	14 Ω 41
4/30 Su	6 Ω 25	5 ♈ 50	13 ♋ 32	14 Ω 40 D
5/07 Su	6 Ω 28	5 ♈ 54	13 ♋ 37	14 Ω 41
5/14 Su	6 Ω 32	5 ♈ 58	13 ♋ 44	14 Ω 42
5/21 Su	6 Ω 37	6 ♈ 01	13 ♋ 51	14 Ω 45
5/28 Su	6 Ω 44	6 ♈ 04	13 ♋ 59	14 Ω 49
6/04 Su	6 Ω 51	6 ♈ 06	14 ♋ 08	14 Ω 53
6/11 Su	6 Ω 59	6 ♈ 08	14 ♋ 18	14 Ω 58
6/18 Su	7 Ω 09	6 ♈ 10	14 ♋ 27	15 Ω 05
6/25 Su	7 Ω 19	6 ♈ 11	14 ♋ 38	15 Ω 12
7/02 Su	7 Ω 30	6 ♈ 11	14 ♋ 48	15 Ω 19
7/09 Su	7 Ω 41	6 ♈ 11 R	14 ♋ 58	15 Ω 27
7/16 Su	7 Ω 53	6 ♈ 10	15 ♋ 09	15 Ω 36
7/23 Su	8 Ω 05	6 ♈ 09	15 ♋ 19	15 Ω 45
7/30 Su	8 Ω 17	6 ♈ 07	15 ♋ 29	15 Ω 54
8/06 Su	8 Ω 29	6 ♈ 05	15 ♋ 39	16 Ω 03
8/13 Su	8 Ω 41	6 ♈ 02	15 ♋ 48	16 Ω 12
8/20 Su	8 Ω 53	5 ♈ 59	15 ♋ 56	16 Ω 22
8/27 Su	9 Ω 05	5 ♈ 55	16 ♋ 04	16 Ω 31
9/03 Su	9 Ω 16	5 ♈ 51	16 ♋ 11	16 Ω 40
9/10 Su	9 Ω 26	5 ♈ 47	16 ♋ 17	16 Ω 48
9/17 Su	9 Ω 36	5 ♈ 43	16 ♋ 23	16 Ω 56
9/24 Su	9 Ω 45	5 ♈ 38	16 ♋ 27	17 Ω 04
10/01 Su	9 Ω 53	5 ♈ 34	16 ♋ 30	17 Ω 10
10/08 Su	10 Ω 00	5 ♈ 29	16 ♋ 32	17 Ω 16
10/15 Su	10 Ω 05	5 ♈ 25	16 ♋ 33	17 Ω 21
10/22 Su	10 Ω 10	5 ♈ 21	16 ♋ 33 R	17 Ω 26
10/29 Su	10 Ω 13	5 ♈ 17	16 ♋ 31	17 Ω 29
11/05 Su	10 Ω 15	5 ♈ 13	16 ♋ 29	17 Ω 31
11/12 Su	10 Ω 16 R	5 ♈ 10	16 ♋ 25	17 Ω 32
11/19 Su	10 Ω 15	5 ♈ 07	16 ♋ 21	17 Ω 33 R
11/26 Su	10 Ω 13	5 ♈ 04	16 ♋ 15	17 Ω 32
12/03 Su	10 Ω 09	5 ♈ 02	16 ♋ 09	17 Ω 30
12/10 Su	10 Ω 05	5 ♈ 01	16 ♋ 02	17 Ω 27
12/17 Su	9 Ω 59	5 ♈ 00	15 ♋ 54	17 Ω 23
12/24 Su	9 Ω 52	5 ♈ 00 D	15 ♋ 46	17 Ω 18
12/31 Su	9 Ω 44	5 ♈ 00	15 ♋ 38	17 Ω 12

Astro Data

1943

10/16 Sa	19:23	♋ SR	15 ♋ 25	35.8 (35:50)	
11/10 We	09:00	♇ SR	8 Ω 45	23.2 (23:15)	
11/16 Tu	09:04	♋ SR	16 Ω 38	23.0 (23:02)	
12/24 Fr	02:50	♀ SD	4 ♈ 44	-21.6 (-21:35)	

1944

3/27 Mo	12:38	♋ SD	13 ♋ 19	36.4 (36:22)	

1944

4/18 Tu	19:22	♀ SD	6 Ω 24	24.1 (24:04)	
4/29 Sa	04:56	♋ SD	14 Ω 40	23.9 (23:51)	
7/02 Su	13:48	♀ SR	6 ♈ 11	-20.9 (-20:55)	
10/17 Tu	01:43	♋ SR	16 ♋ 33	36.2 (36:14)	
11/11 Sa	05:11	♇ SR	10 Ω 16	23.2 (23:14)	
11/16 Th	11:15	♋ SR	17 Ω 33	23.2 (23:10)	
12/23 Sa	17:45	♀ SD	5 ♈ 00	-21.3 (-21:19)	

1945		♇	♀	♈	♎
	1/07 Su	9 ♌ 36 ℞	5 ♈ 01 D	15 ♋ 29 ℞	17 ♌ 06 ℞
	1/14 Su	9 ♌ 27	5 ♈ 03	15 ♋ 21	16 ♌ 59
	1/21 Su	9 ♌ 17	5 ♈ 05	15 ♋ 12	16 ♌ 52
	1/28 Su	9 ♌ 08	5 ♈ 07	15 ♋ 04	16 ♌ 44
	2/04 Su	8 ♌ 58	5 ♈ 10	14 ♋ 57	16 ♌ 37
	2/11 Su	8 ♌ 48	5 ♈ 14	14 ♋ 50	16 ♌ 29
	2/18 Su	8 ♌ 39	5 ♈ 18	14 ♋ 44	16 ♌ 21
	2/25 Su	8 ♌ 30	5 ♈ 22	14 ♋ 38	16 ♌ 13
	3/04 Su	8 ♌ 22	5 ♈ 26	14 ♋ 34	16 ♌ 06
	3/11 Su	8 ♌ 15	5 ♈ 31	14 ♋ 30	16 ♌ 00
	3/18 Su	8 ♌ 08	5 ♈ 36	14 ♋ 28	15 ♌ 53
	3/25 Su	8 ♌ 03	5 ♈ 41	14 ♋ 17	15 ♌ 48
	4/01 Su	7 ♌ 59	5 ♈ 46	14 ♋ 27 D	15 ♌ 44
	4/08 Su	7 ♌ 56	5 ♈ 51	14 ♋ 28	15 ♌ 40
	4/15 Su	7 ♌ 54	5 ♈ 56	14 ♋ 30	15 ♌ 37
	4/22 Su	7 ♌ 54 D	6 ♈ 00	14 ♋ 33	15 ♌ 36
	4/29 Su	7 ♌ 55	6 ♈ 05	14 ♋ 38	15 ♌ 35
	5/06 Su	7 ♌ 57	6 ♈ 09	14 ♋ 43	15 ♌ 35 D
	5/13 Su	8 ♌ 01	6 ♈ 13	14 ♋ 49	15 ♌ 36
	5/20 Su	8 ♌ 05	6 ♈ 16	14 ♋ 56	15 ♌ 39
	5/27 Su	8 ♌ 11	6 ♈ 19	15 ♋ 04	15 ♌ 42
	6/03 Su	8 ♌ 18	6 ♈ 22	15 ♋ 13	15 ♌ 46
	6/10 Su	8 ♌ 27	6 ♈ 24	15 ♋ 22	15 ♌ 51
	6/17 Su	8 ♌ 36	6 ♈ 25	15 ♋ 32	15 ♌ 57
	6/24 Su	8 ♌ 45	6 ♈ 26	15 ♋ 42	16 ♌ 04
	7/01 Su	8 ♌ 56	6 ♈ 27	15 ♋ 52	16 ♌ 11
	7/08 Su	9 ♌ 07	6 ♈ 27 ℞	16 ♋ 02	16 ♌ 19
	7/15 Su	9 ♌ 19	6 ♈ 26	16 ♋ 13	16 ♌ 28
	7/22 Su	9 ♌ 31	6 ♈ 25	16 ♋ 23	16 ♌ 36
	7/29 Su	9 ♌ 43	6 ♈ 23	16 ♋ 33	16 ♌ 45
	8/05 Su	9 ♌ 56	6 ♈ 21	16 ♋ 43	16 ♌ 55
	8/12 Su	10 ♌ 08	6 ♈ 18	16 ♋ 52	17 ♌ 04
	8/19 Su	10 ♌ 20	6 ♈ 15	17 ♋ 01	17 ♌ 13
	8/26 Su	10 ♌ 32	6 ♈ 12	17 ♋ 09	17 ♌ 23
	9/02 Su	10 ♌ 43	6 ♈ 08	17 ♋ 16	17 ♌ 31
	9/09 Su	10 ♌ 54	6 ♈ 04	17 ♋ 23	17 ♌ 40
	9/16 Su	11 ♌ 04	6 ♈ 00	17 ♋ 29	17 ♌ 48
	9/23 Su	11 ♌ 14	5 ♈ 55	17 ♋ 33	17 ♌ 56
	9/30 Su	11 ♌ 22	5 ♈ 51	17 ♋ 37	18 ♌ 03
	10/07 Su	11 ♌ 29	5 ♈ 46	17 ♋ 39	18 ♌ 09

1945		♇	♀	♈	♎
	10/14 Su	11 ♌ 36 D	5 ♈ 42 ℞	17 ♋ 40 D	18 ♌ 14 D
	10/21 Su	11 ♌ 41	5 ♈ 37	17 ♋ 41 ℞	18 ♌ 19
	10/28 Su	11 ♌ 44	5 ♈ 33	17 ♋ 40	18 ♌ 22
	11/04 Su	11 ♌ 47	5 ♈ 30	17 ♋ 37	18 ♌ 25
	11/11 Su	11 ♌ 48	5 ♈ 26	17 ♋ 34	18 ♌ 26
	11/18 Su	11 ♌ 48 ℞	5 ♈ 23	17 ♋ 30	18 ♌ 27 ℞
	11/25 Su	11 ♌ 46	5 ♈ 21	17 ♋ 25	18 ♌ 26
	12/02 Su	11 ♌ 43	5 ♈ 19	17 ♋ 19	18 ♌ 25
	12/09 Su	11 ♌ 39	5 ♈ 17	17 ♋ 12	18 ♌ 22
	12/16 Su	11 ♌ 33	5 ♈ 16	17 ♋ 04	18 ♌ 18
	12/23 Su	11 ♌ 27	5 ♈ 16	16 ♋ 57	18 ♌ 14
	12/30 Su	11 ♌ 20	5 ♈ 16 D	16 ♋ 48	18 ♌ 09

1946		♇	♀	♈	♎
	1/06 Su	11 ♌ 11	5 ♈ 17	16 ♋ 40	18 ♌ 03
	1/13 Su	11 ♌ 02	5 ♈ 18	16 ♋ 31	17 ♌ 56
	1/20 Su	10 ♌ 53	5 ♈ 20	16 ♋ 23	17 ♌ 49
	1/27 Su	10 ♌ 43	5 ♈ 22	16 ♋ 15	17 ♌ 41
	2/03 Su	10 ♌ 34	5 ♈ 25	16 ♋ 07	17 ♌ 33
	2/10 Su	10 ♌ 24	5 ♈ 29	16 ♋ 00	17 ♌ 25
	2/17 Su	10 ♌ 14	5 ♈ 33	15 ♋ 53	17 ♌ 18
	2/24 Su	10 ♌ 05	5 ♈ 37	15 ♋ 47	17 ♌ 10
	3/03 Su	9 ♌ 57	5 ♈ 41	15 ♋ 43	17 ♌ 03
	3/10 Su	9 ♌ 49	5 ♈ 46	15 ♋ 39	16 ♌ 56
	3/17 Su	9 ♌ 42	5 ♈ 51	15 ♋ 36	16 ♌ 50
	3/24 Su	9 ♌ 37	5 ♈ 56	15 ♋ 35	16 ♌ 44
	3/31 Su	9 ♌ 32	6 ♈ 01	15 ♋ 34 D	16 ♌ 39
	4/07 Su	9 ♌ 29	6 ♈ 06	15 ♋ 35	16 ♌ 35
	4/14 Su	9 ♌ 26	6 ♈ 11	15 ♋ 37	16 ♌ 32
	4/21 Su	9 ♌ 26	6 ♈ 15	15 ♋ 40	16 ♌ 30
	4/28 Su	9 ♌ 26 D	6 ♈ 20	15 ♋ 44	16 ♌ 29
	5/05 Su	9 ♌ 28	6 ♈ 24	15 ♋ 49	16 ♌ 29 D
	5/12 Su	9 ♌ 31	6 ♈ 28	15 ♋ 55	16 ♌ 30
	5/19 Su	9 ♌ 35	6 ♈ 31	16 ♋ 01	16 ♌ 32
	5/26 Su	9 ♌ 41	6 ♈ 34	16 ♋ 09	16 ♌ 35
	6/02 Su	9 ♌ 47	6 ♈ 37	16 ♋ 18	16 ♌ 39
	6/09 Su	9 ♌ 55	6 ♈ 39	16 ♋ 27	16 ♌ 44
	6/16 Su	10 ♌ 04	6 ♈ 41	16 ♋ 36	16 ♌ 50
	6/23 Su	10 ♌ 13	6 ♈ 42	16 ♋ 46	16 ♌ 56

Astro Data

1945

3/29 Th	00:17	♈	SD	14 ♋ 27	36.8 (36:46)
4/20 Fr	10:21	♇	SD	7 ♌ 54	24.1 (24:06)
4/30 Mo	10:06	♎	SD	15 ♌ 35	24.0 (24:00)
7/02 Mo	23:01	♀	SR	6 ♈ 27	-20.7 (-20:39)

1945

10/18 Th	10:12	♈	SR	17 ♋ 41	36.6 (36:34)
11/13 Tu	01:54	♀	SR	11 ♌ 48	23.2 (23:14)
11/17 Sa	12:26	♎	SR	18 ♌ 27	23.3 (23:18)
12/24 Mo	06:01	♀	SD	5 ♈ 16	-21.0 (-21:02)

1946

3/30 Sa	09:18	♈	SD	15 ♋ 34	37.2 (37:09)
4/22 Mo	03:51	♇	SD	9 ♌ 25	24.1 (24:06)
5/01 We	15:42	♎	SD	16 ♌ 29	24.1 (24:08)

Year	Date	⚵	⚶	⚷	⚸
1946	6/30 Su	10 ♌ 34 D	6 ♈ 43 D	16 ♋ 56 D	17 ♌ 03 D
	7/07 Su	10 ♌ 35	6 ♈ 43 R	17 ♋ 06	17 ♌ 11
	7/14 Su	10 ♌ 47	6 ♈ 42	17 ♋ 17	17 ♌ 19
	7/21 Su	10 ♌ 59	6 ♈ 41	17 ♋ 27	17 ♌ 28
	7/28 Su	11 ♌ 11	6 ♈ 39	17 ♋ 37	17 ♌ 37
	8/04 Su	11 ♌ 23	6 ♈ 37	17 ♋ 47	17 ♌ 46
	8/11 Su	11 ♌ 36	6 ♈ 35	17 ♋ 57	17 ♌ 55
	8/18 Su	11 ♌ 48	6 ♈ 32	18 ♋ 05	18 ♌ 05
	8/25 Su	12 ♌ 00	6 ♈ 28	18 ♋ 14	18 ♌ 14
	9/01 Su	12 ♌ 12	6 ♈ 24	18 ♋ 21	18 ♌ 23
	9/08 Su	12 ♌ 23	6 ♈ 20	18 ♋ 28	18 ♌ 32
	9/15 Su	12 ♌ 34	6 ♈ 16	18 ♋ 34	18 ♌ 40
	9/22 Su	12 ♌ 43	6 ♈ 12	18 ♋ 39	18 ♌ 48
	9/29 Su	12 ♌ 52	6 ♈ 07	18 ♋ 43	18 ♌ 55
	10/06 Su	13 ♌ 00	6 ♈ 03	18 ♋ 46	19 ♌ 01
	10/13 Su	13 ♌ 07	5 ♈ 59	18 ♋ 47	19 ♌ 07
	10/20 Su	13 ♌ 12	5 ♈ 54	18 ♋ 48 R	19 ♌ 12
	10/27 Su	13 ♌ 17	5 ♈ 50	18 ♋ 47	19 ♌ 16
	11/03 Su	13 ♌ 20	5 ♈ 46	18 ♋ 46	19 ♌ 18
	11/10 Su	13 ♌ 21	5 ♈ 43	18 ♋ 43	19 ♌ 20
	11/17 Su	13 ♌ 22 R	5 ♈ 40	18 ♋ 39	19 ♌ 21
	11/24 Su	13 ♌ 21	5 ♈ 37	18 ♋ 34	19 ♌ 21 R
	12/01 Su	13 ♌ 18	5 ♈ 35	18 ♋ 28	19 ♌ 19
	12/08 Su	13 ♌ 14	5 ♈ 33	18 ♋ 22	19 ♌ 17
	12/15 Su	13 ♌ 09	5 ♈ 32	18 ♋ 14	19 ♌ 14
	12/22 Su	13 ♌ 03	5 ♈ 32	18 ♋ 07	19 ♌ 10
	12/29 Su	12 ♌ 56	5 ♈ 31 D	17 ♋ 58	19 ♌ 04
1947	1/05 Su	12 ♌ 48	5 ♈ 32	17 ♋ 50	18 ♌ 59
	1/12 Su	12 ♌ 40	5 ♈ 34	17 ♋ 41	18 ♌ 52
	1/19 Su	12 ♌ 30	5 ♈ 35	17 ♋ 33	18 ♌ 45
	1/26 Su	12 ♌ 21	5 ♈ 38	17 ♋ 25	18 ♌ 38
	2/02 Su	12 ♌ 11	5 ♈ 41	17 ♋ 17	18 ♌ 30
	2/09 Su	12 ♌ 01	5 ♈ 44	17 ♋ 09	18 ♌ 22
	2/16 Su	11 ♌ 51	5 ♈ 48	17 ♋ 03	18 ♌ 14
	2/23 Su	11 ♌ 42	5 ♈ 52	16 ♋ 57	18 ♌ 07
	3/02 Su	11 ♌ 33	5 ♈ 56	16 ♋ 52	17 ♌ 59
	3/09 Su	11 ♌ 25	6 ♈ 01	16 ♋ 48	17 ♌ 52

Year	Date	⚵	⚶	⚷	⚸
1947	3/16 Su	11 ♌ 18 R	6 ♈ 06 D	16 ♋ 44 R	17 ♌ 46 R
	3/23 Su	11 ♌ 12	6 ♈ 10	16 ♋ 43	17 ♌ 40
	3/30 Su	11 ♌ 07	6 ♈ 15	16 ♋ 42	17 ♌ 35
	4/06 Su	11 ♌ 03	6 ♈ 20	16 ♋ 42 D	17 ♌ 31
	4/13 Su	11 ♌ 00	6 ♈ 25	16 ♋ 43	17 ♌ 28
	4/20 Su	10 ♌ 59	6 ♈ 30	16 ♋ 46	17 ♌ 25
	4/27 Su	10 ♌ 59 D	6 ♈ 35	16 ♋ 50	17 ♌ 24
	5/04 Su	11 ♌ 00	6 ♈ 39	16 ♋ 54	17 ♌ 24 D
	5/11 Su	11 ♌ 02	6 ♈ 43	17 ♋ 00	17 ♌ 24
	5/18 Su	11 ♌ 06	6 ♈ 46	17 ♋ 06	17 ♌ 26
	5/25 Su	11 ♌ 11	6 ♈ 50	17 ♋ 14	17 ♌ 29
	6/01 Su	11 ♌ 18	6 ♈ 52	17 ♋ 22	17 ♌ 32
	6/08 Su	11 ♌ 25	6 ♈ 55	17 ♋ 31	17 ♌ 37
	6/15 Su	11 ♌ 33	6 ♈ 56	17 ♋ 40	17 ♌ 42
	6/22 Su	11 ♌ 43	6 ♈ 57	17 ♋ 50	17 ♌ 48
	6/29 Su	11 ♌ 53	6 ♈ 58	18 ♋ 00	17 ♌ 55
	7/06 Su	12 ♌ 04	6 ♈ 58 R	18 ♋ 10	18 ♌ 03
	7/13 Su	12 ♌ 15	6 ♈ 58	18 ♋ 20	18 ♌ 11
	7/20 Su	12 ♌ 27	6 ♈ 57	18 ♋ 31	18 ♌ 19
	7/27 Su	12 ♌ 40	6 ♈ 55	18 ♋ 41	18 ♌ 28
	8/03 Su	12 ♌ 52	6 ♈ 53	18 ♋ 51	18 ♌ 37
	8/10 Su	13 ♌ 05	6 ♈ 51	19 ♋ 01	18 ♌ 47
	8/17 Su	13 ♌ 17	6 ♈ 48	19 ♋ 10	18 ♌ 56
	8/24 Su	13 ♌ 30	6 ♈ 45	19 ♋ 18	19 ♌ 05
	8/31 Su	13 ♌ 42	6 ♈ 41	19 ♋ 26	19 ♌ 14
	9/07 Su	13 ♌ 53	6 ♈ 37	19 ♋ 33	19 ♌ 23
	9/14 Su	14 ♌ 04	6 ♈ 33	19 ♋ 39	19 ♌ 32
	9/21 Su	14 ♌ 14	6 ♈ 29	19 ♋ 45	19 ♌ 39
	9/28 Su	14 ♌ 23	6 ♈ 24	19 ♋ 49	19 ♌ 47
	10/05 Su	14 ♌ 32	6 ♈ 20	19 ♋ 52	19 ♌ 53
	10/12 Su	14 ♌ 39	6 ♈ 15	19 ♋ 54	19 ♌ 59
	10/19 Su	14 ♌ 45	6 ♈ 11	19 ♋ 55	20 ♌ 04
	10/26 Su	14 ♌ 50	6 ♈ 07	19 ♋ 55 R	20 ♌ 08
	11/02 Su	14 ♌ 54	6 ♈ 03	19 ♋ 54	20 ♌ 12
	11/09 Su	14 ♌ 56	5 ♈ 59	19 ♋ 51	20 ♌ 14
	11/16 Su	14 ♌ 57	5 ♈ 56	19 ♋ 48	20 ♌ 15
	11/23 Su	14 ♌ 56 R	5 ♈ 54	19 ♋ 43	20 ♌ 15 R
	11/30 Su	14 ♌ 54	5 ♈ 51	19 ♋ 37	20 ♌ 14
	12/07 Su	14 ♌ 51	5 ♈ 50	19 ♋ 31	20 ♌ 12
	12/14 Su	14 ♌ 47	5 ♈ 48	19 ♋ 24	20 ♌ 09

Astro Data

1946

Date	Time	Body	Type	Position	Value
7/03 We	11:30	♀	SR	6 ♈ 43	-20.4 (-20:23)
10/19 Sa	20:45	⚷	SR	18 ♋ 48	36.9 (36:54)
11/15 Fr	00:41	⚵	SR	13 ♌ 22	23.2 (23:11)
11/18 Mo	15:51	⚸	SR	19 ♌ 21	23.5 (23:27)
12/24 Tu	12:53	♀	SD	5 ♈ 32	-20.8 (-20:47)

1947

Date	Time	Body	Type	Position	Value
3/31 Mo	15:51	⚷	SD	16 ♋ 42	37.5 (37:28)
4/23 We	20:47	⚵	SD	10 ♌ 58	24.1 (24:05)
5/02 Fr	21:20	⚸	SD	17 ♌ 24	24.3 (24:17)
7/04 Fr	05:11	♀	SR	6 ♈ 58	-20.1 (-20:08)
10/21 Tu	05:55	⚷	SR	19 ♋ 55	37.2 (37:15)
11/16 Su	21:42	⚵	SR	14 ♌ 57	23.1 (23:08)
11/19 We	19:58	⚸	SR	20 ♌ 15	23.6 (23:34)

LONGITUDE

	♇	♀	♇	♇			♇	♀	♇	♇
1947	12/21 Su	14 ♌ 41 R	5 ♈ 48 R	19 ♋ 16 R	20 ♌ 05 R	**1948**	9/05 Su	15 ♌ 24 D	6 ♈ 54 R	20 ♋ 38 D	20 ♌ 14 D
	12/28 Su	14 ♌ 34	5 ♈ 48 D	19 ♋ 08	20 ♌ 00		9/12 Su	15 ♌ 36	6 ♈ 50	20 ♋ 44	20 ♌ 23
							9/19 Su	15 ♌ 46	6 ♈ 45	20 ♋ 50	20 ♌ 31
							9/26 Su	15 ♌ 56	6 ♈ 41	20 ♋ 55	20 ♌ 38
							10/03 Su	16 ♌ 05	6 ♈ 37	20 ♋ 58	20 ♌ 45
1948	1/04 Su	14 ♌ 27	5 ♈ 48	19 ♋ 00	19 ♌ 54		10/10 Su	16 ♌ 13	6 ♈ 32	21 ♋ 01	20 ♌ 51
	1/11 Su	14 ♌ 18	5 ♈ 49	18 ♋ 51	19 ♌ 48		10/17 Su	16 ♌ 19	6 ♈ 28	21 ♋ 02	20 ♌ 57
	1/18 Su	14 ♌ 09	5 ♈ 51	18 ♋ 43	19 ♌ 41		10/24 Su	16 ♌ 25	6 ♈ 24	21 ♋ 02 R	21 ♌ 01
	1/25 Su	13 ♌ 59	5 ♈ 53	18 ♋ 35	19 ♌ 34		10/31 Su	16 ♌ 29	6 ♈ 20	21 ♋ 01	21 ♌ 05
	2/01 Su	13 ♌ 50	5 ♈ 56	18 ♋ 27	19 ♌ 26		11/07 Su	16 ♌ 32	6 ♈ 16	20 ♋ 59	21 ♌ 07
	2/08 Su	13 ♌ 40	5 ♈ 59	18 ♋ 19	19 ♌ 19		11/14 Su	16 ♌ 33	6 ♈ 13	20 ♋ 56	21 ♌ 08
	2/15 Su	13 ♌ 30	6 ♈ 03	18 ♋ 12	19 ♌ 11		11/21 Su	16 ♌ 33 R	6 ♈ 10	20 ♋ 52	21 ♌ 09 R
	2/22 Su	13 ♌ 20	6 ♈ 07	18 ♋ 06	19 ♌ 03		11/28 Su	16 ♌ 32	6 ♈ 08	20 ♋ 46	21 ♌ 08
	2/29 Su	13 ♌ 11	6 ♈ 11	18 ♋ 00	18 ♌ 55		12/05 Su	16 ♌ 29	6 ♈ 06	20 ♋ 40	21 ♌ 06
	3/07 Su	13 ♌ 03	6 ♈ 16	17 ♋ 56	18 ♌ 48		12/12 Su	16 ♌ 25	6 ♈ 04	20 ♋ 34	21 ♌ 04
	3/14 Su	12 ♌ 55	6 ♈ 20	17 ♋ 53	18 ♌ 42		12/19 Su	16 ♌ 20	6 ♈ 04	20 ♋ 26	21 ♌ 00
	3/21 Su	12 ♌ 49	6 ♈ 25	17 ♋ 50	18 ♌ 36		12/26 Su	16 ♌ 14	6 ♈ 03 D	20 ♋ 18	20 ♌ 55
	3/28 Su	12 ♌ 43	6 ♈ 30	17 ♋ 49	18 ♌ 31						
	4/04 Su	12 ♌ 38	6 ♈ 35	17 ♋ 49 D	18 ♌ 26						
	4/11 Su	12 ♌ 35	6 ♈ 40	17 ♋ 50	18 ♌ 23						
	4/18 Su	12 ♌ 33	6 ♈ 45	17 ♋ 52	18 ♌ 20	**1949**	1/02 Su	16 ♌ 06	6 ♈ 04	20 ♋ 10	20 ♌ 50
	4/25 Su	12 ♌ 33 D	6 ♈ 49	17 ♋ 55	18 ♌ 18		1/09 Su	15 ♌ 58	6 ♈ 05	20 ♋ 01	20 ♌ 44
	5/02 Su	12 ♌ 33	6 ♈ 54	18 ♋ 00	18 ♌ 18		1/16 Su	15 ♌ 49	6 ♈ 06	19 ♋ 53	20 ♌ 37
	5/09 Su	12 ♌ 35	6 ♈ 58	18 ♋ 05	18 ♌ 18 D		1/23 Su	15 ♌ 40	6 ♈ 09	19 ♋ 44	20 ♌ 30
	5/16 Su	12 ♌ 39	7 ♈ 01	18 ♋ 11	18 ♌ 19		1/30 Su	15 ♌ 30	6 ♈ 11	19 ♋ 36	20 ♌ 23
	5/23 Su	12 ♌ 43	7 ♈ 05	18 ♋ 18	18 ♌ 22		2/06 Su	15 ♌ 20	6 ♈ 14	19 ♋ 29	20 ♌ 15
	5/30 Su	12 ♌ 49	7 ♈ 07	18 ♋ 26	18 ♌ 25		2/13 Su	15 ♌ 10	6 ♈ 18	19 ♋ 21	20 ♌ 07
	6/06 Su	12 ♌ 56	7 ♈ 10	18 ♋ 35	18 ♌ 29		2/20 Su	15 ♌ 00	6 ♈ 22	19 ♋ 15	19 ♌ 59
	6/13 Su	13 ♌ 04	7 ♈ 12	18 ♋ 44	18 ♌ 34		2/27 Su	14 ♌ 51	6 ♈ 26	19 ♋ 09	19 ♌ 52
	6/20 Su	13 ♌ 14	7 ♈ 13	18 ♋ 54	18 ♌ 40		3/06 Su	14 ♌ 42	6 ♈ 30	19 ♋ 05	19 ♌ 44
	6/27 Su	13 ♌ 24	7 ♈ 14	19 ♋ 04	18 ♌ 47		3/13 Su	14 ♌ 34	6 ♈ 35	19 ♋ 01	19 ♌ 38
	7/04 Su	13 ♌ 34	7 ♈ 14 R	19 ♋ 14	18 ♌ 54		3/20 Su	14 ♌ 27	6 ♈ 40	18 ♋ 58	19 ♌ 31
	7/11 Su	13 ♌ 46	7 ♈ 14	19 ♋ 24	19 ♌ 02		3/27 Su	14 ♌ 21	6 ♈ 45	18 ♋ 56	19 ♌ 26
	7/18 Su	13 ♌ 57	7 ♈ 13	19 ♋ 34	19 ♌ 11		4/03 Su	14 ♌ 16	6 ♈ 50	18 ♋ 56 D	19 ♌ 21
	7/25 Su	14 ♌ 10	7 ♈ 12	19 ♋ 45	19 ♌ 19		4/10 Su	14 ♌ 12	6 ♈ 55	18 ♋ 57	19 ♌ 17
	8/01 Su	14 ♌ 22	7 ♈ 10	19 ♋ 55	19 ♌ 29		4/17 Su	14 ♌ 10	7 ♈ 00	18 ♋ 58	19 ♌ 15
	8/08 Su	14 ♌ 35	7 ♈ 07	20 ♋ 04	19 ♌ 38		4/24 Su	14 ♌ 08	7 ♈ 04	19 ♋ 01	19 ♌ 13
	8/15 Su	14 ♌ 48	7 ♈ 04	20 ♋ 14	19 ♌ 47		5/01 Su	14 ♌ 09 D	7 ♈ 09	19 ♋ 05	19 ♌ 12
	8/22 Su	15 ♌ 00	7 ♈ 01	20 ♋ 22	19 ♌ 56		5/08 Su	14 ♌ 10	7 ♈ 13	19 ♋ 10	19 ♌ 12 D
	8/29 Su	15 ♌ 12	6 ♈ 58	20 ♋ 31	20 ♌ 05		5/15 Su	14 ♌ 13	7 ♈ 16	19 ♋ 16	19 ♌ 13

Astro Data

1947

12/25 Th	01:42	♀	SD	5 ♈ 48	-20.5 (-20:32)	

1948

4/01 Th	01:52	♇	SD	17 ♋ 49	37.8 (37:49)
4/24 Sa	16:58	♇	SD	12 ♌ 33	24.1 (24:03)
5/03 Mo	01:46	♇	SD	18 ♌ 18	24.4 (24:25)
7/03 Sa	17:45	♀	SR	7 ♈ 14	-19.9 (-19:52)

1948

10/21 Th	15:36	♇	SR	21 ♋ 02	37.5 (37:31)
11/17 We	20:18	♇	SR	16 ♌ 33	23.1 (23:03)
11/20 Sa	02:34	♇	SR	21 ♌ 09	13.7 (23:40)
12/24 Fr	18:52	♀	SD	6 ♈ 03	-20.3 (-20:17)

1949

4/02 Sa	11:28	♇	SD	18 ♋ 56	38.2 (38:09)
4/26 Tu	14:00	♇	SD	14 ♌ 08	24.0 (24:00)
5/04 We	01:38	♇	SD	19 ♌ 12	24.5 (24:32)

LONGITUDE

Year	Date	♇	♀	⚵	⚶
1949	5/22 Su	14♌17 D	7♈20 D	19♋23 D	19♌15 D
	5/29 Su	14♌23	7♈23	19♋31	19♌18
	6/05 Su	14♌29	7♈25	19♋39	19♌22
	6/12 Su	14♌37	7♈27	19♋48	19♌27
	6/19 Su	14♌46	7♈29	19♋57	19♌32
	6/26 Su	14♌56	7♈29	20♋07	19♌39
	7/03 Su	15♌06	7♈30	20♋17	19♌46
	7/10 Su	15♌17	7♈30 ℞	20♋27	19♌54
	7/17 Su	15♌29	7♈29	20♋38	20♌02
	7/24 Su	15♌41	7♈28	20♋48	20♌11
	7/31 Su	15♌54	7♈26	20♋58	20♌19
	8/07 Su	16♌07	7♈24	21♋08	20♌29
	8/14 Su	16♌19	7♈21	21♋18	20♌38
	8/21 Su	16♌32	7♈18	21♋26	20♌47
	8/28 Su	16♌45	7♈14	21♋35	20♌56
	9/04 Su	16♌57	7♈10	21♋42	21♌05
	9/11 Su	17♌08	7♈06	21♋49	21♌14
	9/18 Su	17♌19	7♈02	21♋55	21♌22
	9/25 Su	17♌30	6♈58	22♋00	21♌30
	10/02 Su	17♌39	6♈53	22♋04	21♌37
	10/09 Su	17♌47	6♈49	22♋07	21♌43
	10/16 Su	17♌55	6♈45	22♋08	21♌49
	10/23 Su	18♌01	6♈40	22♋09 ℞	21♌54
	10/30 Su	18♌05	6♈36	22♋08	21♌57
	11/06 Su	18♌09	6♈33	22♋07	22♌00
	11/13 Su	18♌11	6♈29	22♋04	22♌02
	11/20 Su	18♌11 ℞	6♈26	22♋00	22♌02
	11/27 Su	18♌11	6♈24	21♋55	22♌02 ℞
	12/04 Su	18♌09	6♈22	21♋49	22♌01
	12/11 Su	18♌05	6♈21	21♋43	21♌58
	12/18 Su	18♌00	6♈20	21♋36	21♌55
	12/25 Su	17♌54	6♈19	21♋28	21♌51
1950	1/01 Su	17♌47	6♈20 D	21♋20	21♌45
	1/08 Su	17♌39	6♈21	21♋11	21♌40
	1/15 Su	17♌31	6♈22	21♋03	21♌33
	1/22 Su	17♌21	6♈24	20♋54	21♌26
	1/29 Su	17♌12	6♈26	20♋46	21♌19
1950	2/05 Su	17♌02 ℞	6♈29 D	20♋38 ℞	21♌11 ℞
	2/12 Su	16♌52	6♈33	20♋31	21♌03
	2/19 Su	16♌42	6♈37	20♋24	20♌55
	2/26 Su	16♌32	6♈41	20♋18	20♌48
	3/05 Su	16♌23	6♈45	20♋13	20♌40
	3/12 Su	16♌15	6♈50	20♋09	20♌33
	3/19 Su	16♌07	6♈55	20♋06	20♌27
	3/26 Su	16♌00	7♈00	20♋04	20♌21
	4/02 Su	15♌55	7♈05	20♋03	20♌16
	4/09 Su	15♌51	7♈10	20♋03 D	20♌12
	4/16 Su	15♌48	7♈14	20♋05	20♌09
	4/23 Su	15♌46	7♈19	20♋07	20♌07
	4/30 Su	15♌46 D	7♈23	20♋11	20♌06
	5/07 Su	15♌47	7♈28	20♋15	20♌05 D
	5/14 Su	15♌49	7♈31	20♋21	20♌06
	5/21 Su	15♌53	7♈35	20♋27	20♌08
	5/28 Su	15♌58	7♈38	20♋35	20♌10
	6/04 Su	16♌04	7♈40	20♋43	20♌14
	6/11 Su	16♌11	7♈42	20♋52	20♌19
	6/18 Su	16♌20	7♈44	21♋01	20♌24
	6/25 Su	16♌29	7♈45	21♋11	20♌30
	7/02 Su	16♌39	7♈46	21♋21	20♌37
	7/09 Su	16♌50	7♈45 ℞	21♋31	20♌45
	7/16 Su	17♌02	7♈45	21♋41	20♌53
	7/23 Su	17♌14	7♈44	21♋52	21♌01
	7/30 Su	17♌27	7♈42	22♋02	21♌10
	8/06 Su	17♌40	7♈40	22♋12	21♌19
	8/13 Su	17♌53	7♈37	22♋21	21♌29
	8/20 Su	18♌05	7♈34	22♋30	21♌38
	8/27 Su	18♌18	7♈31	22♋39	21♌47
	9/03 Su	18♌31	7♈27	22♋47	21♌56
	9/10 Su	18♌43	7♈23	22♋54	22♌05
	9/17 Su	18♌54	7♈19	23♋00	22♌13
	9/24 Su	19♌05	7♈15	23♋05	22♌21
	10/01 Su	19♌14	7♈10	23♋10	22♌28
	10/08 Su	19♌23	7♈06	23♋13	22♌35
	10/15 Su	19♌31	7♈01	23♋15	22♌41
	10/22 Su	19♌38	6♈57	23♋16	22♌46
	10/29 Su	19♌43	6♈53	23♋16 ℞	22♌50
	11/05 Su	19♌47	6♈49	23♋14	22♌53

Astro Data

Year	Date	Time	Body	Station	Position	Value
1949	7/03 Su	23:51	♀	SR	7♈30	-19.6 (-19:37)
	10/22 Sa	22:36	⚵	SR	22♋09	37.8 (37:46)
	11/19 Sa	18:23	♇	SR	18♌11	23.0 (22:57)
	11/21 Mo	05:01	⚶	SR	22♌03	23.8 (23:48)
	12/25 Su	06:08	♀	SD	6♈19	-20.0 (-20:00)
1950	4/03 Mo	22:10	⚵	SD	20♋03	38.4 (38:25)
	4/28 Fr	08:40	♇	SD	15♌46	23.9 (23:56)
	5/05 Fr	05:13	⚶	SD	20♌05	24.7 (24:39)
	7/04 Tu	13:04	♀	SR	7♈46	-19.4 (-19:22)
	10/24 Tu	05:08	⚵	SR	23♋16	38.1 (38:04)

1950	⚷	♀	⯓	⯓
11/12 Su	19 ♌ 50 D	6 ♈ 46 R	23 ⊕ 12 R	22 ♌ 55 D
11/19 Su	19 ♌ 51	6 ♈ 43	23 ⊕ 08	22 ♌ 56
11/26 Su	19 ♌ 51 R	6 ♈ 40	23 ⊕ 04	22 ♌ 56 R
12/03 Su	19 ♌ 49	6 ♈ 38	22 ⊕ 58	22 ♌ 55
12/10 Su	19 ♌ 46	6 ♈ 37	22 ⊕ 52	22 ♌ 53
12/17 Su	19 ♌ 42	6 ♈ 36	22 ⊕ 45	22 ♌ 50
12/24 Su	19 ♌ 37	6 ♈ 35	22 ⊕ 37	22 ♌ 46
12/31 Su	19 ♌ 30	6 ♈ 35 D	22 ⊕ 29	22 ♌ 41

1951	⚷	♀	⯓	⯓
1/07 Su	19 ♌ 22	6 ♈ 36	22 ⊕ 21	22 ♌ 35
1/14 Su	19 ♌ 14	6 ♈ 37	22 ⊕ 12	22 ♌ 29
1/21 Su	19 ♌ 05	6 ♈ 39	22 ⊕ 04	22 ♌ 22
1/28 Su	18 ♌ 55	6 ♈ 42	21 ⊕ 56	22 ♌ 14
2/04 Su	18 ♌ 45	6 ♈ 45	21 ⊕ 48	22 ♌ 07
2/11 Su	18 ♌ 35	6 ♈ 48	21 ⊕ 40	21 ♌ 59
2/18 Su	18 ♌ 25	6 ♈ 52	21 ⊕ 33	21 ♌ 51
2/25 Su	18 ♌ 15	6 ♈ 56	21 ⊕ 27	21 ♌ 43
3/04 Su	18 ♌ 06	7 ♈ 00	21 ⊕ 21	21 ♌ 36
3/11 Su	17 ♌ 57	7 ♈ 05	21 ⊕ 17	21 ♌ 29
3/18 Su	17 ♌ 49	7 ♈ 10	21 ⊕ 14	21 ♌ 22
3/25 Su	17 ♌ 42	7 ♈ 14	21 ⊕ 11	21 ♌ 17
4/01 Su	17 ♌ 36	7 ♈ 19	21 ⊕ 10	21 ♌ 11
4/08 Su	17 ♌ 31	7 ♈ 24	21 ⊕ 10 D	21 ♌ 07
4/15 Su	17 ♌ 28	7 ♈ 29	21 ⊕ 11	21 ♌ 04
4/22 Su	17 ♌ 25	7 ♈ 34	21 ⊕ 13	21 ♌ 01
4/29 Su	17 ♌ 24	7 ♈ 38	21 ⊕ 16	20 ♌ 59
5/06 Su	17 ♌ 25 D	7 ♈ 42	21 ⊕ 21	20 ♌ 59
5/13 Su	17 ♌ 27	7 ♈ 46	21 ⊕ 36	20 ♌ 59 D
5/20 Su	17 ♌ 30	7 ♈ 50	21 ⊕ 32	21 ♌ 01
5/27 Su	17 ♌ 34	7 ♈ 53	21 ⊕ 39	21 ♌ 03
6/03 Su	17 ♌ 40	7 ♈ 56	21 ⊕ 47	21 ♌ 07
6/10 Su	17 ♌ 47	7 ♈ 58	21 ⊕ 55	21 ♌ 11
6/17 Su	17 ♌ 55	7 ♈ 59	22 ⊕ 05	21 ♌ 16
6/24 Su	18 ♌ 04	8 ♈ 01	22 ⊕ 14	21 ♌ 22
7/01 Su	18 ♌ 14	8 ♈ 01	22 ⊕ 24	21 ♌ 29
7/08 Su	18 ♌ 25	8 ♈ 01 R	22 ⊕ 34	21 ♌ 36
7/15 Su	18 ♌ 37	8 ♈ 01	22 ⊕ 44	21 ♌ 44
7/22 Su	18 ♌ 49	8 ♈ 00	22 ⊕ 55	21 ♌ 52
7/29 Su	19 ♌ 01	7 ♈ 58	23 ⊕ 05	22 ♌ 01

1951	⚷	♀	⯓	⯓
8/05 Su	19 ♌ 14 D	7 ♈ 56 R	23 ⊕ 15 D	22 ♌ 10 D
8/12 Su	19 ♌ 27	7 ♈ 54	23 ⊕ 25	22 ♌ 19
8/19 Su	19 ♌ 40	7 ♈ 51	23 ⊕ 34	22 ♌ 29
8/26 Su	19 ♌ 53	7 ♈ 47	23 ⊕ 43	22 ♌ 38
9/02 Su	20 ♌ 06	7 ♈ 44	23 ⊕ 51	22 ♌ 47
9/09 Su	20 ♌ 18	7 ♈ 40	23 ⊕ 58	22 ♌ 56
9/16 Su	20 ♌ 30	7 ♈ 36	24 ⊕ 05	23 ♌ 04
9/23 Su	20 ♌ 41	7 ♈ 31	24 ⊕ 10	23 ♌ 12
9/30 Su	20 ♌ 51	7 ♈ 27	24 ⊕ 15	23 ♌ 20
10/07 Su	21 ♌ 01	7 ♈ 22	24 ⊕ 18	23 ♌ 27
10/14 Su	21 ♌ 09	7 ♈ 18	24 ⊕ 21	23 ♌ 33
10/21 Su	21 ♌ 16	7 ♈ 14	24 ⊕ 22	23 ♌ 38
10/28 Su	21 ♌ 22	7 ♈ 10	24 ⊕ 22 R	23 ♌ 42
11/04 Su	21 ♌ 27	7 ♈ 06	24 ⊕ 22	23 ♌ 45
11/11 Su	21 ♌ 30	7 ♈ 02	24 ⊕ 19	23 ♌ 48
11/18 Su	21 ♌ 32	6 ♈ 59	24 ⊕ 16	23 ♌ 49
11/25 Su	21 ♌ 33 R	6 ♈ 57	24 ⊕ 12	23 ♌ 49 R
12/02 Su	21 ♌ 32	6 ♈ 55	24 ⊕ 07	23 ♌ 49
12/09 Su	21 ♌ 29	6 ♈ 53	24 ⊕ 01	23 ♌ 47
12/16 Su	21 ♌ 25	6 ♈ 52	23 ⊕ 54	23 ♌ 44
12/23 Su	21 ♌ 20	6 ♈ 51	23 ⊕ 47	23 ♌ 40
12/30 Su	21 ♌ 14	6 ♈ 51 D	23 ⊕ 39	23 ♌ 36

1952	⚷	♀	⯓	⯓
1/06 Su	21 ♌ 07	6 ♈ 52	23 ⊕ 31	23 ♌ 30
1/13 Su	20 ♌ 59	6 ♈ 53	23 ⊕ 22	23 ♌ 24
1/20 Su	20 ♌ 50	6 ♈ 55	23 ⊕ 14	23 ♌ 17
1/27 Su	20 ♌ 40	6 ♈ 57	23 ⊕ 05	23 ♌ 10
2/03 Su	20 ♌ 30	7 ♈ 00	22 ⊕ 57	23 ♌ 03
2/10 Su	20 ♌ 20	7 ♈ 03	22 ⊕ 49	22 ♌ 55
2/17 Su	20 ♌ 10	7 ♈ 07	22 ⊕ 42	22 ♌ 47
2/24 Su	20 ♌ 00	7 ♈ 11	22 ⊕ 36	22 ♌ 39
3/02 Su	19 ♌ 50	7 ♈ 15	22 ⊕ 30	22 ♌ 32
3/09 Su	19 ♌ 41	7 ♈ 20	22 ⊕ 25	22 ♌ 25
3/16 Su	19 ♌ 33	7 ♈ 24	22 ⊕ 22	22 ♌ 18
3/23 Su	19 ♌ 25	7 ♈ 29	22 ⊕ 19	22 ♌ 12
3/30 Su	19 ♌ 19	7 ♈ 34	22 ⊕ 17	22 ♌ 06
4/06 Su	19 ♌ 14	7 ♈ 39	22 ⊕ 17 D	22 ♌ 02
4/13 Su	19 ♌ 10	7 ♈ 44	22 ⊕ 17	21 ♌ 58

Astro Data

1950

11/21 Tu	15:56	⚷	SR	19 ♌ 51	22.9 (22:51)
11/22 We	04:28	⯓	SR	22 ♌ 56	23.9 (23:53)
12/25 Mo	12:59	♀	SD	6 ♈ 35	-19.8 (-19:45)

1951

4/05 Th	08:20	⯓	SD	21 ⊕ 10	38.7 (38:42)
4/30 Mo	05:19	⚷	SD	17 ♌ 24	23.8 (23:49)
5/06 Su	11:47	⯓	SD	20 ♌ 59	24.8 (24:45)
7/05 Th	06:15	♀	SR	8 ♈ 01	-19.1 (-19:06)

1951

10/25 Th	15:15	⯓	SR	24 ⊕ 23	38.3 (38:17)
11/23 Fr	16:28	⚷	SR	21 ♌ 33	22.7 (22:41)
11/23 Fr	07:27	⯓	SR	23 ♌ 49	24.0 (23:58)
12/26 We	01:01	♀	SD	6 ♈ 51	-19.5 (-19:30)

1952

4/05 Sa	14:59	⯓	SD	22 ⊕ 17	39.0 (38:57)

LONGITUDE

		♇	♀	⚷	⚷			♇	♀	⚷	⚷
1952	4/20 Su	19 ♌ 07 ℞	7 ♈ 49 D	22 ♋ 19 D	21 ♌ 55 ℞	1953	1/04 Su	22 ♌ 53 ℞	7 ♈ 07 D	24 ♋ 40 ℞	24 ♌ 25 ℞
	4/27 Su	19 ♌ 05	7 ♈ 53	22 ♋ 22	21 ♌ 53		1/11 Su	22 ♌ 45	7 ♈ 08	24 ♋ 32	24 ♌ 19
	5/04 Su	19 ♌ 05 D	7 ♈ 57	22 ♋ 26	21 ♌ 52		1/18 Su	22 ♌ 37	7 ♈ 10	24 ♋ 23	24 ♌ 13
	5/11 Su	19 ♌ 06	8 ♈ 01	22 ♋ 31	21 ♌ 53 D		1/25 Su	22 ♌ 27	7 ♈ 12	24 ♋ 15	24 ♌ 06
	5/18 Su	19 ♌ 09	8 ♈ 05	22 ♋ 37	21 ♌ 54		2/01 Su	22 ♌ 17	7 ♈ 15	24 ♋ 07	23 ♌ 58
	5/25 Su	19 ♌ 13	8 ♈ 08	22 ♋ 43	21 ♌ 56		2/08 Su	22 ♌ 07	7 ♈ 18	23 ♋ 59	23 ♌ 51
	6/01 Su	19 ♌ 18	8 ♈ 11	22 ♋ 51	21 ♌ 59		2/15 Su	21 ♌ 57	7 ♈ 22	23 ♋ 51	23 ♌ 43
	6/08 Su	19 ♌ 25	8 ♈ 13	22 ♋ 59	22 ♌ 03		2/22 Su	21 ♌ 47	7 ♈ 26	23 ♋ 45	23 ♌ 35
	6/15 Su	19 ♌ 33	8 ♈ 15	23 ♋ 08	22 ♌ 08		3/01 Su	21 ♌ 37	7 ♈ 30	23 ♋ 39	23 ♌ 28
	6/22 Su	19 ♌ 41	8 ♈ 16	23 ♋ 18	22 ♌ 14		3/08 Su	21 ♌ 28	7 ♈ 34	23 ♋ 34	23 ♌ 20
	6/29 Su	19 ♌ 51	8 ♈ 17	23 ♋ 27	22 ♌ 20		3/15 Su	21 ♌ 19	7 ♈ 39	23 ♋ 30	23 ♌ 13
	7/06 Su	20 ♌ 02	8 ♈ 17 ℞	23 ♋ 37	22 ♌ 27		3/22 Su	21 ♌ 11	7 ♈ 44	23 ♋ 26	23 ♌ 07
	7/13 Su	20 ♌ 13	8 ♈ 17	23 ♋ 48	22 ♌ 35		3/29 Su	21 ♌ 04	7 ♈ 49	23 ♋ 24	23 ♌ 02
	7/20 Su	20 ♌ 25	8 ♈ 16	23 ♋ 58	22 ♌ 43		4/05 Su	20 ♌ 58	7 ♈ 54	23 ♋ 24	22 ♌ 57
	7/27 Su	20 ♌ 38	8 ♈ 14	24 ♋ 08	22 ♌ 52		4/12 Su	20 ♌ 53	7 ♈ 59	23 ♋ 24 D	22 ♌ 53
	8/03 Su	20 ♌ 50	8 ♈ 12	24 ♋ 19	23 ♌ 01		4/19 Su	20 ♌ 50	8 ♈ 03	23 ♋ 25	22 ♌ 50
	8/10 Su	21 ♌ 03	8 ♈ 10	24 ♋ 28	23 ♌ 10		4/26 Su	20 ♌ 48	8 ♈ 08	23 ♋ 28	22 ♌ 47
	8/17 Su	21 ♌ 17	8 ♈ 07	24 ♋ 38	23 ♌ 19		5/03 Su	20 ♌ 47 D	8 ♈ 12	23 ♋ 31	22 ♌ 46
	8/24 Su	21 ♌ 30	8 ♈ 04	24 ♋ 47	23 ♌ 29		5/10 Su	20 ♌ 48	8 ♈ 16	23 ♋ 36	22 ♌ 46 D
	8/31 Su	21 ♌ 43	8 ♈ 00	24 ♋ 55	23 ♌ 38		5/17 Su	20 ♌ 50	8 ♈ 20	23 ♋ 41	22 ♌ 47
	9/07 Su	21 ♌ 55	7 ♈ 56	25 ♋ 03	23 ♌ 47		5/24 Su	20 ♌ 54	8 ♈ 23	23 ♋ 48	22 ♌ 49
	9/14 Su	22 ♌ 07	7 ♈ 52	25 ♋ 09	23 ♌ 55		5/31 Su	20 ♌ 58	8 ♈ 26	23 ♋ 55	22 ♌ 51
	9/21 Su	22 ♌ 19	7 ♈ 48	25 ♋ 15	24 ♌ 03		6/07 Su	21 ♌ 05	8 ♈ 28	24 ♋ 03	22 ♌ 55
	9/28 Su	22 ♌ 30	7 ♈ 44	25 ♋ 30	24 ♌ 11		6/14 Su	21 ♌ 12	8 ♈ 30	24 ♋ 12	23 ♌ 00
	10/05 Su	22 ♌ 40	7 ♈ 39	25 ♋ 24	24 ♌ 18		6/21 Su	21 ♌ 20	8 ♈ 31	24 ♋ 21	23 ♌ 05
	10/12 Su	22 ♌ 48	7 ♈ 35	25 ♋ 27	24 ♌ 24		6/28 Su	21 ♌ 30	8 ♈ 32	24 ♋ 31	23 ♌ 12
	10/19 Su	22 ♌ 56	7 ♈ 30	25 ♋ 29	24 ♌ 30		7/05 Su	21 ♌ 40	8 ♈ 33	24 ♋ 41	23 ♌ 18
	10/26 Su	23 ♌ 03	7 ♈ 26	25 ♋ 29	24 ♌ 34		7/12 Su	21 ♌ 51	8 ♈ 32 ℞	24 ♋ 51	23 ♌ 26
	11/02 Su	23 ♌ 08	7 ♈ 23	25 ♋ 29 ℞	24 ♌ 38		7/19 Su	22 ♌ 03	8 ♈ 32	25 ♋ 01	23 ♌ 34
	11/09 Su	23 ♌ 12	7 ♈ 19	25 ♋ 27	24 ♌ 41		7/26 Su	22 ♌ 15	8 ♈ 30	25 ♋ 12	23 ♌ 43
	11/16 Su	23 ♌ 15	7 ♈ 16	25 ♋ 24	24 ♌ 42		8/02 Su	22 ♌ 28	8 ♈ 28	25 ♋ 22	23 ♌ 52
	11/23 Su	23 ♌ 16	7 ♈ 13	25 ♋ 20	24 ♌ 43		8/09 Su	22 ♌ 41	8 ♈ 26	25 ♋ 32	24 ♌ 01
	11/30 Su	23 ♌ 15 ℞	7 ♈ 11	25 ♋ 16	24 ♌ 42 ℞		8/16 Su	22 ♌ 55	8 ♈ 23	25 ♋ 41	24 ♌ 10
	12/07 Su	23 ♌ 14	7 ♈ 09	25 ♋ 10	24 ♌ 41		8/23 Su	23 ♌ 08	8 ♈ 20	25 ♋ 50	24 ♌ 19
	12/14 Su	23 ♌ 10	7 ♈ 08	25 ♋ 03	24 ♌ 38		8/30 Su	23 ♌ 21	8 ♈ 17	25 ♋ 59	24 ♌ 28
	12/21 Su	23 ♌ 06	7 ♈ 07	24 ♋ 56	24 ♌ 35		9/06 Su	23 ♌ 34	8 ♈ 13	26 ♋ 07	24 ♌ 37
	12/28 Su	23 ♌ 00	7 ♈ 07 D	24 ♋ 48	24 ♌ 31		9/13 Su	23 ♌ 46	8 ♈ 09	26 ♋ 14	24 ♌ 46
							9/20 Su	23 ♌ 58	8 ♈ 04	26 ♋ 20	24 ♌ 54
							9/27 Su	24 ♌ 10	8 ♈ 00	26 ♋ 25	25 ♌ 02
							10/04 Su	24 ♌ 20	7 ♈ 56	26 ♋ 30	25 ♌ 09

Astro Data

1952

4/30 We	23:20	♇	SD	19 ♌ 05	23.7 (23:43)
5/06 Tu	17:17	⚷	SD	21 ♌ 52	24.9 (24:51)
7/04 Fr	20:01	♀	SR	8 ♈ 17	-18.8 (-18:50)
10/26 Su	01:22	⚷	SR	25 ♋ 29	38.5 (38:32)
11/24 Mo	17:04	♇	SR	23 ♌ 16	22.5 (22:31)
11/23 Su	11:31	⚷	SR	24 ♌ 43	24.1 (24:05)
12/25 Th	17:28	♀	SD	7 ♈ 07	-19.2 (-19:15)

1953

4/06 Mo	12:13	⚷	SD	13 ♋ 24	39.2 (39:10)
5/02 Sa	10:21	♇	SD	20 ♌ 47	23.6 (23:34)
5/07 Th	21:17	⚷	SD	12 ♌ 46	15.0 (24:57)
7/05 Su	03:07	♀	SR	8 ♈ 33	-18.6 (-18:36)

58

1953	♇	♇	♇	♇
10/11 Su	24 ♌ 29 D	7 ♈ 51 R	26 ♋ 33 D	25 ♌ 16 D
10/18 Su	24 ♌ 38	7 ♈ 47	26 ♋ 35	25 ♌ 22
10/25 Su	24 ♌ 45	7 ♈ 43	26 ♋ 36	25 ♌ 26
11/01 Su	24 ♌ 51	7 ♈ 39	26 ♋ 36 R	25 ♌ 30
11/08 Su	24 ♌ 55	7 ♈ 35	26 ♋ 34	25 ♌ 33
11/15 Su	24 ♌ 59	7 ♈ 32	26 ♋ 32	25 ♌ 35
11/22 Su	25 ♌ 00	7 ♈ 29	26 ♋ 29	25 ♌ 36
11/29 Su	25 ♌ 01 R	7 ♈ 27	26 ♋ 24	25 ♌ 36 R
12/06 Su	24 ♌ 59	7 ♈ 25	26 ♋ 19	25 ♌ 35
12/13 Su	24 ♌ 57	7 ♈ 24	26 ♋ 12	25 ♌ 33
12/20 Su	24 ♌ 53	7 ♈ 23	26 ♋ 05	25 ♌ 30
12/27 Su	24 ♌ 48	7 ♈ 23 D	25 ♋ 58	25 ♌ 25

1954	♇	♇	♇	♇
1/03 Su	24 ♌ 41	7 ♈ 23	25 ♋ 50	25 ♌ 20
1/10 Su	24 ♌ 34	7 ♈ 24	25 ♋ 41	25 ♌ 15
1/17 Su	24 ♌ 25	7 ♈ 25	25 ♋ 33	25 ♌ 08
1/24 Su	24 ♌ 16	7 ♈ 27	25 ♋ 24	25 ♌ 01
1/31 Su	24 ♌ 06	7 ♈ 30	25 ♋ 16	24 ♌ 54
2/07 Su	23 ♌ 56	7 ♈ 33	25 ♋ 08	24 ♌ 46
2/14 Su	23 ♌ 46	7 ♈ 36	25 ♋ 01	24 ♌ 39
2/21 Su	23 ♌ 36	7 ♈ 40	24 ♋ 54	24 ♌ 31
2/28 Su	23 ♌ 26	7 ♈ 44	24 ♋ 47	24 ♌ 23
3/07 Su	23 ♌ 16	7 ♈ 49	24 ♋ 42	24 ♌ 16
3/14 Su	23 ♌ 07	7 ♈ 54	24 ♋ 38	24 ♌ 09
3/21 Su	22 ♌ 58	7 ♈ 58	24 ♋ 34	24 ♌ 03
3/28 Su	22 ♌ 51	8 ♈ 03	24 ♋ 32	23 ♌ 57
4/04 Su	22 ♌ 45	8 ♈ 08	24 ♋ 31	23 ♌ 52
4/11 Su	22 ♌ 39	8 ♈ 13	24 ♋ 30 D	23 ♌ 47
4/18 Su	22 ♌ 36	8 ♈ 18	24 ♋ 31	23 ♌ 44
4/25 Su	22 ♌ 33	8 ♈ 22	24 ♋ 34	23 ♌ 41
5/02 Su	22 ♌ 32	8 ♈ 27	24 ♋ 37	23 ♌ 40
5/09 Su	22 ♌ 32 D	8 ♈ 31	24 ♋ 41	23 ♌ 39 D
5/16 Su	22 ♌ 33	8 ♈ 34	24 ♋ 46	23 ♌ 40
5/23 Su	22 ♌ 36	8 ♈ 38	24 ♋ 52	23 ♌ 41
5/30 Su	22 ♌ 41	8 ♈ 41	24 ♋ 59	23 ♌ 44
6/06 Su	22 ♌ 46	8 ♈ 43	25 ♋ 07	23 ♌ 47
6/13 Su	22 ♌ 53	8 ♈ 45	25 ♋ 16	23 ♌ 52
6/20 Su	23 ♌ 01	8 ♈ 47	25 ♋ 25	23 ♌ 57

1954	♇	♇	♇	♇
6/27 Su	23 ♌ 10 D	8 ♈ 48 D	25 ♋ 34 D	24 ♌ 03 D
7/04 Su	23 ♌ 20	8 ♈ 48	25 ♋ 44	24 ♌ 10
7/11 Su	23 ♌ 31	8 ♈ 48 R	25 ♋ 54	24 ♌ 17
7/18 Su	23 ♌ 43	8 ♈ 47	26 ♋ 05	24 ♌ 25
7/25 Su	23 ♌ 55	8 ♈ 46	26 ♋ 15	24 ♌ 33
8/01 Su	24 ♌ 08	8 ♈ 44	26 ♋ 25	24 ♌ 42
8/08 Su	24 ♌ 21	8 ♈ 42	26 ♋ 35	24 ♌ 51
8/15 Su	24 ♌ 34	8 ♈ 39	26 ♋ 45	25 ♌ 01
8/22 Su	24 ♌ 48	8 ♈ 36	26 ♋ 54	25 ♌ 10
8/29 Su	25 ♌ 01	8 ♈ 33	27 ♋ 03	25 ♌ 19
9/05 Su	25 ♌ 14	8 ♈ 29	27 ♋ 11	25 ♌ 28
9/12 Su	25 ♌ 27	8 ♈ 25	27 ♋ 18	25 ♌ 37
9/19 Su	25 ♌ 39	8 ♈ 21	27 ♋ 25	25 ♌ 45
9/26 Su	25 ♌ 51	8 ♈ 17	27 ♋ 30	25 ♌ 53
10/03 Su	26 ♌ 02	8 ♈ 12	27 ♋ 35	26 ♌ 01
10/10 Su	26 ♌ 12	8 ♈ 08	27 ♋ 39	26 ♌ 07
10/17 Su	26 ♌ 21	8 ♈ 03	27 ♋ 41	26 ♌ 13
10/24 Su	26 ♌ 29	7 ♈ 59	27 ♋ 42	26 ♌ 18
10/31 Su	26 ♌ 35	7 ♈ 55	27 ♋ 43 R	26 ♌ 23
11/07 Su	26 ♌ 40	7 ♈ 52	27 ♋ 42	26 ♌ 26
11/14 Su	26 ♌ 44	7 ♈ 48	27 ♋ 40	26 ♌ 28
11/21 Su	26 ♌ 47	7 ♈ 45	27 ♋ 37	26 ♌ 29
11/28 Su	26 ♌ 48	7 ♈ 43	27 ♋ 32	26 ♌ 30 R
12/05 Su	26 ♌ 47 R	7 ♈ 41	27 ♋ 27	26 ♌ 29
12/12 Su	26 ♌ 45	7 ♈ 39	27 ♋ 21	26 ♌ 27
12/19 Su	26 ♌ 42	7 ♈ 38	27 ♋ 14	26 ♌ 24
12/26 Su	26 ♌ 37	7 ♈ 38	27 ♋ 07	26 ♌ 20

1955	♇	♇	♇	♇
1/02 Su	26 ♌ 31	7 ♈ 38 D	26 ♋ 59	26 ♌ 16
1/09 Su	26 ♌ 24	7 ♈ 39	26 ♋ 51	26 ♌ 10
1/16 Su	26 ♌ 16	7 ♈ 41	26 ♋ 42	26 ♌ 04
1/23 Su	26 ♌ 07	7 ♈ 42	26 ♋ 34	25 ♌ 57
1/30 Su	25 ♌ 57	7 ♈ 45	26 ♋ 26	25 ♌ 50
2/06 Su	25 ♌ 47	7 ♈ 48	26 ♋ 17	25 ♌ 42
2/13 Su	25 ♌ 37	7 ♈ 51	26 ♋ 10	25 ♌ 35
2/20 Su	25 ♌ 26	7 ♈ 55	26 ♋ 03	25 ♌ 27
2/27 Su	25 ♌ 16	7 ♈ 59	25 ♋ 56	25 ♌ 19
3/06 Su	25 ♌ 06	8 ♈ 03	25 ♋ 50	25 ♌ 12

Astro Data

1953

10/27 Tu	11:54	♇	SR	26 ♋ 36	38.7	(38:43)
11/26 Th	20:44	♇	SR	25 ♌ 01	22.3	(22:19)
11/24 Tu	17:27	♇	SR	25 ♌ 36	24.1	(24:08)
12/26 Sa	08:49	♀	SD	7 ♈ 23	-19.0	(-19:00)

1954

4/08 Th	05:43	♇	SD	24 ♋ 30	39.4	(39:23)
5/04 Tu	17:45	♇	SD	22 ♌ 32	23.4	(23:23)
5/08 Sa	22:01	♇	SD	23 ♌ 39	25.0	(25:01)

1954

7/05 Mo	11:31	♀	SR	8 ♈ 48	-18.3	(-18:20)
10/28 Th	18:32	♇	SR	27 ♋ 43	38.9	(38:52)
11/25 Th	19:54	♇	SR	26 ♌ 30	34.2	(24:12)
11/28 Su	23:44	♇	SR	26 ♌ 48	22.1	(12:07)
12/26 Su	15:22	♀	SD	7 ♈ 38	-18.7	(-18:43)

1955		♇	♀	♇	♇
	3/13 Su	24♌57 R	8♈08 D	25♋46 R	25♌05 R
	3/20 Su	24♌48	8♈13	25♋42	24♌58
	3/27 Su	24♌40	8♈18	25♋39	24♌52
	4/03 Su	24♌33	8♈23	25♋38	24♌47
	4/10 Su	24♌28	8♈27	25♋37 D	24♌42
	4/17 Su	24♌23	8♈32	25♋38	24♌38
	4/24 Su	24♌20	8♈37	25♋39	24♌36
	5/01 Su	24♌18	8♈41	25♋42	24♌34
	5/08 Su	24♌18 D	8♈45	25♋46	24♌33
	5/15 Su	24♌18	8♈49	25♋51	24♌33 D
	5/22 Su	24♌21	8♈52	25♋57	24♌34
	5/29 Su	24♌25	8♈56	26♋04	24♌37
	6/05 Su	24♌30	8♈58	26♋11	24♌40
	6/12 Su	24♌36	9♈00	26♋19	24♌44
	6/19 Su	24♌44	9♈02	26♋28	24♌49
	6/26 Su	24♌52	9♈03	26♋38	24♌55
	7/03 Su	25♌02	9♈03	26♋47	25♌01
	7/10 Su	25♌13	9♈03 R	26♋58	25♌08
	7/17 Su	25♌24	9♈03	27♋08	25♌16
	7/24 Su	25♌36	9♈02	27♋18	25♌24
	7/31 Su	25♌49	9♈00	27♋28	25♌33
	8/07 Su	26♌02	8♈58	27♋38	25♌42
	8/14 Su	26♌16	8♈55	27♋48	25♌51
	8/21 Su	26♌29	8♈52	27♋58	26♌00
	8/28 Su	26♌43	8♈49	28♋07	26♌10
	9/04 Su	26♌56	8♈45	28♋15	26♌19
	9/11 Su	27♌09	8♈41	28♋23	26♌28
	9/18 Su	27♌22	8♈37	28♋29	26♌36
	9/25 Su	27♌34	8♈33	28♋35	26♌44
	10/02 Su	27♌45	8♈28	28♋40	26♌52
	10/09 Su	27♌56	8♈24	28♋44	26♌59
	10/16 Su	28♌05	8♈20	28♋47	27♌05
	10/23 Su	28♌14	8♈16	28♋49	27♌10
	10/30 Su	28♌21	8♈12	28♋49	27♌15
	11/06 Su	28♌27	8♈08	28♋49 R	27♌18
	11/13 Su	28♌31	8♈04	28♋47	27♌21
	11/20 Su	28♌34	8♈01	28♋44	27♌23
	11/27 Su	28♌36	7♈59	28♋40	27♌23 R
	12/04 Su	28♌36 R	7♈57	28♋36	27♌23
	12/11 Su	28♌35	7♈55	28♋30	27♌21

1955		♇	♀	♇	♇
	12/18 Su	28♌32 R	7♈54 R	28♋23 R	27♌18 R
	12/25 Su	28♌28	7♈54	28♋16	27♌15
1956	1/01 Su	28♌22	7♈54 D	28♋08	27♌10
	1/08 Su	28♌16	7♈54	28♋00	27♌05
	1/15 Su	28♌08	7♈56	27♋52	26♌59
	1/22 Su	27♌59	7♈57	27♋43	26♌53
	1/29 Su	27♌50	8♈00	27♋35	26♌45
	2/05 Su	27♌40	8♈03	27♋27	26♌38
	2/12 Su	27♌30	8♈06	27♋19	26♌30
	2/19 Su	27♌19	8♈09	27♋12	26♌23
	2/26 Su	27♌09	8♈13	27♋05	26♌15
	3/04 Su	26♌59	8♈18	26♋59	26♌07
	3/11 Su	26♌49	8♈22	26♋54	26♌00
	3/18 Su	26♌40	8♈27	26♋50	25♌53
	3/25 Su	26♌31	8♈32	26♋47	25♌47
	4/01 Su	26♌24	8♈37	26♋45	25♌42
	4/08 Su	26♌18	8♈42	26♋44	25♌37
	4/15 Su	26♌13	8♈46	26♋44 D	25♌33
	4/22 Su	26♌09	8♈51	26♋45	25♌30
	4/29 Su	26♌06	8♈56	26♋48	25♌28
	5/06 Su	26♌05	9♈00	26♋51	25♌27
	5/13 Su	26♌06 D	9♈04	26♋56	25♌26 D
	5/20 Su	26♌08	9♈07	27♋01	25♌27
	5/27 Su	26♌11	9♈10	27♋08	25♌29
	6/03 Su	26♌15	9♈13	27♋15	25♌32
	6/10 Su	26♌21	9♈15	27♋23	25♌36
	6/17 Su	26♌28	9♈17	27♋32	25♌41
	6/24 Su	26♌37	9♈18	27♋41	25♌46
	7/01 Su	26♌46	9♈18	27♋51	25♌52
	7/08 Su	26♌56	9♈19 R	28♋01	25♌59
	7/15 Su	27♌08	9♈18	28♋11	26♌07
	7/22 Su	27♌20	9♈17	28♋21	26♌15
	7/29 Su	27♌32	9♈16	28♋31	26♌24
	8/05 Su	27♌45	9♈14	28♋42	26♌33
	8/12 Su	27♌59	9♈11	28♋51	26♌42
	8/19 Su	28♌12	9♈08	29♋01	26♌51
	8/26 Su	28♌26	9♈05	29♋10	27♌00

Astro Data

1955

4/09 Sa	17:35	♇	SD	25♋37	39.6 (39:35)
5/06 Fr	18:29	♇	SD	24♌18	23.2 (23:12)
5/10 Tu	01:09	♇	SD	24♌33	25.1 (25:06)
7/06 We	04:40	♀	SR	9♈03	-18.1 (-18:04)
10/30 Su	01:22	♇	SR	28♋49	39.1 (39:04)
11/26 Sa	20:49	♇	SR	27♌23	24.3 (24:15)
12/01 Th	04:47	♇	SR	28♌36	21.9 (21:52)

1955

12/27 Tu	01:34	♀	SD	7♈54	-18.5 (-18:28)

1956

4/10 Tu	04:30	♇	SD	26♋44	39.7 (39:44)
5/07 Mo	19:59	♇	SD	26♌05	23.0 (22:57)
5/10 Th	05:45	♇	SD	25♌26	25.2 (25:10)
7/05 Th	19:30	♀	SR	9♈19	-17.8 (-17:49)

	♇	♇	♇	♇
1956				
9/02 Su	28 ♌ 40 D	9 ♈ 01 R	29 ♋ 19 D	27 ♌ 09 D
9/09 Su	28 ♌ 53	8 ♈ 57	29 ♋ 27	27 ♌ 18
9/16 Su	29 ♌ 06	8 ♈ 53	29 ♋ 34	27 ♌ 27
9/23 Su	29 ♌ 19	8 ♈ 49	29 ♋ 40	27 ♌ 35
9/30 Su	29 ♌ 30	8 ♈ 45	29 ♋ 45	27 ♌ 43
10/07 Su	29 ♌ 41	8 ♈ 40	29 ♋ 49	27 ♌ 50
10/14 Su	29 ♌ 51	8 ♈ 36	29 ♋ 53	27 ♌ 56
10/21 Su	0 ♍ 00	8 ♈ 32	29 ♋ 55	28 ♌ 02
10/28 Su	0 ♍ 08	8 ♈ 28	29 ♋ 56	28 ♌ 07
11/04 Su	0 ♍ 15	8 ♈ 24	29 ♋ 55 R	28 ♌ 11
11/11 Su	0 ♍ 20	8 ♈ 20	29 ♋ 54	28 ♌ 14
11/18 Su	0 ♍ 24	8 ♈ 17	29 ♋ 52	28 ♌ 16
11/25 Su	0 ♍ 26	8 ♈ 15	29 ♋ 48	28 ♌ 16
12/02 Su	0 ♍ 27	8 ♈ 12	29 ♋ 44	28 ♌ 16 R
12/09 Su	0 ♍ 26 R	8 ♈ 11	29 ♋ 38	28 ♌ 15
12/16 Su	0 ♍ 24	8 ♈ 09	29 ♋ 32	28 ♌ 13
12/23 Su	0 ♍ 20	8 ♈ 09	29 ♋ 25	28 ♌ 09
12/30 Su	0 ♍ 15	8 ♈ 09 D	29 ♋ 17	28 ♌ 05
1957				
1/06 Su	0 ♍ 09	8 ♈ 09	29 ♋ 09	28 ♌ 00
1/13 Su	0 ♍ 02	8 ♈ 11	29 ♋ 01	27 ♌ 54
1/20 Su	29 ♌ 54	8 ♈ 12	28 ♋ 53	27 ♌ 48
1/27 Su	29 ♌ 44	8 ♈ 14	28 ♋ 44	27 ♌ 41
2/03 Su	29 ♌ 35	8 ♈ 17	28 ♋ 36	27 ♌ 34
2/10 Su	29 ♌ 24	8 ♈ 20	28 ♋ 28	27 ♌ 26
2/17 Su	29 ♌ 14	8 ♈ 24	28 ♋ 20	27 ♌ 18
2/24 Su	29 ♌ 03	8 ♈ 28	28 ♋ 13	27 ♌ 10
3/03 Su	28 ♌ 53	8 ♈ 32	28 ♋ 07	27 ♌ 03
3/10 Su	28 ♌ 43	8 ♈ 37	28 ♋ 02	26 ♌ 56
3/17 Su	28 ♌ 34	8 ♈ 41	27 ♋ 57	26 ♌ 49
3/24 Su	28 ♌ 25	8 ♈ 46	27 ♋ 54	26 ♌ 42
3/31 Su	28 ♌ 17	8 ♈ 51	27 ♋ 52	26 ♌ 36
4/07 Su	28 ♌ 10	8 ♈ 56	27 ♋ 50	26 ♌ 31
4/14 Su	28 ♌ 04	9 ♈ 01	27 ♋ 50 D	26 ♌ 27
4/21 Su	28 ♌ 00	9 ♈ 05	27 ♋ 51	26 ♌ 24
4/28 Su	27 ♌ 57	9 ♈ 10	27 ♋ 53	26 ♌ 22
5/05 Su	27 ♌ 55	9 ♈ 14	27 ♋ 56	26 ♌ 20
5/12 Su	27 ♌ 55 D	9 ♈ 18	28 ♋ 01	26 ♌ 20 D
5/19 Su	27 ♌ 56	9 ♈ 21	28 ♋ 06	26 ♌ 20

	♇	♇	♇	♇
1957				
5/26 Su	27 ♌ 59 D	9 ♈ 25 D	28 ♋ 12 D	26 ♌ 22 D
6/02 Su	28 ♌ 03	9 ♈ 27	28 ♋ 19	26 ♌ 24
6/09 Su	28 ♌ 08	9 ♈ 30	28 ♋ 27	26 ♌ 28
6/16 Su	28 ♌ 15	9 ♈ 31	28 ♋ 35	26 ♌ 32
6/23 Su	28 ♌ 23	9 ♈ 33	28 ♋ 44	26 ♌ 38
6/30 Su	28 ♌ 32	9 ♈ 33	28 ♋ 54	26 ♌ 44
7/07 Su	28 ♌ 42	9 ♈ 34 R	29 ♋ 04	26 ♌ 50
7/14 Su	28 ♌ 53	9 ♈ 33	29 ♋ 14	26 ♌ 58
7/21 Su	29 ♌ 05	9 ♈ 32	29 ♋ 24	27 ♌ 06
7/28 Su	29 ♌ 17	9 ♈ 31	29 ♋ 34	27 ♌ 14
8/04 Su	29 ♌ 30	9 ♈ 29	29 ♋ 44	27 ♌ 23
8/11 Su	29 ♌ 43	9 ♈ 27	29 ♋ 54	27 ♌ 32
8/18 Su	29 ♌ 57	9 ♈ 24	0 ♌ 04	27 ♌ 41
8/25 Su	0 ♍ 11	9 ♈ 21	0 ♌ 13	27 ♌ 51
9/01 Su	0 ♍ 25	9 ♈ 17	0 ♌ 22	28 ♌ 00
9/08 Su	0 ♍ 38	9 ♈ 13	0 ♌ 30	28 ♌ 09
9/15 Su	0 ♍ 52	9 ♈ 09	0 ♌ 38	28 ♌ 18
9/22 Su	1 ♍ 05	9 ♈ 05	0 ♌ 44	28 ♌ 26
9/29 Su	1 ♍ 17	9 ♈ 01	0 ♌ 50	28 ♌ 34
10/06 Su	1 ♍ 28	8 ♈ 56	0 ♌ 54	28 ♌ 41
10/13 Su	1 ♍ 39	8 ♈ 52	0 ♌ 58	28 ♌ 48
10/20 Su	1 ♍ 49	8 ♈ 48	1 ♌ 00	28 ♌ 54
10/27 Su	1 ♍ 57	8 ♈ 44	1 ♌ 02	28 ♌ 59
11/03 Su	2 ♍ 04	8 ♈ 40	1 ♌ 02 R	29 ♌ 03
11/10 Su	2 ♍ 10	8 ♈ 36	1 ♌ 01	29 ♌ 06
11/17 Su	2 ♍ 15	8 ♈ 33	0 ♌ 59	29 ♌ 08
11/24 Su	2 ♍ 18	8 ♈ 30	0 ♌ 56	29 ♌ 09
12/01 Su	2 ♍ 19	8 ♈ 28	0 ♌ 52	29 ♌ 10 R
12/08 Su	2 ♍ 19 R	8 ♈ 26	0 ♌ 46	29 ♌ 09
12/15 Su	2 ♍ 18	8 ♈ 25	0 ♌ 40	29 ♌ 07
12/22 Su	2 ♍ 15	8 ♈ 24	0 ♌ 34	29 ♌ 04
12/29 Su	2 ♍ 10	8 ♈ 24 D	0 ♌ 26	29 ♌ 00
1958				
1/05 Su	2 ♍ 04	8 ♈ 24	0 ♌ 18	28 ♌ 55
1/12 Su	1 ♍ 58	8 ♈ 25	0 ♌ 10	28 ♌ 49
1/19 Su	1 ♍ 50	8 ♈ 27	0 ♌ 02	28 ♌ 43
1/26 Su	1 ♍ 41	8 ♈ 29	29 ♋ 53	28 ♌ 36
2/02 Su	1 ♍ 31	8 ♈ 32	29 ♋ 45	28 ♌ 29

Astro Data

1956

10/20 Sa	06:20	♇ → ♍			21.5 (21:32)
10/30 Tu	09:30	♇ SR	29 ♋ 56		39.2 (39:12)
11/26 Mo	23:43	♇ SR	28 ♌ 16		24.3 (24:20)
12/02 Su	07:16	♇ SR	0 ♍ 27		21.6 (21:37)
12/26 We	19:29	♀ SD	8 ♈ 09		-18.2 (-18:13)

1957

1/15 Tu	02:37	♇ → ♌ R			21.0 (22:00)
4/11 Th	12:54	♇ SD	27 ♋ 50		39.9 (39:54)
5/09 Th	19:50	♇ SD	27 ♌ 55		21.7 (22:43)
5/11 Sa	11:03	♇ SD	26 ♌ 20		25.2 (25:14)

1957

7/06 Sa	01:11	♀ SR	9 ♈ 34		-17.6 (-17:33)
8/14 We	14:31	♇ → ♌			39.1 (39:05)
8/19 Mo	04:28	♇ → ♍			21.7 (21:43)
10/31 Th	17:43	♇ SR	1 ♌ 02		39.3 (39:17)
11/28 Th	02:35	♇ SR	29 ♌ 10		24.4 (24:22)
12/04 We	10:31	♇ SR	2 ♍ 19		21.3 (21:17)
12/27 Fr	08:56	♀ SD	8 ♈ 24		-18.0 (-17:58)

1958

1/20 Mo	20:41	♇ → ♋ R			40.0 (40:01)

1958		♇	♀	⚷	⚷
2/09 Su	1 ♍ 21 ℞	8 ♈ 35 D	29 ♋ 37 ℞	28 ♌ 22 ℞
2/16 Su	1 ♍ 11	8 ♈ 38	29 ♋ 29	28 ♌ 14
2/23 Su	1 ♍ 00	8 ♈ 42	29 ♋ 22	28 ♌ 06
3/02 Su	0 ♍ 49	8 ♈ 46	29 ♋ 16	27 ♌ 58
3/09 Su	0 ♍ 39	8 ♈ 51	29 ♋ 10	27 ♌ 51
3/16 Su	0 ♍ 29	8 ♈ 55	29 ♋ 05	27 ♌ 44
3/23 Su	0 ♍ 20	9 ♈ 00	29 ♋ 01	27 ♌ 37
3/30 Su	0 ♍ 12	9 ♈ 05	28 ♋ 59	27 ♌ 31
4/06 Su	0 ♍ 05	9 ♈ 10	28 ♋ 57	27 ♌ 26
4/13 Su	29 ♌ 58	9 ♈ 15	28 ♋ 56 D	27 ♌ 22
4/20 Su	29 ♌ 53	9 ♈ 19	28 ♋ 57	27 ♌ 18
4/27 Su	29 ♌ 50	9 ♈ 24	28 ♋ 59	27 ♌ 15
5/04 Su	29 ♌ 47	9 ♈ 28	29 ♋ 01	27 ♌ 14
5/11 Su	29 ♌ 46	9 ♈ 32	29 ♋ 05	27 ♌ 13
5/18 Su	29 ♌ 47 D	9 ♈ 36	29 ♋ 10	27 ♌ 13 D
5/25 Su	29 ♌ 49	9 ♈ 39	29 ♋ 16	27 ♌ 14
6/01 Su	29 ♌ 52	9 ♈ 42	29 ♋ 23	27 ♌ 17
6/08 Su	29 ♌ 57	9 ♈ 44	29 ♋ 30	27 ♌ 20
6/15 Su	0 ♍ 03	9 ♈ 46	29 ♋ 38	27 ♌ 24
6/22 Su	0 ♍ 11	9 ♈ 48	29 ♋ 47	27 ♌ 29
6/29 Su	0 ♍ 19	9 ♈ 48	29 ♋ 57	27 ♌ 35
7/06 Su	0 ♍ 29	9 ♈ 49	0 ♌ 06	27 ♌ 41
7/13 Su	0 ♍ 40	9 ♈ 48 ℞	0 ♌ 16	27 ♌ 49
7/20 Su	0 ♍ 51	9 ♈ 48	0 ♌ 27	27 ♌ 57
7/27 Su	1 ♍ 04	9 ♈ 46	0 ♌ 37	28 ♌ 05
8/03 Su	1 ♍ 16	9 ♈ 45	0 ♌ 47	28 ♌ 13
8/10 Su	1 ♍ 30	9 ♈ 42	0 ♌ 57	28 ♌ 22
8/17 Su	1 ♍ 44	9 ♈ 40	1 ♌ 07	28 ♌ 32
8/24 Su	1 ♍ 58	9 ♈ 37	1 ♌ 16	28 ♌ 41
8/31 Su	2 ♍ 12	9 ♈ 33	1 ♌ 25	28 ♌ 50
9/07 Su	2 ♍ 25	9 ♈ 29	1 ♌ 34	28 ♌ 59
9/14 Su	2 ♍ 39	9 ♈ 25	1 ♌ 41	29 ♌ 08
9/21 Su	2 ♍ 52	9 ♈ 21	1 ♌ 48	29 ♌ 17
9/28 Su	3 ♍ 05	9 ♈ 17	1 ♌ 54	29 ♌ 25
10/05 Su	3 ♍ 17	9 ♈ 12	1 ♌ 59	29 ♌ 32
10/12 Su	3 ♍ 28	9 ♈ 08	2 ♌ 03	29 ♌ 39
10/19 Su	3 ♍ 38	9 ♈ 04	2 ♌ 06	29 ♌ 45
10/26 Su	3 ♍ 47	9 ♈ 00	2 ♌ 07	29 ♌ 50
11/02 Su	3 ♍ 55	8 ♈ 56	2 ♌ 08	29 ♌ 55
11/09 Su	4 ♍ 02	8 ♈ 52	2 ♌ 08 ℞	29 ♌ 58

1958		♇	♀	⚷	⚷
11/16 Su	4 ♍ 07 D	8 ♈ 49 ℞	2 ♌ 06 ℞	0 ♍ 01 D
11/23 Su	4 ♍ 11	8 ♈ 46	2 ♌ 03	0 ♍ 02
11/30 Su	4 ♍ 13	8 ♈ 44	1 ♌ 59	0 ♍ 03 ℞
12/07 Su	4 ♍ 13 ℞	8 ♈ 42	1 ♌ 54	0 ♍ 02
12/14 Su	4 ♍ 13	8 ♈ 40	1 ♌ 49	0 ♍ 00
12/21 Su	4 ♍ 10	8 ♈ 39	1 ♌ 42	29 ♌ 58
12/28 Su	4 ♍ 07	8 ♈ 39 D	1 ♌ 35	29 ♌ 54

1959		♇	♀	⚷	⚷
1/04 Su	4 ♍ 01	8 ♈ 39	1 ♌ 27	29 ♌ 50
1/11 Su	3 ♍ 55	8 ♈ 40	1 ♌ 19	29 ♌ 44
1/18 Su	3 ♍ 47	8 ♈ 42	1 ♌ 11	29 ♌ 38
1/25 Su	3 ♍ 39	8 ♈ 44	1 ♌ 02	29 ♌ 32
2/01 Su	3 ♍ 30	8 ♈ 46	0 ♌ 54	29 ♌ 24
2/08 Su	3 ♍ 20	8 ♈ 49	0 ♌ 46	29 ♌ 17
2/15 Su	3 ♍ 09	8 ♈ 53	0 ♌ 38	29 ♌ 09
2/22 Su	2 ♍ 59	8 ♈ 56	0 ♌ 30	29 ♌ 02
3/01 Su	2 ♍ 48	9 ♈ 00	0 ♌ 24	28 ♌ 54
3/08 Su	2 ♍ 37	9 ♈ 05	0 ♌ 18	28 ♌ 46
3/15 Su	2 ♍ 27	9 ♈ 09	0 ♌ 13	28 ♌ 39
3/22 Su	2 ♍ 18	9 ♈ 14	0 ♌ 09	28 ♌ 32
3/29 Su	2 ♍ 09	9 ♈ 19	0 ♌ 05	28 ♌ 26
4/05 Su	2 ♍ 01	9 ♈ 24	0 ♌ 03	28 ♌ 21
4/12 Su	1 ♍ 54	9 ♈ 29	0 ♌ 03	28 ♌ 16
4/19 Su	1 ♍ 49	9 ♈ 33	0 ♌ 03 D	28 ♌ 12
4/26 Su	1 ♍ 44	9 ♈ 38	0 ♌ 04	28 ♌ 09
5/03 Su	1 ♍ 41	9 ♈ 42	0 ♌ 06	28 ♌ 07
5/10 Su	1 ♍ 40	9 ♈ 46	0 ♌ 10	28 ♌ 06
5/17 Su	1 ♍ 40 D	9 ♈ 50	0 ♌ 15	28 ♌ 06 D
5/24 Su	1 ♍ 41	9 ♈ 53	0 ♌ 20	28 ♌ 07
5/31 Su	1 ♍ 44	9 ♈ 56	0 ♌ 26	28 ♌ 09
6/07 Su	1 ♍ 48	9 ♈ 59	0 ♌ 34	28 ♌ 12
6/14 Su	1 ♍ 54	10 ♈ 01	0 ♌ 42	28 ♌ 16
6/21 Su	2 ♍ 01	10 ♈ 02	0 ♌ 50	28 ♌ 21
6/28 Su	2 ♍ 09	10 ♈ 03	0 ♌ 59	28 ♌ 26
7/05 Su	2 ♍ 18	10 ♈ 04	1 ♌ 09	28 ♌ 32
7/12 Su	2 ♍ 29	10 ♈ 04 ℞	1 ♌ 19	28 ♌ 39
7/19 Su	2 ♍ 40	10 ♈ 03	1 ♌ 29	28 ♌ 47
7/26 Su	2 ♍ 52	10 ♈ 02	1 ♌ 39	28 ♌ 55

Astro Data

1958

4/11 Fr	14:48	♇	→ ♌ ℞		22.4 (22:26)
4/12 Sa	21:57	⚷	SD	28 ♋ 56	40.1 (40:03)
5/11 Su	22:01	♇	SD	29 ♌ 46	22.4 (22:25)
5/12 Mo	16:18	⚷	SD	27 ♌ 13	25.3 (25:16)
6/10 Tu	19:00	♇	→ ♍		22.2 (22:14)
7/01 Tu	02:25	⚷	→ ♌		39.4 (39:26)
7/06 Su	11:45	♀	SR	9 ♈ 49	-17.3 (-17:19)
11/02 Su	04:38	⚷	SR	2 ♌ 08	39.5 (39:27)
11/11 Tu	19:14	⚷	→ ♍		24.4 (24:21)

1958

11/29 Sa	08:18	⚷	SR	0 ♍ 03	24.4 (24:24)
12/06 Sa	15:42	♇	SR	4 ♍ 13	21.0 (20:57)
12/16 Tu	19:37	⚷	→ ♌ ℞		24.5 (24:31)
12/27 Sa	16:49	♀	SD	8 ♈ 39	-17.7 (-17:43)

1959

4/14 Tu	04:34	⚷	SD	0 ♌ 02	40.2 (40:09)
5/13 We	21:51	♇	SD	1 ♍ 40	22.1 (22:07)
5/13 We	16:52	⚷	SD	28 ♌ 06	25.3 (25:19)
7/07 Tu	03:41	♀	SR	10 ♈ 04	-17.1 (-17:04)

1959		♇	♇	♇	♇	1960		♇	♇	♇	♇
	8/02 Su	3 ♍ 05 D	10 ♈ 00 ℞	1 ♌ 50 D	29 ♌ 04 D		4/17 Su	3 ♍ 46 ℞	9 ♈ 47 D	1 ♌ 08 D	29 ♌ 06 ℞
	8/09 Su	3 ♍ 18	9 ♈ 58	2 ♌ 00	29 ♌ 13		4/24 Su	3 ♍ 41	9 ♈ 52	1 ♌ 09	29 ♌ 03
	8/16 Su	3 ♍ 32	9 ♈ 55	2 ♌ 10	29 ♌ 22		5/01 Su	3 ♍ 38	9 ♈ 56	1 ♌ 11	29 ♌ 01
	8/23 Su	3 ♍ 46	9 ♈ 52	2 ♌ 19	29 ♌ 31		5/08 Su	3 ♍ 36	10 ♈ 00	1 ♌ 15	28 ♌ 59
	8/30 Su	4 ♍ 00	9 ♈ 49	2 ♌ 28	29 ♌ 40		5/15 Su	3 ♍ 35	10 ♈ 04	1 ♌ 19	28 ♌ 59 D
	9/06 Su	4 ♍ 14	9 ♈ 45	2 ♌ 37	29 ♌ 49		5/22 Su	3 ♍ 36 D	10 ♈ 08	1 ♌ 24	29 ♌ 00
	9/13 Su	4 ♍ 28	9 ♈ 41	2 ♌ 45	29 ♌ 58		5/29 Su	3 ♍ 38	10 ♈ 11	1 ♌ 30	29 ♌ 01
	9/20 Su	4 ♍ 41	9 ♈ 37	2 ♌ 52	0 ♍ 07		6/05 Su	3 ♍ 41	10 ♈ 13	1 ♌ 37	29 ♌ 04
	9/27 Su	4 ♍ 54	9 ♈ 33	2 ♌ 58	0 ♍ 15		6/12 Su	3 ♍ 46	10 ♈ 15	1 ♌ 45	29 ♌ 07
	10/04 Su	5 ♍ 07	9 ♈ 28	3 ♌ 03	0 ♍ 23		6/19 Su	3 ♍ 53	10 ♈ 17	1 ♌ 53	29 ♌ 12
	10/11 Su	5 ♍ 19	9 ♈ 24	3 ♌ 08	0 ♍ 30		6/26 Su	4 ♍ 00	10 ♈ 18	2 ♌ 02	29 ♌ 17
	10/18 Su	5 ♍ 29	9 ♈ 20	3 ♌ 11	0 ♍ 36		7/03 Su	4 ♍ 09	10 ♈ 19	2 ♌ 12	29 ♌ 23
	10/25 Su	5 ♍ 39	9 ♈ 16	3 ♌ 13	0 ♍ 42		7/10 Su	4 ♍ 19	10 ♈ 19 ℞	2 ♌ 21	29 ♌ 30
	11/01 Su	5 ♍ 47	9 ♈ 12	3 ♌ 14	0 ♍ 47		7/17 Su	4 ♍ 30	10 ♈ 18	2 ♌ 31	29 ♌ 38
	11/08 Su	5 ♍ 55	9 ♈ 08	3 ♌ 14 ℞	0 ♍ 50		7/24 Su	4 ♍ 42	10 ♈ 17	2 ♌ 42	29 ♌ 46
	11/15 Su	6 ♍ 01	9 ♈ 05	3 ♌ 12	0 ♍ 53		7/31 Su	4 ♍ 55	10 ♈ 15	2 ♌ 52	29 ♌ 54
	11/22 Su	6 ♍ 05	9 ♈ 02	3 ♌ 10	0 ♍ 55		8/07 Su	5 ♍ 08	10 ♈ 13	3 ♌ 02	0 ♍ 03
	11/29 Su	6 ♍ 08	8 ♈ 59	3 ♌ 07	0 ♍ 56		8/14 Su	5 ♍ 22	10 ♈ 11	3 ♌ 12	0 ♍ 12
	12/06 Su	6 ♍ 09	8 ♈ 57	3 ♌ 02	0 ♍ 55 ℞		8/21 Su	5 ♍ 36	10 ♈ 08	3 ♌ 21	0 ♍ 21
	12/13 Su	6 ♍ 09 ℞	8 ♈ 56	2 ♌ 57	0 ♍ 54		8/28 Su	5 ♍ 50	10 ♈ 05	3 ♌ 31	0 ♍ 30
	12/20 Su	6 ♍ 08	8 ♈ 55	2 ♌ 50	0 ♍ 52		9/04 Su	6 ♍ 04	10 ♈ 01	3 ♌ 40	0 ♍ 40
	12/27 Su	6 ♍ 04	8 ♈ 54	2 ♌ 43	0 ♍ 48		9/11 Su	6 ♍ 18	9 ♈ 57	3 ♌ 48	0 ♍ 49
							9/18 Su	6 ♍ 32	9 ♈ 53	3 ♌ 55	0 ♍ 57
							9/25 Su	6 ♍ 46	9 ♈ 49	4 ♌ 01	1 ♍ 06
							10/02 Su	6 ♍ 58	9 ♈ 44	4 ♌ 07	1 ♍ 14
1960	1/03 Su	6 ♍ 00	8 ♈ 54 D	2 ♌ 36	0 ♍ 44		10/09 Su	7 ♍ 11	9 ♈ 40	4 ♌ 12	1 ♍ 21
	1/10 Su	5 ♍ 54	8 ♈ 55	2 ♌ 28	0 ♍ 39		10/16 Su	7 ♍ 22	9 ♈ 36	4 ♌ 16	1 ♍ 27
	1/17 Su	5 ♍ 47	8 ♈ 57	2 ♌ 19	0 ♍ 33		10/23 Su	7 ♍ 32	9 ♈ 31	4 ♌ 18	1 ♍ 33
	1/24 Su	5 ♍ 39	8 ♈ 58	2 ♌ 11	0 ♍ 27		10/30 Su	7 ♍ 41	9 ♈ 27	4 ♌ 19	1 ♍ 38
	1/31 Su	5 ♍ 30	9 ♈ 01	2 ♌ 02	0 ♍ 20		11/06 Su	7 ♍ 49	9 ♈ 24	4 ♌ 20 ℞	1 ♍ 42
	2/07 Su	5 ♍ 20	9 ♈ 04	1 ♌ 54	0 ♍ 12		11/13 Su	7 ♍ 56	9 ♈ 20	4 ♌ 19	1 ♍ 45
	2/14 Su	5 ♍ 10	9 ♈ 07	1 ♌ 46	0 ♍ 05		11/20 Su	8 ♍ 01	9 ♈ 17	4 ♌ 17	1 ♍ 47
	2/21 Su	4 ♍ 59	9 ♈ 11	1 ♌ 39	29 ♌ 57		11/27 Su	8 ♍ 05	9 ♈ 15	4 ♌ 14	1 ♍ 49
	2/28 Su	4 ♍ 48	9 ♈ 15	1 ♌ 32	29 ♌ 49		12/04 Su	8 ♍ 07	9 ♈ 13	4 ♌ 09	1 ♍ 49 ℞
	3/06 Su	4 ♍ 38	9 ♈ 19	1 ♌ 26	29 ♌ 41		12/11 Su	8 ♍ 07 ℞	9 ♈ 11	4 ♌ 04	1 ♍ 47
	3/13 Su	4 ♍ 27	9 ♈ 24	1 ♌ 20	29 ♌ 34		12/18 Su	8 ♍ 07	9 ♈ 10	3 ♌ 58	1 ♍ 45
	3/20 Su	4 ♍ 17	9 ♈ 28	1 ♌ 16	29 ♌ 27		12/25 Su	8 ♍ 04	9 ♈ 09	3 ♌ 51	1 ♍ 42
	3/27 Su	4 ♍ 08	9 ♈ 33	1 ♌ 12	29 ♌ 21						
	4/03 Su	4 ♍ 00	9 ♈ 38	1 ♌ 10	29 ♌ 15						
	4/10 Su	3 ♍ 52	9 ♈ 43	1 ♌ 09	29 ♌ 10						

Astro Data

1959

9/13 Su	21:12	♇	→ ♍			24.5	(24:28)
11/03 Tu	12:32	♇	SR	3 ♌ 14		39.5	(39:31)
11/30 Mo	11:17	♇	SR	0 ♍ 56		24.5	(24:28)
12/08 Tu	20:26	♇	SR	6 ♍ 10		20.6	(20:37)
12/28 Mo	02:59	♇	SD	8 ♈ 54		-17.4	(-17:26)

1960

2/18 Th	14:36	♇	→ ♌ ℞			25.1	(25:06)
4/14 Th	14:12	♇	SD	1 ♌ 08		40.3	(40:16)

1960

5/13 Fr	19:47	♇	SD	28 ♌ 59		25.4	(25:22)
5/15 Su	00:48	♇	SD	3 ♍ 35		21.8	(21:46)
7/06 We	18:09	♇	SR	10 ♈ 19		-16.8	(-16:48)
8/04 Th	08:22	♇	→ ♍			24.8	(24:49)
11/03 Th	19:01	♇	SR	4 ♌ 20		39.6	(39:34)
11/30 We	11:23	♇	SR	1 ♍ 49		24.5	(24:28)
12/10 Sa	04:38	♇	SR	8 ♍ 07		20.2	(20:13)
12/27 Tu	18:32	♇	SD	9 ♈ 09		-17.2	(-17:11)

1961	⚷	♀	⚴	⚶
1/01 Su	8 ♍ 00 R	9 ♈ 09 D	3 ♌ 44 R	1 ♍ 38 R
1/08 Su	7 ♍ 55	9 ♈ 10	3 ♌ 36	1 ♍ 33
1/15 Su	7 ♍ 48	9 ♈ 11	3 ♌ 28	1 ♍ 28
1/22 Su	7 ♍ 40	9 ♈ 13	3 ♌ 20	1 ♍ 22
1/29 Su	7 ♍ 32	9 ♈ 15	3 ♌ 11	1 ♍ 15
2/05 Su	7 ♍ 22	9 ♈ 18	3 ♌ 03	1 ♍ 07
2/12 Su	7 ♍ 12	9 ♈ 21	2 ♌ 55	1 ♍ 00
2/19 Su	7 ♍ 01	9 ♈ 25	2 ♌ 47	0 ♍ 52
2/26 Su	6 ♍ 51	9 ♈ 29	2 ♌ 40	0 ♍ 44
3/05 Su	6 ♍ 40	9 ♈ 33	2 ♌ 33	0 ♍ 37
3/12 Su	6 ♍ 29	9 ♈ 38	2 ♌ 28	0 ♍ 29
3/19 Su	6 ♍ 19	9 ♈ 42	2 ♌ 23	0 ♍ 22
3/26 Su	6 ♍ 09	9 ♈ 47	2 ♌ 19	0 ♍ 16
4/02 Su	6 ♍ 01	9 ♈ 52	2 ♌ 16	0 ♍ 10
4/09 Su	5 ♍ 53	9 ♈ 57	2 ♌ 15	0 ♍ 05
4/16 Su	5 ♍ 46	10 ♈ 01	2 ♌ 14	0 ♍ 00
4/23 Su	5 ♍ 40	10 ♈ 06	2 ♌ 15 D	29 ♌ 57
4/30 Su	5 ♍ 36	10 ♈ 10	2 ♌ 16	29 ♌ 54
5/07 Su	5 ♍ 33	10 ♈ 15	2 ♌ 19	29 ♌ 52
5/14 Su	5 ♍ 32	10 ♈ 18	2 ♌ 23	29 ♌ 52
5/21 Su	5 ♍ 32 D	10 ♈ 22	2 ♌ 28	29 ♌ 52 D
5/28 Su	5 ♍ 34	10 ♈ 25	2 ♌ 34	29 ♌ 53
6/04 Su	5 ♍ 37	10 ♈ 28	2 ♌ 40	29 ♌ 56
6/11 Su	5 ♍ 41	10 ♈ 30	2 ♌ 48	29 ♌ 59
6/18 Su	5 ♍ 47	10 ♈ 32	2 ♌ 56	0 ♍ 03
6/25 Su	5 ♍ 54	10 ♈ 33	3 ♌ 05	0 ♍ 08
7/02 Su	6 ♍ 02	10 ♈ 33	3 ♌ 14	0 ♍ 14
7/09 Su	6 ♍ 12	10 ♈ 34 R	3 ♌ 24	0 ♍ 21
7/16 Su	6 ♍ 23	10 ♈ 33	3 ♌ 34	0 ♍ 28
7/23 Su	6 ♍ 34	10 ♈ 32	3 ♌ 44	0 ♍ 36
7/30 Su	6 ♍ 47	10 ♈ 31	3 ♌ 54	0 ♍ 44
8/06 Su	7 ♍ 00	10 ♈ 29	4 ♌ 05	0 ♍ 53
8/13 Su	7 ♍ 13	10 ♈ 26	4 ♌ 15	1 ♍ 02
8/20 Su	7 ♍ 27	10 ♈ 24	4 ♌ 24	1 ♍ 11
8/27 Su	7 ♍ 42	10 ♈ 20	4 ♌ 34	1 ♍ 20
9/03 Su	7 ♍ 56	10 ♈ 17	4 ♌ 43	1 ♍ 30
9/10 Su	8 ♍ 10	10 ♈ 13	4 ♌ 51	1 ♍ 39
9/17 Su	8 ♍ 25	10 ♈ 09	4 ♌ 59	1 ♍ 48
9/24 Su	8 ♍ 38	10 ♈ 05	5 ♌ 05	1 ♍ 56
10/01 Su	8 ♍ 52	10 ♈ 00	5 ♌ 11	2 ♍ 04

1961	⚷	♀	⚴	⚶
10/08 Su	9 ♍ 04 D	9 ♈ 56 R	5 ♌ 16 D	2 ♍ 12 D
10/15 Su	9 ♍ 16	9 ♈ 52	5 ♌ 20	2 ♍ 18
10/22 Su	9 ♍ 27	9 ♈ 47	5 ♌ 23	2 ♍ 24
10/29 Su	9 ♍ 37	9 ♈ 43	5 ♌ 25	2 ♍ 30
11/05 Su	9 ♍ 45	9 ♈ 40	5 ♌ 25	2 ♍ 34
11/12 Su	9 ♍ 53	9 ♈ 36	5 ♌ 25 R	2 ♍ 37
11/19 Su	9 ♍ 59	9 ♈ 33	5 ♌ 23	2 ♍ 40
11/26 Su	10 ♍ 03	9 ♈ 30	5 ♌ 20	2 ♍ 41
12/03 Su	10 ♍ 06	9 ♈ 28	5 ♌ 17	2 ♍ 41 R
12/10 Su	10 ♍ 07	9 ♈ 26	5 ♌ 12	2 ♍ 41
12/17 Su	10 ♍ 07 R	9 ♈ 25	5 ♌ 06	2 ♍ 39
12/24 Su	10 ♍ 05	9 ♈ 25	5 ♌ 00	2 ♍ 36
12/31 Su	10 ♍ 02	9 ♈ 25 D	4 ♌ 52	2 ♍ 32
1962				
1/07 Su	9 ♍ 57	9 ♈ 25	4 ♌ 45	2 ♍ 28
1/14 Su	9 ♍ 51	9 ♈ 26	4 ♌ 36	2 ♍ 22
1/21 Su	9 ♍ 44	9 ♈ 28	4 ♌ 28	2 ♍ 16
1/28 Su	9 ♍ 36	9 ♈ 30	4 ♌ 20	2 ♍ 10
2/04 Su	9 ♍ 26	9 ♈ 33	4 ♌ 11	2 ♍ 03
2/11 Su	9 ♍ 16	9 ♈ 36	4 ♌ 03	1 ♍ 55
2/18 Su	9 ♍ 06	9 ♈ 39	3 ♌ 55	1 ♍ 47
2/25 Su	8 ♍ 55	9 ♈ 43	3 ♌ 48	1 ♍ 40
3/04 Su	8 ♍ 44	9 ♈ 47	3 ♌ 41	1 ♍ 32
3/11 Su	8 ♍ 33	9 ♈ 52	3 ♌ 35	1 ♍ 24
3/18 Su	8 ♍ 23	9 ♈ 56	3 ♌ 30	1 ♍ 17
3/25 Su	8 ♍ 13	10 ♈ 01	3 ♌ 26	1 ♍ 10
4/01 Su	8 ♍ 04	10 ♈ 06	3 ♌ 23	1 ♍ 04
4/08 Su	7 ♍ 55	10 ♈ 11	3 ♌ 21	0 ♍ 59
4/15 Su	7 ♍ 48	10 ♈ 16	3 ♌ 20	0 ♍ 54
4/22 Su	7 ♍ 42	10 ♈ 20	3 ♌ 20 D	0 ♍ 51
4/29 Su	7 ♍ 37	10 ♈ 25	3 ♌ 21	0 ♍ 48
5/06 Su	7 ♍ 33	10 ♈ 29	3 ♌ 24	0 ♍ 46
5/13 Su	7 ♍ 31	10 ♈ 33	3 ♌ 27	0 ♍ 45
5/20 Su	7 ♍ 31 D	10 ♈ 36	3 ♌ 32	0 ♍ 45 D
5/27 Su	7 ♍ 32	10 ♈ 39	3 ♌ 37	0 ♍ 46
6/03 Su	7 ♍ 34	10 ♈ 42	3 ♌ 44	0 ♍ 48
6/10 Su	7 ♍ 38	10 ♈ 45	3 ♌ 51	0 ♍ 51
6/17 Su	7 ♍ 43	10 ♈ 46	3 ♌ 59	0 ♍ 55
6/24 Su	7 ♍ 50	10 ♈ 48	4 ♌ 07	1 ♍ 00

Astro Data

1961

4/16 Su	00:30	⚶	SD	2 ♌ 14	40.3 (40:19)
4/17 Mo	07:41	♌	→ ♌ R		25.4 (25:25)
5/17 We	04:23	♀	SD	5 ♍ 32	21.4 (21:25)
5/15 Mo	01:09	♌	SD	29 ♌ 52	25.4 (25:23)
6/11 Su	17:02	♌	→ ♍		25.2 (25:14)
7/07 Fr	02:20	♀	SR	10 ♈ 34	-16.5 (-16:32)

1961

11/05 Su	02:03	⚶	SR	5 ♌ 25	39.7 (39:40)
12/01 Fr	14:04	⚴	SR	2 ♍ 41	24.5 (24:29)
12/12 Tu	11:54	⚷	SR	10 ♍ 07	19.8 (19:50)
12/28 Th	08:42	♀	SD	9 ♈ 24	-16.9 (-16:55)

1962

4/17 Tu	09:43	⚶	SD	3 ♌ 20	40.4 (40:24)
5/19 Sa	09:38	⚷	SD	7 ♍ 31	21.0 (21:02)
5/16 We	06:28	⚴	SD	0 ♍ 45	25.4 (25:25)

		♇	♀	♈	♈				♇	♀	♈	♈
1962	7/01 Su	7 ♏ 58 D	10 ♈ 48 D	4 ♌ 17 D	1 ♏ 05 D	1963	3/17 Su	10 ♏ 29 R	10 ♈ 10 D	4 ♌ 37 R	2 ♏ 12 R
	7/08 Su	8 ♏ 07	10 ♈ 49 R	4 ♌ 26	1 ♏ 12		3/24 Su	10 ♏ 19	10 ♈ 15	4 ♌ 33	2 ♏ 05
	7/15 Su	8 ♏ 17	10 ♈ 48	4 ♌ 36	1 ♏ 19		3/31 Su	10 ♏ 09	10 ♈ 20	4 ♌ 30	1 ♏ 59
	7/22 Su	8 ♏ 28	10 ♈ 48	4 ♌ 46	1 ♏ 26		4/07 Su	10 ♏ 00	10 ♈ 25	4 ♌ 27	1 ♏ 53
	7/29 Su	8 ♏ 40	10 ♈ 46	4 ♌ 57	1 ♏ 35		4/14 Su	9 ♏ 52	10 ♈ 30	4 ♌ 26	1 ♏ 48
	8/05 Su	8 ♏ 53	10 ♈ 44	5 ♌ 07	1 ♏ 43		4/21 Su	9 ♏ 46	10 ♈ 34	4 ♌ 26 D	1 ♏ 44
	8/12 Su	9 ♏ 07	10 ♈ 42	5 ♌ 17	1 ♏ 52		4/28 Su	9 ♏ 40	10 ♈ 39	4 ♌ 27	1 ♏ 41
	8/19 Su	9 ♏ 21	10 ♈ 39	5 ♌ 27	2 ♏ 01		5/05 Su	9 ♏ 36	10 ♈ 43	4 ♌ 29	1 ♏ 39
	8/26 Su	9 ♏ 35	10 ♈ 36	5 ♌ 36	2 ♏ 10		5/12 Su	9 ♏ 33	10 ♈ 47	4 ♌ 32	1 ♏ 38
	9/02 Su	9 ♏ 50	10 ♈ 33	5 ♌ 45	2 ♏ 20		5/19 Su	9 ♏ 32	10 ♈ 51	4 ♌ 36	1 ♏ 37 D
	9/09 Su	10 ♏ 04	10 ♈ 29	5 ♌ 54	2 ♏ 29		5/26 Su	9 ♏ 32 D	10 ♈ 54	4 ♌ 41	1 ♏ 38
	9/16 Su	10 ♏ 19	10 ♈ 25	6 ♌ 02	2 ♏ 38		6/02 Su	9 ♏ 34	10 ♈ 57	4 ♌ 47	1 ♏ 40
	9/23 Su	10 ♏ 33	10 ♈ 21	6 ♌ 09	2 ♏ 46		6/09 Su	9 ♏ 37	10 ♈ 59	4 ♌ 54	1 ♏ 43
	9/30 Su	10 ♏ 46	10 ♈ 16	6 ♌ 15	2 ♏ 54		6/16 Su	9 ♏ 42	11 ♈ 01	5 ♌ 02	1 ♏ 46
	10/07 Su	10 ♏ 59	10 ♈ 12	6 ♌ 20	3 ♏ 02		6/23 Su	9 ♏ 48	11 ♈ 02	5 ♌ 10	1 ♏ 51
	10/14 Su	11 ♏ 12	10 ♈ 08	6 ♌ 25	3 ♏ 09		6/30 Su	9 ♏ 55	11 ♈ 03	5 ♌ 19	1 ♏ 56
	10/21 Su	11 ♏ 23	10 ♈ 03	6 ♌ 28	3 ♏ 15		7/07 Su	10 ♏ 04	11 ♈ 04	5 ♌ 29	2 ♏ 02
	10/28 Su	11 ♏ 34	9 ♈ 59	6 ♌ 30	3 ♏ 21		7/14 Su	10 ♏ 13	11 ♈ 03 R	5 ♌ 38	2 ♏ 09
	11/04 Su	11 ♏ 43	9 ♈ 56	6 ♌ 31	3 ♏ 26		7/21 Su	10 ♏ 24	11 ♈ 03	5 ♌ 49	2 ♏ 17
	11/11 Su	11 ♏ 51	9 ♈ 52	6 ♌ 31 R	3 ♏ 29		7/28 Su	10 ♏ 36	11 ♈ 02	5 ♌ 59	2 ♏ 25
	11/18 Su	11 ♏ 58	9 ♈ 49	6 ♌ 30	3 ♏ 32		8/04 Su	10 ♏ 49	11 ♈ 00	6 ♌ 09	2 ♏ 33
	11/25 Su	12 ♏ 03	9 ♈ 46	6 ♌ 27	3 ♏ 34		8/11 Su	11 ♏ 02	10 ♈ 58	6 ♌ 19	2 ♏ 42
	12/02 Su	12 ♏ 07	9 ♈ 44	6 ♌ 24	3 ♏ 34		8/18 Su	11 ♏ 16	10 ♈ 55	6 ♌ 29	2 ♏ 51
	12/09 Su	12 ♏ 09	9 ♈ 42	6 ♌ 19	3 ♏ 34 R		8/25 Su	11 ♏ 31	10 ♈ 52	6 ♌ 39	3 ♏ 00
	12/16 Su	12 ♏ 09 R	9 ♈ 41	6 ♌ 14	3 ♏ 32		9/01 Su	11 ♏ 45	10 ♈ 49	6 ♌ 48	3 ♏ 10
	12/23 Su	12 ♏ 08	9 ♈ 40	6 ♌ 07	3 ♏ 30		9/08 Su	12 ♏ 00	10 ♈ 45	6 ♌ 57	3 ♏ 19
	12/30 Su	12 ♏ 06	9 ♈ 40 D	6 ♌ 00	3 ♏ 27		9/15 Su	12 ♏ 14	10 ♈ 41	7 ♌ 05	3 ♏ 28
							9/22 Su	12 ♏ 29	10 ♈ 37	7 ♌ 12	3 ♏ 37
							9/29 Su	12 ♏ 43	10 ♈ 32	7 ♌ 19	3 ♏ 45
							10/06 Su	12 ♏ 56	10 ♈ 28	7 ♌ 24	3 ♏ 53
1963	1/06 Su	12 ♏ 02	9 ♈ 40	5 ♌ 53	3 ♏ 22		10/13 Su	13 ♏ 09	10 ♈ 24	7 ♌ 29	4 ♏ 00
	1/13 Su	11 ♏ 56	9 ♈ 41	5 ♌ 45	3 ♏ 17		10/20 Su	13 ♏ 21	10 ♈ 19	7 ♌ 33	4 ♏ 07
	1/20 Su	11 ♏ 49	9 ♈ 42	5 ♌ 37	3 ♏ 11		10/27 Su	13 ♏ 32	10 ♈ 15	7 ♌ 35	4 ♏ 12
	1/27 Su	11 ♏ 41	9 ♈ 45	5 ♌ 28	3 ♏ 05		11/03 Su	13 ♏ 42	10 ♈ 11	7 ♌ 37	4 ♏ 17
	2/03 Su	11 ♏ 32	9 ♈ 47	5 ♌ 20	2 ♏ 58		11/10 Su	13 ♏ 51	10 ♈ 08	7 ♌ 37 R	4 ♏ 21
	2/10 Su	11 ♏ 23	9 ♈ 50	5 ♌ 11	2 ♏ 50		11/17 Su	13 ♏ 58	10 ♈ 05	7 ♌ 36	4 ♏ 24
	2/17 Su	11 ♏ 12	9 ♈ 54	5 ♌ 03	2 ♏ 42		11/24 Su	14 ♏ 04	10 ♈ 02	7 ♌ 34	4 ♏ 26
	2/24 Su	11 ♏ 02	9 ♈ 57	4 ♌ 56	2 ♏ 35		12/01 Su	14 ♏ 09	9 ♈ 59	7 ♌ 31	4 ♏ 27
	3/03 Su	10 ♏ 51	10 ♈ 01	4 ♌ 49	2 ♏ 27		12/08 Su	14 ♏ 12	9 ♈ 57	7 ♌ 26	4 ♏ 27 R
	3/10 Su	10 ♏ 40	10 ♈ 06	4 ♌ 43	2 ♏ 19		12/15 Su	14 ♏ 13	9 ♈ 56	7 ♌ 21	4 ♏ 26

Astro Data

1962

7/07 Sa	11:44	♀	SR	10 ♈ 49	-16.3 (-16:17)
11/06 Tu	10:46	♈	SR	6 ♌ 31	39.7 (39:40)
12/02 Su	18:04	♌	SR	3 ♏ 34	24.5 (24:31)
12/14 Fr	21:45	♇	SR	12 ♏ 09	19.4 (19:22)
12/28 Fr	14:29	♀	SD	9 ♈ 40	-16.7 (-16:40)

1963

4/18 Th	17:06	♈	SD	4 ♌ 26	40.5 (40:38)
5/17 Fr	10:04	♌	SD	1 ♏ 37	25.4 (25:26)
5/21 Tu	15:41	♇	SD	9 ♏ 32	20.6 (20:36)
7/08 Mo	05:43	♀	SR	11 ♈ 04	-16.0 (-16:02)
11/07 Th	21:28	♈	SR	7 ♌ 37	39.7 (39:41)
12/04 We	00:02	♌	SR	4 ♏ 27	24.5 (24:31)
12/17 Tu	07:07	♇	SR	14 ♏ 13	18.9 (18:55)

LONGITUDE

	♇	♀	♇	♇
1963 12/22 Su	14 ♍ 13 ℞	9 ♈ 55 ℞	7 ♌ 15 ℞	4 ♍ 24 ℞
12/29 Su	14 ♍ 11	9 ♈ 55	7 ♌ 09	4 ♍ 21
1964 1/05 Su	14 ♍ 08	9 ♈ 55 D	7 ♌ 01	4 ♍ 17
1/12 Su	14 ♍ 03	9 ♈ 56	6 ♌ 53	4 ♍ 12
1/19 Su	13 ♍ 57	9 ♈ 57	6 ♌ 45	4 ♍ 06
1/26 Su	13 ♍ 49	9 ♈ 59	6 ♌ 37	4 ♍ 00
2/02 Su	13 ♍ 41	10 ♈ 02	6 ♌ 28	3 ♍ 53
2/09 Su	13 ♍ 31	10 ♈ 05	6 ♌ 20	3 ♍ 45
2/16 Su	13 ♍ 21	10 ♈ 08	6 ♌ 12	3 ♍ 38
2/23 Su	13 ♍ 10	10 ♈ 12	6 ♌ 04	3 ♍ 30
3/01 Su	12 ♍ 59	10 ♈ 16	5 ♌ 57	3 ♍ 22
3/08 Su	12 ♍ 48	10 ♈ 20	5 ♌ 51	3 ♍ 15
3/15 Su	12 ♍ 38	10 ♈ 25	5 ♌ 45	3 ♍ 07
3/22 Su	12 ♍ 27	10 ♈ 29	5 ♌ 40	3 ♍ 00
3/29 Su	12 ♍ 17	10 ♈ 34	5 ♌ 36	2 ♍ 54
4/05 Su	12 ♍ 08	10 ♈ 39	5 ♌ 34	2 ♍ 48
4/12 Su	11 ♍ 59	10 ♈ 44	5 ♌ 32	2 ♍ 43
4/19 Su	11 ♍ 52	10 ♈ 48	5 ♌ 31 D	2 ♍ 39
4/26 Su	11 ♍ 46	10 ♈ 53	5 ♌ 32	2 ♍ 35
5/03 Su	11 ♍ 41	10 ♈ 57	5 ♌ 34	2 ♍ 33
5/10 Su	11 ♍ 37	11 ♈ 01	5 ♌ 36	2 ♍ 31
5/17 Su	11 ♍ 35	11 ♈ 05	5 ♌ 40	2 ♍ 30
5/24 Su	11 ♍ 35 D	11 ♈ 08	5 ♌ 45	2 ♍ 31 D
5/31 Su	11 ♍ 36	11 ♈ 11	5 ♌ 51	2 ♍ 32
6/07 Su	11 ♍ 38	11 ♈ 14	5 ♌ 57	2 ♍ 35
6/14 Su	11 ♍ 42	11 ♈ 16	6 ♌ 05	2 ♍ 38
6/21 Su	11 ♍ 48	11 ♈ 17	6 ♌ 13	2 ♍ 42
6/28 Su	11 ♍ 55	11 ♈ 18	6 ♌ 22	2 ♍ 47
7/05 Su	12 ♍ 03	11 ♈ 19	6 ♌ 31	2 ♍ 53
7/12 Su	12 ♍ 12	11 ♈ 19 ℞	6 ♌ 41	3 ♍ 00
7/19 Su	12 ♍ 23	11 ♈ 18	6 ♌ 51	3 ♍ 07
7/26 Su	12 ♍ 34	11 ♈ 17	7 ♌ 01	3 ♍ 15
8/02 Su	12 ♍ 47	11 ♈ 15	7 ♌ 11	3 ♍ 24
8/09 Su	13 ♍ 00	11 ♈ 13	7 ♌ 22	3 ♍ 32
8/16 Su	13 ♍ 14	11 ♈ 11	7 ♌ 32	3 ♍ 41
8/23 Su	13 ♍ 28	11 ♈ 08	7 ♌ 41	3 ♍ 51
8/30 Su	13 ♍ 43	11 ♈ 04	7 ♌ 51	4 ♍ 00

	♇	♀	♇	♇
1964 9/06 Su	13 ♍ 57 D	11 ♈ 01 ℞	8 ♌ 00 D	4 ♍ 09 D
9/13 Su	14 ♍ 12	10 ♈ 57	8 ♌ 08	4 ♍ 18
9/20 Su	14 ♍ 27	10 ♈ 53	8 ♌ 16	4 ♍ 27
9/27 Su	14 ♍ 41	10 ♈ 48	8 ♌ 23	4 ♍ 35
10/04 Su	14 ♍ 55	10 ♈ 44	8 ♌ 28	4 ♍ 43
10/11 Su	15 ♍ 09	10 ♈ 40	8 ♌ 33	4 ♍ 51
10/18 Su	15 ♍ 21	10 ♈ 35	8 ♌ 37	4 ♍ 58
10/25 Su	15 ♍ 33	10 ♈ 31	8 ♌ 40	5 ♍ 04
11/01 Su	15 ♍ 43	10 ♈ 27	8 ♌ 42	5 ♍ 09
11/08 Su	15 ♍ 53	10 ♈ 24	8 ♌ 43	5 ♍ 13
11/15 Su	16 ♍ 01	10 ♈ 20	8 ♌ 42 ℞	5 ♍ 16
11/22 Su	16 ♍ 08	10 ♈ 17	8 ♌ 40	5 ♍ 19
11/29 Su	16 ♍ 13	10 ♈ 15	8 ♌ 38	5 ♍ 20
12/06 Su	16 ♍ 17	10 ♈ 13	8 ♌ 34	5 ♍ 20 ℞
12/13 Su	16 ♍ 19	10 ♈ 11	8 ♌ 29	5 ♍ 19
12/20 Su	16 ♍ 19 ℞	10 ♈ 10	8 ♌ 23	5 ♍ 18
12/27 Su	16 ♍ 18	10 ♈ 10	8 ♌ 17	5 ♍ 15
1965 1/03 Su	16 ♍ 16	10 ♈ 10 D	8 ♌ 10	5 ♍ 11
1/10 Su	16 ♍ 11	10 ♈ 11	8 ♌ 02	5 ♍ 06
1/17 Su	16 ♍ 06	10 ♈ 12	7 ♌ 54	5 ♍ 01
1/24 Su	15 ♍ 59	10 ♈ 14	7 ♌ 45	4 ♍ 55
1/31 Su	15 ♍ 51	10 ♈ 16	7 ♌ 37	4 ♍ 48
2/07 Su	15 ♍ 42	10 ♈ 19	7 ♌ 28	4 ♍ 41
2/14 Su	15 ♍ 32	10 ♈ 22	7 ♌ 20	4 ♍ 33
2/21 Su	15 ♍ 21	10 ♈ 26	7 ♌ 13	4 ♍ 25
2/28 Su	15 ♍ 11	10 ♈ 30	7 ♌ 05	4 ♍ 18
3/07 Su	14 ♍ 59	10 ♈ 34	6 ♌ 59	4 ♍ 10
3/14 Su	14 ♍ 48	10 ♈ 39	6 ♌ 53	4 ♍ 03
3/21 Su	14 ♍ 38	10 ♈ 43	6 ♌ 48	3 ♍ 55
3/28 Su	14 ♍ 27	10 ♈ 48	6 ♌ 43	3 ♍ 49
4/04 Su	14 ♍ 17	10 ♈ 53	6 ♌ 40	3 ♍ 43
4/11 Su	14 ♍ 09	10 ♈ 58	6 ♌ 38	3 ♍ 37
4/18 Su	14 ♍ 01	11 ♈ 02	6 ♌ 37	3 ♍ 33
4/25 Su	13 ♍ 54	11 ♈ 07	6 ♌ 38 D	3 ♍ 29
5/02 Su	13 ♍ 48	11 ♈ 11	6 ♌ 39	3 ♍ 26
5/09 Su	13 ♍ 44	11 ♈ 15	6 ♌ 41	3 ♍ 24
5/16 Su	13 ♍ 42	11 ♈ 19	6 ♌ 45	3 ♍ 24

Astro Data

1963
12/29 Su 00:34 ♀ SD 9 ♈ 55 -16.4 (-16:23)
1964
4/18 Sa 22:53 ♇ SD 5 ♌ 31 40.5 (40:30)
5/22 Fr 21:29 ♇ SD 11 ♍ 35 20.1 (20:08)
5/17 Su 10:25 ♇ SD 2 ♍ 30 25.4 (25:26)
7/07 Tu 21:00 ♀ SR 11 ♈ 19 -15.8 (-15:46)

1964
11/08 Su 05:46 ♇ SR 8 ♌ 43 39.7 (39:43)
12/04 Fr 01:58 ♇ SR 5 ♍ 20 24.5 (34:31)
12/18 Fr 18:38 ♇ SR 16 ♍ 19 18.4 (18:24)
12/28 Mo 18:51 ♀ SD 10 ♈ 10 -16.1 (-16:08)
1965
4/20 Tu 08:23 ♇ SD 6 ♌ 37 40.5 (40:30)
5/18 Tu 13:23 ♇ SD 3 ♍ 13 25.5 (25:27)

	♇	♀	♃	♃
1965 5/23 Su	13 ♍ 40 ℞	11 ♈ 23 D	6 ♌ 49 D	3 ♍ 24 D
5/30 Su	13 ♍ 41 D	11 ♈ 26	6 ♌ 55	3 ♍ 25
6/06 Su	13 ♍ 42	11 ♈ 28	7 ♌ 01	3 ♍ 27
6/13 Su	13 ♍ 46	11 ♈ 30	7 ♌ 08	3 ♍ 30
6/20 Su	13 ♍ 51	11 ♈ 32	7 ♌ 16	3 ♍ 34
6/27 Su	13 ♍ 57	11 ♈ 33	7 ♌ 25	3 ♍ 39
7/04 Su	14 ♍ 04	11 ♈ 34	7 ♌ 34	3 ♍ 45
7/11 Su	14 ♍ 13	11 ♈ 34 ℞	7 ♌ 43	3 ♍ 51
7/18 Su	14 ♍ 23	11 ♈ 33	7 ♌ 53	3 ♍ 58
7/25 Su	14 ♍ 35	11 ♈ 32	8 ♌ 03	4 ♍ 06
8/01 Su	14 ♍ 47	11 ♈ 31	8 ♌ 14	4 ♍ 14
8/08 Su	15 ♍ 00	11 ♈ 29	8 ♌ 24	4 ♍ 23
8/15 Su	15 ♍ 13	11 ♈ 26	8 ♌ 34	4 ♍ 32
8/22 Su	15 ♍ 28	11 ♈ 23	8 ♌ 44	4 ♍ 41
8/29 Su	15 ♍ 42	11 ♈ 20	8 ♌ 54	4 ♍ 50
9/05 Su	15 ♍ 57	11 ♈ 16	9 ♌ 03	4 ♍ 59
9/12 Su	16 ♍ 12	11 ♈ 13	9 ♌ 11	5 ♍ 09
9/19 Su	16 ♍ 27	11 ♈ 09	9 ♌ 19	5 ♍ 17
9/26 Su	16 ♍ 42	11 ♈ 04	9 ♌ 26	5 ♍ 26
10/03 Su	16 ♍ 56	11 ♈ 00	9 ♌ 32	5 ♍ 34
10/10 Su	17 ♍ 10	10 ♈ 56	9 ♌ 38	5 ♍ 42
10/17 Su	17 ♍ 23	10 ♈ 51	9 ♌ 42	5 ♍ 49
10/24 Su	17 ♍ 35	10 ♈ 47	9 ♌ 45	5 ♍ 55
10/31 Su	17 ♍ 46	10 ♈ 43	9 ♌ 47	6 ♍ 01
11/07 Su	17 ♍ 56	10 ♈ 40	9 ♌ 48	6 ♍ 05
11/14 Su	18 ♍ 05	10 ♈ 36	9 ♌ 48 ℞	6 ♍ 09
11/21 Su	18 ♍ 13	10 ♈ 33	9 ♌ 47	6 ♍ 11
11/28 Su	18 ♍ 19	10 ♈ 30	9 ♌ 45	6 ♍ 13
12/05 Su	18 ♍ 23	10 ♈ 28	9 ♌ 41	6 ♍ 13
12/12 Su	18 ♍ 26	10 ♈ 27	9 ♌ 37	6 ♍ 13 ℞
12/19 Su	18 ♍ 28	10 ♈ 26	9 ♌ 31	6 ♍ 11
12/26 Su	18 ♍ 27 ℞	10 ♈ 25	9 ♌ 25	6 ♍ 09
1966 1/02 Su	18 ♍ 25	10 ♈ 25 D	9 ♌ 18	6 ♍ 05
1/09 Su	18 ♍ 22	10 ♈ 26	9 ♌ 10	6 ♍ 01
1/16 Su	18 ♍ 17	10 ♈ 27	9 ♌ 02	5 ♍ 56
1/23 Su	18 ♍ 11	10 ♈ 29	8 ♌ 54	5 ♍ 50
1/30 Su	18 ♍ 03	10 ♈ 31	8 ♌ 46	5 ♍ 43

	♇	♀	♃	♃
1966 2/06 Su	17 ♍ 55 ℞	10 ♈ 33 D	8 ♌ 37 ℞	5 ♍ 36 ℞
2/13 Su	17 ♍ 45	10 ♈ 37	8 ♌ 29	5 ♍ 29
2/20 Su	17 ♍ 35	10 ♈ 40	8 ♌ 21	5 ♍ 21
2/27 Su	17 ♍ 24	10 ♈ 44	8 ♌ 14	5 ♍ 13
3/06 Su	17 ♍ 13	10 ♈ 48	8 ♌ 07	5 ♍ 06
3/13 Su	17 ♍ 02	10 ♈ 53	8 ♌ 00	4 ♍ 58
3/20 Su	16 ♍ 51	10 ♈ 57	7 ♌ 55	4 ♍ 51
3/27 Su	16 ♍ 40	11 ♈ 02	7 ♌ 51	4 ♍ 44
4/03 Su	16 ♍ 30	11 ♈ 07	7 ♌ 47	4 ♍ 38
4/10 Su	16 ♍ 21	11 ♈ 12	7 ♌ 45	4 ♍ 32
4/17 Su	16 ♍ 12	11 ♈ 16	7 ♌ 44	4 ♍ 27
4/24 Su	16 ♍ 05	11 ♈ 21	7 ♌ 43 D	4 ♍ 23
5/01 Su	15 ♍ 59	11 ♈ 25	7 ♌ 44	4 ♍ 20
5/08 Su	15 ♍ 54	11 ♈ 30	7 ♌ 46	4 ♍ 18
5/15 Su	15 ♍ 50	11 ♈ 33	7 ♌ 49	4 ♍ 17
5/22 Su	15 ♍ 48	11 ♈ 37	7 ♌ 54	4 ♍ 17 D
5/29 Su	15 ♍ 48 D	11 ♈ 40	7 ♌ 59	4 ♍ 18
6/05 Su	15 ♍ 49	11 ♈ 43	8 ♌ 05	4 ♍ 19
6/12 Su	15 ♍ 52	11 ♈ 45	8 ♌ 12	4 ♍ 22
6/19 Su	15 ♍ 56	11 ♈ 47	8 ♌ 19	4 ♍ 26
6/26 Su	16 ♍ 01	11 ♈ 48	8 ♌ 28	4 ♍ 31
7/03 Su	16 ♍ 08	11 ♈ 48	8 ♌ 37	4 ♍ 36
7/10 Su	16 ♍ 17	11 ♈ 49 ℞	8 ♌ 46	4 ♍ 42
7/17 Su	16 ♍ 26	11 ♈ 48	8 ♌ 56	4 ♍ 49
7/24 Su	16 ♍ 37	11 ♈ 47	9 ♌ 06	4 ♍ 57
7/31 Su	16 ♍ 49	11 ♈ 46	9 ♌ 16	5 ♍ 05
8/07 Su	17 ♍ 02	11 ♈ 44	9 ♌ 26	5 ♍ 13
8/14 Su	17 ♍ 15	11 ♈ 42	9 ♌ 37	5 ♍ 22
8/21 Su	17 ♍ 29	11 ♈ 39	9 ♌ 47	5 ♍ 31
8/28 Su	17 ♍ 44	11 ♈ 36	9 ♌ 56	5 ♍ 41
9/04 Su	17 ♍ 59	11 ♈ 32	10 ♌ 06	5 ♍ 50
9/11 Su	18 ♍ 14	11 ♈ 28	10 ♌ 14	5 ♍ 59
9/18 Su	18 ♍ 29	11 ♈ 24	10 ♌ 22	6 ♍ 08
9/25 Su	18 ♍ 44	11 ♈ 20	10 ♌ 30	6 ♍ 17
10/02 Su	18 ♍ 59	11 ♈ 16	10 ♌ 36	6 ♍ 25
10/09 Su	19 ♍ 13	11 ♈ 12	10 ♌ 42	6 ♍ 33
10/16 Su	19 ♍ 26	11 ♈ 07	10 ♌ 47	6 ♍ 40
10/23 Su	19 ♍ 39	11 ♈ 03	10 ♌ 50	6 ♍ 47
10/30 Su	19 ♍ 51	10 ♈ 59	10 ♌ 53	6 ♍ 52
11/06 Su	20 ♍ 02	10 ♈ 55	10 ♌ 54	6 ♍ 57

Astro Data

1965

5/25 Tu	05:21	♇	SD	13 ♍ 40	19.6 (19:38)
7/08 Th	01:43	♀	SR	11 ♈ 34	-15.5 (-15:31)
11/09 Tu	13:53	♃	SR	9 ♌ 48	39.7 (39:41)
12/05 Su	02:44	♃	SR	6 ♍ 13	24.5 (24:32)
12/21 Tu	05:05	♇	SR	18 ♍ 28	17.9 (17:53)
12/29 We	08:02	♀	SD	10 ♈ 25	-15.9 (-15:53)

1966

4/21 Th	18:19	♃	SD	7 ♌ 43	40.5 (40:30)
5/19 Th	18:00	♃	SD	4 ♍ 17	25.5 (25:27)
5/27 Fr	11:12	♇	SD	15 ♍ 48	19.1 (19:07)
7/08 Fr	11:41	♀	SR	11 ♈ 49	-15.3 (-15:15)
11/10 Th	20:42	♃	SR	10 ♌ 54	39.6 (39:38)

LONGITUDE

Year	Date	♇	⯰	🝼	🝻
1966	11/13 Su	20 ♍ 11 D	10 ♈ 52 ℞	10 ♌ 54 ℞	7 ♍ 01 D
	11/20 Su	20 ♍ 20	10 ♈ 49	10 ♌ 53	7 ♍ 04
	11/27 Su	20 ♍ 27	10 ♈ 46	10 ♌ 51	7 ♍ 06
	12/04 Su	20 ♍ 32	10 ♈ 44	10 ♌ 48	7 ♍ 07
	12/11 Su	20 ♍ 36	10 ♈ 42	10 ♌ 44	7 ♍ 07 ℞
	12/18 Su	20 ♍ 38	10 ♈ 41	10 ♌ 39	7 ♍ 05
	12/25 Su	20 ♍ 38 ℞	10 ♈ 40	10 ♌ 33	7 ♍ 03
1967	1/01 Su	20 ♍ 37	10 ♈ 40 D	10 ♌ 26	7 ♍ 00
	1/08 Su	20 ♍ 35	10 ♈ 41	10 ♌ 19	6 ♍ 56
	1/15 Su	20 ♍ 30	10 ♈ 42	10 ♌ 11	6 ♍ 51
	1/22 Su	20 ♍ 25	10 ♈ 43	10 ♌ 03	6 ♍ 45
	1/29 Su	20 ♍ 18	10 ♈ 45	9 ♌ 54	6 ♍ 39
	2/05 Su	20 ♍ 09	10 ♈ 48	9 ♌ 46	6 ♍ 32
	2/12 Su	20 ♍ 00	10 ♈ 51	9 ♌ 38	6 ♍ 24
	2/19 Su	19 ♍ 50	10 ♈ 54	9 ♌ 30	6 ♍ 17
	2/26 Su	19 ♍ 40	10 ♈ 58	9 ♌ 22	6 ♍ 09
	3/05 Su	19 ♍ 29	11 ♈ 02	9 ♌ 15	6 ♍ 01
	3/12 Su	19 ♍ 17	11 ♈ 07	9 ♌ 08	5 ♍ 54
	3/19 Su	19 ♍ 06	11 ♈ 11	9 ♌ 03	5 ♍ 46
	3/26 Su	18 ♍ 55	11 ♈ 16	8 ♌ 58	5 ♍ 39
	4/02 Su	18 ♍ 45	11 ♈ 21	8 ♌ 54	5 ♍ 33
	4/09 Su	18 ♍ 35	11 ♈ 26	8 ♌ 52	5 ♍ 27
	4/16 Su	18 ♍ 26	11 ♈ 30	8 ♌ 50	5 ♍ 22
	4/23 Su	18 ♍ 18	11 ♈ 35	8 ♌ 49	5 ♍ 18
	4/30 Su	18 ♍ 11	11 ♈ 39	8 ♌ 50 D	5 ♍ 15
	5/07 Su	18 ♍ 06	11 ♈ 44	8 ♌ 52	5 ♍ 12
	5/14 Su	18 ♍ 02	11 ♈ 47	8 ♌ 54	5 ♍ 11
	5/21 Su	17 ♍ 59	11 ♈ 51	8 ♌ 58	5 ♍ 10 D
	5/28 Su	17 ♍ 58	11 ♈ 54	9 ♌ 03	5 ♍ 11
	6/04 Su	17 ♍ 58 D	11 ♈ 57	9 ♌ 09	5 ♍ 12
	6/11 Su	18 ♍ 00	11 ♈ 59	9 ♌ 15	5 ♍ 15
	6/18 Su	18 ♍ 04	12 ♈ 01	9 ♌ 23	5 ♍ 18
	6/25 Su	18 ♍ 09	12 ♈ 02	9 ♌ 31	5 ♍ 22
	7/02 Su	18 ♍ 15	12 ♈ 03	9 ♌ 40	5 ♍ 28
	7/09 Su	18 ♍ 23	12 ♈ 04	9 ♌ 49	5 ♍ 34
	7/16 Su	18 ♍ 32	12 ♈ 03 ℞	9 ♌ 59	5 ♍ 40
	7/23 Su	18 ♍ 42	12 ♈ 03	10 ♌ 09	5 ♍ 48
1967	7/30 Su	18 ♍ 53 D	12 ♈ 01 ℞	10 ♌ 19 D	5 ♍ 56 D
	8/06 Su	19 ♍ 06	11 ♈ 59	10 ♌ 29	6 ♍ 04
	8/13 Su	19 ♍ 19	11 ♈ 57	10 ♌ 39	6 ♍ 13
	8/20 Su	19 ♍ 33	11 ♈ 54	10 ♌ 49	6 ♍ 22
	8/27 Su	19 ♍ 47	11 ♈ 51	10 ♌ 59	6 ♍ 31
	9/03 Su	20 ♍ 02	11 ♈ 48	11 ♌ 09	6 ♍ 40
	9/10 Su	20 ♍ 18	11 ♈ 44	11 ♌ 17	6 ♍ 50
	9/17 Su	20 ♍ 33	11 ♈ 40	11 ♌ 26	6 ♍ 59
	9/24 Su	20 ♍ 48	11 ♈ 36	11 ♌ 33	7 ♍ 08
	10/01 Su	21 ♍ 03	11 ♈ 32	11 ♌ 40	7 ♍ 16
	10/08 Su	21 ♍ 18	11 ♈ 27	11 ♌ 46	7 ♍ 24
	10/15 Su	21 ♍ 32	11 ♈ 23	11 ♌ 51	7 ♍ 31
	10/22 Su	21 ♍ 45	11 ♈ 19	11 ♌ 55	7 ♍ 38
	10/29 Su	21 ♍ 58	11 ♈ 15	11 ♌ 58	7 ♍ 44
	11/05 Su	22 ♍ 09	11 ♈ 11	12 ♌ 00	7 ♍ 49
	11/12 Su	22 ♍ 19	11 ♈ 07	12 ♌ 00	7 ♍ 53
	11/19 Su	22 ♍ 28	11 ♈ 04	12 ♌ 00 ℞	7 ♍ 57
	11/26 Su	22 ♍ 36	11 ♈ 01	11 ♌ 58	7 ♍ 59
	12/03 Su	22 ♍ 42	10 ♈ 59	11 ♌ 55	8 ♍ 00
	12/10 Su	22 ♍ 47	10 ♈ 57	11 ♌ 52	8 ♍ 00 ℞
	12/17 Su	22 ♍ 50	10 ♈ 56	11 ♌ 47	7 ♍ 59
	12/24 Su	22 ♍ 51	10 ♈ 55	11 ♌ 41	7 ♍ 57
	12/31 Su	22 ♍ 51 ℞	10 ♈ 55 D	11 ♌ 35	7 ♍ 55
1968	1/07 Su	22 ♍ 49	10 ♈ 55	11 ♌ 27	7 ♍ 51
	1/14 Su	22 ♍ 45	10 ♈ 56	11 ♌ 20	7 ♍ 46
	1/21 Su	22 ♍ 40	10 ♈ 58	11 ♌ 12	7 ♍ 40
	1/28 Su	22 ♍ 34	11 ♈ 00	11 ♌ 03	7 ♍ 34
	2/04 Su	22 ♍ 26	11 ♈ 02	10 ♌ 55	7 ♍ 27
	2/11 Su	22 ♍ 18	11 ♈ 05	10 ♌ 46	7 ♍ 20
	2/18 Su	22 ♍ 08	11 ♈ 09	10 ♌ 38	7 ♍ 13
	2/25 Su	21 ♍ 58	11 ♈ 12	10 ♌ 31	7 ♍ 05
	3/03 Su	21 ♍ 47	11 ♈ 16	10 ♌ 23	6 ♍ 57
	3/10 Su	21 ♍ 35	11 ♈ 21	10 ♌ 17	6 ♍ 49
	3/17 Su	21 ♍ 24	11 ♈ 25	10 ♌ 11	6 ♍ 42
	3/24 Su	21 ♍ 13	11 ♈ 30	10 ♌ 06	6 ♍ 35
	3/31 Su	21 ♍ 02	11 ♈ 35	10 ♌ 01	6 ♍ 28
	4/07 Su	20 ♍ 52	11 ♈ 39	9 ♌ 58	6 ♍ 22
	4/14 Su	20 ♍ 43	11 ♈ 44	9 ♌ 56	6 ♍ 17

Astro Data

Year	Date	Time	Body	Station	Position	Value
1966	12/06 Tu	06:31	🝻	SR	7 ♍ 07	24.5 (24:30)
	12/23 Fr	15:37	♇	SR	20 ♍ 38	17.3 (17:18)
	12/29 Th	14:28	⯰	SD	10 ♈ 40	-15.6 (-15:38)
1967	4/23 Su	04:02	🝼	SD	8 ♌ 49	40.5 (40:27)
	5/20 Sa	22:45	🝻	SD	5 ♍ 10	25.4 (25:26)
	5/29 Mo	20:30	♇	SD	17 ♍ 58	18.6 (18:33)
	7/09 Su	04:36	⯰	SR	12 ♈ 04	-15.0 (-15:01)
1967	11/12 Su	03:46	🝼	SR	12 ♌ 00	39.6 (39:37)
	12/07 Th	10:01	🝻	SR	8 ♍ 00	24.5 (24:28)
	12/26 Tu	04:47	♇	SR	22 ♍ 51	16.8 (16:45)
	12/30 Sa	00:04	⯰	SD	10 ♈ 55	-15.4 (-15:23)

1968	⚷	⚶	⚴	⚵
4/21 Su	20 ♍ 34 ℞	11 ♈ 49 D	9 ♌ 55 ℞	6 ♍ 13 ℞
4/28 Su	20 ♍ 27	11 ♈ 53	9 ♌ 56 D	6 ♍ 09
5/05 Su	20 ♍ 20	11 ♈ 58	9 ♌ 57	6 ♍ 06
5/12 Su	20 ♍ 16	12 ♈ 01	9 ♌ 59	6 ♍ 04
5/19 Su	20 ♍ 12	12 ♈ 05	10 ♌ 03	6 ♍ 04
5/26 Su	20 ♍ 10	12 ♈ 08	10 ♌ 07	6 ♍ 04 D
6/02 Su	20 ♍ 10 D	12 ♈ 11	10 ♌ 13	6 ♍ 05
6/09 Su	20 ♍ 11	12 ♈ 14	10 ♌ 19	6 ♍ 07
6/16 Su	20 ♍ 14	12 ♈ 16	10 ♌ 26	6 ♍ 10
6/23 Su	20 ♍ 18	12 ♈ 17	10 ♌ 34	6 ♍ 14
6/30 Su	20 ♍ 24	12 ♈ 18	10 ♌ 42	6 ♍ 19
7/07 Su	20 ♍ 31	12 ♈ 18	10 ♌ 52	6 ♍ 25
7/14 Su	20 ♍ 39	12 ♈ 18 ℞	11 ♌ 01	6 ♍ 32
7/21 Su	20 ♍ 49	12 ♈ 18	11 ♌ 11	6 ♍ 39
7/28 Su	21 ♍ 00	12 ♈ 16	11 ♌ 21	6 ♍ 47
8/04 Su	21 ♍ 12	12 ♈ 15	11 ♌ 31	6 ♍ 55
8/11 Su	21 ♍ 25	12 ♈ 13	11 ♌ 42	7 ♍ 04
8/18 Su	21 ♍ 39	12 ♈ 10	11 ♌ 52	7 ♍ 13
8/25 Su	21 ♍ 53	12 ♈ 07	12 ♌ 02	7 ♍ 22
9/01 Su	22 ♍ 08	12 ♈ 04	12 ♌ 11	7 ♍ 31
9/08 Su	22 ♍ 23	12 ♈ 00	12 ♌ 20	7 ♍ 40
9/15 Su	22 ♍ 39	11 ♈ 56	12 ♌ 29	7 ♍ 50
9/22 Su	22 ♍ 54	11 ♈ 52	12 ♌ 37	7 ♍ 58
9/29 Su	23 ♍ 09	11 ♈ 48	12 ♌ 44	8 ♍ 07
10/06 Su	23 ♍ 24	11 ♈ 43	12 ♌ 50	8 ♍ 15
10/13 Su	23 ♍ 39	11 ♈ 39	12 ♌ 55	8 ♍ 23
10/20 Su	23 ♍ 53	11 ♈ 35	13 ♌ 00	8 ♍ 30
10/27 Su	24 ♍ 06	11 ♈ 31	13 ♌ 03	8 ♍ 36
11/03 Su	24 ♍ 18	11 ♈ 27	13 ♌ 05	8 ♍ 41
11/10 Su	24 ♍ 29	11 ♈ 23	13 ♌ 06	8 ♍ 46
11/17 Su	24 ♍ 39	11 ♈ 20	13 ♌ 06 ℞	8 ♍ 49
11/24 Su	24 ♍ 47	11 ♈ 17	13 ♌ 05	8 ♍ 52
12/01 Su	24 ♍ 54	11 ♈ 15	13 ♌ 02	8 ♍ 54
12/08 Su	24 ♍ 59	11 ♈ 13	12 ♌ 59	8 ♍ 54 ℞
12/15 Su	25 ♍ 03	11 ♈ 11	12 ♌ 54	8 ♍ 53
12/22 Su	25 ♍ 06	11 ♈ 10	12 ♌ 49	8 ♍ 52
12/29 Su	25 ♍ 06 ℞	11 ♈ 10	12 ♌ 43	8 ♍ 49

1969	⚷	⚶	⚴	⚵
1/05 Su	25 ♍ 05 ℞	11 ♈ 10 D	12 ♌ 36 ℞	8 ♍ 46 ℞
1/12 Su	25 ♍ 02	11 ♈ 11	12 ♌ 28	8 ♍ 41
1/19 Su	24 ♍ 58	11 ♈ 12	12 ♌ 20	8 ♍ 36
1/26 Su	24 ♍ 52	11 ♈ 14	12 ♌ 12	8 ♍ 30
2/02 Su	24 ♍ 45	11 ♈ 16	12 ♌ 04	8 ♍ 23
2/09 Su	24 ♍ 37	11 ♈ 19	11 ♌ 55	8 ♍ 16
2/16 Su	24 ♍ 28	11 ♈ 23	11 ♌ 47	8 ♍ 09
2/23 Su	24 ♍ 18	11 ♈ 26	11 ♌ 39	8 ♍ 01
3/02 Su	24 ♍ 07	11 ♈ 30	11 ♌ 32	7 ♍ 53
3/09 Su	23 ♍ 56	11 ♈ 35	11 ♌ 25	7 ♍ 45
3/16 Su	23 ♍ 44	11 ♈ 39	11 ♌ 18	7 ♍ 38
3/23 Su	23 ♍ 33	11 ♈ 44	11 ♌ 13	7 ♍ 31
3/30 Su	23 ♍ 22	11 ♈ 48	11 ♌ 09	7 ♍ 24
4/06 Su	23 ♍ 11	11 ♈ 53	11 ♌ 05	7 ♍ 18
4/13 Su	23 ♍ 02	11 ♈ 58	11 ♌ 03	7 ♍ 12
4/20 Su	22 ♍ 52	12 ♈ 03	11 ♌ 02	7 ♍ 07
4/27 Su	22 ♍ 44	12 ♈ 07	11 ♌ 01 D	7 ♍ 04
5/04 Su	22 ♍ 38	12 ♈ 11	11 ♌ 02	7 ♍ 01
5/11 Su	22 ♍ 32	12 ♈ 15	11 ♌ 04	6 ♍ 58
5/18 Su	22 ♍ 28	12 ♈ 19	11 ♌ 07	6 ♍ 57
5/25 Su	22 ♍ 25	12 ♈ 23	11 ♌ 11	6 ♍ 57 D
6/01 Su	22 ♍ 24	12 ♈ 25	11 ♌ 16	6 ♍ 58
6/08 Su	22 ♍ 24 D	12 ♈ 28	11 ♌ 22	7 ♍ 00
6/15 Su	22 ♍ 26	12 ♈ 30	11 ♌ 29	7 ♍ 03
6/22 Su	22 ♍ 30	12 ♈ 32	11 ♌ 37	7 ♍ 07
6/29 Su	22 ♍ 35	12 ♈ 33	11 ♌ 45	7 ♍ 11
7/06 Su	22 ♍ 41	12 ♈ 33	11 ♌ 54	7 ♍ 17
7/13 Su	22 ♍ 49	12 ♈ 33 ℞	12 ♌ 04	7 ♍ 23
7/20 Su	22 ♍ 59	12 ♈ 32	12 ♌ 13	7 ♍ 30
7/27 Su	23 ♍ 09	12 ♈ 31	12 ♌ 24	7 ♍ 38
8/03 Su	23 ♍ 21	12 ♈ 30	12 ♌ 34	7 ♍ 46
8/10 Su	23 ♍ 33	12 ♈ 28	12 ♌ 44	7 ♍ 55
8/17 Su	23 ♍ 47	12 ♈ 25	12 ♌ 54	8 ♍ 03
8/24 Su	24 ♍ 01	12 ♈ 22	13 ♌ 04	8 ♍ 13
8/31 Su	24 ♍ 16	12 ♈ 19	13 ♌ 14	8 ♍ 22
9/07 Su	24 ♍ 31	12 ♈ 15	13 ♌ 23	8 ♍ 31
9/14 Su	24 ♍ 46	12 ♈ 12	13 ♌ 32	8 ♍ 40
9/21 Su	25 ♍ 02	12 ♈ 07	13 ♌ 40	8 ♍ 49
9/28 Su	25 ♍ 17	12 ♈ 03	13 ♌ 47	8 ♍ 58
10/05 Su	25 ♍ 33	11 ♈ 59	13 ♌ 54	9 ♍ 06

Astro Data

1968

4/23 Tu	13:27	⚴	SD	9 ♌ 55	40.4 (40:25)
5/21 Tu	03:37	⚵	SD	6 ♍ 04	25.4 (25:23)
5/31 Fr	04:01	⚷	SD	20 ♍ 10	18.0 (17:58)
7/08 Mo	20:20	⚶	SR	12 ♈ 18	-14.8 (-14:45)
11/12 Tu	14:58	⚴	SR	13 ♌ 06	39.5 (39:32)
12/07 Sa	16:37	⚵	SR	8 ♍ 54	24.4 (24:25)
12/27 Fr	17:05	⚷	SR	25 ♍ 06	16.1 (16:06)
12/29 Su	17:21	⚶	SD	11 ♈ 10	-15.1 (-15:07)

1969

4/24 Th	18:52	⚴	SD	11 ♌ 01	40.4 (40:23)
5/12 Th	03:36	⚵	SD	6 ♍ 57	25.4 (25:22)
6/02 Mo	14:00	⚷	SD	22 ♍ 24	17.3 (17:20)
7/09 We	02:20	⚶	SR	12 ♈ 33	-14.5 (-14:30)

LONGITUDE

1969

Date	♇	♀	♃	♄
10/12 Su	25 ♍ 48 D	11 ♈ 55 ℞	14 ♌ 00 D	9 ♍ 14 D
10/19 Su	26 ♍ 02	11 ♈ 50	14 ♌ 04	9 ♍ 21
10/26 Su	26 ♍ 15	11 ♈ 46	14 ♌ 08	9 ♍ 28
11/02 Su	26 ♍ 28	11 ♈ 42	14 ♌ 10	9 ♍ 33
11/09 Su	26 ♍ 40	11 ♈ 39	14 ♌ 12	9 ♍ 38
11/16 Su	26 ♍ 50	11 ♈ 35	14 ♌ 12 ℞	9 ♍ 42
11/23 Su	27 ♍ 00	11 ♈ 32	14 ♌ 11	9 ♍ 45
11/30 Su	27 ♍ 07	11 ♈ 30	14 ♌ 09	9 ♍ 47
12/07 Su	27 ♍ 14	11 ♈ 28	14 ♌ 06	9 ♍ 48
12/14 Su	27 ♍ 18	11 ♈ 26	14 ♌ 02	9 ♍ 47 ℞
12/21 Su	27 ♍ 22	11 ♈ 25	13 ♌ 57	9 ♍ 46
12/28 Su	27 ♍ 23	11 ♈ 25	13 ♌ 51	9 ♍ 44

1970

Date	♇	♀	♃	♄
1/04 Su	27 ♍ 23 ℞	11 ♈ 25 D	13 ♌ 44	9 ♍ 40
1/11 Su	27 ♍ 21	11 ♈ 26	13 ♌ 37	9 ♍ 36
1/18 Su	27 ♍ 17	11 ♈ 27	13 ♌ 29	9 ♍ 31
1/25 Su	27 ♍ 12	11 ♈ 28	13 ♌ 21	9 ♍ 25
2/01 Su	27 ♍ 06	11 ♈ 31	13 ♌ 12	9 ♍ 19
2/08 Su	26 ♍ 58	11 ♈ 34	13 ♌ 04	9 ♍ 12
2/15 Su	26 ♍ 49	11 ♈ 37	12 ♌ 55	9 ♍ 04
2/22 Su	26 ♍ 40	11 ♈ 40	12 ♌ 47	8 ♍ 57
3/01 Su	26 ♍ 29	11 ♈ 44	12 ♌ 40	8 ♍ 49
3/08 Su	26 ♍ 18	11 ♈ 48	12 ♌ 33	8 ♍ 41
3/15 Su	26 ♍ 07	11 ♈ 53	12 ♌ 26	8 ♍ 34
3/22 Su	25 ♍ 55	11 ♈ 58	12 ♌ 21	8 ♍ 26
3/29 Su	25 ♍ 44	12 ♈ 02	12 ♌ 16	8 ♍ 20
4/05 Su	25 ♍ 33	12 ♈ 07	12 ♌ 12	8 ♍ 13
4/12 Su	25 ♍ 23	12 ♈ 12	12 ♌ 09	8 ♍ 07
4/19 Su	25 ♍ 13	12 ♈ 16	12 ♌ 08	8 ♍ 02
4/26 Su	25 ♍ 05	12 ♈ 21	12 ♌ 07	7 ♍ 58
5/03 Su	24 ♍ 57	12 ♈ 25	12 ♌ 08 D	7 ♍ 55
5/10 Su	24 ♍ 51	12 ♈ 29	12 ♌ 09	7 ♍ 53
5/17 Su	24 ♍ 46	12 ♈ 33	12 ♌ 12	7 ♍ 51
5/24 Su	24 ♍ 43	12 ♈ 37	12 ♌ 16	7 ♍ 51 D
5/31 Su	24 ♍ 41	12 ♈ 40	12 ♌ 20	7 ♍ 51
6/07 Su	24 ♍ 40 D	12 ♈ 42	12 ♌ 26	7 ♍ 53
6/14 Su	24 ♍ 41	12 ♈ 44	12 ♌ 33	7 ♍ 55
6/21 Su	24 ♍ 44	12 ♈ 46	12 ♌ 40	7 ♍ 59

1970

Date	♇	♀	♃	♄
6/28 Su	24 ♍ 49 D	12 ♈ 47 D	12 ♌ 48 D	8 ♍ 03 D
7/05 Su	24 ♍ 54	12 ♈ 48	12 ♌ 57	8 ♍ 09
7/12 Su	25 ♍ 02	12 ♈ 48 ℞	13 ♌ 06	8 ♍ 15
7/19 Su	25 ♍ 10	12 ♈ 47	13 ♌ 16	8 ♍ 22
7/26 Su	25 ♍ 20	12 ♈ 46	13 ♌ 26	8 ♍ 29
8/02 Su	25 ♍ 31	12 ♈ 45	13 ♌ 36	8 ♍ 37
8/09 Su	25 ♍ 44	12 ♈ 43	13 ♌ 46	8 ♍ 45
8/16 Su	25 ♍ 57	12 ♈ 41	13 ♌ 57	8 ♍ 54
8/23 Su	26 ♍ 11	12 ♈ 38	14 ♌ 07	9 ♍ 03
8/30 Su	26 ♍ 25	12 ♈ 35	14 ♌ 16	9 ♍ 13
9/06 Su	26 ♍ 40	12 ♈ 31	14 ♌ 26	9 ♍ 22
9/13 Su	26 ♍ 56	12 ♈ 27	14 ♌ 35	9 ♍ 31
9/20 Su	27 ♍ 11	12 ♈ 23	14 ♌ 43	9 ♍ 40
9/27 Su	27 ♍ 27	12 ♈ 19	14 ♌ 51	9 ♍ 49
10/04 Su	27 ♍ 43	12 ♈ 15	14 ♌ 58	9 ♍ 58
10/11 Su	27 ♍ 58	12 ♈ 10	15 ♌ 03	10 ♍ 05
10/18 Su	28 ♍ 13	12 ♈ 06	15 ♌ 08	10 ♍ 13
10/25 Su	28 ♍ 27	12 ♈ 02	15 ♌ 12	10 ♍ 20
11/01 Su	28 ♍ 40	11 ♈ 58	15 ♌ 15	10 ♍ 25
11/08 Su	28 ♍ 52	11 ♈ 54	15 ♌ 17	10 ♍ 31
11/15 Su	29 ♍ 04	11 ♈ 51	15 ♌ 18	10 ♍ 35
11/22 Su	29 ♍ 14	11 ♈ 48	15 ♌ 17 ℞	10 ♍ 38
11/29 Su	29 ♍ 22	11 ♈ 45	15 ♌ 15	10 ♍ 40
12/06 Su	29 ♍ 29	11 ♈ 43	15 ♌ 13	10 ♍ 41
12/13 Su	29 ♍ 35	11 ♈ 41	15 ♌ 09	10 ♍ 41 ℞
12/20 Su	29 ♍ 39	11 ♈ 40	15 ♌ 04	10 ♍ 40
12/27 Su	29 ♍ 41	11 ♈ 40	14 ♌ 58	10 ♍ 38

1971

Date	♇	♀	♃	♄
1/03 Su	29 ♍ 42 ℞	11 ♈ 40 D	14 ♌ 52	10 ♍ 35
1/10 Su	29 ♍ 41	11 ♈ 40	14 ♌ 45	10 ♍ 31
1/17 Su	29 ♍ 38	11 ♈ 41	14 ♌ 37	10 ♍ 26
1/24 Su	29 ♍ 34	11 ♈ 43	14 ♌ 29	10 ♍ 21
1/31 Su	29 ♍ 28	11 ♈ 45	14 ♌ 21	10 ♍ 15
2/07 Su	29 ♍ 21	11 ♈ 48	14 ♌ 12	10 ♍ 08
2/14 Su	29 ♍ 13	11 ♈ 51	14 ♌ 04	10 ♍ 00
2/21 Su	29 ♍ 03	11 ♈ 54	13 ♌ 56	9 ♍ 53
2/28 Su	28 ♍ 53	11 ♈ 58	13 ♌ 48	9 ♍ 45
3/07 Su	28 ♍ 42	12 ♈ 02	13 ♌ 41	9 ♍ 37

Astro Data

1969

Date	Time			Position	
11/14 Fr	00:02	♎	SR	14 ♌ 12	39.5 (39:27)
12/08 Mo	20:34	♄	SR	9 ♍ 48	24.4 (24:25)
12/30 Tu	08:07	♇	SR	27 ♍ 23	15.5 (15:28)
12/30 Tu	09:24	♀	SD	11 ♈ 25	-14.9 (-14:52)

1970

Date	Time			Position	
4/26 Su	02:42	♎	SD	12 ♌ 07	40.3 (40:17)
5/23 Sa	05:35	♄	SD	7 ♍ 51	25.4 (25:21)
6/05 Fr	02:24	♇	SD	24 ♍ 40	16.7 (16:42)

1970

Date	Time			Position	
7/09 Th	08:58	♀	SR	12 ♈ 48	-14.2 (-14:14)
11/15 Su	08:18	♎	SR	15 ♌ 18	39.4 (39:24)
12/09 We	20:48	♄	SR	10 ♍ 41	24.4 (24:22)

1971

Date	Time			Position	
1/01 Fr	21:59	♇	SR	29 ♍ 42	14.8 (14:45)
12/30 We	14:55	♀	SD	11 ♈ 40	-14.6 (-14:37)

	♇	♀	⚸	⚵
1971				
3/14 Su	28 ♍ 31 ℞	12 ♈ 07 D	13 ♌ 34 ℞	9 ♍ 30 ℞
3/21 Su	28 ♍ 20	12 ♈ 11	13 ♌ 28	9 ♍ 22
3/28 Su	28 ♍ 08	12 ♈ 16	13 ♌ 23	9 ♍ 15
4/04 Su	27 ♍ 57	12 ♈ 21	13 ♌ 19	9 ♍ 09
4/11 Su	27 ♍ 46	12 ♈ 25	13 ♌ 16	9 ♍ 03
4/18 Su	27 ♍ 36	12 ♈ 30	13 ♌ 14	8 ♍ 57
4/25 Su	27 ♍ 27	12 ♈ 35	13 ♌ 13	8 ♍ 53
5/02 Su	27 ♍ 19	12 ♈ 39	13 ♌ 13 D	8 ♍ 49
5/09 Su	27 ♍ 12	12 ♈ 43	13 ♌ 14	8 ♍ 47
5/16 Su	27 ♍ 06	12 ♈ 47	13 ♌ 17	8 ♍ 45
5/23 Su	27 ♍ 02	12 ♈ 51	13 ♌ 20	8 ♍ 44
5/30 Su	26 ♍ 59	12 ♈ 54	13 ♌ 24	8 ♍ 45 D
6/06 Su	26 ♍ 58	12 ♈ 56	13 ♌ 30	8 ♍ 46
6/13 Su	26 ♍ 59 D	12 ♈ 59	13 ♌ 36	8 ♍ 48
6/20 Su	27 ♍ 01	13 ♈ 00	13 ♌ 43	8 ♍ 51
6/27 Su	27 ♍ 04	13 ♈ 02	13 ♌ 51	8 ♍ 56
7/04 Su	27 ♍ 09	13 ♈ 02	14 ♌ 00	9 ♍ 01
7/11 Su	27 ♍ 16	13 ♈ 03 ℞	14 ♌ 09	9 ♍ 06
7/18 Su	27 ♍ 24	13 ♈ 02	14 ♌ 18	9 ♍ 13
7/25 Su	27 ♍ 33	13 ♈ 01	14 ♌ 28	9 ♍ 20
8/01 Su	27 ♍ 44	13 ♈ 00	14 ♌ 38	9 ♍ 28
8/08 Su	27 ♍ 56	12 ♈ 58	14 ♌ 48	9 ♍ 36
8/15 Su	28 ♍ 09	12 ♈ 56	14 ♌ 59	9 ♍ 45
8/22 Su	28 ♍ 22	12 ♈ 53	15 ♌ 09	9 ♍ 54
8/29 Su	28 ♍ 37	12 ♈ 50	15 ♌ 19	10 ♍ 03
9/05 Su	28 ♍ 52	12 ♈ 46	15 ♌ 28	10 ♍ 13
9/12 Su	29 ♍ 07	12 ♈ 43	15 ♌ 37	10 ♍ 22
9/19 Su	29 ♍ 23	12 ♈ 39	15 ♌ 46	10 ♍ 31
9/26 Su	29 ♍ 39	12 ♈ 35	15 ♌ 54	10 ♍ 40
10/03 Su	29 ♍ 54	12 ♈ 30	16 ♌ 01	10 ♍ 49
10/10 Su	0 ♎ 10	12 ♈ 26	16 ♌ 07	10 ♍ 57
10/17 Su	0 ♎ 25	12 ♈ 22	16 ♌ 12	11 ♍ 04
10/24 Su	0 ♎ 40	12 ♈ 18	16 ♌ 17	11 ♍ 11
10/31 Su	0 ♎ 53	12 ♈ 14	16 ♌ 20	11 ♍ 17
11/07 Su	1 ♎ 07	12 ♈ 10	16 ♌ 22	11 ♍ 23
11/14 Su	1 ♎ 18	12 ♈ 06	16 ♌ 23	11 ♍ 27
11/21 Su	1 ♎ 29	12 ♈ 03	16 ♌ 23 ℞	11 ♍ 31
11/28 Su	1 ♎ 39	12 ♈ 00	16 ♌ 22	11 ♍ 33
12/05 Su	1 ♎ 47	11 ♈ 58	16 ♌ 19	11 ♍ 35
12/12 Su	1 ♎ 53	11 ♈ 56	16 ♌ 16	11 ♍ 35 ℞

	♇	♀	⚸	⚵
1971				
12/19 Su	1 ♎ 58 D	11 ♈ 55 ℞	16 ♌ 11 ℞	11 ♍ 34 ℞
12/26 Su	2 ♎ 01	11 ♈ 54	16 ♌ 06	11 ♍ 33
1972				
1/02 Su	2 ♎ 03	11 ♈ 54 D	16 ♌ 00	11 ♍ 30
1/09 Su	2 ♎ 02 ℞	11 ♈ 55	15 ♌ 53	11 ♍ 26
1/16 Su	2 ♎ 00	11 ♈ 56	15 ♌ 45	11 ♍ 22
1/23 Su	1 ♎ 57	11 ♈ 57	15 ♌ 37	11 ♍ 16
1/30 Su	1 ♎ 52	11 ♈ 59	15 ♌ 29	11 ♍ 10
2/06 Su	1 ♎ 45	12 ♈ 02	15 ♌ 20	11 ♍ 03
2/13 Su	1 ♎ 38	12 ♈ 05	15 ♌ 12	10 ♍ 56
2/20 Su	1 ♎ 29	12 ♈ 08	15 ♌ 04	10 ♍ 49
2/27 Su	1 ♎ 19	12 ♈ 12	14 ♌ 56	10 ♍ 41
3/05 Su	1 ♎ 08	12 ♈ 16	14 ♌ 48	10 ♍ 33
3/12 Su	0 ♎ 57	12 ♈ 21	14 ♌ 42	10 ♍ 26
3/19 Su	0 ♎ 46	12 ♈ 25	14 ♌ 35	10 ♍ 18
3/26 Su	0 ♎ 34	12 ♈ 30	14 ♌ 30	10 ♍ 11
4/02 Su	0 ♎ 23	12 ♈ 34	14 ♌ 26	10 ♍ 04
4/09 Su	0 ♎ 12	12 ♈ 39	14 ♌ 22	9 ♍ 58
4/16 Su	0 ♎ 01	12 ♈ 44	14 ♌ 20	9 ♍ 53
4/23 Su	29 ♍ 52	12 ♈ 49	14 ♌ 18	9 ♍ 48
4/30 Su	29 ♍ 43	12 ♈ 53	14 ♌ 18 D	9 ♍ 44
5/07 Su	29 ♍ 35	12 ♈ 57	14 ♌ 19	9 ♍ 41
5/14 Su	29 ♍ 29	13 ♈ 01	14 ♌ 21	9 ♍ 39
5/21 Su	29 ♍ 24	13 ♈ 05	14 ♌ 24	9 ♍ 38
5/28 Su	29 ♍ 21	13 ♈ 08	14 ♌ 28	9 ♍ 38 D
6/04 Su	29 ♍ 19	13 ♈ 11	14 ♌ 33	9 ♍ 39
6/11 Su	29 ♍ 18 D	13 ♈ 13	14 ♌ 39	9 ♍ 41
6/18 Su	29 ♍ 19	13 ♈ 15	14 ♌ 46	9 ♍ 44
6/25 Su	29 ♍ 22	13 ♈ 16	14 ♌ 54	9 ♍ 48
7/02 Su	29 ♍ 27	13 ♈ 17	15 ♌ 02	9 ♍ 53
7/09 Su	29 ♍ 33	13 ♈ 17	15 ♌ 11	9 ♍ 58
7/16 Su	29 ♍ 40	13 ♈ 17 ℞	15 ♌ 20	10 ♍ 04
7/23 Su	29 ♍ 49	13 ♈ 16	15 ♌ 30	10 ♍ 12
7/30 Su	29 ♍ 59	13 ♈ 15	15 ♌ 40	10 ♍ 19
8/06 Su	0 ♎ 10	13 ♈ 13	15 ♌ 50	10 ♍ 27
8/13 Su	0 ♎ 22	13 ♈ 11	16 ♌ 01	10 ♍ 36
8/20 Su	0 ♎ 36	13 ♈ 08	16 ♌ 11	10 ♍ 45
8/27 Su	0 ♎ 50	13 ♈ 05	16 ♌ 21	10 ♍ 54

Astro Data

1971

4/27 Tu	11:19	⚵	SD	13 ♌ 13	40.2	(40:13)
5/24 Mo	10:24	⚸	SD	8 ♍ 44	25.3	(25:17)
6/07 Mo	15:16	♇	SD	26 ♍ 58	16.0	(16:00)
7/10 Sa	02:42	♀	SR	13 ♈ 03	-14.0	(-13:58)
10/05 Tu	06:18	♇	→ ♎		14.4	(14:21)
11/16 Tu	13:21	⚵	SR	16 ♌ 23	39.3	(39:16)
12/10 Fr	12:49	⚸	SR	11 ♍ 35	24.3	(24:18)

1971

12/30 Th	23:12	♀	SD	11 ♈ 54	-14.4	(-14:22)
1972						
1/04 Tu	14:44	♇	SR	2 ♎ 03	14.1	(14:04)
4/17 Mo	07:44	♀	→ ♍ ℞		15.3	(15:18)
4/27 Th	23:08	⚵	SD	14 ♌ 18	40.1	(40:08)
5/24 We	17:01	⚸	SD	9 ♍ 38	25.3	(25:15)
6/09 Fr	05:44	♇	SD	29 ♍ 18	15.3	(15:18)
7/09 Su	18:51	♀	SR	13 ♈ 17	-13.7	(-13:44)
7/30 Su	11:44	♇	→ ♎		14.7	(14:39)

LONGITUDE

1972	9/03 Su	1♎05 D	13♈02 R	16♌31 D	11♍03 D	1973	5/27 Su	1♎44 R	13♈22 D	15♌32 D	10♍31 D

Left (1972):

	⚷	♀	⚷	⚶
1972 9/03 Su	1♎05 D	13♈02 R	16♌31 D	11♍03 D
9/10 Su	1♎20	12♈58	16♌40	11♍13
9/17 Su	1♎36	12♈54	16♌49	11♍22
9/24 Su	1♎52	12♈50	16♌57	11♍31
10/01 Su	2♎08	12♈46	17♌04	11♍40
10/08 Su	2♎23	12♈42	17♌11	11♍48
10/15 Su	2♎39	12♈37	17♌16	11♍56
10/22 Su	2♎54	12♈33	17♌21	12♍03
10/29 Su	3♎08	12♈29	17♌24	12♍09
11/05 Su	3♎22	12♈25	17♌27	12♍15
11/12 Su	3♎34	12♈22	17♌28	12♍20
11/19 Su	3♎46	12♈18	17♌29 R	12♍23
11/26 Su	3♎56	12♈16	17♌28	12♍26
12/03 Su	4♎05	12♈13	17♌26	12♍28
12/10 Su	4♎12	12♈11	17♌22	12♍29
12/17 Su	4♎18	12♈10	17♌18	12♍28 R
12/24 Su	4♎22	12♈09	17♌13	12♍27
12/31 Su	4♎24	12♈09 D	17♌07	12♍24
1973 1/07 Su	4♎25 R	12♈09	17♌00	12♍21
1/14 Su	4♎24	12♈10	16♌53	12♍17
1/21 Su	4♎21	12♈12	16♌45	12♍12
1/28 Su	4♎17	12♈14	16♌37	12♍06
2/04 Su	4♎11	12♈16	16♌29	11♍59
2/11 Su	4♎04	12♈19	16♌20	11♍52
2/18 Su	3♎56	12♈22	16♌12	11♍45
2/25 Su	3♎46	12♈26	16♌04	11♍37
3/04 Su	3♎36	12♈30	15♌56	11♍29
3/11 Su	3♎25	12♈34	15♌49	11♍21
3/18 Su	3♎14	12♈39	15♌43	11♍14
3/25 Su	3♎02	12♈43	15♌37	11♍07
4/01 Su	2♎51	12♈48	15♌32	11♍00
4/08 Su	2♎39	12♈53	15♌29	10♍53
4/15 Su	2♎29	12♈58	15♌26	10♍48
4/22 Su	2♎18	13♈02	15♌24	10♍43
4/29 Su	2♎09	13♈07	15♌24	10♍39
5/06 Su	2♎01	13♈11	15♌24 D	10♍35
5/13 Su	1♎54	13♈15	15♌26	10♍33
5/20 Su	1♎48	13♈18	15♌28	10♍32

Right (1973):

	⚷	♀	⚷	⚶
1973 5/27 Su	1♎44 R	13♈22 D	15♌32 D	10♍31 D
6/03 Su	1♎41	13♈25	15♌37	10♍32
6/10 Su	1♎40	13♈27	15♌43	10♍34
6/17 Su	1♎40 D	13♈29	15♌49	10♍36
6/24 Su	1♎42	13♈30	15♌57	10♍40
7/01 Su	1♎46	13♈31	16♌05	10♍45
7/08 Su	1♎51	13♈32	16♌13	10♍50
7/15 Su	1♎58	13♈32 R	16♌23	10♍56
7/22 Su	2♎06	13♈31	16♌32	11♍03
7/29 Su	2♎15	13♈30	16♌42	11♍10
8/05 Su	2♎26	13♈28	16♌52	11♍18
8/12 Su	2♎38	13♈26	17♌03	11♍27
8/19 Su	2♎51	13♈24	17♌13	11♍36
8/26 Su	3♎05	13♈21	17♌23	11♍45
9/02 Su	3♎19	13♈17	17♌33	11♍54
9/09 Su	3♎35	13♈14	17♌42	12♍04
9/16 Su	3♎50	13♈10	17♌51	12♍13
9/23 Su	4♎06	13♈06	17♌59	12♍22
9/30 Su	4♎22	13♈01	18♌07	12♍31
10/07 Su	4♎38	12♈57	18♌14	12♍39
10/14 Su	4♎54	12♈53	18♌20	12♍47
10/21 Su	5♎09	12♈49	18♌25	12♍54
10/28 Su	5♎24	12♈45	18♌29	13♍01
11/04 Su	5♎38	12♈41	18♌31	13♍07
11/11 Su	5♎52	12♈37	18♌33	13♍12
11/18 Su	6♎04	12♈34	18♌34	13♍16
11/25 Su	6♎15	12♈31	18♌33 R	13♍19
12/02 Su	6♎24	12♈29	18♌32	13♍21
12/09 Su	6♎33	12♈27	18♌29	13♍22
12/16 Su	6♎39	12♈25	18♌25	13♍22 R
12/23 Su	6♎44	12♈24	18♌20	13♍21
12/30 Su	6♎47	12♈24	18♌15	13♍19
1974 1/06 Su	6♎49	12♈24 D	18♌08	13♍16
1/13 Su	6♎49 R	12♈25	18♌01	13♍12
1/20 Su	6♎47	12♈26	17♌53	13♍07
1/27 Su	6♎44	12♈28	17♌45	13♍01
2/03 Su	6♎39	12♈30	17♌37	12♍55

Astro Data

1972

11/16 Th	19:04	⚷ SR	17♌29	39.1 (39:08)
12/11 Mo	02:23	⚶ SR	12♍29	24.3 (24:17)
12/30 Sa	16:34	♀ SD	12♈09	-14.1 (-14:06)

1973

1/06 Sa	06:56	⚷ SR	4♎25	13.3 (13:19)
4/29 Su	09:36	⚷ SD	15♌24	40.0 (40:00)
5/25 Fr	22:35	⚶ SD	10♍31	25.2 (25:13)

1973

6/11 Mo	20:11	♀ SD	1♎40	14.5 (14:32)
7/10 Tu	01:06	♀ SR	13♈32	-13.5 (-13:28)
11/18 Su	04:22	⚷ SR	18♌34	39.0 (39:02)
12/12 We	08:48	⚶ SR	13♍22	24.2 (24:12)
12/31 Mo	07:03	♀ SD	12♈24	-13.8 (-13:50)

1974

1/09 We	00:53	⚷ SR	6♎49	12.6 (12:34)

1974		♇	♀	♈	♎		1974		♇	♀	♈	♎
	2/10 Su	6♎32 R	12♈33 D	17♌28 R	12♍48 R			11/17 Su	8♎23 D	12♈49 R	19♌39 D	14♍09 D
	2/17 Su	6♎24	12♈36	17♌20	12♍41			11/24 Su	8♎34	12♈46	19♌39 R	14♍12
	2/24 Su	6♎15	12♈40	17♌12	12♍33			12/01 Su	8♎45	12♈44	19♌37	14♍14
	3/03 Su	6♎05	12♈44	17♌04	12♍25			12/08 Su	8♎54	12♈42	19♌35	14♍16
	3/10 Su	5♎55	12♈48	16♌57	12♍17			12/15 Su	9♎01	12♈40	19♌32	14♍16 R
	3/17 Su	5♎44	12♈53	16♌50	12♍10			12/22 Su	9♎07	12♈39	19♌27	14♍15
	3/24 Su	5♎32	12♈57	16♌44	12♍02			12/29 Su	9♎12	12♈39	19♌22	14♍13
	3/31 Su	5♎20	13♈02	16♌39	11♍55							
	4/07 Su	5♎09	13♈07	16♌35	11♍49							
	4/14 Su	4♎58	13♈11	16♌32	11♍43							
							1975	1/05 Su	9♎14	12♈39 D	19♌15	14♍11
	4/21 Su	4♎47	13♈16	16♌30	11♍38			1/12 Su	9♎15 R	12♈39	19♌08	14♍07
	4/28 Su	4♎37	13♈20	16♌29	11♍33			1/19 Su	9♎14	12♈40	19♌01	14♍02
	5/05 Su	4♎29	13♈25	16♌29 D	11♍30			1/26 Su	9♎11	12♈42	18♌53	13♍57
	5/12 Su	4♎21	13♈29	16♌30	11♍27			2/02 Su	9♎07	12♈44	18♌45	13♍51
	5/19 Su	4♎14	13♈32	16♌33	11♍26							
								2/09 Su	9♎01	12♈47	18♌36	13♍44
	5/26 Su	4♎09	13♈36	16♌36	11♍25			2/16 Su	8♎54	12♈50	18♌28	13♍37
	6/02 Su	4♎06	13♈39	16♌40	11♍25 D			2/23 Su	8♎46	12♈54	18♌20	13♍29
	6/09 Su	4♎04	13♈41	16♌46	11♍27			3/02 Su	8♎36	12♈58	18♌12	13♍21
	6/16 Su	4♎03 D	13♈43	16♌52	11♍29			3/09 Su	8♎26	13♈02	18♌04	13♍14
	6/23 Su	4♎05	13♈45	16♌59	11♍32							
								3/16 Su	8♎15	13♈06	17♌57	13♍06
	6/30 Su	4♎07	13♈46	17♌07	11♍37			3/23 Su	8♎04	13♈11	17♌51	12♍58
	7/07 Su	4♎12	13♈46	17♌16	11♍42			3/30 Su	7♎52	13♈15	17♌46	12♍51
	7/14 Su	4♎18	13♈46 R	17♌25	11♍48			4/06 Su	7♎40	13♈20	17♌42	12♍44
	7/21 Su	4♎25	13♈46	17♌34	11♍54			4/13 Su	7♎29	13♈25	17♌38	12♍38
	7/28 Su	4♎34	13♈45	17♌44	12♍02							
								4/20 Su	7♎18	13♈30	17♌36	12♍33
	8/04 Su	4♎44	13♈43	17♌54	12♍09			4/27 Su	7♎08	13♈34	17♌34	12♍28
	8/11 Su	4♎55	13♈41	18♌04	12♍18			5/04 Su	6♎58	13♈38	17♌34 D	12♍24
	8/18 Su	5♎08	13♈39	18♌15	12♍27			5/11 Su	6♎50	13♈42	17♌35	12♍22
	8/25 Su	5♎21	13♈36	18♌25	12♍36			5/18 Su	6♎43	13♈46	17♌37	12♍20
	9/01 Su	5♎36	13♈33	18♌35	12♍45							
								5/25 Su	6♎37	13♈50	17♌40	12♍19
	9/08 Su	5♎51	13♈29	18♌44	12♍54			6/01 Su	6♎33	13♈53	17♌44	12♍19 D
	9/15 Su	6♎06	13♈25	18♌53	13♍04			6/08 Su	6♎30	13♈55	17♌49	12♍20
	9/22 Su	6♎22	13♈21	19♌02	13♍13			6/15 Su	6♎28	13♈57	17♌55	12♍22
	9/29 Su	6♎38	13♈17	19♌10	13♍22			6/22 Su	6♎29 D	13♈59	18♌02	12♍25
	10/06 Su	6♎55	13♈13	19♌17	13♍30							
								6/29 Su	6♎31	14♈00	18♌10	12♍29
	10/13 Su	7♎11	13♈08	19♌23	13♍38			7/06 Su	6♎34	14♈01	18♌18	12♍34
	10/20 Su	7♎26	13♈04	19♌28	13♍46			7/13 Su	6♎39	14♈01 R	18♌27	12♍39
	10/27 Su	7♎42	13♈00	19♌33	13♍53			7/20 Su	6♎46	14♈01	18♌36	12♍46
	11/03 Su	7♎56	12♈56	19♌36	13♍59			7/27 Su	6♎54	14♈00	18♌46	12♍53
	11/10 Su	8♎10	12♈53	19♌38	14♍04							

Astro Data

1974

4/30 Tu	16:10	♈	SD	16♌29	39.9 (39:53)
5/26 Su	23:31	♌	SD	11♍25	25.1 (25:08)
6/14 Fr	13:17	♇	SD	4♎03	13.8 (13:47)
7/10 We	09:31	♀	SR	13♈46	-13.2 (-13:13)

1974

11/19 Tu	12:57	♈	SR	19♌39	38.9 (38:52)
12/13 Fr	11:39	♎	SR	14♍16	24.1 (24:08)
12/31 Tu	15:53	♀	SD	12♈38	-13.6 (-13:35)

1975

1/11 Sa	17:39	♇	SR	9♎15	11.8 (11:46)
5/02 Fr	00:12	♈	SD	17♌34	39.8 (39:45)
5/28 We	02:25	♌	SD	12♍19	25.1 (25:05)
6/17 Tu	04:03	♇	SD	6♎28	13.0 (12:58)
7/11 Fr	00:34	♀	SR	14♈01	-13.0 (-12:57)

1975	♇	♀	♇	♀
8/03 Su	7♎04 D	13♈58 ℞	18♌56 D	13♍01 D
8/10 Su	7♎15	13♈56	19♌06	13♍09
8/17 Su	7♎27	13♈54	19♌16	13♍18
8/24 Su	7♎40	13♈51	19♌26	13♍27
8/31 Su	7♎54	13♈48	19♌36	13♍36
9/07 Su	8♎08	13♈44	19♌46	13♍45
9/14 Su	8♎24	13♈41	19♌55	13♍54
9/21 Su	8♎40	13♈37	20♌04	14♍04
9/28 Su	8♎56	13♈33	20♌12	14♍13
10/05 Su	9♎12	13♈28	20♌20	14♍21
10/12 Su	9♎28	13♈24	20♌26	14♍30
10/19 Su	9♎44	13♈20	20♌32	14♍37
10/26 Su	10♎00	13♈16	20♌36	14♍45
11/02 Su	10♎15	13♈12	20♌40	14♍51
11/09 Su	10♎30	13♈08	20♌42	14♍56
11/16 Su	10♎43	13♈05	20♌44	15♍01
11/23 Su	10♎55	13♈01	20♌44 ℞	15♍05
11/30 Su	11♎07	12♈59	20♌43	15♍08
12/07 Su	11♎16	12♈57	20♌41	15♍09
12/14 Su	11♎25	12♈55	20♌38	15♍10
12/21 Su	11♎32	12♈54	20♌34	15♍09 ℞
12/28 Su	11♎37	12♈53	20♌29	15♍08
1976				
1/04 Su	11♎40	12♈53 D	20♌23	15♍05
1/11 Su	11♎42	12♈54	20♌16	15♍02
1/18 Su	11♎42 ℞	12♈55	20♌09	14♍58
1/25 Su	11♎40	12♈56	20♌01	14♍52
2/01 Su	11♎37	12♈58	19♌53	14♍46
2/08 Su	11♎32	13♈01	19♌44	14♍40
2/15 Su	11♎25	13♈04	19♌36	14♍33
2/22 Su	11♎18	13♈08	19♌28	14♍25
2/29 Su	11♎09	13♈11	19♌20	14♍17
3/07 Su	10♎59	13♈16	19♌12	14♍10
3/14 Su	10♎48	13♈20	19♌05	14♍02
3/21 Su	10♎37	13♈24	18♌58	13♍54
3/28 Su	10♎25	13♈29	18♌53	13♍47
4/04 Su	10♎13	13♈34	18♌48	13♍40
4/11 Su	10♎02	13♈39	18♌44	13♍34

1976	♇	♀	♇	♀
4/18 Su	9♎51 ℞	13♈43 D	18♌42 ℞	13♍28 ℞
4/25 Su	9♎40	13♈48	18♌40	13♍23
5/02 Su	9♎30	13♈52	18♌39	13♍19
5/09 Su	9♎21	13♈56	18♌40 D	13♍16
5/16 Su	9♎13	14♈00	18♌41	13♍14
5/23 Su	9♎07	14♈04	18♌44	13♍13
5/30 Su	9♎01	14♈07	18♌48	13♍12 D
6/06 Su	8♎58	14♈09	18♌52	13♍13
6/13 Su	8♎56	14♈12	18♌58	13♍15
6/20 Su	8♎55 D	14♈13	19♌05	13♍18
6/27 Su	8♎56	14♈15	19♌12	13♍21
7/04 Su	8♎59	14♈15	19♌20	13♍26
7/11 Su	9♎03	14♈16 ℞	19♌29	13♍31
7/18 Su	9♎09	14♈15	19♌38	13♍37
7/25 Su	9♎17	14♈14	19♌48	13♍44
8/01 Su	9♎25	14♈13	19♌58	13♍52
8/08 Su	9♎36	14♈11	20♌08	14♍00
8/15 Su	9♎47	14♈09	20♌18	14♍09
8/22 Su	10♎00	14♈06	20♌28	14♍18
8/29 Su	10♎13	14♈03	20♌38	14♍27
9/05 Su	10♎28	14♈00	20♌48	14♍36
9/12 Su	10♎43	13♈56	20♌57	14♍45
9/19 Su	10♎59	13♈52	21♌06	14♍55
9/26 Su	11♎15	13♈48	21♌15	15♍04
10/03 Su	11♎31	13♈44	21♌22	15♍13
10/10 Su	11♎48	13♈39	21♌29	15♍21
10/17 Su	12♎04	13♈35	21♌35	15♍29
10/24 Su	12♎20	13♈31	21♌40	15♍36
10/31 Su	12♎35	13♈27	21♌44	15♍43
11/07 Su	12♎50	13♈23	21♌47	15♍49
11/14 Su	13♎04	13♈20	21♌49	15♍54
11/21 Su	13♎17	13♈17	21♌49	15♍58
11/28 Su	13♎29	13♈14	21♌49 ℞	16♍01
12/05 Su	13♎40	13♈12	21♌47	16♍03
12/12 Su	13♎49	13♈10	21♌44	16♍04
12/19 Su	13♎57	13♈09	21♌40	16♍04 ℞
12/26 Su	14♎03	13♈08	21♌36	16♍02

Astro Data

1975

11/20 Th	12:59	♇	SR	20♌44	38.7	(38:42)
12/14 Su	12:39	♀	SR	15♍10	24.1	(24:06)

1976

1/01 Th	00:19	♀	SD	12♈53	-13.3	(-13:10)
1/14 We	11:41	♇	SR	11♎42	11.0	(10:58)

1976

5/02 Su	07:06	♇	SD	18♌39	39.6	(39:34)
5/28 Fr	06:44	♀	SD	13♍12	25.0	(25:01)
6/18 Fr	21:43	♇	SD	8♎55	12.2	(12:10)
7/10 Sa	15:38	♀	SR	14♈16	-12.7	(-12:42)
11/21 Su	06:33	♇	SR	21♌49	38.6	(38:33)
12/14 Tu	16:15	♀	SR	16♍04	24.0	(24:00)
12/31 Fr	15:15	♀	SD	13♈08	-13.1	(-13:04)

1977	♇	♇	♇	♇
1/02 Su	14♎07 D	13♈08 D	21♌30 R	16♍00 R
1/09 Su	14♎10	13♈08	21♌23	15♍57
1/16 Su	14♎11	13♈09	21♌16	15♍53
1/23 Su	14♎10 R	13♈11	21♌09	15♍48
1/30 Su	14♎08	13♈13	21♌01	15♍42
2/06 Su	14♎03	13♈15	20♌52	15♍36
2/13 Su	13♎58	13♈18	20♌44	15♍29
2/20 Su	13♎51	13♈21	20♌36	15♍21
2/27 Su	13♎42	13♈25	20♌27	15♍14
3/06 Su	13♎33	13♈29	20♌20	15♍06
3/13 Su	13♎23	13♈33	20♌12	14♍58
3/20 Su	13♎11	13♈38	20♌06	14♍51
3/27 Su	13♎00	13♈43	20♌00	14♍43
4/03 Su	12♎48	13♈47	19♌55	14♍36
4/10 Su	12♎37	13♈52	19♌51	14♍30
4/17 Su	12♎25	13♈57	19♌48	14♍24
4/24 Su	12♎14	14♈01	19♌46	14♍19
5/01 Su	12♎04	14♈06	19♌45	14♍14
5/08 Su	11♎54	14♈10	19♌45 D	14♍11
5/15 Su	11♎46	14♈14	19♌46	14♍08
5/22 Su	11♎38	14♈17	19♌48	14♍07
5/29 Su	11♎32	14♈20	19♌52	14♍06
6/05 Su	11♎28	14♈23	19♌56	14♍07 D
6/12 Su	11♎25	14♈26	20♌01	14♍08
6/19 Su	11♎24	14♈27	20♌08	14♍11
6/26 Su	11♎24 D	14♈29	20♌15	14♍14
7/03 Su	11♎26	14♈30	20♌23	14♍18
7/10 Su	11♎29	14♈30	20♌31	14♍23
7/17 Su	11♎34	14♈30 R	20♌40	14♍29
7/24 Su	11♎41	14♈29	20♌50	14♍36
7/31 Su	11♎49	14♈28	20♌59	14♍44
8/07 Su	11♎59	14♈26	21♌10	14♍51
8/14 Su	12♎09	14♈24	21♌20	15♍00
8/21 Su	12♎22	14♈21	21♌30	15♍09
8/28 Su	12♎35	14♈18	21♌40	15♍18
9/04 Su	12♎49	14♈15	21♌50	15♍27
9/11 Su	13♎04	14♈11	22♌00	15♍37
9/18 Su	13♎19	14♈07	22♌09	15♍46
9/25 Su	13♎35	14♈03	22♌17	15♍55
10/02 Su	13♎52	13♈59	22♌25	16♍04

1977	♇	♇	♇	♇
10/09 Su	14♎08 D	13♈55 R	22♌32 D	16♍13 D
10/16 Su	14♎25	13♈51	22♌38	16♍21
10/23 Su	14♎41	13♈46	22♌44	16♍28
10/30 Su	14♎57	13♈42	22♌48	16♍35
11/06 Su	15♎12	13♈39	22♌51	16♍41
11/13 Su	15♎27	13♈35	22♌53	16♍46
11/20 Su	15♎40	13♈32	22♌54	16♍51
11/27 Su	15♎53	13♈29	22♌54 R	16♍54
12/04 Su	16♎04	13♈27	22♌53	16♍56
12/11 Su	16♎14	13♈25	22♌50	16♍58
12/18 Su	16♎23	13♈23	22♌47	16♍58 R
12/25 Su	16♎30	13♈22	22♌43	16♍57

1978	♇	♇	♇	♇
1/01 Su	16♎35	13♈22	22♌37	16♍55
1/08 Su	16♎39	13♈22 D	22♌31	16♍52
1/15 Su	16♎41	13♈23	22♌24	16♍48
1/22 Su	16♎41 R	13♈25	22♌16	16♍44
1/29 Su	16♎39	13♈27	22♌09	16♍38
2/05 Su	16♎36	13♈29	22♌00	16♍32
2/12 Su	16♎31	13♈32	21♌52	16♍25
2/19 Su	16♎25	13♈35	21♌43	16♍18
2/26 Su	16♎17	13♈39	21♌35	16♍10
3/05 Su	16♎08	13♈43	21♌27	16♍03
3/12 Su	15♎58	13♈47	21♌20	15♍55
3/19 Su	15♎48	13♈51	21♌13	15♍47
3/26 Su	15♎36	13♈56	21♌07	15♍40
4/02 Su	15♎25	14♈01	21♌02	15♍32
4/09 Su	15♎13	14♈05	20♌57	15♍26
4/16 Su	15♎01	14♈10	20♌54	15♍20
4/23 Su	14♎50	14♈15	20♌51	15♍14
4/30 Su	14♎39	14♈19	20♌50	15♍10
5/07 Su	14♎29	14♈23	20♌50 D	15♍06
5/14 Su	14♎20	14♈27	20♌51	15♍03
5/21 Su	14♎12	14♈31	20♌53	15♍01
5/28 Su	14♎05	14♈34	20♌56	15♍00
6/04 Su	14♎00	14♈37	21♌00	15♍01 D
6/11 Su	13♎56	14♈39	21♌05	15♍02
6/18 Su	13♎54	14♈41	21♌11	15♍04

Astro Data

1977

1/16 Su	07:05	♇	SR	14♎11	10.2 (10:10)
5/03 Tu	16:12	♇	SD	19♌45	39.4 (39:25)
5/29 Su	11:27	♇	SD	14♍06	24.9 (24:55)
6/21 Tu	13:21	♇	SD	11♎23	11.3 (11:17)
7/11 Mo	00:06	♇	SR	14♈30	-12.5 (-12:27)

1977

11/22 Tu	12:11	♇	SR	22♌54	38.4 (38:21)
12/15 Th	19:43	♇	SR	16♍58	23.9 (23:54)

1978

1/01 Su	07:18	♇	SD	13♈22	-12.8 (-12:48)
1/19 Th	00:46	♇	SR	16♎41	9.3 (9:17)
5/05 Fr	02:43	♇	SD	20♌50	39.2 (39:15)
5/30 Tu	16:44	♇	SD	15♍00	24.9 (24:51)
6/24 Su	07:42	♇	SD	13♎53	10.4 (10:15)

1978	⚳	⚴	⚵	⚶
6/25 Su	13 ♎ 53 D	14 ♈ 43 D	21 ♌ 18 D	15 ♍ 07 D
7/02 Su	13 ♎ 54	14 ♈ 44	21 ♌ 25	15 ♍ 11
7/09 Su	13 ♎ 57	14 ♈ 44	21 ♌ 33	15 ♍ 16
7/16 Su	14 ♎ 01	14 ♈ 44 ℞	21 ♌ 42	15 ♍ 22
7/23 Su	14 ♎ 07	14 ♈ 44	21 ♌ 52	15 ♍ 28
7/30 Su	14 ♎ 15	14 ♈ 43	22 ♌ 01	15 ♍ 35
8/06 Su	14 ♎ 23	14 ♈ 41	22 ♌ 11	15 ♍ 43
8/13 Su	14 ♎ 34	14 ♈ 39	22 ♌ 22	15 ♍ 51
8/20 Su	14 ♎ 45	14 ♈ 36	22 ♌ 32	16 ♍ 00
8/27 Su	14 ♎ 58	14 ♈ 33	22 ♌ 42	16 ♍ 09
9/03 Su	15 ♎ 11	14 ♈ 30	22 ♌ 52	16 ♍ 19
9/10 Su	15 ♎ 26	14 ♈ 26	23 ♌ 02	16 ♍ 28
9/17 Su	15 ♎ 41	14 ♈ 23	23 ♌ 11	16 ♍ 37
9/24 Su	15 ♎ 57	14 ♈ 19	23 ♌ 20	16 ♍ 47
10/01 Su	16 ♎ 14	14 ♈ 14	23 ♌ 28	16 ♍ 56
10/08 Su	16 ♎ 30	14 ♈ 10	23 ♌ 35	17 ♍ 04
10/15 Su	16 ♎ 47	14 ♈ 06	23 ♌ 42	17 ♍ 13
10/22 Su	17 ♎ 03	14 ♈ 02	23 ♌ 47	17 ♍ 20
10/29 Su	17 ♎ 19	13 ♈ 58	23 ♌ 52	17 ♍ 27
11/05 Su	17 ♎ 35	13 ♈ 54	23 ♌ 55	17 ♍ 34
11/12 Su	17 ♎ 50	13 ♈ 50	23 ♌ 58	17 ♍ 39
11/19 Su	18 ♎ 04	13 ♈ 47	23 ♌ 59	17 ♍ 44
11/26 Su	18 ♎ 18	13 ♈ 44	24 ♌ 00 ℞	17 ♍ 48
12/03 Su	18 ♎ 30	13 ♈ 41	23 ♌ 59	17 ♍ 50
12/10 Su	18 ♎ 41	13 ♈ 39	23 ♌ 57	17 ♍ 52
12/17 Su	18 ♎ 50	13 ♈ 38	23 ♌ 53	17 ♍ 52
12/24 Su	18 ♎ 58	13 ♈ 37	23 ♌ 49	17 ♍ 52 ℞
12/31 Su	19 ♎ 04	13 ♈ 37	23 ♌ 44	17 ♍ 50
1979				
1/07 Su	19 ♎ 09	13 ♈ 37 D	23 ♌ 38	17 ♍ 48
1/14 Su	19 ♎ 12	13 ♈ 37	23 ♌ 32	17 ♍ 44
1/21 Su	19 ♎ 13	13 ♈ 39	23 ♌ 24	17 ♍ 40
1/28 Su	19 ♎ 12 ℞	13 ♈ 40	23 ♌ 16	17 ♍ 34
2/04 Su	19 ♎ 10	13 ♈ 43	23 ♌ 08	17 ♍ 28
2/11 Su	19 ♎ 06	13 ♈ 46	23 ♌ 00	17 ♍ 22
2/18 Su	19 ♎ 00	13 ♈ 49	22 ♌ 51	17 ♍ 15
2/25 Su	18 ♎ 53	13 ♈ 52	22 ♌ 43	17 ♍ 07
3/04 Su	18 ♎ 45	13 ♈ 56	22 ♌ 35	16 ♍ 59
3/11 Su	18 ♎ 36	14 ♈ 00	22 ♌ 28	16 ♍ 51

1979	⚳	⚴	⚵	⚶
3/18 Su	18 ♎ 25 ℞	14 ♈ 05 D	22 ♌ 21 ℞	16 ♍ 44 ℞
3/25 Su	18 ♎ 14	14 ♈ 09	22 ♌ 14	16 ♍ 36
4/01 Su	18 ♎ 03	14 ♈ 14	22 ♌ 09	16 ♍ 29
4/08 Su	17 ♎ 51	14 ♈ 19	22 ♌ 04	16 ♍ 22
4/15 Su	17 ♎ 39	14 ♈ 23	22 ♌ 00	16 ♍ 16
4/22 Su	17 ♎ 28	14 ♈ 28	21 ♌ 57	16 ♍ 10
4/29 Su	17 ♎ 16	14 ♈ 32	21 ♌ 56	16 ♍ 05
5/06 Su	17 ♎ 06	14 ♈ 37	21 ♌ 55	16 ♍ 01
5/13 Su	16 ♎ 56	14 ♈ 41	21 ♌ 56 D	15 ♍ 58
5/20 Su	16 ♎ 48	14 ♈ 44	21 ♌ 57	15 ♍ 56
5/27 Su	16 ♎ 40	14 ♈ 48	22 ♌ 00	15 ♍ 55
6/03 Su	16 ♎ 34	14 ♈ 51	22 ♌ 03	15 ♍ 55 D
6/10 Su	16 ♎ 30	14 ♈ 53	22 ♌ 08	15 ♍ 56
6/17 Su	16 ♎ 27	14 ♈ 55	22 ♌ 14	15 ♍ 57
6/24 Su	16 ♎ 25	14 ♈ 57	22 ♌ 20	16 ♍ 00
7/01 Su	16 ♎ 25 D	14 ♈ 58	22 ♌ 28	16 ♍ 04
7/08 Su	16 ♎ 27	14 ♈ 59	22 ♌ 36	16 ♍ 09
7/15 Su	16 ♎ 30	14 ♈ 59 ℞	22 ♌ 44	16 ♍ 14
7/22 Su	16 ♎ 35	14 ♈ 58	22 ♌ 54	16 ♍ 20
7/29 Su	16 ♎ 42	14 ♈ 57	23 ♌ 03	16 ♍ 27
8/05 Su	16 ♎ 50	14 ♈ 56	23 ♌ 13	16 ♍ 35
8/12 Su	16 ♎ 59	14 ♈ 54	23 ♌ 23	16 ♍ 43
8/19 Su	17 ♎ 10	14 ♈ 51	23 ♌ 34	16 ♍ 52
8/26 Su	17 ♎ 22	14 ♈ 48	23 ♌ 44	17 ♍ 01
9/02 Su	17 ♎ 36	14 ♈ 45	23 ♌ 54	17 ♍ 10
9/09 Su	17 ♎ 50	14 ♈ 42	24 ♌ 04	17 ♍ 20
9/16 Su	18 ♎ 05	14 ♈ 38	24 ♌ 13	17 ♍ 29
9/23 Su	18 ♎ 21	14 ♈ 34	24 ♌ 22	17 ♍ 38
9/30 Su	18 ♎ 37	14 ♈ 30	24 ♌ 30	17 ♍ 47
10/07 Su	18 ♎ 53	14 ♈ 25	24 ♌ 38	17 ♍ 56
10/14 Su	19 ♎ 10	14 ♈ 21	24 ♌ 45	18 ♍ 05
10/21 Su	19 ♎ 27	14 ♈ 17	24 ♌ 51	18 ♍ 13
10/28 Su	19 ♎ 43	14 ♈ 13	24 ♌ 56	18 ♍ 20
11/04 Su	19 ♎ 59	14 ♈ 09	25 ♌ 00	18 ♍ 27
11/11 Su	20 ♎ 15	14 ♈ 05	25 ♌ 02	18 ♍ 32
11/18 Su	20 ♎ 29	14 ♈ 02	25 ♌ 04	18 ♍ 37
11/25 Su	20 ♎ 43	13 ♈ 59	25 ♌ 05	18 ♍ 41
12/02 Su	20 ♎ 56	13 ♈ 56	25 ♌ 04 ℞	18 ♍ 44
12/09 Su	21 ♎ 08	13 ♈ 54	25 ♌ 03	18 ♍ 46
12/16 Su	21 ♎ 18	13 ♈ 53	25 ♌ 00	18 ♍ 47

Astro Data

1978

7/11 Tu	07:02	⚴	SR	14 ♈ 44	-12.2 (-12:12)
11/23 Th	20:51	⚵	SR	24 ♌ 00	38.1 (38:08)
12/17 Su	02:20	⚶	SR	17 ♍ 52	23.9 (23:51)

1979

1/01 Mo	15:24	⚴	SD	13 ♈ 37	-12.6 (-12:33)
1/21 Su	20:46	⚳	SR	19 ♎ 13	8.4 (8:25)

1979

5/06 Su	10:12	⚵	SD	21 ♌ 55	39.0 (39:01)
5/31 Th	17:48	⚶	SD	15 ♍ 55	24.8 (24:46)
6/27 We	01:26	⚳	SD	16 ♎ 25	9.5 (9:30)
7/11 We	22:47	⚴	SR	14 ♈ 59	-11.9 (-11:56)
11/25 Su	05:29	⚵	SR	25 ♌ 05	38.0 (37:58)
12/18 Tu	06:45	⚶	SR	18 ♍ 47	23.7 (23:44)

	♇	♀	♣	♣
1979				
12/23 Su	21 ♎ 27 D	13 ♈ 51 ℞	24 ♌ 56 ℞	18 ♍ 47 ℞
12/30 Su	21 ♎ 34	13 ♈ 51	24 ♌ 51	18 ♍ 46
1980				
1/06 Su	21 ♎ 40	13 ♈ 51 D	24 ♌ 46	18 ♍ 43
1/13 Su	21 ♎ 44	13 ♈ 52	24 ♌ 39	18 ♍ 40
1/20 Su	21 ♎ 46	13 ♈ 53	24 ♌ 32	18 ♍ 36
1/27 Su	21 ♎ 46 ℞	13 ♈ 54	24 ♌ 24	18 ♍ 31
2/03 Su	21 ♎ 45	13 ♈ 57	24 ♌ 16	18 ♍ 25
2/10 Su	21 ♎ 41	13 ♈ 59	24 ♌ 08	18 ♍ 18
2/17 Su	21 ♎ 37	14 ♈ 02	23 ♌ 59	18 ♍ 11
2/24 Su	21 ♎ 30	14 ♈ 06	23 ♌ 51	18 ♍ 04
3/02 Su	21 ♎ 23	14 ♈ 10	23 ♌ 43	17 ♍ 56
3/09 Su	21 ♎ 14	14 ♈ 14	23 ♌ 35	17 ♍ 48
3/16 Su	21 ♎ 04	14 ♈ 18	23 ♌ 28	17 ♍ 41
3/23 Su	20 ♎ 53	14 ♈ 23	23 ♌ 21	17 ♍ 33
3/30 Su	20 ♎ 42	14 ♈ 27	23 ♌ 16	17 ♍ 26
4/06 Su	20 ♎ 30	14 ♈ 32	23 ♌ 11	17 ♍ 19
4/13 Su	20 ♎ 19	14 ♈ 37	23 ♌ 06	17 ♍ 12
4/20 Su	20 ♎ 07	14 ♈ 41	23 ♌ 03	17 ♍ 06
4/27 Su	19 ♎ 55	14 ♈ 46	23 ♌ 01	17 ♍ 01
5/04 Su	19 ♎ 45	14 ♈ 50	23 ♌ 00	16 ♍ 57
5/11 Su	19 ♎ 34	14 ♈ 54	23 ♌ 00 D	16 ♍ 54
5/18 Su	19 ♎ 25	14 ♈ 58	23 ♌ 02	16 ♍ 51
5/25 Su	19 ♎ 17	15 ♈ 01	23 ♌ 04	16 ♍ 50
6/01 Su	19 ♎ 10	15 ♈ 04	23 ♌ 07	16 ♍ 49 D
6/08 Su	19 ♎ 05	15 ♈ 07	23 ♌ 12	16 ♍ 50
6/15 Su	19 ♎ 01	15 ♈ 09	23 ♌ 17	16 ♍ 51
6/22 Su	18 ♎ 58	15 ♈ 11	23 ♌ 23	16 ♍ 54
6/29 Su	18 ♎ 58 D	15 ♈ 12	23 ♌ 30	16 ♍ 57
7/06 Su	18 ♎ 58	15 ♈ 13	23 ♌ 38	17 ♍ 02
7/13 Su	19 ♎ 01	15 ♈ 13 ℞	23 ♌ 47	17 ♍ 07
7/20 Su	19 ♎ 05	15 ♈ 12	23 ♌ 56	17 ♍ 13
7/27 Su	19 ♎ 11	15 ♈ 12	24 ♌ 05	17 ♍ 20
8/03 Su	19 ♎ 18	15 ♈ 10	24 ♌ 15	17 ♍ 27
8/10 Su	19 ♎ 27	15 ♈ 08	24 ♌ 25	17 ♍ 35
8/17 Su	19 ♎ 37	15 ♈ 06	24 ♌ 35	17 ♍ 44
8/24 Su	19 ♎ 49	15 ♈ 03	24 ♌ 45	17 ♍ 53
8/31 Su	20 ♎ 01	15 ♈ 00	24 ♌ 56	18 ♍ 02

	♇	♀	♣	♣
1980				
9/07 Su	20 ♎ 15 D	14 ♈ 57 ℞	25 ♌ 05 D	18 ♍ 11 D
9/14 Su	20 ♎ 30	14 ♈ 53	25 ♌ 15	18 ♍ 21
9/21 Su	20 ♎ 45	14 ♈ 49	25 ♌ 24	18 ♍ 30
9/28 Su	21 ♎ 01	14 ♈ 45	25 ♌ 33	18 ♍ 39
10/05 Su	21 ♎ 18	14 ♈ 40	25 ♌ 40	18 ♍ 48
10/12 Su	21 ♎ 34	14 ♈ 36	25 ♌ 48	18 ♍ 57
10/19 Su	21 ♎ 51	14 ♈ 32	25 ♌ 54	19 ♍ 05
10/26 Su	22 ♎ 08	14 ♈ 28	25 ♌ 59	19 ♍ 12
11/02 Su	22 ♎ 24	14 ♈ 24	26 ♌ 03	19 ♍ 19
11/09 Su	22 ♎ 40	14 ♈ 20	26 ♌ 07	19 ♍ 25
11/16 Su	22 ♎ 55	14 ♈ 17	26 ♌ 09	19 ♍ 31
11/23 Su	23 ♎ 10	14 ♈ 14	26 ♌ 10	19 ♍ 35
11/30 Su	23 ♎ 23	14 ♈ 11	26 ♌ 10 ℞	19 ♍ 38
12/07 Su	23 ♎ 36	14 ♈ 09	26 ♌ 08	19 ♍ 40
12/14 Su	23 ♎ 47	14 ♈ 07	26 ♌ 06	19 ♍ 42
12/21 Su	23 ♎ 56	14 ♈ 06	26 ♌ 02	19 ♍ 42 ℞
12/28 Su	24 ♎ 05	14 ♈ 05	25 ♌ 58	19 ♍ 41
1981				
1/04 Su	24 ♎ 11	14 ♈ 05 D	25 ♌ 53	19 ♍ 39
1/11 Su	24 ♎ 16	14 ♈ 06	25 ♌ 46	19 ♍ 36
1/18 Su	24 ♎ 19	14 ♈ 07	25 ♌ 39	19 ♍ 32
1/25 Su	24 ♎ 20	14 ♈ 08	25 ♌ 32	19 ♍ 27
2/01 Su	24 ♎ 20 ℞	14 ♈ 10	25 ♌ 24	19 ♍ 21
2/08 Su	24 ♎ 17	14 ♈ 13	25 ♌ 16	19 ♍ 15
2/15 Su	24 ♎ 14	14 ♈ 16	25 ♌ 07	19 ♍ 08
2/22 Su	24 ♎ 08	14 ♈ 19	24 ♌ 59	19 ♍ 01
3/01 Su	24 ♎ 01	14 ♈ 23	24 ♌ 51	18 ♍ 53
3/08 Su	23 ♎ 53	14 ♈ 27	24 ♌ 43	18 ♍ 46
3/15 Su	23 ♎ 44	14 ♈ 31	24 ♌ 36	18 ♍ 38
3/22 Su	23 ♎ 33	14 ♈ 36	24 ♌ 29	18 ♍ 30
3/29 Su	23 ♎ 22	14 ♈ 41	24 ♌ 23	18 ♍ 23
4/05 Su	23 ♎ 11	14 ♈ 45	24 ♌ 17	18 ♍ 15
4/12 Su	22 ♎ 59	14 ♈ 50	24 ♌ 13	18 ♍ 09
4/19 Su	22 ♎ 47	14 ♈ 55	24 ♌ 09	18 ♍ 03
4/26 Su	22 ♎ 36	14 ♈ 59	24 ♌ 07	17 ♍ 57
5/03 Su	22 ♎ 24	15 ♈ 03	24 ♌ 06	17 ♍ 53
5/10 Su	22 ♎ 14	15 ♈ 08	24 ♌ 05 D	17 ♍ 49
5/17 Su	22 ♎ 04	15 ♈ 11	24 ♌ 06	17 ♍ 46

Astro Data

1980

1/02 We	00:29	♀	SD	13 ♈ 51	-12.3 (-12:18)
1/24 Th	15:49	♇	SR	21 ♎ 46	7.5 (7:30)
5/06 Tu	17:45	♣	SD	23 ♌ 00	38.8 (38:49)
5/31 Su	20:27	♣	SD	16 ♍ 49	24.7 (24:40)
6/28 Su	20:09	♇	SD	18 ♎ 58	8.6 (8:36)
7/11 Fr	13:12	♀	SR	15 ♈ 13	-11.7 (-11:41)

1980

11/25 Tu	15:18	♣	SR	26 ♌ 10	37.7 (37:43)
12/18 Th	08:36	♣	SR	19 ♍ 42	23.6 (23:37)

1981

1/26 Mo	12:51	♇	SR	24 ♎ 20	6.6 (6:36)
5/08 Fr	00:21	♣	SD	24 ♌ 05	38.6 (38:37)

	Date	⯓	♀	⯗	⯘
1981	5/24 Su	21 ♎ 55 ℞	15 ♈ 15 D	24 ♌ 08 D	17 ♍ 45 ℞
	5/31 Su	21 ♎ 48	15 ♈ 18	24 ♌ 11	17 ♍ 44
	6/07 Su	21 ♎ 42	15 ♈ 21	24 ♌ 15	17 ♍ 44 D
	6/14 Su	21 ♎ 37	15 ♈ 23	24 ♌ 20	17 ♍ 45
	6/21 Su	21 ♎ 33	15 ♈ 25	24 ♌ 26	17 ♍ 48
	6/28 Su	21 ♎ 32	15 ♈ 26	24 ♌ 33	17 ♍ 51
	7/05 Su	21 ♎ 32 D	15 ♈ 27	24 ♌ 41	17 ♍ 55
	7/12 Su	21 ♎ 33	15 ♈ 27 ℞	24 ♌ 49	18 ♍ 00
	7/19 Su	21 ♎ 37	15 ♈ 27	24 ♌ 58	18 ♍ 06
	7/26 Su	21 ♎ 41	15 ♈ 26	25 ♌ 07	18 ♍ 12
	8/02 Su	21 ♎ 48	15 ♈ 25	25 ♌ 17	18 ♍ 20
	8/09 Su	21 ♎ 56	15 ♈ 23	25 ♌ 27	18 ♍ 27
	8/16 Su	22 ♎ 06	15 ♈ 21	25 ♌ 37	18 ♍ 36
	8/23 Su	22 ♎ 16	15 ♈ 18	25 ♌ 47	18 ♍ 45
	8/30 Su	22 ♎ 28	15 ♈ 15	25 ♌ 57	18 ♍ 54
	9/06 Su	22 ♎ 42	15 ♈ 11	26 ♌ 07	19 ♍ 03
	9/13 Su	22 ♎ 56	15 ♈ 08	26 ♌ 17	19 ♍ 13
	9/20 Su	23 ♎ 11	15 ♈ 04	26 ♌ 26	19 ♍ 22
	9/27 Su	23 ♎ 27	15 ♈ 00	26 ♌ 35	19 ♍ 31
	10/04 Su	23 ♎ 43	14 ♈ 56	26 ♌ 43	19 ♍ 40
	10/11 Su	24 ♎ 00	14 ♈ 51	26 ♌ 50	19 ♍ 49
	10/18 Su	24 ♎ 16	14 ♈ 47	26 ♌ 57	19 ♍ 57
	10/25 Su	24 ♎ 33	14 ♈ 43	27 ♌ 02	20 ♍ 05
	11/01 Su	24 ♎ 50	14 ♈ 39	27 ♌ 07	20 ♍ 12
	11/08 Su	25 ♎ 06	14 ♈ 35	27 ♌ 11	20 ♍ 18
	11/15 Su	25 ♎ 22	14 ♈ 32	27 ♌ 13	20 ♍ 24
	11/22 Su	25 ♎ 37	14 ♈ 28	27 ♌ 15	20 ♍ 29
	11/29 Su	25 ♎ 51	14 ♈ 26	27 ♌ 15 ℞	20 ♍ 32
	12/06 Su	26 ♎ 04	14 ♈ 23	27 ♌ 14	20 ♍ 35
	12/13 Su	26 ♎ 16	14 ♈ 22	27 ♌ 12	20 ♍ 36
	12/20 Su	26 ♎ 26	14 ♈ 20	27 ♌ 09	20 ♍ 37 ℞
	12/27 Su	26 ♎ 35	14 ♈ 20	27 ♌ 05	20 ♍ 36
1982	1/03 Su	26 ♎ 43	14 ♈ 19 D	26 ♌ 59	20 ♍ 34
	1/10 Su	26 ♎ 49	14 ♈ 20	26 ♌ 54	20 ♍ 32
	1/17 Su	26 ♎ 53	14 ♈ 21	26 ♌ 47	20 ♍ 28
	1/24 Su	26 ♎ 55	14 ♈ 22	26 ♌ 40	20 ♍ 24
	1/31 Su	26 ♎ 55 ℞	14 ♈ 24	26 ♌ 32	20 ♍ 18

	Date	⯓	♀	⯗	⯘
1982	2/07 Su	26 ♎ 54 ℞	14 ♈ 27 D	26 ♌ 24 ℞	20 ♍ 12 ℞
	2/14 Su	26 ♎ 51	14 ♈ 29	26 ♌ 15	20 ♍ 05
	2/21 Su	26 ♎ 46	14 ♈ 33	26 ♌ 07	19 ♍ 58
	2/28 Su	26 ♎ 40	14 ♈ 36	25 ♌ 59	19 ♍ 51
	3/07 Su	26 ♎ 33	14 ♈ 40	25 ♌ 51	19 ♍ 43
	3/14 Su	26 ♎ 24	14 ♈ 45	25 ♌ 43	19 ♍ 35
	3/21 Su	26 ♎ 14	14 ♈ 49	25 ♌ 36	19 ♍ 27
	3/28 Su	26 ♎ 04	14 ♈ 54	25 ♌ 30	19 ♍ 20
	4/04 Su	25 ♎ 52	14 ♈ 58	25 ♌ 24	19 ♍ 12
	4/11 Su	25 ♎ 41	15 ♈ 03	25 ♌ 19	19 ♍ 06
	4/18 Su	25 ♎ 29	15 ♈ 08	25 ♌ 16	18 ♍ 59
	4/25 Su	25 ♎ 17	15 ♈ 12	25 ♌ 13	18 ♍ 54
	5/02 Su	25 ♎ 06	15 ♈ 17	25 ♌ 11	18 ♍ 49
	5/09 Su	24 ♎ 55	15 ♈ 21	25 ♌ 10	18 ♍ 45
	5/16 Su	24 ♎ 44	15 ♈ 25	25 ♌ 11 D	18 ♍ 42
	5/23 Su	24 ♎ 35	15 ♈ 28	25 ♌ 12	18 ♍ 40
	5/30 Su	24 ♎ 27	15 ♈ 31	25 ♌ 15	18 ♍ 39
	6/06 Su	24 ♎ 20	15 ♈ 34	25 ♌ 19	18 ♍ 39 D
	6/13 Su	24 ♎ 14	15 ♈ 37	25 ♌ 23	18 ♍ 40
	6/20 Su	24 ♎ 10	15 ♈ 39	25 ♌ 29	18 ♍ 42
	6/27 Su	24 ♎ 07	15 ♈ 40	25 ♌ 36	18 ♍ 44
	7/04 Su	24 ♎ 06	15 ♈ 41	25 ♌ 43	18 ♍ 48
	7/11 Su	24 ♎ 07 D	15 ♈ 41	25 ♌ 51	18 ♍ 53
	7/18 Su	24 ♎ 09	15 ♈ 41 ℞	26 ♌ 00	18 ♍ 59
	7/25 Su	24 ♎ 14	15 ♈ 40	26 ♌ 09	19 ♍ 05
	8/01 Su	24 ♎ 19	15 ♈ 39	26 ♌ 18	19 ♍ 12
	8/08 Su	24 ♎ 26	15 ♈ 37	26 ♌ 28	19 ♍ 20
	8/15 Su	24 ♎ 35	15 ♈ 35	26 ♌ 38	19 ♍ 28
	8/22 Su	24 ♎ 45	15 ♈ 33	26 ♌ 49	19 ♍ 37
	8/29 Su	24 ♎ 57	15 ♈ 30	26 ♌ 59	19 ♍ 46
	9/05 Su	25 ♎ 09	15 ♈ 26	27 ♌ 09	19 ♍ 55
	9/12 Su	25 ♎ 23	15 ♈ 23	27 ♌ 19	20 ♍ 05
	9/19 Su	25 ♎ 38	15 ♈ 19	27 ♌ 28	20 ♍ 14
	9/26 Su	25 ♎ 53	15 ♈ 15	27 ♌ 37	20 ♍ 23
	10/03 Su	26 ♎ 09	15 ♈ 11	27 ♌ 45	20 ♍ 33
	10/10 Su	26 ♎ 26	15 ♈ 06	27 ♌ 53	20 ♍ 41
	10/17 Su	26 ♎ 42	15 ♈ 02	28 ♌ 00	20 ♍ 50
	10/24 Su	26 ♎ 59	14 ♈ 58	28 ♌ 06	20 ♍ 58
	10/31 Su	27 ♎ 16	14 ♈ 54	28 ♌ 11	21 ♍ 05
	11/07 Su	27 ♎ 33	14 ♈ 50	28 ♌ 15	21 ♍ 12

Astro Data

1981

6/02 Tu	00:45	⯘	SD	17 ♍ 44	24.6 (24:33)
7/01 We	16:12	⯓	SD	21 ♎ 32	7.6 (7:37)
7/11 Sa	20:12	♀	SR	15 ♈ 27	-11.4 (-11:25)
11/26 Th	21:29	⯗	SR	27 ♌ 15	37.5 (37:28)
12/19 Sa	12:08	⯘	SR	20 ♍ 37	23.5 (23:30)

1982

1/02 Sa	05:39	♀	SD	14 ♈ 19	-11.8 (-11:48)
1/29 Fr	08:18	⯓	SR	26 ♎ 55	5.6 (5:38)

1982

5/09 Su	10:59	⯗	SD	25 ♌ 10	38.4 (38:22)
6/03 Th	06:57	⯘	SD	18 ♍ 39	24.5 (24:27)
7/04 Su	13:11	⯓	SD	24 ♎ 06	6.6 (6:38)
7/12 Mo	05:52	♀	SR	15 ♈ 41	-11.2 (-11:11)

		♀	♀	♠	♠
1982	11/14 Su	27 ♎ 49 D	14 ♈ 47 ℞	28 ♌ 17 D	21 ♍ 17 D
	11/21 Su	28 ♎ 04	14 ♈ 43	28 ♌ 19	21 ♍ 22
	11/28 Su	28 ♎ 19	14 ♈ 41	28 ♌ 20	21 ♍ 26
	12/05 Su	28 ♎ 33	14 ♈ 38	28 ♌ 19 ℞	21 ♍ 29
	12/12 Su	28 ♎ 45	14 ♈ 36	28 ♌ 18	21 ♍ 31
	12/19 Su	28 ♎ 57	14 ♈ 35	28 ♌ 15	21 ♍ 32
	12/26 Su	29 ♎ 06	14 ♈ 34	28 ♌ 11	21 ♍ 32 ℞
1983	1/02 Su	29 ♎ 15	14 ♈ 34	28 ♌ 06	21 ♍ 30
	1/09 Su	29 ♎ 21	14 ♈ 34 D	28 ♌ 00	21 ♍ 28
	1/16 Su	29 ♎ 26	14 ♈ 35	27 ♌ 54	21 ♍ 24
	1/23 Su	29 ♎ 30	14 ♈ 36	27 ♌ 47	21 ♍ 20
	1/30 Su	29 ♎ 31	14 ♈ 38	27 ♌ 39	21 ♍ 15
	2/06 Su	29 ♎ 31 ℞	14 ♈ 40	27 ♌ 31	21 ♍ 09
	2/13 Su	29 ♎ 29	14 ♈ 43	27 ♌ 23	21 ♍ 03
	2/20 Su	29 ♎ 25	14 ♈ 46	27 ♌ 14	20 ♍ 56
	2/27 Su	29 ♎ 20	14 ♈ 50	27 ♌ 06	20 ♍ 48
	3/06 Su	29 ♎ 13	14 ♈ 54	26 ♌ 58	20 ♍ 40
	3/13 Su	29 ♎ 05	14 ♈ 58	26 ♌ 50	20 ♍ 33
	3/20 Su	28 ♎ 56	15 ♈ 02	26 ♌ 43	20 ♍ 25
	3/27 Su	28 ♎ 45	15 ♈ 07	26 ♌ 37	20 ♍ 17
	4/03 Su	28 ♎ 34	15 ♈ 12	26 ♌ 31	20 ♍ 10
	4/10 Su	28 ♎ 23	15 ♈ 16	26 ♌ 26	20 ♍ 03
	4/17 Su	28 ♎ 11	15 ♈ 21	26 ♌ 22	19 ♍ 56
	4/24 Su	27 ♎ 59	15 ♈ 26	26 ♌ 18	19 ♍ 50
	5/01 Su	27 ♎ 48	15 ♈ 30	26 ♌ 16	19 ♍ 45
	5/08 Su	27 ♎ 36	15 ♈ 34	26 ♌ 15	19 ♍ 41
	5/15 Su	27 ♎ 26	15 ♈ 38	26 ♌ 16 D	19 ♍ 38
	5/22 Su	27 ♎ 16	15 ♈ 42	26 ♌ 17	19 ♍ 35
	5/29 Su	27 ♎ 07	15 ♈ 45	26 ♌ 19	19 ♍ 34
	6/05 Su	26 ♎ 59	15 ♈ 48	26 ♌ 22	19 ♍ 34 D
	6/12 Su	26 ♎ 53	15 ♈ 50	26 ♌ 27	19 ♍ 34
	6/19 Su	26 ♎ 48	15 ♈ 52	26 ♌ 32	19 ♍ 36
	6/26 Su	26 ♎ 44	15 ♈ 54	26 ♌ 38	19 ♍ 38
	7/03 Su	26 ♎ 42	15 ♈ 55	26 ♌ 45	19 ♍ 42
	7/10 Su	26 ♎ 42 D	15 ♈ 55	26 ♌ 53	19 ♍ 46
	7/17 Su	26 ♎ 44	15 ♈ 55 ℞	27 ♌ 01	19 ♍ 52
	7/24 Su	26 ♎ 47	15 ♈ 55	27 ♌ 10	19 ♍ 58

		♀	♀	♠	♠
1983	7/31 Su	26 ♎ 52 D	15 ♈ 54 ℞	27 ♌ 20 D	20 ♍ 05 D
	8/07 Su	26 ♎ 58	15 ♈ 52	27 ♌ 30	20 ♍ 12
	8/14 Su	27 ♎ 06	15 ♈ 50	27 ♌ 40	20 ♍ 20
	8/21 Su	27 ♎ 15	15 ♈ 48	27 ♌ 50	20 ♍ 29
	8/28 Su	27 ♎ 26	15 ♈ 45	28 ♌ 00	20 ♍ 38
	9/04 Su	27 ♎ 38	15 ♈ 41	28 ♌ 10	20 ♍ 47
	9/11 Su	27 ♎ 51	15 ♈ 38	28 ♌ 20	20 ♍ 57
	9/18 Su	28 ♎ 05	15 ♈ 34	28 ♌ 30	21 ♍ 06
	9/25 Su	28 ♎ 20	15 ♈ 30	28 ♌ 39	21 ♍ 16
	10/02 Su	28 ♎ 36	15 ♈ 26	28 ♌ 47	21 ♍ 25
	10/09 Su	28 ♎ 52	15 ♈ 22	28 ♌ 55	21 ♍ 34
	10/16 Su	29 ♎ 09	15 ♈ 17	29 ♌ 02	21 ♍ 42
	10/23 Su	29 ♎ 26	15 ♈ 13	29 ♌ 08	21 ♍ 51
	10/30 Su	29 ♎ 43	15 ♈ 09	29 ♌ 14	21 ♍ 58
	11/06 Su	0 ♏ 00	15 ♈ 05	29 ♌ 18	22 ♍ 05
	11/13 Su	0 ♏ 16	15 ♈ 02	29 ♌ 21	22 ♍ 11
	11/20 Su	0 ♏ 32	14 ♈ 58	29 ♌ 23	22 ♍ 16
	11/27 Su	0 ♏ 47	14 ♈ 55	29 ♌ 24	22 ♍ 20
	12/04 Su	1 ♏ 02	14 ♈ 53	29 ♌ 24 ℞	22 ♍ 24
	12/11 Su	1 ♏ 15	14 ♈ 51	29 ♌ 23	22 ♍ 26
	12/18 Su	1 ♏ 27	14 ♈ 49	29 ♌ 21	22 ♍ 27
	12/25 Su	1 ♏ 38	14 ♈ 48	29 ♌ 17	22 ♍ 27 ℞
1984	1/01 Su	1 ♏ 47	14 ♈ 48	29 ♌ 13	22 ♍ 26
	1/08 Su	1 ♏ 54	14 ♈ 48 D	29 ♌ 07	22 ♍ 24
	1/15 Su	2 ♏ 00	14 ♈ 49	29 ♌ 01	22 ♍ 21
	1/22 Su	2 ♏ 05	14 ♈ 50	28 ♌ 54	22 ♍ 17
	1/29 Su	2 ♏ 07	14 ♈ 52	28 ♌ 47	22 ♍ 12
	2/05 Su	2 ♏ 08 ℞	14 ♈ 54	28 ♌ 39	22 ♍ 06
	2/12 Su	2 ♏ 07	14 ♈ 57	28 ♌ 30	22 ♍ 00
	2/19 Su	2 ♏ 04	15 ♈ 00	28 ♌ 22	21 ♍ 53
	2/26 Su	1 ♏ 59	15 ♈ 03	28 ♌ 14	21 ♍ 46
	3/04 Su	1 ♏ 53	15 ♈ 07	28 ♌ 05	21 ♍ 38
	3/11 Su	1 ♏ 46	15 ♈ 11	27 ♌ 58	21 ♍ 30
	3/18 Su	1 ♏ 37	15 ♈ 16	27 ♌ 50	21 ♍ 22
	3/25 Su	1 ♏ 28	15 ♈ 20	27 ♌ 43	21 ♍ 14
	4/01 Su	1 ♏ 17	15 ♈ 25	27 ♌ 37	21 ♍ 07
	4/08 Su	1 ♏ 06	15 ♈ 30	27 ♌ 32	21 ♍ 00

Astro Data

1982

| 11/28 Su | 02:50 | ♠ | SR | 28 ♌ 20 | 37.3 (37:16) |
| 12/20 Mo | 16:15 | ♠ | SR | 21 ♍ 32 | 23.4 (23:25) |

1983

1/03 Mo	00:00	♀	SD	14 ♈ 34	-11.5 (-11:31)
2/01 Tu	05:53	♀	SR	29 ♎ 31	4.7 (4:43)
5/10 Tu	21:53	♠	SD	26 ♌ 15	38.2 (38:09)
6/04 Sa	13:03	♠	SD	19 ♍ 34	24.4 (24:21)
7/07 Th	11:15	♀	SD	26 ♎ 42	5.7 (5:41)
7/12 Tu	20:52	♀	SR	15 ♈ 55	-10.9 (-10:55)

1983

11/05 Sa	21:09	♀	→ ♏		4.0 (3:58)
11/29 Tu	10:26	♠	SR	29 ♌ 24	37.0 (37:00)
12/21 We	23:34	♠	SR	12 ♍ 27	23.3 (23:16)

1984

| 1/03 Tu | 00:00 | ♀ | SD | 14 ♈ 48 | -11.3 (-11:16) |
| 2/04 Sa | 02:06 | ♀ | SR | 2 ♏ 08 | 3.7 (3:43) |

LONGITUDE

1984	♇	♀	⚷	⚳	1985	♇	♀	⚷	⚳
4/15 Su	0 ♏ 54 R	15 ♈ 34 D	27 ♌ 28 R	20 ♍ 53 R	1/06 Su	4 ♏ 27 D	15 ♈ 02 D	0 ♍ 14 R	23 ♍ 20 R
4/22	0 ♏ 42	15 ♈ 39	27 ♌ 24	20 ♍ 47	1/13	4 ♏ 34	15 ♈ 03	0 ♍ 08	23 ♍ 17
4/29	0 ♏ 30	15 ♈ 43	27 ♌ 22	20 ♍ 42	1/20	4 ♏ 39	15 ♈ 04	0 ♍ 01	23 ♍ 13
5/06	0 ♏ 19	15 ♈ 48	27 ♌ 20	20 ♍ 37	1/27	4 ♏ 43	15 ♈ 06	29 ♌ 54	23 ♍ 09
5/13	0 ♏ 08	15 ♈ 52	27 ♌ 20 D	20 ♍ 34	2/03	4 ♏ 44	15 ♈ 08	29 ♌ 46	23 ♍ 03
5/20 Su	29 ♎ 58	15 ♈ 55	27 ♌ 21	20 ♍ 31	2/10 Su	4 ♏ 44 R	15 ♈ 10	29 ♌ 38	22 ♍ 57
5/27	29 ♎ 48	15 ♈ 59	27 ♌ 23	20 ♍ 29	2/17	4 ♏ 42	15 ♈ 13	29 ♌ 29	22 ♍ 50
6/03	29 ♎ 40	16 ♈ 02	27 ♌ 26	20 ♍ 29	2/24	4 ♏ 39	15 ♈ 17	29 ♌ 21	22 ♍ 43
6/10	29 ♎ 32	16 ♈ 04	27 ♌ 30	20 ♍ 29 D	3/03	4 ♏ 34	15 ♈ 21	29 ♌ 13	22 ♍ 35
6/17	29 ♎ 27	16 ♈ 06	27 ♌ 35	20 ♍ 30	3/10	4 ♏ 27	15 ♈ 25	29 ♌ 05	22 ♍ 28
6/24 Su	29 ♎ 22	16 ♈ 08	27 ♌ 41	20 ♍ 32	3/17	4 ♏ 19	15 ♈ 29	28 ♌ 57	22 ♍ 20
7/01	29 ♎ 20	16 ♈ 09	27 ♌ 48	20 ♍ 36	3/24	4 ♏ 10	15 ♈ 34	28 ♌ 50	22 ♍ 12
7/08	29 ♎ 18	16 ♈ 10	27 ♌ 55	20 ♍ 40	3/31	4 ♏ 00	15 ♈ 38	28 ♌ 44	22 ♍ 04
7/15	29 ♎ 19 D	16 ♈ 10 R	28 ♌ 03	20 ♍ 45	4/07	3 ♏ 49	15 ♈ 43	28 ♌ 38	21 ♍ 57
7/22	29 ♎ 21	16 ♈ 09	28 ♌ 12	20 ♍ 51	4/14	3 ♏ 37	15 ♈ 48	28 ♌ 34	21 ♍ 50
7/29	29 ♎ 25	16 ♈ 08	28 ♌ 21	20 ♍ 58	4/21	3 ♏ 26	15 ♈ 52	28 ♌ 30	21 ♍ 44
8/05	29 ♎ 30	16 ♈ 07	28 ♌ 31	21 ♍ 05	4/28	3 ♏ 14	15 ♈ 57	28 ♌ 27	21 ♍ 39
8/12	29 ♎ 37	16 ♈ 05	28 ♌ 41	21 ♍ 13	5/05	3 ♏ 02	16 ♈ 01	28 ♌ 25	21 ♍ 34
8/19	29 ♎ 46	16 ♈ 02	28 ♌ 51	21 ♍ 21	5/12	2 ♏ 51	16 ♈ 05	28 ♌ 25	21 ♍ 30
8/26	29 ♎ 56	16 ♈ 00	29 ♌ 01	21 ♍ 30	5/19 Su	2 ♏ 40	16 ♈ 09	28 ♌ 25 D	21 ♍ 27
9/02 Su	0 ♏ 07	15 ♈ 56	29 ♌ 12	21 ♍ 39	5/26	2 ♏ 30	16 ♈ 12	28 ♌ 27	21 ♍ 25
9/09	0 ♏ 20	15 ♈ 53	29 ♌ 22	21 ♍ 49	6/02	2 ♏ 21	16 ♈ 15	28 ♌ 29	21 ♍ 24
9/16	0 ♏ 34	15 ♈ 49	29 ♌ 31	21 ♍ 58	6/09 Su	2 ♏ 13	16 ♈ 18	28 ♌ 33	21 ♍ 24 D
9/23	0 ♏ 48	15 ♈ 45	29 ♌ 40	22 ♍ 08	6/16	2 ♏ 06	16 ♈ 20	28 ♌ 38	21 ♍ 25
9/30	1 ♏ 04	15 ♈ 41	29 ♌ 49	22 ♍ 17	6/23	2 ♏ 01	16 ♈ 22	28 ♌ 43	21 ♍ 27
10/07	1 ♏ 20	15 ♈ 37	29 ♌ 57	22 ♍ 26	6/30 Su	1 ♏ 58	16 ♈ 23	28 ♌ 50	21 ♍ 30
10/14	1 ♏ 36	15 ♈ 32	0 ♍ 05	22 ♍ 35	7/07	1 ♏ 55	16 ♈ 24	28 ♌ 57	21 ♍ 34
10/21	1 ♏ 53	15 ♈ 28	0 ♍ 11	22 ♍ 43	7/14	1 ♏ 55 D	16 ♈ 24 R	29 ♌ 05	21 ♍ 38
10/28	2 ♏ 10	15 ♈ 24	0 ♍ 17	22 ♍ 51	7/21	1 ♏ 56	16 ♈ 24	29 ♌ 14	21 ♍ 44
11/04	2 ♏ 27	15 ♈ 20	0 ♍ 21	22 ♍ 58	7/28	1 ♏ 59	16 ♈ 23	29 ♌ 23	21 ♍ 51
11/11 Su	2 ♏ 44	15 ♈ 17	0 ♍ 25	23 ♍ 04	8/04	2 ♏ 04	16 ♈ 21	29 ♌ 32	21 ♍ 58
11/18	3 ♏ 00	15 ♈ 13	0 ♍ 27	23 ♍ 10	8/11	2 ♏ 10	16 ♈ 20	29 ♌ 42	22 ♍ 06
11/25	3 ♏ 16	15 ♈ 10	0 ♍ 29	23 ♍ 14	8/18	2 ♏ 18	16 ♈ 17	29 ♌ 52	22 ♍ 14
12/02	3 ♏ 30	15 ♈ 08	0 ♍ 29 R	23 ♍ 18	8/25	2 ♏ 27	16 ♈ 14	0 ♍ 03	22 ♍ 23
12/09	3 ♏ 44	15 ♈ 06	0 ♍ 28	23 ♍ 20	9/01 Su	2 ♏ 38	16 ♈ 11	0 ♍ 13	22 ♍ 32
12/16 Su	3 ♏ 57	15 ♈ 04	0 ♍ 26	23 ♍ 22	9/08	2 ♏ 49	16 ♈ 08	0 ♍ 23	22 ♍ 41
12/23	4 ♏ 09	15 ♈ 03	0 ♍ 23	23 ♍ 22 R	9/15	3 ♏ 03	16 ♈ 04	0 ♍ 33	22 ♍ 51
12/30	4 ♏ 19	15 ♈ 02	0 ♍ 19	23 ♍ 22	9/22	3 ♏ 17	16 ♈ 00	0 ♍ 42	23 ♍ 00
					9/29	3 ♏ 32	15 ♈ 56	0 ♍ 51	23 ♍ 10
					10/06 Su	3 ♏ 48	15 ♈ 52	0 ♍ 59	23 ♍ 19

Astro Data

1984

5/11 Fr	06:08	⚷	SD	27 ♌ 20	37.9	(37:54)
5/18 Fr	14:33	♇	→ ♎ R		4.8	(4:47)
6/04 Mo	14:02	⚳	SD	20 ♍ 29	24.2	(24:13)
7/09 Mo	08:22	♀	SD	29 ♎ 18	4.7	(4:40)
7/12 Th	12:39	♀	SR	16 ♈ 10	-10.7	(-10:40)
8/28 Tu	04:46	♇	→ ♏		4.0	(4:02)
10/09 Tu	01:25	⚷	→ ♍		36.5	(36:32)
11/29 Th	17:47	⚷	SR	0 ♍ 29	36.7	(36:43)
12/22 Sa	03:31	⚳	SR	23 ♍ 22	23.1	(23:08)

1985

1/03 Th	00:00	♀	SD	15 ♈ 02	-11.0	(-11:01)

1985

1/21 Mo	11:21	⚷	→ ♌ R		37.3	(37:18)
2/05 Tu	23:58	♇	SR	4 ♏ 44	2.8	(2:47)
5/12 Su	14:48	⚷	SD	28 ♌ 25	37.6	(37:37)
6/05 We	17:20	⚳	SD	21 ♍ 24	24.1	(24:06)
7/12 Fr	08:41	♇	SD	1 ♏ 55	3.7	(3:42)
7/12 Fr	21:36	♀	SR	16 ♈ 24	-10.4	(-10:24)
8/22 Th	21:04	⚷	→ ♍		36.6	(36:33)

		♇	♀	♇	♇
1985	10/13 Su	4 ♏ 04 D	15 ♈ 48 ℞	1 ♍ 07 D	23 ♍ 28 D
	10/20 Su	4 ♏ 21	15 ♈ 44	1 ♍ 14	23 ♍ 36
	10/27 Su	4 ♏ 38	15 ♈ 39	1 ♍ 19	23 ♍ 44
	11/03 Su	4 ♏ 55	15 ♈ 35	1 ♍ 24	23 ♍ 51
	11/10 Su	5 ♏ 11	15 ♈ 32	1 ♍ 28	23 ♍ 58
	11/17 Su	5 ♏ 28	15 ♈ 28	1 ♍ 31	24 ♍ 04
	11/24 Su	5 ♏ 44	15 ♈ 25	1 ♍ 33	24 ♍ 08
	12/01 Su	5 ♏ 59	15 ♈ 23	1 ♍ 34	24 ♍ 12
	12/08 Su	6 ♏ 14	15 ♈ 20	1 ♍ 33 ℞	24 ♍ 15
	12/15 Su	6 ♏ 27	15 ♈ 19	1 ♍ 31	24 ♍ 17
	12/22 Su	6 ♏ 39	15 ♈ 17	1 ♍ 29	24 ♍ 18
	12/29 Su	6 ♏ 50	15 ♈ 17	1 ♍ 25	24 ♍ 17 ℞
1986	1/05 Su	6 ♏ 59	15 ♈ 17 D	1 ♍ 20	24 ♍ 16
	1/12 Su	7 ♏ 07	15 ♈ 17	1 ♍ 14	24 ♍ 13
	1/19 Su	7 ♏ 13	15 ♈ 18	1 ♍ 08	24 ♍ 10
	1/26 Su	7 ♏ 18	15 ♈ 20	1 ♍ 01	24 ♍ 06
	2/02 Su	7 ♏ 20	15 ♈ 22	0 ♍ 53	24 ♍ 00
	2/09 Su	7 ♏ 21 ℞	15 ♈ 24	0 ♍ 45	23 ♍ 54
	2/16 Su	7 ♏ 20	15 ♈ 27	0 ♍ 37	23 ♍ 48
	2/23 Su	7 ♏ 18	15 ♈ 31	0 ♍ 28	23 ♍ 41
	3/02 Su	7 ♏ 13	15 ♈ 34	0 ♍ 20	23 ♍ 33
	3/09 Su	7 ♏ 08	15 ♈ 38	0 ♍ 12	23 ♍ 25
	3/16 Su	7 ♏ 00	15 ♈ 43	0 ♍ 04	23 ♍ 18
	3/23 Su	6 ♏ 52	15 ♈ 47	29 ♌ 57	23 ♍ 10
	3/30 Su	6 ♏ 42	15 ♈ 52	29 ♌ 50	23 ♍ 03
	4/06 Su	6 ♏ 32	15 ♈ 56	29 ♌ 45	22 ♍ 55
	4/13 Su	6 ♏ 21	16 ♈ 01	29 ♌ 40	22 ♍ 48
	4/20 Su	6 ♏ 09	16 ♈ 06	29 ♌ 35	22 ♍ 41
	4/27 Su	5 ♏ 57	16 ♈ 10	29 ♌ 32	22 ♍ 36
	5/04 Su	5 ♏ 45	16 ♈ 14	29 ♌ 30	22 ♍ 31
	5/11 Su	5 ♏ 34	16 ♈ 19	29 ♌ 29	22 ♍ 26
	5/18 Su	5 ♏ 23	16 ♈ 22	29 ♌ 29 D	22 ♍ 23
	5/25 Su	5 ♏ 12	16 ♈ 26	29 ♌ 31	22 ♍ 21
	6/01 Su	5 ♏ 02	16 ♈ 29	29 ♌ 33	22 ♍ 19
	6/08 Su	4 ♏ 54	16 ♈ 32	29 ♌ 36	22 ♍ 19 D
	6/15 Su	4 ♏ 47	16 ♈ 34	29 ♌ 41	22 ♍ 20
	6/22 Su	4 ♏ 41	16 ♈ 36	29 ♌ 46	22 ♍ 21

		♇	♀	♇	♇
1986	6/29 Su	4 ♏ 36 ℞	16 ♈ 37 D	29 ♌ 52 D	22 ♍ 24 D
	7/06 Su	4 ♏ 33	16 ♈ 38	29 ♌ 59	22 ♍ 28
	7/13 Su	4 ♏ 32	16 ♈ 38	0 ♍ 07	22 ♍ 32
	7/20 Su	4 ♏ 32 D	16 ♈ 38 ℞	0 ♍ 15	22 ♍ 38
	7/27 Su	4 ♏ 34	16 ♈ 37	0 ♍ 24	22 ♍ 44
	8/03 Su	4 ♏ 38	16 ♈ 36	0 ♍ 34	22 ♍ 51
	8/10 Su	4 ♏ 43	16 ♈ 34	0 ♍ 43	22 ♍ 58
	8/17 Su	4 ♏ 50	16 ♈ 32	0 ♍ 53	23 ♍ 07
	8/24 Su	4 ♏ 58	16 ♈ 29	1 ♍ 04	23 ♍ 15
	8/31 Su	5 ♏ 08	16 ♈ 26	1 ♍ 14	23 ♍ 24
	9/07 Su	5 ♏ 19	16 ♈ 23	1 ♍ 24	23 ♍ 34
	9/14 Su	5 ♏ 32	16 ♈ 19	1 ♍ 34	23 ♍ 43
	9/21 Su	5 ♏ 45	16 ♈ 16	1 ♍ 43	23 ♍ 53
	9/28 Su	6 ♏ 00	16 ♈ 11	1 ♍ 52	24 ♍ 02
	10/05 Su	6 ♏ 15	16 ♈ 07	2 ♍ 01	24 ♍ 11
	10/12 Su	6 ♏ 31	16 ♈ 03	2 ♍ 09	24 ♍ 20
	10/19 Su	6 ♏ 48	15 ♈ 59	2 ♍ 16	24 ♍ 29
	10/26 Su	7 ♏ 05	15 ♈ 55	2 ♍ 22	24 ♍ 37
	11/02 Su	7 ♏ 22	15 ♈ 51	2 ♍ 27	24 ♍ 45
	11/09 Su	7 ♏ 39	15 ♈ 47	2 ♍ 32	24 ♍ 51
	11/16 Su	7 ♏ 56	15 ♈ 43	2 ♍ 35	24 ♍ 57
	11/23 Su	8 ♏ 12	15 ♈ 40	2 ♍ 37	25 ♍ 03
	11/30 Su	8 ♏ 28	15 ♈ 38	2 ♍ 38	25 ♍ 07
	12/07 Su	8 ♏ 43	15 ♈ 35	2 ♍ 38 ℞	25 ♍ 10
	12/14 Su	8 ♏ 57	15 ♈ 33	2 ♍ 36	25 ♍ 12
	12/21 Su	9 ♏ 09	15 ♈ 32	2 ♍ 34	25 ♍ 13
	12/28 Su	9 ♏ 21	15 ♈ 31	2 ♍ 30	25 ♍ 13 ℞
1987	1/04 Su	9 ♏ 31	15 ♈ 31 D	2 ♍ 26	25 ♍ 12
	1/11 Su	9 ♏ 40	15 ♈ 31	2 ♍ 21	25 ♍ 10
	1/18 Su	9 ♏ 47	15 ♈ 32	2 ♍ 14	25 ♍ 07
	1/25 Su	9 ♏ 52	15 ♈ 34	2 ♍ 07	25 ♍ 03
	2/01 Su	9 ♏ 56	15 ♈ 36	2 ♍ 00	24 ♍ 58
	2/08 Su	9 ♏ 58	15 ♈ 38	1 ♍ 52	24 ♍ 52
	2/15 Su	9 ♏ 58 ℞	15 ♈ 41	1 ♍ 44	24 ♍ 45
	2/22 Su	9 ♏ 56	15 ♈ 44	1 ♍ 35	24 ♍ 38
	3/01 Su	9 ♏ 53	15 ♈ 48	1 ♍ 27	24 ♍ 31
	3/08 Su	9 ♏ 48	15 ♈ 52	1 ♍ 19	24 ♍ 23

Astro Data

1985

Date	Time			Pos	Value
12/01 Su	04:23	♇	SR	1 ♍ 34	36.5 (36:29)
12/23 Mo	04:20	♇	SR	24 ♍ 18	23.0 (23:02)

1986

1/03 Fr	04:20	♀	SD	15 ♈ 17	-10.8 (-10:46)
2/08 Sa	20:16	♇	SR	7 ♏ 21	1.8 (1:47)
3/20 Th	12:29	♇	→ ♌ ℞		37.5 (37:28)
5/13 Tu	19:42	♇	SD	29 ♌ 29	37.4 (37:21)
6/06 Fr	22:53	♇	SD	22 ♍ 19	24.0 (23:58)

1986

7/06 Su	11:04	♇	→ ♍		36.8 (36:46)
7/15 Tu	06:32	♇	SD	4 ♏ 32	2.7 (2:39)
7/13 Su	04:03	♀	SR	16 ♈ 38	-10.2 (-10:09)
12/02 Tu	12:53	♇	SR	2 ♍ 38	36.2 (36:10)
12/24 We	07:35	♇	SR	25 ♍ 13	22.9 (22:53)

1987

| 1/03 Sa | 12:16 | ♀ | SD | 15 ♈ 31 | -10.5 (-10:31) |
| 2/11 We | 16:56 | ♀ | SR | 9 ♏ 58 | 0.8 (0:50) |

1987		♇	♀	♀	♀
	3/15 Su	9 ♏ 41 ℞	15 ♈ 56 D	1 ♍ 11 ℞	24 ♍ 15 ℞
	3/22 Su	9 ♏ 33	16 ♈ 01	1 ♍ 04	24 ♍ 08
	3/29 Su	9 ♏ 24	16 ♈ 05	0 ♍ 57	24 ♍ 00
	4/05 Su	9 ♏ 14	16 ♈ 10	0 ♍ 51	23 ♍ 52
	4/12 Su	9 ♏ 04	16 ♈ 14	0 ♍ 46	23 ♍ 45
	4/19 Su	8 ♏ 52	16 ♈ 19	0 ♍ 41	23 ♍ 39
	4/26 Su	8 ♏ 40	16 ♈ 24	0 ♍ 38	23 ♍ 33
	5/03 Su	8 ♏ 29	16 ♈ 18	0 ♍ 35	23 ♍ 27
	5/10 Su	8 ♏ 17	16 ♈ 32	0 ♍ 34	23 ♍ 23
	5/17 Su	8 ♏ 05	16 ♈ 36	0 ♍ 34 D	23 ♍ 19
	5/24 Su	7 ♏ 55	16 ♈ 40	0 ♍ 35	23 ♍ 17
	5/31 Su	7 ♏ 44	16 ♈ 43	0 ♍ 36	23 ♍ 15
	6/07 Su	7 ♏ 35	16 ♈ 46	0 ♍ 39	23 ♍ 14
	6/14 Su	7 ♏ 27	16 ♈ 48	0 ♍ 43	23 ♍ 15 D
	6/21 Su	7 ♏ 21	16 ♈ 50	0 ♍ 48	23 ♍ 16
	6/28 Su	7 ♏ 15	16 ♈ 51	0 ♍ 54	23 ♍ 18
	7/05 Su	7 ♏ 11	16 ♈ 52	1 ♍ 01	23 ♍ 22
	7/12 Su	7 ♏ 09	16 ♈ 53	1 ♍ 09	23 ♍ 26
	7/19 Su	7 ♏ 08 D	16 ♈ 52 ℞	1 ♍ 17	23 ♍ 31
	7/26 Su	7 ♏ 09	16 ♈ 52	1 ♍ 26	23 ♍ 37
	8/02 Su	7 ♏ 12	16 ♈ 51	1 ♍ 35	23 ♍ 44
	8/09 Su	7 ♏ 17	16 ♈ 49	1 ♍ 45	23 ♍ 51
	8/16 Su	7 ♏ 23	16 ♈ 47	1 ♍ 54	23 ♍ 59
	8/23 Su	7 ♏ 30	16 ♈ 44	2 ♍ 05	24 ♍ 08
	8/30 Su	7 ♏ 39	16 ♈ 42	2 ♍ 15	24 ♍ 17
	9/06 Su	7 ♏ 50	16 ♈ 38	2 ♍ 25	24 ♍ 26
	9/13 Su	8 ♏ 01	16 ♈ 35	2 ♍ 35	24 ♍ 36
	9/20 Su	8 ♏ 14	16 ♈ 31	2 ♍ 44	24 ♍ 45
	9/27 Su	8 ♏ 29	16 ♈ 27	2 ♍ 54	24 ♍ 55
	10/04 Su	8 ♏ 43	16 ♈ 23	3 ♍ 02	25 ♍ 04
	10/11 Su	8 ♏ 59	16 ♈ 18	3 ♍ 10	25 ♍ 13
	10/18 Su	9 ♏ 15	16 ♈ 14	3 ♍ 18	25 ♍ 22
	10/25 Su	9 ♏ 32	16 ♈ 10	3 ♍ 24	25 ♍ 30
	11/01 Su	9 ♏ 49	16 ♈ 06	3 ♍ 30	25 ♍ 38
	11/08 Su	10 ♏ 06	16 ♈ 02	3 ♍ 35	25 ♍ 45
	11/15 Su	10 ♏ 23	15 ♈ 59	3 ♍ 38	25 ♍ 51
	11/22 Su	10 ♏ 40	15 ♈ 55	3 ♍ 41	25 ♍ 57
	11/29 Su	10 ♏ 56	15 ♈ 53	3 ♍ 42	26 ♍ 01
	12/06 Su	11 ♏ 11	15 ♈ 50	3 ♍ 42 ℞	26 ♍ 05
	12/13 Su	11 ♏ 26	15 ♈ 48	3 ♍ 41	26 ♍ 07

1987		♇	♀	♀	♀
	12/20 Su	11 ♏ 39 D	15 ♈ 47 ℞	3 ♍ 39 ℞	26 ♍ 09 D
	12/27 Su	11 ♏ 51	15 ♈ 46	3 ♍ 36	26 ♍ 09 ℞
1988	1/03 Su	12 ♏ 02	15 ♈ 46	3 ♍ 32	26 ♍ 08
	1/10 Su	12 ♏ 12	15 ♈ 46 D	3 ♍ 27	26 ♍ 06
	1/17 Su	12 ♏ 20	15 ♈ 47	3 ♍ 21	26 ♍ 04
	1/24 Su	12 ♏ 26	15 ♈ 48	3 ♍ 14	26 ♍ 00
	1/31 Su	12 ♏ 31	15 ♈ 50	3 ♍ 07	25 ♍ 55
	2/07 Su	12 ♏ 34	15 ♈ 52	2 ♍ 59	25 ♍ 49
	2/14 Su	12 ♏ 35	15 ♈ 55	2 ♍ 51	25 ♍ 43
	2/21 Su	12 ♏ 34 ℞	15 ♈ 58	2 ♍ 43	25 ♍ 36
	2/28 Su	12 ♏ 31	16 ♈ 02	2 ♍ 34	25 ♍ 29
	3/06 Su	12 ♏ 27	16 ♈ 05	2 ♍ 26	25 ♍ 21
	3/13 Su	12 ♏ 22	16 ♈ 10	2 ♍ 18	25 ♍ 14
	3/20 Su	12 ♏ 14	16 ♈ 14	2 ♍ 11	25 ♍ 06
	3/27 Su	12 ♏ 06	16 ♈ 19	2 ♍ 04	24 ♍ 58
	4/03 Su	11 ♏ 57	16 ♈ 23	1 ♍ 57	24 ♍ 50
	4/10 Su	11 ♏ 46	16 ♈ 28	1 ♍ 52	24 ♍ 43
	4/17 Su	11 ♏ 35	16 ♈ 32	1 ♍ 47	24 ♍ 36
	4/24 Su	11 ♏ 24	16 ♈ 37	1 ♍ 43	24 ♍ 30
	5/01 Su	11 ♏ 12	16 ♈ 41	1 ♍ 40	24 ♍ 25
	5/08 Su	11 ♏ 00	16 ♈ 46	1 ♍ 39	24 ♍ 20
	5/15 Su	10 ♏ 48	16 ♈ 50	1 ♍ 38	24 ♍ 16
	5/22 Su	10 ♏ 37	16 ♈ 53	1 ♍ 39 D	24 ♍ 13
	5/29 Su	10 ♏ 27	16 ♈ 57	1 ♍ 40	24 ♍ 11
	6/05 Su	10 ♏ 17	16 ♈ 59	1 ♍ 43	24 ♍ 10
	6/12 Su	10 ♏ 08	17 ♈ 02	1 ♍ 46	24 ♍ 10 D
	6/19 Su	10 ♏ 01	17 ♈ 04	1 ♍ 51	24 ♍ 11
	6/26 Su	9 ♏ 55	17 ♈ 05	1 ♍ 57	24 ♍ 13
	7/03 Su	9 ♏ 50	17 ♈ 06	2 ♍ 03	24 ♍ 16
	7/10 Su	9 ♏ 47	17 ♈ 07	2 ♍ 10	24 ♍ 20
	7/17 Su	9 ♏ 45	17 ♈ 07 ℞	2 ♍ 18	24 ♍ 25
	7/24 Su	9 ♏ 45 D	17 ♈ 06	2 ♍ 27	24 ♍ 31
	7/31 Su	9 ♏ 47	17 ♈ 05	2 ♍ 36	24 ♍ 37
	8/07 Su	9 ♏ 51	17 ♈ 04	2 ♍ 46	24 ♍ 45
	8/14 Su	9 ♏ 56	17 ♈ 02	2 ♍ 55	24 ♍ 52
	8/21 Su	10 ♏ 02	16 ♈ 59	3 ♍ 06	25 ♍ 01
	8/28 Su	10 ♏ 11	16 ♈ 57	3 ♍ 16	25 ♍ 10

Astro Data

1987						
5/15 Fr	03:05	♎	SD	0 ♍ 34	37.1 (37:05)
6/08 Mo	04:48	♇	SD	23 ♍ 14	23.8 (23:49)
7/18 Sa	06:11	♇	SD	7 ♏ 08	1.7 (1:40)
7/13 Mo	19:36	♀	SR	16 ♈ 53	-9.9 (-9:53)
12/03 Th	18:00	♎	SR	3 ♍ 41	35.9 (35:52)

1987						
12/25 Fr	11:32	♎	SR	26 ♍ 09	12.7 (22:44)
1988						
1/03 Su	19:18	♀	SD	15 ♈ 46	-10.2 (-10:14)
2/14 Su	14:51	♇	SR	12 ♏ 35	-0.1 (0:06)
5/15 Su	13:14	♎	SD	1 ♍ 38	36.8 (36:46)
6/08 We	11:10	♎	SD	24 ♍ 10	23.7 (23:41)
7/13 We	11:34	♀	SR	17 ♈ 07	-9.6 (-9:38)
7/20 We	04:21	♇	SD	9 ♏ 45	0.6 (0:37)

LONGITUDE

		♇	♇	♇	♇
1988	9/04 Su	10 ♏ 20 D	16 ♈ 53 ℞	3 ♍ 26 D	25 ♍ 19 D
	9/11 Su	10 ♏ 31	16 ♈ 50	3 ♍ 36	25 ♍ 28
	9/18 Su	10 ♏ 44	16 ♈ 46	3 ♍ 46	25 ♍ 38
	9/25 Su	10 ♏ 57	16 ♈ 42	3 ♍ 55	25 ♍ 48
	10/02 Su	11 ♏ 12	16 ♈ 38	4 ♍ 04	25 ♍ 57
	10/09 Su	11 ♏ 27	16 ♈ 34	4 ♍ 12	26 ♍ 06
	10/16 Su	11 ♏ 43	16 ♈ 29	4 ♍ 20	26 ♍ 15
	10/23 Su	11 ♏ 59	16 ♈ 25	4 ♍ 27	26 ♍ 24
	10/30 Su	12 ♏ 16	16 ♈ 21	4 ♍ 32	26 ♍ 32
	11/06 Su	12 ♏ 33	16 ♈ 17	4 ♍ 37	26 ♍ 39
	11/13 Su	12 ♏ 50	16 ♈ 14	4 ♍ 41	26 ♍ 45
	11/20 Su	13 ♏ 07	16 ♈ 10	4 ♍ 44	26 ♍ 51
	11/27 Su	13 ♏ 13	16 ♈ 08	4 ♍ 46	26 ♍ 56
	12/04 Su	13 ♏ 39	16 ♈ 05	4 ♍ 47 ℞	27 ♍ 00
	12/11 Su	13 ♏ 54	16 ♈ 03	4 ♍ 46	27 ♍ 03
	12/18 Su	14 ♏ 08	16 ♈ 01	4 ♍ 44	27 ♍ 04
	12/25 Su	14 ♏ 21	16 ♈ 00	4 ♍ 41	27 ♍ 05
1989	1/01 Su	14 ♏ 33	16 ♈ 00	4 ♍ 38	27 ♍ 04 ℞
	1/08 Su	14 ♏ 43	16 ♈ 00 D	4 ♍ 33	27 ♍ 03
	1/15 Su	14 ♏ 52	16 ♈ 01	4 ♍ 27	27 ♍ 00
	1/22 Su	14 ♏ 59	16 ♈ 02	4 ♍ 21	26 ♍ 57
	1/29 Su	15 ♏ 05	16 ♈ 04	4 ♍ 14	26 ♍ 52
	2/05 Su	15 ♏ 09	16 ♈ 06	4 ♍ 06	26 ♍ 47
	2/12 Su	15 ♏ 11	16 ♈ 08	3 ♍ 58	26 ♍ 41
	2/19 Su	15 ♏ 11 ℞	16 ♈ 12	3 ♍ 50	26 ♍ 34
	2/26 Su	15 ♏ 09	16 ♈ 15	3 ♍ 41	26 ♍ 27
	3/05 Su	15 ♏ 06	16 ♈ 19	3 ♍ 33	26 ♍ 20
	3/12 Su	15 ♏ 01	16 ♈ 23	3 ♍ 25	26 ♍ 12
	3/19 Su	14 ♏ 55	16 ♈ 27	3 ♍ 17	26 ♍ 04
	3/26 Su	14 ♏ 47	16 ♈ 32	3 ♍ 10	25 ♍ 56
	4/02 Su	14 ♏ 38	16 ♈ 37	3 ♍ 04	25 ♍ 48
	4/09 Su	14 ♏ 28	16 ♈ 41	2 ♍ 58	25 ♍ 41
	4/16 Su	14 ♏ 18	16 ♈ 46	2 ♍ 53	25 ♍ 34
	4/23 Su	14 ♏ 06	16 ♈ 50	2 ♍ 49	25 ♍ 28
	4/30 Su	13 ♏ 55	16 ♈ 55	2 ♍ 46	25 ♍ 22
	5/07 Su	13 ♏ 43	16 ♈ 59	2 ♍ 44	25 ♍ 17
	5/14 Su	13 ♏ 31	17 ♈ 03	2 ♍ 43	25 ♍ 13

		♇	♇	♇	♇
1989	5/21 Su	13 ♏ 20 ℞	17 ♈ 07 D	2 ♍ 43 D	25 ♍ 10 ℞
	5/28 Su	13 ♏ 09	17 ♈ 10	2 ♍ 44	25 ♍ 07
	6/04 Su	12 ♏ 59	17 ♈ 13	2 ♍ 46	25 ♍ 06
	6/11 Su	12 ♏ 49	17 ♈ 16	2 ♍ 49	25 ♍ 06 D
	6/18 Su	12 ♏ 41	17 ♈ 18	2 ♍ 54	25 ♍ 06
	6/25 Su	12 ♏ 34	17 ♈ 19	2 ♍ 59	25 ♍ 08
	7/02 Su	12 ♏ 29	17 ♈ 21	3 ♍ 05	25 ♍ 11
	7/09 Su	12 ♏ 25	17 ♈ 21	3 ♍ 12	25 ♍ 15
	7/16 Su	12 ♏ 22	17 ♈ 21 ℞	3 ♍ 20	25 ♍ 19
	7/23 Su	12 ♏ 21	17 ♈ 21	3 ♍ 28	25 ♍ 25
	7/30 Su	12 ♏ 22 D	17 ♈ 20	3 ♍ 37	25 ♍ 31
	8/06 Su	12 ♏ 25	17 ♈ 18	3 ♍ 47	25 ♍ 38
	8/13 Su	12 ♏ 29	17 ♈ 17	3 ♍ 57	25 ♍ 46
	8/20 Su	12 ♏ 35	17 ♈ 14	4 ♍ 07	25 ♍ 54
	8/27 Su	12 ♏ 42	17 ♈ 11	4 ♍ 17	26 ♍ 03
	9/03 Su	12 ♏ 51	17 ♈ 08	4 ♍ 27	26 ♍ 12
	9/10 Su	13 ♏ 01	17 ♈ 05	4 ♍ 37	26 ♍ 21
	9/17 Su	13 ♏ 13	17 ♈ 01	4 ♍ 47	26 ♍ 31
	9/24 Su	13 ♏ 26	16 ♈ 57	4 ♍ 56	26 ♍ 41
	10/01 Su	13 ♏ 40	16 ♈ 53	5 ♍ 05	26 ♍ 50
	10/08 Su	13 ♏ 55	16 ♈ 49	5 ♍ 14	26 ♍ 59
	10/15 Su	14 ♏ 10	16 ♈ 45	5 ♍ 22	27 ♍ 08
	10/22 Su	14 ♏ 26	16 ♈ 40	5 ♍ 29	27 ♍ 17
	10/29 Su	14 ♏ 43	16 ♈ 36	5 ♍ 35	27 ♍ 25
	11/05 Su	15 ♏ 00	16 ♈ 32	5 ♍ 40	27 ♍ 33
	11/12 Su	15 ♏ 17	16 ♈ 29	5 ♍ 44	27 ♍ 40
	11/19 Su	15 ♏ 34	16 ♈ 25	5 ♍ 48	27 ♍ 46
	11/26 Su	15 ♏ 50	16 ♈ 22	5 ♍ 50	27 ♍ 51
	12/03 Su	16 ♏ 07	16 ♈ 20	5 ♍ 51	27 ♍ 55
	12/10 Su	16 ♏ 22	16 ♈ 18	5 ♍ 51 ℞	27 ♍ 58
	12/17 Su	16 ♏ 37	16 ♈ 16	5 ♍ 49	28 ♍ 00
	12/24 Su	16 ♏ 50	16 ♈ 15	5 ♍ 47	28 ♍ 01
	12/31 Su	17 ♏ 03	16 ♈ 14	5 ♍ 43	28 ♍ 01 ℞
1990	1/07 Su	17 ♏ 14	16 ♈ 14 D	5 ♍ 39	28 ♍ 00
	1/14 Su	17 ♏ 23	16 ♈ 15	5 ♍ 33	27 ♍ 58
	1/21 Su	17 ♏ 31	16 ♈ 16	5 ♍ 27	27 ♍ 54
	1/28 Su	17 ♏ 38	16 ♈ 18	5 ♍ 20	27 ♍ 50
	2/04 Su	17 ♏ 43	16 ♈ 20	5 ♍ 13	27 ♍ 45

Astro Data

1988

12/03 Sa	23:51	♇	SR	4 ♍ 47	35.5 (35:32)
12/25 Su	18:55	♇	SR	27 ♍ 05	21.6 (22:37)

1989

1/03 Tu	10:16	♀	SD	16 ♈ 00	-10.0 (-9:59)
2/16 Th	09:47	♇	SR	15 ♏ 11	-1.1 (-1:07)
5/16 Tu	23:08	♇	SD	2 ♍ 43	36.5 (36:28)

1989

6/09 Fr	13:20	♇	SD	25 ♍ 06	13.5 (23:32)
7/13 Th	20:15	♀	SR	17 ♈ 21	-9.4 (-9:22)
7/23 Su	03:55	♇	SD	12 ♏ 21	-0.4 (0:25)
12/05 Tu	07:00	♇	SR	5 ♍ 51	35.3 (35:16)
12/17 We	00:42	♇	SR	28 ♍ 01	22.5 (22:27)

1990

1/04 Th	01:31	♀	SD	16 ♈ 14	-9.7 (-9:44)

1990		♇	♀	⚷	⚸
	2/11 Su	17 ♏ 46 D	16 ♈ 22 D	5 ♍ 05 ℞	27 ♍ 39 ℞
	2/18 Su	17 ♏ 47	16 ♈ 25	4 ♍ 57	27 ♍ 33
	2/25 Su	17 ♏ 46 ℞	16 ♈ 29	4 ♍ 48	27 ♍ 26
	3/04 Su	17 ♏ 44	16 ♈ 32	4 ♍ 40	27 ♍ 18
	3/11 Su	17 ♏ 40	16 ♈ 36	4 ♍ 32	27 ♍ 11
	3/18 Su	17 ♏ 34	16 ♈ 41	4 ♍ 24	27 ♍ 03
	3/25 Su	17 ♏ 27	16 ♈ 45	4 ♍ 17	26 ♍ 55
	4/01 Su	17 ♏ 19	16 ♈ 50	4 ♍ 10	26 ♍ 47
	4/08 Su	17 ♏ 10	16 ♈ 54	4 ♍ 04	26 ♍ 39
	4/15 Su	17 ♏ 00	16 ♈ 59	3 ♍ 59	26 ♍ 32
	4/22 Su	16 ♏ 49	17 ♈ 04	3 ♍ 54	26 ♍ 26
	4/29 Su	16 ♏ 37	17 ♈ 08	3 ♍ 51	26 ♍ 20
	5/06 Su	16 ♏ 25	17 ♈ 12	3 ♍ 49	26 ♍ 15
	5/13 Su	16 ♏ 14	17 ♈ 17	3 ♍ 47	26 ♍ 10
	5/20 Su	16 ♏ 02	17 ♈ 20	3 ♍ 47 D	26 ♍ 07
	5/27 Su	15 ♏ 51	17 ♈ 24	3 ♍ 48	26 ♍ 04
	6/03 Su	15 ♏ 40	17 ♈ 27	3 ♍ 50	26 ♍ 02
	6/10 Su	15 ♏ 31	17 ♈ 29	3 ♍ 53	26 ♍ 02
	6/17 Su	15 ♏ 22	17 ♈ 32	3 ♍ 57	26 ♍ 02 D
	6/24 Su	15 ♏ 14	17 ♈ 33	4 ♍ 02	26 ♍ 04
	7/01 Su	15 ♏ 08	17 ♈ 35	4 ♍ 07	26 ♍ 06
	7/08 Su	15 ♏ 03	17 ♈ 35	4 ♍ 14	26 ♍ 10
	7/15 Su	15 ♏ 00	17 ♈ 36 ℞	4 ♍ 22	26 ♍ 14
	7/22 Su	14 ♏ 58	17 ♈ 35	4 ♍ 30	26 ♍ 19
	7/29 Su	14 ♏ 58 D	17 ♈ 34	4 ♍ 39	26 ♍ 25
	8/05 Su	14 ♏ 59	17 ♈ 33	4 ♍ 48	26 ♍ 32
	8/12 Su	15 ♏ 03	17 ♈ 31	4 ♍ 58	26 ♍ 40
	8/19 Su	15 ♏ 07	17 ♈ 29	5 ♍ 08	26 ♍ 48
	8/26 Su	15 ♏ 14	17 ♈ 26	5 ♍ 18	26 ♍ 56
	9/02 Su	15 ♏ 22	17 ♈ 23	5 ♍ 28	27 ♍ 05
	9/09 Su	15 ♏ 31	17 ♈ 20	5 ♍ 38	27 ♍ 15
	9/16 Su	15 ♏ 42	17 ♈ 16	5 ♍ 48	27 ♍ 24
	9/23 Su	15 ♏ 55	17 ♈ 12	5 ♍ 57	27 ♍ 34
	9/30 Su	16 ♏ 08	17 ♈ 08	6 ♍ 07	27 ♍ 43
	10/07 Su	16 ♏ 22	17 ♈ 04	6 ♍ 15	27 ♍ 53
	10/14 Su	16 ♏ 37	17 ♈ 00	6 ♍ 23	28 ♍ 02
	10/21 Su	16 ♏ 53	16 ♈ 56	6 ♍ 31	28 ♍ 11
	10/28 Su	17 ♏ 10	16 ♈ 51	6 ♍ 37	28 ♍ 19
	11/04 Su	17 ♏ 26	16 ♈ 47	6 ♍ 43	28 ♍ 27
	11/11 Su	17 ♏ 43	16 ♈ 44	6 ♍ 47	28 ♍ 34

1990		♇	♀	⚷	⚸
	11/18 Su	18 ♏ 00 D	16 ♈ 40 ℞	6 ♍ 51 D	28 ♍ 40 D
	11/25 Su	18 ♏ 17	16 ♈ 37	6 ♍ 53	28 ♍ 46
	12/02 Su	18 ♏ 33	16 ♈ 35	6 ♍ 55	28 ♍ 50
	12/09 Su	18 ♏ 49	16 ♈ 32	6 ♍ 55 ℞	28 ♍ 54
	12/16 Su	19 ♏ 04	16 ♈ 31	6 ♍ 54	28 ♍ 56
	12/23 Su	19 ♏ 18	16 ♈ 29	6 ♍ 52	28 ♍ 57
	12/30 Su	19 ♏ 31	16 ♈ 29	6 ♍ 49	28 ♍ 58 ℞
1991	1/06 Su	19 ♏ 43	16 ♈ 29 D	6 ♍ 45	28 ♍ 57
	1/13 Su	19 ♏ 54	16 ♈ 29	6 ♍ 40	28 ♍ 55
	1/20 Su	20 ♏ 03	16 ♈ 30	6 ♍ 34	28 ♍ 52
	1/27 Su	20 ♏ 10	16 ♈ 31	6 ♍ 27	28 ♍ 48
	2/03 Su	20 ♏ 16	16 ♈ 33	6 ♍ 20	28 ♍ 43
	2/10 Su	20 ♏ 20	16 ♈ 36	6 ♍ 12	28 ♍ 38
	2/17 Su	20 ♏ 22	16 ♈ 39	6 ♍ 04	28 ♍ 31
	2/24 Su	20 ♏ 22 ℞	16 ♈ 42	5 ♍ 56	28 ♍ 24
	3/03 Su	20 ♏ 21	16 ♈ 46	5 ♍ 47	28 ♍ 17
	3/10 Su	20 ♏ 18	16 ♈ 50	5 ♍ 39	28 ♍ 09
	3/17 Su	20 ♏ 13	16 ♈ 54	5 ♍ 31	28 ♍ 02
	3/24 Su	20 ♏ 07	16 ♈ 58	5 ♍ 24	27 ♍ 54
	3/31 Su	19 ♏ 59	17 ♈ 03	5 ♍ 17	27 ♍ 46
	4/07 Su	19 ♏ 51	17 ♈ 08	5 ♍ 10	27 ♍ 38
	4/14 Su	19 ♏ 41	17 ♈ 12	5 ♍ 05	27 ♍ 31
	4/21 Su	19 ♏ 30	17 ♈ 17	5 ♍ 00	27 ♍ 24
	4/28 Su	19 ♏ 19	17 ♈ 21	4 ♍ 56	27 ♍ 18
	5/05 Su	19 ♏ 08	17 ♈ 26	4 ♍ 54	27 ♍ 13
	5/12 Su	18 ♏ 56	17 ♈ 30	4 ♍ 52	27 ♍ 08
	5/19 Su	18 ♏ 44	17 ♈ 34	4 ♍ 51	27 ♍ 04
	5/26 Su	18 ♏ 33	17 ♈ 37	4 ♍ 52 D	27 ♍ 01
	6/02 Su	18 ♏ 22	17 ♈ 40	4 ♍ 53	26 ♍ 59
	6/09 Su	18 ♏ 12	17 ♈ 43	4 ♍ 56	26 ♍ 58
	6/16 Su	18 ♏ 02	17 ♈ 45	5 ♍ 00	26 ♍ 58 D
	6/23 Su	17 ♏ 54	17 ♈ 47	5 ♍ 04	26 ♍ 59
	6/30 Su	17 ♏ 47	17 ♈ 49	5 ♍ 10	27 ♍ 02
	7/07 Su	17 ♏ 41	17 ♈ 49	5 ♍ 16	27 ♍ 05
	7/14 Su	17 ♏ 37	17 ♈ 50	5 ♍ 23	27 ♍ 09
	7/21 Su	17 ♏ 34	17 ♈ 49 ℞	5 ♍ 31	27 ♍ 14
	7/28 Su	17 ♏ 33	17 ♈ 49	5 ♍ 40	27 ♍ 20

Astro Data

1990

2/19 Mo	06:31	♇	SR	17 ♏ 47	-2.1	(-2:04)
5/18 Fr	07:46	⚷	SD	3 ♍ 47	36.2	(36:11)
6/10 Su	15:30	⚸	SD	26 ♍ 02	23.4	(23:22)
7/14 Sa	03:13	♀	SR	17 ♈ 36	-9.1	(-9:07)
7/26 Th	01:26	♇	SD	14 ♏ 58	-1.4	(-1:25)

1990

12/06 Th	16:47	⚷	SR	6 ♍ 55	34.9	(34:56)
12/18 Fr	03:56	⚸	SR	28 ♍ 58	22.3	(22:17)

1991

1/04 Fr	13:26	♀	SD	16 ♈ 29	-9.5	(-9:28)
2/22 Fr	01:28	♇	SR	20 ♏ 22	-3.1	(-3:04)
5/19 Su	13:20	⚷	SD	4 ♍ 51	35.8	(35:49)
6/11 Tu	18:50	⚸	SD	26 ♍ 58	23.2	(23:13)
7/14 Su	15:05	♀	SR	17 ♈ 50	-8.9	(-8:52)
7/28 Su	23:48	♇	SD	17 ♏ 33	-2.5	(-2:28)

LONGITUDE

		♇	♀	♆	♎			♇	♀	♆	♎
1991	8/04 Su	17 ♏ 34 D	17 ♈ 48 ℞	5 ♍ 49 D	27 ♍ 26 D	1992	4/19 Su	22 ♏ 11 ℞	17 ♈ 30 D	6 ♍ 06 ℞	28 ♍ 23 ℞
	8/11 Su	17 ♏ 36	17 ♈ 46	5 ♍ 59	27 ♍ 34		4/26 Su	22 ♏ 00	17 ♈ 35	6 ♍ 02	28 ♍ 16
	8/18 Su	17 ♏ 40	17 ♈ 44	6 ♍ 08	27 ♍ 42		5/03 Su	21 ♏ 49	17 ♈ 39	5 ♍ 59	28 ♍ 11
	8/25 Su	17 ♏ 46	17 ♈ 41	6 ♍ 18	27 ♍ 50		5/10 Su	21 ♏ 37	17 ♈ 43	5 ♍ 57	28 ♍ 06
	9/01 Su	17 ♏ 53	17 ♈ 38	6 ♍ 29	27 ♍ 59		5/17 Su	21 ♏ 26	17 ♈ 47	5 ♍ 56	28 ♍ 02
	9/08 Su	18 ♏ 02	17 ♈ 35	6 ♍ 39	28 ♍ 08		5/24 Su	21 ♏ 14	17 ♈ 51	5 ♍ 56 D	27 ♍ 59
	9/15 Su	18 ♏ 12	17 ♈ 31	6 ♍ 49	28 ♍ 18		5/31 Su	21 ♏ 03	17 ♈ 54	5 ♍ 57	27 ♍ 56
	9/22 Su	18 ♏ 23	17 ♈ 27	6 ♍ 58	28 ♍ 27		6/07 Su	20 ♏ 52	17 ♈ 57	5 ♍ 59	27 ♍ 55
	9/29 Su	18 ♏ 36	17 ♈ 23	7 ♍ 08	28 ♍ 37		6/14 Su	20 ♏ 42	17 ♈ 59	6 ♍ 02	27 ♍ 55 D
	10/06 Su	18 ♏ 50	17 ♈ 19	7 ♍ 17	28 ♍ 46		6/21 Su	20 ♏ 33	18 ♈ 01	6 ♍ 07	27 ♍ 56
	10/13 Su	19 ♏ 04	17 ♈ 15	7 ♍ 25	28 ♍ 56		6/28 Su	20 ♏ 26	18 ♈ 02	6 ♍ 12	27 ♍ 57
	10/20 Su	19 ♏ 20	17 ♈ 11	7 ♍ 33	29 ♍ 05		7/05 Su	20 ♏ 19	18 ♈ 03	6 ♍ 18	28 ♍ 00
	10/27 Su	19 ♏ 36	17 ♈ 06	7 ♍ 39	29 ♍ 13		7/12 Su	20 ♏ 14	18 ♈ 04	6 ♍ 25	28 ♍ 04
	11/03 Su	19 ♏ 53	17 ♈ 02	7 ♍ 45	29 ♍ 21		7/19 Su	20 ♏ 11	18 ♈ 04 ℞	6 ♍ 33	28 ♍ 09
	11/10 Su	20 ♏ 09	16 ♈ 59	7 ♍ 50	29 ♍ 28		7/26 Su	20 ♏ 09	18 ♈ 03	6 ♍ 41	28 ♍ 14
	11/17 Su	20 ♏ 26	16 ♈ 55	7 ♍ 54	29 ♍ 35		8/02 Su	20 ♏ 08 D	18 ♈ 02	6 ♍ 50	28 ♍ 21
	11/24 Su	20 ♏ 43	16 ♈ 52	7 ♍ 57	29 ♍ 41		8/09 Su	20 ♏ 10	18 ♈ 00	6 ♍ 59	28 ♍ 28
	12/01 Su	21 ♏ 00	16 ♈ 49	7 ♍ 59	29 ♍ 45		8/16 Su	20 ♏ 13	17 ♈ 58	7 ♍ 09	28 ♍ 36
	12/08 Su	21 ♏ 16	16 ♈ 47	7 ♍ 59	29 ♍ 49		8/23 Su	20 ♏ 17	17 ♈ 56	7 ♍ 19	28 ♍ 44
	12/15 Su	21 ♏ 31	16 ♈ 45	7 ♍ 59 ℞	29 ♍ 52		8/30 Su	20 ♏ 24	17 ♈ 53	7 ♍ 29	28 ♍ 53
	12/22 Su	21 ♏ 46	16 ♈ 44	7 ♍ 57	29 ♍ 54		9/06 Su	20 ♏ 32	17 ♈ 50	7 ♍ 40	29 ♍ 02
	12/29 Su	21 ♏ 59	16 ♈ 43	7 ♍ 54	29 ♍ 54		9/13 Su	20 ♏ 41	17 ♈ 46	7 ♍ 50	29 ♍ 11
1992	1/05 Su	22 ♏ 12	16 ♈ 43 D	7 ♍ 50	29 ♍ 54 ℞		9/20 Su	20 ♏ 52	17 ♈ 42	7 ♍ 59	29 ♍ 21
	1/12 Su	22 ♏ 23	16 ♈ 43	7 ♍ 46	29 ♍ 52		9/27 Su	21 ♏ 04	17 ♈ 38	8 ♍ 09	29 ♍ 31
	1/19 Su	22 ♏ 33	16 ♈ 44	7 ♍ 40	29 ♍ 50		10/04 Su	21 ♏ 17	17 ♈ 34	8 ♍ 18	29 ♍ 40
	1/26 Su	22 ♏ 41	16 ♈ 45	7 ♍ 33	29 ♍ 46		10/11 Su	21 ♏ 31	17 ♈ 30	8 ♍ 26	29 ♍ 50
	2/02 Su	22 ♏ 48	16 ♈ 47	7 ♍ 26	29 ♍ 42		10/18 Su	21 ♏ 46	17 ♈ 26	8 ♍ 34	29 ♍ 59
	2/09 Su	22 ♏ 52	16 ♈ 49	7 ♍ 19	29 ♍ 36		10/25 Su	22 ♏ 02	17 ♈ 21	8 ♍ 41	0 ♎ 07
	2/16 Su	22 ♏ 55	16 ♈ 52	7 ♍ 11	29 ♍ 30		11/01 Su	22 ♏ 18	17 ♈ 17	8 ♍ 47	0 ♎ 16
	2/23 Su	22 ♏ 57	16 ♈ 55	7 ♍ 02	29 ♍ 23		11/08 Su	22 ♏ 35	17 ♈ 14	8 ♍ 53	0 ♎ 23
	3/01 Su	22 ♏ 56 ℞	16 ♈ 59	6 ♍ 54	29 ♍ 16		11/15 Su	22 ♏ 52	17 ♈ 10	8 ♍ 57	0 ♎ 30
	3/08 Su	22 ♏ 54	17 ♈ 03	6 ♍ 46	29 ♍ 08		11/22 Su	23 ♏ 08	17 ♈ 07	9 ♍ 00	0 ♎ 36
	3/15 Su	22 ♏ 51	17 ♈ 07	6 ♍ 38	29 ♍ 01		11/29 Su	23 ♏ 25	17 ♈ 04	9 ♍ 02	0 ♎ 41
	3/22 Su	22 ♏ 45	17 ♈ 12	6 ♍ 30	28 ♍ 53		12/06 Su	23 ♏ 41	17 ♈ 01	9 ♍ 03	0 ♎ 45
	3/29 Su	22 ♏ 38	17 ♈ 16	6 ♍ 23	28 ♍ 45		12/13 Su	23 ♏ 57	17 ♈ 00	9 ♍ 03 ℞	0 ♎ 48
	4/05 Su	22 ♏ 30	17 ♈ 21	6 ♍ 17	28 ♍ 37		12/20 Su	24 ♏ 12	16 ♈ 58	9 ♍ 02	0 ♎ 50
	4/12 Su	22 ♏ 21	17 ♈ 25	6 ♍ 11	28 ♍ 30		12/27 Su	24 ♏ 26	16 ♈ 57	8 ♍ 59	0 ♎ 51

Astro Data

1991						
12/08 Su	00:40	♆	SR	7 ♍ 59	34.7 (34:39)	
1992						
1/04 Sa	19:48	♀	SD	16 ♈ 43	-9.1 (-9:13)	
12/29 Su	07:46	♎	SR	29 ♍ 54	22.2 (22:09)	
2/24 Mo	21:33	♇	SR	22 ♏ 57	-4.0 (-4:01)	

1992						
5/19 Tu	21:11	♆	SD	5 ♍ 56	35.5 (35:31)	
6/12 Fr	01:23	♎	SD	27 ♍ 55	23.1 (23:04)	
7/14 Tu	07:19	♀	SR	18 ♈ 04	-8.6 (-8:37)	
7/30 Th	21:35	♇	SD	20 ♏ 08	-3.5 (-3:27)	
10/18 Su	13:47	♎	→ ♎		21.9 (21:52)	
12/08 Tu	07:32	♆	SR	9 ♍ 03	34.3 (34:17)	
12/29 Tu	11:06	♎	SR	0 ♎ 51	22.0 (21:58)	
1993						
1/04 Mo	08:02	♀	SR	16 ♈ 57	-9.0 (-8:57)	

1993	♇	♀	⚳	⚴
1/03 Su	24 ♏ 39 D	16 ♈ 57 R	8 ♍ 56 R	0 ♎ 51 R
1/10 Su	24 ♏ 51	16 ♈ 57 D	8 ♍ 51	0 ♎ 50
1/17 Su	25 ♏ 02	16 ♈ 58	8 ♍ 46	0 ♎ 48
1/24 Su	25 ♏ 11	16 ♈ 59	8 ♍ 40	0 ♎ 44
1/31 Su	25 ♏ 18	17 ♈ 01	8 ♍ 33	0 ♎ 40
2/07 Su	25 ♏ 24	17 ♈ 03	8 ♍ 25	0 ♎ 35
2/14 Su	25 ♏ 28	17 ♈ 06	8 ♍ 17	0 ♎ 29
2/21 Su	25 ♏ 30	17 ♈ 09	8 ♍ 09	0 ♎ 22
2/28 Su	25 ♏ 31 R	17 ♈ 12	8 ♍ 01	0 ♎ 15
3/07 Su	25 ♏ 30	17 ♈ 16	7 ♍ 53	0 ♎ 08
3/14 Su	25 ♏ 27	17 ♈ 20	7 ♍ 45	0 ♎ 00
3/21 Su	25 ♏ 22	17 ♈ 25	7 ♍ 37	29 ♍ 52
3/28 Su	25 ♏ 16	17 ♈ 29	7 ♍ 29	29 ♍ 44
4/04 Su	25 ♏ 09	17 ♈ 34	7 ♍ 23	29 ♍ 36
4/11 Su	25 ♏ 00	17 ♈ 39	7 ♍ 17	29 ♍ 29
4/18 Su	24 ♏ 51	17 ♈ 43	7 ♍ 11	29 ♍ 22
4/25 Su	24 ♏ 40	17 ♈ 48	7 ♍ 07	29 ♍ 15
5/02 Su	24 ♏ 29	17 ♈ 52	7 ♍ 04	29 ♍ 09
5/09 Su	24 ♏ 18	17 ♈ 56	7 ♍ 01	29 ♍ 04
5/16 Su	24 ♏ 06	18 ♈ 00	7 ♍ 00	29 ♍ 00
5/23 Su	23 ♏ 55	18 ♈ 04	7 ♍ 00 D	28 ♍ 56
5/30 Su	23 ♏ 43	18 ♈ 07	7 ♍ 00	28 ♍ 54
6/06 Su	23 ♏ 32	18 ♈ 10	7 ♍ 02	28 ♍ 52
6/13 Su	23 ♏ 22	18 ♈ 12	7 ♍ 05	28 ♍ 51
6/20 Su	23 ♏ 13	18 ♈ 15	7 ♍ 09	28 ♍ 52 D
6/27 Su	23 ♏ 04	18 ♈ 16	7 ♍ 14	28 ♍ 53
7/04 Su	22 ♏ 57	18 ♈ 17	7 ♍ 20	28 ♍ 56
7/11 Su	22 ♏ 51	18 ♈ 18	7 ♍ 27	28 ♍ 59
7/18 Su	22 ♏ 47	18 ♈ 18 R	7 ♍ 34	29 ♍ 04
7/25 Su	22 ♏ 44	18 ♈ 17	7 ♍ 42	29 ♍ 09
8/01 Su	22 ♏ 43	18 ♈ 16	7 ♍ 51	29 ♍ 15
8/08 Su	22 ♏ 43 D	18 ♈ 15	8 ♍ 00	29 ♍ 22
8/15 Su	22 ♏ 45	18 ♈ 13	8 ♍ 10	29 ♍ 30
8/22 Su	22 ♏ 49	18 ♈ 10	8 ♍ 20	29 ♍ 38
8/29 Su	22 ♏ 54	18 ♈ 07	8 ♍ 30	29 ♍ 47
9/05 Su	23 ♏ 01	18 ♈ 04	8 ♍ 40	29 ♍ 56
9/12 Su	23 ♏ 10	18 ♈ 01	8 ♍ 50	0 ♎ 05
9/19 Su	23 ♏ 20	17 ♈ 57	9 ♍ 00	0 ♎ 15
9/26 Su	23 ♏ 31	17 ♈ 53	9 ♍ 10	0 ♎ 25
10/03 Su	23 ♏ 43	17 ♈ 49	9 ♍ 19	0 ♎ 34

1993	♇	♀	⚳	⚴
10/10 Su	23 ♏ 57 D	17 ♈ 45 R	9 ♍ 28 D	0 ♎ 44 D
10/17 Su	24 ♏ 12	17 ♈ 40	9 ♍ 36	0 ♎ 53
10/24 Su	24 ♏ 27	17 ♈ 36	9 ♍ 43	1 ♎ 02
10/31 Su	24 ♏ 43	17 ♈ 32	9 ♍ 49	1 ♎ 10
11/07 Su	24 ♏ 59	17 ♈ 28	9 ♍ 55	1 ♎ 18
11/14 Su	25 ♏ 16	17 ♈ 25	10 ♍ 00	1 ♎ 25
11/21 Su	25 ♏ 33	17 ♈ 21	10 ♍ 03	1 ♎ 31
11/28 Su	25 ♏ 50	17 ♈ 18	10 ♍ 05	1 ♎ 37
12/05 Su	26 ♏ 06	17 ♈ 16	10 ♍ 07	1 ♎ 41
12/12 Su	26 ♏ 22	17 ♈ 14	10 ♍ 07 R	1 ♎ 44
12/19 Su	26 ♏ 38	17 ♈ 12	10 ♍ 06	1 ♎ 47
12/26 Su	26 ♏ 52	17 ♈ 11	10 ♍ 04	1 ♎ 48

1994	♇	♀	⚳	⚴
1/02 Su	27 ♏ 06	17 ♈ 11	10 ♍ 01	1 ♎ 48 R
1/09 Su	27 ♏ 18	17 ♈ 11 D	9 ♍ 57	1 ♎ 47
1/16 Su	27 ♏ 30	17 ♈ 11	9 ♍ 52	1 ♎ 45
1/23 Su	27 ♏ 39	17 ♈ 13	9 ♍ 46	1 ♎ 42
1/30 Su	27 ♏ 48	17 ♈ 14	9 ♍ 39	1 ♎ 38
2/06 Su	27 ♏ 54	17 ♈ 16	9 ♍ 32	1 ♎ 34
2/13 Su	27 ♏ 59	17 ♈ 19	9 ♍ 24	1 ♎ 28
2/20 Su	28 ♏ 02	17 ♈ 22	9 ♍ 16	1 ♎ 22
2/27 Su	28 ♏ 04	17 ♈ 26	9 ♍ 08	1 ♎ 15
3/06 Su	28 ♏ 04 R	17 ♈ 29	8 ♍ 59	1 ♎ 07
3/13 Su	28 ♏ 02	17 ♈ 33	8 ♍ 51	0 ♎ 59
3/20 Su	27 ♏ 58	17 ♈ 38	8 ♍ 43	0 ♎ 52
3/27 Su	27 ♏ 53	17 ♈ 42	8 ♍ 36	0 ♎ 44
4/03 Su	27 ♏ 46	17 ♈ 47	8 ♍ 29	0 ♎ 36
4/10 Su	27 ♏ 38	17 ♈ 51	8 ♍ 22	0 ♎ 28
4/17 Su	27 ♏ 29	17 ♈ 56	8 ♍ 17	0 ♎ 21
4/24 Su	27 ♏ 19	18 ♈ 01	8 ♍ 12	0 ♎ 14
5/01 Su	27 ♏ 09	18 ♈ 05	8 ♍ 09	0 ♎ 08
5/08 Su	26 ♏ 57	18 ♈ 09	8 ♍ 06	0 ♎ 02
5/15 Su	26 ♏ 46	18 ♈ 13	8 ♍ 04	29 ♍ 58
5/22 Su	26 ♏ 34	18 ♈ 17	8 ♍ 03	29 ♍ 54
5/29 Su	26 ♏ 23	18 ♈ 20	8 ♍ 04 D	29 ♍ 51
6/05 Su	26 ♏ 12	18 ♈ 23	8 ♍ 05	29 ♍ 49
6/12 Su	26 ♏ 01	18 ♈ 26	8 ♍ 08	29 ♍ 48
6/19 Su	25 ♏ 51	18 ♈ 28	8 ♍ 12	29 ♍ 49 D

Astro Data

1993

2/26 Fr	14:30	♀	SR	25 ♏ 31	-5.0 (-5:01)
3/14 Su	10:25	⚴	→ ♍ R		22.7 (22:43)
5/21 Fr	06:08	⚳	SD	7 ♍ 00	35.2 (35:12)
6/13 Su	09:31	⚴	SD	28 ♍ 51	22.9 (22:52)
7/14 We	18:29	♀	SR	18 ♈ 18	-8.4 (-8:21)
8/02 Mo	19:29	♇	SD	22 ♏ 43	-4.5 (-4:30)
9/07 Tu	17:09	⚴	→ ♎		21.0 (22:02)

1993

12/09 Th	13:21	⚳	SR	10 ♍ 07	33.9 (33:55)
12/30 Th	18:45	⚴	SR	1 ♎ 48	21.8 (21:47)

1994

1/05 We	00:36	♀	SD	17 ♈ 11	-8.7 (-8:41)
3/01 Tu	10:01	♇	SR	28 ♏ 04	-5.9 (-5:56)
5/12 Th	08:18	⚴	→ ♍ R		22.8 (22:49)
5/22 Su	15:33	⚳	SD	8 ♍ 03	34.8 (34:49)
6/14 Tu	12:40	⚴	SD	29 ♍ 48	22.7 (22:42)

1994

Date	♇	♀	♎	♏
6/26 Su	25 ♏ 42 R	18 ♈ 30 D	8 ♍ 16 D	29 ♍ 50 D
7/03 Su	25 ♏ 34	18 ♈ 31	8 ♍ 22	29 ♍ 52
7/10 Su	25 ♏ 28	18 ♈ 32	8 ♍ 28	29 ♍ 55
7/17 Su	25 ♏ 23	18 ♈ 32 R	8 ♍ 35	29 ♍ 59
7/24 Su	25 ♏ 19	18 ♈ 31	8 ♍ 43	0 ♎ 04
7/31 Su	25 ♏ 17	18 ♈ 30	8 ♍ 52	0 ♎ 10
8/07 Su	25 ♏ 16 D	18 ♈ 29	9 ♍ 01	0 ♎ 17
8/14 Su	25 ♏ 17	18 ♈ 27	9 ♍ 10	0 ♎ 24
8/21 Su	25 ♏ 20	18 ♈ 25	9 ♍ 20	0 ♎ 32
8/28 Su	25 ♏ 25	18 ♈ 22	9 ♍ 30	0 ♎ 41
9/04 Su	25 ♏ 31	18 ♈ 19	9 ♍ 40	0 ♎ 50
9/11 Su	25 ♏ 38	18 ♈ 15	9 ♍ 51	0 ♎ 59
9/18 Su	25 ♏ 47	18 ♈ 12	10 ♍ 01	1 ♎ 09
9/25 Su	25 ♏ 58	18 ♈ 08	10 ♍ 10	1 ♎ 19
10/02 Su	26 ♏ 10	18 ♈ 04	10 ♍ 20	1 ♎ 28
10/09 Su	26 ♏ 23	17 ♈ 59	10 ♍ 28	1 ♎ 38
10/16 Su	26 ♏ 37	17 ♈ 55	10 ♍ 37	1 ♎ 47
10/23 Su	26 ♏ 51	17 ♈ 51	10 ♍ 44	1 ♎ 56
10/30 Su	27 ♏ 07	17 ♈ 47	10 ♍ 51	2 ♎ 05
11/06 Su	27 ♏ 23	17 ♈ 43	10 ♍ 57	2 ♎ 13
11/13 Su	27 ♏ 40	17 ♈ 39	11 ♍ 02	2 ♎ 20
11/20 Su	27 ♏ 56	17 ♈ 36	11 ♍ 06	2 ♎ 26
11/27 Su	28 ♏ 13	17 ♈ 33	11 ♍ 08	2 ♎ 32
12/04 Su	28 ♏ 30	17 ♈ 30	11 ♍ 10	2 ♎ 37
12/11 Su	28 ♏ 46	17 ♈ 28	11 ♍ 11 R	2 ♎ 41
12/18 Su	29 ♏ 02	17 ♈ 17	11 ♍ 10	2 ♎ 43
12/25 Su	29 ♏ 17	17 ♈ 25	11 ♍ 08	2 ♎ 45

1995

Date	♇	♀	♎	♏
1/01 Su	29 ♏ 31	17 ♈ 25	11 ♍ 06	2 ♎ 46
1/08 Su	29 ♏ 44	17 ♈ 25 D	11 ♍ 02	2 ♎ 45 R
1/15 Su	29 ♏ 56	17 ♈ 15	10 ♍ 57	2 ♎ 43
1/22 Su	0 ♐ 06	17 ♈ 26	10 ♍ 51	2 ♎ 41
1/29 Su	0 ♐ 15	17 ♈ 28	10 ♍ 45	2 ♎ 37
2/05 Su	0 ♐ 23	17 ♈ 30	10 ♍ 38	2 ♎ 32
2/12 Su	0 ♐ 29	17 ♈ 32	10 ♍ 30	2 ♎ 27
2/19 Su	0 ♐ 33	17 ♈ 35	10 ♍ 22	2 ♎ 21
2/26 Su	0 ♐ 35	17 ♈ 39	10 ♍ 14	2 ♎ 14
3/05 Su	0 ♐ 36 R	17 ♈ 43	10 ♍ 06	2 ♎ 07
3/12 Su	0 ♐ 35 R	17 ♈ 47 D	9 ♍ 57 R	1 ♎ 59 R
3/19 Su	0 ♐ 32	17 ♈ 51	9 ♍ 49	1 ♎ 51
3/26 Su	0 ♐ 28	17 ♈ 55	9 ♍ 42	1 ♎ 43
4/02 Su	0 ♐ 22	18 ♈ 00	9 ♍ 35	1 ♎ 35
4/09 Su	0 ♐ 15	18 ♈ 04	9 ♍ 28	1 ♎ 28
4/16 Su	0 ♐ 06	18 ♈ 09	9 ♍ 22	1 ♎ 20
4/23 Su	29 ♏ 57	18 ♈ 14	9 ♍ 17	1 ♎ 13
4/30 Su	29 ♏ 47	18 ♈ 18	9 ♍ 13	1 ♎ 07
5/07 Su	29 ♏ 36	18 ♈ 22	9 ♍ 10	1 ♎ 01
5/14 Su	29 ♏ 24	18 ♈ 26	9 ♍ 08	0 ♎ 56
5/21 Su	29 ♏ 13	18 ♈ 30	9 ♍ 07	0 ♎ 52
5/28 Su	29 ♏ 01	18 ♈ 34	9 ♍ 07 D	0 ♎ 49
6/04 Su	28 ♏ 50	18 ♈ 37	9 ♍ 08	0 ♎ 47
6/11 Su	28 ♏ 39	18 ♈ 39	9 ♍ 11	0 ♎ 46
6/18 Su	28 ♏ 29	18 ♈ 42	9 ♍ 14	0 ♎ 45 D
6/25 Su	28 ♏ 19	18 ♈ 43	9 ♍ 18	0 ♎ 46
7/02 Su	28 ♏ 11	18 ♈ 45	9 ♍ 23	0 ♎ 48
7/09 Su	28 ♏ 03	18 ♈ 45	9 ♍ 30	0 ♎ 51
7/16 Su	27 ♏ 58	18 ♈ 46 R	9 ♍ 37	0 ♎ 55
7/23 Su	27 ♏ 53	18 ♈ 45	9 ♍ 44	1 ♎ 00
7/30 Su	27 ♏ 50	18 ♈ 44	9 ♍ 53	1 ♎ 05
8/06 Su	27 ♏ 49	18 ♈ 43	10 ♍ 01	1 ♎ 12
8/13 Su	27 ♏ 49 D	18 ♈ 41	10 ♍ 11	1 ♎ 19
8/20 Su	27 ♏ 51	18 ♈ 39	10 ♍ 21	1 ♎ 27
8/27 Su	27 ♏ 54	18 ♈ 37	10 ♍ 30	1 ♎ 35
9/03 Su	27 ♏ 59	18 ♈ 33	10 ♍ 41	1 ♎ 44
9/10 Su	28 ♏ 06	18 ♈ 30	10 ♍ 51	1 ♎ 53
9/17 Su	28 ♏ 14	18 ♈ 26	11 ♍ 01	2 ♎ 03
9/24 Su	28 ♏ 34	18 ♈ 23	11 ♍ 11	2 ♎ 13
10/01 Su	28 ♏ 35	18 ♈ 18	11 ♍ 20	2 ♎ 22
10/08 Su	28 ♏ 47	18 ♈ 14	11 ♍ 29	2 ♎ 32
10/15 Su	29 ♏ 01	18 ♈ 10	11 ♍ 37	2 ♎ 41
10/22 Su	29 ♏ 15	18 ♈ 06	11 ♍ 45	2 ♎ 51
10/29 Su	29 ♏ 30	18 ♈ 02	11 ♍ 52	2 ♎ 59
11/05 Su	29 ♏ 46	17 ♈ 58	11 ♍ 58	3 ♎ 07
11/12 Su	0 ♐ 02	17 ♈ 54	12 ♍ 04	3 ♎ 15
11/19 Su	0 ♐ 19	17 ♈ 51	12 ♍ 08	3 ♎ 22
11/26 Su	0 ♐ 36	17 ♈ 48	12 ♍ 11	3 ♎ 28
12/03 Su	0 ♐ 52	17 ♈ 45	12 ♍ 13	3 ♎ 33
12/10 Su	1 ♐ 09	17 ♈ 43	12 ♍ 14	3 ♎ 37

Astro Data

1994

Date	Time	Planet	Event	Position	Value
7/15 Fr	00:08	♀	SR	18 ♈ 32	-8.1 (-8:06)
7/17 Su	08:58	♏	→ ♎		22.4 (22:24)
8/05 Fr	17:07	♀	SD	25 ♏ 16	-5.5 (-5:28)
12/10 Sa	18:15	♏	SR	11 ♍ 11	33.6 (33:33)

1995

Date	Time	Planet	Event	Position	Value
1/05 Th	11:04	♀	SD	17 ♈ 25	-8.4 (-8:16)
1/01 Su	00:49	♎	SR	2 ♎ 46	21.6 (21:38)
1/17 Tu	09:16	♀	→ ♐		-7.0 (-7:01)
3/04 Sa	02:34	♀	SR	0 ♐ 36	-6.9 (-6:54)

1995

Date	Time	Planet	Event	Position	Value
4/21 Fr	02:57	♀	→ ♏ R		-6.6 (-6:33)
5/24 We	01:50	♏	SD	9 ♍ 07	34.5 (34:28)
6/15 Th	16:41	♎	SD	0 ♎ 45	22.5 (22:32)
7/15 Sa	13:28	♀	SR	18 ♈ 46	-7.8 (-7:50)
8/08 Tu	13:34	♀	SD	27 ♏ 48	-6.5 (-6:28)
11/10 Fr	19:12	♀	→ ♐		-7.5 (-7:30)
12/12 Tu	03:16	♏	SR	12 ♍ 14	33.2 (33:14)

LONGITUDE

		♇	♀	⯓	⯔
1995	12/17 Su	1 ♐ 25 D	17 ♈ 41 ℞	12 ♍ 14 ℞	3 ♎ 40 D
	12/24 Su	1 ♐ 40	17 ♈ 40	12 ♍ 12	3 ♎ 42
	12/31 Su	1 ♐ 54	17 ♈ 39	12 ♍ 10	3 ♎ 43
1996	1/07 Su	2 ♐ 08	17 ♈ 39 D	12 ♍ 06	3 ♎ 43 ℞
	1/14 Su	2 ♐ 20	17 ♈ 39	12 ♍ 02	3 ♎ 41
	1/21 Su	2 ♐ 32	17 ♈ 40	11 ♍ 57	3 ♎ 39
	1/28 Su	2 ♐ 41	17 ♈ 41	11 ♍ 50	3 ♎ 36
	2/04 Su	2 ♐ 50	17 ♈ 43	11 ♍ 43	3 ♎ 31
	2/11 Su	2 ♐ 56	17 ♈ 46	11 ♍ 36	3 ♎ 26
	2/18 Su	3 ♐ 01	17 ♈ 49	11 ♍ 28	3 ♎ 20
	2/25 Su	3 ♐ 05	17 ♈ 52	11 ♍ 20	3 ♎ 13
	3/03 Su	3 ♐ 06	17 ♈ 56	11 ♍ 12	3 ♎ 06
	3/10 Su	3 ♐ 06 ℞	18 ♈ 00	11 ♍ 03	2 ♎ 59
	3/17 Su	3 ♐ 04	18 ♈ 04	10 ♍ 55	2 ♎ 51
	3/24 Su	3 ♐ 01	18 ♈ 08	10 ♍ 48	2 ♎ 43
	3/31 Su	2 ♐ 56	18 ♈ 13	10 ♍ 40	2 ♎ 35
	4/07 Su	2 ♐ 49	18 ♈ 17	10 ♍ 34	2 ♎ 27
	4/14 Su	2 ♐ 42	18 ♈ 22	10 ♍ 28	2 ♎ 20
	4/21 Su	2 ♐ 33	18 ♈ 27	10 ♍ 22	2 ♎ 13
	4/28 Su	2 ♐ 23	18 ♈ 31	10 ♍ 18	2 ♎ 06
	5/05 Su	2 ♐ 12	18 ♈ 35	10 ♍ 15	2 ♎ 00
	5/12 Su	2 ♐ 01	18 ♈ 40	10 ♍ 12	1 ♎ 55
	5/19 Su	1 ♐ 50	18 ♈ 43	10 ♍ 11	1 ♎ 50
	5/26 Su	1 ♐ 38	18 ♈ 47	10 ♍ 11 D	1 ♎ 47
	6/02 Su	1 ♐ 27	18 ♈ 50	10 ♍ 11	1 ♎ 44
	6/09 Su	1 ♐ 16	18 ♈ 53	10 ♍ 13	1 ♎ 43
	6/16 Su	1 ♐ 05	18 ♈ 55	10 ♍ 16	1 ♎ 42 D
	6/23 Su	0 ♐ 55	18 ♈ 57	10 ♍ 20	1 ♎ 43
	6/30 Su	0 ♐ 46	18 ♈ 58	10 ♍ 25	1 ♎ 45
	7/07 Su	0 ♐ 38	18 ♈ 59	10 ♍ 31	1 ♎ 47
	7/14 Su	0 ♐ 32	18 ♈ 59	10 ♍ 37	1 ♎ 51
	7/21 Su	0 ♐ 26	18 ♈ 59 ℞	10 ♍ 45	1 ♎ 55
	7/28 Su	0 ♐ 23	18 ♈ 59	10 ♍ 53	2 ♎ 01
	8/04 Su	0 ♐ 20	18 ♈ 57	11 ♍ 02	2 ♎ 07
	8/11 Su	0 ♐ 20 D	18 ♈ 56	11 ♍ 11	2 ♎ 14
	8/18 Su	0 ♐ 20	18 ♈ 54	11 ♍ 21	2 ♎ 21
	8/25 Su	0 ♐ 23	18 ♈ 51	11 ♍ 30	2 ♎ 30
	9/01 Su	0 ♐ 27	18 ♈ 48	11 ♍ 41	2 ♎ 39

		♇	♀	⯓	⯔
1996	9/08 Su	0 ♐ 33 D	18 ♈ 45 ℞	11 ♍ 51 D	2 ♎ 48 D
	9/15 Su	0 ♐ 40	18 ♈ 41	12 ♍ 01	2 ♎ 57
	9/22 Su	0 ♐ 49	18 ♈ 37	12 ♍ 11	3 ♎ 07
	9/29 Su	1 ♐ 00	18 ♈ 33	12 ♍ 20	3 ♎ 17
	10/06 Su	1 ♐ 11	18 ♈ 29	12 ♍ 29	3 ♎ 26
	10/13 Su	1 ♐ 24	18 ♈ 25	12 ♍ 38	3 ♎ 36
	10/20 Su	1 ♐ 38	18 ♈ 21	12 ♍ 46	3 ♎ 45
	10/27 Su	1 ♐ 52	18 ♈ 17	12 ♍ 53	3 ♎ 54
	11/03 Su	2 ♐ 08	18 ♈ 13	13 ♍ 00	4 ♎ 02
	11/10 Su	2 ♐ 24	18 ♈ 09	13 ♍ 05	4 ♎ 10
	11/17 Su	2 ♐ 40	18 ♈ 05	13 ♍ 10	4 ♎ 17
	11/24 Su	2 ♐ 57	18 ♈ 02	13 ♍ 13	4 ♎ 23
	12/01 Su	3 ♐ 13	17 ♈ 59	13 ♍ 16	4 ♎ 29
	12/08 Su	3 ♐ 30	17 ♈ 57	13 ♍ 17	4 ♎ 33
	12/15 Su	3 ♐ 46	17 ♈ 55	13 ♍ 17 ℞	4 ♎ 37
	12/22 Su	4 ♐ 02	17 ♈ 54	13 ♍ 16	4 ♎ 39
	12/29 Su	4 ♐ 17	17 ♈ 53	13 ♍ 14	4 ♎ 40
1997	1/05 Su	4 ♐ 31	17 ♈ 53	13 ♍ 11	4 ♎ 40 ℞
	1/12 Su	4 ♐ 44	17 ♈ 53 D	13 ♍ 07	4 ♎ 39
	1/19 Su	4 ♐ 55	17 ♈ 54	13 ♍ 02	4 ♎ 37
	1/26 Su	5 ♐ 06	17 ♈ 55	12 ♍ 56	4 ♎ 34
	2/02 Su	5 ♐ 15	17 ♈ 57	12 ♍ 49	4 ♎ 30
	2/09 Su	5 ♐ 22	17 ♈ 59	12 ♍ 42	4 ♎ 25
	2/16 Su	5 ♐ 28	18 ♈ 02	12 ♍ 34	4 ♎ 19
	2/23 Su	5 ♐ 32	18 ♈ 05	12 ♍ 26	4 ♎ 13
	3/02 Su	5 ♐ 35	18 ♈ 09	12 ♍ 18	4 ♎ 06
	3/09 Su	5 ♐ 36 ℞	18 ♈ 13	12 ♍ 09	3 ♎ 59
	3/16 Su	5 ♐ 35	18 ♈ 17	12 ♍ 01	3 ♎ 51
	3/23 Su	5 ♐ 32	18 ♈ 21	11 ♍ 53	3 ♎ 43
	3/30 Su	5 ♐ 28	18 ♈ 26	11 ♍ 46	3 ♎ 35
	4/06 Su	5 ♐ 22	18 ♈ 30	11 ♍ 39	3 ♎ 27
	4/13 Su	5 ♐ 15	18 ♈ 35	11 ♍ 33	3 ♎ 19
	4/20 Su	5 ♐ 07	18 ♈ 40	11 ♍ 27	3 ♎ 12
	4/27 Su	4 ♐ 58	18 ♈ 44	11 ♍ 23	3 ♎ 05
	5/04 Su	4 ♐ 48	18 ♈ 49	11 ♍ 19	2 ♎ 59
	5/11 Su	4 ♐ 37	18 ♈ 53	11 ♍ 16	2 ♎ 54
	5/18 Su	4 ♐ 26	18 ♈ 57	11 ♍ 14	2 ♎ 49

Astro Data

1996

1/05 Fr	18:17	♀	SD	17 ♈ 39	-8.2 (-8:11)
1/02 Tu	03:35	⯔	SR	3 ♎ 43	21.5 (21:27)
3/05 Tu	20:18	♇	SR	3 ♐ 06	-7.8 (-7:48)
5/24 Fr	08:02	⯓	SD	10 ♍ 11	34.1 (34:08)
6/15 Sa	21:50	⯔	SD	1 ♎ 42	22.4 (22:22)
7/15 Mo	05:07	♀	SR	18 ♈ 59	-7.6 (-7:35)
8/10 Sa	12:35	♇	SD	0 ♐ 20	-7.4 (-7:25)

1996

12/12 Th	11:12	⯓	SR	13 ♍ 17	32.9 (32:51)

1997

1/03 Fr	00:00	⯔	SR	4 ♎ 40	21.2 (21:14)
1/05 Su	06:53	♀	SD	17 ♈ 53	-7.9 (-7:55)
3/08 Sa	12:54	♇	SR	5 ♐ 36	-8.7 (-8:43)
5/25 Su	14:58	⯓	SD	11 ♍ 14	33.7 (33:44)

LONGITUDE

1997		♇	♀	♎	♎
	5/25 Su	4 ♐ 14 ℞	19 ♈ 00 D	11 ♍ 14 ℞	2 ♎ 45 ℞
	6/01 Su	4 ♐ 03	19 ♈ 03	11 ♍ 14 D	2 ♎ 42
	6/08 Su	3 ♐ 51	19 ♈ 06	11 ♍ 16	2 ♎ 41
	6/15 Su	3 ♐ 40	19 ♈ 09	11 ♍ 18	2 ♎ 40
	6/22 Su	3 ♐ 30	19 ♈ 11	11 ♍ 22	2 ♎ 40 D
	6/29 Su	3 ♐ 21	19 ♈ 12	11 ♍ 26	2 ♎ 41
	7/06 Su	3 ♐ 12	19 ♈ 13	11 ♍ 32	2 ♎ 43
	7/13 Su	3 ♐ 05	19 ♈ 13	11 ♍ 38	2 ♎ 47
	7/20 Su	2 ♐ 59	19 ♈ 13 ℞	11 ♍ 45	2 ♎ 51
	7/27 Su	2 ♐ 54	19 ♈ 13	11 ♍ 53	2 ♎ 56
	8/03 Su	2 ♐ 51	19 ♈ 12	12 ♍ 02	3 ♎ 02
	8/10 Su	2 ♐ 49	19 ♈ 10	12 ♍ 11	3 ♎ 09
	8/17 Su	2 ♐ 49 D	19 ♈ 08	12 ♍ 20	3 ♎ 16
	8/24 Su	2 ♐ 51	19 ♈ 06	12 ♍ 30	3 ♎ 24
	8/31 Su	2 ♐ 54	19 ♈ 03	12 ♍ 40	3 ♎ 33
	9/07 Su	2 ♐ 59	18 ♈ 59	12 ♍ 50	3 ♎ 42
	9/14 Su	3 ♐ 06	18 ♈ 56	13 ♍ 00	3 ♎ 51
	9/21 Su	3 ♐ 14	18 ♈ 52	13 ♍ 10	4 ♎ 01
	9/28 Su	3 ♐ 23	18 ♈ 48	13 ♍ 20	4 ♎ 11
	10/05 Su	3 ♐ 34	18 ♈ 44	13 ♍ 29	4 ♎ 21
	10/12 Su	3 ♐ 46	18 ♈ 40	13 ♍ 38	4 ♎ 30
	10/19 Su	3 ♐ 59	18 ♈ 36	13 ♍ 46	4 ♎ 40
	10/26 Su	4 ♐ 14	18 ♈ 31	13 ♍ 54	4 ♎ 49
	11/02 Su	4 ♐ 28	18 ♈ 27	14 ♍ 01	4 ♎ 57
	11/09 Su	4 ♐ 44	18 ♈ 24	14 ♍ 06	5 ♎ 05
	11/16 Su	5 ♐ 00	18 ♈ 20	14 ♍ 11	5 ♎ 13
	11/23 Su	5 ♐ 17	18 ♈ 17	14 ♍ 15	5 ♎ 19
	11/30 Su	5 ♐ 33	18 ♈ 14	14 ♍ 18	5 ♎ 25
	12/07 Su	5 ♐ 50	18 ♈ 12	14 ♍ 20	5 ♎ 29
	12/14 Su	6 ♐ 06	18 ♈ 10	14 ♍ 20 ℞	5 ♎ 33
	12/21 Su	6 ♐ 22	18 ♈ 08	14 ♍ 19	5 ♎ 36
	12/28 Su	6 ♐ 37	18 ♈ 07	14 ♍ 18	5 ♎ 37
1998	1/04 Su	6 ♐ 51	18 ♈ 07	14 ♍ 15	5 ♎ 38 ℞
	1/11 Su	7 ♐ 05	18 ♈ 07 D	14 ♍ 11	5 ♎ 37
	1/18 Su	7 ♐ 17	18 ♈ 08	14 ♍ 06	5 ♎ 36
	1/25 Su	7 ♐ 28	18 ♈ 09	14 ♍ 01	5 ♎ 33
	2/01 Su	7 ♐ 38	18 ♈ 11	13 ♍ 54	5 ♎ 29

1998		♇	♀	♎	♎
	2/08 Su	7 ♐ 46 D	18 ♈ 13 D	13 ♍ 47 ℞	5 ♎ 24 ℞
	2/15 Su	7 ♐ 53	18 ♈ 15	13 ♍ 39	5 ♎ 19
	2/22 Su	7 ♐ 58	18 ♈ 19	13 ♍ 31	5 ♎ 13
	3/01 Su	8 ♐ 01	18 ♈ 22	13 ♍ 23	5 ♎ 06
	3/08 Su	8 ♐ 03	18 ♈ 26	13 ♍ 15	4 ♎ 58
	3/15 Su	8 ♐ 03 ℞	18 ♈ 30	13 ♍ 07	4 ♎ 51
	3/22 Su	8 ♐ 01	18 ♈ 34	12 ♍ 59	4 ♎ 43
	3/29 Su	7 ♐ 58	18 ♈ 39	12 ♍ 51	4 ♎ 35
	4/05 Su	7 ♐ 53	18 ♈ 43	12 ♍ 44	4 ♎ 27
	4/12 Su	7 ♐ 47	18 ♈ 48	12 ♍ 38	4 ♎ 19
	4/19 Su	7 ♐ 39	18 ♈ 53	12 ♍ 32	4 ♎ 12
	4/26 Su	7 ♐ 31	18 ♈ 57	12 ♍ 27	4 ♎ 05
	5/03 Su	7 ♐ 21	19 ♈ 02	12 ♍ 23	3 ♎ 58
	5/10 Su	7 ♐ 10	19 ♈ 06	12 ♍ 20	3 ♎ 53
	5/17 Su	6 ♐ 59	19 ♈ 10	12 ♍ 18	3 ♎ 48
	5/24 Su	6 ♐ 48	19 ♈ 13	12 ♍ 17	3 ♎ 44
	5/31 Su	6 ♐ 37	19 ♈ 17	12 ♍ 17 D	3 ♎ 41
	6/07 Su	6 ♐ 25	19 ♈ 20	12 ♍ 18	3 ♎ 38
	6/14 Su	6 ♐ 14	19 ♈ 22	12 ♍ 20	3 ♎ 37
	6/21 Su	6 ♐ 04	19 ♈ 24	12 ♍ 24	3 ♎ 37 D
	6/28 Su	5 ♐ 54	19 ♈ 26	12 ♍ 28	3 ♎ 38
	7/05 Su	5 ♐ 45	19 ♈ 27	12 ♍ 33	3 ♎ 40
	7/12 Su	5 ♐ 37	19 ♈ 27	12 ♍ 39	3 ♎ 43
	7/19 Su	5 ♐ 30	19 ♈ 27 ℞	12 ♍ 46	3 ♎ 47
	7/26 Su	5 ♐ 25	19 ♈ 27	12 ♍ 54	3 ♎ 52
	8/02 Su	5 ♐ 21	19 ♈ 26	13 ♍ 02	3 ♎ 57
	8/09 Su	5 ♐ 18	19 ♈ 24	13 ♍ 11	4 ♎ 04
	8/16 Su	5 ♐ 17	19 ♈ 23	13 ♍ 20	4 ♎ 11
	8/23 Su	5 ♐ 18 D	19 ♈ 20	13 ♍ 30	4 ♎ 19
	8/30 Su	5 ♐ 20	19 ♈ 17	13 ♍ 40	4 ♎ 28
	9/06 Su	5 ♐ 24	19 ♈ 14	13 ♍ 50	4 ♎ 37
	9/13 Su	5 ♐ 30	19 ♈ 11	14 ♍ 00	4 ♎ 46
	9/20 Su	5 ♐ 37	19 ♈ 07	14 ♍ 10	4 ♎ 56
	9/27 Su	5 ♐ 46	19 ♈ 03	14 ♍ 20	5 ♎ 05
	10/04 Su	5 ♐ 56	18 ♈ 59	14 ♍ 29	5 ♎ 15
	10/11 Su	6 ♐ 07	18 ♈ 55	14 ♍ 38	5 ♎ 25
	10/18 Su	6 ♐ 20	18 ♈ 51	14 ♍ 47	5 ♎ 34
	10/25 Su	6 ♐ 33	18 ♈ 46	14 ♍ 54	5 ♎ 43
	11/01 Su	6 ♐ 48	18 ♈ 42	15 ♍ 01	5 ♎ 52
	11/08 Su	7 ♐ 03	18 ♈ 38	15 ♍ 07	6 ♎ 00

Astro Data

1997

6/17 Tu	04:13	♎	SD	2 ♎ 40	22.1 (22:08)
7/15 Tu	15:37	♀	SR	19 ♈ 13	-7.3 (-7:19)
8/13 We	08:32	♇	SD	2 ♐ 49	-8.4 (-8:24)
12/13 Sa	17:56	♎	SR	14 ♍ 20	32.5 (32:28)

1998

1/03 Sa	11:13	♎	SR	5 ♎ 38	21.0 (21:02)
1/05 Mo	20:40	♀	SD	18 ♈ 07	-7.7 (-7:40)

1998

3/11 We	04:55	♇	SR	8 ♐ 03	-9.6 (-9:36)
5/26 Tu	12:15	♎	SD	12 ♍ 17	33.4 (33:23)
6/18 Th	11:50	♎	SD	3 ♎ 37	22.0 (21:58)
7/16 Th	00:30	♀	SR	19 ♈ 27	-7.1 (-7:04)
8/16 Su	06:09	♇	SD	5 ♐ 17	-9.4 (-9:22)

		⯓	♀	⯗	⯘
1998	11/15 Su	7 ♐ 19 D	18 ♈ 35 ℞	15 ♍ 13 D	6 ♎ 08 D
	11/22 Su	7 ♐ 35	18 ♈ 32	15 ♍ 17	6 ♎ 15
	11/29 Su	7 ♐ 52	18 ♈ 29	15 ♍ 20	6 ♎ 21
	12/06 Su	8 ♐ 08	18 ♈ 26	15 ♍ 22	6 ♎ 26
	12/13 Su	8 ♐ 24	18 ♈ 24	15 ♍ 23	6 ♎ 30
	12/20 Su	8 ♐ 40	18 ♈ 22	15 ♍ 23 ℞	6 ♎ 33
	12/27 Su	8 ♐ 56	18 ♈ 21	15 ♍ 21	6 ♎ 35
1999	1/03 Su	9 ♐ 11	18 ♈ 21	15 ♍ 19	6 ♎ 36
	1/10 Su	9 ♐ 24	18 ♈ 21 D	15 ♍ 15	6 ♎ 35 ℞
	1/17 Su	9 ♐ 37	18 ♈ 21	15 ♍ 11	6 ♎ 34
	1/24 Su	9 ♐ 49	18 ♈ 23	15 ♍ 05	6 ♎ 32
	1/31 Su	9 ♐ 59	18 ♈ 24	14 ♍ 59	6 ♎ 28
	2/07 Su	10 ♐ 08	18 ♈ 26	14 ♍ 52	6 ♎ 24
	2/14 Su	10 ♐ 16	18 ♈ 29	14 ♍ 45	6 ♎ 18
	2/21 Su	10 ♐ 22	18 ♈ 32	14 ♍ 37	6 ♎ 12
	2/28 Su	10 ♐ 26	18 ♈ 35	14 ♍ 29	6 ♎ 06
	3/07 Su	10 ♐ 28	18 ♈ 39	14 ♍ 21	5 ♎ 58
	3/14 Su	10 ♐ 29 ℞	18 ♈ 43	14 ♍ 12	5 ♎ 51
	3/21 Su	10 ♐ 28	18 ♈ 47	14 ♍ 04	5 ♎ 43
	3/28 Su	10 ♐ 26	18 ♈ 52	13 ♍ 57	5 ♎ 35
	4/04 Su	10 ♐ 22	18 ♈ 57	13 ♍ 49	5 ♎ 27
	4/11 Su	10 ♐ 16	19 ♈ 01	13 ♍ 43	5 ♎ 19
	4/18 Su	10 ♐ 09	19 ♈ 06	13 ♍ 37	5 ♎ 12
	4/25 Su	10 ♐ 01	19 ♈ 10	13 ♍ 31	5 ♎ 04
	5/02 Su	9 ♐ 52	19 ♈ 15	13 ♍ 27	4 ♎ 58
	5/09 Su	9 ♐ 42	19 ♈ 19	13 ♍ 24	4 ♎ 52
	5/16 Su	9 ♐ 32	19 ♈ 23	13 ♍ 21	4 ♎ 47
	5/23 Su	9 ♐ 20	19 ♈ 27	13 ♍ 20	4 ♎ 42
	5/30 Su	9 ♐ 09	19 ♈ 30	13 ♍ 20 D	4 ♎ 39
	6/06 Su	8 ♐ 58	19 ♈ 33	13 ♍ 20	4 ♎ 37
	6/13 Su	8 ♐ 46	19 ♈ 36	13 ♍ 22	4 ♎ 35
	6/20 Su	8 ♐ 36	19 ♈ 38	13 ♍ 25	4 ♎ 35 D
	6/27 Su	8 ♐ 25	19 ♈ 39	13 ♍ 29	4 ♎ 35
	7/04 Su	8 ♐ 16	19 ♈ 41	13 ♍ 34	4 ♎ 37
	7/11 Su	8 ♐ 07	19 ♈ 41	13 ♍ 40	4 ♎ 39
	7/18 Su	8 ♐ 00	19 ♈ 41 ℞	13 ♍ 47	4 ♎ 43
	7/25 Su	7 ♐ 54	19 ♈ 41	13 ♍ 54	4 ♎ 48
1999	8/01 Su	7 ♐ 49 ℞	19 ♈ 40 ℞	14 ♍ 02 D	4 ♎ 53 D
	8/08 Su	7 ♐ 46	19 ♈ 39	14 ♍ 11	4 ♎ 59
	8/15 Su	7 ♐ 44	19 ♈ 37	14 ♍ 20	5 ♎ 06
	8/22 Su	7 ♐ 44 D	19 ♈ 35	14 ♍ 29	5 ♎ 14
	8/29 Su	7 ♐ 45	19 ♈ 32	14 ♍ 39	5 ♎ 23
	9/05 Su	7 ♐ 49	19 ♈ 29	14 ♍ 49	5 ♎ 31
	9/12 Su	7 ♐ 53	19 ♈ 26	14 ♍ 59	5 ♎ 41
	9/19 Su	8 ♐ 00	19 ♈ 22	15 ♍ 09	5 ♎ 50
	9/26 Su	8 ♐ 07	19 ♈ 18	15 ♍ 19	6 ♎ 00
	10/03 Su	8 ♐ 17	19 ♈ 14	15 ♍ 29	6 ♎ 10
	10/10 Su	8 ♐ 27	19 ♈ 10	15 ♍ 38	6 ♎ 20
	10/17 Su	8 ♐ 39	19 ♈ 05	15 ♍ 47	6 ♎ 29
	10/24 Su	8 ♐ 52	19 ♈ 01	15 ♍ 55	6 ♎ 38
	10/31 Su	9 ♐ 06	18 ♈ 57	16 ♍ 02	6 ♎ 47
	11/07 Su	9 ♐ 21	18 ♈ 53	16 ♍ 08	6 ♎ 56
	11/14 Su	9 ♐ 36	18 ♈ 50	16 ♍ 14	7 ♎ 04
	11/21 Su	9 ♐ 52	18 ♈ 46	16 ♍ 18	7 ♎ 11
	11/28 Su	10 ♐ 08	18 ♈ 43	16 ♍ 22	7 ♎ 17
	12/05 Su	10 ♐ 25	18 ♈ 41	16 ♍ 24	7 ♎ 22
	12/12 Su	10 ♐ 41	18 ♈ 38	16 ♍ 25	7 ♎ 27
	12/19 Su	10 ♐ 57	18 ♈ 37	16 ♍ 25 ℞	7 ♎ 30
	12/26 Su	11 ♐ 13	18 ♈ 36	16 ♍ 24	7 ♎ 32
2000	1/02 Su	11 ♐ 28	18 ♈ 35	16 ♍ 22	7 ♎ 33
	1/09 Su	11 ♐ 42	18 ♈ 35 D	16 ♍ 19	7 ♎ 34 ℞
	1/16 Su	11 ♐ 55	18 ♈ 35	16 ♍ 15	7 ♎ 32
	1/23 Su	12 ♐ 08	18 ♈ 36	16 ♍ 10	7 ♎ 30
	1/30 Su	12 ♐ 19	18 ♈ 38	16 ♍ 04	7 ♎ 27
	2/06 Su	12 ♐ 28	18 ♈ 40	15 ♍ 57	7 ♎ 23
	2/13 Su	12 ♐ 37	18 ♈ 42	15 ♍ 50	7 ♎ 18
	2/20 Su	12 ♐ 43	18 ♈ 45	15 ♍ 42	7 ♎ 12
	2/27 Su	12 ♐ 48	18 ♈ 49	15 ♍ 34	7 ♎ 06
	3/05 Su	12 ♐ 52	18 ♈ 52	15 ♍ 26	6 ♎ 59
	3/12 Su	12 ♐ 53	18 ♈ 56	15 ♍ 18	6 ♎ 51
	3/19 Su	12 ♐ 53 ℞	19 ♈ 01	15 ♍ 10	6 ♎ 43
	3/26 Su	12 ♐ 52	19 ♈ 05	15 ♍ 02	6 ♎ 35
	4/02 Su	12 ♐ 49	19 ♈ 10	14 ♍ 54	6 ♎ 27
	4/09 Su	12 ♐ 44	19 ♈ 14	14 ♍ 48	6 ♎ 19

Astro Data

1998						
12/14 Mo	22:56	⯗	SR	15 ♍ 23	32.1	(32:07)
1999						
1/06 We	08:28	♀	SD	18 ♈ 21	-7.4	(-7:24)
1/04 Mo	18:36	⯘	SR	6 ♎ 36	20.9	(20:52)
3/13 Sa	21:34	⯓	SR	10 ♐ 29	-10.5	(-10:28)
5/28 Fr	08:01	⯗	SD	13 ♍ 20	33.0	(33:01)
6/19 Sa	15:38	⯘	SD	4 ♎ 35	21.8	(21:46)
7/16 Fr	12:16	♀	SR	19 ♈ 41	-6.8	(-6:48)
1999						
8/19 Th	01:46	⯓	SD	7 ♐ 44	-10.3	(-10:15)
12/16 Th	04:01	⯗	SR	16 ♍ 26	31.7	(31:43)
2000						
1/06 Th	15:04	♀	SD	18 ♈ 35	-7.2	(-7:09)
1/06 Th	00:51	⯘	SR	7 ♎ 34	20.7	(20:39)
3/15 We	11:51	⯓	SR	12 ♐ 54	-11.3	(-11:18)

2000	♇	♇	♇	♇		2001	♇	♇	♇	♇
4/16 Su	12 ✗ 38 R	19 ♈ 19 D	14 ♍ 41 R	6 ♎ 12 R		1/07 Su	13 ✗ 58 D	18 ♈ 49 D	17 ♍ 23 R	8 ♎ 32 R
4/23 Su	12 ✗ 30	19 ♈ 23	14 ♍ 36	6 ♎ 05		1/14 Su	14 ✗ 12	18 ♈ 49	17 ♍ 19	8 ♎ 31
4/30 Su	12 ✗ 22	19 ♈ 28	14 ♍ 31	5 ♎ 58		1/21 Su	14 ✗ 25	18 ♈ 50	17 ♍ 14	8 ♎ 29
5/07 Su	12 ✗ 12	19 ♈ 32	14 ♍ 28	5 ♎ 52		1/28 Su	14 ✗ 36	18 ♈ 52	17 ♍ 09	8 ♎ 27
5/14 Su	12 ✗ 02	19 ♈ 36	14 ♍ 25	5 ♎ 46		2/04 Su	14 ✗ 47	18 ♈ 53	17 ♍ 02	8 ♎ 23
5/21 Su	11 ✗ 51	19 ♈ 40	14 ♍ 23	5 ♎ 42		2/11 Su	14 ✗ 55	18 ♈ 56	16 ♍ 55	8 ♎ 18
5/28 Su	11 ✗ 40	19 ♈ 43	14 ♍ 23	5 ♎ 38		2/18 Su	15 ✗ 03	18 ♈ 59	16 ♍ 48	8 ♎ 13
6/04 Su	11 ✗ 28	19 ♈ 46	14 ♍ 23 D	5 ♎ 35		2/25 Su	15 ✗ 09	19 ♈ 02	16 ♍ 40	8 ♎ 06
6/11 Su	11 ✗ 17	19 ♈ 49	14 ♍ 24	5 ♎ 33		3/04 Su	15 ✗ 13	19 ♈ 06	16 ♍ 32	7 ♎ 59
6/18 Su	11 ✗ 06	19 ♈ 51	14 ♍ 27	5 ♎ 32		3/11 Su	15 ✗ 15	19 ♈ 10	16 ♍ 23	7 ♎ 52
6/25 Su	10 ✗ 55	19 ♈ 53	14 ♍ 31	5 ♎ 33 D		3/18 Su	15 ✗ 16	19 ♈ 14	16 ♍ 15	7 ♎ 44
7/02 Su	10 ✗ 46	19 ♈ 54	14 ♍ 35	5 ♎ 34		3/25 Su	15 ✗ 15 R	19 ♈ 18	16 ♍ 07	7 ♎ 36
7/09 Su	10 ✗ 37	19 ♈ 55	14 ♍ 41	5 ♎ 36		4/01 Su	15 ✗ 13	19 ♈ 23	16 ♍ 00	7 ♎ 28
7/16 Su	10 ✗ 29	19 ♈ 56	14 ♍ 47	5 ♎ 40		4/08 Su	15 ✗ 09	19 ♈ 27	15 ♍ 53	7 ♎ 20
7/23 Su	10 ✗ 22	19 ♈ 55 R	14 ♍ 54	5 ♎ 44		4/15 Su	15 ✗ 04	19 ♈ 32	15 ♍ 46	7 ♎ 12
7/30 Su	10 ✗ 16	19 ♈ 54	15 ♍ 02	5 ♎ 49		4/22 Su	14 ✗ 57	19 ♈ 36	15 ♍ 40	7 ♎ 05
8/06 Su	10 ✗ 12	19 ♈ 53	15 ♍ 11	5 ♎ 55		4/29 Su	14 ✗ 49	19 ♈ 41	15 ♍ 36	6 ♎ 58
8/13 Su	10 ✗ 10	19 ♈ 51	15 ♍ 20	6 ♎ 02		5/06 Su	14 ✗ 40	19 ♈ 45	15 ♍ 32	6 ♎ 52
8/20 Su	10 ✗ 09	19 ♈ 49	15 ♍ 29	6 ♎ 10		5/13 Su	14 ✗ 30	19 ♈ 49	15 ♍ 28	6 ♎ 46
8/27 Su	10 ✗ 09 D	19 ♈ 47	15 ♍ 39	6 ♎ 18		5/20 Su	14 ✗ 19	19 ♈ 53	15 ♍ 26	6 ♎ 41
9/03 Su	10 ✗ 11	19 ♈ 44	15 ♍ 49	6 ♎ 27		5/27 Su	14 ✗ 08	19 ♈ 57	15 ♍ 25	6 ♎ 37
9/10 Su	10 ✗ 15	19 ♈ 40	15 ♍ 59	6 ♎ 36		6/03 Su	13 ✗ 57	20 ♈ 00	15 ♍ 26 D	6 ♎ 34
9/17 Su	10 ✗ 21	19 ♈ 37	16 ♍ 09	6 ♎ 45		6/10 Su	13 ✗ 46	20 ♈ 03	15 ♍ 27	6 ♎ 32
9/24 Su	10 ✗ 28	19 ♈ 33	16 ♍ 19	6 ♎ 55		6/17 Su	13 ✗ 35	20 ♈ 05	15 ♍ 29	6 ♎ 31
10/01 Su	10 ✗ 36	19 ♈ 29	16 ♍ 28	7 ♎ 05		6/24 Su	13 ✗ 24	20 ♈ 07	15 ♍ 32	6 ♎ 31 D
10/08 Su	10 ✗ 46	19 ♈ 25	16 ♍ 38	7 ♎ 15		7/01 Su	13 ✗ 14	20 ♈ 08	15 ♍ 36	6 ♎ 32
10/15 Su	10 ✗ 57	19 ♈ 20	16 ♍ 47	7 ♎ 24		7/08 Su	13 ✗ 04	20 ♈ 09	15 ♍ 42	6 ♎ 34
10/22 Su	11 ✗ 10	19 ♈ 16	16 ♍ 55	7 ♎ 34		7/15 Su	12 ✗ 56	20 ♈ 10	15 ♍ 48	6 ♎ 37
10/29 Su	11 ✗ 23	19 ♈ 12	17 ♍ 02	7 ♎ 43		7/22 Su	12 ✗ 48	20 ♈ 09 R	15 ♍ 55	6 ♎ 41
11/05 Su	11 ✗ 37	19 ♈ 08	17 ♍ 09	7 ♎ 51		7/29 Su	12 ✗ 42	20 ♈ 09	16 ♍ 02	6 ♎ 46
11/12 Su	11 ✗ 52	19 ♈ 04	17 ♍ 15	7 ♎ 59		8/05 Su	12 ✗ 37	20 ♈ 08	16 ♍ 11	6 ♎ 51
11/19 Su	12 ✗ 08	19 ♈ 01	17 ♍ 20	8 ♎ 07		8/12 Su	12 ✗ 34	20 ♈ 06	16 ♍ 19	6 ♎ 58
11/26 Su	12 ✗ 24	18 ♈ 58	17 ♍ 23	8 ♎ 13		8/19 Su	12 ✗ 31	20 ♈ 04	16 ♍ 29	7 ♎ 05
12/03 Su	12 ✗ 40	18 ♈ 55	17 ♍ 26	8 ♎ 19		8/26 Su	12 ✗ 32 D	20 ♈ 01	16 ♍ 38	7 ♎ 13
12/10 Su	12 ✗ 56	18 ♈ 53	17 ♍ 28	8 ♎ 24		9/02 Su	12 ✗ 33	19 ♈ 58	16 ♍ 48	7 ♎ 22
12/17 Su	13 ✗ 12	18 ♈ 51	17 ♍ 28 R	8 ♎ 27		9/09 Su	12 ✗ 36	19 ♈ 55	16 ♍ 58	7 ♎ 31
12/24 Su	13 ✗ 28	18 ♈ 50	17 ♍ 28	8 ♎ 30		9/16 Su	12 ✗ 41	19 ♈ 51	17 ♍ 08	7 ♎ 41
12/31 Su	13 ✗ 43	18 ♈ 49	17 ♍ 26	8 ♎ 31		9/23 Su	12 ✗ 47	19 ♈ 48	17 ♍ 18	7 ♎ 50
							9/30 Su	12 ✗ 55	19 ♈ 44	17 ♍ 28	8 ♎ 00
							10/07 Su	13 ✗ 04	19 ♈ 40	17 ♍ 37	8 ♎ 10

Astro Data

2000

5/28 Su	17:47	♎	SD	14 ♍ 23	31.6 (32:35)
6/19 Mo	19:17	♇	SD	5 ♎ 32	21.5 (21:32)
7/16 Su	04:41	♀	SR	19 ♈ 55	-6.6 (-6:33)
8/20 Su	12:43	♇	SD	10 ✗ 09	-11.2 (-11:10)
12/16 Sa	12:56	♎	SR	17 ♍ 28	31.3 (31:19)

2001

1/06 Sa	03:22	♀	SD	18 ♈ 49	-6.9 (-6:54)
1/06 Sa	05:34	♇	SR	8 ♎ 32	20.4 (20:25)

2001

3/18 Su	02:38	♇	SR	15 ✗ 16	-12.1 (-12:06)
5/29 Tu	13:23	♎	SD	15 ♍ 25	32.2 (32:13)
6/20 We	22:47	♇	SD	6 ♎ 31	21.4 (21:21)
7/16 Mo	15:46	♀	SR	20 ♈ 10	-6.3 (-6:18)
8/23 Th	16:07	♇	SD	12 ✗ 32	-12.0 (-12:01)

2001	♇	♀	⚷	⚸
10/14 Su	13 ♐ 14 D	19 ♈ 35 ℞	17 ♍ 46 D	8 ♎ 20 D
10/21 Su	13 ♐ 26	19 ♈ 31	17 ♍ 55	8 ♎ 29
10/28 Su	13 ♐ 39	19 ♈ 27	18 ♍ 03	8 ♎ 38
11/04 Su	13 ♐ 52	19 ♈ 23	18 ♍ 09	8 ♎ 47
11/11 Su	14 ♐ 07	19 ♈ 19	18 ♍ 16	8 ♎ 55
11/18 Su	14 ♐ 22	19 ♈ 16	18 ♍ 21	9 ♎ 03
11/25 Su	14 ♐ 38	19 ♈ 13	18 ♍ 25	9 ♎ 10
12/02 Su	14 ♐ 54	19 ♈ 10	18 ♍ 28	9 ♎ 16
12/09 Su	15 ♐ 10	19 ♈ 07	18 ♍ 30	9 ♎ 21
12/16 Su	15 ♐ 26	19 ♈ 06	18 ♍ 31	9 ♎ 25
12/23 Su	15 ♐ 42	19 ♈ 04	18 ♍ 31 ℞	9 ♎ 28
12/30 Su	15 ♐ 57	19 ♈ 03	18 ♍ 29	9 ♎ 30

2002	♇	♀	⚷	⚸
1/06 Su	16 ♐ 12	19 ♈ 03	18 ♍ 27	9 ♎ 31
1/13 Su	16 ♐ 26	19 ♈ 03 D	18 ♍ 23	9 ♎ 30 ℞
1/20 Su	16 ♐ 40	19 ♈ 04	18 ♍ 19	9 ♎ 29
1/27 Su	16 ♐ 52	19 ♈ 05	18 ♍ 13	9 ♎ 26
2/03 Su	17 ♐ 03	19 ♈ 07	18 ♍ 07	9 ♎ 23
2/10 Su	17 ♐ 12	19 ♈ 09	18 ♍ 00	9 ♎ 18
2/17 Su	17 ♐ 20	19 ♈ 12	17 ♍ 53	9 ♎ 13
2/24 Su	17 ♐ 27	19 ♈ 15	17 ♍ 45	9 ♎ 07
3/03 Su	17 ♐ 32	19 ♈ 19	17 ♍ 37	9 ♎ 00
3/10 Su	17 ♐ 35	19 ♈ 23	17 ♍ 29	8 ♎ 53
3/17 Su	17 ♐ 37	19 ♈ 27	17 ♍ 21	8 ♎ 45
3/24 Su	17 ♐ 37 ℞	19 ♈ 31	17 ♍ 13	8 ♎ 37
3/31 Su	17 ♐ 35	19 ♈ 36	17 ♍ 05	8 ♎ 29
4/07 Su	17 ♐ 32	19 ♈ 40	16 ♍ 58	8 ♎ 21
4/14 Su	17 ♐ 28	19 ♈ 45	16 ♍ 51	8 ♎ 13
4/21 Su	17 ♐ 22	19 ♈ 50	16 ♍ 45	8 ♎ 06
4/28 Su	17 ♐ 14	19 ♈ 54	16 ♍ 40	7 ♎ 59
5/05 Su	17 ♐ 06	19 ♈ 58	16 ♍ 36	7 ♎ 52
5/12 Su	16 ♐ 56	20 ♈ 03	16 ♍ 32	7 ♎ 46
5/19 Su	16 ♐ 46	20 ♈ 06	16 ♍ 30	7 ♎ 41
5/26 Su	16 ♐ 36	20 ♈ 10	16 ♍ 29	7 ♎ 37
6/02 Su	16 ♐ 24	20 ♈ 13	16 ♍ 28 D	7 ♎ 33
6/09 Su	16 ♐ 13	20 ♈ 16	16 ♍ 29	7 ♎ 31
6/16 Su	16 ♐ 02	20 ♈ 19	16 ♍ 31	7 ♎ 30
6/23 Su	15 ♐ 51	20 ♈ 20	16 ♍ 34	7 ♎ 29 D

2002	♇	♀	⚷	⚸
6/30 Su	15 ♐ 41 ℞	20 ♈ 22 D	16 ♍ 38 D	7 ♎ 30 D
7/07 Su	15 ♐ 31	20 ♈ 23	16 ♍ 43	7 ♎ 31
7/14 Su	15 ♐ 22	20 ♈ 23	16 ♍ 48	7 ♎ 34
7/21 Su	15 ♐ 14	20 ♈ 23 ℞	16 ♍ 55	7 ♎ 38
7/28 Su	15 ♐ 07	20 ♈ 23	17 ♍ 02	7 ♎ 42
8/04 Su	15 ♐ 01	20 ♈ 22	17 ♍ 10	7 ♎ 48
8/11 Su	14 ♐ 57	20 ♈ 20	17 ♍ 19	7 ♎ 54
8/18 Su	14 ♐ 55	20 ♈ 18	17 ♍ 28	8 ♎ 02
8/25 Su	14 ♐ 54	20 ♈ 16	17 ♍ 38	8 ♎ 09
9/01 Su	14 ♐ 54 D	20 ♈ 13	17 ♍ 48	8 ♎ 18
9/08 Su	14 ♐ 56	20 ♈ 10	17 ♍ 58	8 ♎ 27
9/15 Su	15 ♐ 00	20 ♈ 06	18 ♍ 08	8 ♎ 36
9/22 Su	15 ♐ 05	20 ♈ 02	18 ♍ 18	8 ♎ 46
9/29 Su	15 ♐ 12	19 ♈ 59	18 ♍ 28	8 ♎ 56
10/06 Su	15 ♐ 20	19 ♈ 54	18 ♍ 37	9 ♎ 06
10/13 Su	15 ♐ 30	19 ♈ 50	18 ♍ 46	9 ♎ 15
10/20 Su	15 ♐ 41	19 ♈ 46	18 ♍ 55	9 ♎ 25
10/27 Su	15 ♐ 53	19 ♈ 42	19 ♍ 03	9 ♎ 34
11/03 Su	16 ♐ 06	19 ♈ 38	19 ♍ 10	9 ♎ 43
11/10 Su	16 ♐ 20	19 ♈ 34	19 ♍ 16	9 ♎ 52
11/17 Su	16 ♐ 35	19 ♈ 30	19 ♍ 22	10 ♎ 00
11/24 Su	16 ♐ 50	19 ♈ 27	19 ♍ 26	10 ♎ 07
12/01 Su	17 ♐ 06	19 ♈ 24	19 ♍ 30	10 ♎ 13
12/08 Su	17 ♐ 21	19 ♈ 22	19 ♍ 32	10 ♎ 18
12/15 Su	17 ♐ 38	19 ♈ 20	19 ♍ 33	10 ♎ 23
12/22 Su	17 ♐ 54	19 ♈ 18	19 ♍ 33 ℞	10 ♎ 26
12/29 Su	18 ♐ 10	19 ♈ 17	19 ♍ 32	10 ♎ 28

2003	♇	♀	⚷	⚸
1/05 Su	18 ♐ 25	19 ♈ 17	19 ♍ 30	10 ♎ 29
1/12 Su	18 ♐ 39	19 ♈ 17 D	19 ♍ 27	10 ♎ 29 ℞
1/19 Su	18 ♐ 53	19 ♈ 18	19 ♍ 23	10 ♎ 28
1/26 Su	19 ♐ 05	19 ♈ 19	19 ♍ 18	10 ♎ 26
2/02 Su	19 ♐ 17	19 ♈ 21	19 ♍ 12	10 ♎ 23
2/09 Su	19 ♐ 27	19 ♈ 23	19 ♍ 05	10 ♎ 19
2/16 Su	19 ♐ 36	19 ♈ 26	18 ♍ 58	10 ♎ 14
2/23 Su	19 ♐ 43	19 ♈ 29	18 ♍ 50	10 ♎ 08
3/02 Su	19 ♐ 49	19 ♈ 32	18 ♍ 42	10 ♎ 01
3/09 Su	19 ♐ 53	19 ♈ 36	18 ♍ 34	9 ♎ 54

Astro Data

2001
| 12/17 Mo | 20:46 | ♎ | SR | 18 ♍ 31 | 31.0 (30:57) |

2002
1/06 Su	19:55	♀	SD	19 ♈ 03	-6.6 (-6:37)
1/07 Mo	10:52	♇	SR	9 ♎ 31	20.2 (20:15)
3/20 We	14:55	♇	SR	17 ♐ 37	-12.9 (-12:55)
5/31 Fr	06:07	♎	SD	16 ♍ 28	31.8 (31:50)
6/22 Sa	04:53	♇	SD	7 ♎ 29	21.1 (21:08)

2002
7/16 Tu	21:04	♀	SR	20 ♈ 24	-6.0 (-6:02)
8/26 Mo	11:01	♇	SD	14 ♐ 54	-12.9 (-12:52)
12/19 Th	04:37	♎	SR	19 ♍ 34	30.5 (30:32)

2003
| 1/07 Tu | 06:24 | ♀ | SD | 19 ♈ 17 | -6.4 (-6:22) |
| 1/08 We | 14:52 | ♇ | SR | 10 ♎ 30 | 20.0 (20:01) |

		♇	♀	♎	♎			♇	♀	♎	♎
2003	3/16 Su	19 ♐ 56 D	19 ♈ 40 D	18 ♍ 26 R	9 ♎ 47 R	**2003**	12/21 Su	20 ♐ 05 D	19 ♈ 33 R	20 ♍ 36 R	11 ♎ 24 D
	3/23 Su	19 ♐ 57	19 ♈ 44	18 ♍ 18	9 ♎ 39		12/28 Su	20 ♐ 21	19 ♈ 32	20 ♍ 35	11 ♎ 27
	3/30 Su	19 ♐ 56 R	19 ♈ 49	18 ♍ 10	9 ♎ 31						
	4/06 Su	19 ♐ 53	19 ♈ 53	18 ♍ 03	9 ♎ 23						
	4/13 Su	19 ♐ 50	19 ♈ 58	17 ♍ 56	9 ♎ 15						
	4/20 Su	19 ♐ 44	20 ♈ 03	17 ♍ 50	9 ♎ 07	**2004**	1/04 Su	20 ♐ 36	19 ♈ 31	20 ♍ 34	11 ♎ 29
	4/27 Su	19 ♐ 38	20 ♈ 07	17 ♍ 44	9 ♎ 00		1/11 Su	20 ♐ 50	19 ♈ 31 D	20 ♍ 31	11 ♎ 29 R
	5/04 Su	19 ♐ 30	20 ♈ 11	17 ♍ 40	8 ♎ 53		1/18 Su	21 ♐ 04	19 ♈ 32	20 ♍ 27	11 ♎ 28
	5/11 Su	19 ♐ 21	20 ♈ 16	17 ♍ 36	8 ♎ 47		1/25 Su	21 ♐ 17	19 ♈ 33	20 ♍ 22	11 ♎ 26
	5/18 Su	19 ♐ 11	20 ♈ 20	17 ♍ 33	8 ♎ 42		2/01 Su	21 ♐ 29	19 ♈ 34	20 ♍ 16	11 ♎ 24
	5/25 Su	19 ♐ 01	20 ♈ 23	17 ♍ 32	8 ♎ 37		2/08 Su	21 ♐ 40	19 ♈ 36	20 ♍ 10	11 ♎ 20
	6/01 Su	18 ♐ 50	20 ♈ 27	17 ♍ 31	8 ♎ 33		2/15 Su	21 ♐ 50	19 ♈ 39	20 ♍ 03	11 ♎ 15
	6/08 Su	18 ♐ 39	20 ♈ 30	17 ♍ 31 D	8 ♎ 31		2/22 Su	21 ♐ 58	19 ♈ 42	19 ♍ 55	11 ♎ 09
	6/15 Su	18 ♐ 28	20 ♈ 32	17 ♍ 33	8 ♎ 29		2/29 Su	22 ♐ 04	19 ♈ 45	19 ♍ 48	11 ♎ 03
	6/22 Su	18 ♐ 17	20 ♈ 34	17 ♍ 36	8 ♎ 28		3/07 Su	22 ♐ 09	19 ♈ 49	19 ♍ 39	10 ♎ 56
	6/29 Su	18 ♐ 06	20 ♈ 36	17 ♍ 39	8 ♎ 28 D		3/14 Su	22 ♐ 12	19 ♈ 53	19 ♍ 31	10 ♎ 49
	7/06 Su	17 ♐ 56	20 ♈ 37	17 ♍ 44	8 ♎ 30		3/21 Su	22 ♐ 14	19 ♈ 57	19 ♍ 23	10 ♎ 41
	7/13 Su	17 ♐ 46	20 ♈ 37	17 ♍ 49	8 ♎ 32		3/28 Su	22 ♐ 14 R	20 ♈ 02	19 ♍ 15	10 ♎ 33
	7/20 Su	17 ♐ 38	20 ♈ 37 R	17 ♍ 56	8 ♎ 35		4/04 Su	22 ♐ 13	20 ♈ 06	19 ♍ 08	10 ♎ 25
	7/27 Su	17 ♐ 30	20 ♈ 37	18 ♍ 03	8 ♎ 40		4/11 Su	22 ♐ 09	20 ♈ 11	19 ♍ 01	10 ♎ 17
	8/03 Su	17 ♐ 24	20 ♈ 36	18 ♍ 11	8 ♎ 45		4/18 Su	22 ♐ 05	20 ♈ 16	18 ♍ 54	10 ♎ 09
	8/10 Su	17 ♐ 19	20 ♈ 35	18 ♍ 19	8 ♎ 51		4/25 Su	21 ♐ 59	20 ♈ 20	18 ♍ 49	10 ♎ 02
	8/17 Su	17 ♐ 16	20 ♈ 33	18 ♍ 28	8 ♎ 58		5/02 Su	21 ♐ 52	20 ♈ 24	18 ♍ 44	9 ♎ 55
	8/24 Su	17 ♐ 14	20 ♈ 30	18 ♍ 37	9 ♎ 06		5/09 Su	21 ♐ 43	20 ♈ 29	18 ♍ 40	9 ♎ 48
	8/31 Su	17 ♐ 14 D	20 ♈ 28	18 ♍ 47	9 ♎ 14		5/16 Su	21 ♐ 34	20 ♈ 33	18 ♍ 37	9 ♎ 43
	9/07 Su	17 ♐ 15	20 ♈ 24	18 ♍ 57	9 ♎ 23		5/23 Su	21 ♐ 24	20 ♈ 36	18 ♍ 35	9 ♎ 38
	9/14 Su	17 ♐ 18	20 ♈ 21	19 ♍ 07	9 ♎ 32		5/30 Su	21 ♐ 14	20 ♈ 40	18 ♍ 34	9 ♎ 34
	9/21 Su	17 ♐ 22	20 ♈ 17	19 ♍ 17	9 ♎ 42		6/06 Su	21 ♐ 03	20 ♈ 43	18 ♍ 34 D	9 ♎ 31
	9/28 Su	17 ♐ 28	20 ♈ 13	19 ♍ 27	9 ♎ 52		6/13 Su	20 ♐ 51	20 ♈ 45	18 ♍ 35	9 ♎ 29
	10/05 Su	17 ♐ 36	20 ♈ 09	19 ♍ 37	10 ♎ 02		6/20 Su	20 ♐ 40	20 ♈ 48	18 ♍ 37	9 ♎ 27
	10/12 Su	17 ♐ 45	20 ♈ 05	19 ♍ 46	10 ♎ 11		6/27 Su	20 ♐ 30	20 ♈ 49	18 ♍ 41	9 ♎ 27 D
	10/19 Su	17 ♐ 55	20 ♈ 01	19 ♍ 55	10 ♎ 21		7/04 Su	20 ♐ 19	20 ♈ 51	18 ♍ 45	9 ♎ 28
	10/26 Su	18 ♐ 06	19 ♈ 57	20 ♍ 03	10 ♎ 31		7/11 Su	20 ♐ 09	20 ♈ 51	18 ♍ 50	9 ♎ 30
	11/02 Su	18 ♐ 19	19 ♈ 53	20 ♍ 10	10 ♎ 40		7/18 Su	20 ♐ 00	20 ♈ 51 R	18 ♍ 56	9 ♎ 34
	11/09 Su	18 ♐ 32	19 ♈ 49	20 ♍ 17	10 ♎ 48		7/25 Su	19 ♐ 53	20 ♈ 51	19 ♍ 03	9 ♎ 38
	11/16 Su	18 ♐ 47	19 ♈ 45	20 ♍ 23	10 ♎ 57		8/01 Su	19 ♐ 46	20 ♈ 50	19 ♍ 11	9 ♎ 43
	11/23 Su	19 ♐ 02	19 ♈ 42	20 ♍ 28	11 ♎ 04		8/08 Su	19 ♐ 40	20 ♈ 49	19 ♍ 19	9 ♎ 49
	11/30 Su	19 ♐ 17	19 ♈ 39	20 ♍ 31	11 ♎ 10		8/15 Su	19 ♐ 36	20 ♈ 47	19 ♍ 28	9 ♎ 55
	12/07 Su	19 ♐ 33	19 ♈ 36	20 ♍ 34	11 ♎ 16		8/22 Su	19 ♐ 33	20 ♈ 45	19 ♍ 37	10 ♎ 03
	12/14 Su	19 ♐ 49	19 ♈ 34	20 ♍ 36	11 ♎ 21		8/29 Su	19 ♐ 32	20 ♈ 42	19 ♍ 47	10 ♎ 11

Astro Data

2003

3/23 Su	05:13	♀	SR	19 ♐ 57	-13.7	(-13:40)
6/01 Su	12:03	♎	SD	17 ♍ 31	31.4	(31:23)
6/23 Mo	13:38	♀	SD	8 ♎ 28	20.9	(20:52)
7/17 Th	09:57	♀	SR	20 ♈ 37	-5.8	(-5:46)
8/29 Fr	03:34	♀	SD	17 ♐ 14	-13.7	(-13:40)
12/20 Sa	10:32	♎	SR	20 ♍ 36	30.1	(30:06)

2004

1/07 We	12:26	♀	SD	19 ♈ 31	-6.1	(-6:06)
1/09 Fr	23:46	♎	SR	11 ♎ 29	19.8	(19:46)
3/24 We	15:08	♀	SR	22 ♐ 14	-14.4	(-14:25)
6/01 Tu	20:09	♎	SD	18 ♍ 34	31.0	(31:00)
6/23 We	17:59	♀	SD	9 ♎ 27	20.7	(20:40)
7/17 Sa	02:40	♀	SR	20 ♈ 51	-5.5	(-5:30)
8/30 Mo	19:38	♀	SD	19 ♐ 32	-14.5	(-14:28)

Year	Date	♇	⯰	🝼	🝻
2004	9/05 Su	19 ♐ 33 D	20 ♈ 39 ℞	19 ♍ 56 D	10 ♎ 19 D
	9/12 Su	19 ♐ 35	20 ♈ 36	20 ♍ 06	10 ♎ 29
	9/19 Su	19 ♐ 38	20 ♈ 32	20 ♍ 16	10 ♎ 38
	9/26 Su	19 ♐ 43	20 ♈ 28	20 ♍ 26	10 ♎ 48
	10/03 Su	19 ♐ 50	20 ♈ 24	20 ♍ 36	10 ♎ 58
	10/10 Su	19 ♐ 58	20 ♈ 20	20 ♍ 45	11 ♎ 08
	10/17 Su	20 ♐ 08	20 ♈ 16	20 ♍ 54	11 ♎ 18
	10/24 Su	20 ♐ 18	20 ♈ 12	21 ♍ 03	11 ♎ 27
	10/31 Su	20 ♐ 30	20 ♈ 07	21 ♍ 10	11 ♎ 37
	11/07 Su	20 ♐ 43	20 ♈ 04	21 ♍ 17	11 ♎ 45
	11/14 Su	20 ♐ 57	20 ♈ 00	21 ♍ 23	11 ♎ 54
	11/21 Su	21 ♐ 12	19 ♈ 56	21 ♍ 29	12 ♎ 01
	11/28 Su	21 ♐ 27	19 ♈ 53	21 ♍ 33	12 ♎ 08
	12/05 Su	21 ♐ 42	19 ♈ 51	21 ♍ 36	12 ♎ 14
	12/12 Su	21 ♐ 58	19 ♈ 49	21 ♍ 38	12 ♎ 19
	12/19 Su	22 ♐ 14	19 ♈ 47	21 ♍ 39	12 ♎ 23
	12/26 Su	22 ♐ 30	19 ♈ 46	21 ♍ 38 ℞	12 ♎ 26
2005	1/02 Su	22 ♐ 45	19 ♈ 45	21 ♍ 37	12 ♎ 28
	1/09 Su	23 ♐ 00	19 ♈ 45 D	21 ♍ 34	12 ♎ 29
	1/16 Su	23 ♐ 14	19 ♈ 45	21 ♍ 31	12 ♎ 28 ℞
	1/23 Su	23 ♐ 28	19 ♈ 46	21 ♍ 26	12 ♎ 27
	1/30 Su	23 ♐ 40	19 ♈ 48	21 ♍ 21	12 ♎ 24
	2/06 Su	23 ♐ 51	19 ♈ 50	21 ♍ 15	12 ♎ 21
	2/13 Su	24 ♐ 01	19 ♈ 52	21 ♍ 08	12 ♎ 16
	2/20 Su	24 ♐ 10	19 ♈ 55	21 ♍ 01	12 ♎ 11
	2/27 Su	24 ♐ 17	19 ♈ 58	20 ♍ 53	12 ♎ 05
	3/06 Su	24 ♐ 23	20 ♈ 02	20 ♍ 45	11 ♎ 58
	3/13 Su	24 ♐ 27	20 ♈ 06	20 ♍ 37	11 ♎ 51
	3/20 Su	24 ♐ 30	20 ♈ 10	20 ♍ 28	11 ♎ 43
	3/27 Su	24 ♐ 30	20 ♈ 15	20 ♍ 20	11 ♎ 35
	4/03 Su	24 ♐ 30 ℞	20 ♈ 19	20 ♍ 13	11 ♎ 27
	4/10 Su	24 ♐ 27	20 ♈ 24	20 ♍ 06	11 ♎ 19
	4/17 Su	24 ♐ 23	20 ♈ 29	19 ♍ 59	11 ♎ 11
	4/24 Su	24 ♐ 18	20 ♈ 33	19 ♍ 53	11 ♎ 03
	5/01 Su	24 ♐ 12	20 ♈ 38	19 ♍ 48	10 ♎ 56
	5/08 Su	24 ♐ 04	20 ♈ 42	19 ♍ 44	10 ♎ 50
	5/15 Su	23 ♐ 55	20 ♈ 46	19 ♍ 40	10 ♎ 44
2005	5/22 Su	23 ♐ 46 ℞	20 ♈ 50 D	19 ♍ 38 ℞	10 ♎ 39 ℞
	5/29 Su	23 ♐ 35	20 ♈ 53	19 ♍ 37	10 ♎ 34
	6/05 Su	23 ♐ 25	20 ♈ 56	19 ♍ 36 D	10 ♎ 31
	6/12 Su	23 ♐ 14	20 ♈ 59	19 ♍ 37	10 ♎ 29
	6/19 Su	23 ♐ 03	21 ♈ 01	19 ♍ 39	10 ♎ 27
	6/26 Su	22 ♐ 52	21 ♈ 03	19 ♍ 42	10 ♎ 27 D
	7/03 Su	22 ♐ 41	21 ♈ 04	19 ♍ 46	10 ♎ 28
	7/10 Su	22 ♐ 31	21 ♈ 05	19 ♍ 51	10 ♎ 29
	7/17 Su	22 ♐ 22	21 ♈ 05	19 ♍ 56	10 ♎ 32
	7/24 Su	22 ♐ 13	21 ♈ 05 ℞	20 ♍ 03	10 ♎ 36
	7/31 Su	22 ♐ 06	21 ♈ 04	20 ♍ 10	10 ♎ 40
	8/07 Su	22 ♐ 00	21 ♈ 03	20 ♍ 19	10 ♎ 46
	8/14 Su	21 ♐ 55	21 ♈ 01	20 ♍ 27	10 ♎ 53
	8/21 Su	21 ♐ 51	20 ♈ 59	20 ♍ 36	11 ♎ 00
	8/28 Su	21 ♐ 49	20 ♈ 57	20 ♍ 46	11 ♎ 08
	9/04 Su	21 ♐ 49 D	20 ♈ 54	20 ♍ 56	11 ♎ 16
	9/11 Su	21 ♐ 50	20 ♈ 50	21 ♍ 06	11 ♎ 25
	9/18 Su	21 ♐ 53	20 ♈ 47	21 ♍ 16	11 ♎ 35
	9/25 Su	21 ♐ 57	20 ♈ 43	21 ♍ 26	11 ♎ 44
	10/02 Su	22 ♐ 03	20 ♈ 39	21 ♍ 35	11 ♎ 54
	10/09 Su	22 ♐ 10	20 ♈ 35	21 ♍ 45	12 ♎ 04
	10/16 Su	22 ♐ 19	20 ♈ 30	21 ♍ 54	12 ♎ 14
	10/23 Su	22 ♐ 29	20 ♈ 26	22 ♍ 02	12 ♎ 24
	10/30 Su	22 ♐ 40	20 ♈ 22	22 ♍ 10	12 ♎ 33
	11/06 Su	22 ♐ 53	20 ♈ 18	22 ♍ 18	12 ♎ 42
	11/13 Su	23 ♐ 06	20 ♈ 15	22 ♍ 24	12 ♎ 51
	11/20 Su	23 ♐ 20	20 ♈ 11	22 ♍ 29	12 ♎ 59
	11/27 Su	23 ♐ 35	20 ♈ 08	22 ♍ 34	13 ♎ 06
	12/04 Su	23 ♐ 50	20 ♈ 05	22 ♍ 37	13 ♎ 12
	12/11 Su	24 ♐ 06	20 ♈ 03	22 ♍ 39	13 ♎ 18
	12/18 Su	24 ♐ 22	20 ♈ 01	22 ♍ 41	13 ♎ 22
	12/25 Su	24 ♐ 37	20 ♈ 00	22 ♍ 41 ℞	13 ♎ 25
2006	1/01 Su	24 ♐ 53	19 ♈ 59	22 ♍ 40	13 ♎ 27
	1/08 Su	25 ♐ 08	19 ♈ 59 D	22 ♍ 38	13 ♎ 29
	1/15 Su	25 ♐ 22	19 ♈ 59	22 ♍ 34	13 ♎ 29 ℞
	1/22 Su	25 ♐ 36	20 ♈ 00	22 ♍ 30	13 ♎ 27
	1/29 Su	25 ♐ 49	20 ♈ 01	22 ♍ 25	13 ♎ 25

Astro Data

Year	Date	Time	Body	Station	Position	Value
2004	12/20 Mo	14:20	🝼	SR	21 ♍ 39	29.7 (29:43)
2005	1/07 Fr	00:47	⯰	SD	19 ♈ 45	-5.8 (-5:50)
	1/10 Mo	08:14	🝻	SR	12 ♎ 29	19.6 (19:34)
	3/27 Su	02:29	♇	SR	24 ♐ 30	-15.1 (-15:07)
2005	6/03 Fr	06:50	🝼	SD	19 ♍ 36	30.6 (30:35)
	6/24 Fr	22:11	🝻	SD	10 ♎ 27	20.5 (20:27)
	7/17 Su	14:09	⯰	SR	21 ♈ 05	-5.3 (-5:15)
	9/02 Fr	10:52	♇	SD	21 ♐ 49	-15.2 (-15:13)
	12/21 We	21:44	🝼	SR	22 ♍ 41	29.3 (29:17)
2006	1/07 Sa	16:00	⯰	SD	19 ♈ 59	-5.6 (-5:35)
	1/11 We	12:58	🝻	SR	13 ♎ 29	19.3 (19:19)

2006	♇	♀	⚳	⚴		2006	♇	♀	⚳	⚴
2/05 Su	26 ♐ 01 D	20 ♈ 03 D	22 ♍ 19 ℞	13 ♎ 22 ℞		11/12 Su	25 ♐ 14 D	20 ♈ 29 ℞	23 ♍ 24 D	13 ♎ 48 D
2/12 Su	26 ♐ 11	20 ♈ 06	22 ♍ 13	13 ♎ 18		11/19 Su	25 ♐ 28	20 ♈ 26	23 ♍ 30	13 ♎ 56
2/19 Su	26 ♐ 21	20 ♈ 08	22 ♍ 05	13 ♎ 13		11/26 Su	25 ♐ 43	20 ♈ 23	23 ♍ 35	14 ♎ 04
2/26 Su	26 ♐ 28	20 ♈ 12	21 ♍ 58	13 ♎ 07		12/03 Su	25 ♐ 57	20 ♈ 20	23 ♍ 38	14 ♎ 10
3/05 Su	26 ♐ 35	20 ♈ 15	21 ♍ 50	13 ♎ 00		12/10 Su	26 ♐ 12	20 ♈ 17	23 ♍ 41	14 ♎ 16
3/12 Su	26 ♐ 40	20 ♈ 19	21 ♍ 42	12 ♎ 53		12/17 Su	26 ♐ 28	20 ♈ 15	23 ♍ 43	14 ♎ 21
3/19 Su	26 ♐ 43	20 ♈ 23	21 ♍ 33	12 ♎ 45		12/24 Su	26 ♐ 43	20 ♈ 14	23 ♍ 43 ℞	14 ♎ 24
3/26 Su	26 ♐ 45	20 ♈ 28	21 ♍ 25	12 ♎ 37		12/31 Su	26 ♐ 59	20 ♈ 13	23 ♍ 42	14 ♎ 27
4/02 Su	26 ♐ 45 ℞	20 ♈ 32	21 ♍ 18	12 ♎ 29						
4/09 Su	26 ♐ 43	20 ♈ 37	21 ♍ 10	12 ♎ 21						
						2007				
4/16 Su	26 ♐ 40	20 ♈ 41	21 ♍ 03	12 ♎ 13		1/07 Su	27 ♐ 14	20 ♈ 13	23 ♍ 40	14 ♎ 29
4/23 Su	26 ♐ 35	20 ♈ 46	20 ♍ 57	12 ♎ 06		1/14 Su	27 ♐ 29	20 ♈ 13 D	23 ♍ 38	14 ♎ 29 ℞
4/30 Su	26 ♐ 30	20 ♈ 50	20 ♍ 52	11 ♎ 58		1/21 Su	27 ♐ 43	20 ♈ 14	23 ♍ 34	14 ♎ 28
5/07 Su	26 ♐ 22	20 ♈ 55	20 ♍ 47	11 ♎ 52		1/28 Su	27 ♐ 56	20 ♈ 15	23 ♍ 29	14 ♎ 26
5/14 Su	26 ♐ 14	20 ♈ 59	20 ♍ 44	11 ♎ 45		2/04 Su	28 ♐ 08	20 ♈ 17	23 ♍ 23	14 ♎ 23
5/21 Su	26 ♐ 05	21 ♈ 03	20 ♍ 41	11 ♎ 40		2/11 Su	28 ♐ 19	20 ♈ 19	23 ♍ 17	14 ♎ 19
5/28 Su	25 ♐ 55	21 ♈ 06	20 ♍ 39	11 ♎ 35		2/18 Su	28 ♐ 29	20 ♈ 22	23 ♍ 10	14 ♎ 15
6/04 Su	25 ♐ 45	21 ♈ 09	20 ♍ 39	11 ♎ 32		2/25 Su	28 ♐ 38	20 ♈ 25	23 ♍ 02	14 ♎ 09
6/11 Su	25 ♐ 34	21 ♈ 12	20 ♍ 39 D	11 ♎ 29		3/04 Su	28 ♐ 45	20 ♈ 28	22 ♍ 54	14 ♎ 02
6/18 Su	25 ♐ 23	21 ♈ 15	20 ♍ 41	11 ♎ 27		3/11 Su	28 ♐ 50	20 ♈ 32	22 ♍ 46	13 ♎ 55
6/25 Su	25 ♐ 12	21 ♈ 16	20 ♍ 43	11 ♎ 27		3/18 Su	28 ♐ 54	20 ♈ 36	22 ♍ 38	13 ♎ 48
7/02 Su	25 ♐ 01	21 ♈ 18	20 ♍ 47	11 ♎ 27 D		3/25 Su	28 ♐ 57	20 ♈ 41	22 ♍ 30	13 ♎ 40
7/09 Su	24 ♐ 51	21 ♈ 19	20 ♍ 51	11 ♎ 28		4/01 Su	28 ♐ 58 ℞	20 ♈ 45	22 ♍ 22	13 ♎ 32
7/16 Su	24 ♐ 41	21 ♈ 19	20 ♍ 57	11 ♎ 31		4/08 Su	28 ♐ 57	20 ♈ 50	22 ♍ 15	13 ♎ 24
7/23 Su	24 ♐ 33	21 ♈ 19 ℞	21 ♍ 03	11 ♎ 34		4/15 Su	28 ♐ 54	20 ♈ 54	22 ♍ 08	13 ♎ 16
7/30 Su	24 ♐ 25	21 ♈ 18	21 ♍ 10	11 ♎ 39		4/22 Su	28 ♐ 51	20 ♈ 59	22 ♍ 01	13 ♎ 08
8/06 Su	24 ♐ 18	21 ♈ 17	21 ♍ 18	11 ♎ 44		4/29 Su	28 ♐ 45	21 ♈ 03	21 ♍ 56	13 ♎ 01
8/13 Su	24 ♐ 12	21 ♈ 16	21 ♍ 27	11 ♎ 50		5/06 Su	28 ♐ 39	21 ♈ 08	21 ♍ 51	12 ♎ 54
8/20 Su	24 ♐ 08	21 ♈ 14	21 ♍ 36	11 ♎ 57		5/13 Su	28 ♐ 31	21 ♈ 12	21 ♍ 47	12 ♎ 47
8/27 Su	24 ♐ 05	21 ♈ 11	21 ♍ 45	12 ♎ 05		5/20 Su	28 ♐ 23	21 ♈ 16	21 ♍ 44	12 ♎ 42
9/03 Su	24 ♐ 04	21 ♈ 08	21 ♍ 55	12 ♎ 13		5/27 Su	28 ♐ 13	21 ♈ 19	21 ♍ 42	12 ♎ 37
9/10 Su	24 ♐ 05 D	21 ♈ 05	22 ♍ 05	12 ♎ 22		6/03 Su	28 ♐ 03	21 ♈ 23	21 ♍ 41	12 ♎ 33
9/17 Su	24 ♐ 06	21 ♈ 01	22 ♍ 15	12 ♎ 32		6/10 Su	27 ♐ 52	21 ♈ 26	21 ♍ 41 D	12 ♎ 30
9/24 Su	24 ♐ 10	20 ♈ 58	22 ♍ 25	12 ♎ 41		6/17 Su	27 ♐ 42	21 ♈ 28	21 ♍ 42	12 ♎ 28
10/01 Su	24 ♐ 15	20 ♈ 54	22 ♍ 34	12 ♎ 51		6/24 Su	27 ♐ 31	21 ♈ 30	21 ♍ 45	12 ♎ 27
10/08 Su	24 ♐ 21	20 ♈ 49	22 ♍ 44	13 ♎ 01		7/01 Su	27 ♐ 20	21 ♈ 32	21 ♍ 48	12 ♎ 27 D
10/15 Su	24 ♐ 29	20 ♈ 45	22 ♍ 53	13 ♎ 11		7/08 Su	27 ♐ 09	21 ♈ 33	21 ♍ 52	12 ♎ 28
10/22 Su	24 ♐ 39	20 ♈ 41	23 ♍ 02	13 ♎ 21		7/15 Su	26 ♐ 59	21 ♈ 33	21 ♍ 57	12 ♎ 30
10/29 Su	24 ♐ 49	20 ♈ 37	23 ♍ 10	13 ♎ 31		7/22 Su	26 ♐ 50	21 ♈ 33 ℞	22 ♍ 03	12 ♎ 33
11/05 Su	25 ♐ 01	20 ♈ 33	23 ♍ 17	13 ♎ 40		7/29 Su	26 ♐ 42	21 ♈ 33	22 ♍ 10	12 ♎ 37

Astro Data

2006

3/29 We	12:40	♇	SR	26 ♐ 45	-15.8 (-15:48)
6/04 Su	14:26	⚳	SD	20 ♍ 39	30.1 (30:07)
6/26 Mo	03:04	⚴	SD	11 ♎ 27	20.2 (20:10)
7/17 Mo	21:02	♀	SR	21 ♈ 19	-5.0 (-5:00)
9/04 Mo	23:21	♇	SD	24 ♐ 04	-16.0 (-15:57)

2006

12/23 Sa	05:31	⚳	SR	23 ♍ 43	28.9 (28:51)

2007

1/08 Mo	05:28	♀	SD	20 ♈ 13	-5.3 (-5:19)
1/12 Fr	17:16	⚴	SR	14 ♎ 29	19.1 (19:04)
3/31 Sa	22:45	♇	SR	28 ♐ 58	-16.5 (-16:27)
6/05 Tu	20:59	⚳	SD	21 ♍ 41	29.7 (29:43)
6/27 We	10:07	⚴	SD	12 ♎ 27	20.0 (19:57)
7/18 We	06:31	♀	SR	21 ♈ 33	-4.7 (-4:43)

	♇	♀	♠	♣
2007 8/05 Su	26 ♐ 35 ℞	21 ♈ 32 ℞	22 ♍ 18 D	12 ♎ 42 D
8/12 Su	26 ♐ 28	21 ♈ 30	22 ♍ 26	12 ♎ 48
8/19 Su	26 ♐ 34	21 ♈ 28	22 ♍ 35	12 ♎ 55
8/26 Su	26 ♐ 20	21 ♈ 26	22 ♍ 44	13 ♎ 02
9/02 Su	26 ♐ 18	21 ♈ 23	22 ♍ 53	13 ♎ 11
9/09 Su	26 ♐ 18 D	21 ♈ 20	23 ♍ 03	13 ♎ 19
9/16 Su	26 ♐ 19	21 ♈ 16	23 ♍ 13	13 ♎ 29
9/23 Su	26 ♐ 21	21 ♈ 12	23 ♍ 23	13 ♎ 38
9/30 Su	26 ♐ 26	21 ♈ 08	23 ♍ 33	13 ♎ 48
10/07 Su	26 ♐ 31	21 ♈ 04	23 ♍ 43	13 ♎ 58
10/14 Su	26 ♐ 39	21 ♈ 00	23 ♍ 52	14 ♎ 08
10/21 Su	26 ♐ 47	20 ♈ 56	24 ♍ 01	14 ♎ 18
10/28 Su	26 ♐ 57	20 ♈ 52	24 ♍ 09	14 ♎ 28
11/04 Su	27 ♐ 08	20 ♈ 48	24 ♍ 17	14 ♎ 37
11/11 Su	27 ♐ 20	20 ♈ 44	24 ♍ 24	14 ♎ 46
11/18 Su	27 ♐ 33	20 ♈ 40	24 ♍ 30	14 ♎ 54
11/25 Su	27 ♐ 47	20 ♈ 37	24 ♍ 35	15 ♎ 02
12/02 Su	28 ♐ 02	20 ♈ 34	24 ♍ 39	15 ♎ 09
12/09 Su	28 ♐ 17	20 ♈ 32	24 ♍ 42	15 ♎ 15
12/16 Su	28 ♐ 32	20 ♈ 30	24 ♍ 44	15 ♎ 20
12/23 Su	28 ♐ 48	20 ♈ 28	24 ♍ 45	15 ♎ 24
12/30 Su	29 ♐ 03	20 ♈ 27	24 ♍ 44 ℞	15 ♎ 27
2008 1/06 Su	29 ♐ 19	20 ♈ 27	24 ♍ 43	15 ♎ 29
1/13 Su	29 ♐ 33	20 ♈ 27 D	24 ♍ 40	15 ♎ 29
1/20 Su	29 ♐ 48	20 ♈ 27	24 ♍ 37	15 ♎ 29 ℞
1/27 Su	0 ♑ 01	20 ♈ 29	24 ♍ 32	15 ♎ 27
2/03 Su	0 ♑ 14	20 ♈ 30	24 ♍ 27	15 ♎ 25
2/10 Su	0 ♑ 25	20 ♈ 32	24 ♍ 21	15 ♎ 21
2/17 Su	0 ♑ 36	20 ♈ 35	24 ♍ 14	15 ♎ 17
2/24 Su	0 ♑ 45	20 ♈ 38	24 ♍ 07	15 ♎ 11
3/02 Su	0 ♑ 53	20 ♈ 42	23 ♍ 59	15 ♎ 05
3/09 Su	0 ♑ 59	20 ♈ 45	23 ♍ 51	14 ♎ 58
3/16 Su	1 ♑ 04	20 ♈ 49	23 ♍ 43	14 ♎ 51
3/23 Su	1 ♑ 07	20 ♈ 54	23 ♍ 35	14 ♎ 43
3/30 Su	1 ♑ 08	20 ♈ 58	23 ♍ 27	14 ♎ 35
4/06 Su	1 ♑ 08 ℞	21 ♈ 03	23 ♍ 19	14 ♎ 27
4/13 Su	1 ♑ 07	21 ♈ 07	23 ♍ 12	14 ♎ 19

	♇	♀	♠	♣
2008 4/20 Su	1 ♑ 04 ℞	21 ♈ 12 D	23 ♍ 05 ℞	14 ♎ 11 ℞
4/27 Su	0 ♑ 59	21 ♈ 17	22 ♍ 59	14 ♎ 03
5/04 Su	0 ♑ 53	21 ♈ 21	22 ♍ 54	13 ♎ 56
5/11 Su	0 ♑ 46	21 ♈ 25	22 ♍ 50	13 ♎ 50
5/18 Su	0 ♑ 38	21 ♈ 29	22 ♍ 47	13 ♎ 44
5/25 Su	0 ♑ 29	21 ♈ 33	22 ♍ 44	13 ♎ 39
6/01 Su	0 ♑ 19	21 ♈ 36	22 ♍ 43	13 ♎ 34
6/08 Su	0 ♑ 09	21 ♈ 39	22 ♍ 43 D	13 ♎ 31
6/15 Su	29 ♐ 58	21 ♈ 42	22 ♍ 44	13 ♎ 28
6/22 Su	29 ♐ 47	21 ♈ 44	22 ♍ 46	13 ♎ 27
6/29 Su	29 ♐ 37	21 ♈ 45	22 ♍ 48	13 ♎ 27 D
7/06 Su	29 ♐ 26	21 ♈ 46	22 ♍ 52	13 ♎ 27
7/13 Su	29 ♐ 16	21 ♈ 47	22 ♍ 57	13 ♎ 29
7/20 Su	29 ♐ 06	21 ♈ 47 ℞	23 ♍ 03	13 ♎ 32
7/27 Su	28 ♐ 58	21 ♈ 47	23 ♍ 10	13 ♎ 36
8/03 Su	28 ♐ 50	21 ♈ 46	23 ♍ 17	13 ♎ 41
8/10 Su	28 ♐ 43	21 ♈ 44	23 ♍ 25	13 ♎ 46
8/17 Su	28 ♐ 37	21 ♈ 42	23 ♍ 33	13 ♎ 53
8/24 Su	28 ♐ 33	21 ♈ 40	23 ♍ 43	14 ♎ 00
8/31 Su	28 ♐ 31	21 ♈ 37	23 ♍ 52	14 ♎ 08
9/07 Su	28 ♐ 29	21 ♈ 34	24 ♍ 02	14 ♎ 17
9/14 Su	28 ♐ 30 D	21 ♈ 31	24 ♍ 12	14 ♎ 26
9/21 Su	28 ♐ 31	21 ♈ 27	24 ♍ 22	14 ♎ 35
9/28 Su	28 ♐ 35	21 ♈ 23	24 ♍ 32	14 ♎ 45
10/05 Su	28 ♐ 40	21 ♈ 19	24 ♍ 41	14 ♎ 55
10/12 Su	28 ♐ 46	21 ♈ 15	24 ♍ 51	15 ♎ 05
10/19 Su	28 ♐ 54	21 ♈ 11	25 ♍ 00	15 ♎ 15
10/26 Su	29 ♐ 03	21 ♈ 07	25 ♍ 08	15 ♎ 25
11/02 Su	29 ♐ 14	21 ♈ 03	25 ♍ 16	15 ♎ 34
11/09 Su	29 ♐ 25	20 ♈ 59	25 ♍ 23	15 ♎ 44
11/16 Su	29 ♐ 38	20 ♈ 55	25 ♍ 30	15 ♎ 52
11/23 Su	29 ♐ 51	20 ♈ 52	25 ♍ 35	16 ♎ 00
11/30 Su	0 ♑ 06	20 ♈ 49	25 ♍ 39	16 ♎ 07
12/07 Su	0 ♑ 20	20 ♈ 46	25 ♍ 43	16 ♎ 13
12/14 Su	0 ♑ 35	20 ♈ 44	25 ♍ 45	16 ♎ 19
12/21 Su	0 ♑ 51	20 ♈ 42	25 ♍ 46	16 ♎ 23
12/28 Su	1 ♑ 06	20 ♈ 41	25 ♍ 46 ℞	16 ♎ 26

Astro Data

2007

9/07 Fr	14:55	♇	SD	26 ♐ 18	-16.6 (-16:38)
12/24 Mo	13:33	♠	SR	24 ♍ 45	28.5 (28:27)

2008

1/08 Tu	09:53	♀	SD	20 ♈ 27	-5.1 (-5:03)
1/13 Su	20:50	♣	SR	15 ♎ 29	18.9 (18:52)
1/26 Sa	02:38	♇ → ♑			-17.2 (-17:09)
4/02 We	09:23	♀	SR	1 ♑ 08	-17.1 (-17:04)

2008

6/06 Fr	01:56	♠	SD	22 ♍ 43	29.3 (29:17)
6/14 Sa	05:13	♇ → ♐ ℞			-17.0 (-17:01)
6/27 Fr	19:45	♣	SD	13 ♎ 27	19.7 (19:42)
7/18 Fr	00:30	♀	SR	21 ♈ 47	-4.5 (-4:28)
9/09 Tu	03:14	♇	SD	28 ♐ 29	-17.3 (-17:19)
11/27 Th	01:04	♇ → ♑			-17.7 (-17:39)
12/24 We	17:51	♠	SR	25 ♍ 46	28.0 (28:00)

2009

1/07 We	19:40	♀	SD	20 ♈ 41	-4.8 (-4:48)

LONGITUDE

		♇	♀	⯓	⯔
2009	1/04 Su	1 ♑ 21 D	20 ♈ 41 ℞	25 ♍ 45 ℞	16 ♎ 29 D
	1/11 Su	1 ♑ 36	20 ♈ 41 D	25 ♍ 43	16 ♎ 30
	1/18 Su	1 ♑ 51	20 ♈ 41	25 ♍ 40	16 ♎ 30 ℞
	1/25 Su	2 ♑ 04	20 ♈ 42	25 ♍ 36	16 ♎ 28
	2/01 Su	2 ♑ 17	20 ♈ 44	25 ♍ 30	16 ♎ 26
	2/08 Su	2 ♑ 29	20 ♈ 46	25 ♍ 24	16 ♎ 23
	2/15 Su	2 ♑ 40	20 ♈ 48	25 ♍ 18	16 ♎ 19
	2/22 Su	2 ♑ 50	20 ♈ 51	25 ♍ 11	16 ♎ 13
	3/01 Su	2 ♑ 58	20 ♈ 55	25 ♍ 03	16 ♎ 08
	3/08 Su	3 ♑ 05	20 ♈ 59	24 ♍ 55	16 ♎ 01
	3/15 Su	3 ♑ 11	21 ♈ 03	24 ♍ 47	15 ♎ 54
	3/22 Su	3 ♑ 15	21 ♈ 07	24 ♍ 39	15 ♎ 46
	3/29 Su	3 ♑ 17	21 ♈ 11	24 ♍ 31	15 ♎ 38
	4/05 Su	3 ♑ 18 ℞	21 ♈ 16	24 ♍ 23	15 ♎ 30
	4/12 Su	3 ♑ 17	21 ♈ 20	24 ♍ 16	15 ♎ 22
	4/19 Su	3 ♑ 14	21 ♈ 25	24 ♍ 09	15 ♎ 14
	4/26 Su	3 ♑ 11	21 ♈ 30	24 ♍ 03	15 ♎ 06
	5/03 Su	3 ♑ 05	21 ♈ 34	23 ♍ 58	14 ♎ 59
	5/10 Su	2 ♑ 59	21 ♈ 38	23 ♍ 53	14 ♎ 52
	5/17 Su	2 ♑ 51	21 ♈ 42	23 ♍ 49	14 ♎ 46
	5/24 Su	2 ♑ 43	21 ♈ 46	23 ♍ 47	14 ♎ 40
	5/31 Su	2 ♑ 33	21 ♈ 49	23 ♍ 45	14 ♎ 36
	6/07 Su	2 ♑ 23	21 ♈ 52	23 ♍ 45	14 ♎ 32
	6/14 Su	2 ♑ 13	21 ♈ 55	23 ♍ 45 D	14 ♎ 29
	6/21 Su	2 ♑ 02	21 ♈ 57	23 ♍ 46	14 ♎ 28
	6/28 Su	1 ♑ 51	21 ♈ 59	23 ♍ 49	14 ♎ 27
	7/05 Su	1 ♑ 41	22 ♈ 00	23 ♍ 53	14 ♎ 27 D
	7/12 Su	1 ♑ 30	22 ♈ 01	23 ♍ 57	14 ♎ 29
	7/19 Su	1 ♑ 21	22 ♈ 01 ℞	24 ♍ 03	14 ♎ 31
	7/26 Su	1 ♑ 11	22 ♈ 01	24 ♍ 09	14 ♎ 35
	8/02 Su	1 ♑ 03	22 ♈ 00	24 ♍ 16	14 ♎ 39
	8/09 Su	0 ♑ 56	21 ♈ 59	24 ♍ 24	14 ♎ 45
	8/16 Su	0 ♑ 50	21 ♈ 57	24 ♍ 32	14 ♎ 51
	8/23 Su	0 ♑ 45	21 ♈ 55	24 ♍ 41	14 ♎ 58
	8/30 Su	0 ♑ 42	21 ♈ 52	24 ♍ 50	15 ♎ 06
	9/06 Su	0 ♑ 40	21 ♈ 49	25 ♍ 00	15 ♎ 14
	9/13 Su	0 ♑ 39 D	21 ♈ 46	25 ♍ 10	15 ♎ 23
	9/20 Su	0 ♑ 40	21 ♈ 42	25 ♍ 20	15 ♎ 33
	9/27 Su	0 ♑ 43	21 ♈ 38	25 ♍ 30	15 ♎ 42
	10/04 Su	0 ♑ 47	21 ♈ 34	25 ♍ 40	15 ♎ 52

		♇	♀	⯓	⯔
2009	10/11 Su	0 ♑ 52 D	21 ♈ 30 ℞	25 ♍ 49 D	16 ♎ 02 D
	10/18 Su	1 ♑ 00	21 ♈ 26	25 ♍ 58	16 ♎ 12
	10/25 Su	1 ♑ 08	21 ♈ 21	26 ♍ 07	16 ♎ 22
	11/01 Su	1 ♑ 18	21 ♈ 17	26 ♍ 15	16 ♎ 32
	11/08 Su	1 ♑ 29	21 ♈ 13	26 ♍ 22	16 ♎ 41
	11/15 Su	1 ♑ 41	21 ♈ 10	26 ♍ 29	16 ♎ 50
	11/22 Su	1 ♑ 54	21 ♈ 06	26 ♍ 35	16 ♎ 58
	11/29 Su	2 ♑ 08	21 ♈ 03	26 ♍ 39	17 ♎ 05
	12/06 Su	2 ♑ 22	21 ♈ 01	26 ♍ 43	17 ♎ 12
	12/13 Su	2 ♑ 37	20 ♈ 58	26 ♍ 46	17 ♎ 18
	12/20 Su	2 ♑ 52	20 ♈ 57	26 ♍ 47	17 ♎ 22
	12/27 Su	3 ♑ 07	20 ♈ 56	26 ♍ 48 ℞	17 ♎ 26
2010	1/03 Su	3 ♑ 22	20 ♈ 55	26 ♍ 47	17 ♎ 29
	1/10 Su	3 ♑ 37	20 ♈ 55 D	26 ♍ 45	17 ♎ 30
	1/17 Su	3 ♑ 52	20 ♈ 55	26 ♍ 42	17 ♎ 30 ℞
	1/24 Su	4 ♑ 06	20 ♈ 56	26 ♍ 38	17 ♎ 30
	1/31 Su	4 ♑ 19	20 ♈ 57	26 ♍ 33	17 ♎ 28
	2/07 Su	4 ♑ 31	20 ♈ 59	26 ♍ 28	17 ♎ 25
	2/14 Su	4 ♑ 43	21 ♈ 02	26 ♍ 21	17 ♎ 21
	2/21 Su	4 ♑ 53	21 ♈ 05	26 ♍ 14	17 ♎ 16
	2/28 Su	5 ♑ 02	21 ♈ 08	26 ♍ 07	17 ♎ 10
	3/07 Su	5 ♑ 09	21 ♈ 12	25 ♍ 59	17 ♎ 04
	3/14 Su	5 ♑ 16	21 ♈ 16	25 ♍ 51	16 ♎ 57
	3/21 Su	5 ♑ 20	21 ♈ 20	25 ♍ 43	16 ♎ 49
	3/28 Su	5 ♑ 23	21 ♈ 24	25 ♍ 35	16 ♎ 41
	4/04 Su	5 ♑ 25	21 ♈ 29	25 ♍ 27	16 ♎ 33
	4/11 Su	5 ♑ 24 ℞	21 ♈ 33	25 ♍ 20	16 ♎ 25
	4/18 Su	5 ♑ 23	21 ♈ 38	25 ♍ 13	16 ♎ 17
	4/25 Su	5 ♑ 20	21 ♈ 43	25 ♍ 06	16 ♎ 09
	5/02 Su	5 ♑ 15	21 ♈ 47	25 ♍ 01	16 ♎ 02
	5/09 Su	5 ♑ 09	21 ♈ 51	24 ♍ 56	15 ♎ 55
	5/16 Su	5 ♑ 02	21 ♈ 55	24 ♍ 52	15 ♎ 48
	5/23 Su	4 ♑ 54	21 ♈ 59	24 ♍ 49	15 ♎ 43
	5/30 Su	4 ♑ 45	22 ♈ 03	24 ♍ 47	15 ♎ 38
	6/06 Su	4 ♑ 36	22 ♈ 06	24 ♍ 46	15 ♎ 34
	6/13 Su	4 ♑ 26	22 ♈ 08	24 ♍ 46 D	15 ♎ 31
	6/20 Su	4 ♑ 15	22 ♈ 11	24 ♍ 47	15 ♎ 29

Astro Data

2009						
1/14 We	04:23	⯔	SR	16 ♎ 30	18.6	(18:36)
4/04 Sa	17:35	♇	SR	3 ♑ 18	-17.7	(-17:39)
6/07 Su	10:39	⯓	SD	23 ♍ 45	28.8	(28:49)
6/29 Mo	01:57	⯔	SD	14 ♎ 27	19.4	(19:25)
7/18 Sa	15:11	♀	SR	22 ♈ 01	-4.2	(-4:12)
9/11 Fr	16:57	♇	SD	0 ♑ 39	-17.9	(-17:55)
2009						
12/25 Fr	20:24	⯓	SR	26 ♍ 48	27.6	(27:33)
2010						
1/08 Fr	13:05	♀	SD	20 ♈ 55	-4.6	(-4:33)
1/15 Fr	11:57	⯔	SR	17 ♎ 30	18.3	(18:20)
4/07 We	02:34	♇	SR	5 ♑ 25	-18.2	(-18:12)
6/08 Tu	20:53	⯓	SD	24 ♍ 46	28.4	(28:24)

	♇	♀	♇	♎
2010				
6/27 Su	4 ♑ 04 ℞	22 ♈ 13 D	24 ♍ 49 D	15 ♎ 28 ℞
7/04 Su	3 ♑ 54	22 ♈ 14	24 ♍ 53	15 ♎ 28 D
7/11 Su	3 ♑ 43	22 ♈ 15	24 ♍ 57	15 ♎ 29
7/18 Su	3 ♑ 33	22 ♈ 15	25 ♍ 02	15 ♎ 31
7/25 Su	3 ♑ 24	22 ♈ 15 ℞	25 ♍ 08	15 ♎ 34
8/01 Su	3 ♑ 15	22 ♈ 14	25 ♍ 15	15 ♎ 38
8/08 Su	3 ♑ 07	22 ♈ 13	25 ♍ 22	15 ♎ 43
8/15 Su	3 ♑ 00	22 ♈ 11	25 ♍ 31	15 ♎ 49
8/22 Su	2 ♑ 55	22 ♈ 09	25 ♍ 39	15 ♎ 56
8/29 Su	2 ♑ 51	22 ♈ 07	25 ♍ 49	16 ♎ 04
9/05 Su	2 ♑ 48	22 ♈ 04	25 ♍ 58	16 ♎ 12
9/12 Su	2 ♑ 47	22 ♈ 00	26 ♍ 08	16 ♎ 21
9/19 Su	2 ♑ 47 D	21 ♈ 57	26 ♍ 18	16 ♎ 30
9/26 Su	2 ♑ 49	21 ♈ 53	26 ♍ 28	16 ♎ 40
10/03 Su	2 ♑ 52	21 ♈ 49	26 ♍ 38	16 ♎ 50
10/10 Su	2 ♑ 57	21 ♈ 45	26 ♍ 47	17 ♎ 00
10/17 Su	3 ♑ 04	21 ♈ 41	26 ♍ 57	17 ♎ 10
10/24 Su	3 ♑ 11	21 ♈ 36	27 ♍ 05	17 ♎ 20
10/31 Su	3 ♑ 20	21 ♈ 32	27 ♍ 14	17 ♎ 30
11/07 Su	3 ♑ 31	21 ♈ 28	27 ♍ 21	17 ♎ 39
11/14 Su	3 ♑ 42	21 ♈ 25	27 ♍ 28	17 ♎ 48
11/21 Su	3 ♑ 55	21 ♈ 21	27 ♍ 34	17 ♎ 56
11/28 Su	4 ♑ 08	21 ♈ 18	27 ♍ 39	18 ♎ 04
12/05 Su	4 ♑ 22	21 ♈ 15	27 ♍ 43	18 ♎ 11
12/12 Su	4 ♑ 36	21 ♈ 13	27 ♍ 46	18 ♎ 17
12/19 Su	4 ♑ 51	21 ♈ 11	27 ♍ 48	18 ♎ 22
12/26 Su	5 ♑ 06	21 ♈ 10	27 ♍ 49	18 ♎ 26
2011				
1/02 Su	5 ♑ 22	21 ♈ 09	27 ♍ 48 ℞	18 ♎ 29
1/09 Su	5 ♑ 37	21 ♈ 09	27 ♍ 47	18 ♎ 31
1/16 Su	5 ♑ 51	21 ♈ 09 D	27 ♍ 44	18 ♎ 31
1/23 Su	6 ♑ 05	21 ♈ 10	27 ♍ 41	18 ♎ 31 ℞
1/30 Su	6 ♑ 19	21 ♈ 11	27 ♍ 36	18 ♎ 29
2/06 Su	6 ♑ 32	21 ♈ 13	27 ♍ 31	18 ♎ 27
2/13 Su	6 ♑ 43	21 ♈ 15	27 ♍ 25	18 ♎ 23
2/20 Su	6 ♑ 54	21 ♈ 18	27 ♍ 18	18 ♎ 18
2/27 Su	7 ♑ 03	21 ♈ 21	27 ♍ 10	18 ♎ 13
3/06 Su	7 ♑ 11	21 ♈ 25	27 ♍ 03	18 ♎ 07

	♇	♀	♇	♎
2011				
3/13 Su	7 ♑ 18 D	21 ♈ 29 D	26 ♍ 55 ℞	18 ♎ 00 ℞
3/20 Su	7 ♑ 23	21 ♈ 33	26 ♍ 47	17 ♎ 52
3/27 Su	7 ♑ 27	21 ♈ 37	26 ♍ 38	17 ♎ 44
4/03 Su	7 ♑ 29	21 ♈ 42	26 ♍ 31	17 ♎ 36
4/10 Su	7 ♑ 30 ℞	21 ♈ 46	26 ♍ 23	17 ♎ 28
4/17 Su	7 ♑ 29	21 ♈ 51	26 ♍ 16	17 ♎ 20
4/24 Su	7 ♑ 27	21 ♈ 56	26 ♍ 09	17 ♎ 12
5/01 Su	7 ♑ 23	22 ♈ 00	26 ♍ 04	17 ♎ 05
5/08 Su	7 ♑ 18	22 ♈ 04	25 ♍ 58	16 ♎ 57
5/15 Su	7 ♑ 11	22 ♈ 08	25 ♍ 54	16 ♎ 51
5/22 Su	7 ♑ 04	22 ♈ 12	25 ♍ 51	16 ♎ 45
5/29 Su	6 ♑ 55	22 ♈ 16	25 ♍ 49	16 ♎ 40
6/05 Su	6 ♑ 46	22 ♈ 19	25 ♍ 47	16 ♎ 35
6/12 Su	6 ♑ 36	22 ♈ 22	25 ♍ 47 D	16 ♎ 32
6/19 Su	6 ♑ 26	22 ♈ 24	25 ♍ 48	16 ♎ 30
6/26 Su	6 ♑ 15	22 ♈ 26	25 ♍ 50	16 ♎ 28
7/03 Su	6 ♑ 04	22 ♈ 28	25 ♍ 53	16 ♎ 28 D
7/10 Su	5 ♑ 54	22 ♈ 29	25 ♍ 57	16 ♎ 29
7/17 Su	5 ♑ 44	22 ♈ 29	26 ♍ 01	16 ♎ 31
7/24 Su	5 ♑ 34	22 ♈ 29 ℞	26 ♍ 07	16 ♎ 33
7/31 Su	5 ♑ 25	22 ♈ 28	26 ♍ 14	16 ♎ 37
8/07 Su	5 ♑ 17	22 ♈ 27	26 ♍ 21	16 ♎ 42
8/14 Su	5 ♑ 09	22 ♈ 26	26 ♍ 29	16 ♎ 48
8/21 Su	5 ♑ 03	22 ♈ 24	26 ♍ 38	16 ♎ 54
8/28 Su	4 ♑ 59	22 ♈ 21	26 ♍ 47	17 ♎ 02
9/04 Su	4 ♑ 55	22 ♈ 18	26 ♍ 56	17 ♎ 10
9/11 Su	4 ♑ 53	22 ♈ 15	27 ♍ 06	17 ♎ 19
9/18 Su	4 ♑ 53 D	22 ♈ 11	27 ♍ 16	17 ♎ 28
9/25 Su	4 ♑ 54	22 ♈ 08	27 ♍ 26	17 ♎ 37
10/02 Su	4 ♑ 56	22 ♈ 04	27 ♍ 35	17 ♎ 47
10/09 Su	5 ♑ 01	22 ♈ 00	27 ♍ 45	17 ♎ 57
10/16 Su	5 ♑ 06	21 ♈ 55	27 ♍ 55	18 ♎ 07
10/23 Su	5 ♑ 13	21 ♈ 51	28 ♍ 03	18 ♎ 17
10/30 Su	5 ♑ 21	21 ♈ 47	28 ♍ 12	18 ♎ 27
11/06 Su	5 ♑ 31	21 ♈ 43	28 ♍ 20	18 ♎ 37
11/13 Su	5 ♑ 42	21 ♈ 39	28 ♍ 27	18 ♎ 46
11/20 Su	5 ♑ 54	21 ♈ 36	28 ♍ 33	18 ♎ 55
11/27 Su	6 ♑ 07	21 ♈ 33	28 ♍ 38	19 ♎ 02
12/04 Su	6 ♑ 20	21 ♈ 30	28 ♍ 43	19 ♎ 10
12/11 Su	6 ♑ 34	21 ♈ 27	28 ♍ 46	19 ♎ 16

Astro Data

2010

6/30 We	08:20	♎	SD	15 ♎ 27	19.2	(19:11)
7/18 Su	19:47	♀	SR	22 ♈ 15	-4.0	(-3:57)
9/14 Tu	04:36	♇	SD	2 ♑ 47	-18.5	(-18:32)
12/27 Mo	02:50	♎	SR	27 ♍ 49	27.1	(27:08)

2011

1/09 Su	01:46	♀	SD	21 ♈ 09	-4.3	(-4:16)
1/16 Su	19:16	♎	SR	18 ♎ 31	18.1	(18:07)

2011

4/09 Sa	08:50	♇	SR	7 ♑ 30	-18.7	(-18:43)
6/10 Fr	04:19	♎	SD	25 ♍ 47	28.0	(27:58)
7/01 Fr	11:56	♎	SD	16 ♎ 28	18.9	(18:56)
7/19 Tu	05:44	♀	SR	22 ♈ 29	-3.7	(-3:41)
9/16 Fr	18:24	♇	SD	4 ♑ 53	-19.1	(-19:04)

		♇	♀	♀	♇				♇	♀	♀	♇
2011	12/18 Su	6 ♑ 49 D	21 ♈ 15 R	28 ♍ 48 D	19 ♎ 21 D	2012	9/02 Su	7 ♑ 01 R	22 ♈ 33 R	27 ♍ 54 D	18 ♎ 08 D
	12/25 Su	7 ♑ 04	21 ♈ 24	28 ♍ 49	19 ♎ 26		9/09 Su	6 ♑ 58	22 ♈ 30	28 ♍ 03	18 ♎ 17
							9/16 Su	6 ♑ 57	22 ♈ 26	28 ♍ 13	18 ♎ 26
							9/23 Su	6 ♑ 57 D	22 ♈ 22	28 ♍ 23	18 ♎ 35
							9/30 Su	6 ♑ 59	22 ♈ 18	28 ♍ 33	18 ♎ 45
2012	1/01 Su	7 ♑ 19	21 ♈ 23	28 ♍ 49 R	19 ♎ 29		10/07 Su	7 ♑ 02	22 ♈ 14	28 ♍ 43	18 ♎ 55
	1/08 Su	7 ♑ 34	21 ♈ 23	28 ♍ 48	19 ♎ 31		10/14 Su	7 ♑ 07	22 ♈ 10	28 ♍ 52	19 ♎ 05
	1/15 Su	7 ♑ 49	21 ♈ 23 D	28 ♍ 46	19 ♎ 32		10/21 Su	7 ♑ 13	22 ♈ 06	29 ♍ 01	19 ♎ 15
	1/22 Su	8 ♑ 03	21 ♈ 23	28 ♍ 43	19 ♎ 32 R		10/28 Su	7 ♑ 21	22 ♈ 02	29 ♍ 10	19 ♎ 25
	1/29 Su	8 ♑ 17	21 ♈ 25	28 ♍ 38	19 ♎ 31		11/04 Su	7 ♑ 30	21 ♈ 58	29 ♍ 18	19 ♎ 35
	2/05 Su	8 ♑ 30	21 ♈ 26	28 ♍ 33	19 ♎ 29		11/11 Su	7 ♑ 40	21 ♈ 54	29 ♍ 25	19 ♎ 44
	2/12 Su	8 ♑ 42	21 ♈ 29	28 ♍ 27	19 ♎ 25		11/18 Su	7 ♑ 52	21 ♈ 50	29 ♍ 32	19 ♎ 53
	2/19 Su	8 ♑ 53	21 ♈ 31	28 ♍ 21	19 ♎ 21		11/25 Su	8 ♑ 04	21 ♈ 47	29 ♍ 37	20 ♎ 01
	2/26 Su	9 ♑ 03	21 ♈ 35	28 ♍ 14	19 ♎ 16		12/02 Su	8 ♑ 17	21 ♈ 44	29 ♍ 42	20 ♎ 09
	3/04 Su	9 ♑ 11	21 ♈ 38	28 ♍ 06	19 ♎ 10		12/09 Su	8 ♑ 31	21 ♈ 42	29 ♍ 46	20 ♎ 15
	3/11 Su	9 ♑ 19	21 ♈ 42	27 ♍ 58	19 ♎ 03		12/16 Su	8 ♑ 45	21 ♈ 40	29 ♍ 48	20 ♎ 21
	3/18 Su	9 ♑ 25	21 ♈ 46	27 ♍ 50	18 ♎ 56		12/23 Su	9 ♑ 00	21 ♈ 38	29 ♍ 50	20 ♎ 26
	3/25 Su	9 ♑ 29	21 ♈ 50	27 ♍ 42	18 ♎ 48		12/30 Su	9 ♑ 15	21 ♈ 37	29 ♍ 50 R	20 ♎ 29
	4/01 Su	9 ♑ 32	21 ♈ 55	27 ♍ 34	18 ♎ 40	2013	1/06 Su	9 ♑ 29	21 ♈ 37	29 ♍ 49	20 ♎ 32
	4/08 Su	9 ♑ 33	21 ♈ 59	27 ♍ 26	18 ♎ 32		1/13 Su	9 ♑ 44	21 ♈ 37 D	29 ♍ 47	20 ♎ 33
	4/15 Su	9 ♑ 33 R	22 ♈ 04	27 ♍ 19	18 ♎ 24		1/20 Su	9 ♑ 59	21 ♈ 37	29 ♍ 45	20 ♎ 34 R
	4/22 Su	9 ♑ 31	22 ♈ 09	27 ♍ 12	18 ♎ 16		1/27 Su	10 ♑ 12	21 ♈ 38	29 ♍ 41	20 ♎ 33
	4/29 Su	9 ♑ 28	22 ♈ 13	27 ♍ 06	18 ♎ 08		2/03 Su	10 ♑ 26	21 ♈ 40	29 ♍ 36	20 ♎ 31
	5/06 Su	9 ♑ 24	22 ♈ 17	27 ♍ 01	18 ♎ 01		2/10 Su	10 ♑ 38	21 ♈ 42	29 ♍ 30	20 ♎ 28
	5/13 Su	9 ♑ 18	22 ♈ 22	26 ♍ 56	17 ♎ 54		2/17 Su	10 ♑ 50	21 ♈ 45	29 ♍ 24	20 ♎ 24
	5/20 Su	9 ♑ 11	22 ♈ 25	26 ♍ 53	17 ♎ 48		2/24 Su	11 ♑ 00	21 ♈ 48	29 ♍ 17	20 ♎ 19
	5/27 Su	9 ♑ 03	22 ♈ 29	26 ♍ 50	17 ♎ 42		3/03 Su	11 ♑ 09	21 ♈ 51	29 ♍ 09	20 ♎ 13
	6/03 Su	8 ♑ 54	22 ♈ 32	26 ♍ 49	17 ♎ 38		3/10 Su	11 ♑ 17	21 ♈ 55	29 ♍ 01	20 ♎ 06
	6/10 Su	8 ♑ 44	22 ♈ 35	26 ♍ 48	17 ♎ 34		3/17 Su	11 ♑ 24	21 ♈ 59	28 ♍ 53	19 ♎ 59
	6/17 Su	8 ♑ 34	22 ♈ 38	26 ♍ 48 D	17 ♎ 31		3/24 Su	11 ♑ 29	22 ♈ 03	28 ♍ 45	19 ♎ 52
	6/24 Su	8 ♑ 24	22 ♈ 40	26 ♍ 50	17 ♎ 29		3/31 Su	11 ♑ 32	22 ♈ 08	28 ♍ 37	19 ♎ 44
	7/01 Su	8 ♑ 13	22 ♈ 41	26 ♍ 53	17 ♎ 29		4/07 Su	11 ♑ 34	22 ♈ 12	28 ♍ 30	19 ♎ 36
	7/08 Su	8 ♑ 03	22 ♈ 42	26 ♍ 56	17 ♎ 29 D		4/14 Su	11 ♑ 35 R	22 ♈ 17	28 ♍ 22	19 ♎ 27
	7/15 Su	7 ♑ 52	22 ♈ 43	27 ♍ 01	17 ♎ 31		4/21 Su	11 ♑ 34	22 ♈ 21	28 ♍ 15	19 ♎ 19
	7/22 Su	7 ♑ 42	22 ♈ 43 R	27 ♍ 06	17 ♎ 33		4/28 Su	11 ♑ 31	22 ♈ 26	28 ♍ 09	19 ♎ 12
	7/29 Su	7 ♑ 33	22 ♈ 42	27 ♍ 12	17 ♎ 37		5/05 Su	11 ♑ 27	22 ♈ 30	28 ♍ 03	19 ♎ 04
	8/05 Su	7 ♑ 24	22 ♈ 41	27 ♍ 19	17 ♎ 41		5/12 Su	11 ♑ 22	22 ♈ 35	27 ♍ 59	18 ♎ 57
	8/12 Su	7 ♑ 17	22 ♈ 40	27 ♍ 27	17 ♎ 47		5/19 Su	11 ♑ 16	22 ♈ 39	27 ♍ 55	18 ♎ 51
	8/19 Su	7 ♑ 10	22 ♈ 38	27 ♍ 36	17 ♎ 53						
	8/26 Su	7 ♑ 05	22 ♈ 36	27 ♍ 44	18 ♎ 00						

Astro Data

2011						
12/28 We	08:55	♇	SR	28 ♍ 49	26.7 (26:41)
2012						
1/09 Mo	07:51	♀	SD	21 ♈ 23	-4.0 (-4:00)
1/18 We	01:33	♇	SR	19 ♎ 32	17.8 (17:50)
4/10 Tu	16:24	♇	SR	9 ♑ 33	-19.2 (-19:12)
6/10 Su	12:18	♇	SD	26 ♍ 48	27.5 (27:29)
7/01 Su	17:27	♇	SD	17 ♎ 29	18.6 (18:38)
7/18 We	22:03	♀	SR	22 ♈ 43	-3.4 (-3:25)

2012						
9/18 Tu	05:07	♀	SD	6 ♑ 57	-19.6 (-19:37)
12/28 Fr	17:08	♇	SR	29 ♍ 50	26.2 (26:13)
2013						
1/08 Tu	18:38	♀	SD	21 ♈ 37	-3.8 (-3:45)
1/18 Fr	05:13	♇	SR	20 ♎ 34	17.6 (17:33)
4/12 Fr	19:34	♀	SR	11 ♑ 35	-19.7 (-19:39)

		♇	⯰	🝼	🝻
2013	5/26 Su	11 ♑ 08 ℞	22 ♈ 42 D	27 ♍ 52 ℞	18 ♎ 45 ℞
	6/02 Su	11 ♑ 00	22 ♈ 46	27 ♍ 50	18 ♎ 40
	6/09 Su	10 ♑ 51	22 ♈ 49	27 ♍ 49	18 ♎ 36
	6/16 Su	10 ♑ 41	22 ♈ 51	27 ♍ 49 D	18 ♎ 33
	6/23 Su	10 ♑ 31	22 ♈ 53	27 ♍ 50	18 ♎ 31
	6/30 Su	10 ♑ 20	22 ♈ 55	27 ♍ 52	18 ♎ 30
	7/07 Su	10 ♑ 09	22 ♈ 56	27 ♍ 56	18 ♎ 30 D
	7/14 Su	9 ♑ 59	22 ♈ 57	28 ♍ 00	18 ♎ 31
	7/21 Su	9 ♑ 49	22 ♈ 57 ℞	28 ♍ 05	18 ♎ 33
	7/28 Su	9 ♑ 39	22 ♈ 56	28 ♍ 11	18 ♎ 37
	8/04 Su	9 ♑ 30	22 ♈ 56	28 ♍ 18	18 ♎ 41
	8/11 Su	9 ♑ 22	22 ♈ 54	28 ♍ 25	18 ♎ 46
	8/18 Su	9 ♑ 15	22 ♈ 52	28 ♍ 34	18 ♎ 52
	8/25 Su	9 ♑ 09	22 ♈ 50	28 ♍ 42	18 ♎ 59
	9/01 Su	9 ♑ 05	22 ♈ 47	28 ♍ 51	19 ♎ 07
	9/08 Su	9 ♑ 01	22 ♈ 44	29 ♍ 01	19 ♎ 15
	9/15 Su	8 ♑ 59	22 ♈ 41	29 ♍ 11	19 ♎ 24
	9/22 Su	8 ♑ 59 D	22 ♈ 37	29 ♍ 21	19 ♎ 33
	9/29 Su	9 ♑ 00	22 ♈ 33	29 ♍ 31	19 ♎ 43
	10/06 Su	9 ♑ 03	22 ♈ 29	29 ♍ 40	19 ♎ 53
	10/13 Su	9 ♑ 07	22 ♈ 25	29 ♍ 50	20 ♎ 03
	10/20 Su	9 ♑ 12	22 ♈ 21	29 ♍ 59	20 ♎ 13
	10/27 Su	9 ♑ 19	22 ♈ 17	0 ♎ 08	20 ♎ 23
	11/03 Su	9 ♑ 27	22 ♈ 12	0 ♎ 16	20 ♎ 33
	11/10 Su	9 ♑ 37	22 ♈ 09	0 ♎ 24	20 ♎ 43
	11/17 Su	9 ♑ 48	22 ♈ 05	0 ♎ 30	20 ♎ 52
	11/24 Su	9 ♑ 59	22 ♈ 02	0 ♎ 36	21 ♎ 00
	12/01 Su	10 ♑ 12	21 ♈ 59	0 ♎ 41	21 ♎ 08
	12/08 Su	10 ♑ 25	21 ♈ 56	0 ♎ 45	21 ♎ 15
	12/15 Su	10 ♑ 39	21 ♈ 54	0 ♎ 48	21 ♎ 21
	12/22 Su	10 ♑ 54	21 ♈ 52	0 ♎ 50	21 ♎ 26
	12/29 Su	11 ♑ 09	21 ♈ 51	0 ♎ 51	21 ♎ 30
2014	1/05 Su	11 ♑ 23	21 ♈ 50	0 ♎ 50 ℞	21 ♎ 33
	1/12 Su	11 ♑ 38	21 ♈ 50 D	0 ♎ 49	21 ♎ 34
	1/19 Su	11 ♑ 52	21 ♈ 51	0 ♎ 46	21 ♎ 35
	1/26 Su	12 ♑ 07	21 ♈ 52	0 ♎ 43	21 ♎ 35 ℞
	2/02 Su	12 ♑ 20	21 ♈ 53	0 ♎ 38	21 ♎ 33
2014	2/09 Su	12 ♑ 33 D	21 ♈ 55 D	0 ♎ 33 ℞	21 ♎ 30 ℞
	2/16 Su	12 ♑ 45	21 ♈ 58	0 ♎ 26	21 ♎ 27
	2/23 Su	12 ♑ 55	22 ♈ 01	0 ♎ 20	21 ♎ 22
	3/02 Su	13 ♑ 05	22 ♈ 04	0 ♎ 12	21 ♎ 16
	3/09 Su	13 ♑ 13	22 ♈ 08	0 ♎ 05	21 ♎ 10
	3/16 Su	13 ♑ 20	22 ♈ 12	29 ♍ 57	21 ♎ 03
	3/23 Su	13 ♑ 26	22 ♈ 16	29 ♍ 49	20 ♎ 56
	3/30 Su	13 ♑ 30	22 ♈ 21	29 ♍ 41	20 ♎ 48
	4/06 Su	13 ♑ 33	22 ♈ 25	29 ♍ 33	20 ♎ 40
	4/13 Su	13 ♑ 34	22 ♈ 30	29 ♍ 25	20 ♎ 32
	4/20 Su	13 ♑ 34 ℞	22 ♈ 34	29 ♍ 18	20 ♎ 23
	4/27 Su	13 ♑ 32	22 ♈ 39	29 ♍ 12	20 ♎ 16
	5/04 Su	13 ♑ 29	22 ♈ 43	29 ♍ 06	20 ♎ 08
	5/11 Su	13 ♑ 24	22 ♈ 48	29 ♍ 01	20 ♎ 01
	5/18 Su	13 ♑ 19	22 ♈ 52	28 ♍ 57	19 ♎ 54
	5/25 Su	13 ♑ 12	22 ♈ 55	28 ♍ 53	19 ♎ 48
	6/01 Su	13 ♑ 04	22 ♈ 59	28 ♍ 51	19 ♎ 43
	6/08 Su	12 ♑ 55	23 ♈ 02	28 ♍ 50	19 ♎ 39
	6/15 Su	12 ♑ 45	23 ♈ 04	28 ♍ 50 D	19 ♎ 35
	6/22 Su	12 ♑ 35	23 ♈ 07	28 ♍ 51	19 ♎ 33
	6/29 Su	12 ♑ 25	23 ♈ 08	28 ♍ 52	19 ♎ 32
	7/06 Su	12 ♑ 14	23 ♈ 10	28 ♍ 55	19 ♎ 31 D
	7/13 Su	12 ♑ 04	23 ♈ 10	28 ♍ 59	19 ♎ 32
	7/20 Su	11 ♑ 54	23 ♈ 11 ℞	29 ♍ 04	19 ♎ 34
	7/27 Su	11 ♑ 44	23 ♈ 10	29 ♍ 10	19 ♎ 37
	8/03 Su	11 ♑ 35	23 ♈ 10	29 ♍ 16	19 ♎ 41
	8/10 Su	11 ♑ 26	23 ♈ 08	29 ♍ 24	19 ♎ 46
	8/17 Su	11 ♑ 19	23 ♈ 06	29 ♍ 31	19 ♎ 51
	8/24 Su	11 ♑ 12	23 ♈ 04	29 ♍ 40	19 ♎ 58
	8/31 Su	11 ♑ 07	23 ♈ 02	29 ♍ 49	20 ♎ 06
	9/07 Su	11 ♑ 03	22 ♈ 59	29 ♍ 58	20 ♎ 14
	9/14 Su	11 ♑ 00	22 ♈ 55	0 ♎ 08	20 ♎ 23
	9/21 Su	10 ♑ 59	22 ♈ 52	0 ♎ 18	20 ♎ 32
	9/28 Su	11 ♑ 00 D	22 ♈ 48	0 ♎ 28	20 ♎ 41
	10/05 Su	11 ♑ 01	22 ♈ 44	0 ♎ 38	20 ♎ 51
	10/12 Su	11 ♑ 05	22 ♈ 40	0 ♎ 47	21 ♎ 02
	10/19 Su	11 ♑ 10	22 ♈ 35	0 ♎ 57	21 ♎ 12
	10/26 Su	11 ♑ 16	22 ♈ 31	1 ♎ 06	21 ♎ 22
	11/02 Su	11 ♑ 24	22 ♈ 27	1 ♎ 14	21 ♎ 32
	11/09 Su	11 ♑ 32	22 ♈ 23	1 ♎ 22	21 ♎ 41

Astro Data

2013						
6/11 Tu	16:20	🝼	SD	27 ♍ 49	27.0 (27:02)
7/03 We	03:14	🝻	SD	18 ♎ 30	18.4 (18:23)
7/19 Fr	11:16	⯰	SR	22 ♈ 57	-3.2 (-3:09)
9/20 Fr	15:29	♇	SD	8 ♑ 59	-20.1 (-20:06)
10/20 Su	06:41	🝼	→ ♎		25.7 (25:40)
12/29 Su	23:51	🝼	SR	0 ♎ 51	25.8 (25:47)
2014						
1/09 Th	10:15	⯰	SD	21 ♈ 50	-3.5 (-3:29)
1/19 Su	13:02	🝻	SR	21 ♎ 35	17.3 (17:19)

2014					
3/13 Th	12:34	🝼	→ ♍ ℞		26.5 (26:29)
4/14 Mo	23:47	♇	SR	13 ♑ 34	-20.1 (-20:04)
6/12 Th	21:45	🝼	SD	28 ♍ 50	26.6 (26:36)
7/04 Fr	10:17	🝻	SD	19 ♎ 31	18.1 (18:07)
7/19 Sa	18:15	⯰	SR	23 ♈ 11	-2.9 (-2:54)
9/07 Su	17:30	🝼	→ ♎		25.6 (25:35)
9/23 Tu	00:36	♇	SD	10 ♑ 59	-20.6 (-20:34)

	♇	♀	♇	♇

2014

Date				
11/16 Su	11 ♑ 43 D	22 ♈ 19 ℞	1 ♎ 29 D	21 ♎ 51 D
11/23 Su	11 ♑ 54	22 ♈ 16	1 ♎ 35	21 ♎ 59
11/30 Su	12 ♑ 06	22 ♈ 13	1 ♎ 40	22 ♎ 07
12/07 Su	12 ♑ 19	22 ♈ 10	1 ♎ 45	22 ♎ 14
12/14 Su	12 ♑ 32	22 ♈ 08	1 ♎ 48	22 ♎ 21
12/21 Su	12 ♑ 47	22 ♈ 06	1 ♎ 50	22 ♎ 26
12/28 Su	13 ♑ 01	22 ♈ 05	1 ♎ 51	22 ♎ 30

2015

Date				
1/04 Su	13 ♑ 16	22 ♈ 04	1 ♎ 51 ℞	22 ♎ 34
1/11 Su	13 ♑ 30	22 ♈ 04 D	1 ♎ 50	22 ♎ 36
1/18 Su	13 ♑ 45	22 ♈ 04	1 ♎ 48	22 ♎ 37
1/25 Su	13 ♑ 59	22 ♈ 05	1 ♎ 44	22 ♎ 37 ℞
2/01 Su	14 ♑ 13	22 ♈ 07	1 ♎ 40	22 ♎ 36
2/08 Su	14 ♑ 25	22 ♈ 09	1 ♎ 35	22 ♎ 33
2/15 Su	14 ♑ 38	22 ♈ 11	1 ♎ 29	22 ♎ 30
2/22 Su	14 ♑ 49	22 ♈ 14	1 ♎ 22	22 ♎ 26
3/01 Su	14 ♑ 59	22 ♈ 17	1 ♎ 15	22 ♎ 20
3/08 Su	15 ♑ 08	22 ♈ 21	1 ♎ 08	22 ♎ 14
3/15 Su	15 ♑ 16	22 ♈ 25	1 ♎ 00	22 ♎ 07
3/22 Su	15 ♑ 22	22 ♈ 29	0 ♎ 52	22 ♎ 00
3/29 Su	15 ♑ 27	22 ♈ 33	0 ♎ 44	21 ♎ 52
4/05 Su	15 ♑ 30	22 ♈ 38	0 ♎ 36	21 ♎ 44
4/12 Su	15 ♑ 32	22 ♈ 43	0 ♎ 28	21 ♎ 36
4/19 Su	15 ♑ 32 ℞	22 ♈ 47	0 ♎ 21	21 ♎ 28
4/26 Su	15 ♑ 31	22 ♈ 52	0 ♎ 14	21 ♎ 20
5/03 Su	15 ♑ 29	22 ♈ 56	0 ♎ 08	21 ♎ 12
5/10 Su	15 ♑ 25	23 ♈ 00	0 ♎ 03	21 ♎ 05
5/17 Su	15 ♑ 19	23 ♈ 04	29 ♍ 59	20 ♎ 58
5/24 Su	15 ♑ 13	23 ♈ 08	29 ♍ 55	20 ♎ 52
5/31 Su	15 ♑ 06	23 ♈ 12	29 ♍ 52	20 ♎ 46
6/07 Su	14 ♑ 57	23 ♈ 15	29 ♍ 51	20 ♎ 42
6/14 Su	14 ♑ 48	23 ♈ 18	29 ♍ 50	20 ♎ 38
6/21 Su	14 ♑ 38	23 ♈ 20	29 ♍ 51 D	20 ♎ 35
6/28 Su	14 ♑ 28	23 ♈ 22	29 ♍ 52	20 ♎ 34
7/05 Su	14 ♑ 18	23 ♈ 23	29 ♍ 55	20 ♎ 33
7/12 Su	14 ♑ 07	23 ♈ 24	29 ♍ 58	20 ♎ 34 D
7/19 Su	13 ♑ 57	23 ♈ 24	0 ♎ 03	20 ♎ 35
7/26 Su	13 ♑ 47	23 ♈ 24 ℞	0 ♎ 08	20 ♎ 38

2015

Date				
8/02 Su	13 ♑ 38 ℞	23 ♈ 23 ℞	0 ♎ 15 D	20 ♎ 41 D
8/09 Su	13 ♑ 29	23 ♈ 22	0 ♎ 22	20 ♎ 46
8/16 Su	13 ♑ 21	23 ♈ 21	0 ♎ 29	20 ♎ 51
8/23 Su	13 ♑ 14	23 ♈ 19	0 ♎ 38	20 ♎ 58
8/30 Su	13 ♑ 08	23 ♈ 16	0 ♎ 47	21 ♎ 05
9/06 Su	13 ♑ 03	23 ♈ 13	0 ♎ 56	21 ♎ 13
9/13 Su	13 ♑ 00	23 ♈ 10	1 ♎ 05	21 ♎ 21
9/20 Su	12 ♑ 58	23 ♈ 06	1 ♎ 15	21 ♎ 31
9/27 Su	12 ♑ 58 D	23 ♈ 02	1 ♎ 25	21 ♎ 40
10/04 Su	12 ♑ 59	22 ♈ 58	1 ♎ 35	21 ♎ 50
10/11 Su	13 ♑ 02	22 ♈ 54	1 ♎ 45	22 ♎ 00
10/18 Su	13 ♑ 06	22 ♈ 50	1 ♎ 54	22 ♎ 10
10/25 Su	13 ♑ 11	22 ♈ 46	2 ♎ 03	22 ♎ 21
11/01 Su	13 ♑ 18	22 ♈ 42	2 ♎ 12	22 ♎ 31
11/08 Su	13 ♑ 27	22 ♈ 38	2 ♎ 20	22 ♎ 40
11/15 Su	13 ♑ 36	22 ♈ 34	2 ♎ 27	22 ♎ 50
11/22 Su	13 ♑ 47	22 ♈ 30	2 ♎ 33	22 ♎ 59
11/29 Su	13 ♑ 58	22 ♈ 27	2 ♎ 39	23 ♎ 07
12/06 Su	14 ♑ 11	22 ♈ 25	2 ♎ 44	23 ♎ 14
12/13 Su	14 ♑ 24	22 ♈ 22	2 ♎ 47	23 ♎ 21
12/20 Su	14 ♑ 38	22 ♈ 20	2 ♎ 50	23 ♎ 27
12/27 Su	14 ♑ 52	22 ♈ 19	2 ♎ 51	23 ♎ 31

2016

Date				
1/03 Su	15 ♑ 07	22 ♈ 18	2 ♎ 51 ℞	23 ♎ 35
1/10 Su	15 ♑ 21	22 ♈ 18	2 ♎ 51	23 ♎ 38
1/17 Su	15 ♑ 36	22 ♈ 18 D	2 ♎ 49	23 ♎ 39
1/24 Su	15 ♑ 50	22 ♈ 19	2 ♎ 46	23 ♎ 39 ℞
1/31 Su	16 ♑ 03	22 ♈ 20	2 ♎ 42	23 ♎ 38
2/07 Su	16 ♑ 17	22 ♈ 22	2 ♎ 37	23 ♎ 36
2/14 Su	16 ♑ 29	22 ♈ 24	2 ♎ 31	23 ♎ 33
2/21 Su	16 ♑ 41	22 ♈ 27	2 ♎ 25	23 ♎ 29
2/28 Su	16 ♑ 51	22 ♈ 30	2 ♎ 18	23 ♎ 24
3/06 Su	17 ♑ 01	22 ♈ 34	2 ♎ 10	23 ♎ 18
3/13 Su	17 ♑ 09	22 ♈ 38	2 ♎ 03	23 ♎ 12
3/20 Su	17 ♑ 16	22 ♈ 42	1 ♎ 55	23 ♎ 05
3/27 Su	17 ♑ 21	22 ♈ 46	1 ♎ 47	22 ♎ 57
4/03 Su	17 ♑ 25	22 ♈ 51	1 ♎ 39	22 ♎ 49
4/10 Su	17 ♑ 28	22 ♈ 55	1 ♎ 31	22 ♎ 41

Astro Data

2014

12/31 We	03:11	♎ SR	1 ♎ 51	25.3 (25:19)	

2015

1/10 Sa	00:40	♀ SD	22 ♈ 04	-3.2 (-3:13)
1/20 Tu	21:42	♋ SR	22 ♎ 37	17.0 (17:01)
4/17 Fr	03:54	♀ SR	15 ♑ 32	-20.5 (-20:38)
5/15 Fr	10:07	♎ → ♍ ℞		26.3 (26:16)
6/14 Su	06:38	♎ SD	29 ♍ 50	26.1 (26:06)
7/05 Su	17:08	♋ SD	20 ♎ 33	17.8 (17:47)
7/13 Mo	21:38	♎ → ♎		25.8 (25:49)
7/20 Mo	02:29	♀ SR	23 ♈ 24	-2.6 (-2:38)

2015

| 9/25 Fr | 06:58 | ♀ SD | 12 ♑ 58 | -21.0 (-20:59) |

2016

1/01 Fr	08:35	♎ SR	2 ♎ 51	24.8 (24:50)
1/10 Su	06:36	♀ SD	22 ♈ 18	-3.0 (-2:57)
1/22 Fr	05:27	♋ SR	23 ♎ 39	16.7 (16:43)

2016	♇	♆		
4/17 Su	17 ♑ 29 D	23 ♈ 00 D	1 ♎ 24 R	22 ♎ 33 R
4/24 Su	17 ♑ 28 R	23 ♈ 04	1 ♎ 17	22 ♎ 25
5/01 Su	17 ♑ 26	23 ♈ 09	1 ♎ 11	22 ♎ 17
5/08 Su	17 ♑ 23	23 ♈ 13	1 ♎ 05	22 ♎ 09
5/15 Su	17 ♑ 18	23 ♈ 17	1 ♎ 00	22 ♎ 02
5/22 Su	17 ♑ 13	23 ♈ 21	0 ♎ 57	21 ♎ 56
5/29 Su	17 ♑ 06	23 ♈ 25	0 ♎ 54	21 ♎ 50
6/05 Su	16 ♑ 58	23 ♈ 28	0 ♎ 52	21 ♎ 45
6/12 Su	16 ♑ 49	23 ♈ 31	0 ♎ 51	21 ♎ 41
6/19 Su	16 ♑ 39	23 ♈ 33	0 ♎ 51 D	21 ♎ 38
6/26 Su	16 ♑ 30	23 ♈ 35	0 ♎ 52	21 ♎ 36
7/03 Su	16 ♑ 19	23 ♈ 37	0 ♎ 54	21 ♎ 35
7/10 Su	16 ♑ 09	23 ♈ 38	0 ♎ 58	21 ♎ 35 D
7/17 Su	15 ♑ 59	23 ♈ 38	1 ♎ 02	21 ♎ 36
7/24 Su	15 ♑ 48	23 ♈ 38 R	1 ♎ 07	21 ♎ 39
7/31 Su	15 ♑ 39	23 ♈ 37	1 ♎ 13	21 ♎ 42
8/07 Su	15 ♑ 30	23 ♈ 36	1 ♎ 20	21 ♎ 46
8/14 Su	15 ♑ 21	23 ♈ 35	1 ♎ 27	21 ♎ 51
8/21 Su	15 ♑ 14	23 ♈ 33	1 ♎ 35	21 ♎ 58
8/28 Su	15 ♑ 08	23 ♈ 30	1 ♎ 44	22 ♎ 05
9/04 Su	15 ♑ 03	23 ♈ 27	1 ♎ 53	22 ♎ 12
9/11 Su	14 ♑ 59	23 ♈ 24	2 ♎ 03	22 ♎ 21
9/18 Su	14 ♑ 56	23 ♈ 21	2 ♎ 12	22 ♎ 30
9/25 Su	14 ♑ 55	23 ♈ 17	2 ♎ 22	22 ♎ 39
10/02 Su	14 ♑ 56 D	23 ♈ 13	2 ♎ 32	22 ♎ 49
10/09 Su	14 ♑ 57	23 ♈ 09	2 ♎ 42	22 ♎ 59
10/16 Su	15 ♑ 01	23 ♈ 05	2 ♎ 51	23 ♎ 09
10/23 Su	15 ♑ 06	23 ♈ 00	3 ♎ 01	23 ♎ 20
10/30 Su	15 ♑ 12	22 ♈ 56	3 ♎ 09	23 ♎ 30
11/06 Su	15 ♑ 20	22 ♈ 52	3 ♎ 17	23 ♎ 40
11/13 Su	15 ♑ 28	22 ♈ 48	3 ♎ 25	23 ♎ 49
11/20 Su	15 ♑ 38	22 ♈ 45	3 ♎ 32	23 ♎ 58
11/27 Su	15 ♑ 50	22 ♈ 42	3 ♎ 37	24 ♎ 07
12/04 Su	16 ♑ 02	22 ♈ 39	3 ♎ 42	24 ♎ 14
12/11 Su	16 ♑ 14	22 ♈ 36	3 ♎ 46	24 ♎ 21
12/18 Su	16 ♑ 28	22 ♈ 34	3 ♎ 49	24 ♎ 27
12/25 Su	16 ♑ 42	22 ♈ 33	3 ♎ 51	24 ♎ 32

2017	♇	♆		
1/01 Su	16 ♑ 56 D	22 ♈ 32 R	3 ♎ 52 D	24 ♎ 36 D
1/08 Su	17 ♑ 10	22 ♈ 32	3 ♎ 51 R	24 ♎ 39
1/15 Su	17 ♑ 25	22 ♈ 32 D	3 ♎ 50	24 ♎ 41
1/22 Su	17 ♑ 39	22 ♈ 32	3 ♎ 47	24 ♎ 42
1/29 Su	17 ♑ 53	22 ♈ 34	3 ♎ 43	24 ♎ 41 R
2/05 Su	18 ♑ 06	22 ♈ 35	3 ♎ 39	24 ♎ 40
2/12 Su	18 ♑ 19	22 ♈ 38	3 ♎ 33	24 ♎ 37
2/19 Su	18 ♑ 31	22 ♈ 40	3 ♎ 27	24 ♎ 33
2/26 Su	18 ♑ 42	22 ♈ 43	3 ♎ 20	24 ♎ 29
3/05 Su	18 ♑ 52	22 ♈ 47	3 ♎ 13	24 ♎ 23
3/12 Su	19 ♑ 00	22 ♈ 51	3 ♎ 05	24 ♎ 17
3/19 Su	19 ♑ 08	22 ♈ 55	2 ♎ 57	24 ♎ 10
3/26 Su	19 ♑ 14	22 ♈ 59	2 ♎ 49	24 ♎ 02
4/02 Su	19 ♑ 18	23 ♈ 03	2 ♎ 42	23 ♎ 54
4/09 Su	19 ♑ 21	23 ♈ 08	2 ♎ 34	23 ♎ 46
4/16 Su	19 ♑ 23	23 ♈ 13	2 ♎ 26	23 ♎ 38
4/23 Su	19 ♑ 23 R	23 ♈ 17	2 ♎ 19	23 ♎ 30
4/30 Su	19 ♑ 22	23 ♈ 22	2 ♎ 13	23 ♎ 22
5/07 Su	19 ♑ 19	23 ♈ 26	2 ♎ 07	23 ♎ 14
5/14 Su	19 ♑ 15	23 ♈ 30	2 ♎ 02	23 ♎ 07
5/21 Su	19 ♑ 10	23 ♈ 34	1 ♎ 58	23 ♎ 00
5/28 Su	19 ♑ 04	23 ♈ 38	1 ♎ 55	22 ♎ 54
6/04 Su	18 ♑ 56	23 ♈ 41	1 ♎ 53	22 ♎ 49
6/11 Su	18 ♑ 48	23 ♈ 44	1 ♎ 51	22 ♎ 45
6/18 Su	18 ♑ 39	23 ♈ 46	1 ♎ 51 D	22 ♎ 41
6/25 Su	18 ♑ 29	23 ♈ 48	1 ♎ 52	22 ♎ 39
7/02 Su	18 ♑ 19	23 ♈ 50	1 ♎ 54	22 ♎ 38
7/09 Su	18 ♑ 09	23 ♈ 51	1 ♎ 57	22 ♎ 38 D
7/16 Su	17 ♑ 59	23 ♈ 52	2 ♎ 01	22 ♎ 38
7/23 Su	17 ♑ 48	23 ♈ 52 R	2 ♎ 05	22 ♎ 40
7/30 Su	17 ♑ 39	23 ♈ 51	2 ♎ 11	22 ♎ 43
8/06 Su	17 ♑ 29	23 ♈ 50	2 ♎ 18	22 ♎ 47
8/13 Su	17 ♑ 21	23 ♈ 49	2 ♎ 25	22 ♎ 52
8/20 Su	17 ♑ 13	23 ♈ 47	2 ♎ 33	22 ♎ 58
8/27 Su	17 ♑ 06	23 ♈ 44	2 ♎ 41	23 ♎ 05
9/03 Su	17 ♑ 00	23 ♈ 42	2 ♎ 50	23 ♎ 12
9/10 Su	16 ♑ 56	23 ♈ 39	3 ♎ 00	23 ♎ 20
9/17 Su	16 ♑ 53	23 ♈ 35	3 ♎ 09	23 ♎ 29
9/24 Su	16 ♑ 51	23 ♈ 31	3 ♎ 19	23 ♎ 39
10/01 Su	16 ♑ 51 D	23 ♈ 27	3 ♎ 29	23 ♎ 48

Astro Data

2016

Date	Time			Position	
4/18 Mo	07:26	♇	SR	17 ♑ 29	-20.8 (-20:49)
6/14 Tu	14:43		SD	0 ♎ 51	25.6 (25:38)
7/05 Tu	22:00		SD	21 ♎ 35	17.5 (17:31)
7/19 Tu	19:13	♆	SR	23 ♈ 38	-2.4 (-2:22)
9/26 Mo	15:02	♇	SD	14 ♑ 55	-21.4 (-21:23)

2017

Date	Time			Position	
1/01 Su	14:39		SR	3 ♎ 52	24.4 (24:24)

2017

Date	Time			Position	
1/09 Mo	16:43	♆	SD	22 ♈ 32	-2.7 (-2:42)
1/22 Su	12:15		SR	24 ♎ 42	16.5 (16:29)
4/20 Th	12:49	♇	SR	19 ♑ 23	-21.2 (-21:09)
6/15 Th	22:15		SD	1 ♎ 51	25.2 (25:11)
7/07 Fr	04:36		SD	22 ♎ 37	17.3 (17:15)
7/20 Th	08:55	♆	SR	23 ♈ 52	-2.1 (-2:06)
9/28 Th	19:36	♇	SD	16 ♑ 51	-21.7 (-21:44)

	♇	♀	♣	♣
2017				
10/08 Su	16 ♑ 52 D	23 ♈ 23 ℞	3 ♎ 39 D	23 ♎ 58 D
10/15 Su	16 ♑ 55	23 ♈ 19	3 ♎ 48	24 ♎ 09
10/22 Su	16 ♑ 59	23 ♈ 15	3 ♎ 58	24 ♎ 19
10/29 Su	17 ♑ 04	23 ♈ 11	4 ♎ 07	24 ♎ 29
11/05 Su	17 ♑ 11	23 ♈ 07	4 ♎ 15	24 ♎ 39
11/12 Su	17 ♑ 20	23 ♈ 03	4 ♎ 23	24 ♎ 49
11/19 Su	17 ♑ 29	22 ♈ 59	4 ♎ 30	24 ♎ 58
11/26 Su	17 ♑ 40	22 ♈ 56	4 ♎ 36	25 ♎ 07
12/03 Su	17 ♑ 51	22 ♈ 53	4 ♎ 41	25 ♎ 15
12/10 Su	18 ♑ 03	22 ♈ 51	4 ♎ 45	25 ♎ 12
12/17 Su	18 ♑ 17	22 ♈ 48	4 ♎ 48	25 ♎ 28
12/24 Su	18 ♑ 30	22 ♈ 47	4 ♎ 50	25 ♎ 34
12/31 Su	18 ♑ 44	22 ♈ 46	4 ♎ 51	25 ♎ 38
2018				
1/07 Su	18 ♑ 58	22 ♈ 45	4 ♎ 51 ℞	25 ♎ 41
1/14 Su	19 ♑ 13	22 ♈ 45 D	4 ♎ 50	25 ♎ 43
1/21 Su	19 ♑ 27	22 ♈ 46	4 ♎ 48	25 ♎ 45
1/28 Su	19 ♑ 41	22 ♈ 47	4 ♎ 45	25 ♎ 44 ℞
2/04 Su	19 ♑ 54	22 ♈ 49	4 ♎ 40	25 ♎ 43
2/11 Su	20 ♑ 07	22 ♈ 51	4 ♎ 35	25 ♎ 41
2/18 Su	20 ♑ 19	22 ♈ 53	4 ♎ 29	25 ♎ 37
2/25 Su	20 ♑ 31	22 ♈ 56	4 ♎ 23	25 ♎ 33
3/04 Su	20 ♑ 41	23 ♈ 00	4 ♎ 15	25 ♎ 28
3/11 Su	20 ♑ 50	23 ♈ 03	4 ♎ 08	25 ♎ 22
3/18 Su	20 ♑ 58	23 ♈ 07	4 ♎ 00	25 ♎ 15
3/25 Su	21 ♑ 05	23 ♈ 12	3 ♎ 52	25 ♎ 07
4/01 Su	21 ♑ 10	23 ♈ 16	3 ♎ 44	25 ♎ 00
4/08 Su	21 ♑ 14	23 ♈ 21	3 ♎ 36	24 ♎ 52
4/15 Su	21 ♑ 16	23 ♈ 25	3 ♎ 29	24 ♎ 43
4/22 Su	21 ♑ 17	23 ♈ 30	3 ♎ 22	24 ♎ 35
4/29 Su	21 ♑ 16 ℞	23 ♈ 34	3 ♎ 15	24 ♎ 27
5/06 Su	21 ♑ 14	23 ♈ 39	3 ♎ 09	24 ♎ 19
5/13 Su	21 ♑ 11	23 ♈ 43	3 ♎ 04	24 ♎ 12
5/20 Su	21 ♑ 06	23 ♈ 47	2 ♎ 59	24 ♎ 05
5/27 Su	21 ♑ 00	23 ♈ 51	2 ♎ 56	23 ♎ 59
6/03 Su	20 ♑ 53	23 ♈ 54	2 ♎ 53	23 ♎ 53
6/10 Su	20 ♑ 45	23 ♈ 57	2 ♎ 52	23 ♎ 49
6/17 Su	20 ♑ 37	24 ♈ 00	2 ♎ 51	23 ♎ 45
6/24 Su	20 ♑ 27	24 ♈ 02	2 ♎ 52 D	23 ♎ 42

	♇	♀	♣	♣
2018				
7/01 Su	20 ♑ 17 ℞	24 ♈ 03 D	2 ♎ 53 D	23 ♎ 41 ℞
7/08 Su	20 ♑ 07	24 ♈ 05	2 ♎ 56	23 ♎ 40
7/15 Su	19 ♑ 57	24 ♈ 05	2 ♎ 59	23 ♎ 41 D
7/22 Su	19 ♑ 47	24 ♈ 05 ℞	3 ♎ 04	23 ♎ 42
7/29 Su	19 ♑ 37	24 ♈ 05	3 ♎ 09	23 ♎ 45
8/05 Su	19 ♑ 27	24 ♈ 04	3 ♎ 15	23 ♎ 48
8/12 Su	19 ♑ 18	24 ♈ 03	3 ♎ 22	23 ♎ 53
8/19 Su	19 ♑ 10	24 ♈ 01	3 ♎ 30	23 ♎ 59
8/26 Su	19 ♑ 03	23 ♈ 59	3 ♎ 38	24 ♎ 05
9/02 Su	18 ♑ 57	23 ♈ 56	3 ♎ 47	24 ♎ 12
9/09 Su	18 ♑ 52	23 ♈ 53	3 ♎ 57	24 ♎ 20
9/16 Su	18 ♑ 48	23 ♈ 50	4 ♎ 06	24 ♎ 29
9/23 Su	18 ♑ 46	23 ♈ 46	4 ♎ 16	24 ♎ 38
9/30 Su	18 ♑ 45	23 ♈ 42	4 ♎ 26	24 ♎ 48
10/07 Su	18 ♑ 45 D	23 ♈ 38	4 ♎ 36	24 ♎ 58
10/14 Su	18 ♑ 47	23 ♈ 34	4 ♎ 45	25 ♎ 08
10/21 Su	18 ♑ 51	23 ♈ 30	4 ♎ 55	25 ♎ 18
10/28 Su	18 ♑ 56	23 ♈ 25	5 ♎ 04	25 ♎ 29
11/04 Su	19 ♑ 02	23 ♈ 21	5 ♎ 12	25 ♎ 39
11/11 Su	19 ♑ 10	23 ♈ 17	5 ♎ 20	25 ♎ 49
11/18 Su	19 ♑ 18	23 ♈ 14	5 ♎ 27	25 ♎ 58
11/25 Su	19 ♑ 28	23 ♈ 10	5 ♎ 34	26 ♎ 07
12/02 Su	19 ♑ 39	23 ♈ 07	5 ♎ 39	26 ♎ 15
12/09 Su	19 ♑ 51	23 ♈ 05	5 ♎ 44	26 ♎ 23
12/16 Su	20 ♑ 04	23 ♈ 03	5 ♎ 47	26 ♎ 29
12/23 Su	20 ♑ 17	23 ♈ 01	5 ♎ 50	26 ♎ 35
12/30 Su	20 ♑ 31	23 ♈ 00	5 ♎ 51	26 ♎ 40
2019				
1/06 Su	20 ♑ 45	22 ♈ 59	5 ♎ 51 ℞	26 ♎ 43
1/13 Su	20 ♑ 59	22 ♈ 59 D	5 ♎ 50	26 ♎ 46
1/20 Su	21 ♑ 14	22 ♈ 59	5 ♎ 48	26 ♎ 47
1/27 Su	21 ♑ 27	23 ♈ 00	5 ♎ 45	26 ♎ 48 ℞
2/03 Su	21 ♑ 41	23 ♈ 02	5 ♎ 41	26 ♎ 47
2/10 Su	21 ♑ 54	23 ♈ 04	5 ♎ 37	26 ♎ 45
2/17 Su	22 ♑ 07	23 ♈ 06	5 ♎ 31	26 ♎ 42
2/24 Su	22 ♑ 18	23 ♈ 09	5 ♎ 24	26 ♎ 38
3/03 Su	22 ♑ 29	23 ♈ 13	5 ♎ 18	26 ♎ 33
3/10 Su	22 ♑ 38	23 ♈ 16	5 ♎ 10	26 ♎ 27

Astro Data

2018

1/02 Tu	22:39	♣	SR	4 ♎ 51	23.9 (23:55)
1/10 We	09:44	♀	SD	22 ♈ 45	-2.4 (-2:26)
1/23 Tu	16:44	♣	SR	25 ♎ 45	16.2 (16:10)
4/22 Su	15:26	♇	SR	21 ♑ 17	-21.5 (-21:27)
6/17 Su	02:36	♣	SD	2 ♎ 51	24.7 (24:40)

2018

7/08 Su	14:10	♣	SD	23 ♎ 40	16.9 (16:55)
7/20 Fr	13:57	♀	SR	24 ♈ 05	-1.9 (-1:51)
10/01 Mo	02:03	♇	SD	18 ♑ 45	-22.1 (-22:04)

2019

1/04 Fr	03:12	♣	SR	5 ♎ 51	23.4 (23:26)
1/10 Th	20:52	♀	SD	22 ♈ 59	-2.2 (-2:10)
1/25 Fr	00:45	♣	SR	16 ♎ 48	15.9 (15:52)

2019	♇	♀	♇	♇
3/17 Su	22 ♑ 47 D	23 ♈ 20 D	5 ♎ 02 ℞	26 ♎ 20 ℞
3/24 Su	22 ♑ 54	23 ♈ 25	4 ♎ 54	26 ♎ 13
3/31 Su	23 ♑ 00	23 ♈ 29	4 ♎ 46	26 ♎ 05
4/07 Su	23 ♑ 04	23 ♈ 33	4 ♎ 39	25 ♎ 57
4/14 Su	23 ♑ 07	23 ♈ 38	4 ♎ 31	25 ♎ 49
4/21 Su	23 ♑ 08	23 ♈ 43	4 ♎ 24	25 ♎ 41
4/28 Su	23 ♑ 08 ℞	23 ♈ 47	4 ♎ 17	25 ♎ 33
5/05 Su	23 ♑ 07	23 ♈ 52	4 ♎ 11	25 ♎ 25
5/12 Su	23 ♑ 04	23 ♈ 56	4 ♎ 05	25 ♎ 17
5/19 Su	23 ♑ 00	24 ♈ 00	4 ♎ 00	25 ♎ 10
5/26 Su	22 ♑ 55	24 ♈ 04	3 ♎ 57	25 ♎ 04
6/02 Su	22 ♑ 48	24 ♈ 07	3 ♎ 54	24 ♎ 58
6/09 Su	22 ♑ 41	24 ♈ 10	3 ♎ 52	24 ♎ 53
6/16 Su	22 ♑ 33	24 ♈ 13	3 ♎ 51	24 ♎ 49
6/23 Su	22 ♑ 24	24 ♈ 15	3 ♎ 51 D	24 ♎ 46
6/30 Su	22 ♑ 14	24 ♈ 17	3 ♎ 52	24 ♎ 44
7/07 Su	22 ♑ 04	24 ♈ 18	3 ♎ 55	24 ♎ 43
7/14 Su	21 ♑ 54	24 ♈ 19	3 ♎ 58	24 ♎ 43 D
7/21 Su	21 ♑ 44	24 ♈ 19	4 ♎ 02	24 ♎ 44
7/28 Su	21 ♑ 34	24 ♈ 19 ℞	4 ♎ 07	24 ♎ 47
8/04 Su	21 ♑ 24	24 ♈ 18	4 ♎ 13	24 ♎ 50
8/11 Su	21 ♑ 15	24 ♈ 17	4 ♎ 20	24 ♎ 54
8/18 Su	21 ♑ 06	24 ♈ 15	4 ♎ 27	24 ♎ 59
8/25 Su	20 ♑ 59	24 ♈ 13	4 ♎ 35	25 ♎ 06
9/01 Su	20 ♑ 52	24 ♈ 10	4 ♎ 44	25 ♎ 13
9/08 Su	20 ♑ 47	24 ♈ 07	4 ♎ 53	25 ♎ 21
9/15 Su	20 ♑ 42	24 ♈ 04	5 ♎ 03	25 ♎ 29
9/22 Su	20 ♑ 39	24 ♈ 00	5 ♎ 12	25 ♎ 38
9/29 Su	20 ♑ 38	23 ♈ 57	5 ♎ 22	25 ♎ 48
10/06 Su	20 ♑ 38 D	23 ♈ 53	5 ♎ 32	25 ♎ 58
10/13 Su	20 ♑ 39	23 ♈ 48	5 ♎ 42	26 ♎ 08
10/20 Su	20 ♑ 42	23 ♈ 44	5 ♎ 51	26 ♎ 18
10/27 Su	20 ♑ 46	23 ♈ 40	6 ♎ 00	26 ♎ 28
11/03 Su	20 ♑ 51	23 ♈ 36	6 ♎ 09	26 ♎ 39
11/10 Su	20 ♑ 58	23 ♈ 32	6 ♎ 17	26 ♎ 48
11/17 Su	21 ♑ 07	23 ♈ 28	6 ♎ 24	26 ♎ 58
11/24 Su	21 ♑ 16	23 ♈ 25	6 ♎ 31	27 ♎ 07
12/01 Su	21 ♑ 27	23 ♈ 22	6 ♎ 37	27 ♎ 16
12/08 Su	21 ♑ 38	23 ♈ 19	6 ♎ 42	27 ♎ 23
12/15 Su	21 ♑ 50	23 ♈ 17	6 ♎ 46	27 ♎ 30

	♇	♀	♇	♇
2019				
12/22 Su	22 ♑ 03 D	23 ♈ 15 ℞	6 ♎ 48 D	27 ♎ 36 D
12/29 Su	22 ♑ 17	23 ♈ 14	6 ♎ 50	27 ♎ 42
2020				
1/05 Su	22 ♑ 31	23 ♈ 13	6 ♎ 51	27 ♎ 46
1/12 Su	22 ♑ 45	23 ♈ 13 D	6 ♎ 50 ℞	27 ♎ 48
1/19 Su	22 ♑ 59	23 ♈ 13	6 ♎ 49	27 ♎ 50
1/26 Su	23 ♑ 13	23 ♈ 14	6 ♎ 46	27 ♎ 51
2/02 Su	23 ♑ 26	23 ♈ 15	6 ♎ 42	27 ♎ 50 ℞
2/09 Su	23 ♑ 40	23 ♈ 17	6 ♎ 38	27 ♎ 49
2/16 Su	23 ♑ 52	23 ♈ 20	6 ♎ 32	27 ♎ 46
2/23 Su	24 ♑ 04	23 ♈ 23	6 ♎ 26	27 ♎ 42
3/01 Su	24 ♑ 15	23 ♈ 26	6 ♎ 19	27 ♎ 38
3/08 Su	24 ♑ 25	23 ♈ 29	6 ♎ 12	27 ♎ 32
3/15 Su	24 ♑ 34	23 ♈ 33	6 ♎ 04	27 ♎ 26
3/22 Su	24 ♑ 41	23 ♈ 37	5 ♎ 56	27 ♎ 19
3/29 Su	24 ♑ 48	23 ♈ 42	5 ♎ 48	27 ♎ 11
4/05 Su	24 ♑ 53	23 ♈ 46	5 ♎ 41	27 ♎ 03
4/12 Su	24 ♑ 56	23 ♈ 51	5 ♎ 33	26 ♎ 55
4/19 Su	24 ♑ 58	23 ♈ 56	5 ♎ 25	26 ♎ 47
4/26 Su	24 ♑ 59 ℞	24 ♈ 00	5 ♎ 18	26 ♎ 38
5/03 Su	24 ♑ 58	24 ♈ 05	5 ♎ 12	26 ♎ 30
5/10 Su	24 ♑ 56	24 ♈ 09	5 ♎ 06	26 ♎ 23
5/17 Su	24 ♑ 53	24 ♈ 13	5 ♎ 01	26 ♎ 15
5/24 Su	24 ♑ 48	24 ♈ 17	4 ♎ 57	26 ♎ 09
5/31 Su	24 ♑ 42	24 ♈ 20	4 ♎ 54	26 ♎ 03
6/07 Su	24 ♑ 35	24 ♈ 23	4 ♎ 52	25 ♎ 58
6/14 Su	24 ♑ 27	24 ♈ 26	4 ♎ 51	25 ♎ 53
6/21 Su	24 ♑ 18	24 ♈ 28	4 ♎ 51 D	25 ♎ 50
6/28 Su	24 ♑ 09	24 ♈ 30	4 ♎ 51	25 ♎ 48
7/05 Su	23 ♑ 59	24 ♈ 32	4 ♎ 53	25 ♎ 46
7/12 Su	23 ♑ 49	24 ♈ 33	4 ♎ 56	25 ♎ 46 D
7/19 Su	23 ♑ 39	24 ♈ 33	5 ♎ 00	25 ♎ 47
7/26 Su	23 ♑ 29	24 ♈ 33 ℞	5 ♎ 05	25 ♎ 49
8/02 Su	23 ♑ 19	24 ♈ 32	5 ♎ 11	25 ♎ 52
8/09 Su	23 ♑ 10	24 ♈ 31	5 ♎ 17	25 ♎ 56
8/16 Su	23 ♑ 01	24 ♈ 29	5 ♎ 24	26 ♎ 01
8/23 Su	22 ♑ 53	24 ♈ 27	5 ♎ 32	26 ♎ 07
8/30 Su	22 ♑ 46	24 ♈ 25	5 ♎ 41	26 ♎ 13

Astro Data

2019

4/24 We	18:48	♇	SR	23 ♑ 09	-21.7 (-21:43)
6/18 Tu	09:03	♇	SD	3 ♎ 51	24.2 (24:12)
7/09 Tu	21:39	♇	SD	24 ♎ 43	16.6 (16:38)
7/21 Su	01:29	♀	SR	24 ♈ 19	-1.6 (-1:35)
10/03 Th	06:39	♇	SD	20 ♑ 38	-22.4 (-22:22)

2020

1/11 Sa	01:44	♀	SD	23 ♈ 13	-1.9 (-1:54)
1/05 Su	05:26	♇	SR	6 ♎ 51	23.0 (22:59)
1/26 Su	08:44	♇	SR	27 ♎ 51	15.6 (15:36)
4/25 Sa	18:54	♇	SR	24 ♑ 59	-22.0 (-21:57)
6/18 Th	17:38	♇	SD	4 ♎ 50	23.8 (23:45)
7/10 Fr	06:33	♇	SD	25 ♎ 46	16.4 (16:21)
7/20 Mo	19:13	♀	SR	24 ♈ 33	-1.3 (-1:19)

	Date	♇	♀	♇	♇		Date	♇	♀	♇	♇
2020	9/06 Su	22 ♑ 40 ℞	24 ♈ 22 ℞	5 ♎ 50 D	26 ♎ 21 D	2021	5/23 Su	26 ♑ 39 ℞	24 ♈ 30 D	5 ♎ 58 ℞	27 ♎ 14 ℞
	9/13 Su	22 ♑ 35	24 ♈ 19	5 ♎ 59	26 ♎ 29		5/30 Su	26 ♑ 34	24 ♈ 33	5 ♎ 54	27 ♎ 08
	9/20 Su	22 ♑ 32	24 ♈ 15	6 ♎ 09	26 ♎ 38		6/06 Su	26 ♑ 27	24 ♈ 37	5 ♎ 52	27 ♎ 03
	9/27 Su	22 ♑ 30	24 ♈ 11	6 ♎ 18	26 ♎ 48		6/13 Su	26 ♑ 20	24 ♈ 40	5 ♎ 50	26 ♎ 58
	10/04 Su	22 ♑ 29	24 ♈ 07	6 ♎ 28	26 ♎ 57		6/20 Su	26 ♑ 11	24 ♈ 42	5 ♎ 50	26 ♎ 54
	10/11 Su	22 ♑ 29 D	24 ♈ 03	6 ♎ 38	27 ♎ 08		6/27 Su	26 ♑ 03	24 ♈ 44	5 ♎ 50 D	26 ♎ 52
	10/18 Su	22 ♑ 31	23 ♈ 59	6 ♎ 47	27 ♎ 18		7/04 Su	25 ♑ 53	24 ♈ 45	5 ♎ 52	26 ♎ 50
	10/25 Su	22 ♑ 35	23 ♈ 55	6 ♎ 57	27 ♎ 28		7/11 Su	25 ♑ 43	24 ♈ 46	5 ♎ 54	26 ♎ 49
	11/01 Su	22 ♑ 40	23 ♈ 51	7 ♎ 06	27 ♎ 38		7/18 Su	25 ♑ 33	24 ♈ 47	5 ♎ 58	26 ♎ 50 D
	11/08 Su	22 ♑ 46	23 ♈ 47	7 ♎ 14	27 ♎ 49		7/25 Su	25 ♑ 23	24 ♈ 47 ℞	6 ♎ 02	26 ♎ 51
	11/15 Su	22 ♑ 54	23 ♈ 43	7 ♎ 21	27 ♎ 58		8/01 Su	25 ♑ 13	24 ♈ 46	6 ♎ 08	26 ♎ 54
	11/22 Su	23 ♑ 03	23 ♈ 39	7 ♎ 28	28 ♎ 08		8/08 Su	25 ♑ 04	24 ♈ 45	6 ♎ 14	26 ♎ 58
	11/29 Su	23 ♑ 13	23 ♈ 36	7 ♎ 34	28 ♎ 16		8/15 Su	24 ♑ 55	24 ♈ 44	6 ♎ 21	27 ♎ 02
	12/06 Su	23 ♑ 24	23 ♈ 33	7 ♎ 39	28 ♎ 24		8/22 Su	24 ♑ 46	24 ♈ 42	6 ♎ 29	27 ♎ 08
	12/13 Su	23 ♑ 35	23 ♈ 31	7 ♎ 44	28 ♎ 32		8/29 Su	24 ♑ 39	24 ♈ 39	6 ♎ 37	27 ♎ 14
	12/20 Su	23 ♑ 48	23 ♈ 29	7 ♎ 47	28 ♎ 38		9/05 Su	24 ♑ 32	24 ♈ 37	6 ♎ 46	27 ♎ 22
	12/27 Su	24 ♑ 01	23 ♈ 28	7 ♎ 49	28 ♎ 43		9/12 Su	24 ♑ 27	24 ♈ 33	6 ♎ 55	27 ♎ 30
							9/19 Su	24 ♑ 23	24 ♈ 30	7 ♎ 05	27 ♎ 39
							9/26 Su	24 ♑ 20	24 ♈ 26	7 ♎ 14	27 ♎ 48
							10/03 Su	24 ♑ 19	24 ♈ 22	7 ♎ 24	27 ♎ 58
2021	1/03 Su	24 ♑ 15	23 ♈ 27	7 ♎ 50	28 ♎ 48		10/10 Su	24 ♑ 19 D	24 ♈ 18	7 ♎ 34	28 ♎ 08
	1/10 Su	24 ♑ 29	23 ♈ 27	7 ♎ 50 ℞	28 ♎ 51		10/17 Su	24 ♑ 20	24 ♈ 14	7 ♎ 44	28 ♎ 18
	1/17 Su	24 ♑ 43	23 ♈ 27 D	7 ♎ 48	28 ♎ 53		10/24 Su	24 ♑ 23	24 ♈ 10	7 ♎ 53	28 ♎ 28
	1/24 Su	24 ♑ 56	23 ♈ 28	7 ♎ 46	28 ♎ 54		10/31 Su	24 ♑ 27	24 ♈ 05	8 ♎ 02	28 ♎ 39
	1/31 Su	25 ♑ 10	23 ♈ 29	7 ♎ 43	28 ♎ 54 ℞		11/07 Su	24 ♑ 33	24 ♈ 01	8 ♎ 10	28 ♎ 49
	2/07 Su	25 ♑ 24	23 ♈ 31	7 ♎ 38	28 ♎ 53		11/14 Su	24 ♑ 40	23 ♈ 58	8 ♎ 18	28 ♎ 59
	2/14 Su	25 ♑ 36	23 ♈ 33	7 ♎ 33	28 ♎ 51		11/21 Su	24 ♑ 48	23 ♈ 54	8 ♎ 25	29 ♎ 08
	2/21 Su	25 ♑ 48	23 ♈ 36	7 ♎ 27	28 ♎ 47		11/28 Su	24 ♑ 57	23 ♈ 51	8 ♎ 31	29 ♎ 17
	2/28 Su	26 ♑ 00	23 ♈ 39	7 ♎ 21	28 ♎ 43		12/05 Su	25 ♑ 08	23 ♈ 48	8 ♎ 37	29 ♎ 25
	3/07 Su	26 ♑ 10	23 ♈ 42	7 ♎ 14	28 ♎ 37		12/12 Su	25 ♑ 19	23 ♈ 46	8 ♎ 41	29 ♎ 33
	3/14 Su	26 ♑ 19	23 ♈ 46	7 ♎ 06	28 ♎ 31		12/19 Su	25 ♑ 31	23 ♈ 44	8 ♎ 45	29 ♎ 40
	3/21 Su	26 ♑ 27	23 ♈ 50	6 ♎ 58	28 ♎ 24		12/26 Su	25 ♑ 44	23 ♈ 42	8 ♎ 47	29 ♎ 45
	3/28 Su	26 ♑ 34	23 ♈ 55	6 ♎ 50	28 ♎ 17						
	4/04 Su	26 ♑ 40	23 ♈ 59	6 ♎ 42	28 ♎ 09						
	4/11 Su	26 ♑ 44	24 ♈ 04	6 ♎ 35	28 ♎ 01						
	4/18 Su	26 ♑ 47	24 ♈ 08	6 ♎ 27	27 ♎ 53	2022	1/02 Su	25 ♑ 58	23 ♈ 41	8 ♎ 48	29 ♎ 50
	4/25 Su	26 ♑ 48	24 ♈ 13	6 ♎ 20	27 ♎ 44		1/09 Su	26 ♑ 11	23 ♈ 41	8 ♎ 49 ℞	29 ♎ 54
	5/02 Su	26 ♑ 48 ℞	24 ♈ 18	6 ♎ 13	27 ♎ 36		1/16 Su	26 ♑ 25	23 ♈ 41 D	8 ♎ 48	29 ♎ 56
	5/09 Su	26 ♑ 46	24 ♈ 22	6 ♎ 07	27 ♎ 29		1/23 Su	26 ♑ 39	23 ♈ 41	8 ♎ 46	29 ♎ 58
	5/16 Su	26 ♑ 43	24 ♈ 26	6 ♎ 02	27 ♎ 21		1/30 Su	26 ♑ 53	23 ♈ 43	8 ♎ 43	29 ♎ 58 ℞

Astro Data

2020

Date	Time	Planet	Event	Longitude	Decl.
10/04 Su	13:32	♇	SD	22 ♑ 29	-22.6 (-22:38)

2021

Date	Time	Planet	Event	Longitude	Decl.
1/05 Tu	10:21	♈	SR	7 ♎ 50	22.5 (22:30)
1/10 Su	12:43	♀	SD	23 ♈ 27	-1.6 (-1:37)
1/26 Tu	18:00	♎	SR	28 ♎ 54	15.3 (15:17)
4/27 Tu	20:02	♇	SR	26 ♑ 48	-22.2 (-22:10)

2021

Date	Time	Planet	Event	Longitude	Decl.
6/20 Su	01:27	♈	SD	5 ♎ 50	23.2 (23:13)
7/11 Su	11:25	♎	SD	26 ♎ 49	16.0 (16:00)
7/21 We	09:08	♀	SR	24 ♈ 47	-1.0 (-1:02)
10/06 We	18:29	♇	SD	24 ♑ 18	-21.9 (-22:52)

2022

Date	Time	Planet	Event	Longitude	Decl.
1/06 Th	14:56	♈	SR	8 ♎ 49	22.0 (22:00)
1/11 Tu	04:42	♀	SD	23 ♈ 41	-1.4 (-1:22)
1/28 Fr	02:16	♎	SR	29 ♎ 58	15.0 (14:57)

2022		♇	⯰	🝼	🝻
2022	2/06 Su	27♑06 D	23♈44 D	8♎39 ℞	29♎57 ℞
	2/13 Su	27♑19	23♈46	8♎34	29♎55
	2/20 Su	27♑31	23♈49	8♎28	29♎52
	2/27 Su	27♑43	23♈52	8♎22	29♎48
	3/06 Su	27♑53	23♈56	8♎15	29♎43
	3/13 Su	28♑03	24♈00	8♎07	29♎37
	3/20 Su	28♑12	24♈04	8♎00	29♎30
	3/27 Su	28♑19	24♈08	7♎52	29♎23
	4/03 Su	28♑25	24♈12	7♎44	29♎15
	4/10 Su	28♑30	24♈17	7♎36	29♎07
	4/17 Su	28♑33	24♈21	7♎28	28♎59
	4/24 Su	28♑35	24♈26	7♎21	28♎51
	5/01 Su	28♑35 ℞	24♈31	7♎14	28♎43
	5/08 Su	28♑34	24♈35	7♎08	28♎35
	5/15 Su	28♑32	24♈39	7♎03	28♎27
	5/22 Su	28♑29	24♈43	6♎58	28♎20
	5/29 Su	28♑24	24♈47	6♎54	28♎13
	6/05 Su	28♑18	24♈50	6♎52	28♎08
	6/12 Su	28♑11	24♈53	6♎50	28♎03
	6/19 Su	28♑03	24♈56	6♎49	27♎59
	6/26 Su	27♑54	24♈58	6♎49 D	27♎56
	7/03 Su	27♑45	24♈59	6♎50	27♎54
	7/10 Su	27♑35	25♈00	6♎53	27♎53
	7/17 Su	27♑25	25♈01	6♎56	27♎53 D
	7/24 Su	27♑15	25♈01 ℞	7♎00	27♎54
	7/31 Su	27♑05	25♈01	7♎05	27♎56
	8/07 Su	26♑56	25♈00	7♎11	28♎00
	8/14 Su	26♑46	24♈58	7♎18	28♎04
	8/21 Su	26♑38	24♈56	7♎25	28♎09
	8/28 Su	26♑30	24♈54	7♎33	28♎16
	9/04 Su	26♑23	24♈51	7♎42	28♎23
	9/11 Su	26♑17	24♈48	7♎51	28♎31
	9/18 Su	26♑13	24♈45	8♎01	28♎39
	9/25 Su	26♑09	24♈41	8♎10	28♎48
	10/02 Su	26♑07	24♈37	8♎20	28♎58
	10/09 Su	26♑06 D	24♈33	8♎30	29♎08
	10/16 Su	26♑07	24♈29	8♎39	29♎18
	10/23 Su	26♑09	24♈25	8♎49	29♎28
	10/30 Su	26♑13	24♈20	8♎58	29♎39
	11/06 Su	26♑18	24♈16	9♎06	29♎49

		♇	⯰	🝼	🝻
2022	11/13 Su	26♑24 D	24♈12 ℞	9♎14 D	29♎59 D
	11/20 Su	26♑32	24♈09	9♎22	0♏09
	11/27 Su	26♑41	24♈06	9♎28	0♏18
	12/04 Su	26♑51	24♈03	9♎34	0♏26
	12/11 Su	27♑02	24♈00	9♎39	0♏34
	12/18 Su	27♑13	23♈58	9♎43	0♏41
	12/25 Su	27♑26	23♈56	9♎45	0♏47
2023	1/01 Su	27♑39	23♈55	9♎47	0♏52
	1/08 Su	27♑52	23♈55	9♎47 ℞	0♏56
	1/15 Su	28♑06	23♈55 D	9♎47	0♏59
	1/22 Su	28♑20	23♈55	9♎45	1♏01
	1/29 Su	28♑34	23♈56	9♎43	1♏02
	2/05 Su	28♑47	23♈58	9♎39	1♏01 ℞
	2/12 Su	29♑00	24♈00	9♎34	1♏00
	2/19 Su	29♑13	24♈03	9♎29	0♏57
	2/26 Su	29♑24	24♈06	9♎23	0♏53
	3/05 Su	29♑35	24♈09	9♎16	0♏48
	3/12 Su	29♑45	24♈13	9♎09	0♏43
	3/19 Su	29♑54	24♈17	9♎01	0♏36
	3/26 Su	0♒02	24♈21	8♎53	0♏29
	4/02 Su	0♒09	24♈25	8♎45	0♏22
	4/09 Su	0♒14	24♈30	8♎37	0♏14
	4/16 Su	0♒18	24♈35	8♎30	0♏05
	4/23 Su	0♒20	24♈39	8♎22	29♎57
	4/30 Su	0♒21	24♈44	8♎15	29♎49
	5/07 Su	0♒21 ℞	24♈48	8♎09	29♎41
	5/14 Su	0♒19	24♈52	8♎03	29♎33
	5/21 Su	0♒16	24♈56	7♎58	29♎26
	5/28 Su	0♒12	25♈00	7♎54	29♎19
	6/04 Su	0♒06	25♈03	7♎51	29♎13
	6/11 Su	0♒00	25♈06	7♎49	29♎08
	6/18 Su	29♑52	25♈09	7♎48	29♎04
	6/25 Su	29♑44	25♈11	7♎48 D	29♎00
	7/02 Su	29♑35	25♈13	7♎49	28♎58
	7/09 Su	29♑26	25♈14	7♎51	28♎57
	7/16 Su	29♑16	25♈15	7♎53	28♎56 D
	7/23 Su	29♑06	25♈15 ℞	7♎57	28♎57

Astro Data

2022

4/29 Fr	18:36	♇	SR	28♑35	-22.3 (-22:20)
6/21 Tu	09:41	🝼	SD	6♎49	22.8 (22:45)
7/12 Tu	16:31	🝻	SD	27♎53	15.7 (15:42)
7/21 Th	15:19	⯰	SR	25♈01	-0.8 (0:47)
10/08 Sa	21:56	♇	SD	26♑06	-23.1 (-23:04)
11/13 Su	07:21	🝻	→ ♏		14.5 (14:29)

2023

1/07 Sa	22:34	🝼	SR	9♎47	21.5 (21:30)
1/11 We	18:16	⯰	SD	23♈55	-1.1 (-1:06)
1/29 Su	06:42	🝻	SR	1♏02	14.7 (14:41)
3/23 Th	12:23	♇	→ ♒		-22.5 (-22:30)
4/21 Fr	00:36	🝻	→ ♎ ℞		15.4 (15:26)
5/01 Mo	17:08	♇	SR	0♒21	-22.5 (-22:30)
6/11 Su	09:37	♇	→ ♑ ℞		-22.7 (-22:41)
6/22 Th	13:18	🝼	SD	7♎48	22.3 (22:16)
7/14 Fr	02:52	🝻	SD	28♎56	15.4 (15:24)
7/21 Fr	23:41	⯰	SR	25♈15	-0.5 (0:31)

2023	♇	♇	♇	♇
7/30 Su	28 ♑ 56 R	25 ♈ 15 R	8 ♎ 02 D	28 ♎ 59 D
8/06 Su	28 ♑ 46	25 ♈ 14	8 ♎ 08	29 ♎ 02
8/13 Su	28 ♑ 37	25 ♈ 13	8 ♎ 14	29 ♎ 06
8/20 Su	28 ♑ 28	25 ♈ 11	8 ♎ 22	29 ♎ 11
8/27 Su	28 ♑ 20	25 ♈ 09	8 ♎ 29	29 ♎ 17
9/03 Su	28 ♑ 13	25 ♈ 06	8 ♎ 38	29 ♎ 24
9/10 Su	28 ♑ 06	25 ♈ 03	8 ♎ 47	29 ♎ 31
9/17 Su	28 ♑ 01	24 ♈ 59	8 ♎ 56	29 ♎ 40
9/24 Su	27 ♑ 57	24 ♈ 56	9 ♎ 06	29 ♎ 49
10/01 Su	27 ♑ 54	24 ♈ 52	9 ♎ 16	29 ♎ 58
10/08 Su	27 ♑ 53	24 ♈ 48	9 ♎ 25	0 ♏ 08
10/15 Su	27 ♑ 53 D	24 ♈ 44	9 ♎ 35	0 ♏ 18
10/22 Su	27 ♑ 55	24 ♈ 39	9 ♎ 44	0 ♏ 29
10/29 Su	27 ♑ 58	24 ♈ 35	9 ♎ 54	0 ♏ 39
11/05 Su	28 ♑ 02	24 ♈ 31	10 ♎ 02	0 ♏ 50
11/12 Su	28 ♑ 08	24 ♈ 27	10 ♎ 11	1 ♏ 00
11/19 Su	28 ♑ 15	24 ♈ 24	10 ♎ 18	1 ♏ 09
11/26 Su	28 ♑ 23	24 ♈ 20	10 ♎ 25	1 ♏ 19
12/03 Su	28 ♑ 33	24 ♈ 17	10 ♎ 31	1 ♏ 28
12/10 Su	28 ♑ 43	24 ♈ 15	10 ♎ 36	1 ♏ 36
12/17 Su	28 ♑ 54	24 ♈ 12	10 ♎ 40	1 ♏ 43
12/24 Su	29 ♑ 06	24 ♈ 11	10 ♎ 43	1 ♏ 49
12/31 Su	29 ♑ 19	24 ♈ 10	10 ♎ 45	1 ♏ 55
2024				
1/07 Su	29 ♑ 32	24 ♈ 09	10 ♎ 46	1 ♏ 59
1/14 Su	29 ♑ 46	24 ♈ 09 D	10 ♎ 46 R	2 ♏ 03
1/21 Su	29 ♑ 59	24 ♈ 09	10 ♎ 44	2 ♏ 05
1/28 Su	0 ♒ 13	24 ♈ 10	10 ♎ 42	2 ♏ 06
2/04 Su	0 ♒ 27	24 ♈ 12	10 ♎ 39	2 ♏ 06 R
2/11 Su	0 ♒ 40	24 ♈ 14	10 ♎ 34	2 ♏ 04
2/18 Su	0 ♒ 52	24 ♈ 16	10 ♎ 29	2 ♏ 02
2/25 Su	1 ♒ 04	24 ♈ 19	10 ♎ 23	1 ♏ 58
3/03 Su	1 ♒ 16	24 ♈ 22	10 ♎ 17	1 ♏ 54
3/10 Su	1 ♒ 26	24 ♈ 26	10 ♎ 10	1 ♏ 49
3/17 Su	1 ♒ 35	24 ♈ 30	10 ♎ 02	1 ♏ 42
3/24 Su	1 ♒ 44	24 ♈ 34	9 ♎ 54	1 ♏ 36
3/31 Su	1 ♒ 51	24 ♈ 39	9 ♎ 46	1 ♏ 28
4/07 Su	1 ♒ 56	24 ♈ 43	9 ♎ 38	1 ♏ 20
4/14 Su	2 ♒ 01	24 ♈ 48	9 ♎ 31	1 ♏ 12

2024	♇	♇	♇	♇
4/21 Su	2 ♒ 04 D	24 ♈ 52 D	9 ♎ 23 R	1 ♏ 04 R
4/28 Su	2 ♒ 05	24 ♈ 57	9 ♎ 16	0 ♏ 56
5/05 Su	2 ♒ 06 R	25 ♈ 01	9 ♎ 10	0 ♏ 47
5/12 Su	2 ♒ 05	25 ♈ 06	9 ♎ 04	0 ♏ 40
5/19 Su	2 ♒ 02	25 ♈ 10	8 ♎ 59	0 ♏ 32
5/26 Su	1 ♒ 58	25 ♈ 13	8 ♎ 54	0 ♏ 25
6/02 Su	1 ♒ 53	25 ♈ 17	8 ♎ 51	0 ♏ 19
6/09 Su	1 ♒ 47	25 ♈ 20	8 ♎ 48	0 ♏ 13
6/16 Su	1 ♒ 40	25 ♈ 23	8 ♎ 47	0 ♏ 09
6/23 Su	1 ♒ 32	25 ♈ 25	8 ♎ 46 D	0 ♏ 05
6/30 Su	1 ♒ 24	25 ♈ 27	8 ♎ 47	0 ♏ 02
7/07 Su	1 ♒ 14	25 ♈ 28	8 ♎ 49	0 ♏ 01
7/14 Su	1 ♒ 05	25 ♈ 29	8 ♎ 51	0 ♏ 00
7/21 Su	0 ♒ 55	25 ♈ 29	8 ♎ 55	0 ♏ 01 D
7/28 Su	0 ♒ 45	25 ♈ 29 R	8 ♎ 59	0 ♏ 02
8/04 Su	0 ♒ 35	25 ♈ 28	9 ♎ 05	0 ♏ 05
8/11 Su	0 ♒ 26	25 ♈ 27	9 ♎ 11	0 ♏ 08
8/18 Su	0 ♒ 17	25 ♈ 25	9 ♎ 18	0 ♏ 13
8/25 Su	0 ♒ 08	25 ♈ 23	9 ♎ 26	0 ♏ 19
9/01 Su	0 ♒ 01	25 ♈ 21	9 ♎ 34	0 ♏ 25
9/08 Su	29 ♑ 54	25 ♈ 18	9 ♎ 43	0 ♏ 33
9/15 Su	29 ♑ 48	25 ♈ 14	9 ♎ 52	0 ♏ 41
9/22 Su	29 ♑ 44	25 ♈ 11	10 ♎ 01	0 ♏ 50
9/29 Su	29 ♑ 40	25 ♈ 07	10 ♎ 11	0 ♏ 59
10/06 Su	29 ♑ 39	25 ♈ 03	10 ♎ 21	1 ♏ 09
10/13 Su	29 ♑ 38 D	24 ♈ 59	10 ♎ 30	1 ♏ 19
10/20 Su	29 ♑ 39	24 ♈ 54	10 ♎ 40	1 ♏ 29
10/27 Su	29 ♑ 41	24 ♈ 50	10 ♎ 49	1 ♏ 40
11/03 Su	29 ♑ 45	24 ♈ 46	10 ♎ 58	1 ♏ 50
11/10 Su	29 ♑ 50	24 ♈ 42	11 ♎ 06	2 ♏ 01
11/17 Su	29 ♑ 56	24 ♈ 39	11 ♎ 14	2 ♏ 10
11/24 Su	0 ♒ 04	24 ♈ 35	11 ♎ 21	2 ♏ 20
12/01 Su	0 ♒ 13	24 ♈ 32	11 ♎ 27	2 ♏ 29
12/08 Su	0 ♒ 23	24 ♈ 29	11 ♎ 33	2 ♏ 37
12/15 Su	0 ♒ 34	24 ♈ 27	11 ♎ 37	2 ♏ 45
12/22 Su	0 ♒ 46	24 ♈ 25	11 ♎ 41	2 ♏ 52
12/29 Su	0 ♒ 58	24 ♈ 24	11 ♎ 43	2 ♏ 57

Astro Data

2023

10/01 Su	20:10	♎ → ♏			14.5 (14:30)
10/11 We	01:10	♇ SD		27 ♑ 53	-23.3 (-23:15)

2024

1/11 Th	21:49	♀ SD		24 ♈ 09	-0.8 (0:50)
1/09 Tu	05:01	♎ SR		10 ♎ 46	21.0 (21:02)
1/21 Su	00:56	♇ → ♒			-22.9 (-22:52)
1/30 Tu	13:31	♏ SR		2 ♏ 06	14.4 (14:21)

2024

5/02 Th	17:46	♇ SR		2 ♒ 06	-22.6 (-22:37)
6/22 Sa	16:50	♎ SD		8 ♎ 46	21.8 (21:47)
7/14 Su	12:10	♏ SD		0 ♏ 00	15.0 (15:02)
7/21 Su	18:16	♀ SR		25 ♈ 29	-0.2 (0:15)
9/01 Su	23:59	♇ → ♑ R			-23.3 (-23:19)
10/12 Sa	00:33	♇ SD		29 ♑ 38	-23.4 (-23:24)
11/19 Tu	20:39	♇ → ♒			-23.3 (-23:20)

2025

1/11 Sa	08:09	♀ SD		24 ♈ 23	-0.6 (0:34)
1/09 Th	07:46	♎ SR		11 ♎ 44	20.5 (20:31)

		♇	♀	♀	♀
2025	1/05 Su	1 ≈ 11 D	24 ♈ 23 ℞	11 ♎ 44 D	3 ♏ 02 D
	1/12 Su	1 ≈ 24	24 ♈ 23 D	11 ♎ 44 ℞	3 ♏ 06
	1/19 Su	1 ≈ 38	24 ♈ 23	11 ♎ 43	3 ♏ 08
	1/26 Su	1 ≈ 51	24 ♈ 24	11 ♎ 41	3 ♏ 10
	2/02 Su	2 ≈ 05	24 ♈ 25	11 ♎ 38	3 ♏ 10 ℞
	2/09 Su	2 ≈ 18	24 ♈ 27	11 ♎ 34	3 ♏ 09
	2/16 Su	2 ≈ 31	24 ♈ 30	11 ♎ 29	3 ♏ 07
	2/23 Su	2 ≈ 43	24 ♈ 32	11 ♎ 24	3 ♏ 04
	3/02 Su	2 ≈ 54	24 ♈ 36	11 ♎ 17	3 ♏ 00
	3/09 Su	3 ≈ 05	24 ♈ 39	11 ♎ 10	2 ♏ 55
	3/16 Su	3 ≈ 15	24 ♈ 43	11 ♎ 03	2 ♏ 49
	3/23 Su	3 ≈ 23	24 ♈ 47	10 ♎ 55	2 ♏ 42
	3/30 Su	3 ≈ 31	24 ♈ 52	10 ♎ 47	2 ♏ 35
	4/06 Su	3 ≈ 37	24 ♈ 56	10 ♎ 39	2 ♏ 27
	4/13 Su	3 ≈ 42	25 ♈ 01	10 ♎ 32	2 ♏ 19
	4/20 Su	3 ≈ 46	25 ♈ 05	10 ♎ 24	2 ♏ 11
	4/27 Su	3 ≈ 48	25 ♈ 10	10 ♎ 17	2 ♏ 03
	5/04 Su	3 ≈ 49	25 ♈ 14	10 ♎ 10	1 ♏ 54
	5/11 Su	3 ≈ 48 ℞	25 ♈ 19	10 ♎ 04	1 ♏ 46
	5/18 Su	3 ≈ 46	25 ♈ 23	9 ♎ 59	1 ♏ 39
	5/25 Su	3 ≈ 43	25 ♈ 27	9 ♎ 54	1 ♏ 32
	6/01 Su	3 ≈ 39	25 ♈ 30	9 ♎ 50	1 ♏ 25
	6/08 Su	3 ≈ 33	25 ♈ 33	9 ♎ 48	1 ♏ 19
	6/15 Su	3 ≈ 26	25 ♈ 36	9 ♎ 46	1 ♏ 14
	6/22 Su	3 ≈ 19	25 ♈ 39	9 ♎ 45	1 ♏ 10
	6/29 Su	3 ≈ 10	25 ♈ 40	9 ♎ 45 D	1 ♏ 07
	7/06 Su	3 ≈ 01	25 ♈ 42	9 ♎ 47	1 ♏ 05
	7/13 Su	2 ≈ 52	25 ♈ 43	9 ♎ 49	1 ♏ 04
	7/20 Su	2 ≈ 42	25 ♈ 43	9 ♎ 52	1 ♏ 04 D
	7/27 Su	2 ≈ 32	25 ♈ 43 ℞	9 ♎ 56	1 ♏ 06
	8/03 Su	2 ≈ 23	25 ♈ 42	10 ♎ 01	1 ♏ 08
	8/10 Su	2 ≈ 13	25 ♈ 41	10 ♎ 07	1 ♏ 11
	8/17 Su	2 ≈ 04	25 ♈ 40	10 ♎ 14	1 ♏ 16
	8/24 Su	1 ≈ 55	25 ♈ 38	10 ♎ 22	1 ♏ 21
	8/31 Su	1 ≈ 47	25 ♈ 35	10 ♎ 30	1 ♏ 27
	9/07 Su	1 ≈ 40	25 ♈ 32	10 ♎ 38	1 ♏ 35
	9/14 Su	1 ≈ 34	25 ♈ 29	10 ♎ 47	1 ♏ 42
	9/21 Su	1 ≈ 29	25 ♈ 26	10 ♎ 57	1 ♏ 51
	9/28 Su	1 ≈ 25	25 ♈ 22	11 ♎ 06	2 ♏ 00
	10/05 Su	1 ≈ 23	25 ♈ 18	11 ♎ 16	2 ♏ 10
2025	10/12 Su	1 ≈ 22 ℞	25 ♈ 14 ℞	11 ♎ 26 D	2 ♏ 20 D
	10/19 Su	1 ≈ 22 D	25 ♈ 09	11 ♎ 35	2 ♏ 30
	10/26 Su	1 ≈ 24	25 ♈ 05	11 ♎ 45	2 ♏ 41
	11/02 Su	1 ≈ 27	25 ♈ 01	11 ♎ 54	2 ♏ 51
	11/09 Su	1 ≈ 31	24 ♈ 57	12 ♎ 02	3 ♏ 02
	11/16 Su	1 ≈ 37	24 ♈ 53	12 ♎ 10	3 ♏ 12
	11/23 Su	1 ≈ 44	24 ♈ 50	12 ♎ 17	3 ♏ 21
	11/30 Su	1 ≈ 52	24 ♈ 47	12 ♎ 24	3 ♏ 31
	12/07 Su	2 ≈ 02	24 ♈ 44	12 ♎ 30	3 ♏ 39
	12/14 Su	2 ≈ 12	24 ♈ 41	12 ♎ 34	3 ♏ 47
	12/21 Su	2 ≈ 23	24 ♈ 40	12 ♎ 38	3 ♏ 54
	12/28 Su	2 ≈ 35	24 ♈ 38	12 ♎ 41	4 ♏ 00
2026	1/04 Su	2 ≈ 48	24 ♈ 37	12 ♎ 42	4 ♏ 05
	1/11 Su	3 ≈ 01	24 ♈ 37	12 ♎ 43 ℞	4 ♏ 09
	1/18 Su	3 ≈ 14	24 ♈ 37 D	12 ♎ 42	4 ♏ 12
	1/25 Su	3 ≈ 28	24 ♈ 38	12 ♎ 40	4 ♏ 14
	2/01 Su	3 ≈ 41	24 ♈ 39	12 ♎ 38	4 ♏ 15
	2/08 Su	3 ≈ 55	24 ♈ 41	12 ♎ 34	4 ♏ 14 ℞
	2/15 Su	4 ≈ 07	24 ♈ 43	12 ♎ 29	4 ♏ 13
	2/22 Su	4 ≈ 20	24 ♈ 46	12 ♎ 24	4 ♏ 10
	3/01 Su	4 ≈ 32	24 ♈ 49	12 ♎ 18	4 ♏ 06
	3/08 Su	4 ≈ 42	24 ♈ 53	12 ♎ 11	4 ♏ 01
	3/15 Su	4 ≈ 53	24 ♈ 56	12 ♎ 04	3 ♏ 56
	3/22 Su	5 ≈ 02	25 ♈ 00	11 ♎ 56	3 ♏ 49
	3/29 Su	5 ≈ 09	25 ♈ 05	11 ♎ 48	3 ♏ 42
	4/05 Su	5 ≈ 16	25 ♈ 09	11 ♎ 40	3 ♏ 34
	4/12 Su	5 ≈ 22	25 ♈ 14	11 ♎ 32	3 ♏ 26
	4/19 Su	5 ≈ 26	25 ♈ 18	11 ♎ 25	3 ♏ 18
	4/26 Su	5 ≈ 29	25 ♈ 23	11 ♎ 18	3 ♏ 10
	5/03 Su	5 ≈ 30	25 ♈ 28	11 ♎ 11	3 ♏ 02
	5/10 Su	5 ≈ 30 ℞	25 ♈ 32	11 ♎ 04	2 ♏ 54
	5/17 Su	5 ≈ 29	25 ♈ 36	10 ♎ 59	2 ♏ 46
	5/24 Su	5 ≈ 26	25 ♈ 40	10 ♎ 54	2 ♏ 38
	5/31 Su	5 ≈ 22	25 ♈ 44	10 ♎ 50	2 ♏ 32
	6/07 Su	5 ≈ 17	25 ♈ 47	10 ♎ 47	2 ♏ 26
	6/14 Su	5 ≈ 11	25 ♈ 50	10 ♎ 45	2 ♏ 21
	6/21 Su	5 ≈ 04	25 ♈ 52	10 ♎ 44	2 ♏ 16

Astro Data

2025

1/30 Th	21:58	♇	SR	3 ♏ 10	14.0 (14:01)
5/04 Su	15:26	♇	SR	3 ≈ 49	-12.7 (-12:44)
6/23 Mo	22:53	♇	SD	9 ♎ 45	21.3 (21:15)
7/15 Tu	21:46	♇	SD	1 ♏ 04	14.7 (14:43)
7/21 Tu	09:01	♀	SR	25 ♈ 43	0.0 (0:00)

2025

10/14 Tu	02:53	♇	SD	1 ≈ 22	-23.5 (-23:31)

2026

1/10 Sa	11:25	♇	SR	12 ♎ 43	20.0 (20:01)
1/12 Mo	02:48	♀	SD	24 ♈ 37	-0.3 (0:17)
2/01 Su	08:09	♇	SR	4 ♏ 15	13.7 (13:44)
5/06 We	15:34	♇	SR	5 ≈ 30	-21.8 (-22:48)
6/25 Th	06:59	♇	SD	10 ♎ 44	20.8 (20:46)

		♇	♀	♎	♏			♇	♀	♎	♏
2026	6/28 Su	4≈56 R	25♈54 D	10♎44 D	2♏13 R	2027	3/14 Su	6≈29 D	25♈10 D	13♎04 R	5♏03 R
	7/05 Su	4≈47	25♈56	10♎45	2♏10		3/21 Su	6≈38	25♈14	12♎57	4♏56
	7/12 Su	4≈38	25♈57	10♎46	2♏09		3/28 Su	6≈47	25♈18	12♎49	4♏49
	7/19 Su	4≈28	25♈57	10♎49	2♏09 D		4/04 Su	6≈54	25♈22	12♎41	4♏42
	7/26 Su	4≈18	25♈57 R	10♎53	2♏10		4/11 Su	7≈00	25♈27	12♎33	4♏34
	8/02 Su	4≈09	25♈57	10♎58	2♏12		4/18 Su	7≈04	25♈31	12♎26	4♏26
	8/09 Su	3≈59	25♈56	11♎04	2♏15		4/25 Su	7≈08	25♈36	12♎18	4♏18
	8/16 Su	3≈50	25♈54	11♎10	2♏19		5/02 Su	7≈10	25♈41	12♎11	4♏09
	8/23 Su	3≈41	25♈52	11♎17	2♏24		5/09 Su	7≈10 R	25♈45	12♎05	4♏01
	8/30 Su	3≈32	25♈50	11♎25	2♏30		5/16 Su	7≈09	25♈49	11♎59	3♏53
	9/06 Su	3≈25	25♈47	11♎34	2♏37		5/23 Su	7≈07	25♈53	11♎54	3♏46
	9/13 Su	3≈18	25♈44	11♎43	2♏44		5/30 Su	7≈04	25♈57	11♎50	3♏39
	9/20 Su	3≈13	25♈40	11♎52	2♏53		6/06 Su	6≈59	26♈00	11♎46	3♏33
	9/27 Su	3≈09	25♈37	12♎02	3♏02		6/13 Su	6≈54	26♈03	11♎44	3♏27
	10/04 Su	3≈06	25♈33	12♎11	3♏11		6/20 Su	6≈47	26♈06	11♎42	3♏22
	10/11 Su	3≈04	25♈28	12♎21	3♏21		6/27 Su	6≈39	26♈08	11♎42 D	3♏19
	10/18 Su	3≈04 D	25♈24	12♎31	3♏32		7/04 Su	6≈31	26♈09	11♎42	3♏16
	10/25 Su	3≈05	25♈20	12♎40	3♏42		7/11 Su	6≈22	26♈10	11♎44	3♏14
	11/01 Su	3≈07	25♈16	12♎49	3♏53		7/18 Su	6≈13	26♈11	11♎47	3♏14
	11/08 Su	3≈11	25♈12	12♎58	4♏03		7/25 Su	6≈03	26♈11 R	11♎50	3♏14 D
	11/15 Su	3≈16	25♈08	13♎06	4♏13		8/01 Su	5≈53	26♈11	11♎55	3♏16
	11/22 Su	3≈23	25♈05	13♎13	4♏23		8/08 Su	5≈44	26♈10	12♎00	3♏18
	11/29 Su	3≈31	25♈01	13♎20	4♏32		8/15 Su	5≈34	26♈09	12♎06	3♏22
	12/06 Su	3≈39	24♈58	13♎26	4♏41		8/22 Su	5≈25	26♈07	12♎13	3♏27
	12/13 Su	3≈49	24♈56	13♎31	4♏49		8/29 Su	5≈16	26♈04	12♎21	3♏32
	12/20 Su	4≈00	24♈54	13♎35	4♏57		9/05 Su	5≈09	26♈02	12♎29	3♏39
	12/27 Su	4≈12	24♈52	13♎38	5♏03		9/12 Su	5≈02	25♈58	12♎38	3♏47
							9/19 Su	4≈56	25♈55	12♎47	3♏55
							9/26 Su	4≈51	25♈51	12♎57	4♏04
							10/03 Su	4≈48	25♈47	13♎06	4♏13
2027	1/03 Su	4≈24	24♈51	13♎40	5♏09		10/10 Su	4≈45	25♈43	13♎16	4♏23
	1/10 Su	4≈37	24♈51	13♎41	5♏13		10/17 Su	4≈44	25♈39	13♎26	4♏33
	1/17 Su	4≈50	24♈51 D	13♎40 R	5♏16		10/24 Su	4≈45 D	25♈35	13♎35	4♏44
	1/24 Su	5≈03	24♈52	13♎39	5♏19		10/31 Su	4≈47	25♈31	13♎44	4♏54
	1/31 Su	5≈17	24♈53	13♎37	5♏20		11/07 Su	4≈50	25♈27	13♎53	5♏05
	2/07 Su	5≈30	24♈54	13♎33	5♏20 R		11/14 Su	4≈55	25♈23	14♎01	5♏15
	2/14 Su	5≈43	24♈57	13♎29	5♏18		11/21 Su	5≈01	25♈19	14♎09	5♏25
	2/21 Su	5≈55	24♈59	13♎24	5♏16		11/28 Su	5≈08	25♈16	14♎16	5♏35
	2/28 Su	6≈07	25♈02	13♎18	5♏12		12/05 Su	5≈16	25♈13	14♎22	5♏44
	3/07 Su	6≈19	25♈06	13♎11	5♏08		12/12 Su	5≈26	25♈10	14♎28	5♏52

Astro Data

2026

7/17 Fr	03:54	♎	SD	2♏09	14.4	(14:24)
7/22 We	12:48	♀	SR	25♈57	0.3	(0:16)
10/16 Fr	02:39	♇	SD	3≈04	-23.6	(-23:37)

2027

1/12 Tu	16:06	♀	SD	24♈51	-0.0	(0:01)
1/11 Mo	15:37	♎	SR	13♎41	19.6	(19:33)
2/02 Tu	17:13	♏	SR	5♏20	13.4	(13:23)

2027

5/08 Sa	12:56	♇	SR	7≈10	-22.9	(-22:51)
6/26 Sa	15:54	♎	SD	11♎42	20.3	(20:16)
7/22 Th	21:25	♀	SR	26♈11	0.5	(0:32)
7/18 Su	09:50	♏	SD	3♏14	14.0	(14:01)
10/18 Mo	03:50	♇	SD	4≈44	-23.7	(-23:42)

	♀	♀	⚷	⚷
2027				
12/19 Su	5 ♒ 36 D	25 ♈ 08 ℞	14 ♎ 32 D	6 ♏ 00 D
12/26 Su	5 ♒ 47	25 ♈ 07	14 ♎ 35	6 ♏ 06
2028				
1/02 Su	5 ♒ 59	25 ♈ 05	14 ♎ 37	6 ♏ 12
1/09 Su	6 ♒ 12	25 ♈ 05	14 ♎ 39	6 ♏ 17
1/16 Su	6 ♒ 25	25 ♈ 05 D	14 ♎ 39 ℞	6 ♏ 21
1/23 Su	6 ♒ 38	25 ♈ 05	14 ♎ 38	6 ♏ 23
1/30 Su	6 ♒ 51	25 ♈ 06	14 ♎ 36	6 ♏ 25
2/06 Su	7 ♒ 04	25 ♈ 08	14 ♎ 32	6 ♏ 25 ℞
2/13 Su	7 ♒ 17	25 ♈ 10	14 ♎ 28	6 ♏ 24
2/20 Su	7 ♒ 30	25 ♈ 13	14 ♎ 24	6 ♏ 22
2/27 Su	7 ♒ 42	25 ♈ 16	14 ♎ 18	6 ♏ 19
3/05 Su	7 ♒ 53	25 ♈ 19	14 ♎ 11	6 ♏ 15
3/12 Su	8 ♒ 04	25 ♈ 23	14 ♎ 05	6 ♏ 10
3/19 Su	8 ♒ 14	25 ♈ 27	13 ♎ 57	6 ♏ 04
3/26 Su	8 ♒ 22	25 ♈ 31	13 ♎ 49	5 ♏ 57
4/02 Su	8 ♒ 30	25 ♈ 35	13 ♎ 42	5 ♏ 50
4/09 Su	8 ♒ 36	25 ♈ 40	13 ♎ 34	5 ♏ 42
4/16 Su	8 ♒ 42	25 ♈ 44	13 ♎ 26	5 ♏ 34
4/23 Su	8 ♒ 45	25 ♈ 49	13 ♎ 19	5 ♏ 26
4/30 Su	8 ♒ 48	25 ♈ 54	13 ♎ 11	5 ♏ 17
5/07 Su	8 ♒ 49	25 ♈ 58	13 ♎ 05	5 ♏ 09
5/14 Su	8 ♒ 49 ℞	26 ♈ 02	12 ♎ 59	5 ♏ 01
5/21 Su	8 ♒ 47	26 ♈ 06	12 ♎ 54	4 ♏ 53
5/28 Su	8 ♒ 44	26 ♈ 10	12 ♎ 49	4 ♏ 46
6/04 Su	8 ♒ 40	26 ♈ 13	12 ♎ 45	4 ♏ 40
6/11 Su	8 ♒ 35	26 ♈ 16	12 ♎ 43	4 ♏ 34
6/18 Su	8 ♒ 29	26 ♈ 19	12 ♎ 41	4 ♏ 29
6/25 Su	8 ♒ 22	26 ♈ 21	12 ♎ 40	4 ♏ 25
7/02 Su	8 ♒ 14	26 ♈ 23	12 ♎ 40 D	4 ♏ 22
7/09 Su	8 ♒ 05	26 ♈ 24	12 ♎ 42	4 ♏ 20
7/16 Su	7 ♒ 56	26 ♈ 25	12 ♎ 44	4 ♏ 19
7/23 Su	7 ♒ 46	26 ♈ 25 ℞	12 ♎ 47	4 ♏ 19 D
7/30 Su	7 ♒ 37	26 ♈ 25	12 ♎ 51	4 ♏ 20
8/06 Su	7 ♒ 27	26 ♈ 24	12 ♎ 56	4 ♏ 21
8/13 Su	7 ♒ 17	26 ♈ 23	13 ♎ 02	4 ♏ 26
8/20 Su	7 ♒ 08	26 ♈ 21	13 ♎ 09	4 ♏ 30
8/27 Su	6 ♒ 59	26 ♈ 19	13 ♎ 17	4 ♏ 36
2028				
9/03 Su	6 ♒ 51 ℞	26 ♈ 16 ℞	13 ♎ 25 D	4 ♏ 42 D
9/10 Su	6 ♒ 44	26 ♈ 13	13 ♎ 33	4 ♏ 49
9/17 Su	6 ♒ 38	26 ♈ 10	13 ♎ 42	4 ♏ 57
9/24 Su	6 ♒ 33	26 ♈ 06	13 ♎ 52	5 ♏ 06
10/01 Su	6 ♒ 28	26 ♈ 02	14 ♎ 01	5 ♏ 15
10/08 Su	6 ♒ 26	25 ♈ 58	14 ♎ 11	5 ♏ 25
10/15 Su	6 ♒ 24	25 ♈ 54	14 ♎ 21	5 ♏ 35
10/22 Su	6 ♒ 24 D	25 ♈ 50	14 ♎ 30	5 ♏ 45
10/29 Su	6 ♒ 25	25 ♈ 46	14 ♎ 39	5 ♏ 56
11/05 Su	6 ♒ 28	25 ♈ 41	14 ♎ 48	6 ♏ 06
11/12 Su	6 ♒ 32	25 ♈ 38	14 ♎ 57	6 ♏ 17
11/19 Su	6 ♒ 37	25 ♈ 34	15 ♎ 05	6 ♏ 27
11/26 Su	6 ♒ 44	25 ♈ 30	15 ♎ 12	6 ♏ 37
12/03 Su	6 ♒ 52	25 ♈ 27	15 ♎ 18	6 ♏ 46
12/10 Su	7 ♒ 01	25 ♈ 25	15 ♎ 24	6 ♏ 55
12/17 Su	7 ♒ 11	25 ♈ 23	15 ♎ 28	7 ♏ 03
12/24 Su	7 ♒ 22	25 ♈ 21	15 ♎ 32	7 ♏ 10
12/31 Su	7 ♒ 33	25 ♈ 20	15 ♎ 35	7 ♏ 16
2029				
1/07 Su	7 ♒ 45	25 ♈ 19	15 ♎ 36	7 ♏ 21
1/14 Su	7 ♒ 58	25 ♈ 19 D	15 ♎ 37 ℞	7 ♏ 25
1/21 Su	8 ♒ 11	25 ♈ 19	15 ♎ 36	7 ♏ 28
1/28 Su	8 ♒ 24	25 ♈ 20	15 ♎ 34	7 ♏ 30
2/04 Su	8 ♒ 37	25 ♈ 21	15 ♎ 31	7 ♏ 31
2/11 Su	8 ♒ 50	25 ♈ 23	15 ♎ 28	7 ♏ 30 ℞
2/18 Su	9 ♒ 03	25 ♈ 26	15 ♎ 23	7 ♏ 28
2/25 Su	9 ♒ 15	25 ♈ 29	15 ♎ 18	7 ♏ 26
3/04 Su	9 ♒ 27	25 ♈ 32	15 ♎ 11	7 ♏ 22
3/11 Su	9 ♒ 38	25 ♈ 36	15 ♎ 05	7 ♏ 17
3/18 Su	9 ♒ 48	25 ♈ 40	14 ♎ 57	7 ♏ 11
3/25 Su	9 ♒ 57	25 ♈ 44	14 ♎ 50	7 ♏ 05
4/01 Su	10 ♒ 05	25 ♈ 48	14 ♎ 42	6 ♏ 58
4/08 Su	10 ♒ 12	25 ♈ 53	14 ♎ 34	6 ♏ 50
4/15 Su	10 ♒ 17	25 ♈ 57	14 ♎ 26	6 ♏ 42
4/22 Su	10 ♒ 22	26 ♈ 02	14 ♎ 19	6 ♏ 34
4/29 Su	10 ♒ 25	26 ♈ 07	14 ♎ 12	6 ♏ 26
5/06 Su	10 ♒ 26	26 ♈ 11	14 ♎ 05	6 ♏ 17
5/13 Su	10 ♒ 27 ℞	26 ♈ 15	13 ♎ 59	6 ♏ 09
5/20 Su	10 ♒ 26	26 ♈ 19	13 ♎ 53	6 ♏ 01

Astro Data

2028

1/12 We	21:52	♀ SD	25 ♈ 05	0.2	(0:13)
1/12 We	23:32	⚷ SR	14 ♎ 39	19.0	(19:02)
2/03 Th	23:35	♃ SR	6 ♏ 25	13.0	(13:01)
5/09 Tu	09:33	♀ SR	8 ♒ 49	-22.9	(-22:53)
6/26 Mo	20:00	⚷ SD	12 ♎ 40	19.7	(19:43)
7/22 Sa	13:57	♀ SR	26 ♈ 25	0.8	(0:48)
7/18 Tu	17:34	♃ SD	4 ♏ 19	13.7	(13:42)

2028

10/19 Th	03:42	♀ SD	6 ♒ 24	-23.8	(-23:45)

2029

1/12 Fr	08:02	♀ SD	25 ♈ 19	0.5	(0:30)
1/13 Sa	04:52	⚷ SR	15 ♎ 37	18.5	(18:31)
2/04 Su	07:56	♃ SR	7 ♏ 31	12.7	(12:43)
5/11 Fr	04:17	♀ SR	10 ♒ 27	-22.9	(-22:53)

	♇	♀	⚷	⚶
2029 5/27 Su	10 ≈ 23 R	26 ♈ 23 D	13 ♎ 48 R	5 ♏ 54 R
6/03 Su	10 ≈ 20	26 ♈ 27	13 ♎ 44	5 ♏ 47
6/10 Su	10 ≈ 15	26 ♈ 30	13 ♎ 41	5 ♏ 41
6/17 Su	10 ≈ 09	26 ♈ 32	13 ♎ 39	5 ♏ 36
6/24 Su	10 ≈ 02	26 ♈ 35	13 ♎ 38	5 ♏ 32
7/01 Su	9 ≈ 55	26 ♈ 37	13 ♎ 38 D	5 ♏ 28
7/08 Su	9 ≈ 46	26 ♈ 38	13 ♎ 39	5 ♏ 26
7/15 Su	9 ≈ 38	26 ♈ 39	13 ♎ 41	5 ♏ 24
7/22 Su	9 ≈ 28	26 ♈ 39	13 ♎ 44	5 ♏ 24 D
7/29 Su	9 ≈ 19	26 ♈ 39 R	13 ♎ 48	5 ♏ 25
8/05 Su	9 ≈ 09	26 ♈ 38	13 ♎ 53	5 ♏ 27
8/12 Su	8 ≈ 59	26 ♈ 37	13 ♎ 58	5 ♏ 30
8/19 Su	8 ≈ 50	26 ♈ 35	14 ♎ 05	5 ♏ 34
8/26 Su	8 ≈ 41	26 ♈ 33	14 ♎ 12	5 ♏ 39
9/02 Su	8 ≈ 33	26 ♈ 31	14 ♎ 20	5 ♏ 45
9/09 Su	8 ≈ 25	26 ♈ 28	14 ♎ 28	5 ♏ 52
9/16 Su	8 ≈ 19	26 ♈ 24	14 ♎ 37	6 ♏ 00
9/23 Su	8 ≈ 13	26 ♈ 21	14 ♎ 47	6 ♏ 08
9/30 Su	8 ≈ 08	26 ♈ 17	14 ♎ 56	6 ♏ 17
10/07 Su	8 ≈ 05	26 ♈ 13	15 ♎ 06	6 ♏ 27
10/14 Su	8 ≈ 03	26 ♈ 09	15 ♎ 15	6 ♏ 37
10/21 Su	8 ≈ 02	26 ♈ 04	15 ♎ 25	6 ♏ 47
10/28 Su	8 ≈ 03 D	26 ♈ 00	15 ♎ 34	6 ♏ 58
11/04 Su	8 ≈ 05	25 ♈ 56	15 ♎ 43	7 ♏ 09
11/11 Su	8 ≈ 08	25 ♈ 52	15 ♎ 52	7 ♏ 19
11/18 Su	8 ≈ 13	25 ♈ 48	16 ♎ 00	7 ♏ 29
11/25 Su	8 ≈ 19	25 ♈ 45	16 ♎ 07	7 ♏ 39
12/02 Su	8 ≈ 27	25 ♈ 42	16 ♎ 14	7 ♏ 49
12/09 Su	8 ≈ 35	25 ♈ 39	16 ♎ 20	7 ♏ 58
12/16 Su	8 ≈ 44	25 ♈ 37	16 ♎ 25	8 ♏ 06
12/23 Su	8 ≈ 55	25 ♈ 35	16 ♎ 29	8 ♏ 13
12/30 Su	9 ≈ 06	25 ♈ 34	16 ♎ 32	8 ♏ 20
2030 1/06 Su	9 ≈ 18	25 ♈ 33	16 ♎ 33	8 ♏ 25
1/13 Su	9 ≈ 30	25 ♈ 33 D	16 ♎ 34	8 ♏ 30
1/20 Su	9 ≈ 43	25 ♈ 33	16 ♎ 34 R	8 ♏ 33
1/27 Su	9 ≈ 56	25 ♈ 34	16 ♎ 32	8 ♏ 35
2/03 Su	10 ≈ 09	25 ♈ 35	16 ♎ 30	8 ♏ 36

	♇	♀	⚷	⚶
2030 2/10 Su	10 ≈ 22 D	25 ♈ 37 D	16 ♎ 27 R	8 ♏ 36 R
2/17 Su	10 ≈ 35	25 ♈ 39	16 ♎ 22	8 ♏ 35
2/24 Su	10 ≈ 47	25 ♈ 42	16 ♎ 17	8 ♏ 32
3/03 Su	10 ≈ 59	25 ♈ 45	16 ♎ 11	8 ♏ 29
3/10 Su	11 ≈ 10	25 ♈ 49	16 ♎ 04	8 ♏ 24
3/17 Su	11 ≈ 21	25 ♈ 53	15 ♎ 57	8 ♏ 19
3/24 Su	11 ≈ 30	25 ♈ 57	15 ♎ 50	8 ♏ 13
3/31 Su	11 ≈ 38	26 ♈ 01	15 ♎ 42	8 ♏ 06
4/07 Su	11 ≈ 46	26 ♈ 06	15 ♎ 34	7 ♏ 58
4/14 Su	11 ≈ 52	26 ♈ 10	15 ♎ 27	7 ♏ 51
4/21 Su	11 ≈ 57	26 ♈ 15	15 ♎ 19	7 ♏ 42
4/28 Su	12 ≈ 00	26 ♈ 19	15 ♎ 12	7 ♏ 34
5/05 Su	12 ≈ 02	26 ♈ 24	15 ♎ 05	7 ♏ 26
5/12 Su	12 ≈ 03	26 ♈ 28	14 ♎ 58	7 ♏ 17
5/19 Su	12 ≈ 03 R	26 ♈ 32	14 ♎ 53	7 ♏ 10
5/26 Su	12 ≈ 01	26 ♈ 36	14 ♎ 48	7 ♏ 02
6/02 Su	11 ≈ 58	26 ♈ 40	14 ♎ 43	6 ♏ 55
6/09 Su	11 ≈ 54	26 ♈ 43	14 ♎ 40	6 ♏ 49
6/16 Su	11 ≈ 48	26 ♈ 46	14 ♎ 38	6 ♏ 43
6/23 Su	11 ≈ 42	26 ♈ 48	14 ♎ 36	6 ♏ 39
6/30 Su	11 ≈ 35	26 ♈ 50	14 ♎ 36 D	6 ♏ 35
7/07 Su	11 ≈ 27	26 ♈ 52	14 ♎ 36	6 ♏ 32
7/14 Su	11 ≈ 18	26 ♈ 53	14 ♎ 38	6 ♏ 30
7/21 Su	11 ≈ 09	26 ♈ 53	14 ♎ 41	6 ♏ 30
7/28 Su	10 ≈ 59	26 ♈ 53 R	14 ♎ 44	6 ♏ 30 D
8/04 Su	10 ≈ 50	26 ♈ 52	14 ♎ 49	6 ♏ 32
8/11 Su	10 ≈ 40	26 ♈ 51	14 ♎ 54	6 ♏ 34
8/18 Su	10 ≈ 31	26 ♈ 50	15 ♎ 00	6 ♏ 38
8/25 Su	10 ≈ 22	26 ♈ 48	15 ♎ 07	6 ♏ 43
9/01 Su	10 ≈ 13	26 ♈ 45	15 ♎ 15	6 ♏ 49
9/08 Su	10 ≈ 05	26 ♈ 42	15 ♎ 23	6 ♏ 55
9/15 Su	9 ≈ 58	26 ♈ 39	15 ♎ 32	7 ♏ 03
9/22 Su	9 ≈ 52	26 ♈ 35	15 ♎ 41	7 ♏ 11
9/29 Su	9 ≈ 47	26 ♈ 32	15 ♎ 51	7 ♏ 20
10/06 Su	9 ≈ 43	26 ♈ 28	16 ♎ 00	7 ♏ 30
10/13 Su	9 ≈ 41	26 ♈ 23	16 ♎ 10	7 ♏ 39
10/20 Su	9 ≈ 40	26 ♈ 19	16 ♎ 19	7 ♏ 50
10/27 Su	9 ≈ 40 D	26 ♈ 15	16 ♎ 29	8 ♏ 00
11/03 Su	9 ≈ 41	26 ♈ 11	16 ♎ 38	8 ♏ 11
11/10 Su	9 ≈ 44	26 ♈ 07	16 ♎ 47	8 ♏ 21

Astro Data

2029

6/28 Th	00:42	♇	SD	13 ♎ 38	19.2	(19:14)
7/20 Fr	02:07	⚶	SD	5 ♏ 24	13.4	(13:21)
7/23 Mo	04:06	♀	SR	26 ♈ 39	1.1	(1:04)
10/21 Su	03:53	♇	SD	8 ≈ 02	-23.8	(-23:46)

2030

1/12 Sa	23:36	♀	SD	25 ♈ 33	0.8	(0:45)
1/14 Mo	07:12	⚷	SR	16 ♎ 34	18.0	(18:02)
2/05 Tu	14:30	⚶	SR	8 ♏ 36	12.4	(12:21)

2030

5/12 Su	23:12	♇	SR	12 ≈ 03	-21.9	(-22:54)
6/29 Sa	06:15	⚷	SD	14 ♎ 36	18.7	(18:44)
7/23 Tu	11:34	♀	SR	26 ♈ 53	1.4	(1:21)
7/21 Su	13:49	⚶	SD	6 ♏ 30	13.0	(12:59)
10/23 We	03:05	♇	SD	9 ≈ 39	-23.8	(-23:46)

	⚷	♀	⚷	⚷
2030				
11/17 Su	9 ≈ 48 D	26 ♈ 03 R	16 ♎ 55 D	8 ♏ 32 D
11/24 Su	9 ≈ 54	26 ♈ 00	17 ♎ 03	8 ♏ 42
12/01 Su	10 ≈ 00	25 ♈ 56	17 ♎ 09	8 ♏ 52
12/08 Su	10 ≈ 08	25 ♈ 54	17 ♎ 15	9 ♏ 01
12/15 Su	10 ≈ 17	25 ♈ 51	17 ♎ 21	9 ♏ 09
12/22 Su	10 ≈ 27	25 ♈ 49	17 ♎ 25	9 ♏ 17
12/29 Su	10 ≈ 38	25 ♈ 48	17 ♎ 28	9 ♏ 24
2031				
1/05 Su	10 ≈ 50	25 ♈ 47	17 ♎ 30	9 ♏ 29
1/12 Su	11 ≈ 02	25 ♈ 46	17 ♎ 31	9 ♏ 34
1/19 Su	11 ≈ 14	25 ♈ 47 D	17 ♎ 31 R	9 ♏ 38
1/26 Su	11 ≈ 27	25 ♈ 47	17 ♎ 30	9 ♏ 41
2/02 Su	11 ≈ 40	25 ♈ 48	17 ♎ 28	9 ♏ 42
2/09 Su	11 ≈ 53	25 ♈ 50	17 ♎ 25	9 ♏ 42 R
2/16 Su	12 ≈ 06	25 ♈ 52	17 ♎ 21	9 ♏ 41
2/23 Su	12 ≈ 18	25 ♈ 55	17 ♎ 16	9 ♏ 39
3/02 Su	12 ≈ 30	25 ♈ 58	17 ♎ 10	9 ♏ 36
3/09 Su	12 ≈ 42	26 ♈ 02	17 ♎ 04	9 ♏ 32
3/16 Su	12 ≈ 52	26 ♈ 06	16 ♎ 57	9 ♏ 27
3/23 Su	13 ≈ 02	26 ♈ 10	16 ♎ 50	9 ♏ 21
3/30 Su	13 ≈ 11	26 ♈ 14	16 ♎ 42	9 ♏ 14
4/06 Su	13 ≈ 18	26 ♈ 19	16 ♎ 34	9 ♏ 07
4/13 Su	13 ≈ 25	26 ♈ 23	16 ♎ 26	8 ♏ 59
4/20 Su	13 ≈ 30	26 ♈ 28	16 ♎ 19	8 ♏ 51
4/27 Su	13 ≈ 34	26 ♈ 32	16 ♎ 11	8 ♏ 43
5/04 Su	13 ≈ 37	26 ♈ 37	16 ♎ 04	8 ♏ 34
5/11 Su	13 ≈ 38	26 ♈ 41	15 ♎ 58	8 ♏ 26
5/18 Su	13 ≈ 38 R	26 ♈ 45	15 ♎ 52	8 ♏ 18
5/25 Su	13 ≈ 37	26 ♈ 49	15 ♎ 46	8 ♏ 10
6/01 Su	13 ≈ 35	26 ♈ 53	15 ♎ 42	8 ♏ 03
6/08 Su	13 ≈ 31	26 ♈ 56	15 ♎ 38	7 ♏ 57
6/15 Su	13 ≈ 26	26 ♈ 59	15 ♎ 36	7 ♏ 51
6/22 Su	13 ≈ 20	27 ♈ 02	15 ♎ 34	7 ♏ 46
6/29 Su	13 ≈ 13	27 ♈ 04	15 ♎ 33	7 ♏ 42
7/06 Su	13 ≈ 06	27 ♈ 05	15 ♎ 34 D	7 ♏ 39
7/13 Su	12 ≈ 57	27 ♈ 06	15 ♎ 35	7 ♏ 37
7/20 Su	12 ≈ 48	27 ♈ 07	15 ♎ 37	7 ♏ 36
7/27 Su	12 ≈ 39	27 ♈ 07 R	15 ♎ 40	7 ♏ 36 D

	⚷	♀	⚷	⚷
2031				
8/03 Su	12 ≈ 29 R	27 ♈ 06 R	15 ♎ 45 D	7 ♏ 37 D
8/10 Su	12 ≈ 20	27 ♈ 05	15 ♎ 50	7 ♏ 39
8/17 Su	12 ≈ 10	27 ♈ 04	15 ♎ 56	7 ♏ 43
8/24 Su	12 ≈ 01	27 ♈ 02	16 ♎ 02	7 ♏ 47
8/31 Su	11 ≈ 52	27 ♈ 00	16 ♎ 10	7 ♏ 52
9/07 Su	11 ≈ 44	26 ♈ 57	16 ♎ 18	7 ♏ 59
9/14 Su	11 ≈ 37	26 ♈ 54	16 ♎ 27	8 ♏ 06
9/21 Su	11 ≈ 31	26 ♈ 50	16 ♎ 36	8 ♏ 14
9/28 Su	11 ≈ 25	26 ♈ 46	16 ♎ 45	8 ♏ 23
10/05 Su	11 ≈ 21	26 ♈ 42	16 ♎ 54	8 ♏ 32
10/12 Su	11 ≈ 18	26 ♈ 38	17 ♎ 04	8 ♏ 42
10/19 Su	11 ≈ 16	26 ♈ 34	17 ♎ 14	8 ♏ 52
10/26 Su	11 ≈ 15 D	26 ♈ 30	17 ♎ 23	9 ♏ 03
11/02 Su	11 ≈ 16	26 ♈ 26	17 ♎ 32	9 ♏ 13
11/09 Su	11 ≈ 19	26 ♈ 22	17 ♎ 41	9 ♏ 24
11/16 Su	11 ≈ 22	26 ♈ 18	17 ♎ 50	9 ♏ 34
11/23 Su	11 ≈ 27	26 ♈ 14	17 ♎ 57	9 ♏ 45
11/30 Su	11 ≈ 33	26 ♈ 11	18 ♎ 04	9 ♏ 54
12/07 Su	11 ≈ 41	26 ♈ 08	18 ♎ 11	10 ♏ 04
12/14 Su	11 ≈ 49	26 ♈ 05	18 ♎ 16	10 ♏ 12
12/21 Su	11 ≈ 59	26 ♈ 03	18 ♎ 21	10 ♏ 20
12/28 Su	12 ≈ 09	26 ♈ 02	18 ♎ 24	10 ♏ 28
2032				
1/04 Su	12 ≈ 20	26 ♈ 01	18 ♎ 27	10 ♏ 34
1/11 Su	12 ≈ 32	26 ♈ 00	18 ♎ 28	10 ♏ 39
1/18 Su	12 ≈ 45	26 ♈ 00 D	18 ♎ 29 R	10 ♏ 43
1/25 Su	12 ≈ 57	26 ♈ 01	18 ♎ 28	10 ♏ 46
2/01 Su	13 ≈ 10	26 ♈ 02	18 ♎ 26	10 ♏ 48
2/08 Su	13 ≈ 23	26 ♈ 04	18 ♎ 23	10 ♏ 49
2/15 Su	13 ≈ 36	26 ♈ 06	18 ♎ 19	10 ♏ 48 R
2/22 Su	13 ≈ 48	26 ♈ 08	18 ♎ 15	10 ♏ 46
2/29 Su	14 ≈ 00	26 ♈ 12	18 ♎ 09	10 ♏ 44
3/07 Su	14 ≈ 12	26 ♈ 15	18 ♎ 03	10 ♏ 40
3/14 Su	14 ≈ 23	26 ♈ 19	17 ♎ 56	10 ♏ 35
3/21 Su	14 ≈ 33	26 ♈ 23	17 ♎ 49	10 ♏ 29
3/28 Su	14 ≈ 42	26 ♈ 27	17 ♎ 42	10 ♏ 23
4/04 Su	14 ≈ 50	26 ♈ 31	17 ♎ 34	10 ♏ 16
4/11 Su	14 ≈ 57	26 ♈ 36	17 ♎ 26	10 ♏ 08

Astro Data

2031

1/13 Mo	14:41	♀	SD	25 ♈ 46	1.0	(1:02)
1/15 We	10:21	⚷	SR	17 ♎ 32	17.5	(17:31)
2/07 Fr	00:44	⚵	SR	9 ♏ 42	12.0	(12:00)
5/14 We	20:27	⚷	SR	13 ≈ 39	-12.9	(-22:51)
6/30 Mo	12:51	⚷	SD	15 ♎ 33	18.2	(18:11)
7/23 We	18:44	♀	SR	27 ♈ 07	1.6	(1:37)
7/21 Tu	22:04	⚵	SD	7 ♏ 35	12.6	(12:38)

2031

10/24 Fr	23:13	⚷	SD	11 ≈ 15	-23.8	(-23:46)

2032

1/13 Tu	20:50	♀	SD	26 ♈ 00	1.3	(1:18)
1/16 Fr	13:08	⚷	SR	18 ♎ 29	17.0	(16:59)
2/08 Su	11:34	⚵	SR	10 ♏ 49	11.7	(11:41)

2032

Date	♇	♀	♎	♏
4/18 Su	15 ≈ 03 D	26 ♈ 41 D	17 ♎ 18 R	10 ♏ 00 R
4/25 Su	15 ≈ 07	26 ♈ 45	17 ♎ 11	9 ♏ 52
5/02 Su	15 ≈ 10	26 ♈ 50	17 ♎ 04	9 ♏ 43
5/09 Su	15 ≈ 12	26 ♈ 54	16 ♎ 57	9 ♏ 35
5/16 Su	15 ≈ 13 R	26 ♈ 58	16 ♎ 51	9 ♏ 27
5/23 Su	15 ≈ 12	27 ♈ 02	16 ♎ 45	9 ♏ 19
5/30 Su	15 ≈ 10	27 ♈ 06	16 ♎ 40	9 ♏ 12
6/06 Su	15 ≈ 07	27 ♈ 09	16 ♎ 37	9 ♏ 05
6/13 Su	15 ≈ 02	27 ♈ 12	16 ♎ 34	8 ♏ 59
6/20 Su	14 ≈ 57	27 ♈ 15	16 ♎ 32	8 ♏ 53
6/27 Su	14 ≈ 51	27 ♈ 17	16 ♎ 31	8 ♏ 49
7/04 Su	14 ≈ 43	27 ♈ 19	16 ♎ 30 D	8 ♏ 45
7/11 Su	14 ≈ 35	27 ♈ 20	16 ♎ 31	8 ♏ 43
7/18 Su	14 ≈ 26	27 ♈ 21	16 ♎ 33	8 ♏ 42
7/25 Su	14 ≈ 17	27 ♈ 21 R	16 ♎ 36	8 ♏ 41 D
8/01 Su	14 ≈ 08	27 ♈ 20	16 ♎ 40	8 ♏ 42
8/08 Su	13 ≈ 58	27 ♈ 19	16 ♎ 45	8 ♏ 44
8/15 Su	13 ≈ 49	27 ♈ 18	16 ♎ 51	8 ♏ 47
8/22 Su	13 ≈ 40	27 ♈ 16	16 ♎ 57	8 ♏ 51
8/29 Su	13 ≈ 31	27 ♈ 14	17 ♎ 05	8 ♏ 56
9/05 Su	13 ≈ 22	27 ♈ 11	17 ♎ 12	9 ♏ 02
9/12 Su	13 ≈ 15	27 ♈ 08	17 ♎ 21	9 ♏ 09
9/19 Su	13 ≈ 08	27 ♈ 05	17 ♎ 30	9 ♏ 17
9/26 Su	13 ≈ 02	27 ♈ 01	17 ♎ 39	9 ♏ 26
10/03 Su	12 ≈ 57	26 ♈ 57	17 ♎ 48	9 ♏ 35
10/10 Su	12 ≈ 54	26 ♈ 53	17 ♎ 58	9 ♏ 45
10/17 Su	12 ≈ 51	26 ♈ 49	18 ♎ 08	9 ♏ 55
10/24 Su	12 ≈ 50	26 ♈ 45	18 ♎ 17	10 ♏ 05
10/31 Su	12 ≈ 51 D	26 ♈ 40	18 ♎ 26	10 ♏ 16
11/07 Su	12 ≈ 52	26 ♈ 36	18 ♎ 35	10 ♏ 26
11/14 Su	12 ≈ 55	26 ♈ 32	18 ♎ 44	10 ♏ 37
11/21 Su	13 ≈ 00	26 ♈ 29	18 ♎ 52	10 ♏ 47
11/28 Su	13 ≈ 05	26 ♈ 25	18 ♎ 59	10 ♏ 57
12/05 Su	13 ≈ 12	26 ♈ 22	19 ♎ 06	11 ♏ 07
12/12 Su	13 ≈ 20	26 ♈ 20	19 ♎ 11	11 ♏ 16
12/19 Su	13 ≈ 29	26 ♈ 18	19 ♎ 16	11 ♏ 24
12/26 Su	13 ≈ 39	26 ♈ 16	19 ♎ 20	11 ♏ 31

2033

Date	♇	♀	♎	♏
1/02 Su	13 ≈ 50 D	26 ♈ 15 R	19 ♎ 23 D	11 ♏ 38 D
1/09 Su	14 ≈ 02	26 ♈ 14	19 ♎ 25	11 ♏ 44
1/16 Su	14 ≈ 14	26 ♈ 14 D	19 ♎ 25	11 ♏ 48
1/23 Su	14 ≈ 26	26 ♈ 15	19 ♎ 25 R	11 ♏ 51
1/30 Su	14 ≈ 39	26 ♈ 16	19 ♎ 23	11 ♏ 54
2/06 Su	14 ≈ 52	26 ♈ 17	19 ♎ 21	11 ♏ 55
2/13 Su	15 ≈ 04	26 ♈ 19	19 ♎ 17	11 ♏ 55 R
2/20 Su	15 ≈ 17	26 ♈ 22	19 ♎ 13	11 ♏ 53
2/27 Su	15 ≈ 29	26 ♈ 25	19 ♎ 08	11 ♏ 51
3/06 Su	15 ≈ 41	26 ♈ 28	19 ♎ 02	11 ♏ 47
3/13 Su	15 ≈ 52	26 ♈ 32	18 ♎ 55	11 ♏ 43
3/20 Su	16 ≈ 02	26 ♈ 36	18 ♎ 48	11 ♏ 37
3/27 Su	16 ≈ 12	26 ♈ 40	18 ♎ 41	11 ♏ 31
4/03 Su	16 ≈ 20	26 ♈ 44	18 ♎ 33	11 ♏ 24
4/10 Su	16 ≈ 27	26 ♈ 49	18 ♎ 25	11 ♏ 17
4/17 Su	16 ≈ 34	26 ♈ 54	18 ♎ 17	11 ♏ 09
4/24 Su	16 ≈ 39	26 ♈ 58	18 ♎ 10	11 ♏ 01
5/01 Su	16 ≈ 42	27 ♈ 03	18 ♎ 03	10 ♏ 52
5/08 Su	16 ≈ 45	27 ♈ 07	17 ♎ 56	10 ♏ 44
5/15 Su	16 ≈ 46	27 ♈ 11	17 ♎ 49	10 ♏ 36
5/22 Su	16 ≈ 46 R	27 ♈ 15	17 ♎ 44	10 ♏ 28
5/29 Su	16 ≈ 44	27 ♈ 19	17 ♎ 39	10 ♏ 20
6/05 Su	16 ≈ 41	27 ♈ 23	17 ♎ 35	10 ♏ 13
6/12 Su	16 ≈ 38	27 ♈ 26	17 ♎ 31	10 ♏ 07
6/19 Su	16 ≈ 33	27 ♈ 28	17 ♎ 29	10 ♏ 01
6/26 Su	16 ≈ 26	27 ♈ 31	17 ♎ 28	9 ♏ 56
7/03 Su	16 ≈ 19	27 ♈ 32	17 ♎ 27 D	9 ♏ 53
7/10 Su	16 ≈ 12	27 ♈ 34	17 ♎ 28	9 ♏ 50
7/17 Su	16 ≈ 03	27 ♈ 34	17 ♎ 30	9 ♏ 48
7/24 Su	15 ≈ 54	27 ♈ 35	17 ♎ 32	9 ♏ 47
7/31 Su	15 ≈ 45	27 ♈ 34 R	17 ♎ 36	9 ♏ 48 D
8/07 Su	15 ≈ 36	27 ♈ 34	17 ♎ 40	9 ♏ 49
8/14 Su	15 ≈ 26	27 ♈ 32	17 ♎ 46	9 ♏ 52
8/21 Su	15 ≈ 17	27 ♈ 31	17 ♎ 52	9 ♏ 56
8/28 Su	15 ≈ 08	27 ♈ 28	17 ♎ 59	10 ♏ 01
9/04 Su	14 ≈ 59	27 ♈ 26	18 ♎ 07	10 ♏ 06
9/11 Su	14 ≈ 51	27 ♈ 23	18 ♎ 15	10 ♏ 13
9/18 Su	14 ≈ 44	27 ♈ 19	18 ♎ 24	10 ♏ 21
9/25 Su	14 ≈ 38	27 ♈ 16	18 ♎ 33	10 ♏ 29
10/02 Su	14 ≈ 33	27 ♈ 12	18 ♎ 42	10 ♏ 38

Astro Data

2032

5/15 Sa	15:53	♇	SR	15 ≈ 13	-22.8	(-22:47)
6/30 We	21:25	♎	SD	16 ♎ 30	17.7	(17:41)
7/23 Fr	11:18	♀	SR	27 ♈ 21	1.9	(1:53)
7/23 Fr	05:16	♏	SD	8 ♏ 41	12.3	(12:18)
10/25 Mo	21:09	♇	SD	12 ≈ 50	-23.7	(-23:43)

2033

1/13 Th	05:59	♀	SD	26 ♈ 14	1.6	(1:34)
1/16 Su	19:15	♎	SR	19 ♎ 25	16.5	(16:30)
2/08 Tu	18:31	♏	SR	11 ♏ 55	11.3	(11:19)
5/17 Tu	12:59	♇	SR	16 ≈ 46	-22.8	(-22:45)
7/02 Sa	02:31	♎	SD	17 ♎ 27	17.2	(17:10)
7/24 Su	01:45	♀	SR	27 ♈ 35	2.2	(2:09)
7/24 Su	13:59	♏	SD	9 ♏ 47	11.9	(11:53)

2033		♅	♆	♇	⚷
	10/09 Su	14 ♒ 29 ℞	27 ♈ 08 ℞	18 ♎ 52 D	10 ♏ 47 D
	10/16 Su	14 ♒ 26	27 ♈ 04	19 ♎ 01	10 ♏ 57
	10/23 Su	14 ♒ 24	26 ♈ 59	19 ♎ 11	11 ♏ 08
	10/30 Su	14 ♒ 24 D	26 ♈ 55	19 ♎ 20	11 ♏ 18
	11/06 Su	14 ♒ 25	26 ♈ 51	19 ♎ 29	11 ♏ 29
	11/13 Su	14 ♒ 28	26 ♈ 47	19 ♎ 38	11 ♏ 40
	11/20 Su	14 ♒ 31	26 ♈ 43	19 ♎ 46	11 ♏ 50
	11/27 Su	14 ♒ 37	26 ♈ 40	19 ♎ 53	12 ♏ 00
	12/04 Su	14 ♒ 43	26 ♈ 37	20 ♎ 00	12 ♏ 10
	12/11 Su	14 ♒ 50	26 ♈ 34	20 ♎ 06	12 ♏ 19
	12/18 Su	14 ♒ 59	26 ♈ 32	20 ♎ 11	12 ♏ 28
	12/25 Su	15 ♒ 09	26 ♈ 30	20 ♎ 15	12 ♏ 35
2034	1/01 Su	15 ♒ 19	26 ♈ 29	20 ♎ 19	12 ♏ 42
	1/08 Su	15 ♒ 30	26 ♈ 28	20 ♎ 21	12 ♏ 48
	1/15 Su	15 ♒ 42	26 ♈ 28 D	20 ♎ 22	12 ♏ 53
	1/22 Su	15 ♒ 54	26 ♈ 28	20 ♎ 22 ℞	12 ♏ 57
	1/29 Su	16 ♒ 07	26 ♈ 29	20 ♎ 20	12 ♏ 59
	2/05 Su	16 ♒ 20	26 ♈ 31	20 ♎ 18	13 ♏ 01
	2/12 Su	16 ♒ 32	26 ♈ 33	20 ♎ 15	13 ♏ 01 ℞
	2/19 Su	16 ♒ 45	26 ♈ 35	20 ♎ 11	13 ♏ 00
	2/26 Su	16 ♒ 57	26 ♈ 38	20 ♎ 06	12 ♏ 58
	3/05 Su	17 ♒ 09	26 ♈ 41	20 ♎ 00	12 ♏ 55
	3/12 Su	17 ♒ 20	26 ♈ 45	19 ♎ 54	12 ♏ 51
	3/19 Su	17 ♒ 31	26 ♈ 49	19 ♎ 47	12 ♏ 46
	3/26 Su	17 ♒ 40	26 ♈ 53	19 ♎ 40	12 ♏ 40
	4/02 Su	17 ♒ 49	26 ♈ 57	19 ♎ 32	12 ♏ 33
	4/09 Su	17 ♒ 57	27 ♈ 02	19 ♎ 24	12 ♏ 26
	4/16 Su	18 ♒ 03	27 ♈ 07	19 ♎ 16	12 ♏ 18
	4/23 Su	18 ♒ 09	27 ♈ 11	19 ♎ 09	12 ♏ 10
	4/30 Su	18 ♒ 13	27 ♈ 16	19 ♎ 01	12 ♏ 01
	5/07 Su	18 ♒ 16	27 ♈ 20	18 ♎ 54	11 ♏ 53
	5/14 Su	18 ♒ 18	27 ♈ 25	18 ♎ 48	11 ♏ 45
	5/21 Su	18 ♒ 18 ℞	27 ♈ 29	18 ♎ 42	11 ♏ 37
	5/28 Su	18 ♒ 17	27 ♈ 32	18 ♎ 37	11 ♏ 29
	6/04 Su	18 ♒ 15	27 ♈ 36	18 ♎ 32	11 ♏ 22
	6/11 Su	18 ♒ 11	27 ♈ 39	18 ♎ 29	11 ♏ 15
	6/18 Su	18 ♒ 07	27 ♈ 42	18 ♎ 26	11 ♏ 09

2034		♅	♆	♇	⚷
	6/25 Su	18 ♒ 01 ℞	27 ♈ 44 D	18 ♎ 25 ℞	11 ♏ 04 ℞
	7/02 Su	17 ♒ 54	27 ♈ 46	18 ♎ 24	11 ♏ 00
	7/09 Su	17 ♒ 47	27 ♈ 47	18 ♎ 24 D	10 ♏ 57
	7/16 Su	17 ♒ 39	27 ♈ 48	18 ♎ 25	10 ♏ 55
	7/23 Su	17 ♒ 30	27 ♈ 49	18 ♎ 28	10 ♏ 54
	7/30 Su	17 ♒ 21	27 ♈ 49 ℞	18 ♎ 31	10 ♏ 54 D
	8/06 Su	17 ♒ 12	27 ♈ 48	18 ♎ 35	10 ♏ 55
	8/13 Su	17 ♒ 02	27 ♈ 47	18 ♎ 40	10 ♏ 57
	8/20 Su	16 ♒ 53	27 ♈ 45	18 ♎ 46	11 ♏ 01
	8/27 Su	16 ♒ 44	27 ♈ 43	18 ♎ 53	11 ♏ 05
	9/03 Su	16 ♒ 35	27 ♈ 40	19 ♎ 01	11 ♏ 11
	9/10 Su	16 ♒ 27	27 ♈ 37	19 ♎ 09	11 ♏ 17
	9/17 Su	16 ♒ 20	27 ♈ 34	19 ♎ 17	11 ♏ 24
	9/24 Su	16 ♒ 13	27 ♈ 31	19 ♎ 26	11 ♏ 32
	10/01 Su	16 ♒ 07	27 ♈ 27	19 ♎ 35	11 ♏ 41
	10/08 Su	16 ♒ 03	27 ♈ 23	19 ♎ 45	11 ♏ 50
	10/15 Su	15 ♒ 59	27 ♈ 18	19 ♎ 55	12 ♏ 00
	10/22 Su	15 ♒ 57	27 ♈ 14	20 ♎ 04	12 ♏ 11
	10/29 Su	15 ♒ 57	27 ♈ 10	20 ♎ 13	12 ♏ 21
	11/05 Su	15 ♒ 57 D	27 ♈ 06	20 ♎ 23	12 ♏ 32
	11/12 Su	15 ♒ 59	27 ♈ 02	20 ♎ 31	12 ♏ 42
	11/19 Su	16 ♒ 02	26 ♈ 58	20 ♎ 40	12 ♏ 53
	11/26 Su	16 ♒ 07	26 ♈ 55	20 ♎ 47	13 ♏ 03
	12/03 Su	16 ♒ 13	26 ♈ 52	20 ♎ 54	13 ♏ 13
	12/10 Su	16 ♒ 20	26 ♈ 49	21 ♎ 01	13 ♏ 23
	12/17 Su	16 ♒ 28	26 ♈ 46	21 ♎ 06	13 ♏ 31
	12/24 Su	16 ♒ 37	26 ♈ 45	21 ♎ 10	13 ♏ 39
	12/31 Su	16 ♒ 47	26 ♈ 43	21 ♎ 14	13 ♏ 47
2035	1/07 Su	16 ♒ 58	26 ♈ 42	21 ♎ 16	13 ♏ 53
	1/14 Su	17 ♒ 09	26 ♈ 42	21 ♎ 18	13 ♏ 58
	1/21 Su	17 ♒ 21	26 ♈ 42 D	21 ♎ 18 ℞	14 ♏ 02
	1/28 Su	17 ♒ 34	26 ♈ 43	21 ♎ 17	14 ♏ 05
	2/04 Su	17 ♒ 46	26 ♈ 44	21 ♎ 15	14 ♏ 07
	2/11 Su	17 ♒ 59	26 ♈ 46	21 ♎ 12	14 ♏ 08
	2/18 Su	18 ♒ 11	26 ♈ 49	21 ♎ 08	14 ♏ 07 ℞
	2/25 Su	18 ♒ 24	26 ♈ 51	21 ♎ 04	14 ♏ 05
	3/04 Su	18 ♒ 36	26 ♈ 55	20 ♎ 58	14 ♏ 03
	3/11 Su	18 ♒ 47	26 ♈ 58	20 ♎ 52	13 ♏ 59

Astro Data

2033

10/27 Th	16:40	♅	SD	14 ♒ 24	-23.7 (-23:40)

2034

1/13 Fr	22:00	♆	SD	26 ♈ 28	1.9 (1:51)
1/18 We	00:43	♇	SR	20 ♎ 22	16.0 (15:58)
2/10 Fr	02:08	⚷	SR	13 ♏ 01	10.9 (10:56)
5/19 Fr	06:59	♅	SR	18 ♒ 18	-22.7 (-22:39)

2034

7/03 Mo	06:29	♇	SD	18 ♎ 24	16.6 (16:37)
7/24 Mo	08:41	♆	SR	27 ♈ 49	2.4 (2:25)
7/25 Tu	23:01	⚷	SD	10 ♏ 54	11.6 (11:33)
10/29 Su	13:42	♅	SD	15 ♒ 57	-23.6 (-23:35)

2035

1/14 Su	10:11	♆	SD	26 ♈ 42	2.1 (2:07)
1/19 Fr	03:09	♇	SR	21 ♎ 18	15.4 (15:26)
2/11 Su	08:52	⚷	SR	14 ♏ 08	10.6 (10:37)

		♇	♀	♇	♇			♇	♀	♇	♇
2035	3/18 Su	18♒58 D	27♈02 D	20♎45 ℞	13♏54 ℞	2035	12/23 Su	18♒04 D	26♈59 ℞	22♎05 D	14♏43 D
	3/25 Su	19♒08	27♈06	20♎38	13♏48		12/30 Su	18♒14	26♈57	22♎09	14♏51
	4/01 Su	19♒17	27♈10	20♎31	13♏42						
	4/08 Su	19♒25	27♈15	20♎23	13♏35						
	4/15 Su	19♒32	27♈20	20♎15	13♏27						
	4/22 Su	19♒38	27♈24	20♎07	13♏19	2036	1/06 Su	18♒24	26♈56	22♎12	14♏57
	4/29 Su	19♒42	27♈29	20♎00	13♏11		1/13 Su	18♒36	26♈56	22♎13	15♏03
	5/06 Su	19♒46	27♈33	19♎53	13♏02		1/20 Su	18♒47	26♈56 D	22♎14	15♏08
	5/13 Su	19♒48	27♈38	19♎46	12♏54		1/27 Su	18♒59	26♈57	22♎13 ℞	15♏11
	5/20 Su	19♒49	27♈42	19♎40	12♏46		2/03 Su	19♒12	26♈58	22♎12	15♏13
	5/27 Su	19♒48 ℞	27♈46	19♎35	12♏38		2/10 Su	19♒24	27♈00	22♎09	15♏14
	6/03 Su	19♒47	27♈49	19♎30	12♏30		2/17 Su	19♒37	27♈02	22♎06	15♏14 ℞
	6/10 Su	19♒44	27♈53	19♎26	12♏23		2/24 Su	19♒49	27♈05	22♎01	15♏13
	6/17 Su	19♒40	27♈55	19♎23	12♏17		3/02 Su	20♒01	27♈08	21♎56	15♏10
	6/24 Su	19♒34	27♈58	19♎21	12♏12		3/09 Su	20♒13	27♈11	21♎50	15♏07
	7/01 Su	19♒28	28♈00	19♎20	12♏08		3/16 Su	20♒24	27♈15	21♎44	15♏02
	7/08 Su	19♒21	28♈01	19♎20 D	12♏04		3/23 Su	20♒34	27♈19	21♎37	14♏57
	7/15 Su	19♒13	28♈02	19♎21	12♏02		3/30 Su	20♒43	27♈24	21♎29	14♏51
	7/22 Su	19♒05	28♈03	19♎23	12♏00		4/06 Su	20♒52	27♈28	21♎21	14♏44
	7/29 Su	18♒56	28♈03 ℞	19♎26	12♏00 D		4/13 Su	20♒59	27♈33	21♎14	14♏36
	8/05 Su	18♒47	28♈02	19♎30	12♏01		4/20 Su	21♒05	27♈37	21♎06	14♏28
	8/12 Su	18♒37	28♈01	19♎35	12♏03		4/27 Su	21♒11	27♈42	20♎58	14♏20
	8/19 Su	18♒28	27♈59	19♎41	12♏06		5/04 Su	21♒14	27♈46	20♎51	14♏12
	8/26 Su	18♒19	27♈57	19♎47	12♏10		5/11 Su	21♒17	27♈51	20♎44	14♏03
	9/02 Su	18♒10	27♈55	19♎54	12♏15		5/18 Su	21♒18	27♈55	20♎38	13♏55
	9/09 Su	18♒01	27♈52	20♎02	12♏21		5/25 Su	21♒18 ℞	27♈59	20♎33	13♏47
	9/16 Su	17♒54	27♈49	20♎11	12♏28		6/01 Su	21♒17	28♈03	20♎28	13♏39
	9/23 Su	17♒47	27♈45	20♎20	12♏36		6/08 Su	21♒15	28♈06	20♎24	13♏32
	9/30 Su	17♒41	27♈42	20♎29	12♏44		6/15 Su	21♒11	28♈09	20♎20	13♏26
	10/07 Su	17♒36	27♈37	20♎38	12♏54		6/22 Su	21♒06	28♈11	20♎18	13♏20
	10/14 Su	17♒32	27♈33	20♎48	13♏03		6/29 Su	21♒00	28♈13	20♎17	13♏16
	10/21 Su	17♒29	27♈29	20♎57	13♏14		7/06 Su	20♒54	28♈15	20♎16 D	13♏12
	10/28 Su	17♒28	27♈25	21♎07	13♏24		7/13 Su	20♒46	28♈16	20♎17	13♏09
	11/04 Su	17♒28 D	27♈21	21♎16	13♏35		7/20 Su	20♒38	28♈17	20♎19	13♏07
	11/11 Su	17♒30	27♈17	21♎25	13♏45		7/27 Su	20♒29	28♈17 ℞	20♎21	13♏07
	11/18 Su	17♒32	27♈13	21♎33	13♏56		8/03 Su	20♒20	28♈16	20♎25	13♏07 D
	11/25 Su	17♒36	27♈09	21♎41	14♏06		8/10 Su	20♒11	28♈15	20♎30	13♏08
	12/02 Su	17♒41	27♈06	21♎48	14♏16		8/17 Su	20♒02	28♈14	20♎35	13♏11
	12/09 Su	17♒48	27♈03	21♎55	14♏26		8/24 Su	19♒52	28♈12	20♎41	13♏15
	12/16 Su	17♒56	27♈01	22♎01	14♏35		8/31 Su	19♒43	28♈10	20♎48	13♏20

Astro Data

2035

5/20 Su	13:00	♇	SR	19♒49	-22.6	(-22:34)
7/04 We	10:16	♇	SD	19♎20	16.1	(16:06)
7/24 Tu	18:58	♀	SR	28♈03	2.7	(2:42)
7/27 Fr	10:42	♇	SD	12♏00	11.2	(11:11)
10/31 We	11:34	♇	SD	17♒28	-23.5	(-23:30)

2036

1/14 Mo	17:42	♀	SD	26♈56	2.4	(2:24)
1/20 Su	06:38	♇	SR	22♎14	15.0	(14:57)
2/12 Tu	19:02	♇	SR	15♏14	10.2	(10:14)
5/21 We	15:37	♇	SR	21♒19	-22.4	(-22:26)
7/04 Fr	16:38	♇	SD	20♎16	15.6	(15:36)
7/24 Th	10:21	♀	SR	28♈17	3.0	(2:58)
7/27 Su	19:08	♇	SD	13♏07	10.8	(10:46)

	♇	♀	⚶	⚶
2036 9/07 Su	19 ≈ 35 R	28 ♈ 07 R	20 ♎ 56 D	13 ♏ 25 D
9/14 Su	19 ≈ 27	28 ♈ 04	21 ♎ 04	13 ♏ 32
9/21 Su	19 ≈ 20	28 ♈ 00	21 ♎ 13	13 ♏ 40
9/28 Su	19 ≈ 13	27 ♈ 56	21 ♎ 12	13 ♏ 48
10/05 Su	19 ≈ 08	27 ♈ 52	21 ♎ 31	13 ♏ 57
10/12 Su	19 ≈ 04	27 ♈ 48	21 ♎ 41	14 ♏ 07
10/19 Su	19 ≈ 01	27 ♈ 44	21 ♎ 50	14 ♏ 17
10/26 Su	18 ≈ 59	27 ♈ 40	22 ♎ 00	14 ♏ 27
11/02 Su	18 ≈ 58 D	27 ♈ 36	22 ♎ 09	14 ♏ 38
11/09 Su	18 ≈ 59	27 ♈ 32	22 ♎ 18	14 ♏ 49
11/16 Su	19 ≈ 01	27 ♈ 28	22 ♎ 27	14 ♏ 59
11/23 Su	19 ≈ 05	27 ♈ 24	22 ♎ 35	15 ♏ 10
11/30 Su	19 ≈ 09	27 ♈ 21	22 ♎ 42	15 ♏ 20
12/07 Su	19 ≈ 15	27 ♈ 18	22 ♎ 49	15 ♏ 30
12/14 Su	19 ≈ 23	27 ♈ 15	22 ♎ 55	15 ♏ 39
12/21 Su	19 ≈ 31	27 ♈ 13	23 ♎ 00	15 ♏ 48
12/28 Su	19 ≈ 40	27 ♈ 12	23 ♎ 04	15 ♏ 55
2037 1/04 Su	19 ≈ 50	27 ♈ 11	23 ♎ 07	16 ♏ 02
1/11 Su	20 ≈ 01	27 ♈ 10	23 ♎ 09	16 ♏ 08
1/18 Su	20 ≈ 12	27 ♈ 10 D	23 ♎ 10	16 ♏ 13
1/25 Su	20 ≈ 24	27 ♈ 11	23 ♎ 10 R	16 ♏ 17
2/01 Su	20 ≈ 37	27 ♈ 12	23 ♎ 08	16 ♏ 20
2/08 Su	20 ≈ 49	27 ♈ 13	23 ♎ 06	16 ♏ 21
2/15 Su	21 ≈ 01	27 ♈ 16	23 ♎ 03	16 ♏ 21 R
2/22 Su	21 ≈ 14	27 ♈ 18	22 ♎ 59	16 ♏ 20
3/01 Su	21 ≈ 26	27 ♈ 21	22 ♎ 54	16 ♏ 18
3/08 Su	21 ≈ 37	27 ♈ 25	22 ♎ 48	16 ♏ 15
3/15 Su	21 ≈ 49	27 ♈ 28	22 ♎ 42	16 ♏ 11
3/22 Su	21 ≈ 59	27 ♈ 32	22 ♎ 35	16 ♏ 06
3/29 Su	22 ≈ 09	27 ♈ 37	22 ♎ 27	16 ♏ 00
4/05 Su	22 ≈ 17	27 ♈ 41	22 ♎ 20	15 ♏ 53
4/12 Su	22 ≈ 25	27 ♈ 46	22 ♎ 12	15 ♏ 46
4/19 Su	22 ≈ 32	27 ♈ 50	22 ♎ 04	15 ♏ 38
4/26 Su	22 ≈ 37	27 ♈ 55	21 ♎ 57	15 ♏ 30
5/03 Su	22 ≈ 42	27 ♈ 59	21 ♎ 50	15 ♏ 22
5/10 Su	22 ≈ 45	28 ♈ 04	21 ♎ 43	15 ♏ 13
5/17 Su	22 ≈ 47	28 ♈ 08	21 ♎ 36	15 ♏ 05

	♇	♀	⚶	⚶
2037 5/24 Su	22 ≈ 47 R	28 ♈ 12 D	21 ♎ 30 R	14 ♏ 57 R
5/31 Su	22 ≈ 46	28 ♈ 16	21 ♎ 25	14 ♏ 49
6/07 Su	22 ≈ 44	28 ♈ 19	21 ♎ 21	14 ♏ 42
6/14 Su	22 ≈ 41	28 ♈ 22	21 ♎ 17	14 ♏ 35
6/21 Su	22 ≈ 37	28 ♈ 25	21 ♎ 15	14 ♏ 29
6/28 Su	22 ≈ 32	28 ♈ 27	21 ♎ 13	14 ♏ 24
7/05 Su	22 ≈ 25	28 ♈ 29	21 ♎ 13	14 ♏ 20
7/12 Su	22 ≈ 18	28 ♈ 30	21 ♎ 13 D	14 ♏ 17
7/19 Su	22 ≈ 10	28 ♈ 31	21 ♎ 14	14 ♏ 15
7/26 Su	22 ≈ 02	28 ♈ 31 R	21 ♎ 17	14 ♏ 13
8/02 Su	21 ≈ 53	28 ♈ 30	21 ♎ 20	14 ♏ 14 D
8/09 Su	21 ≈ 44	28 ♈ 30	21 ♎ 24	14 ♏ 15
8/16 Su	21 ≈ 34	28 ♈ 28	21 ♎ 29	14 ♏ 17
8/23 Su	21 ≈ 25	28 ♈ 26	21 ♎ 35	14 ♏ 20
8/30 Su	21 ≈ 16	28 ♈ 24	21 ♎ 42	14 ♏ 25
9/06 Su	21 ≈ 07	28 ♈ 21	21 ♎ 50	14 ♏ 30
9/13 Su	20 ≈ 59	28 ♈ 18	21 ♎ 58	14 ♏ 37
9/20 Su	20 ≈ 51	28 ♈ 15	22 ♎ 06	14 ♏ 44
9/27 Su	20 ≈ 45	28 ♈ 11	22 ♎ 15	14 ♏ 52
10/04 Su	20 ≈ 39	28 ♈ 07	22 ♎ 24	15 ♏ 01
10/11 Su	20 ≈ 34	28 ♈ 03	22 ♎ 34	15 ♏ 10
10/18 Su	20 ≈ 31	27 ♈ 59	22 ♎ 43	15 ♏ 20
10/25 Su	20 ≈ 28	27 ♈ 55	22 ♎ 53	15 ♏ 31
11/01 Su	20 ≈ 27	27 ♈ 51	23 ♎ 02	15 ♏ 41
11/08 Su	20 ≈ 28 D	27 ♈ 46	23 ♎ 11	15 ♏ 52
11/15 Su	20 ≈ 29	27 ♈ 43	23 ♎ 20	16 ♏ 03
11/22 Su	20 ≈ 32	27 ♈ 39	23 ♎ 28	16 ♏ 13
11/29 Su	20 ≈ 36	27 ♈ 35	23 ♎ 36	16 ♏ 24
12/06 Su	20 ≈ 42	27 ♈ 32	23 ♎ 43	16 ♏ 34
12/13 Su	20 ≈ 49	27 ♈ 30	23 ♎ 49	16 ♏ 43
12/20 Su	20 ≈ 56	27 ♈ 28	23 ♎ 54	16 ♏ 52
12/27 Su	21 ≈ 05	27 ♈ 26	23 ♎ 59	17 ♏ 00
2038 1/03 Su	21 ≈ 15	27 ♈ 25	24 ♎ 02	17 ♏ 07
1/10 Su	21 ≈ 25	27 ♈ 24	24 ♎ 04	17 ♏ 14
1/17 Su	21 ≈ 36	27 ♈ 24 D	24 ♎ 05	17 ♏ 19
1/24 Su	21 ≈ 48	27 ♈ 24	24 ♎ 06 R	17 ♏ 23
1/31 Su	22 ≈ 00	27 ♈ 25	24 ♎ 05	17 ♏ 26

Astro Data

2036

11/01 Sa	07:53	♇	SD	18 ≈ 58	-23.4	(-23:23)

2037

1/14 We	04:15	♀	SD	27 ♈ 10	2.7	(2:40)
1/20 Tu	09:31	⚶	SR	23 ♎ 10	14.4	(14:25)
2/13 Fr	05:30	⚶	SR	16 ♏ 21	9.8	(9:50)
5/23 Sa	07:48	♇	SR	22 ≈ 47	-22.3	(-22:17)

2037

7/06 Mo	00:55	⚶	SD	21 ♎ 13	15.0	(15:01)
7/24 Fr	23:51	♀	SR	28 ♈ 31	3.2	(3:15)
7/29 We	03:31	⚶	SD	14 ♏ 13	10.4	(10:24)
11/03 Tu	03:35	♇	SD	20 ≈ 27	-23.3	(-23:16)

2038

1/14 Th	19:19	♀	SD	27 ♈ 24	2.9	(2:56)
1/21 Th	16:39	⚶	SR	24 ♎ 06	13.9	(13:53)

	♇	♀	⚷	⚷
2038				
2/07 Su	22 ♒ 13 D	27 ♈ 27 D	24 ♎ 03 ℞	17 ♏ 28 D
2/14 Su	22 ♒ 25	27 ♈ 29	24 ♎ 00	17 ♏ 29
2/21 Su	22 ♒ 37	27 ♈ 32	23 ♎ 56	17 ♏ 28 ℞
2/28 Su	22 ♒ 49	27 ♈ 34	23 ♎ 51	17 ♏ 27
3/07 Su	23 ♒ 01	27 ♈ 38	23 ♎ 46	17 ♏ 24
3/14 Su	23 ♒ 12	27 ♈ 41	23 ♎ 40	17 ♏ 20
3/21 Su	23 ♒ 23	27 ♈ 45	23 ♎ 33	17 ♏ 15
3/28 Su	23 ♒ 33	27 ♈ 50	23 ♎ 26	17 ♏ 09
4/04 Su	23 ♒ 42	27 ♈ 54	23 ♎ 18	17 ♏ 03
4/11 Su	23 ♒ 50	27 ♈ 59	23 ♎ 10	16 ♏ 56
4/18 Su	23 ♒ 57	28 ♈ 03	23 ♎ 03	16 ♏ 48
4/25 Su	24 ♒ 03	28 ♈ 08	22 ♎ 55	16 ♏ 40
5/02 Su	24 ♒ 08	28 ♈ 13	22 ♎ 48	16 ♏ 32
5/09 Su	24 ♒ 11	28 ♈ 17	22 ♎ 41	16 ♏ 23
5/16 Su	24 ♒ 14	28 ♈ 21	22 ♎ 34	16 ♏ 15
5/23 Su	24 ♒ 15	28 ♈ 25	22 ♎ 28	16 ♏ 07
5/30 Su	24 ♒ 14 ℞	28 ♈ 29	22 ♎ 23	15 ♏ 59
6/06 Su	24 ♒ 13	28 ♈ 33	22 ♎ 18	15 ♏ 51
6/13 Su	24 ♒ 10	28 ♈ 36	22 ♎ 14	15 ♏ 44
6/20 Su	24 ♒ 06	28 ♈ 38	22 ♎ 12	15 ♏ 38
6/27 Su	24 ♒ 01	28 ♈ 41	22 ♎ 10	15 ♏ 33
7/04 Su	23 ♒ 55	28 ♈ 42	22 ♎ 09	15 ♏ 28
7/11 Su	23 ♒ 49	28 ♈ 44	22 ♎ 09 D	15 ♏ 25
7/18 Su	23 ♒ 41	28 ♈ 45	22 ♎ 10	15 ♏ 22
7/25 Su	23 ♒ 33	28 ♈ 45	22 ♎ 12	15 ♏ 21
8/01 Su	23 ♒ 24	28 ♈ 45 ℞	22 ♎ 15	15 ♏ 21 D
8/08 Su	23 ♒ 15	28 ♈ 44	22 ♎ 19	15 ♏ 21
8/15 Su	23 ♒ 06	28 ♈ 43	22 ♎ 24	15 ♏ 23
8/22 Su	22 ♒ 56	28 ♈ 41	22 ♎ 29	15 ♏ 26
8/29 Su	22 ♒ 47	28 ♈ 39	22 ♎ 36	15 ♏ 30
9/05 Su	22 ♒ 38	28 ♈ 36	22 ♎ 43	15 ♏ 36
9/12 Su	22 ♒ 30	28 ♈ 33	22 ♎ 51	15 ♏ 42
9/19 Su	22 ♒ 22	28 ♈ 30	22 ♎ 59	15 ♏ 49
9/26 Su	22 ♒ 15	28 ♈ 26	23 ♎ 08	15 ♏ 57
10/03 Su	22 ♒ 09	28 ♈ 22	23 ♎ 17	16 ♏ 05
10/10 Su	22 ♒ 04	28 ♈ 18	23 ♎ 27	16 ♏ 15
10/17 Su	22 ♒ 00	28 ♈ 14	23 ♎ 36	16 ♏ 24
10/24 Su	21 ♒ 57	28 ♈ 10	23 ♎ 46	16 ♏ 35
10/31 Su	21 ♒ 56	28 ♈ 05	23 ♎ 55	16 ♏ 45
11/07 Su	21 ♒ 56 D	28 ♈ 01	24 ♎ 04	16 ♏ 56

	♇	♀	⚷	⚷
2038				
11/14 Su	21 ♒ 57 D	27 ♈ 57 ℞	24 ♎ 13 D	17 ♏ 07 D
11/21 Su	21 ♒ 59	27 ♈ 54	24 ♎ 22	17 ♏ 17
11/28 Su	22 ♒ 03	27 ♈ 50	24 ♎ 29	17 ♏ 28
12/05 Su	22 ♒ 08	27 ♈ 47	24 ♎ 37	17 ♏ 38
12/12 Su	22 ♒ 14	27 ♈ 44	24 ♎ 43	17 ♏ 48
12/19 Su	22 ♒ 21	27 ♈ 42	24 ♎ 48	17 ♏ 57
12/26 Su	22 ♒ 29	27 ♈ 40	24 ♎ 53	18 ♏ 05
2039				
1/02 Su	22 ♒ 39	27 ♈ 39	24 ♎ 57	18 ♏ 13
1/09 Su	22 ♒ 49	27 ♈ 38	24 ♎ 59	18 ♏ 19
1/16 Su	23 ♒ 00	27 ♈ 38 D	25 ♎ 01	18 ♏ 25
1/23 Su	23 ♒ 11	27 ♈ 38	25 ♎ 01 ℞	18 ♏ 29
1/30 Su	23 ♒ 23	27 ♈ 39	25 ♎ 01	18 ♏ 33
2/06 Su	23 ♒ 35	27 ♈ 41	24 ♎ 59	18 ♏ 35
2/13 Su	23 ♒ 47	27 ♈ 43	24 ♎ 57	18 ♏ 36
2/20 Su	24 ♒ 00	27 ♈ 45	24 ♎ 53	18 ♏ 36 ℞
2/27 Su	24 ♒ 12	27 ♈ 48	24 ♎ 49	18 ♏ 35
3/06 Su	24 ♒ 24	27 ♈ 51	24 ♎ 43	18 ♏ 32
3/13 Su	24 ♒ 35	27 ♈ 55	24 ♎ 37	18 ♏ 29
3/20 Su	24 ♒ 46	27 ♈ 59	24 ♎ 31	18 ♏ 25
3/27 Su	24 ♒ 56	28 ♈ 03	24 ♎ 24	18 ♏ 19
4/03 Su	25 ♒ 05	28 ♈ 07	24 ♎ 16	18 ♏ 13
4/10 Su	25 ♒ 14	28 ♈ 12	24 ♎ 09	18 ♏ 06
4/17 Su	25 ♒ 21	28 ♈ 16	24 ♎ 01	17 ♏ 58
4/24 Su	25 ♒ 28	28 ♈ 21	23 ♎ 53	17 ♏ 50
5/01 Su	25 ♒ 33	28 ♈ 26	23 ♎ 46	17 ♏ 42
5/08 Su	25 ♒ 37	28 ♈ 30	23 ♎ 39	17 ♏ 34
5/15 Su	25 ♒ 40	28 ♈ 34	23 ♎ 32	17 ♏ 25
5/22 Su	25 ♒ 41	28 ♈ 39	23 ♎ 26	17 ♏ 17
5/29 Su	25 ♒ 41 ℞	28 ♈ 42	23 ♎ 20	17 ♏ 09
6/05 Su	25 ♒ 40	28 ♈ 46	23 ♎ 16	17 ♏ 01
6/12 Su	25 ♒ 38	28 ♈ 49	23 ♎ 12	16 ♏ 54
6/19 Su	25 ♒ 35	28 ♈ 52	23 ♎ 08	16 ♏ 48
6/26 Su	25 ♒ 30	28 ♈ 54	23 ♎ 06	16 ♏ 42
7/03 Su	25 ♒ 24	28 ♈ 56	23 ♎ 05	16 ♏ 37
7/10 Su	25 ♒ 18	28 ♈ 58	23 ♎ 05 D	16 ♏ 34
7/17 Su	25 ♒ 11	28 ♈ 58	23 ♎ 05	16 ♏ 31
7/24 Su	25 ♒ 03	28 ♈ 59	23 ♎ 07	16 ♏ 29

Astro Data

2038

2/14 Su	15:10	⚷	SR	17 ♏ 29	9.5 (9:30)
5/25 Tu	02:10	♇	SR	24 ♒ 15	-22.2 (-22:10)
7/07 We	04:20	⚷	SD	22 ♎ 09	14.5 (14:30)
7/25 Su	07:35	♀	SR	28 ♈ 45	3.5 (3:31)
7/30 Fr	10:10	⚷	SD	15 ♏ 21	10.0 (10:02)
11/04 Th	20:20	♇	SD	21 ♒ 55	-23.1 (-23:08)

2039

1/15 Sa	09:44	♀	SD	27 ♈ 38	3.2 (3:13)
1/22 Sa	12:22	⚷	SR	15 ♎ 02	13.3 (13:20)
2/16 We	01:06	⚷	SR	18 ♏ 36	9.1 (9:06)
5/26 Th	19:19	♇	SR	25 ♒ 41	-23.0 (-22:00)
7/08 Fr	07:58	⚷	SD	23 ♎ 05	14.0 (13:59)
7/25 Mo	15:17	♀	SR	28 ♈ 59	3.8 (3:47)
7/31 Su	17:43	⚷	SD	16 ♏ 28	9.6 (9:36)

2039		♇	♀	♎	♏
	7/31 Su	24≈54 R	28♈59 R	23♎10 D	16♏28 R
	8/07 Su	24≈45	28♈58	23♎13	16♏29 D
	8/14 Su	24≈36	28♈57	23♎18	16♏30
	8/21 Su	24≈27	28♈55	23♎24	16♏33
	8/28 Su	24≈18	28♈53	23♎30	16♏37
	9/04 Su	24≈09	28♈51	23♎37	16♏41
	9/11 Su	24≈00	28♈48	23♎44	16♏47
	9/18 Su	23≈52	28♈44	23♎53	16♏54
	9/25 Su	23≈45	28♈41	24♎01	17♏02
	10/02 Su	23≈39	28♈37	24♎10	17♏10
	10/09 Su	23≈33	28♈33	24♎20	17♏19
	10/16 Su	23≈29	28♈29	24♎29	17♏29
	10/23 Su	23≈25	28♈25	24♎39	17♏39
	10/30 Su	23≈23	28♈20	24♎48	17♏49
	11/06 Su	23≈23	28♈16	24♎57	18♏00
	11/13 Su	23≈23 D	28♈12	25♎06	18♏11
	11/20 Su	23≈25	28♈08	25♎15	18♏21
	11/27 Su	23≈28	28♈05	25♎23	18♏32
	12/04 Su	23≈33	28♈02	25♎30	18♏42
	12/11 Su	23≈38	27♈59	25♎37	18♏52
	12/18 Su	23≈45	27♈56	25♎43	19♏02
	12/25 Su	23≈53	27♈55	25♎48	19♏10
2040	1/01 Su	24≈02	27♈53	25♎51	19♏18
	1/08 Su	24≈12	27♈52	25♎54	19♏25
	1/15 Su	24≈22	27♈52	25♎56	19♏31
	1/22 Su	24≈33	27♈52 D	25♎57	19♏36
	1/29 Su	24≈45	27♈53	25♎57 R	19♏40
	2/05 Su	24≈57	27♈54	25♎56	19♏42
	2/12 Su	25≈09	27♈56	25♎53	19♏44
	2/19 Su	25≈21	27♈58	25♎50	19♏44 R
	2/26 Su	25≈34	28♈01	25♎46	19♏43
	3/04 Su	25≈45	28♈04	25♎41	19♏41
	3/11 Su	25≈57	28♈08	25♎35	19♏38
	3/18 Su	26≈08	28♈12	25♎29	19♏34
	3/25 Su	26≈18	28♈16	25♎22	19♏29
	4/01 Su	26≈28	28♈20	25♎15	19♏23
	4/08 Su	26≈37	28♈25	25♎07	19♏16

2040		♇	♀	♎	♏
	4/15 Su	26≈44 D	28♈29 D	24♎59 R	19♏09 R
	4/22 Su	26≈51	28♈34	24♎52	19♏01
	4/29 Su	26≈57	28♈39	24♎44	18♏53
	5/06 Su	27≈01	28♈43	24♎37	18♏45
	5/13 Su	27≈04	28♈48	24♎30	18♏36
	5/20 Su	27≈06	28♈52	24♎24	18♏28
	5/27 Su	27≈07	28♈56	24♎18	18♏20
	6/03 Su	27≈06 R	28♈59	24♎13	18♏12
	6/10 Su	27≈05	29♈02	24♎09	18♏05
	6/17 Su	27≈02	29♈05	24♎05	17♏58
	6/24 Su	26≈58	29♈08	24♎03	17♏52
	7/01 Su	26≈53	29♈10	24♎01	17♏47
	7/08 Su	26≈46	29♈11	24♎01	17♏43
	7/15 Su	26≈40	29♈12	24♎01 D	17♏39
	7/22 Su	26≈32	29♈13	24♎02	17♏37
	7/29 Su	26≈24	29♈13 R	24♎05	17♏36
	8/05 Su	26≈15	29♈12	24♎08	17♏36 D
	8/12 Su	26≈06	29♈11	24♎12	17♏37
	8/19 Su	25≈57	29♈10	24♎18	17♏40
	8/26 Su	25≈47	29♈08	24♎24	17♏43
	9/02 Su	25≈38	29♈05	24♎30	17♏48
	9/09 Su	25≈30	29♈02	24♎38	17♏53
	9/16 Su	25≈22	28♈59	24♎46	17♏59
	9/23 Su	25≈14	28♈56	24♎54	18♏07
	9/30 Su	25≈07	28♈52	25♎03	18♏15
	10/07 Su	25≈01	28♈48	25♎13	18♏24
	10/14 Su	24≈57	28♈44	25♎22	18♏33
	10/21 Su	24≈53	28♈39	25♎31	18♏43
	10/28 Su	24≈50	28♈35	25♎41	18♏54
	11/04 Su	24≈49	28♈31	25♎50	19♏04
	11/11 Su	24≈49 D	28♈27	25♎59	19♏15
	11/18 Su	24≈50	28♈23	26♎08	19♏26
	11/25 Su	24≈53	28♈20	26♎16	19♏37
	12/02 Su	24≈57	28♈16	26♎24	19♏47
	12/09 Su	25≈02	28♈13	26♎30	19♏57
	12/16 Su	25≈09	28♈11	26♎37	20♏07
	12/23 Su	25≈16	28♈09	26♎42	20♏16
	12/30 Su	25≈25	28♈07	26♎46	20♏24

Astro Data

2039

11/06 Su	13:54	♇	SD	23≈23	-23.0 (-21:58)

2040

1/15 Su	15:46	♀	SD	27♈52	3.5 (3:30)
1/24 Tu	00:01	♎	SR	25♎57	12.8 (12:50)
2/17 Fr	07:48	♏	SR	19♏44	8.7 (8:41)

2040

5/27 Su	13:23	♇	SR	27≈07	-21.9 (-21:51)
7/08 Su	11:50	♎	SD	24♎01	13.4 (13:24)
7/25 We	08:03	♀	SR	29♈13	4.1 (4:04)
8/01 We	06:02	♏	SD	17♏36	9.2 (9:13)
11/07 We	06:02	♇	SD	24≈49	-22.8 (-22:49)

	♇	♀	♀	♀			♇	♀	♀	♀
2041	1/06 Su 25 ≈ 34 D	28 ♈ 06 ℞	26 ♎ 49 D	20 ♏ 31 D	**2041**	10/13 Su 26 ≈ 24 ℞	28 ♈ 59 ℞	26 ♎ 15 D	19 ♏ 38 D
	1/13 Su 25 ≈ 44	28 ♈ 06	26 ♎ 51	20 ♏ 37		10/20 Su 26 ≈ 20	28 ♈ 54	26 ♎ 24	19 ♏ 48
	1/20 Su 25 ≈ 55	28 ♈ 06 D	26 ♎ 53	20 ♏ 43		10/27 Su 26 ≈ 17	28 ♈ 50	26 ♎ 34	19 ♏ 59
	1/27 Su 26 ≈ 06	28 ♈ 07	26 ♎ 53 ℞	20 ♏ 47		11/03 Su 26 ≈ 15	28 ♈ 46	26 ♎ 43	20 ♏ 09
	2/03 Su 26 ≈ 18	28 ♈ 08	26 ♎ 52	20 ♏ 50		11/10 Su 26 ≈ 14 D	28 ♈ 42	26 ♎ 52	20 ♏ 20
	2/10 Su 26 ≈ 30	28 ♈ 10	26 ♎ 50	20 ♏ 52		11/17 Su 26 ≈ 15	28 ♈ 38	27 ♎ 01	20 ♏ 31
	2/17 Su 26 ≈ 42	28 ♈ 12	26 ♎ 47	20 ♏ 53		11/24 Su 26 ≈ 17	28 ♈ 34	27 ♎ 09	20 ♏ 42
	2/24 Su 26 ≈ 54	28 ♈ 15	26 ♎ 43	20 ♏ 52 ℞		12/01 Su 26 ≈ 21	28 ♈ 31	27 ♎ 17	20 ♏ 52
	3/03 Su 27 ≈ 06	28 ♈ 18	26 ♎ 38	20 ♏ 51		12/08 Su 26 ≈ 26	28 ♈ 28	27 ♎ 24	21 ♏ 02
	3/10 Su 27 ≈ 18	28 ♈ 21	26 ♎ 33	20 ♏ 48		12/15 Su 26 ≈ 31	28 ♈ 25	27 ♎ 30	21 ♏ 12
	3/17 Su 27 ≈ 29	28 ♈ 25	26 ♎ 26	20 ♏ 44		12/22 Su 26 ≈ 38	28 ♈ 23	27 ♎ 36	21 ♏ 21
	3/24 Su 27 ≈ 40	28 ♈ 29	26 ♎ 20	20 ♏ 39		12/29 Su 26 ≈ 46	28 ♈ 22	27 ♎ 40	21 ♏ 30
	3/31 Su 27 ≈ 50	28 ♈ 33	26 ♎ 13	20 ♏ 34						
	4/07 Su 27 ≈ 59	28 ♈ 38	26 ♎ 05	20 ♏ 27						
	4/14 Su 28 ≈ 07	28 ♈ 42	25 ♎ 57	20 ♏ 20						
	4/21 Su 28 ≈ 14	28 ♈ 47	25 ♎ 50	20 ♏ 12	**2042**	1/05 Su 26 ≈ 56	28 ♈ 21	27 ♎ 44	21 ♏ 37
	4/28 Su 28 ≈ 20	28 ♈ 52	25 ♎ 42	20 ♏ 04		1/12 Su 27 ≈ 05	28 ♈ 20	27 ♎ 46	21 ♏ 44
	5/05 Su 28 ≈ 25	28 ♈ 56	25 ♎ 35	19 ♏ 56		1/19 Su 27 ≈ 16	28 ♈ 20 D	27 ♎ 48	21 ♏ 50
	5/12 Su 28 ≈ 28	29 ♈ 01	25 ♎ 28	19 ♏ 47		1/26 Su 27 ≈ 27	28 ♈ 21	27 ♎ 48 ℞	21 ♏ 54
	5/19 Su 28 ≈ 31	29 ♈ 05	25 ♎ 21	19 ♏ 39		2/02 Su 27 ≈ 39	28 ♈ 22	27 ♎ 48	21 ♏ 58
	5/26 Su 28 ≈ 32	29 ♈ 09	25 ♎ 15	19 ♏ 31		2/09 Su 27 ≈ 51	28 ♈ 23	27 ♎ 46	22 ♏ 00
	6/02 Su 28 ≈ 32 ℞	29 ♈ 13	25 ♎ 10	19 ♏ 23		2/16 Su 28 ≈ 03	28 ♈ 25	27 ♎ 43	22 ♏ 01
	6/09 Su 28 ≈ 30	29 ♈ 16	25 ♎ 06	19 ♏ 15		2/23 Su 28 ≈ 15	28 ♈ 28	27 ♎ 40	22 ♏ 01 ℞
	6/16 Su 28 ≈ 28	29 ♈ 19	25 ♎ 02	19 ♏ 08		3/02 Su 28 ≈ 27	28 ♈ 31	27 ♎ 35	22 ♏ 00
	6/23 Su 28 ≈ 24	29 ♈ 21	24 ♎ 59	19 ♏ 02		3/09 Su 28 ≈ 38	28 ♈ 34	27 ♎ 30	21 ♏ 58
	6/30 Su 28 ≈ 20	29 ♈ 24	24 ♎ 57	18 ♏ 57		3/16 Su 28 ≈ 50	28 ♈ 38	27 ♎ 24	21 ♏ 54
	7/07 Su 28 ≈ 14	29 ♈ 25	24 ♎ 56	18 ♏ 52		3/23 Su 29 ≈ 00	28 ♈ 42	27 ♎ 17	21 ♏ 50
	7/14 Su 28 ≈ 07	29 ♈ 26	24 ♎ 57 D	18 ♏ 49		3/30 Su 29 ≈ 10	28 ♈ 47	27 ♎ 10	21 ♏ 44
	7/21 Su 28 ≈ 00	29 ♈ 27	24 ♎ 58	18 ♏ 46		4/06 Su 29 ≈ 20	28 ♈ 51	27 ♎ 03	21 ♏ 38
	7/28 Su 27 ≈ 52	29 ♈ 27 ℞	25 ♎ 00	18 ♏ 45		4/13 Su 29 ≈ 28	28 ♈ 56	26 ♎ 55	21 ♏ 31
	8/04 Su 27 ≈ 43	29 ♈ 27	25 ♎ 03	18 ♏ 44 D		4/20 Su 29 ≈ 35	29 ♈ 00	26 ♎ 48	21 ♏ 24
	8/11 Su 27 ≈ 34	29 ♈ 26	25 ♎ 07	18 ♏ 45		4/27 Su 29 ≈ 42	29 ♈ 05	26 ♎ 40	21 ♏ 16
	8/18 Su 27 ≈ 25	29 ♈ 24	25 ♎ 12	18 ♏ 47		5/04 Su 29 ≈ 47	29 ♈ 09	26 ♎ 33	21 ♏ 07
	8/25 Su 27 ≈ 16	29 ♈ 22	25 ♎ 17	18 ♏ 50		5/11 Su 29 ≈ 51	29 ♈ 14	26 ♎ 26	20 ♏ 59
	9/01 Su 27 ≈ 07	29 ♈ 20	25 ♎ 24	18 ♏ 54		5/18 Su 29 ≈ 54	29 ♈ 18	26 ♎ 19	20 ♏ 50
	9/08 Su 26 ≈ 58	29 ♈ 17	25 ♎ 31	18 ♏ 59		5/25 Su 29 ≈ 56	29 ♈ 22	26 ♎ 13	20 ♏ 42
	9/15 Su 26 ≈ 50	29 ♈ 14	25 ♎ 39	19 ♏ 05		6/01 Su 29 ≈ 56 ℞	29 ♈ 26	26 ♎ 07	20 ♏ 34
	9/22 Su 26 ≈ 42	29 ♈ 10	25 ♎ 47	19 ♏ 13		6/08 Su 29 ≈ 55	29 ♈ 29	26 ♎ 03	20 ♏ 26
	9/29 Su 26 ≈ 35	29 ♈ 07	25 ♎ 56	19 ♏ 20		6/15 Su 29 ≈ 53	29 ♈ 32	25 ♎ 59	20 ♏ 19
	10/06 Su 26 ≈ 29	29 ♈ 03	26 ♎ 05	19 ♏ 29		6/22 Su 29 ≈ 50	29 ♈ 35	25 ♎ 56	20 ♏ 13

Astro Data

2041

1/15 Tu	00:52	♀	SD	28 ♈ 06	3.8	(3:46)
1/24 Th	02:24	♀	SR	26 ♎ 53	12.3	(12:17)
2/17 Su	17:50	♀	SR	20 ♏ 53	8.3	(8:20)
5/29 We	03:31	♇	SR	28 ≈ 32	-21.7	(-21:39)
7/09 Tu	17:06	♀	SD	24 ♎ 56	12.9	(12:53)
7/25 Th	22:52	♀	SR	29 ♈ 27	4.3	(4:20)
8/02 Fr	16:35	♀	SD	18 ♏ 44	8.8	(8:49)

2041

11/09 Sa	00:10	♇	SD	26 ≈ 14	-22.6	(-22:38)

2042

1/15 We	17:25	♀	SD	28 ♈ 20	4.1	(4:03)
1/25 Su	04:52	♀	SR	27 ♎ 48	11.7	(11:44)
2/19 We	05:34	♀	SR	22 ♏ 01	7.9	(7:55)
5/30 Fr	16:35	♇	SR	29 ≈ 56	-21.5	(-21:27)

2042	♆	♇	⚷	⚸
6/29 Su	29 ≈ 46 R	29 Υ 37 D	25 ♎ 53 R	20 ♏ 07 R
7/06 Su	29 ≈ 40	29 Υ 39	25 ♎ 52	20 ♏ 02
7/13 Su	29 ≈ 34	29 Υ 40	25 ♎ 52 D	19 ♏ 58
7/20 Su	29 ≈ 27	29 Υ 41	25 ♎ 53	19 ♏ 55
7/27 Su	29 ≈ 19	29 Υ 41 R	25 ♎ 55	19 ♏ 54
8/03 Su	29 ≈ 11	29 Υ 41	25 ♎ 57	19 ♏ 53
8/10 Su	29 ≈ 02	29 Υ 40	26 ♎ 01	19 ♏ 53 D
8/17 Su	28 ≈ 53	29 Υ 39	26 ♎ 06	19 ♏ 55
8/24 Su	28 ≈ 44	29 Υ 37	26 ♎ 11	19 ♏ 57
8/31 Su	28 ≈ 35	29 Υ 35	26 ♎ 17	20 ♏ 01
9/07 Su	28 ≈ 26	29 Υ 32	26 ♎ 24	20 ♏ 06
9/14 Su	28 ≈ 18	29 Υ 29	26 ♎ 32	20 ♏ 12
9/21 Su	28 ≈ 10	29 Υ 25	26 ♎ 40	20 ♏ 19
9/28 Su	28 ≈ 02	29 Υ 22	26 ♎ 49	20 ♏ 26
10/05 Su	27 ≈ 56	29 Υ 18	26 ♎ 58	20 ♏ 35
10/12 Su	27 ≈ 50	29 Υ 14	27 ♎ 07	20 ♏ 44
10/19 Su	27 ≈ 46	29 Υ 09	27 ♎ 17	20 ♏ 53
10/26 Su	27 ≈ 42	29 Υ 05	27 ♎ 26	21 ♏ 04
11/02 Su	27 ≈ 40	29 Υ 01	27 ♎ 36	21 ♏ 14
11/09 Su	27 ≈ 39	28 Υ 57	27 ♎ 45	21 ♏ 25
11/16 Su	27 ≈ 40 D	28 Υ 53	27 ♎ 54	21 ♏ 36
11/23 Su	27 ≈ 41	28 Υ 49	28 ♎ 02	21 ♏ 47
11/30 Su	27 ≈ 44	28 Υ 46	28 ♎ 10	21 ♏ 57
12/07 Su	27 ≈ 48	28 Υ 43	28 ♎ 17	22 ♏ 08
12/14 Su	27 ≈ 54	28 Υ 40	28 ♎ 24	22 ♏ 17
12/21 Su	28 ≈ 00	28 Υ 38	28 ♎ 29	22 ♏ 27
12/28 Su	28 ≈ 08	28 Υ 36	28 ♎ 34	22 ♏ 36
2043				
1/04 Su	28 ≈ 16	28 Υ 35	28 ♎ 38	22 ♏ 43
1/11 Su	28 ≈ 26	28 Υ 34	28 ♎ 41	22 ♏ 51
1/18 Su	28 ≈ 36	28 Υ 34 D	28 ♎ 43	22 ♏ 57
1/25 Su	28 ≈ 47	28 Υ 35	28 ♎ 44	23 ♏ 02
2/01 Su	28 ≈ 58	28 Υ 36	28 ♎ 43 R	23 ♏ 05
2/08 Su	29 ≈ 10	28 Υ 37	28 ♎ 42	23 ♏ 08
2/15 Su	29 ≈ 22	28 Υ 39	28 ♎ 40	23 ♏ 10
2/22 Su	29 ≈ 34	28 Υ 42	28 ♎ 36	23 ♏ 10 R
3/01 Su	29 ≈ 46	28 Υ 44	28 ♎ 32	23 ♏ 09
3/08 Su	29 ≈ 58	28 Υ 48	28 ♎ 27	23 ♏ 07

2043	♆	♇	⚷	⚸
3/15 Su	0 ♓ 09 D	28 Υ 51 D	28 ♎ 21 R	23 ♏ 04 R
3/22 Su	0 ♓ 20	28 Υ 55	28 ♎ 15	23 ♏ 00
3/29 Su	0 ♓ 30	29 Υ 00	28 ♎ 08	22 ♏ 55
4/05 Su	0 ♓ 40	29 Υ 04	28 ♎ 01	22 ♏ 49
4/12 Su	0 ♓ 48	29 Υ 09	27 ♎ 53	22 ♏ 42
4/19 Su	0 ♓ 56	29 Υ 13	27 ♎ 45	22 ♏ 35
4/26 Su	1 ♓ 03	29 Υ 18	27 ♎ 38	22 ♏ 27
5/03 Su	1 ♓ 09	29 Υ 23	27 ♎ 30	22 ♏ 19
5/10 Su	1 ♓ 13	29 Υ 27	27 ♎ 23	22 ♏ 10
5/17 Su	1 ♓ 16	29 Υ 31	27 ♎ 16	22 ♏ 02
5/24 Su	1 ♓ 19	29 Υ 35	27 ♎ 10	21 ♏ 54
5/31 Su	1 ♓ 19	29 Υ 39	27 ♎ 04	21 ♏ 45
6/07 Su	1 ♓ 19 R	29 Υ 43	26 ♎ 59	21 ♏ 38
6/14 Su	1 ♓ 18	29 Υ 46	26 ♎ 55	21 ♏ 30
6/21 Su	1 ♓ 15	29 Υ 49	26 ♎ 52	21 ♏ 24
6/28 Su	1 ♓ 11	29 Υ 51	26 ♎ 49	21 ♏ 18
7/05 Su	1 ♓ 06	29 Υ 53	26 ♎ 48	21 ♏ 12
7/12 Su	1 ♓ 00	29 Υ 54	26 ♎ 47	21 ♏ 08
7/19 Su	0 ♓ 53	29 Υ 55	26 ♎ 48 D	21 ♏ 05
7/26 Su	0 ♓ 46	29 Υ 55	26 ♎ 49	21 ♏ 03
8/02 Su	0 ♓ 38	29 Υ 55 R	26 ♎ 52	21 ♏ 02
8/09 Su	0 ♓ 29	29 Υ 54	26 ♎ 55	21 ♏ 02 D
8/16 Su	0 ♓ 20	29 Υ 53	26 ♎ 59	21 ♏ 03
8/23 Su	0 ♓ 11	29 Υ 51	27 ♎ 05	21 ♏ 05
8/30 Su	0 ♓ 02	29 Υ 49	27 ♎ 11	21 ♏ 08
9/06 Su	29 ≈ 53	29 Υ 47	27 ♎ 17	21 ♏ 13
9/13 Su	29 ≈ 45	29 Υ 44	27 ♎ 25	21 ♏ 18
9/20 Su	29 ≈ 37	29 Υ 40	27 ♎ 33	21 ♏ 25
9/27 Su	29 ≈ 29	29 Υ 37	27 ♎ 41	21 ♏ 32
10/04 Su	29 ≈ 22	29 Υ 33	27 ♎ 50	21 ♏ 40
10/11 Su	29 ≈ 16	29 Υ 29	28 ♎ 00	21 ♏ 49
10/18 Su	29 ≈ 11	29 Υ 24	28 ♎ 09	21 ♏ 59
10/25 Su	29 ≈ 08	29 Υ 20	28 ♎ 18	22 ♏ 09
11/01 Su	29 ≈ 05	29 Υ 16	28 ♎ 28	22 ♏ 19
11/08 Su	29 ≈ 03	29 Υ 12	28 ♎ 37	22 ♏ 30
11/15 Su	29 ≈ 03 D	29 Υ 08	28 ♎ 46	22 ♏ 41
11/22 Su	29 ≈ 04	29 Υ 04	28 ♎ 55	22 ♏ 52
11/29 Su	29 ≈ 07	29 Υ 01	29 ♎ 03	23 ♏ 02
12/06 Su	29 ≈ 10	28 Υ 58	29 ♎ 10	23 ♏ 13
12/13 Su	29 ≈ 15	28 Υ 55	29 ♎ 17	23 ♏ 23

Astro Data

2042

7/11 Fr	01:06	♎	SD	25 ♎ 52	12.4	(12:21)
7/26 Sa	05:40	♀	SR	29 Υ 41	4.6	(4:37)
8/04 Mo	02:41	♇	SD	19 ♏ 53	8.4	(8:22)
11/10 Mo	19:21	♆	SD	27 ≈ 39	-22.4	(-22:26)

2043

1/16 Fr	06:29	♀	SD	28 Υ 34	4.3	(4:19)
1/26 Mo	10:35	♎	SR	28 ♎ 44	11.2	(11:14)
2/20 Fr	15:47	♇	SR	23 ♏ 10	7.5	(7:30)
3/09 Mo	01:02	♆ → ♓			-21.4	(-21:25)

2043

6/01 Mo	08:38	♆	SR	1 ♓ 19	-21.3	(-21:15)
7/12 Su	06:14	♎	SD	26 ♎ 47	11.8	(11:46)
7/26 Su	14:44	♀	SR	29 Υ 55	4.9	(4:54)
8/05 We	10:49	♇	SD	21 ♏ 02	8.0	(7:59)
9/01 Tu	03:12	♆ → ≈ R			-22.0	(-22:01)
11/12 Th	11:26	♆	SD	29 ≈ 03	-22.2	(-22:14)

LONGITUDE

Date	♇	♀	♎	♏
2043				
12/20 Su	29 ≈ 21 D	28 ♈ 52 ℞	29 ♎ 23 D	23 ♏ 33 D
12/27 Su	29 ≈ 29	28 ♈ 51	29 ♎ 28	23 ♏ 42
2044				
1/03 Su	29 ≈ 37	28 ♈ 49	29 ♎ 32	23 ♏ 50
1/10 Su	29 ≈ 46	28 ♈ 48	29 ♎ 35	23 ♏ 57
1/17 Su	29 ≈ 56	28 ♈ 48 D	29 ♎ 37	24 ♏ 04
1/24 Su	0 ♓ 07	28 ♈ 49	29 ♎ 39	24 ♏ 09
1/31 Su	0 ♓ 18	28 ♈ 49	29 ♎ 39 ℞	24 ♏ 13
2/07 Su	0 ♓ 29	28 ♈ 51	29 ♎ 37	24 ♏ 16
2/14 Su	0 ♓ 41	28 ♈ 53	29 ♎ 35	24 ♏ 18
2/21 Su	0 ♓ 53	28 ♈ 55	29 ♎ 32	24 ♏ 19
2/28 Su	1 ♓ 05	28 ♈ 58	29 ♎ 28	24 ♏ 19 ℞
3/06 Su	1 ♓ 17	29 ♈ 01	29 ♎ 24	24 ♏ 17
3/13 Su	1 ♓ 28	29 ♈ 05	29 ♎ 18	24 ♏ 14
3/20 Su	1 ♓ 39	29 ♈ 09	29 ♎ 12	24 ♏ 11
3/27 Su	1 ♓ 49	29 ♈ 13	29 ♎ 05	24 ♏ 06
4/03 Su	1 ♓ 59	29 ♈ 17	28 ♎ 58	24 ♏ 00
4/10 Su	2 ♓ 08	29 ♈ 22	28 ♎ 51	23 ♏ 54
4/17 Su	2 ♓ 16	29 ♈ 27	28 ♎ 43	23 ♏ 47
4/24 Su	2 ♓ 23	29 ♈ 31	28 ♎ 35	23 ♏ 39
5/01 Su	2 ♓ 29	29 ♈ 36	28 ♎ 28	23 ♏ 31
5/08 Su	2 ♓ 34	29 ♈ 40	28 ♎ 20	23 ♏ 22
5/15 Su	2 ♓ 38	29 ♈ 45	28 ♎ 14	23 ♏ 14
5/22 Su	2 ♓ 41	29 ♈ 49	28 ♎ 07	23 ♏ 05
5/29 Su	2 ♓ 42	29 ♈ 53	28 ♎ 01	22 ♏ 57
6/05 Su	2 ♓ 42 ℞	29 ♈ 56	27 ♎ 56	22 ♏ 49
6/12 Su	2 ♓ 41	0 ♉ 00	27 ♎ 52	22 ♏ 42
6/19 Su	2 ♓ 39	0 ♉ 02	27 ♎ 48	22 ♏ 35
6/26 Su	2 ♓ 35	0 ♉ 05	27 ♎ 45	22 ♏ 28
7/03 Su	2 ♓ 31	0 ♉ 07	27 ♎ 43	22 ♏ 23
7/10 Su	2 ♓ 25	0 ♉ 08	27 ♎ 43	22 ♏ 18
7/17 Su	2 ♓ 19	0 ♉ 09	27 ♎ 43 D	22 ♏ 15
7/24 Su	2 ♓ 12	0 ♉ 10	27 ♎ 44	22 ♏ 12
7/31 Su	2 ♓ 04	0 ♉ 09 ℞	27 ♎ 46	22 ♏ 11
8/07 Su	1 ♓ 55	0 ♉ 09	27 ♎ 49	22 ♏ 10 D
8/14 Su	1 ♓ 47	0 ♉ 08	27 ♎ 53	22 ♏ 11
8/21 Su	1 ♓ 38	0 ♉ 06	27 ♎ 58	22 ♏ 13
8/28 Su	1 ♓ 29	0 ♉ 04	28 ♎ 04	22 ♏ 16
2044				
9/04 Su	1 ♓ 20 ℞	0 ♉ 01 ℞	28 ♎ 10 D	22 ♏ 20 D
9/11 Su	1 ♓ 11	29 ♈ 59	28 ♎ 18	22 ♏ 25
9/18 Su	1 ♓ 03	29 ♈ 55	28 ♎ 25	22 ♏ 31
9/25 Su	0 ♓ 55	29 ♈ 52	28 ♎ 34	22 ♏ 38
10/02 Su	0 ♓ 48	29 ♈ 48	28 ♎ 43	22 ♏ 46
10/09 Su	0 ♓ 42	29 ♈ 44	28 ♎ 52	22 ♏ 55
10/16 Su	0 ♓ 36	29 ♈ 40	29 ♎ 01	23 ♏ 04
10/23 Su	0 ♓ 32	29 ♈ 35	29 ♎ 10	23 ♏ 14
10/30 Su	0 ♓ 29	29 ♈ 31	29 ♎ 20	23 ♏ 25
11/06 Su	0 ♓ 27	29 ♈ 27	29 ♎ 29	23 ♏ 35
11/13 Su	0 ♓ 26	29 ♈ 23	29 ♎ 38	23 ♏ 46
11/20 Su	0 ♓ 27 D	29 ♈ 19	29 ♎ 47	23 ♏ 57
11/27 Su	0 ♓ 29	29 ♈ 16	29 ♎ 55	24 ♏ 08
12/04 Su	0 ♓ 32	29 ♈ 12	0 ♏ 03	24 ♏ 18
12/11 Su	0 ♓ 37	29 ♈ 10	0 ♏ 10	24 ♏ 29
12/18 Su	0 ♓ 42	29 ♈ 07	0 ♏ 16	24 ♏ 39
12/25 Su	0 ♓ 49	29 ♈ 05	0 ♏ 21	24 ♏ 48
2045				
1/01 Su	0 ♓ 57	29 ♈ 04	0 ♏ 26	24 ♏ 56
1/08 Su	1 ♓ 05	29 ♈ 03	0 ♏ 29	25 ♏ 04
1/15 Su	1 ♓ 15	29 ♈ 02	0 ♏ 32	25 ♏ 11
1/22 Su	1 ♓ 25	29 ♈ 03 D	0 ♏ 33	25 ♏ 16
1/29 Su	1 ♓ 36	29 ♈ 03	0 ♏ 33 ℞	25 ♏ 21
2/05 Su	1 ♓ 48	29 ♈ 05	0 ♏ 33	25 ♏ 25
2/12 Su	1 ♓ 59	29 ♈ 07	0 ♏ 31	25 ♏ 27
2/19 Su	2 ♓ 11	29 ♈ 09	0 ♏ 28	25 ♏ 28
2/26 Su	2 ♓ 23	29 ♈ 12	0 ♏ 25	25 ♏ 28 ℞
3/05 Su	2 ♓ 35	29 ♈ 15	0 ♏ 20	25 ♏ 27
3/12 Su	2 ♓ 46	29 ♈ 18	0 ♏ 15	25 ♏ 25
3/19 Su	2 ♓ 57	29 ♈ 22	0 ♏ 09	25 ♏ 21
3/26 Su	3 ♓ 08	29 ♈ 26	0 ♏ 02	25 ♏ 17
4/02 Su	3 ♓ 18	29 ♈ 31	29 ♎ 55	25 ♏ 11
4/09 Su	3 ♓ 27	29 ♈ 35	29 ♎ 48	25 ♏ 05
4/16 Su	3 ♓ 35	29 ♈ 40	29 ♎ 40	24 ♏ 58
4/23 Su	3 ♓ 43	29 ♈ 45	29 ♎ 33	24 ♏ 51
4/30 Su	3 ♓ 49	29 ♈ 49	29 ♎ 25	24 ♏ 43
5/07 Su	3 ♓ 55	29 ♈ 54	29 ♎ 18	24 ♏ 34
5/14 Su	3 ♓ 59	29 ♈ 58	29 ♎ 11	24 ♏ 26

Astro Data

2044

Date	Time	Planet	Event	Position	Value
1/16 Sa	14:26	♀	SD	28 ♈ 48	4.6 (4:35)
1/19 Tu	09:49	♇ → ♓			-21.7 (-21:42)
1/27 We	15:54	♎	SR	29 ♎ 39	10.7 (10:40)
2/22 Mo	01:58	♏	SR	24 ♏ 19	7.1 (7:08)
6/01 We	23:11	♇	SR	2 ♓ 42	-21.0 (-21:01)
6/11 Sa	23:14	♀ → ♉			5.1 (5:07)
7/12 Tu	09:56	♎	SD	27 ♎ 43	11.2 (11:15)
7/26 Tu	05:23	♀	SR	0 ♉ 10	5.2 (5:10)
8/05 Fr	19:00	♏	SD	22 ♏ 10	7.6 (7:35)

2044

Date	Time	Planet	Event	Position	Value
9/08 Th	18:59	♀ → ♈ ℞			5.1 (5:07)
11/13 Su	04:07	♇	SD	0 ♓ 26	-22.0 (-22:00)
11/30 We	20:09	♎ → ♏			10.0 (10:02)

2045

Date	Time	Planet	Event	Position	Value
1/15 Su	22:10	♀	SD	29 ♈ 02	4.9 (4:53)
1/27 Fr	18:04	♎	SR	0 ♏ 34	10.1 (10:07)
2/22 We	08:35	♏	SR	25 ♏ 28	6.7 (6:43)
3/28 Tu	16:42	♎ → ♏ ℞			10.6 (10:36)
5/16 Tu	08:52	♀ → ♉			5.3 (5:20)

2045		♆	♇	⚷	⚳
5/21 Su		4 ♓ 02 D	0 ♉ 02 D	29 ♎ 04 ℞	24 ♏ 17 ℞
5/28 Su		4 ♓ 03	0 ♉ 06	28 ♎ 58	24 ♏ 09
6/04 Su		4 ♓ 04 ℞	0 ♉ 10	28 ♎ 52	24 ♏ 01
6/11 Su		4 ♓ 03	0 ♉ 13	28 ♎ 48	23 ♏ 53
6/18 Su		4 ♓ 02	0 ♉ 16	28 ♎ 44	23 ♏ 46
6/25 Su		3 ♓ 59	0 ♉ 19	28 ♎ 41	23 ♏ 39
7/02 Su		3 ♓ 54	0 ♉ 21	28 ♎ 39	23 ♏ 34
7/09 Su		3 ♓ 49	0 ♉ 22	28 ♎ 38	23 ♏ 29
7/16 Su		3 ♓ 43	0 ♉ 23	28 ♎ 37 D	23 ♏ 25
7/23 Su		3 ♓ 36	0 ♉ 24	28 ♎ 38	23 ♏ 22
7/30 Su		3 ♓ 29	0 ♉ 24 ℞	28 ♎ 40	23 ♏ 20
8/06 Su		3 ♓ 21	0 ♉ 23	28 ♎ 43	23 ♏ 19
8/13 Su		3 ♓ 12	0 ♉ 22	28 ♎ 47	23 ♏ 20 D
8/20 Su		3 ♓ 03	0 ♉ 21	28 ♎ 51	23 ♏ 21
8/27 Su		2 ♓ 54	0 ♉ 19	28 ♎ 57	23 ♏ 14
9/03 Su		2 ♓ 45	0 ♉ 16	29 ♎ 03	23 ♏ 27
9/10 Su		2 ♓ 36	0 ♉ 14	29 ♎ 10	23 ♏ 32
9/17 Su		2 ♓ 28	0 ♉ 10	29 ♎ 18	23 ♏ 38
9/24 Su		2 ♓ 20	0 ♉ 07	29 ♎ 26	23 ♏ 45
10/01 Su		2 ♓ 13	0 ♉ 03	29 ♎ 35	23 ♏ 52
10/08 Su		2 ♓ 06	29 ♈ 59	29 ♎ 44	24 ♏ 01
10/15 Su		2 ♓ 01	29 ♈ 55	29 ♎ 53	24 ♏ 10
10/22 Su		1 ♓ 56	29 ♈ 51	0 ♏ 02	24 ♏ 20
10/29 Su		1 ♓ 52	29 ♈ 46	0 ♏ 12	24 ♏ 30
11/05 Su		1 ♓ 50	29 ♈ 42	0 ♏ 21	24 ♏ 41
11/12 Su		1 ♓ 49	29 ♈ 38	0 ♏ 30	24 ♏ 51
11/19 Su		1 ♓ 49 D	29 ♈ 34	0 ♏ 39	25 ♏ 02
11/26 Su		1 ♓ 50	29 ♈ 31	0 ♏ 47	25 ♏ 13
12/03 Su		1 ♓ 53	29 ♈ 27	0 ♏ 55	25 ♏ 24
12/10 Su		1 ♓ 57	29 ♈ 24	1 ♏ 02	25 ♏ 34
12/17 Su		2 ♓ 02	29 ♈ 22	1 ♏ 09	25 ♏ 44
12/24 Su		2 ♓ 09	29 ♈ 20	1 ♏ 14	25 ♏ 54
12/31 Su		2 ♓ 16	29 ♈ 18	1 ♏ 19	26 ♏ 03
2046					
1/07 Su		2 ♓ 24	29 ♈ 17	1 ♏ 23	26 ♏ 11
1/14 Su		2 ♓ 33	29 ♈ 17	1 ♏ 26	26 ♏ 18
1/21 Su		2 ♓ 43	29 ♈ 17 D	1 ♏ 27	26 ♏ 24
1/28 Su		2 ♓ 54	29 ♈ 18	1 ♏ 28	26 ♏ 29
2/04 Su		3 ♓ 05	29 ♈ 19	1 ♏ 28 ℞	26 ♏ 33

2046		♆	♇	⚷	⚳
2/11 Su		3 ♓ 17 D	29 ♈ 20 D	1 ♏ 26 ℞	26 ♏ 35 D
2/18 Su		3 ♓ 28	29 ♈ 23	1 ♏ 24	26 ♏ 37
2/25 Su		3 ♓ 40	29 ♈ 25	1 ♏ 20	26 ♏ 37 ℞
3/04 Su		3 ♓ 52	29 ♈ 28	1 ♏ 16	26 ♏ 37
3/11 Su		4 ♓ 03	29 ♈ 32	1 ♏ 11	26 ♏ 35
3/18 Su		4 ♓ 15	29 ♈ 36	1 ♏ 05	26 ♏ 32
3/25 Su		4 ♓ 25	29 ♈ 40	0 ♏ 59	26 ♏ 28
4/01 Su		4 ♓ 36	29 ♈ 44	0 ♏ 52	26 ♏ 22
4/08 Su		4 ♓ 45	29 ♈ 49	0 ♏ 45	26 ♏ 16
4/15 Su		4 ♓ 54	29 ♈ 53	0 ♏ 37	26 ♏ 10
4/22 Su		5 ♓ 01	29 ♈ 58	0 ♏ 29	26 ♏ 02
4/29 Su		5 ♓ 08	0 ♉ 03	0 ♏ 22	25 ♏ 55
5/06 Su		5 ♓ 14	0 ♉ 07	0 ♏ 14	25 ♏ 46
5/13 Su		5 ♓ 18	0 ♉ 12	0 ♏ 07	25 ♏ 38
5/20 Su		5 ♓ 22	0 ♉ 16	0 ♏ 01	25 ♏ 29
5/27 Su		5 ♓ 24	0 ♉ 20	29 ♎ 54	25 ♏ 21
6/03 Su		5 ♓ 25	0 ♉ 23	29 ♎ 49	25 ♏ 13
6/10 Su		5 ♓ 25 ℞	0 ♉ 27	29 ♎ 44	25 ♏ 05
6/17 Su		5 ♓ 23	0 ♉ 30	29 ♎ 40	24 ♏ 57
6/24 Su		5 ♓ 21	0 ♉ 32	29 ♎ 36	24 ♏ 51
7/01 Su		5 ♓ 17	0 ♉ 35	29 ♎ 34	24 ♏ 45
7/08 Su		5 ♓ 12	0 ♉ 36	29 ♎ 32	24 ♏ 39
7/15 Su		5 ♓ 07	0 ♉ 37	29 ♎ 32 D	24 ♏ 35
7/22 Su		5 ♓ 00	0 ♉ 38	29 ♎ 33	24 ♏ 32
7/29 Su		4 ♓ 53	0 ♉ 38 ℞	29 ♎ 34	24 ♏ 30
8/05 Su		4 ♓ 45	0 ♉ 38	29 ♎ 37	24 ♏ 28
8/12 Su		4 ♓ 37	0 ♉ 37	29 ♎ 40	24 ♏ 28 D
8/19 Su		4 ♓ 28	0 ♉ 36	29 ♎ 44	24 ♏ 29
8/26 Su		4 ♓ 19	0 ♉ 34	29 ♎ 50	24 ♏ 32
9/02 Su		4 ♓ 10	0 ♉ 31	29 ♎ 56	24 ♏ 35
9/09 Su		4 ♓ 01	0 ♉ 29	0 ♏ 02	24 ♏ 39
9/16 Su		3 ♓ 53	0 ♉ 25	0 ♏ 10	24 ♏ 45
9/23 Su		3 ♓ 44	0 ♉ 22	0 ♏ 18	24 ♏ 51
9/30 Su		3 ♓ 37	0 ♉ 18	0 ♏ 26	24 ♏ 59
10/07 Su		3 ♓ 30	0 ♉ 14	0 ♏ 35	25 ♏ 07
10/14 Su		3 ♓ 24	0 ♉ 10	0 ♏ 44	25 ♏ 16
10/21 Su		3 ♓ 19	0 ♉ 06	0 ♏ 54	25 ♏ 26
10/28 Su		3 ♓ 15	0 ♉ 02	1 ♏ 03	25 ♏ 36
11/04 Su		3 ♓ 12	29 ♈ 57	1 ♏ 13	25 ♏ 46
11/11 Su		3 ♓ 11	29 ♈ 53	1 ♏ 22	25 ♏ 57

Astro Data

2045

6/03 Sa	16:35	♆ SR	4 ♓ 04	-20.8	(-20:47)
7/13 Th	11:41	⚷ SD	28 ♎ 37	10.7	(10:42)
7/26 We	21:26	♇ SR	0 ♉ 24	5.5	(5:27)
8/07 Mo	06:19	⚳ SD	23 ♏ 19	7.1	(7:07)
10/07 Sa	01:39	♇ → ♈ ℞		5.3	(5:19)
10/19 Th	21:29	⚷ → ♏		9.8	(9:45)
11/14 Tu	17:33	♆ SD	1 ♓ 49	-21.8	(-21:47)

2046

1/16 Tu	12:18	♇ SD	29 ♈ 17	5.2	(5:10)
1/28 Su	20:27	⚷ SR	1 ♏ 28	9.6	(9:37)

2046

2/23 Fr	18:01	⚳ SR	26 ♏ 38	6.3	(6:17)
4/24 Tu	12:27	♇ → ♉		5.5	(5:31)
5/21 Mo	04:53	⚷ → ♎ ℞		10.3	(10:19)
6/05 Tu	07:25	♆ SR	5 ♓ 25	-20.6	(-20:34)
7/14 Sa	16:45	⚷ SD	29 ♎ 32	10.2	(10:10)
7/27 Fr	07:40	♇ SR	0 ♉ 38	5.7	(5:44)
8/08 We	16:29	⚳ SD	24 ♏ 28	6.7	(6:43)
9/06 Th	00:54	⚷ → ♏		9.7	(9:39)
10/31 We	09:33	♇ → ♈ ℞		5.5	(5:31)
11/16 Fr	08:46	♆ SD	3 ♓ 10	-21.6	(-21:33)

		♇	♀	♈	♈			♇	♀	♈	♈
2046	11/18 Su	3 ⅄ 10 D	29 ♈ 49 ℞	1 ♏ 31 D	26 ♏ 08 D	2047	8/04 Su	6 ⅄ 08 ℞	0 ♉ 52 ℞	0 ♏ 30 D	25 ♏ 38 ℞
	11/25 Su	3 ⅄ 11	29 ♈ 46	1 ♏ 39	26 ♏ 19		8/11 Su	6 ⅄ 00	0 ♉ 52	0 ♏ 33	25 ♏ 37 D
	12/02 Su	3 ⅄ 14	29 ♈ 42	1 ♏ 47	26 ♏ 29		8/18 Su	5 ⅄ 52	0 ♉ 50	0 ♏ 37	25 ♏ 38
	12/09 Su	3 ⅄ 17	29 ♈ 39	1 ♏ 55	26 ♏ 40		8/25 Su	5 ⅄ 43	0 ♉ 48	0 ♏ 42	25 ♏ 40
	12/16 Su	3 ⅄ 22	29 ♈ 37	2 ♏ 01	26 ♏ 50		9/01 Su	5 ⅄ 34	0 ♉ 46	0 ♏ 48	25 ♏ 43
	12/23 Su	3 ⅄ 27	29 ♈ 35	2 ♏ 07	27 ♏ 00		9/08 Su	5 ⅄ 25	0 ♉ 44	0 ♏ 55	25 ♏ 47
	12/30 Su	3 ⅄ 34	29 ♈ 33	2 ♏ 12	27 ♏ 09		9/15 Su	5 ⅄ 16	0 ♉ 40	1 ♏ 02	25 ♏ 52
							9/22 Su	5 ⅄ 08	0 ♉ 37	1 ♏ 10	25 ♏ 58
							9/29 Su	5 ⅄ 00	0 ♉ 33	1 ♏ 18	26 ♏ 05
							10/06 Su	4 ⅄ 53	0 ♉ 29	1 ♏ 27	26 ♏ 13
2047	1/06 Su	3 ⅄ 42	29 ♈ 32	2 ♏ 16	27 ♏ 17		10/13 Su	4 ⅄ 47	0 ♉ 25	1 ♏ 36	26 ♏ 22
	1/13 Su	3 ⅄ 51	29 ♈ 31	2 ♏ 19	27 ♏ 25		10/20 Su	4 ⅄ 41	0 ♉ 21	1 ♏ 45	26 ♏ 31
	1/20 Su	4 ⅄ 01	29 ♈ 31 D	2 ♏ 21	27 ♏ 31		10/27 Su	4 ⅄ 37	0 ♉ 17	1 ♏ 55	26 ♏ 41
	1/27 Su	4 ⅄ 11	29 ♈ 32	2 ♏ 22	27 ♏ 36		11/03 Su	4 ⅄ 34	0 ♉ 13	2 ♏ 04	26 ♏ 52
	2/03 Su	4 ⅄ 22	29 ♈ 33	2 ♏ 21 ℞	27 ♏ 41		11/10 Su	4 ⅄ 32	0 ♉ 08	2 ♏ 13	27 ♏ 02
	2/10 Su	4 ⅄ 33	29 ♈ 34	2 ♏ 21	27 ♏ 44		11/17 Su	4 ⅄ 31	0 ♉ 05	2 ♏ 22	27 ♏ 13
	2/17 Su	4 ⅄ 45	29 ♈ 36	2 ♏ 19	27 ♏ 46		11/24 Su	4 ⅄ 31 D	0 ♉ 01	2 ♏ 31	27 ♏ 24
	2/24 Su	4 ⅄ 57	29 ♈ 39	2 ♏ 16	27 ♏ 47		12/01 Su	4 ⅄ 33	29 ♈ 57	2 ♏ 39	27 ♏ 35
	3/03 Su	5 ⅄ 08	29 ♈ 42	2 ♏ 12	27 ♏ 46 ℞		12/08 Su	4 ⅄ 36	29 ♈ 54	2 ♏ 46	27 ♏ 46
	3/10 Su	5 ⅄ 20	29 ♈ 45	2 ♏ 07	27 ♏ 45		12/15 Su	4 ⅄ 40	29 ♈ 52	2 ♏ 53	27 ♏ 56
	3/17 Su	5 ⅄ 31	29 ♈ 49	2 ♏ 01	27 ♏ 42		12/22 Su	4 ⅄ 46	29 ♈ 49	2 ♏ 59	28 ♏ 06
	3/24 Su	5 ⅄ 42	29 ♈ 53	1 ♏ 55	27 ♏ 38		12/29 Su	4 ⅄ 52	29 ♈ 48	3 ♏ 05	28 ♏ 15
	3/31 Su	5 ⅄ 53	29 ♈ 57	1 ♏ 48	27 ♏ 34						
	4/07 Su	6 ⅄ 02	0 ♉ 02	1 ♏ 41	27 ♏ 28						
	4/14 Su	6 ⅄ 11	0 ♉ 07	1 ♏ 34	27 ♏ 21						
	4/21 Su	6 ⅄ 19	0 ♉ 11	1 ♏ 26	27 ♏ 14	2048	1/05 Su	5 ⅄ 00	29 ♈ 46	3 ♏ 09	28 ♏ 24
	4/28 Su	6 ⅄ 26	0 ♉ 16	1 ♏ 19	27 ♏ 07		1/12 Su	5 ⅄ 08	29 ♈ 46	3 ♏ 12	28 ♏ 31
	5/05 Su	6 ⅄ 32	0 ♉ 20	1 ♏ 11	26 ♏ 58		1/19 Su	5 ⅄ 18	29 ♈ 45 D	3 ♏ 15	28 ♏ 38
	5/12 Su	6 ⅄ 37	0 ♉ 25	1 ♏ 04	26 ♏ 50		1/26 Su	5 ⅄ 28	29 ♈ 46	3 ♏ 16	28 ♏ 44
	5/19 Su	6 ⅄ 41	0 ♉ 29	0 ♏ 57	26 ♏ 42		2/02 Su	5 ⅄ 38	29 ♈ 47	3 ♏ 16 ℞	28 ♏ 49
	5/26 Su	6 ⅄ 44	0 ♉ 33	0 ♏ 51	26 ♏ 33		2/09 Su	5 ⅄ 49	29 ♈ 48	3 ♏ 16	28 ♏ 52
	6/02 Su	6 ⅄ 45	0 ♉ 37	0 ♏ 45	26 ♏ 25		2/16 Su	6 ⅄ 01	29 ♈ 50	3 ♏ 14	28 ♏ 55
	6/09 Su	6 ⅄ 45 ℞	0 ♉ 41	0 ♏ 40	26 ♏ 17		2/23 Su	6 ⅄ 12	29 ♈ 53	3 ♏ 11	28 ♏ 56
	6/16 Su	6 ⅄ 44	0 ♉ 44	0 ♏ 35	26 ♏ 09		3/01 Su	6 ⅄ 24	29 ♈ 56	3 ♏ 07	28 ♏ 56 ℞
	6/23 Su	6 ⅄ 42	0 ♉ 46	0 ♏ 32	26 ♏ 02		3/08 Su	6 ⅄ 36	29 ♈ 59	3 ♏ 03	28 ♏ 55
	6/30 Su	6 ⅄ 39	0 ♉ 49	0 ♏ 29	25 ♏ 56		3/15 Su	6 ⅄ 47	0 ♉ 03	2 ♏ 57	28 ♏ 53
	7/07 Su	6 ⅄ 35	0 ♉ 50	0 ♏ 27	25 ♏ 50		3/22 Su	6 ⅄ 58	0 ♉ 07	2 ♏ 51	28 ♏ 49
	7/14 Su	6 ⅄ 29	0 ♉ 52	0 ♏ 26	25 ♏ 46		3/29 Su	7 ⅄ 08	0 ♉ 11	2 ♏ 45	28 ♏ 45
	7/21 Su	6 ⅄ 23	0 ♉ 52	0 ♏ 27 D	25 ♏ 42		4/05 Su	7 ⅄ 18	0 ♉ 15	2 ♏ 38	28 ♏ 39
	7/28 Su	6 ⅄ 16	0 ♉ 53 ℞	0 ♏ 28	25 ♏ 39		4/12 Su	7 ⅄ 28	0 ♉ 20	2 ♏ 30	28 ♏ 33

Astro Data

2047

1/17 Th	04:08	♀	SD	29 ♈ 31	5.4	(5:26)
1/29 Tu	20:51	♈	SR	2 ♏ 22	9.1	(9:03)
2/25 Mo	03:06	♈	SR	27 ♏ 47	5.9	(5:55)
4/03 We	04:56	♀ → ♉			5.7	(5:41)
6/06 Th	20:52	♇	SR	6 ⅄ 45	-20.3	(-20:18)
7/16 Tu	01:20	♈	SD	0 ♏ 26	9.6	(9:35)
7/27 Sa	13:41	♀	SR	0 ♉ 53	6.0	(6:01)

2047

8/10 Sa	05:39	♈	SD	25 ♏ 37	6.3	(6:19)
11/17 Su	23:54	♇	SD	4 ⅄ 31	-21.3	(-21:17)
11/26 Tu	10:46	♀ → ♈ ℞			5.7	(5:44)

2048

1/17 Fr	12:52	♀	SD	29 ♈ 45	5.7	(5:43)
1/31 Fr	02:21	♈	SR	3 ♏ 16	8.5	(8:30)
2/26 We	14:45	♈	SR	28 ♏ 56	5.5	(5:28)
3/09 Mo	01:58	♀ → ♉			5.9	(5:52)

2048

Date				
4/19 Su	7 ♓ 36 D	0 ♉ 25 D	2 ♏ 23 ℞	28 ♏ 26 ℞
4/26 Su	7 ♓ 43	0 ♉ 29	2 ♏ 15	28 ♏ 19
5/03 Su	7 ♓ 50	0 ♉ 34	2 ♏ 08	28 ♏ 11
5/10 Su	7 ♓ 55	0 ♉ 38	2 ♏ 00	28 ♏ 02
5/17 Su	7 ♓ 59	0 ♉ 43	1 ♏ 53	27 ♏ 54
5/24 Su	8 ♓ 02	0 ♉ 47	1 ♏ 47	27 ♏ 45
5/31 Su	8 ♓ 04	0 ♉ 51	1 ♏ 41	27 ♏ 37
6/07 Su	8 ♓ 05	0 ♉ 54	1 ♏ 35	27 ♏ 29
6/14 Su	8 ♓ 04 ℞	0 ♉ 57	1 ♏ 31	27 ♏ 21
6/21 Su	8 ♓ 03	1 ♉ 00	1 ♏ 27	27 ♏ 14
6/28 Su	8 ♓ 00	1 ♉ 03	1 ♏ 24	27 ♏ 07
7/05 Su	7 ♓ 56	1 ♉ 04	1 ♏ 22	27 ♏ 01
7/12 Su	7 ♓ 51	1 ♉ 06	1 ♏ 21	26 ♏ 56
7/19 Su	7 ♓ 45	1 ♉ 07	1 ♏ 21 D	26 ♏ 52
7/26 Su	7 ♓ 38	1 ♉ 07	1 ♏ 22	26 ♏ 49
8/02 Su	7 ♓ 31	1 ♉ 07 ℞	1 ♏ 23	26 ♏ 47
8/09 Su	7 ♓ 23	1 ♉ 06	1 ♏ 26	26 ♏ 47
8/16 Su	7 ♓ 14	1 ♉ 05	1 ♏ 30	26 ♏ 47 D
8/23 Su	7 ♓ 06	1 ♉ 03	1 ♏ 35	26 ♏ 48
8/30 Su	6 ♓ 57	1 ♉ 01	1 ♏ 40	26 ♏ 51
9/06 Su	6 ♓ 48	0 ♉ 59	1 ♏ 47	26 ♏ 55
9/13 Su	6 ♓ 39	0 ♉ 56	1 ♏ 54	26 ♏ 59
9/20 Su	6 ♓ 31	0 ♉ 52	2 ♏ 01	27 ♏ 05
9/27 Su	6 ♓ 23	0 ♉ 49	2 ♏ 09	27 ♏ 12
10/04 Su	6 ♓ 15	0 ♉ 45	2 ♏ 18	27 ♏ 20
10/11 Su	6 ♓ 09	0 ♉ 41	2 ♏ 27	27 ♏ 28
10/18 Su	6 ♓ 03	0 ♉ 36	2 ♏ 36	27 ♏ 37
10/25 Su	5 ♓ 58	0 ♉ 32	2 ♏ 46	27 ♏ 47
11/01 Su	5 ♓ 55	0 ♉ 28	2 ♏ 55	27 ♏ 57
11/08 Su	5 ♓ 52	0 ♉ 24	3 ♏ 04	28 ♏ 08
11/15 Su	5 ♓ 51	0 ♉ 20	3 ♏ 13	28 ♏ 19
11/22 Su	5 ♓ 51 D	0 ♉ 16	3 ♏ 22	28 ♏ 30
11/29 Su	5 ♓ 52	0 ♉ 12	3 ♏ 30	28 ♏ 41
12/06 Su	5 ♓ 55	0 ♉ 09	3 ♏ 38	28 ♏ 52
12/13 Su	5 ♓ 58	0 ♉ 06	3 ♏ 45	29 ♏ 02
12/20 Su	6 ♓ 03	0 ♉ 04	3 ♏ 52	29 ♏ 12
12/27 Su	6 ♓ 09	0 ♉ 02	3 ♏ 57	29 ♏ 22

2049

Date				
1/03 Su	6 ♓ 17 D	0 ♉ 01 ℞	4 ♏ 02 D	29 ♏ 30 D
1/10 Su	6 ♓ 25	0 ♉ 00	4 ♏ 05	29 ♏ 38
1/17 Su	6 ♓ 34	0 ♉ 00 D	4 ♏ 08	29 ♏ 46
1/24 Su	6 ♓ 43	0 ♉ 00	4 ♏ 10	29 ♏ 52
1/31 Su	6 ♓ 54	0 ♉ 01	4 ♏ 10	29 ♏ 57
2/07 Su	7 ♓ 05	0 ♉ 02	4 ♏ 10 ℞	0 ♐ 01
2/14 Su	7 ♓ 16	0 ♉ 04	4 ♏ 08	0 ♐ 04
2/21 Su	7 ♓ 27	0 ♉ 06	4 ♏ 06	0 ♐ 05
2/28 Su	7 ♓ 39	0 ♉ 09	4 ♏ 02	0 ♐ 06 ℞
3/07 Su	7 ♓ 51	0 ♉ 13	3 ♏ 58	0 ♐ 05
3/14 Su	8 ♓ 02	0 ♉ 16	3 ♏ 53	0 ♐ 03
3/21 Su	8 ♓ 13	0 ♉ 20	3 ♏ 47	0 ♐ 00
3/28 Su	8 ♓ 24	0 ♉ 24	3 ♏ 41	29 ♏ 56
4/04 Su	8 ♓ 34	0 ♉ 29	3 ♏ 34	29 ♏ 51
4/11 Su	8 ♓ 43	0 ♉ 33	3 ♏ 26	29 ♏ 45
4/18 Su	8 ♓ 52	0 ♉ 38	3 ♏ 19	29 ♏ 38
4/25 Su	8 ♓ 59	0 ♉ 43	3 ♏ 11	29 ♏ 31
5/02 Su	9 ♓ 06	0 ♉ 47	3 ♏ 04	29 ♏ 23
5/09 Su	9 ♓ 12	0 ♉ 52	2 ♏ 56	29 ♏ 15
5/16 Su	9 ♓ 16	0 ♉ 56	2 ♏ 49	29 ♏ 06
5/23 Su	9 ♓ 20	1 ♉ 00	2 ♏ 43	28 ♏ 58
5/30 Su	9 ♓ 22	1 ♉ 04	2 ♏ 37	28 ♏ 49
6/06 Su	9 ♓ 23	1 ♉ 08	2 ♏ 31	28 ♏ 41
6/13 Su	9 ♓ 23 ℞	1 ♉ 11	2 ♏ 26	28 ♏ 33
6/20 Su	9 ♓ 22	1 ♉ 14	2 ♏ 22	28 ♏ 26
6/27 Su	9 ♓ 19	1 ♉ 16	2 ♏ 19	28 ♏ 19
7/04 Su	9 ♓ 16	1 ♉ 18	2 ♏ 16	28 ♏ 13
7/11 Su	9 ♓ 11	1 ♉ 20	2 ♏ 15	28 ♏ 07
7/18 Su	9 ♓ 06	1 ♉ 21	2 ♏ 15 D	28 ♏ 03
7/25 Su	8 ♓ 59	1 ♉ 21	2 ♏ 15	28 ♏ 00
8/01 Su	8 ♓ 52	1 ♉ 21 ℞	2 ♏ 17	27 ♏ 57
8/08 Su	8 ♓ 44	1 ♉ 21	2 ♏ 19	27 ♏ 56
8/15 Su	8 ♓ 36	1 ♉ 20	2 ♏ 23	27 ♏ 56 D
8/22 Su	8 ♓ 28	1 ♉ 18	2 ♏ 27	27 ♏ 57
8/29 Su	8 ♓ 19	1 ♉ 16	2 ♏ 33	27 ♏ 59
9/05 Su	8 ♓ 10	1 ♉ 13	2 ♏ 39	28 ♏ 03
9/12 Su	8 ♓ 01	1 ♉ 11	2 ♏ 45	28 ♏ 07
9/19 Su	7 ♓ 53	1 ♉ 07	2 ♏ 53	28 ♏ 13
9/26 Su	7 ♓ 44	1 ♉ 04	3 ♏ 01	28 ♏ 19
10/03 Su	7 ♓ 37	1 ♉ 00	3 ♏ 09	28 ♏ 26

Astro Data

2048

6/07 Su	08:18	⚷	SR	8 ♓ 05	-20.1 (-20:04)
7/16 Th	06:14	♇	SD	1 ♏ 21	9.1 (9:03)
7/27 Mo	03:42	♀	SR	1 ♉ 07	6.3 (6:18)
8/10 Mo	14:54	⚵	SD	26 ♏ 47	5.8 (5:50)
11/18 We	16:53	⚷	SD	5 ♓ 51	-21.0 (-21:02)

2049

1/16 Sa	20:23	♀	SD	0 ♉ 00	6.0 (6:00)
1/31 Su	08:23	♇	SR	4 ♏ 10	8.0 (7:59)
2/04 Th	09:00	⚵	→ ♐		4.9 (4:53)
2/27 Sa	03:15	⚵	SR	0 ♐ 06	5.0 (5:02)
3/21 Su	23:50	⚵	→ ♏ ℞		5.3 (5:16)
6/08 Tu	19:14	⚷	SR	9 ♓ 23	-19.8 (-19:47)
7/17 Sa	10:05	♇	SD	2 ♏ 15	8.5 (8:30)
7/27 Tu	19:25	♀	SR	1 ♉ 21	6.6 (6:34)
8/11 We	22:15	⚵	SD	27 ♏ 56	5.4 (5:25)

		♇	♀	⯙	⯚
2049	10/10 Su	7 ♓ 30 ℞	0 ♉ 56 ℞	3 ♏ 18 D	28 ♏ 35 D
	10/17 Su	7 ♓ 24	0 ♉ 52	3 ♏ 27	28 ♏ 44
	10/24 Su	7 ♓ 19	0 ♉ 47	3 ♏ 37	28 ♏ 53
	10/31 Su	7 ♓ 15	0 ♉ 43	3 ♏ 46	29 ♏ 03
	11/07 Su	7 ♓ 12	0 ♉ 39	3 ♏ 55	29 ♏ 14
	11/14 Su	7 ♓ 10	0 ♉ 35	4 ♏ 05	29 ♏ 25
	11/21 Su	7 ♓ 10 D	0 ♉ 31	4 ♏ 13	29 ♏ 36
	11/28 Su	7 ♓ 10	0 ♉ 27	4 ♏ 22	29 ♏ 47
	12/05 Su	7 ♓ 12	0 ♉ 24	4 ♏ 30	29 ♏ 58
	12/12 Su	7 ♓ 16	0 ♉ 21	4 ♏ 37	0 ♐ 08
	12/19 Su	7 ♓ 20	0 ♉ 19	4 ♏ 44	0 ♐ 18
	12/26 Su	7 ♓ 26	0 ♉ 17	4 ♏ 49	0 ♐ 28
2050	1/02 Su	7 ♓ 33	0 ♉ 15	4 ♏ 54	0 ♐ 37
	1/09 Su	7 ♓ 40	0 ♉ 14	4 ♏ 58	0 ♐ 45
	1/16 Su	7 ♓ 49	0 ♉ 14	5 ♏ 01	0 ♐ 53
	1/23 Su	7 ♓ 58	0 ♉ 14 D	5 ♏ 03	0 ♐ 59
	1/30 Su	8 ♓ 08	0 ♉ 15	5 ♏ 04	1 ♐ 05
	2/06 Su	8 ♓ 19	0 ♉ 16	5 ♏ 04 ℞	1 ♐ 09
	2/13 Su	8 ♓ 30	0 ♉ 18	5 ♏ 03	1 ♐ 13
	2/20 Su	8 ♓ 41	0 ♉ 20	5 ♏ 00	1 ♐ 15
	2/27 Su	8 ♓ 53	0 ♉ 23	4 ♏ 57	1 ♐ 15
	3/06 Su	9 ♓ 05	0 ♉ 26	4 ♏ 53	1 ♐ 15 ℞
	3/13 Su	9 ♓ 16	0 ♉ 30	4 ♏ 48	1 ♐ 14
	3/20 Su	9 ♓ 27	0 ♉ 34	4 ♏ 43	1 ♐ 11
	3/27 Su	9 ♓ 38	0 ♉ 38	4 ♏ 36	1 ♐ 07
	4/03 Su	9 ♓ 48	0 ♉ 42	4 ♏ 30	1 ♐ 02
	4/10 Su	9 ♓ 58	0 ♉ 47	4 ♏ 23	0 ♐ 57
	4/17 Su	10 ♓ 06	0 ♉ 51	4 ♏ 15	0 ♐ 50
	4/24 Su	10 ♓ 14	0 ♉ 56	4 ♏ 08	0 ♐ 43
	5/01 Su	10 ♓ 21	1 ♉ 01	4 ♏ 00	0 ♐ 35
	5/08 Su	10 ♓ 28	1 ♉ 05	3 ♏ 53	0 ♐ 27
	5/15 Su	10 ♓ 32	1 ♉ 10	3 ♏ 45	0 ♐ 19
	5/22 Su	10 ♓ 36	1 ♉ 14	3 ♏ 39	0 ♐ 10
	5/29 Su	10 ♓ 39	1 ♉ 18	3 ♏ 32	0 ♐ 02
	6/05 Su	10 ♓ 41	1 ♉ 21	3 ♏ 27	29 ♏ 53
	6/12 Su	10 ♓ 41 ℞	1 ♉ 25	3 ♏ 21	29 ♏ 45
	6/19 Su	10 ♓ 40	1 ♉ 28	3 ♏ 17	29 ♏ 38
2050	6/26 Su	10 ♓ 38 ℞	1 ♉ 30 D	3 ♏ 14 ℞	29 ♏ 31 ℞
	7/03 Su	10 ♓ 35	1 ♉ 32	3 ♏ 11	29 ♏ 24
	7/10 Su	10 ♓ 31	1 ♉ 34	3 ♏ 09	29 ♏ 19
	7/17 Su	10 ♓ 26	1 ♉ 35	3 ♏ 09	29 ♏ 14
	7/24 Su	10 ♓ 19	1 ♉ 36	3 ♏ 09 D	29 ♏ 10
	7/31 Su	10 ♓ 13	1 ♉ 36 ℞	3 ♏ 10	29 ♏ 08
	8/07 Su	10 ♓ 05	1 ♉ 35	3 ♏ 13	29 ♏ 06
	8/14 Su	9 ♓ 57	1 ♉ 34	3 ♏ 16	29 ♏ 06 D
	8/21 Su	9 ♓ 49	1 ♉ 33	3 ♏ 20	29 ♏ 06
	8/28 Su	9 ♓ 40	1 ♉ 31	3 ♏ 25	29 ♏ 08
	9/04 Su	9 ♓ 31	1 ♉ 28	3 ♏ 31	29 ♏ 11
	9/11 Su	9 ♓ 22	1 ♉ 25	3 ♏ 37	29 ♏ 15
	9/18 Su	9 ♓ 14	1 ♉ 22	3 ♏ 44	29 ♏ 20
	9/25 Su	9 ♓ 05	1 ♉ 19	3 ♏ 52	29 ♏ 26
	10/02 Su	8 ♓ 58	1 ♉ 15	4 ♏ 01	29 ♏ 33
	10/09 Su	8 ♓ 50	1 ♉ 11	4 ♏ 09	29 ♏ 41
	10/16 Su	8 ♓ 44	1 ♉ 07	4 ♏ 19	29 ♏ 50
	10/23 Su	8 ♓ 39	1 ♉ 02	4 ♏ 28	0 ♐ 00
	10/30 Su	8 ♓ 34	0 ♉ 58	4 ♏ 37	0 ♐ 10
	11/06 Su	8 ♓ 31	0 ♉ 54	4 ♏ 46	0 ♐ 20
	11/13 Su	8 ♓ 29	0 ♉ 50	4 ♏ 56	0 ♐ 31
	11/20 Su	8 ♓ 28	0 ♉ 46	5 ♏ 05	0 ♐ 42
	11/27 Su	8 ♓ 28 D	0 ♉ 42	5 ♏ 13	0 ♐ 53
	12/04 Su	8 ♓ 30	0 ♉ 39	5 ♏ 21	1 ♐ 04
	12/11 Su	8 ♓ 32	0 ♉ 36	5 ♏ 29	1 ♐ 14
	12/18 Su	8 ♓ 36	0 ♉ 33	5 ♏ 36	1 ♐ 25
	12/25 Su	8 ♓ 42	0 ♉ 31	5 ♏ 42	1 ♐ 35

Astro Data

2049						
11/20 Sa	09:38	♇	SD	7 ♓ 10	-20.8 (-20:47)
12/06 Mo	06:43	⯚	→ ♐		4.4 (4:22)
2050						
1/17 Mo	11:27	♀	SD	0 ♉ 14	6.3 (6:17)
2/01 Tu	09:53	⯙	SR	5 ♏ 04	7.4 (7:25)
2/28 Mo	11:31	⯚	SR	1 ♐ 16	4.7 (4:39)
5/30 Mo	23:25	⯚	→ ♏ ℞		5.3 (5:16)
6/10 Fr	09:58	♇	SR	10 ♓ 41	-19.5 (-19:31)
2050						
7/18 Mo	12:16	⯙	SD	3 ♏ 09	7.9 (7:55)
7/28 Th	04:37	♀	SR	1 ♉ 36	6.9 (6:52)
8/13 Sa	09:05	⯚	SD	29 ♏ 06	5.0 (5:00)
10/22 Sa	21:49	⯚	→ ♐		4.3 (4:17)
11/21 Mo	22:12	♇	SD	8 ♓ 28	-20.5 (-20:31)

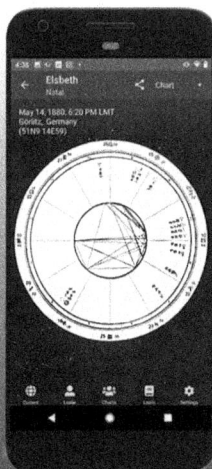

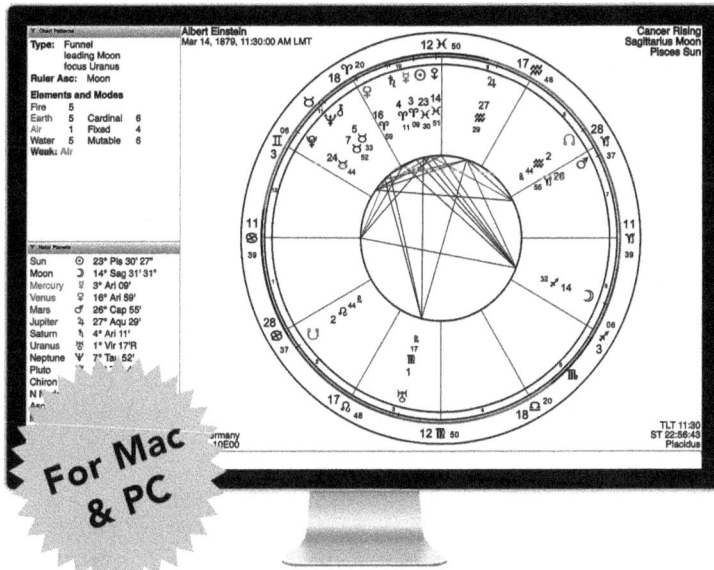

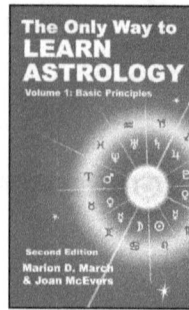

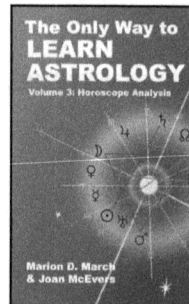